Air War over South Vietnam
1968–1975

Bernard C. Nalty

Air Force History and Museums Program
United States Air Force
Washington, D.C. 2000

Library of Congress Cataloging-in-Publication Data

Nalty, Bernard C.
    Air war over South Vietnam, 1968-1975/Bernard C. Nalty.
        p. 24 cm.
    Includes bibliographical references and index.
    1. Vietnamese Conflict, 1961-1975--Aerial operations, American.
    2. United States. Air Force--History--Vietnamese Conflict, 1961-1975.
    I. Title

DS558.8 .N35 2000
959.704'348--dc21   00-028867

Foreword

This volume covers the period from the Tet offensive and the opening of the road to Khe Sanh in 1968 through the final collapse of South Vietnam in 1975. It deals with the role of the Air Force in advising the South Vietnamese Air Force and waging war in South Vietnam, Cambodia, and Laos. Until the Tet offensive of 1968, the United States hoped to compel North Vietnam, through military operations and negotiations, to call off its war against South Vietnam thus ensuring the survival of an independent South Vietnam. However, the 1973 peace agreement accepted the presence of North Vietnamese forces on territory seized from South Vietnam, and the survival of the Saigon regime depended on the forbearance of the communist leadership or the willingness of the United States to vigorously respond to a new attack. This history includes the so-called Vietnamization of the war, the withdrawal of American forces, American and South Vietnamese operations in Cambodia, the South Vietnamese attack in Laos toward Tchepone, the containment of the invading North Vietnamese forces in 1972, the provision of additional aid from the United States, the military impact of the peace settlement, and the successful communist offensive of 1975. These events took place against the background of deepening American disenchantment with the war, initially voiced by a clamorous antiwar movement but eventually shared by a sizeable segment of the general populace. The unpopularity of the war influenced the decision of the administration of President Richard M. Nixon to minimize American casualties by increasing Vietnamese participation in the fighting and substituting air power, wielded largely by military professionals or volunteers, for American ground troops, who were mostly draftees.

This, in short, is a story of frustration, disillusionment, changing goals, and eventual disengagement that can teach an important lesson to those who would impulsively commit American might without ensuring that the nation's vital interests are involved and that the populace, which supplies the troops and treasure needed for the effort, understands and supports the intervention. The author, Bernard C. Nalty, devoted some thirty years to the Air Force history program.

RICHARD P. HALLION
Air Force Historian

The Author

Before retiring in 1994, Bernard C. Nalty was a senior historian in the Office of Air Force History. He earned a B.A. from Creighton University and an M.A. from Catholic University and served as an officer in the U.S. Army from 1953 to 1955. He was chief editor and coauthor of *Winged Sword, Winged Shield* (1997), the Air Force's two-volume 50th-anniversary history, and has written *Air Power and the Fight for Khe Sanh* (1973), an Air Force monograph on the Vietnam War; *Tigers over Asia* (1978), an account of the Flying Tigers during World War II; *Strength for the Fight: A History of Black Americans in the Military* (1986); and two pamphlets dealing with the Marine Corps in World War II — *Cape Gloucester: The Green Inferno* (1994) and *The Right to Fight: African American Marines in World War II* (1995). He is coauthor with Henry I. Shaw, Jr., and Edwin T. Turnbladh of *Central Pacific Drive* (1996), a history of Marine Corps operations in World War II. With Morris J. MacGregor, Jr., he edited the thirteen-volume *Blacks in the United States Armed Forces: Basic Documents* and its single volume abridgement *Blacks in the Military: Essential Documents* (1981).

Preface

The nature of the Vietnam War changed over the years, reflecting a radical shift in U.S. objectives and prompting an adjustment in the mission of the Air Force. Earlier histories in the United States Air Force in Southeast Asia series describe the shift from a war fought by proxies — the armed forces of the Republic of Vietnam, trained and supplied by the United States, fighting to achieve the American purpose of checking the spread of communism by maintaining an independent South and communist North Vietnam supporting the Viet Cong guerrillas seeking to destroy South Vietnam — to a struggle between the United States and North Vietnam, with the South Vietnamese and Viet Cong relegated to lesser roles.

The Tet offensive of February 1968 altered the nature of the conflict by shaking public confidence in the ability of the United States to force the North Vietnamese, through a combination of military and diplomatic pressure, to abandon their campaign to absorb the South into a unified, communist Vietnam. Disillusionment with the war began to surface during the mid-1960s in two widely different groups — those who argued that the United States was wasting lives and resources in Southeast Asia and those who believed that the nation was not adequately supporting its men sent to fight a decisive battle in the struggle against communism. The sudden and violent attacks that erupted during the Tet holidays of 1968 followed official assurances of progress, timing that increased the corrosive effect of the offensive on national resolve. Negotiation loomed larger in U.S. policy and while military operations continued, South Vietnamese forces began to assume responsibility for fighting the war.

This transfer of the burden of combat, which began in earnest after the inauguration of President Richard M. Nixon in January 1969, came to be called Vietnamization. The United States would supply South Vietnam with weapons to defend itself, provide training, and maintain a shield behind which the South Vietnamese could expand their armed forces. Because the Nixon administration was determined to reduce U.S. casualties, especially among ground troop draftees, Vietnamizing the ground war took priority. Air power, applied by military professionals and volunteers, would have to provide the shield.

The Tet offensive changed the tactics of the war fought by the North Vietnamese, though not Hanoi's ultimate goal of conquering the South. A failure either to exploit the initial successes of the Tet offensive or to break off the fighting and regroup brought crippling losses to Viet Cong units. North Vietnamese troops, deployed and sustained by means of the Ho Chi Minh Trail, took over the war, much as the Americans had taken over from the South Vietnamese between 1965 and 1968. The expanded North Vietnamese role resulted in a shift from unconventional tactics based on mobility and surprise to conventional warfare by massed forces tied to extended supply lines far more fragile than the Ho Chi Minh Trail. An invasion of South Vietnam, launched in March 1972, proved vulnerable to overpowering U.S. aerial strength and ground to a halt with the Saigon government still in at least nominal control of a large portion of the South.

By this time, bringing home the troops took precedence over the survival of an independent South Vietnam in American policy objectives. Even the invasion of Cambodia in 1970 and the U.S.-supported South Vietnamese attack on the Ho Chi Minh Trail a year later served principally to ensure that North Vietnamese forces did not disrupt troop withdrawals. The departures continued, even during the fighting that followed the North Vietnamese invasion of 1972. Over the years, U.S. ground forces left at an accelerating pace that bore scant relationship to the ability of the South Vietnamese to take over their duties.

By late 1972, the United States concentrated on obtaining a cease-fire and the release of American prisoners of war, whatever the cost. To gain Saigon's consent to a settlement that would leave North Vietnamese forces in control of territory captured in 1972, the Nixon administration combined the threat of abandonment with a promise of decisive aerial intervention in the event North Vietnam renewed the war. But when the fighting resumed in the spring of 1975, the United States stood aside as North Vietnam conquered the South, ending, finally, the active involvement of the United States in this long and bloody conflict.

Acknowledgments

In writing this volume, my efforts benefitted from the help of numerous persons. Dr. Wayne Thompson and Mr. Jacob Van Staaveren, authors of a history of the air war against North Vietnam, shared their insights as did Dr. R. Frank Futrell, author of the first volume in this series dealing with the air war in South Vietnam, and Col. John Schlight, author of the second. Especially useful advice came from authors of several of the Office of Air Force History's monographs on the war in Southeast Asia, among them Mr. Van Staaveren, Dr. Elizabeth H. Hartsook, Capt. William A. Buckingham, Jr., Lt. Col. Roger P. Fox, and Capt. Earl H. Tilford, Jr. Two military members of the office, Maj. John F. Kreis and Lt. Col. Vance O. Mitchell, cheerfully shared their first-hand knowledge.

Over the years, almost the entire administrative structure of the Air Force History Support Office and its precursors helped in various ways, including Dr. Stanley L. Falk, Colonel Schlight, Col. Drue L. DeBerry, Mr. Warren Trest, Col. John F. Shiner, Mr. Herman Wolk, Mr. Jacob Neufeld, Dr. B. Franklin Cooling, Dr. Alfred M. Beck, and Mr. R. Cargill Hall. The roster of archivists, librarians, editors, and typists includes Mr. David Schoem, Dr. George M. Watson, Jr., MSgt. Roger Jernigan, MSgt. Barry Spink, CMSgt. Al Hargett, Mr. William C. Heimdahl, Mr. Sheldon Goldberg, Capt. Sue Cober, Maj. Lucinda M. Hackman, Mrs. Yvonne Kincaid, Mr. Lawrence Paszek, Mr. Eugene P. Sagstetter, Mr. Samuel Duncan Miller, Dr. Beck, Mrs. I. Jewell Newman, Mrs. Ann Caudle, SrA. Terry Nance, SrA. James Brannan, and Mrs. Debra Moss.

Writing this volume involved the use of documents not included in the holdings of the Air Force. Dr. R. A. Winnacker and Mr. Charles Pugh of the Office of Secretary of Defense; Mr. George C. McGarrigle, Dr. Ronald Spector, Dr. Richard Hunt, Mr. Vincent Demma, Ms. Geraldine Harcarik, and Ms. Hannah Zeidlik from the Army; Mr. Ben Frank, Dr. Jack Shulimson, Mrs. Joyce Bonnett, and Mr. Frederick Graboske from the Marine Corps; and Dr. Oscar P. Fitzgerald and Dr. Edward Marolda from the Navy all provided information or access to materials relating to their respective offices.

All of these individuals, and probably others I have inadvertently slighted, contributed to the writing and publication of this book, but I take sole responsibility for the narrative and interpretations that shape its conclusions.

Contents

	page
Foreword	iii
Preface	v
Acknowledgments	vii
Introduction	1
1 The Tet Offensive Begins	7
2 The Enemy Repulsed	19
3 Facing Some Hard Decisions	39
4 The Air War from Tet to Mini-Tet	55
5 Above Highlands, Plain, and Delta	75
6 Testing the Single Manager Concept	93
7 Unified Management takes a Final Form	113
8 Secret Bombing and Troop Withdrawals	127
9 The Nature of the Air War, 1969	145
10 Improving the South Vietnamese Air Force	161
11 Storming the Cambodian Bases	179
12 From Incursion to Interdiction	199
13 The Continued Growth of South Vietnam's Air Force	211
14 Further Disengagement	229
15 The South Vietnamese Invasion of Laos: Operation Lam Son 719	247
16 Action in South Vietnam and Cambodia 1971	275
17 Further Vietnamization and Accelerated Withdrawal	293
18 Discipline, Drug Abuse, and Racial Unrest	311
19 Invasion	325
20 Reinforcement, Continuing Withdrawal, and Further Vietnamization	333
21 Military Region I: Quang Tri City Lost and Regained	357
22 Kontum City, An Loc, and the Delta	373
23 After the Truce	403
24 Recapturing *Mayaguez*: An Epilogue	427
Notes	449
Glossary	491
Bibliographic Note	497
Index	513

Illustrations

Maps

Southeast Asia	xiii
South Vietnam	48–49
Lam Son 719 Area	267
Military Region I	362
Military Region II	382
Military Regions III and IV	388
Koh Tang Island	428

Photographs

President Johnson and his military advisers	6
Air Force Security Police and South Vietnamese soldiers guard the perimeter at Tan Son Nhut	9
The U.S. Embassy in Saigon after Tet attacks	11
Bien Hoa bunker after Tet attacks	12
President Lyndon Johnson, Brig. Gen. Robert N. Ginsburgh, and Walt W. Rostow	15
Hue during the Tet fighting	17
Royal Australian Air Force Canberra	21
Cholon district of Saigon after Tet attacks	22
Imperial Palace in Hue after Tet attacks	25
Khe Sanh combat base	29
C–130 delivers cargo at Khe Sanh	33
South Vietnamese UH–1 helicopters	34
Pre-Tet and post-Tet revetments	37
Aircraft destroyed during the Tet attacks at Bien Hoa	40
Burning fuel dump at Khe Sanh	41
New Mexico Air National Guard F–100s at Tuy Hoa Air Base	46
Relief of Khe Sanh during Operation Pegasus	58
Bomb craters in the A Shau valley	60
C–130 dropping supplies at the A Loui airstrip in the A Shau Valley	63
C–123 landing at the A Loui airstrip	65
AC–47 gunships near Saigon	68

Effects of bombing on the Ho Chi Minh Trail 78
South Vietnamese troops in the Mekong Delta 80
Duc Lap Special Forces camp 84
C-7 landing at Duc Lap Special Forces Camp 85
Night observation device on an AC-119 89
North American OV-10 91
Gen. William C. Westmoreland and Gen. William W. Momyer 100
Adm. U. S. Grant Sharp and Lt. Gen. Robert E. Cushman, Jr. 101
Lt. Col. Joe M. Jackson 111
Gen. Leonard F. Chapman, Jr., and Lt. Gen. Victor H. Krulak 115
Gen. Creighton W. Abrams and Gen. George S. Brown 118
Combat Skyspot radar installation 131
Cessna A-37 137
Departing troops board a commercial airliner at Da Nang 138
Cessna O-2 142
McDonnell F-101, McDonnell Douglas F-4, and Grumman OV-1 146
A Military Airlift Command C-141 receives wounded 148
A Marine Corps A-6 at Chu Lai Marine Base 153
Bu Prang Special Forces Camp 160
South Vietnamese A-37 163
Richard M. Nixon and Nguyen Van Thieu 165
South Vietnamese UH-1 helicopter at Binh Thuy Air Base 168
South Vietnamese O-1 near Da Nang 170
South Vietnamese C-119 172
Norodom Sihanouk and Pham Van Dong 181
Lon Nol with Cambodian troops in the field 185
Air Force F-4 over the Fishhook region of Cambodia 190
Rice and ammunition captured in Cambodia 196
C-130 dropping leaflets 201
Cambodian refugees in South Vietnam 204
EC-121D over Southeast Asia 209
Robert C. Seamans and Gen. Cao Van Vien 215
South Vietnamese students at Sheppard Air Force Base 220
South Vietnamese cadet pilots at Nha Trang 221
South Vietnamese UH-1 helicopters loading troops 224
Maj. Gen. Tran Van Minh 227
Airmen loading 500-pound bombs on an F-4 at Phu Cat 233
UC-123s spraying defoliant over South Vietnam 235
Storage site in Gulfport, Mississippi, for herbicides removed
   from Vietnam 236
Martin B-57G 240
Fuel tanks at Cam Ranh Bay destroyed by rocket attacks in 1970 245
C-130 at Khe Sanh during Lam Son 719 251

xi

Air War over South Vietnam, 1968–1975

South Vietnamese personnel carrier in Laos 255
Soviet-built PT–76 tank captured during Lam Son 719 257
Runway matting at Khe Sanh 260
Cambodians training in South Vietnam 277
F–100s at Phan Rang 281
Air Force sentry and dog at Cam Ranh Bay 290
Destroyed trucks on the Ho Chi Minh Trail 296
AC–47, AC–119, and AC–130 gunships 300
South Vietnamese gunner training in UH–1 helicopter 308
Hootches at Tan Son Nhut 316
Inspection of outbound cargo 319
Gates at Tan Son Nhut 321
Gen. John D. Lavelle and Lt. Gen. John W. Vogt 331
Haiphong harbor under attack 336
B–52s at Andersen 338
EB–66s at Takhli 340
Wild Weasel F–105F at Korat 341
F–111s and F–4s at Takhli 347
A–7s at Korat 347
Enhance Plus F–5s 352
SA–2 launcher and SA–2 missile in flight 360
U.S. Army helicopter gunship escorting Marine transport helicopters ... 369
Capt. Steven L. Bennett 370
Installation of a 105-mm howitzer on an AC–130 gunship 376
AC–130 crewmembers at consoles 395
Ex-prisoners of war on a C–141 404
Maintenance on South Vietnamese A–37 408
Phnom Penh evacuation area, April 1975 414
Civilians evacuated from Saigon on the USS Blue Ridge 423
Vietnamese refugees crowd the decks of the USS Pioneer Contender ... 424
Cambodiam patrol boat on bottom 433
U.S. Marines board the Mayaguez 436
Koh Tang Island 438
Air Force HH–53 rescues Marines from Koh Tang Island 444

Air War over South Vietnam
1968–1975

Introduction

A Turning Point

From the establishment of the Republic of Vietnam in 1954 until 1965, the United States gradually increased its efforts to help that nation resist subversion or military attack from communist North Vietnam. The volume of American aid expanded; the number of U.S. troops stationed there grew from fewer than 700 to 23,000; and the distinction between advising and providing combat support blurred, then disappeared. The Air Force, which sent its first detachment to South Vietnam late in 1961, proceeded in a matter of months from training South Vietnamese crews to actual bombing and strafing, though a trainee usually was on board during these first combat missions. By January 1965, Air Force aircraft in South Vietnam had increased from one squadron of thirty-two airplanes — North American T–28 trainers, Douglas B–26 bombers, and Douglas C–47 transports — to 218 aircraft of various types, including twin-jet Martin B–57B bombers.[1]

In spite of expanded American aid, the South Vietnamese government staggered from one crisis to another. Early in 1965, Air Force and Navy planes began bombing North Vietnam, both to punish the communist enemy and to shore up the discouraged and divided leadership in the South. Shortly afterward, American combat troops arrived on the scene. Although initially assigned to protect airfields and supply depots, the Marines and soldiers had by year's end assumed responsibility for waging war throughout the country, shunting the armed forces of the Republic of Vietnam into a subsidiary role. At the beginning of 1968, American combat and logistics operations involved more than 400,000 soldiers, sailors, and Marines and required a wide range of activity by a Vietnam-based Air Force contingent numbering 56,000 men and almost 1,100 planes. Other Air Force units flying from Guam, Okinawa, or Thailand also took part in the conflict.[2]

Because of the limited nature of the war — the objective was to preserve South Vietnamese independence rather than to subjugate the North — the Air Force did not exercise all its normal functions during operations in South Vietnam. For example, as long as the enemy husbanded his aerial strength to defend his homeland, instead of using air power to support his ground forces in

Air War over South Vietnam, 1968–1975

the South, air superiority over the South posed no problem. Therefore, the function of maintaining air supremacy over South Vietnam required no more than the presence of a few fighter-interceptors in case North Vietnam should change its longstanding policy and launch an aerial foray. Another primary function — formulating doctrines and procedures for organizing, training, equipping, and employing forces — continued with Vietnam in mind. New or modified aircraft and other equipment arrived in the battle area, and the senior Air Force officer in the country, who doubled as deputy for air operations to the Army general in overall command, campaigned for the adoption of Air Force doctrine on issues such as the centralized control of tactical aviation, both American and South Vietnamese.

The Vietnam War interfered with a function that had come to dominate Air Force thinking during the intensification of the Cold War — providing strategic forces to deter or, if necessary, to fight a nuclear war. The Air Force had to shift Boeing B–52 bombers and KC–135 tankers from strategic assignments to deliver firepower for the Army and Marine Corps in Vietnam. The worldwide air transport service, yet another Air Force function, rushed men and equipment to Southeast Asia in times of buildup and evacuated the sick and wounded. Because much of South Vietnam was poorly charted, aerial mapping, also an Air Force responsibility, proved essential. So, too, did the intelligence function during a conflict in which rain, cloud, forest, and sometimes the noncombatant populace concealed enemy movement.

The most important function, in terms of effort expended, came to be described as close combat and logistical support to the Army. It included tactical reconnaissance, close air support, tactical airlift, the support and resupply of airborne operations, and the interdiction of enemy lines of communication. The unusual characteristics of the Vietnam war — the absence of strategic targets in South Vietnam, the lack of aerial opposition there, and Army tactics that emphasized finding and destroying hostile troops — compelled the Air Force to concentrate upon the combat and logistic support of ground troops.[3]

The role of the Air Force — not attacking hostile troops in South Vietnam, but bombing urban military targets in the North — created the image of a vast nation using advanced technology to bully, though unsuccessfully, a smaller and comparatively backward nation and aroused the wrath of a group of articulate critics of U.S. involvement in Southeast Asia. The actual number of persons opposing the war was small at the end of 1965, but grew rapidly as U.S. casualty lists grew longer, attracting a varied following. Some adherents saw the war as an immoral effort to uphold a puppet regime at Saigon, while others opposed foreign entanglements as a matter of principle, and still others were dedicated pacifists. The most numerous and active element consisted of college-age people whose lives and careers seemed threatened by military service.[4]

By late 1967, as demonstrations against the war grew larger and more frequent, Alain Enthoven, a systems analyst in the Office of Secretary of

A Turning Point

Defense, warned, "We're up against an enemy who just may have found a dangerously clever strategy for licking the United States." Hanoi, he said, might continue the war over a number of years, keeping its commitment at an acceptable level but forcing the United States to expend lives and money until a disillusioned American public rejected the war.[5]

As the Air Force carried out its several roles in South Vietnam, the massive infusion of U.S. men, equipment, and money that began in earnest during 1965 seemed to be bringing the war effort to the threshold of success, whatever the antiwar activists might say. Early in 1967, Robert W. Komer, a special assistant to President Lyndon B. Johnson, returned brimming with confidence from a visit to South Vietnam. "Wastefully, expensively," he reported, "we are winning the war in the South. Few of our programs — civil or military — are very efficient, but we are grinding the enemy down by sheer weight and mass."[6]

At year's end, prospects seemed, if anything, even brighter. Ellsworth Bunker, U.S. Ambassador to South Vietnam, told the Overseas Press Club at New York City of steady, though not spectacular, progress on the battlefield and elsewhere. South Vietnam verged on becoming a true nation. Representative government seemed to be taking root, and, in Bunker's opinion, "The enemy's attempt to impose a solution by force has run into a stone wall."[7]

Gen. William C. Westmoreland, Commander, U.S. Military Assistance Command, Vietnam — the Army officer responsible for directing American combat, support, and advisory activity in South Vietnam — shared this confidence. A few days after Bunker's New York speech, Westmoreland told the National Press Club at Washington, D.C., "In 1965 the enemy was winning, today he is certainly losing." Although General Westmoreland, like Bunker, refused to predict when the war would end, he did say that January 1968 would mark the beginning of a new phase in the conflict, during which the United States would strengthen South Vietnamese forces, assign them a greater role in defending their country, and in general set the stage for a final phase, sometime in the more distant future, when a strong and stable republic would crush the last communist opposition on its soil.

The year 1968, Westmoreland warned, would see heavy fighting, for the North refused to give up. Even though enemy forces had not won a major battle in more than a year, they continued to infiltrate from sanctuaries outside South Vietnam in an attempt to gain control of the rural populace and rebuild local guerrilla units. He acknowledged that the enemy remained confident of victory, but insisted that a transition to the final stage of the war lay "within our grasp." North Vietnam's hopes of conquest, he declared, were bankrupt.[8]

President Johnson's publicly expressed views coincided with those of his principal subordinates, diplomatic and military, in the conduct of the war. On the same day that Ambassador Bunker spoke in New York, Johnson outlined for the White House press corps the goals of the Vietnam conflict. The main purposes, he suggested, were to demonstrate that the United States intended to

Air War over South Vietnam, 1968–1975

honor its commitments in Southeast Asia and elsewhere; to resist aggression against the South and thus discourage all would-be aggressors; and to enable South Vietnam to chart its own future without fear of domination by the North, a goal that the United States proposed to achieve by doing, in his words, "whatever we think is necessary to protect the security of South Vietnam." The President insisted that American efforts over the years had made progress toward these objectives, though hard work lay ahead. The level of U.S. military power in South Vietnam at last seemed adequate, however, and Johnson told the press that "General Westmoreland . . . anticipates no increase in that level."[9]

Within a few months, claims of progress took on a hollow ring, as the enemy at the end of January and beginning of February 1968 unleashed a series of attacks throughout South Vietnam. The entire American war effort underwent reassessment in the light of a request that General Westmoreland receive substantial reinforcements. The U.S. government, in the process, reached a crossroad and turned onto a tortuous route leading, despite flurries of savage fighting, to a gradually reduced American involvement and ultimately to a negotiated settlement.[10]

For the Seventh Air Force, the principal Air Force command in South Vietnam, these sudden attacks plunged airmen, many of them off duty, into the midst of a ground war, as communist infiltrators raided billets in towns and shelled or stormed crowded air bases. Security troops, including specially trained Air Force detachments, rallied to protect the airfields, so that after only brief disruptions, the strike, reconnaissance, and transport aircraft were back in the skies, giving close combat and logistical support to embattled ground units.

President Johnson and his military advisers in the White House early in 1968.

Chapter One

The Tet Offensive Begins

From the windows of their villa not far from Tan Son Nhut Air Base, 1st Lt. David C. Brown and other off-duty officers of the 12th Tactical Reconnaissance Squadron watched fireworks begin bursting throughout Saigon, welcoming to South Vietnam's capital the lunar new year that began on January 31, 1968. The holiday saluted by these joyous explosions traditionally began with the first new moon after January 20, lasted for three days, and drew together families separated for the rest of the year. During Tet, as this time of celebration was called, a truce normally prevailed between the contending Vietnamese forces, and the Saigon government took advantage of the cease-fire to grant liberal leave to the armed forces.

When the sound of fireworks died away, the airmen went to bed, secure in the knowledge that their quarters, in one of the many buildings leased for American use because the air base had become so crowded, were being protected by South Vietnamese guards. Within a few hours, however, the harsh crack of small-arms fire from the direction of Tan Son Nhut jolted Brown and the others fully awake.[1]

To the south, enemy forces had gathered undetected near the air base, the busiest in South Vietnam and the site of Seventh Air Force headquarters. Across the runways from the Seventh Air Force area, near the civilian air terminal, stood the buildings that housed the headquarters of the U.S. Military Assistance Command, Vietnam, including the command post from which the commander, Gen. William C. Westmoreland, directed U.S. ground forces, obtained air support for them, and maintained communication with his military and civilian superiors. Near the compound of the assistance command lay the headquarters of the South Vietnamese Joint General Staff, patterned after the American Joint Chiefs of Staff. A tempting target for the enemy, Tan Son Nhut and its environs came under attack at about 3:20 a.m. local time on the first day of Tet, when a group of Viet Cong — the communist guerrillas in South Vietnam — opened fire from the darkness beyond the east end of one of two parallel main runways. Besides awakening Lieutenant Brown and the other officers billeted at the nearby villa, this attack diverted attention from the main enemy thrust.

Air War over South Vietnam, 1968–1975

Shortly after the firing broke out, several men materialized from the shadows to hurl hand grenades at a bunker manned by Air Force security police that guarded a gate at the west end of that same runway. At about 3:40 a.m., a taxi stopped not far from the gate and disgorged a Viet Cong assault team that quickly assembled a bangalore torpedo — threaded sections of pipe filled with explosive — ignited the fuse, and blasted a hole in the chain-link fence surrounding the base. Other attackers rushed through the gap to open fire with rocket-propelled grenades that shattered the wall of the bunker, driving out the defenders. The airmen forced from this position had done their assigned job, however, holding off vastly superior numbers until other Air Force security police could join American and South Vietnamese soldiers in setting up a defensive line between the gate, now in enemy hands, and the end of the runway.

The Air Force unit responsible for halting the enemy advance was the 377th Security Police Squadron, on alert since the previous afternoon because of attacks against South Vietnamese towns far to the north of the capital. The squadron had readied its eight thirteen-man quick reaction teams, while U.S. Army signal and transportation battalions stationed on the base prepared to execute their part of the defense plan, organizing three improvised rifle platoons, each numbering about 40 men, to fight alongside the airmen. These soldiers and Air Force security police, numbering fewer than 250 in all, formed the cutting edge of a 900-man security force, composed of South Vietnamese as well as U.S. troops, that now tried to contain and kill the well-trained assault troops entering through the gap blown in the perimeter fence.

The American soldiers and airmen succeeded in stopping the Viet Cong, thanks in part to three light tanks dispatched by the South Vietnamese base commander, who bore formal responsibility for protecting Tan Son Nhut, even though his U.S. tenants had made their own security arrangements. Rocket-propelled grenades disabled two of the armored vehicles, but fire from the survivor helped the Americans hold their ground through the night. Dawn found the attackers in control of an area that measured approximately 1,000 by 2,000 feet, including the west gate but stopping short of the runway. Meanwhile, other groups of Viet Cong were probing the southeastern perimeter of Tan Son Nhut and attacking the Joint General Staff compound, but these forays presented only a minor threat to base security.[2]

Since so many of his own units were short-handed, the South Vietnamese officer responsible for security at Tan Son Nhut and the surrounding area called for help, and elements of the 25th Infantry Division promptly responded. The component closest to the base, not quite eight miles distant, boarded vehicles and drove through the night, its commander dropping flares from his helicopter to illuminate the roadway and reveal any ambush attempt. The relief column encountered no opposition until it approached Tan Son Nhut shortly before dawn, where it clashed with enemy forces massed just outside the base. When additional units arrived, it joined in attacking toward the airfield.[3]

The Tet Offensive Begins

Air Force Security Police and South Vietnamese soldiers
guard the perimeter fence at Tan Son Nhut Air Base.

The arrival of the first contingent of American soldiers triggered savage fighting around Tan Son Nhut, causing explosions that reverberated through the building where Lieutenant Brown was staying. The sounds of battle drew closer until, as he and his fellow officers watched, the enemy occupied a warehouse just a hundred yards from the villa and began setting up machineguns to defend against the rapidly developing American counterattack. Since the airmen living away from the base relied on locally recruited guards for protection, they had no more than a pistol or two among them and could only pile up furniture for a barricade in case the Viet Cong tried to storm the building.

By mid-morning, South Vietnamese troops advanced upon the enemy-held warehouse across the street. Army helicopters laid down a barrage of rockets and machinegun fire, but before being killed or forced to flee, Viet Cong gunners knocked out several vehicles approaching the warehouse. As the fighting neared a climax, sniper fire tore into that wing of the villa where the Americans had taken refuge. A bullet struck Lieutenant Brown in the head. After giving the wounded man what first aid they could, two of the other officers braved stray shots that still came from the direction of the warehouse, commandeered a South Vietnamese truck, and drove him to a U.S. Army field hospital. There, despite the efforts of a neurosurgeon, he died.[4]

Shortly after noon on January 31, at about the time Lieutenant Brown suffered his fatal wound, a mixed force of American and South Vietnamese soldiers and Air Force security police were attacking the Viet Cong's Tan Son Nhut foothold from inside the base, while the recently arrived units from the

Air War over South Vietnam, 1968–1975

25th Infantry Division closed in on the enemy-held western gate. Viet Cong mortar barrages impeded the counterattacks, as enemy gunners tried in vain to screen an orderly withdrawal. An assault that might have crippled, at least temporarily, a vital air base thus ended in failure.[5]

Although over within a half-day, the struggle on Tan Son Nhut airfield had been fierce. The retreating enemy left behind 157 bodies and almost that number of individual and crew-served weapons. Four of the Air Force security police died in the battle and eleven were wounded, while nineteen of the U.S. soldiers fighting beside the airmen lost their lives and seventy-five suffered wounds. South Vietnamese base defense forces sustained comparable losses: five airmen killed and twelve wounded, with twelve soldiers killed and sixty-seven wounded. Despite the shelling that accompanied the Viet Cong assault, only thirteen American planes — eleven Air Force and two Navy — sustained damage; not one was destroyed.[6]

Elsewhere in Saigon and vicinity, other Viet Cong attacks lost momentum and collapsed in defeat, even though the enemy retained control of some residential sections of the city. When the first hostile rounds fell on Tan Son Nhut, shattering the early morning quiet there, an assault team blasted an opening in the masonry wall surrounding the U.S. Embassy and attacked the recently completed chancery building, a suicidal gamble that had far greater impact on public opinion in the United States than on the outcome of the Tet fighting in South Vietnam. None of the attackers — apparently five in number — entered the chancery structure, though one was killed inside a residence within the compound. The fight ended after about four hours, with two wounded Viet Cong in custody and three others dead.[7]

The air base at Bien Hoa, about 15 miles northeast of Tan Son Nhut, also came under attack, as enemy forces converged on Saigon from the north, east, and southwest. A rocket and mortar barrage shook the base only moments before a raiding party penetrated the security fence guarding Bien Hoa's lightly manned eastern boundary. A sentry dog detected the presence of the enemy, and the animal's handler alerted the command post, which sent Air Force security police and additional dog teams to the threatened sector. The Viet Cong, however, bypassed the bunker sited to defend in this direction and rushed onward to occupy an engine test stand located by the near end of a runway overrun.[8]

While the enemy consolidated its hold on the test stand, a hard-surfaced pad protected on three sides by sandbag revetments, a North Vietnamese regiment infiltrated the Bien Hoa perimeter at three different places. As soon as it became light enough to aim, some of the infiltrators began firing into the III Direct Air Support Center, which controlled aerial activity in the III Corps area of central South Vietnam. The center's deputy director, Air Force Lt. Col. John E. Pitts, grabbed a rifle and blazed away at an enemy soldier lying prone on a roof nearby. The North Vietnamese weapon soon fell silent, but Pitts never discovered if he had killed the marksman.[9]

The Tet Offensive Begins

Rubble from the 1968 Tet attack on the U.S. Embassy in Saigon.

However those under fire may have felt, the sniping around the direct air support center was mere harassment compared to the fighting that raged around the engine test stand. Air Force security police worked their way to within grenade-throwing distance of enemy troops firing from behind sandbag barriers and the huge benches upon which jet engines were mounted for testing. At this juncture, unfortunately, an Army helicopter strafed the test stand forcing the airmen to retreat, but inflicting no friendly casualties. The incident occurred because the Army officer assigned to coordinate helicopter support lay wounded inside the bunker and could not contact the aircraft he was supposed to direct. The Air Force security troops then stormed the test stand a second time, killing or driving away the enemy.

The battle now shifted roughly a hundred yards to a shed, protected by an embankment, where Air Force ordnance specialists disarmed live bombs that strike aircraft had been unable to drop. A South Vietnamese security contingent, armed with a 57-mm recoilless rifle, blasted the shed to splinters, Army helicopters strafed the position, but the North Vietnamese and Viet Cong held out until U.S. airmen and South Vietnamese troops killed them with hand grenades and rifle fire.[10]

As at Tan Son Nhut, the first U.S. Army units reached Bien Hoa at about dawn to begin driving the enemy from the outskirts of the airfield. For the Air Force, the battle at Bien Hoa proved more costly than the struggle for the other base. Four airmen were killed in action, another died of a heart attack induced by exertion during the fighting, and twenty-six were wounded. Enemy losses within the base perimeter amounted to 137 killed and 25 captured. Hostile fire

Air War over South Vietnam, 1968–1975

Bunker at Bien Hoa bears the scars of the Tet attack.

destroyed a Cessna A-37 attack plane being evaluated for possible use by the South Vietnamese and a North American F-100 fighter-bomber, while the attack damaged seventeen other planes, four of them heavily.[11]

Although mopping-up continued at Bien Hoa into the afternoon of January 31, limited flight operations got underway by sunrise on that day. Among the first aircraft into the sky was a Cessna O-1 observation plane flown by Maj. James Grant, a forward air controller. He spent three hours searching out enemy units and calling in air strikes or artillery concentrations, then refueled at Bien Hoa for a second sortie. During the afternoon mission, his airplane suddenly heeled, struck by the force of a detonation on the ground more than two miles away. The explosion, he later reported, resembled a small nuclear blast — "a gigantic flash and a rising mushroom cloud that reached 8,000 to 9,000 feet." The enemy had destroyed the ammunition stored by U.S. forces at a vast dump near Long Binh.[12]

Nor were the Tet attacks limited to such vital installations as the Long Binh Army base, Bien Hoa, Tan Son Nhut, and the embassy compound at Saigon. An estimated 67,000 enemy troops, almost 45,000 of them Viet Cong and the remainder North Vietnamese regulars, shelled or tried to seize military facilities, towns, and government administrative offices from Khe Sanh in the north, a base already surrounded by North Vietnamese troops, to Ca Mau in southernmost South Vietnam. Among the objectives were five major cities, including Saigon, the capitals of 27 of the nation's 44 provinces, 58 lesser towns, and some 50 hamlets.[13]

The Tet Offensive Begins

Of the ten major bases used by the Air Force in South Vietnam, only four — Cam Ranh Bay, Phu Cat, Phan Rang, and Tuy Hoa — emerged unscathed from the initial Tet attacks. Enemy troops broke through the defensive perimeters guarding Tan Son Nhut and Bien Hoa, but were expelled, killed, or captured within the day. At other air bases — Pleiku, Nha Trang, Da Nang, and Binh Thuy — the North Vietnamese and Viet Cong merely shelled the installations, using rocket launchers, mortars, or recoilless rifles.[14]

Airmen stationed at Binh Thuy, southernmost of the ten air bases, may not have realized at first that Tet 1968 marked a special enemy effort. Located among the rice fields irrigated by the Bassac River, the airfield had already proved so inviting a target for shells and rockets that explosions shattered the night three or four times each week. Not until February 13 did the Viet Cong launch a ground attack at Binh Thuy, but that effort failed. Air Force security police, two receiving wounds during the skirmish, drove off a demolition team that approached the fence. Heavy defensive fire discouraged other infiltrators who had crept through tall grass to hurl grenades over the barbed wire at a pair of armored personnel carriers parked near the edge of the base perimeter.[15]

From a military standpoint, the enemy achieved his greatest success of the Tet offensive at Hue, formerly the royal capital of Vietnam, a city that symbolized past greatness. At the heart of modern Hue lay the Imperial City or Citadel, walled around with earth and masonry and protected on three sides by a moat. Patterned after the Imperial City at Beijing, China, the Citadel contained almost a hundred buildings, including the palace from which Vietnam once was ruled. Because of its status as a shrine, Hue seemed immune to attack and was lightly held by South Vietnamese units, further reduced in strength by holiday leave. Lax security enabled enemy soldiers, who had arrived amid the Tet throng, to exchange civilian clothes for uniforms, break out concealed weapons, and seize almost all the objectives assigned them. Except for the military assistance command compound in the new city and a South Vietnamese division headquarters inside the Citadel, the North Vietnamese and Viet Cong soon controlled all of Hue.[16]

Only at Da Nang, one of six places attacked on the morning of January 30 rather than on the 31st, did the enemy fail completely. Since General Westmoreland had rejected a Tet cease-fire in the northern provinces, the Marines protecting the town and its airfield remained on full alert. As a result, they intercepted the main North Vietnamese force advancing on Da Nang and, aided by South Vietnamese and U.S. Army units, repulsed a two-pronged thrust toward that city and nearby Hoi An. Enemy forces did not stage an infantry assault, although a rocket barrage temporarily closed one runway. Since flight operations continued without interruption, the Tet attack on the airdrome amounted to little more than a nuisance raid.[17]

In suddenly lashing out against towns and installations throughout the country, the enemy had taken advantage of U.S. preoccupation with the border regions, a reaction to recent battles at Loc Ninh, Dak To, and Bu Doc and to the encirclement of the Marine combat base at Khe Sanh. The military assistance command hoped to seal the borders with U.S. troops, leaving the South Vietnamese — along with the South Koreans, plus the few Australians and New Zealanders serving in the country — to protect the interior, including the vital installations at Tan Son Nhut, Bien Hoa, and Long Binh. Had the enemy been able to conceal the military buildup around the cities more thoroughly, the Tet offensive might have caused far more damage.[18]

As early as mid-December 1967, an informal intelligence group in the basement of the White House had become convinced, mainly on the basis of translations of prisoner of war interrogations and captured documents, that an enemy offensive was in the making. Four individuals made up this group: Walt W. Rostow, special assistant to the President for national security affairs; Brig. Gen. Robert N. Ginsburgh, an Air Force officer serving as a senior member of Dr. Rostow's staff; Art McCafferty, director of the White House situation room; and Mary Lee Chatternuck, secretary for the team, who screened the translations, calling attention to pertinent items. The available evidence indicated an impending "winter/spring campaign" — which turned out to be the Tet offensive — with two possible objectives, either Khe Sanh in the far northwest or "towns like Hue." Although alert to the possibility of an attack, the White House group, like most analysts elsewhere, simply could not believe that the enemy could maintain pressure on the Marine outpost and launch simultaneous assaults throughout South Vietnam.[19]

Meanwhile, isolated bits of intelligence were surfacing in South Vietnam, revealing the possibility of assaults on Tan Son Nhut and Bien Hoa. These clues proved to be fragments of a plan to take advantage of the Tet holiday and seize major U.S. air bases and military installations.[20] Since reports pointing toward an offensive formed but a small fraction of the 600 items that might reach intelligence specialists in a single day, they disappeared in the torrent of data and caused no particular alarm. The assistance command continued planning to use South Vietnamese troops for protecting Saigon, for example, while U.S. forces normally based near the capital took the offensive "in the more remote areas."[21] Early in January 1968, however, General Westmoreland reconsidered the policy of entrusting the defense of Saigon to South Vietnamese units.

His change of plan apparently resulted from a conference on January 10 with Lt. Gen. Frederick G. Weyand, the Army officer in command of II Field Force, who was scheduled to shift the bulk of his forces from the vicinity of the capital to an operating area near the Cambodian border. Intelligence reports received over the weeks had convinced Weyand that Saigon was in danger. He outlined for General Westmoreland the evidence he had found so persuasive, and the senior commander decided to cancel part of the planned deployment, so that about fifteen U.S. Army battalions would be available to defend the city and the nearby installations.[22]

The Tet Offensive Begins

President Lyndon Johnson, Brig. Gen. Robert N. Ginsburgh, and Walt W. Rostow (left to right) examine a terrain map of the Khe Sanh area.

At the approach of Tet, other signs of impending action appeared, as the enemy recruited porters and made his final troop dispositions.[23] Although the various elements of intelligence now gleam like newly washed nuggets, at the time they lay buried among tons of gravel — interrogation reports, captured documents, and other information, some of it contradictory and much of it local in scope. A team of Department of Defense systems analysts, who studied the role of intelligence in the Tet offensive, concluded, "While there were reports of coordinated attacks on cities prior to the commencement of the Tet offensive, they were more like voices in the crowd than a warning of disaster." Indeed, the analysts sympathized with those intelligence specialists whose attention had remained focused on Khe Sanh and the border region. According to the findings of the inquiry, an officer reading the pertinent intelligence documents, though he would have expected "some sort of significant effort by the communists," could not have known where, when, or in what strength. He probably would have "guessed the DMZ" — the demilitarized zone north of Khe Sanh — as the marshaling area, and "shortly after Tet" as the time, but he would have had no idea of "the extent and scope of the effort." Whether in the White House basement, at the Pentagon, or at Westmoreland's headquarters in Saigon, most of those who studied the intelligence data did not grasp the magnitude or timing of the planned offensive.[24]

The military assistance command's attitude toward the 1968 Tet truce reflected an order of priority that emphasized the threat to Khe Sanh. In agreeing reluctantly to a holiday truce, in part to help sustain South Vietnamese morale, General Westmoreland specified that military operations continue in I Corps, where Khe Sanh was located, and in the demilitarized zone just to the north. In the region excluded from the Tet cease-fire, troops and air crews were to take "every precaution" to ensure "an absolute minimum of danger to or involvement

Air War over South Vietnam, 1968–1975

of any civilian populace." Westmoreland tried to limit the cease-fire, where it applied, to just twenty-four hours, but, as a concession to South Vietnam's President, Nguyen Van Thieu, he accepted a 36-hour truce to last from 6:00 p.m. local time on January 29 to 6:00 a.m. on January 31.[25]

Already concerned that the North Vietnamese and Viet Cong would attack Saigon during their self-proclaimed seven-day truce, scheduled to last from January 27 to February 3, General Weyand took note of the continuing hostile activity near the capital and on the evening of the 29th alerted his troops. When the enemy did strike, however, his first blows fell not on Saigon, as Weyand had anticipated, but on Da Nang, Nha Trang, Kontum, Hoi An, Qui Nhon, and Pleiku, all to the north of the capital. These attacks, launched some twenty-four hours before the main effort, prompted the South Vietnamese high command to order an alert throughout the country. Unfortunately, the nation's armed forces had no way to recall the thousands of men given holiday leave, many of whom did not have access to radio or telephone. Most units remained at about half strength when the Tet offensive erupted in full fury. As a result of the early attacks, General Westmoreland summoned all U.S. forces to maximum alert, issuing a last-minute warning that called attention to the danger of raids upon supply depots, troop billets, and population centers.[26]

The full extent of the Tet offensive gradually revealed itself to eyes fixed upon Khe Sanh. Indeed, the belief lingered that the North Vietnamese intended to make Khe Sanh a second Dien Bien Phu, storming the Marine combat base in an attempt to deliver the same devastating blow to American resolve that the fall of Dien Bien Phu, some fourteen years earlier, had inflicted on the French.[27] As late as mid-February, for instance, President Johnson spoke of enemy plans to overrun Khe Sanh and attack eastward to "plant his flag on the free soil of the Republic of Vietnam."[28]

The allocation of air strikes during the crucial first three days of the Tet offensive reflected the importance placed on Khe Sanh. The number of sorties flown in support of the Marine base increased by eighty-eight — fifty-one by fighter-bombers and thirty-seven by B-52s — over the three days preceding the urban attacks.[29] The isolated bastion required a large share of the aerial transport available at this time, for the 6,000 defenders relied almost exclusively on Air Force cargo planes to fly in the food, munitions, and medicine that normally would have come by truck convoy. Luckily, an emergency airlift had already replaced the 1,500 tons of ammunition destroyed on January 21 when North Vietnamese shells detonated the main munitions dump.[30]

Though American planners considered an assault on Khe Sanh understandable, albeit foolhardy, in view of the aerial might available for its defense, the objectives established by the enemy for the Tet offensive all but defied belief. In his Tet exhortation to the Vietnamese, Ho Chi Minh, North Vietnam's chief of state, vowed to "restore power to the people, completely liberate [the] 14 million people of South Vietnam, [and] fulfill our revolutionary task of estab-

The Tet Offensive Begins

Hue, during the Tet fighting, from across the Perfume River.

lishing democracy throughout the country." These spectacular accomplishments — which to American eyes appeared impossible — would result from the "greatest battle ever fought in the history of our country," an engagement requiring "many sacrifices." The victory gained through these efforts, Ho declared, would "decide the fate and survival of our fatherland and ... shake the world and cause the most bitter failure to the imperialist ringleaders."[31]

North Vietnamese military doctrine, rooted in communist ideology rather than military experience, looked to a general uprising in Vietnam's towns and cities, a thunderclap to signal the triumph of communist arms. According to this mythology, which ran counter to actual experience in the war with France, conventional combat units and citizen guerrillas would isolate the population centers, and the oppressed urban masses would then rise up to effect their liberation. This certainly had not happened against the French, who realized after their defeat, largely by regular troops, at Dien Bien Phu in the far-off northwestern highlands that they could not win the long, bloody, and expensive war. Perhaps the enemy, in mounting the 1968 Tet offensive, sought deliberately or instinctively to duplicate the effect of Dien Bien Phu, demoralizing the American people by attacking a number of towns simultaneously instead of overwhelming a single bastion.[32]

If the North Vietnamese and Viet Cong who suddenly appeared on the streets of Saigon actually expected a spontaneous uprising, they encountered cruel disappointment, for few citizens took up arms beside them. On the other hand, government authorities received few warnings of the secret gathering of North Vietnamese and Viet Cong soldiers. Some families sought to ingratiate themselves with the attackers by giving them token assistance, such as food and water, while others shunned any involvement and simply barricaded themselves

Air War over South Vietnam, 1968–1975

in their homes. The communists harangued the citizenry to rise up and sometimes kidnapped or executed previously identified government officials, but neither speeches nor terror had much impact. In general, the inhabitants of Saigon displayed apathy toward both sides, withholding support from the assault forces but also refusing to turn them in.[33]

Although the enemy at Saigon seemed indecisive in trying to marshal popular support, relying mainly on rallies reinforced by occasional terrorism, at Hue he quickly established leadership committees to rule the captured city and then set about killing those who might oppose him. Throughout the Tet offensive, even at Saigon, the attackers seemed to know precisely where to find members of the opposition, but only at Hue did communist cadres systematically ferret them out — American nonmilitary officials, South Vietnamese soldiers or police, several Roman Catholic priests, or other influential persons — and herd them off for re-education, in this case a euphemism for murder. During the weeks that communist forces ruled Hue, executioners killed some 2,800 people, most of them listed by Viet Cong intelligence as being enemies of the new order. In addition to these carefully chosen victims, the number executed almost certainly included relatives or associates of persons on the list, along with some who simply were misidentified. This bloodshed, instead of consolidating the power of the city's conquerors, created a climate of fear and hatred that resulted in acts of revenge after the recapture of Hue, when the communist cadre members in turn became prisoners.[34]

Assisted by underground sympathizers who kept quiet about infiltrating troops and singled out those South Vietnamese hostile to the communist revolution, North Vietnamese regulars and Viet Cong guerrillas suddenly brought the war to South Vietnam's towns and principal cities. No general uprising occurred, however, and Air Force security police helped beat back the initial assaults on key air bases, although hostile gunners continued to harass these installations through February and March. Suddenly caught up in battle, the officers and airmen in these security detachments helped defeat attacks on Tan Son Nhut and Bien Hoa that could have delayed and weakened the Air Force response to the Tet offensive. As it turned out, despite casualties and aircraft losses, the reconnaissance, tactical fighter, observation, bombardment, and transport squadrons promptly carried the war to the enemy, locating and attacking his forces and shuttling troops and cargo among the embattled towns.

Chapter Two

The Enemy Repulsed

Once the American and South Vietnamese forces had beaten back the sudden attacks on the air bases, General Westmoreland sought to defeat the enemy country-wide, systematically using air power to support counterattacks designed to regain total control of Saigon, Hue, and the other cities. To help him achieve his objective, the Seventh Air Force devoted roughly 70 percent of its sorties during February to those activities later categorized as close combat and logistics support of ground forces.

Of some 56,000 operational sorties flown in South Vietnam that month by fixed-wing aircraft of the Seventh Air Force, 43,000 supported the war on the ground, support that included tactical reconnaissance, combat support, airlift, and attack. Tactical reconnaissance accounted for about 10,000 sorties, producing visual sightings by forward air controllers as well as aerial photographs and infrared imagery. Not quite 2,500 were classified as combat support, limited at the time to battlefield illumination, defoliation, and psychological warfare missions. Another 19,000 airlift sorties flown by Air Force transports carried men or material needed by tactical units. The number of attack sorties flown during February exceeded 10,000 — almost one operational sortie in six — with 70 percent of them providing close air support to ground units and the rest attempting to interdict enemy movement. In addition, the 3d Air Division flew 1,291 B–52 sorties against targets in South Vietnam, missions designed to kill enemy troops, destroy supplies, or disrupt lines of supply and communication.

The Tet attacks thus triggered a month of sustained aerial warfare in support of ground operations throughout South Vietnam. Besides the squadrons of the Seventh Air Force, tactical fighters, attack planes, and light bombers of the Navy, Marine Corps, South Vietnamese Air Force, and Royal Australian Air Force participated in the February fighting. The 10,000-odd attack sorties flown by the Air Force represented slightly more than half the monthly total for February. Marine aviators flew about 27 percent of the February attack sorties, Navy airmen 8 percent, the South Vietnamese 11 percent, and the Australians 1 percent. During the response to the Tet offensive, support of ground forces — whether with aerial transport, reconnaissance, dropping flares or propaganda leaflets, close air support, or aerial interdiction — served as the focal point for American air power.[1]

Before joining in this response to the Tet offensive, many Air Force units had to recover from the first stunning blows delivered by the North Vietnamese and Viet Cong. Although a nationwide alert had gone into effect after the January 30 attacks on Da Nang and five other cities north of Saigon, the street fighting that broke out in the capital and elsewhere some 24 hours later prevented airmen who had not yet returned to their posts from getting there. Moreover, some aircraft crews, especially those delivering cargo or on routine courier missions, found themselves either trapped on the ground at bases under attack or unable to land at destinations raked by hostile fire.

Key staff officers in Saigon could not reach Seventh Air Force headquarters at Tan Son Nhut. Such absences hampered the work of the tactical air control center in preparing the daily operations order that specified the number and type of tactical air sorties, the kinds of ordnance, and the times over target. For three days, while fighting raged in Saigon, no more than three officers handled this essential job.[2]

On January 31, Air Force and South Vietnamese airmen attacked their first target, a textile mill not far from Tan Son Nhut that the enemy had converted into a fortress. After the structure had been bombed and recaptured, the battle shifted to an enemy stronghold in the residential area around the Phu Tho racetrack, within striking distance of the air base. Throughout most of February, communist forces clung to the race course and its environs, launching thrusts from this region into Saigon proper and into Cholon, the Chinese quarter south of the airfield. By the end of the month, however, U.S. and South Vietnamese troops had eliminated the pocket and regained control of Saigon and nearby hamlets.[3]

Because the conflict had enveloped populated places, Air Force forward air controllers faced the unpleasant task of directing attacks against enemy forces that had taken over and fortified the homes of South Vietnamese civilians. One Air Force officer acknowledged that he had been reluctant to direct his first strike against a suburb of Saigon. He described the target as "a nice little town, a pretty place, very picturesque," where the Viet Cong had dug in. He experienced this uneasiness even though he was following rules of engagement that required him to have clearance from South Vietnamese authorities before calling down bombs or artillery fire on any inhabited place. In this case, an American ground commander assured him that the local South Vietnamese province chief had evacuated the town, but even so he found "it was difficult to start putting in...ordnance," for he knew, "before the day was out we were going to make a lot of people homeless."[4]

Around Saigon and elsewhere, U.S. airmen observed complicated rules of engagement that, among other things, required that an appropriate South Vietnamese authority approve air strikes or artillery fire in or near population cen-

The Enemy Repulsed

A Royal Australian Air Force Canberra over South Vietnam.

ters or in close proximity to South Vietnamese troops. Even though the rules placed responsibility on officials expected to be concerned about the lives and welfare of their fellow citizens, the enemy had converted the cities into battlefields, at least in part to demonstrate the weakness of the Saigon government, and urban destruction proved unavoidable. Within most of the towns or cities attacked at Tet, American firepower contributed comparatively little to the devastation, for South Vietnamese troops, supported by their own artillery and aviation and acting with the consent of their own authorities, did the greater share of the fighting.[5]

A widely publicized example of urban destruction — the battle for Ben Tre — involved American, rather than South Vietnamese, artillery and air power. Two Viet Cong battalions infiltrated the town, roughly 35 miles southwest of Saigon, and attacked on the morning of January 31, taking the South Vietnamese defenders completely by surprise. When dawn broke, the only friendly forces in Ben Tre were seventy or eighty U.S. advisers and a handful of South Vietnamese soldiers, holding out near the center of town. An American infantry brigade went to the rescue, but became pinned down by Viet Cong troops firing from the cover of houses and other buildings. Realizing that his men had to have additional firepower to fight their way through, the brigade commander obtained approval for the use of mortars, artillery, and air strikes against enemy strongpoints within the town.

One of the forward air controllers working with the brigade, Maj. James Gibson, shared the normal reluctance to attack a populated area. "We would have preferred not to operate within the cities," he said, "and our choice has never been to operate in the cities — that is the philosophy of our brigade, and from what I have been able to read and understand, it is the philosophy of the United States military services in this country." At Ben Tre, however, the enemy had selected the battleground, leaving the brigade commander and South

Air War over South Vietnam, 1968–1975

Devastation from the Tet attacks in the Cholon district of Saigon.

Vietnamese authorities the choice, in Gibson's opinion, of either using overwhelming firepower or allowing the leading elements of the relief force to be "pretty well wiped out."

As Major Gibson remembered the battle, parts of Ben Tre already lay in ruins when he arrived above the town. He and his fellow forward air controllers promptly directed seven strikes against enemy emplacements within an eight-block area in the comparatively untouched eastern section of the city. These attacks, he believed, "killed the VC [Viet Cong] offensive in that part of town." Gibson and the other forward air controllers also called down artillery fire, since they could, from their slow-moving planes, keep track of the advance on the ground and pinpoint the centers of enemy resistance. By the evening of February 2, the Americans controlled the ruins of Ben Tre, but two days of mopping up lay ahead.[6]

After the recapture of Ben Tre, where 500 or more noncombatants may have died, an anonymous "U.S. major" declared: "It became necessary to destroy the town in order to save it." This widely quoted comment, which seemed to summarize the contradiction between American aims and accomplishments in the Vietnam war, riveted attention upon Ben Tre and the death or displacement of civilians. Indeed, at Ben Tre more noncombatants perished than soldiers, though the exact number of civilian deaths could not be verified. Although subsequent news stories challenged the first estimates of property destroyed and spoke of Ben Tre's recovery, the officer's words raised the question whether the United States could build a nation, the Republic of South Vietnam, by waging a destructive war on its territory. At Ben Tre, if not elsewhere, bombs and shells seemed to be destroying the very thing the United States claimed to be trying to nurture, a self-sustaining society. The path to independence dead-ended at the refugee camp.[7]

The Enemy Repulsed

Air power, whether American or South Vietnamese, also lent its destructive might to the recapture of other towns, among them Phuoc Le, the capital of Phuoc Tuy, a coastal province southeast of Saigon. Although the Viet Cong, some 700-strong, did not attack here until the early morning of February 1, air support responded slowly, for by this time it was needed throughout the country. Before dawn, an Air Force O–1 based at the Phuoc Le airstrip took off on a routine patrol and began dropping flares, and soon discovered the approaching enemy, whose fire prevented the aircraft from landing. Meanwhile, hostile fire began grazing the path from the pilots' quarters to their parked planes, a passage that one officer described as "Death Valley." Despite the danger, the controllers crossed Death Valley to reach their O–1s, take off, and continue the battle from a more secure flying field.

The early reports proved so vague that South Vietnamese authorities and American commanders hesitated to approve air strikes on the town. The defenders had to wait some three hours before their request for air support produced a handful of Army helicopter gunships. These aircraft used their multi-barrel machineguns to strafe the Viet Cong who had closed the airstrip and laid siege to the American and South Vietnamese headquarters in the heart of town. For much of the day, one Army and two Air Force observation planes circled overhead, directing both armed helicopters and the fighter-bombers that joined them in attacking targets in and around the provincial capital. Late in the afternoon, the Viet Cong, battered from the air and prodded by South Vietnamese troops entering the town, began to retreat.[8]

Elsewhere, an eleven-day battle raged for control of Da Lat, some 135 miles northeast of Saigon. Since Da Lat had never before come under communist attack, even though it was the site of the national military academy, the Tet assault had shocked the irregular troops and military police defending the town. Before the startled eyes of this small garrison, Viet Cong seemed to appear simultaneously throughout Da Lat, but the attackers could not take full advantage of surprise. Between them and victory stood the first-year students from the military academy, the only class that had not received holiday leave. These young men set up a blocking position in the city, causing the enemy to hesitate long enough for the local commander, Maj. Dao Mong Xuan, to organize the ill-trained students. Legend has it that several American soldiers, spending the night on the upper stories of a downtown bordello, heard firing from the streets below, reached the major by telephone, and alerted him to the direction in which the attackers were moving, enabling him to deploy his force appropriately.

Whether or not he benefitted from this particular intelligence source, the South Vietnamese commander's hurriedly organized defense stopped the Viet Cong, forcing them to dig in and await reinforcements, which unaccountably proved late in arriving. By setting up a perimeter inside the city, the enemy provided a well-defined target for air power and artillery, but forward air controllers to direct this firepower were scarce. To meet the need, Col. Philip Erdle, a pilot as well as a professor at the Air Force Academy, volunteered to help. Erdle had come to Da Lat to advise the staff of the South Vietnamese military academy on organizing an engineering curriculum, but in this emergency he commandeered an O–1 and helped handle the seventy-four sorties flown by Seventh Air Force and South Vietnamese planes.

Aided by these strikes, South Vietnamese rangers and infantrymen drove the Viet Cong from Da Lat. The bombing destroyed about 200 homes and other structures, and perhaps fifty noncombatants died in the battle. The destruction and loss of civilian life here proved far less than at Ben Tre, but more than at Phuoc Le in Phuoc Tuy Province.[9]

If the fighting at Da Lat seemed typical of the Tet offensive — suddenly begun, bitterly fought, but involving comparatively few troops and over in a short time — the battle at Hue more closely resembled the urban combat of World War II in terms of duration, ferocity, and numbers involved. American Marines and soldiers, along with South Vietnamese troops, waged a struggle that began on January 31, the first day of Tet, but did not end until February 24 and the elimination of the last pocket of Viet Cong resistance within the walled city. The unfurling of South Vietnam's red-and-yellow flag over the recaptured palace verified the failure of the entire Tet offensive, though mopping up in and around Hue continued for another week.[10]

During the early days of the fighting at Hue, South Vietnamese officials sought to minimize damage to the city and casualties among its inhabitants by forbidding the use of artillery, napalm, and high-explosive aerial bombs. Through the evening of February 3, the counterattacking forces relied on direct-fire weapons — rifles, machineguns, tank guns, and recoilless rifles — supplemented by tear gas, in a house-by-house battle. The exhausting and bloody struggle, however, prompted the South Vietnamese to lift these restrictions for much of the modern city. Two days later, they lifted restrictions for the ancient Citadel. After February 5, air power could join with artillery in engaging targets throughout most of the city, although certain structures — temples and public or historic buildings — could not be bombed or shelled.

Despite the change of policy, the weather prevented air power from playing a decisive role in the fighting at Hue. Daytime cloud cover and low-lying fog that persisted through most mornings limited the total number of combat sorties by tactical aircraft to about 150, one-third of them by Marine aviators. At night, when fog and cloud usually abated, Marine and Air Force planes flew almost 50 strikes, usually following instructions from radar operators on the ground. To avoid endangering American and South Vietnamese troops fighting in the midst of the city, where only the thickness of a wall might separate friend from enemy, the night strikes engaged targets on the outskirts of Hue where clearly defined radar checkpoints existed or the enemy could otherwise be pinpointed.[11]

Progress on the ground remained slow, however, and South Vietnam's leaders grew impatient. On February 10, Vice President Nguyen Cao Ky, former

The Enemy Repulsed

The Imperial Palace in Hue, damaged during the Tet fighting.

commander of the South Vietnamese Air Force, and a dozen of the country's military and civilian leaders visited the strife-torn city, where they talked with the U.S. officers directing the battle — Gen. Creighton W. Abrams of the Army and two Marines, Lt. Gen. Robert E. Cushman, Jr. and Brig. Gen. Foster C. LaHue. The discussion focused on the enemy's practice of fortifying schools such as Hue University, public buildings like the city post office, and even historic or religious shrines. Vice President Ky weighed the lives of American and South Vietnamese soldiers against the value of such structures and accepted responsibility for the damage that would result from using whatever supporting weapons might be needed to dislodge the enemy. Within the week, the South Vietnamese corps commander for the northern provinces, Lt. Gen. Huong Xuan Lam, specifically authorized air strikes against the historic palace itself, which served as a Viet Cong redoubt. Most of the bombs dropped within the Citadel, however, exploded on targets between the palace and the southwest wall.[12]

The battle for Hue helped alienate an individual uniquely able to shape American public opinion. The members of the press visiting the city included Walter Cronkite, a popular and influential television commentator, who had initially accepted the idea that the United States was successfully waging war to help the South Vietnamese create a nation. By the outbreak of the Tet offensive in 1968, however, he had begun to doubt reports of steady progress, and the house-by-house fighting that he saw at Hue further disillusioned him. He came away convinced not only that the enemy was far more tenacious than American officials had been willing to admit, but also that the conflict was destroying, rather than building, a South Vietnamese nation. His televised "Report from Vietnam," broadcast on February 27, struck a pessimistic note, emphasizing the surprise achieved by the enemy, detailing the havoc caused by the Tet fighting, and predicting that the "bloody experience of Vietnam" would likely "end in a stalemate."[13]

Although the destruction that Cronkite reported, along with the remarks about Ben Tre attributed to the anonymous major, might imply otherwise, U.S. forces continued to observe rules of engagement prescribing the circumstances in which various weapons could be used. As before, South Vietnamese authorities had to approve specific targets, though they might designate general areas subject to aerial attack without further review. Both the South Vietnamese corps commander and his American counterpart had to agree before air strikes could take place within an inhabited place. Psychological warfare planes had to warn civilians to flee, either by dropping leaflets or making loudspeaker broadcasts, before the first bomb fell. The rules also specified that a forward air controller in contact with forces on the ground direct the bombing. If the enemy, as he had during the Tet offensive, took refuge in shrines, temples, or similar buildings, senior American or South Vietnamese commanders on the scene might approve air attacks without consulting a higher headquarters. Should the war return to the Citadel at Hue, however, the allies were to use tear gas and direct-fire weapons before resorting to aerial bombardment or artillery fire.

Such in general were the revised rules of engagement governing combat in towns. Since commanders and local officials had to apply them to specific situations, the regulations could not in themselves prevent the death of noncombatants and the destruction of their property. As had happened during the Tet fighting, the safety of friendly forces or the need to destroy the enemy might again outweigh a genuine desire to protect the civilian populace.[14]

A concern for South Vietnamese noncombatants kept General Westmoreland from using Boeing B–52s in the urban battles, where their large, devastating bombing pattern would have endangered not only civilians but friendly troops, sometimes just a grenade's throw from the enemy. As a result, these planes supported the counteroffensive on the ground by flying some 200 sorties during February against troop concentrations, base areas, and supply routes a safe distance from South Vietnamese towns and villages.

Khe Sanh remained the focus of B–52 activity in South Vietnam during the month. More than 1,000 of the 1,500 sorties flown against targets in the South hit the enemy forces massed in the vicinity of that base. In addition, most of the 170 targets bombed in Laos contributed directly to the security of Khe Sanh.[15]

A key individual in selecting B–52 targets at this time was Marine Lt. Gen. John R. Chaisson, the director of General Westmoreland's combat operations center, a joint organization with Air Force representation. The major ground combat units sent their requests for air support to Chaisson and his staff, who arranged them in order of priority and apportioned the total available sorties, beginning with the most important targets. Although encirclement of Khe Sanh and attacks on the cities triggered additional target nominations, the assistance

The Enemy Repulsed

command had at its disposal a greater number of B–52 sorties than ever before. From 800 per month, the number of sorties authorized by the Joint Chiefs of Staff increased to 1,200 (40 per day) on January 22 and to 1,800 (60 per day) on February 15. In order to fly the approved 60 sorties each day, the Strategic Air Command had to place at General Westmoreland's call a force of 26 B–52s deployed to the Pacific after North Korean motor gunboats captured the U.S. communications intelligence ship *Pueblo* on January 23. By mid-February, 104 B–52 bombers stood ready to support ground operations in Southeast Asia — 66 on Guam; 23 in Thailand; and 15 on Okinawa.[16]

Although under the "command control" of the Strategic Air Command, which could reconvert them in a matter of hours to carry hydrogen bombs in the event of nuclear war, the B–52s stationed in the Far East served as Westmoreland's flying artillery, battering area targets too large for tactical fighters and usually beyond reach of the heaviest guns. After Chaisson's combat operations center had completed a slate of recommended targets for the B–52s, it submitted them for Westmoreland's approval. The recommendations reflected intelligence produced by Seventh Air Force, which in turn benefitted from advice given by the Strategic Air Command Advance Echelon, a liaison agency located at Tan Son Nhut. A list containing proposed times of attack, the targets, and the recommended weight of effort then went to Andersen Air Force Base, Guam, where the 3d Air Division — later redesignated the Eighth Air Force — planned missions that normally hit the selected targets about forty-eight hours after they had been proposed to General Chaisson.[17]

Normally, Westmoreland readily approved the slate of targets presented by Chaisson. In the event the schedule of strikes had to be adjusted in the middle of the night, Chaisson usually did not awaken Westmoreland but made any necessary alteration on his own initiative, waiting to explain the change in the morning when the commander arrived at headquarters. The threat to Khe Sanh, however, and the Tet offensive persuaded Westmoreland to move from his residence to the headquarters, where he began closely supervising B–52 activity. Each evening, after a briefing that covered all four tactical zones or corps areas, he approved a schedule of B–52 strikes, and on the following morning, he reviewed the latest intelligence on previous attacks. In short, Westmoreland was, in Chaisson's phrase, "personally ... fingering the targets." Although Chaisson could offer "side comments and all that," Westmoreland usually "would just say ... these are the ones we are going on." Occasionally, he might establish "a flat priority," directing Chaisson to concentrate the available sorties for a specific purpose — the defense of Khe Sanh, for instance — but allowing his subordinates to select the exact targets.[18]

Upon receipt of the compilation from Westmoreland's headquarters, the 3d Air Division, commanded at the time of the Tet fighting by Maj. Gen. Selmon W. Wells, began planning the attacks, even as higher headquarters were reviewing the targets. The same list that General Wells received, called a strike request, went also to the Commander in Chief, Strategic Air Command, Gen. Joseph J. Nazzaro; to the Commander in Chief, Pacific, Adm. U. S. Grant Sharp; and to the Joint Chiefs of Staff. For some overriding reason, such as interference with another more critical activity, any of the reviewers might veto a strike. If they remained silent, and they usually did, the 3d Air Division headquarters issued an operations order for the specific day, formally authorizing the attacks and establishing takeoff times.

Radar operators in Southeast Asia directed the actual bombing, using the Combat Skyspot radar targeting equipment and techniques developed over the years. After the arrival of the day's operations order issued by the 3d Air Division, the Combat Skyspot radar teams made the necessary calculations that would enable the ground controllers to tell each mission when and where to release its bombs. The considerations in determining a release point included the speed and altitude of the aircraft, ballistic characteristics of the bombs, and nature and location of the target.

The B–52 crews reported the results of their missions — those fires and secondary explosions visible four miles in the air — but the magnitude of effort proved easier to calculate than results, and that sort of data proved essential for logistics and manpower planning. A record of munitions dropped and hours flown entered the maw of a computer in the Pentagon, forming an automated data base used in supplying the 3d Air Division with bombs, fuel, spare parts, and replacement crews.[19]

To help General Westmoreland bring the B–52s to bear against enemy concentrations around Khe Sanh, the Strategic Air Command on February 15 adopted so-called Bugle Note procedures, capable of focusing as many as forty-eight sorties per day against targets near the base. To do so, the 3d Air Division designated two pre-initial points where approaching three-plane B–52 cells came under control of a Combat Skyspot radar that routed each cell to one of several initial points and then to a target. Thailand-based bombers approaching Khe Sanh from the west checked in at one pre-initial point, while those coming from the east, dispatched from Guam or Okinawa, used the other. Cells took off alternately from western and eastern airfields so that the bombers arrived at their pre-initial points about ninety minutes apart throughout the day. By carefully selecting initial points, a radar controller could vary the interval between strikes so that one might follow another by as little as half an hour or as much as two hours, thus avoiding an overly rigid, easily predictable pattern.

As anticipated, Bugle Note demonstrated that maintaining a steady, around-the-clock launch rate eased the burden of arming, fueling, and servicing the bombers, but minor changes in the procedure proved necessary. For example, the arrival at the pre-initial point of two cells every three hours, instead of one every ninety minutes, not only doubled the weight of explosives that could be dropped on a single target box but allowed time to evaluate a strike before the next cells of B–52s arrived. General Westmoreland expressed pleasure with

The Enemy Repulsed

Khe Sanh combat base. The craters in the hills at the top of the picture attest to the intensity and accuracy of the air bombardment at Khe Sanh.

Bugle Note, and soon other pre-initial points were designated for radar controlled B–52 strikes elsewhere in South Vietnam.[20]

In spite of General Westmoreland's satisfaction with B–52 effectiveness, questions persisted concerning the results of their use. After more than two years of bombing, the evidence of success remained tenuous at best, consisting of air crew reports, aerial photographs, some prisoner of war interrogations, and occasional reports from friendly troops following up a raid. Unfortunately, the bombing usually took place deep in enemy territory where ground reconnaissance was impossible or in jungle that impeded photography, and the testimony of thoroughly shaken survivors of B–52 attacks was contradicted by statements from prisoners whose units had evaded the bombers. One Viet Cong defector told an Air Force interrogator, "We always get a two-day warning."[21]

Although that may well have been an exaggeration, several hours' advance notice could have come from agents among the thousands of Vietnamese employed at Tan Son Nhut where the target list was prepared, at bases in Thailand that launched B–52s or those in South Vietnam that provided support aircraft, or at the various American and South Vietnamese headquarters that received notice of B–52 attacks. The enemy, moreover, had other means of learning from thirty minutes to several hours ahead of time that a B–52 strike was imminent. Soviet trawlers off Guam, for instance, reported the takeoff times and numbers of bombers. North Vietnamese or Viet Cong communications analysts might pick up radar jamming signals, indicating that the cells and their escort would pass near radar-controlled guns or missiles. Intercepted radio traffic, using infrequently changed call signs, might reveal the approach of the bombers and

Air War over South Vietnam, 1968–1975

their location at the moment, while the presence of any radar suppression escort was an additional clue to the general course the B–52s were following. Intelligence such as this, combined with the enemy's realization that certain units or base areas were especially vulnerable to pattern bombing, probably enabled the enemy to evade at least some B–52 strikes, provided he was not in actual contact with American or South Vietnamese ground forces and could move.[22]

Photo reconnaissance proved more helpful in defeating the Tet offensive than in obtaining day-to-day evidence of B–52 effectiveness. Reconnaissance crews based at Tan Son Nhut, for example, flew twenty-one missions on February 1, seeking out enemy activity within about an eight-mile radius of the base. Coverage expanded, even as the Tet offensive collapsed, as U.S. intelligence continued to watch for another series of urban attacks. By late April, these Tan Son Nhut airmen had flown ninety-two missions in South Vietnam and produced more than 180,000 feet of film. To help process and analyze this photographic data, along with that obtained outside the country, Seventh Air Force requested the assignment of sixty-four additional technicians, thirty-five of them photo interpreters. These specialists began arriving about March 1 and remained at Tan Son Nhut for sixty days.

Pictures taken during the weeks following Tet revealed hundreds of hastily dug emplacements in the vicinity of Saigon, ranging in purpose from storage pits to individual foxholes, but ground patrols found that some were the work of friendly troops, who had deployed in response to the initial Tet attacks and then moved on. The photo interpreters did, however, detect new hostile deployments, including 37-mm antiaircraft guns dug in along the A Shau Valley infiltration route and around Khe Sanh. In March, after the Tet offensive had ended, General Westmoreland's troops discovered a cache of ammunition for the Soviet-built 23-mm antiaircraft gun, a further indication that the enemy in South Vietnam no longer relied upon concealment, supplemented by light automatic weapons, for defense against air attack.[23]

Before the photo reconnaissance crews had begun systematically seeking out the Tet attackers, forward air controllers went aloft in search of the enemy. Unfortunately, hostile fire forced some controllers to abandon the airstrips from which they usually operated and to find bases less vulnerable to attack. All forward air controllers in the northern provinces of Thua Thien and Quang Tri, where Khe Sanh was located, had to retreat briefly to the comparative safety of Da Nang. As a result, the twin-engine Cessna O–2A observation plane, with five-hour endurance, had to spend two hours flying to and from the surrounded Marine base.[24]

Like the forward air controllers in northernmost South Vietnam, a large number of transport crews found themselves caught up in the fury of the Tet offensive. Maj. Billy G. Gibson, a Lockheed C–130 pilot, took off from Cam Ranh Bay on January 30 to carry men and cargo to several airfields. He arrived over Ban Me Thuot, site of the earliest Tet attack, as enemy fire was scourging

The Enemy Repulsed

the runway. The control tower operator warned him not to descend below 6,000 feet, an altitude safely beyond the effective range of Viet Cong heavy machineguns. Unable to complete the scheduled mission, Gibson returned to the quiet of Cam Ranh Bay and unloaded. For the next few days, he flew from Cam Ranh Bay, easily the most secure of South Vietnamese air bases, to Qui Nhon, Da Nang, and Chu Lai. During each landing, he recalled, his crew could see explosions on the ground and hear artillery at the perimeter, but the airmen were never close to the explosions.[25]

Cam Ranh Bay, where Gibson's plane was based, became a refuge for C–130s that normally operated from Tan Son Nhut. The new arrivals included a transport flown by Capt. Lloyd J. Probst, which had been approaching Tan Son Nhut when the Tet attack began. After circling for what seemed like hours, Probst received instructions to fly to Cam Ranh Bay, which served as his operating base for the next few days.

Crews aloft when the Tet fighting erupted fared better than those who were off-duty in their quarters at hotels like the Marlin, a short distance from the airfield itself. After receiving reports of gunfire near the hotel, a duty officer at Tan Son Nhut told the airmen to return immediately to the airfield. Four officers at the Marlin failed to get the word, however, and were trapped when the Viet Cong attacked the building. Although the enemy killed one guard, others kept the assault team from advancing beyond the lobby, saving the lives of the unarmed crew members barricaded behind a door on an upper floor.[26]

Scattered among several billets in Saigon, the crews of the Fairchild C–123s operating out of Tan Son Nhut did not receive a recall notice and were cut off by the January 31 fighting. Relief crews had to be flown in from Phan Rang for the C–123s, since the 834th Air Division, the headquarters responsible for airlift in South Vietnam, had decided to transfer these aircraft and all other Tan Son Nhut-based transports not parked in protective revetments to safer airfields. Within forty-eight hours, the stranded crewmen made their way to Tan Son Nhut and caught flights to Phan Rang where they rejoined their assigned airplanes.

On the eve of the Tet offensive, a squadron of seventeen UC–123 spray planes stood ready to scatter herbicide that either stripped away the enemy's jungle concealment or destroyed crops that fed Viet Cong guerrillas. When the Tet offensive began, most of the South Vietnamese who pumped herbicide into the aircraft were on holiday leave, and the fighting — Bien Hoa, like Tan Son Nhut, was the objective of direct attack — kept them from returning. Even though defoliation missions might have proved helpful by depriving the enemy of the foliage that screened him, air transport seemed more important. Air Force mechanics therefore began removing the rubber chemical tanks so the UC–123s could again carry supplies and ammunition. By February 5, all had been reconverted to transports, and by the end of the month they had delivered some 3,500 tons of cargo among the various airstrips in South Vietnam.[27]

Air War over South Vietnam, 1968–1975

Reconversion of the UC–123s represented one means of coping with the disruption of tactical airlift caused by the Tet onslaught. Shelling or ground attack forced transports to evacuate or avoid certain airfields at the very time that widespread fighting required the rapid movement of men and cargo throughout the country. In these circumstances, the airlift control center scrapped its usual practice of devoting 90 percent of all cargo missions to routinely scheduled resupply and the remaining 10 percent to emergencies. So many crises arose immediately after the Tet holiday that the center had to establish degrees of emergency. By February 2, however, high priority items jammed the terminals, and organizations filling emergency requests began to assign top priority to every order, frustrating the arrangement. The passage of time and diminution of backlogs, rather than arbitrary priorities, finally sorted things out.

The volume of cargo delivered and number of passengers carried declined sharply in the immediate aftermath of the Tet offensive. Crews could not get to their planes, airfields came under attack and shut down for hours at a time, preventing transports from reaching their destinations, and schedules meant nothing. On January 30, the airlift system had transported the usual 3,500 tons, but on the following day, as widespread fighting disrupted planned flights, the amount of cargo declined by almost 1,500 tons, and the number of passengers underwent a similar reduction. Within four days, however, aerial transport had rebounded, though this recovery did not signal a return to peak efficiency.

With many roads closed, fighting all over the country, and speed of movement the main consideration, Air Force transports took off partially loaded with critical cargo or shuttled frantically between bases instead of making longer flights, touching down at several airfields in succession to unload or take on shipments. The number of sorties therefore rose, although flying hours declined, a combination that indicated inefficient operation. Yet, until the crisis passed, efficiency remained a secondary consideration. C–130s and C–123s were doing the work of trucks, as demonstrated early in the Tet fighting when transports carried troops a mere fourteen miles, flying from Tan Son Nhut to Duc Hoa because the enemy had cut the road.[28]

The need to move troops and cargo as rapidly as possible increased the demand for C–130s, the largest tactical transport flown by the Air Force. Under normal conditions, sixty-odd C–130s could have flown the necessary logistical and troop carrier sorties, operating in a manner that avoided overcrowding air bases, cargo terminals, or aircraft maintenance facilities. The frenzied response to the Tet offensive disrupted efficiency, however, imposing a burden that this number of C–130s simply could not bear.

As a result, a total of ninety-six of these transports operated in South Vietnam during March. The additional C–130s from Japan and the Philippines caused overcrowding and further inefficiency, but in the tactical situation following Tet, more of the planes were needed, regardless of operating theory. Of the March total, sixteen flew down from Tachikawa, Japan, where thirty-two

The Enemy Repulsed

A load of cargo is pulled from an Air Force C–130 at Khe Sanh by a cable attached to the load that has snagged the runway's arrester cable. Using this system, the transport delivered cargo without landing.

C–130s had arrived in February. Half the Tachikawa contingent served in South Vietnam, changing places with the others, so that half remained available in Japan to support the U.S. buildup in South Korea following the North Vietnamese capture of the intelligence ship *Pueblo*.[29]

The South Vietnamese Air Force shared in the airlift and other missions flown in response to the Tet attacks. Fortunately, the headquarters staff heeded a January 31 alert, returning to Tan Son Nhut before the enemy struck. Such was not the case in most tactical units, however. The method of recall used for the squadrons at Tan Son Nhut, for instance, consisted of dispatching couriers on motor bikes, but because of Tet, many South Vietnamese airmen had left their listed billets to attend family reunions at unknown locations. As a result, U.S. Air Force advisers had to take over some maintenance and even flight duties during the three days that elapsed before most South Vietnamese squadrons returned to near-normal strength. Among those rejoining his unit was a squadron commander at Bien Hoa who had been taken prisoner by the Viet Cong, but managed to escape.[30]

South Vietnam's fighter-bomber squadrons, with almost ninety aircraft, entered the battle on the afternoon of January 31, helping U.S. Air Force North American F–100s attack enemy units dug in not far from Tan Son Nhut. By the end of February, South Vietnamese Douglas A–1s and Northrop F–5s had flown some 2,500 operational sorties, about 2,200 close support or interdiction and the others flak suppression or other forms of escort. Using roughly seventy helicopters, the South Vietnamese flew almost 3,200 operational hours during the month, carrying approximately 11,500 men and 220 tons of cargo. Especially valuable during the counterattacks were twenty-eight Douglas C–47 transports

Air War over South Vietnam, 1968–1975

that flew 800 sorties, shuttling 7,600 men and 320 tons of cargo among various airfields. These same transports flew an additional 200 sorties, dropping flares to illuminate battlefields at night or, if suitably modified, engaging in radio direction finding. One AC–47 gunship, used to train South Vietnamese crews in the use of side-firing machineguns, saw extensive action around Saigon.[31]

A high accident rate — during 1967 roughly ten times the U.S. Air Force rate — had become almost a hallmark of South Vietnam's Air Force,[32] but the problem subsided during the Tet counteroffensive, only to emerge again later in the conflict. During the hectic weeks following the enemy attacks, the South Vietnamese flew on weekends — normally a time for relaxation — at night, and in bad weather. "Although such conditions might be expected to increase accidents," wrote Brig. Gen. Donavon F. Smith, chief of the Air Force Advisory Group, he found that the reverse was true. He attributed the improved performance to "increased motivation stimulated by the crisis."[33] Perhaps the importance of these missions prompted inexperienced, careless, or overly bold pilots to fly with greater precision.

All in all, the South Vietnamese sustained few aircraft losses as a result of the Tet offensive. Of some 300 combat and administrative types on hand when it began, seventeen were lost during the following thirty days and two received major damage. Also destroyed was one C–119 transport used for training, while a second plane of this type sustained severe damage. The maximum effort made in response to the Tet offensive did, however, disrupt scheduled training.[34]

South Vietnamese UH–1 helicopters landing to pick up
South Vietnamese troops for an airmobile assault operation.

The Enemy Repulsed

The Tet offensive lasted until the end of February, when South Vietnamese and American troops at last regained control of Hue, its Citadel, and its suburbs. Beating back the enemy had required savage fighting, a fact reflected in the number of U.S. Air Force officers and men killed or wounded during that month, contrasted with the totals for earlier periods. Casualties within South Vietnam for February 1968 were 260, 39 of them killed, compared to 120 killed and wounded during the preceding month and 130 in February 1967. The initial Tet attacks and the fighting that ensued claimed thirty-two U.S. Air Force planes, more than twenty of them destroyed on the ground, compared to a monthly average of seven losses during 1967. Also during February, some 300 Air Force planes sustained battle damage, roughly eighty more than in a typical month of the previous year.[35]

Air Force casualties, though higher than usual, formed but a small fraction of the 450 Americans killed and more than 2,000 wounded each week during the month-long Tet battles.[36] The South Vietnamese, moreover, whether civilians or members of the armed forces, bore an even greater share of the suffering caused by the Tet offensive. After two weeks of fighting, for example, the South Vietnamese army had lost more than twice as many killed as the American ground forces. Although the number of noncombatant casualties remained elusive, an estimated 600,000 persons fled the ruins of their homes during February and sought shelter in refugee camps, some of them forced from one such makeshift haven to another.[37]

From a military standpoint, the enemy suffered grievously during the Tet offensive, gaining no permanent tactical advantage in return. Within thirty days, the South Vietnamese once again controlled the cities and were beginning to reassert their authority in the countryside. Ho Chi Minh's bid for victory might well have cost him half the attacking force, more than 30,000 regulars and guerrillas killed or made prisoner.[38]

Indeed, the Central Office for South Vietnam, the communist headquarters for operations in the South, acknowledged that the Tet offensive had failed to ignite the urban uprising that would have ended the war. Although confident that the South Vietnamese "revolution-minded masses" stood ready "to make any sacrifice in return for the country's genuine freedom and democracy," Ho's lieutenants reluctantly conceded that, "when confronted with the enemy's iron grip and oppressive control," the urban populace proved "hesitant and frightened." As might be expected, headquarters maintained that the offensive would have succeeded, if carried out with the proper military discipline and ideological zeal, and fixed the blame on those who had executed the plan. The cadres assigned to foment the uprising had lacked revolutionary zeal, the critique stated; military operations had received too much emphasis, political indoctrination too little, and control of both had been lax.[39]

Although the overall military results of the Tet offensive disappointed the enemy, the attacks at Tan Son Nhut and Bien Hoa came close enough to success to dramatize a number of weaknesses in air base defenses, including the poor protection afforded parked aircraft. Although existing revetments could absorb shell fragments in their earth-and-steel walls, a rocket or mortar round might plunge through the open top and destroy the airplane within. To correct this deficiency, Deputy Secretary of Defense Paul Nitze on March 6 approved the construction of 165 roofed shelters capable of withstanding hits from mortar shells and from all but the largest rockets. This decision launched a program that completed 373 steel-roofed shelters in South Vietnam by January 1970, when work came to an end. The evidence indicated that the shelters had repaid, in terms of damage prevented, the $15.7 million invested in them. Also 1,000 open revetments, better constructed than those in place at the time of the Tet attacks, complemented the more expensive roofed shelters.[40]

To prevent repetition of the frenzied activity of the morning of January 31, when Army truck drivers and radio technicians had grabbed rifles and deployed in provisional platoons to fight alongside lightly armed security police, the Air Force moved swiftly to strengthen its base defense forces in numbers and firepower. Reinforcements swelled the various base security detachments — at Tan Son Nhut, for example, the number of combat teams more than doubled — and the airmen assigned to them now received mortars, recoilless rifles, and similar light infantry weapons, as well as dependable radios. In April 1968, at Phan Rang Air Base, a 500-man quick reaction force took shape. Besides defending this airfield, its components could deploy by air to any other base in South Vietnam within two hours.[41]

Despite additional men, better weapons, and the construction of aircraft shelters, some aspects of air base security received only a short-lived impetus from the Tet offensive. The building of personnel shelters and the placement of sandbag revetments around the lower floors of barracks proceeded sporadically, prodded along by occasional shellings of a particular base. Other projects, such as installation of floodlights around defensive perimeters, waxed and waned in response to changing perceptions of the threat. The absence of a continuing program reflected the policy of short tours in Southeast Asia, which usually lasted only one year. Base commanders changed frequently and each had to learn for himself the danger on the ground. Also, construction priorities emphasized such morale-sustaining projects as theaters or exchanges, sometimes at the expense of base security.[42]

Besides demonstrating weaknesses in air base defense, the Tet offensive dramatized the importance of local intelligence, such as that provided by the area source program, administered since 1964 by the Air Force Office of Special Investigations. Within an eighteen-mile radius of each base used by the Air Force, the local program director recruited South Vietnamese agents to report suspicious occurrences, such as the sudden appearance of crude aiming stakes that might herald a nighttime rocket or mortar attack. The assaults upon air bases during the 1968 Tet holidays and the frequent shelling of these instal-

The Enemy Repulsed

Revetments built before 1968 (top) were open on top and susceptible to rocket attacks from overhead. Shelters built after the 1968 Tet attacks had steel arches on top, covered with eighteen inches of concrete.

lations in the weeks that followed demonstrated the need for such a program which, at its peak in late 1969, included some 400 civilian sources.[43]

The Tet offensive affected the civic action program, in which U.S. officers and enlisted men carried out inexpensive and informal welfare projects designed to create among the South Vietnamese a sense of loyalty to their government. Air Force personnel provided encouragement, instruction, financial aid, and even labor for a variety of self-help projects undertaken by South Vietnamese living near the air bases. These ventures ranged from aiding refugees to making souvenirs to sell to American troops to assisting in the construction of schools and dispensaries. In the field of medicine, however, emphasis rested on giving basic care to the sick and injured rather than training others to do so, although some South Vietnamese received rudimentary instruction in public health practices like disposing of waste and ensuring clean water.[44]

The Tet fighting, since it brought destruction to many communities near the Air Force bases, created an overriding need for emergency relief, usually in the form of food, cash, medical care, and building materials. American airmen, who recently had been shelled from some of the same villages that now needed their help, at first proved less than eager to volunteer their time or donate money for local relief projects sponsored by their units. Commanders, moreover, showed reluctance to allow those who did volunteer to go very far from base, especially at night, until South Vietnamese authorities restored security. Also, the South Vietnamese government inadvertently delayed recovery by enforcing draft laws so rigidly that many English-speaking interpreters and able-bodied laborers, essential elements of successful civic action, ended up in military units far from their war-ravaged villages.[45]

Although thousands of homes remained in ruins and hundreds of thousands of refugees were being cared for in camps, the military situation in South Vietnam at the end of February 1968 had turned against the North Vietnamese and Viet Cong. The enemy had persisted in fighting pitched battles when he could have pulled back and regrouped, as a result suffering staggering losses without gaining a permanent hold on the towns and cities. In much of the countryside, the South Vietnamese government seemed to be filling a power vacuum created by the Tet attacks, with the bloodied Viet Cong going underground. In the United States, however, the impact of Tet proved more severe, causing the nation's leaders to seek means of limiting the American role in the conflict, thus reducing casualties, even as they dispatched reinforcements, including Air Force squadrons, to meet the immediate threat.

Chapter Three

Facing Some Hard Decisions

Although the Tet offensive caught the U.S. armed forces at a time when they were straining to meet their world-wide obligations, the Air Force had greater depth in terms of readily available units than the other services. To reinforce General Westmoreland, the Army could call on just one fully trained, combat-ready division, the 82d Airborne. The Marine Corps had elements of one division and its aircraft wing available for service in South Vietnam; once these had departed, any further Marine reinforcements would have to come from a division-wing team serving with the Atlantic Command. The Navy could dispatch five aircraft carriers and five cruisers to Southeast Asian waters, but only by redeploying ships committed to the North Atlantic Treaty Organization. In contrast, the Air Force had a dozen tactical fighter squadrons immediately available for service in South Vietnam.[1]

Had it not been for North Korea's recent capture of the intelligence ship *Pueblo*, the Air Force could not have tapped this reservoir of trained units, for President Johnson had mobilized eight Air National Guard tactical fighter squadrons as part of his reaction to that emergency. The eight were among twenty-two Air National Guard and Air Force Reserve units summoned to active duty in response to the *Pueblo* crisis. The mobilization took place on January 26, only three days after North Korean naval forces seized the ship and, providentially, five days before the main Tet attacks. The eight squadrons, each with twenty-five F–100Cs, reconstituted an Air Force strategic reserve depleted by the redeployment to the Far East in the wake of the *Pueblo* incident. Three tactical fighter squadrons, totaling seventy-two McDonnell Douglas F–4Ds, flew from the United States to South Korea, and one squadron of eighteen F–100Ds deployed to South Vietnam, so that an equal number of F–4Cs, better suited than the F–100Ds to the kind of aerial combat likely to erupt over the Korean peninsula, could depart for South Korea.[2]

The Tet offensive, to the surprise of General Westmoreland's superiors, did not trigger a sudden request for air, ground, or naval reinforcements. After a week had passed with no request for more men and machines, Army Gen. Earle G. Wheeler, Joint Chiefs of Staff Chairman, telephoned Saigon and learned that

Air War over South Vietnam, 1968–1975

An aircraft destroyed during the Tet attacks at Bien Hoa.

Westmoreland intended to crush the Tet offensive with the forces he had. He planned to shift more troops to the five northern provinces of I Corps, a move that, in Wheeler's opinion, might expose the cities to further attack.³ "Do you need reinforcements?" Wheeler asked Westmoreland. Acknowledging that "capabilities are limited," Wheeler offered "the 82d Airborne Division and about one-half of a Marine division, both loaded with Vietnam veterans." Confident that the United States was "not prepared to accept defeat in South Vietnam," he urged Westmoreland to ask for as many troops as he might need.⁴

Although he looked upon reinforcements as insurance against "the worst possible contingency" — the unlikely loss of Khe Sanh — General Westmoreland decided to accept the additional troops that Wheeler had offered.⁵ The Joint Chiefs of Staff then began preparations to tap the existing strategic reserve for the promised units. While ground troops formed most of the reinforcements, the plan under consideration by the Joint Chiefs called for as many as five tactical fighter squadrons, plus additional tactical airlift.⁶

As the reinforcement program took shape, Wheeler came to view the Tet offensive as an opportunity not only to punish the enemy on the battlefield but also to reconstitute the dwindling strategic reserve. Motivated by the Tet offensive and the perilous state of the pool of U.S. military manpower, Wheeler again urged Westmoreland to ask for more men. Although Wheeler denied he was "trying to sell" additional troops, he warned that "the critical phase of the war is upon us" and urged Westmoreland not to refrain from asking for "what you believe you need under the circumstances."⁷

Scarcely had General Wheeler sent this advice, when the Joint Chiefs of Staff met with President Johnson and discussed reinforcing General Westmoreland and rebuilding the strategic reserve. In effect, the military leadership

Facing Hard Decisions

A Khe Sanh fuel dump burns after a Viet Cong rocket attack.

proposed sending to South Vietnam almost all the ground troops currently in the manpower reservoir and replacing them with 120,000 mobilized reservists and National Guardsmen. Clearly, the President found the plan unpalatable, for expanding the war in Southeast Asia and increasing the number of Americans under arms would not only fan the flames of opposition to an increasingly unpopular war, but also play havoc with the budget and jeopardize social programs at the heart of his administration. Indeed, later that day, Secretary of Defense Robert S. McNamara formally asked General Wheeler for less ambitious alternatives to large-scale reinforcement and mass mobilization.[8]

Hard upon the President's instructions, as relayed by Secretary McNamara, came Westmoreland's response to Wheeler's thinly veiled invitation to ask for the bulk of the strategic reserve. "Needless to say," he answered, "I would welcome reinforcements at any time," but he stopped short of asking for them.[9] The President's advisers — McNamara, Clark Clifford (who would become Secretary of Defense after McNamara's resignation took effect on February 29), Gen. Maxwell D. Taylor (Wheeler's predecessor, who served for a time as Ambassador to South Vietnam), Walt W. Rostow (who had interpreted the intelligence on Khe Sanh), and Richard M. Helms (director of the Central Intelligence Agency) — interpreted Westmoreland's use of "welcome" as meaning that he could use the additional men but really did not need them to avoid defeat.[10]

Thus alerted to the attitude of Johnson's close advisers, Westmoreland soon was declaring that he "desperately" needed more men to hold the northern provinces without placing the cities in new jeopardy. Specifically, he asked for all

Air War over South Vietnam, 1968–1975

the infantry units in the strategic reserve, in excess of 20,000 men, thus bringing his American forces to their authorized strength of 525,000, a goal approved but not yet reached when Tet fighting broke out.[11]

When Westmoreland called for more men, the administration was already preparing to send him additional battalions from the strategic reserve. On February 12, President Johnson summoned the Chairman of the Joint Chiefs of Staff to the White House and directed that the Air Force fly to South Vietnam the 27th Marines and one brigade from the 82d Airborne Division, roughly 10,500 men, about half the total infantry strength of the strategic reserve. The Marines, based at Camp Pendleton, California, took off from nearby El Toro Marine Corps Air Station and arrived at Da Nang on February 17. The soldiers, from Fort Bragg, North Carolina, disembarked at Chu Lai on the 21st.[12]

This infusion of strength seemed to satisfy Westmoreland, even though he had expressed a desperate need for the 10,000 ground troops remaining in the strategic reserve. He now made it clear that his command did not totter on the brink of disaster. "I am expressing a firm request for additional troops," he told Wheeler, "not because I fear defeat but because I do not feel I can fully grasp the initiative from the recently reinforced enemy without them."[13] If anything, this statement reinforced the idea that Westmoreland could use more troops, but did not really need them.

Such a carefully hedged request could not justify the kind of mobilization that Wheeler believed necessary to provide men to fight the Vietnam War and at the same time rebuild a strategic reserve to meet threats elsewhere. This fact loomed large in his mind as he prepared for the trip that would bring him to Saigon on the morning of February 23. "As you would surmise," he told Westmoreland before departing for Southeast Asia, "the administration must face up to some hard decisions in the near future regarding the possibility of providing you additional troops, recouping our strategic reserves in CONUS [continental United States], and obtaining the necessary legislation in terms of money and authorities." Since the President and Secretary McNamara had thus far avoided large-scale mobilization, General Wheeler apparently hoped to return from South Vietnam with a request from Westmoreland that would enable him to link a massive call-up of reservists to the reinforcement of the military assistance command to deal with the Tet offensive.[14]

During discussions in Saigon, according to Westmoreland's recollection, Wheeler suggested the military assistance command submit "a requirement that would permit the development of a substantial reserve for worldwide use." In carrying out Wheeler's wishes, Westmoreland proposed a bank of reservists from which U.S. forces in South Vietnam could draw over the coming year.[15] Such a bank would contain roughly 176,000 men, selected from among 262,000 mobilized reservists and National Guardsmen, and include two Army brigades and a half dozen Air Force squadrons. Besides obtaining access to the bank of reinforcements, from which he might draw throughout the year, Westmoreland

Facing Some Hard Decisions

would receive 30,000 men during the summer of 1968, some of them mobilized from the reserve components. The immediate reinforcements would include two Air Force tactical fighter squadrons, in addition to two others scheduled to be sent under the 525,000-man ceiling.[16]

The prospect of mobilizing more than a quarter million from reserve components to fulfill General Westmoreland's request for 206,000 men — the 176,000 bank from which he could freely draw plus 30,000 reinforcements during the coming summer — jolted the administration into examining the harsh realities of the Vietnam conflict. President Johnson promptly convened a group of trusted advisers for what came to be called the "A to Z policy review." Clark Clifford, Secretary of Defense-designate, served as the chairman of this panel, which met for the first time on February 28, the day before Secretary McNamara stepped down. As its nickname indicated, the project involved an examination of every aspect of the war effort — military, budgetary and economic, diplomatic, and political.[17]

Prospects for further reinforcement seemed good when the "A to Z" group reported to the President on March 4. These advisers endorsed the mobilization of 262,000 reservists and National Guardsmen to rebuild the strategic manpower pool and recommended sending some 22,000 men to South Vietnam in addition to the 10,500 that had just arrived. The Air Force contribution to the 22,000-man force would be six tactical fighter squadrons, totaling some 3,000 officers and men, in addition to the pair of squadrons authorized before Tet for Vietnam duty, but not yet sent, and the F–100Ds that replaced the F–4Cs transferred to South Korea. The report of the group did not, however, state that these actions would suffice or that nothing further would be necessary.[18]

Opposition to the plan quickly gathered momentum, however, and General Wheeler soon was acknowledging "strong resistance from all quarters to putting more ground forces into South Vietnam." The reinforcement of General Westmoreland's command and the calling up of reserves, Wheeler conceded, seemed certain to "raise unshirted hell in many quarters."[19] Front-page stories in the *New York Times* and *Washington Post*, surely based on leaks from within the Johnson administration, declared that General Westmoreland, who had talked openly of victory as recently as November, now requested 206,000 men. The press combined the bank of 176,000 potential reinforcements with the 30,000 who would be sent to Vietnam during the summer to arrive at a total that shocked a public grown weary of a long and inconclusive war. The efforts since 1965, when the United States took over the war, apparently had accomplished nothing, and the proposed solution seemed to be more of the same.[20]

President Johnson persisted for a time in his efforts to fulfill Westmoreland's request for a total of 30,000 men, though the lack of confidence that characterized the "A to Z" report and the mounting public clamor and growing political opposition to the numbers involved caused him to avoid any extensive mobilization to create a manpower bank for South Vietnam and a strategic reserve available worldwide. The political and economic risks seemed to outweigh the uncertain military and diplomatic results. General Wheeler attributed the President's reluctance to three developments: "leaks in Washington" that created "an extremely difficult political and public atmosphere"; a balance of payments deficit that undermined willingness to face the expense of extensive deployments overseas; and "doom and gloom generated by the Tet offensive" which had cut into public support for the war effort.[21]

The Air Force contribution to the projected 30,000-man force included four F–100C squadrons, manned by Air National Guardsmen mobilized for the *Pueblo* crisis, and two Republic F–84 units that would be called up especially for service in South Vietnam. Admiral Sharp, the Commander in Chief, Pacific, brought about elimination of the F–84s, however, pointing out that age, lack of range, lack of bomb capacity, and dependence on scarce spare parts made the F–84 a liability rather than an asset.[22]

While the 30,000-man contingent took shape, the President received advice that caused him to reconsider the wisdom of sending even this force. Several civilian officials in the Department of Defense called Secretary Clifford's attention to North Vietnam's demonstrated ability to match U.S. reinforcements. Thus far, the enemy had refused to fold, however much the United States raised the ante in terms of manpower and equipment. Another comparatively small increase seemed unlikely to give him pause.

Far more important were the findings of a panel composed of distinguished citizens who had served in the military or in government that met from time to time, with a varying roster of members, to review the conduct of the war. In 1968, the membership included Dean Acheson, Secretary of State to President Harry S. Truman; C. Douglas Dillon, President John F. Kennedy's Secretary of the Treasury; and two former Chairmen of the Joint Chiefs of Staff, Gen. Maxwell Taylor and Gen. Omar N. Bradley. At President Johnson's invitation, the group, nicknamed the "Wise Men," met in Washington in mid-March 1968 to review the progress of the war since their previous session in November 1967. Beginning on March 18, these advisers listened to representatives of the Departments of State and Defense, the Joint Chiefs of Staff, and the Central Intelligence Agency, whose conflicting testimony left at least one critical question unresolved. The experts appearing before the group could not agree whether any reasonable increase in the tempo of the war — one that did not risk intervention by China or the Soviet Union — could compel North Vietnam to abandon its designs on the South. As a result, the group counseled imposing a ceiling on U.S. involvement, believing that no degree of escalation — whether heavier bombing of the North or massive reinforcement in the South — could guarantee that North Vietnam would call off the war.[23]

Within a week of the meeting of the Wise Men, General Wheeler flew to Clark Air Base in the Philippines, where he outlined for General Westmoreland the President's plans for cutting the 30,000-man augmentation by about one-

Facing Some Hard Decisions

third, a reduction accomplished by including almost the entire 10,500 men sent to Vietnam in February as part of the total. Since the Air Force had not contributed to the February build up — save to send the F–100s that replaced F–4s destined for South Korea as part of the *Pueblo* deployments — it would send two tactical fighter squadrons in addition to the two already authorized for duty in South Vietnam when the Tet offensive erupted. The force numbered some 24,500, thus keeping total U.S. strength in the country below a new authorized maximum of 549,000. As it turned out, Gen. Creighton Abrams, who succeeded General Westmoreland in July, decided he did not need all the ground forces the President was willing to send him.[24]

The 24,500 reinforcements approved by the President included five tactical fighter squadrons, four from the Air Force and one from the Marine Corps. First to reach its destination was the Marine unit, which arrived from Iwakuni, Japan, with its McDonnell Douglas A–4s late in April. On May 3, Air Force elements began arriving when the 120th Tactical Fighter Squadron, mobilized in January at Denver, Colorado, reached Phan Rang Air Base. Two days later, another Air National Guard unit, the 174th Tactical Fighter Squadron of Sioux City, Iowa, landed its F–100Cs at Phu Cat. These three squadrons represented the balance of the 525,000-man force authorized for South Vietnam when the Tet fighting began. In June, two more Air National Guard tactical fighter squadrons brought their F–100Cs to Tuy Hoa, including the 188th from Albuquerque, New Mexico, and the 136th from Niagara Falls, New York, both of which had been on extended active duty since January. These two units formed part of the 24,500-man augmentation, and their arrival increased Air Force tactical fighter strength in South Vietnam to twenty-five squadrons.[25]

Besides strengthening U.S. forces in South Vietnam, President Johnson addressed the problem of building a strategic manpower reserve, though without the kind of general mobilization that would disturb the nation's economic and political balance or intensify the existing public opposition to the war. Because of the possible consequences of a major call-up, the administration decided to mobilize no more than 62,000 reservists or National Guardsmen in addition to those already on extended active duty because of the *Pueblo* crisis. The number who reported in May for extended active duty totaled some 57,000; roughly 75 percent of these officers and men reconstituted the strategic reserve, while the remainder went to Southeast Asia. The Air Force's share of the May mobilization numbered about 1,000, all of them members of the Air Force Reserve rather than the Air National Guard. One unit mobilized in May, the 71st Special Operations Squadron, trained in Fairchild AC–119G gunships and served in South Vietnam during the first six months of 1969.[26]

As he weighed the recommendations of his various advisers and worked out this modest program to reinforce General Westmoreland and at the same time rebuild a strategic manpower pool, President Johnson apparently concluded that the escalation of American might in South Vietnam had reached a dead end. As

Air War over South Vietnam, 1968–1975

F–100s of the New Mexico Air National Guard's 188th
Tactical Fighter Squadron lined up at Tuy Hoa Air Base.

he had in the past, the enemy seemed likely to match any military action that the President deemed reasonable. Moreover, the war was rending the fabric of American society, setting supporters and opponents of the war at each other's throats. As the narrowness of his victory over a peace candidate in the New Hampshire Presidential primary seemed to demonstrate, popular support for his policies, which he considered balanced and rational, was rapidly disappearing. On March 31, 1968, during a televised speech, Johnson announced that he would not seek reelection to a second four-year term and called a halt, effective the next day, to aerial and naval bombardment north of the 19th (later the 20th) parallel. His withdrawal from political life, he believed, would help restore national unity, while the restrictions on attacking North Vietnam might lead to a negotiated settlement of the conflict.[27]

The President's decision to limit both reinforcement and bombing signaled abandonment of the idea, expressed by Westmoreland before the National Press Club as recently as November, that limited military action could force North Vietnam to call off the war. It also committed the United States to seek a negotiated peace. Since concessions formed an inescapable part of negotiation, emphasis shifted from fighting a war on behalf of the South Vietnamese to preparing them to take over the conflict and defend their nation after the fighting ended.

Preliminary cease-fire talks began at Paris in May, but quickly bogged down in often pointless detail, such as the shape of the table at the negotiations. In July 1968, while the conversations at Paris droned on, Secretary of Defense Clark Clifford visited Saigon and told South Vietnamese officials that the United States "was greatly interested in what we and the GVN [Government of Vietnam] could do jointly to strengthen the RVNAF [Republic of Vietnam's Armed Forces]." Nguyen Van Thieu, South Vietnam's president, proposed three

Facing Some Hard Decisions

kinds of help that the United States could provide: increasing his nation's military forces, especially irregular local defense units; making better weapons available; and improving housing for servicemen and their families.[28] By year's end, the military assistance command was helping South Vietnam organize, train, and arm a balanced force, regular and paramilitary, slightly in excess of 800,000 men, an increase of roughly 100,000 since Tet.[29] These actions lent substance to President Johnson's statement in his March 31 speech that South Vietnamese forces would "progressively . . . undertake a larger share of combat operations against the Communist invaders."[30]

The restrictions imposed on the bombing of the North, effective April 1, did not result in a reciprocal reduction of North Vietnamese pressure against the government of the South. As a result, the authorization of sixty B–52 sorties per day, approved during the Tet fighting while the fate of Khe Sanh seemed to hang in the balance, remained in effect throughout 1968. By December, however, the Strategic Air Command, now headed by Gen. Bruce K. Holloway, was warning General Abrams, who had taken over the assistance command some five months earlier, that the 106 B–52s in the western Pacific could not continue flying 1,800 sorties per month in Southeast Asia without affecting the nuclear retaliatory force. Intensive use increased the strain on planes, crews, and mechanics, causing bombers to be sidelined frequently for maintenance and repair, thus limiting their versatility. Although the B–52s could readily be modified to carry nuclear weapons, at any given time a variable number remained grounded because of hard usage over South Vietnam or Laos. Using strategic aircraft, refueled by Boeing KC–135 aerial tankers, to shower high explosives on targets in Southeast Asia reduced the number of bombers and tankers available for prompt retaliation in case of all-out war. Since one B–52, with refueling, might have to attack two or more targets in rapid succession, the impact of each lost or delayed sortie was therefore multiplied.[31]

President Johnson's reappraisal of the war effort, though it did not diminish the B–52 bombing campaign, sounded the death knell for an Air Force plan to fight a unified Southeast Asia campaign, combining operations in both Vietnams and much of Laos, in which the focus would shift from ground combat to aerial warfare. During March, as the "A to Z" policy review convened at the President's direction, the Air Force launched its own evaluation in the hope of influencing future strategy, encouraged perhaps by vigorous support of the air war by Senator John C. Stennis, a Mississippi Democrat, and other like-minded legislators. Air Staff agencies and analysts from RAND, a research corporation, conducted studies dealing with intensified bombing of the North, an air offensive against southern North Vietnam and adjacent regions of Laos, and adoption of a new strategy for South Vietnam that made greater use of air power. At the outset, the study teams were considering three closely related campaigns, with success in South Vietnam dependent in large measure upon the impact of air operations in North Vietnam and in southern Laos.

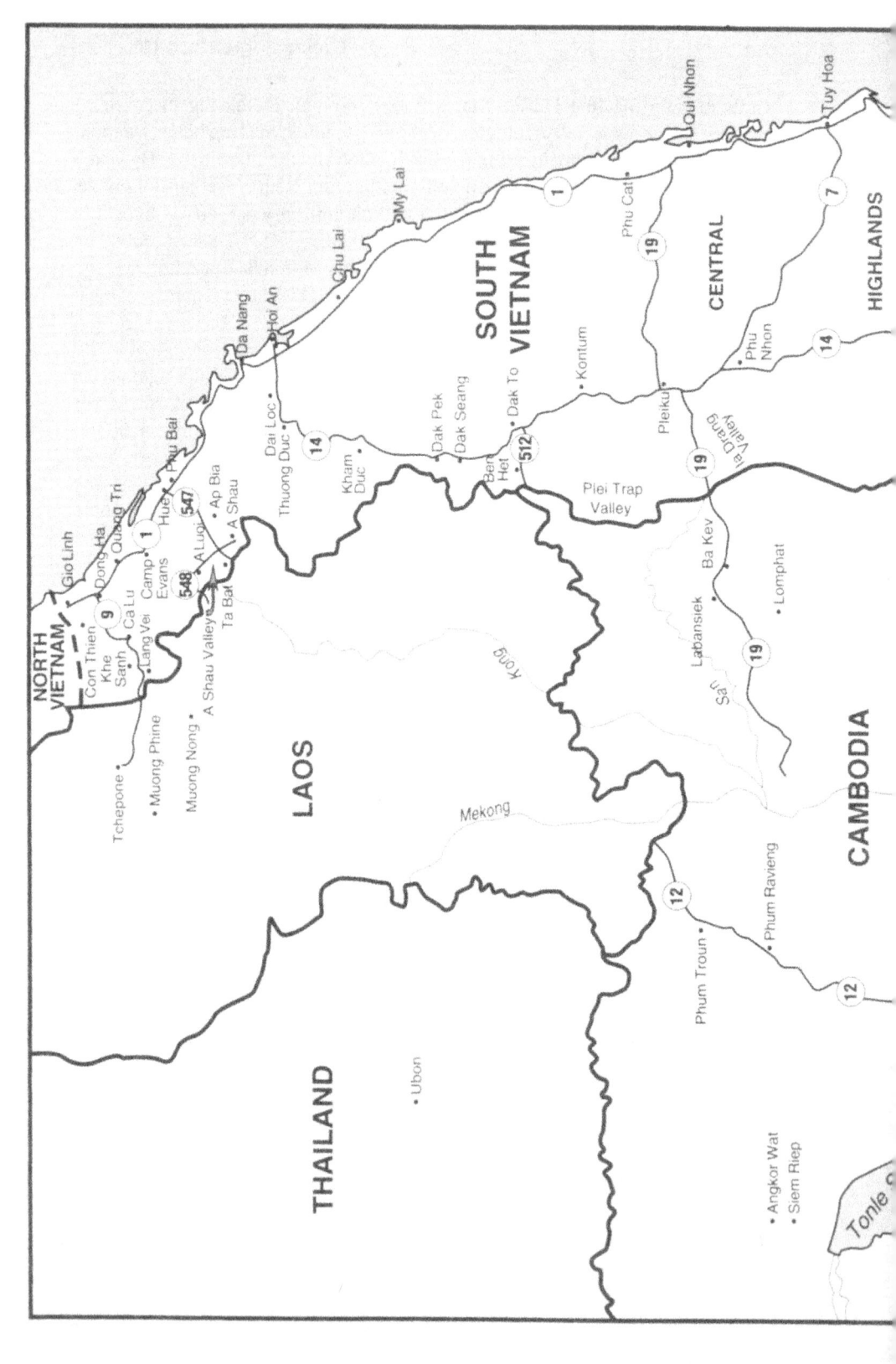

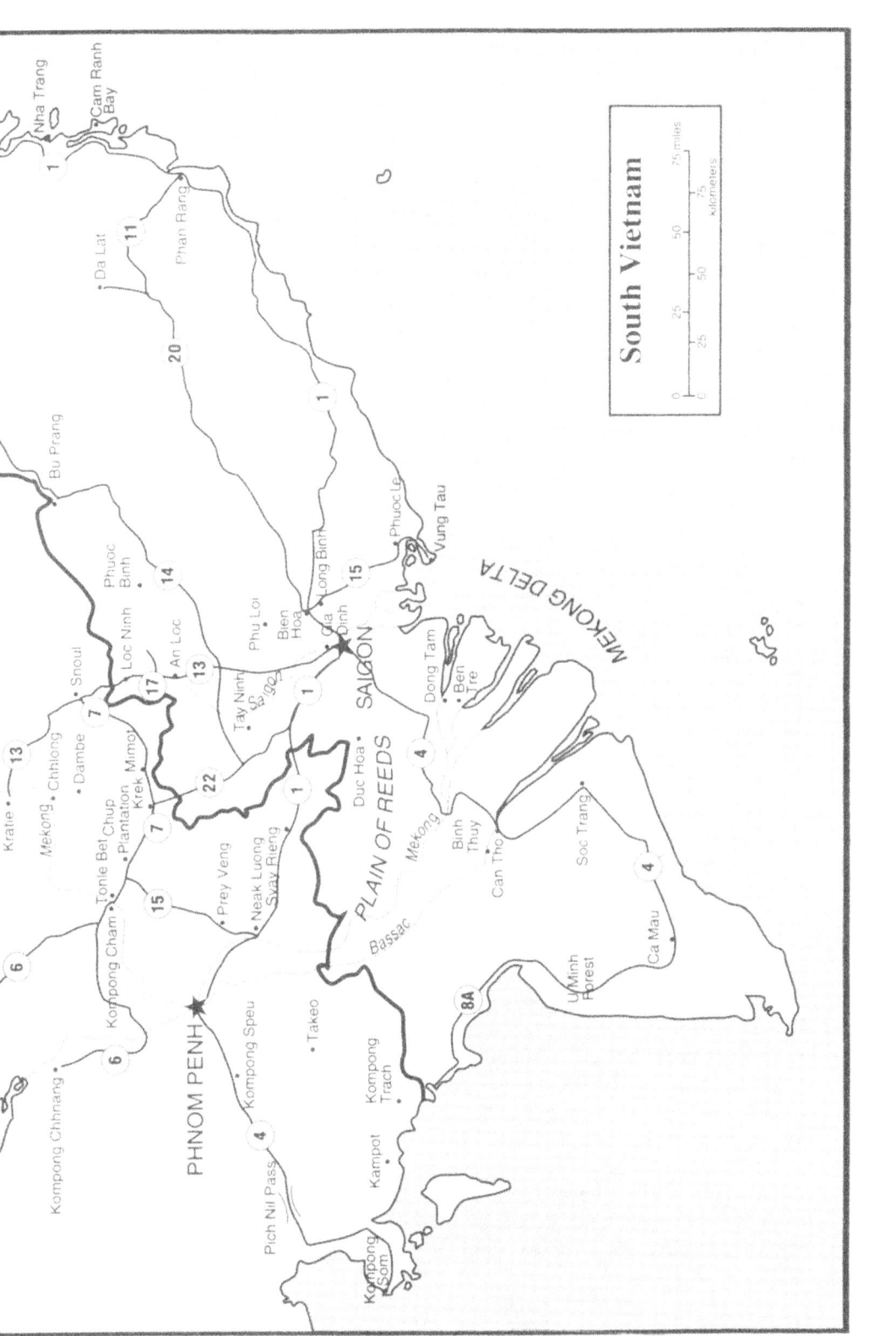

Air War over South Vietnam, 1968–1975

The course of action suggested for the campaign in South Vietnam called for exchanging territory for security, abandoning outlying strongpoints like Khe Sanh (which, by coincidence, soon would be given up) to concentrate on protecting the population, which had resettled within clearly defined defensive zones. Army and Air Force fliers based within these defensive zones would maintain surveillance over the outlying territory and by charting enemy activity determine interdiction areas vulnerable to air attack. American ground units were to engage in what the Air Force planners called "mobile defense," lashing out against hostile concentrations outside the secure region, while training South Vietnamese forces to assume responsibility for the war. Adoption of this scheme of mobile defense would, the planners suggested, reduce casualties among U.S. ground troops by some 41 percent. The proposal, in brief, envisioned air power and limited infantry action as a shield, maintained at a comparatively low cost in Americans killed and wounded, behind which the South Vietnamese could gather strength to take over the war.

After examining the three studies, Gen. John P. McConnell, the Air Force Chief of Staff, concluded that, taken together, they offered a blueprint for decisive aerial action against the North Vietnamese and Viet Cong throughout Southeast Asia. The Vietnam conflict, he believed, would and should become an air war supplemented by ground action instead of the ground war fought with massive but poorly focused aerial support, as had, in his opinion, been the case since 1965. He attempted to persuade his colleagues on the Joint Chiefs of Staff that the war — treated as loosely related efforts in Laos, South Vietnam, and North Vietnam — should be a unified campaign fought from Hanoi in the North to Ca Mau in the South and from the coastline westward through the infiltration routes in southern Laos. His proposal came too late, however, to receive serious consideration. On the basis of his own assessment, the President had decided to exempt much of North Vietnam from aerial attack.[32]

Even as the President and his advisers were beginning the policy review that led to this scaling down of the air war, a new reconnaissance project offered fleeting promise of impeding the enemy's use of Cambodia as a supply route and military staging area. American officials already had obtained evidence of Cambodia's role in supporting North Vietnamese logistics. During the enemy's preparations for what became the Tet offensive, for instance, agents reported that cargo unloaded at the port of Sihanoukville was carried in trucks toward the South Vietnamese border. In addition, General Westmoreland called attention to activity in the Parrot's Beak, a salient of Cambodian territory pointing toward Saigon. Patrolling on their side of the border, South Vietnamese troops discovered numerous arms caches, heard the sound of truck traffic on nearby Cambodian soil, and found indications, later confirmed by aerial reconnaissance, that sampans regularly travelled the waterways in the Plain of Reeds, a swamp south of the Parrot's Beak, delivering cargo to the Viet Cong. The evidence pointed to an offensive but not to a particular objective; indeed, the activity lent credence to the belief that the enemy would strike in the border area rather than attacking the cities at Tet.[33]

Although debate raged among American officials as to the amount of military assistance the communist forces in South Vietnam were receiving through Cambodia, the enemy may well have enjoyed free passage since 1965. During that year, Prince Norodom Sihanouk, who ruled Cambodia, severed diplomatic relations with the United States, alleging that American troops had violated the nation's border, a charge that he had frequently repeated. In January 1968, a U.S. diplomat arrived at Phnom Penh, Cambodia's capital, a sign that the two nations might again cooperate, perhaps to a degree that would impede the passage of supplies to the Viet Cong and the North Vietnamese units in the South.

Some three weeks before the Tet offensive, Sihanouk welcomed Chester Bowles, the U.S. Ambassador to India. During a series of meetings from January 8 through January 12, the Prince and his Prime Minister, Son Sann, discussed with Ambassador Bowles how the Vietnam conflict affected Cambodian independence and territorial integrity. Although Bowles indicated otherwise at a press conference afterward,[34] the topics discussed at Phnom Penh include the "hot pursuit" by U.S. or South Vietnamese forces of hostile troops seeking refuge across the Cambodian border. Sihanouk acknowledged his concern about the use of his country as a safe haven by the communists and said that he did not object to hot pursuit in uninhabited areas, though he could not admit it publicly, for fear of bringing down on Cambodia the wrath of the communists. According to Bowles, Sihanouk said, "If the U.S. engaged the VC/NVA [Viet Cong or North Vietnamese Army] on Cambodian territory, both would be guilty of violating Cambodian soil, but the VC/NVA would be 'more guilty'," because, in his own words, "You would be liberating us from the VC."

The Cambodian ruler, Bowles reported, "did not want Vietnamese of any stripe on Cambodian soil, since they ... were traditional enemies of Cambodia." This did not mean, however, that Sihanouk would turn against the Viet Cong and North Vietnamese. Indeed, he told Bowles that he intended to maintain good relations with the communists because they formally recognized Cambodia's boundaries, which South Vietnam did not, and also, as Bowles reported, "because the future of Southeast Asia was 'Red'."

Nor could Sihanouk accept everything the United States had done. He told Bowles that U.S. troops had to some degree contributed to his problems by attacking communist forces in the border region of South Vietnam, making Cambodia seem an attractive place of refuge. Sihanouk also claimed that previous attempts at hot pursuit, far from exterminating the Viet Cong or North Vietnamese, had killed mostly Cambodians, the very reason that he now hoped to limit the practice to uninhabited areas.

Although willing to permit hot pursuit in the border wilderness, Prince Sihanouk hoped to rein in the Vietnamese intruders using either his own forces or the International Control Commission, a peacekeeping agency dating from the 1954 Geneva settlement that had produced the two Vietnams. To do this, however, he had to locate the North Vietnamese and Viet Cong concentrations and for this information he turned to the United States.[35]

Specifically, he asked to receive on a regular basis whatever information the Americans could obtain on the location of communist forces in northeastern Cambodia. Armed with this data, he could either send his own soldiers to eject the foreigners or appeal to the international body. Unfortunately, either approach seemed utterly unrealistic. Cambodia's army could scarcely maintain order in the country, let alone mount an offensive against the infinitely stronger North Vietnamese and Viet Cong; and the International Control Commission — with one member from a communist nation, one from a pro-western nation, and one from a neutral nation — not only had problems reaching a consensus but also demonstrated an inability to enforce those decisions it did make.[36]

In a later meeting with Son Sann, Ambassador Bowles found the Cambodian official insisting upon restrictions on hot pursuit that Sihanouk had not demanded, including a pledge that neither Americans nor South Vietnamese would ever again bomb or shell Cambodian villages or frontier outposts, the subject of many of Sihanouk's protests over the years. Although Bowles declined to offer such assurances — to do so would have exceeded his authority — Son Sann did not withdraw, contradict, or modify any statements the prince had made.[37]

Prince Sihanouk and Ambassador Bowles then prepared a bland public communiqué that mentioned neither hot pursuit, the Cambodian ruler's worries about Vietnamese on his nation's soil, nor his desire for intelligence on communist bases in the Cambodian wilderness. Instead, the statement focused upon American willingness to provide the International Control Commission with helicopters for its investigations and Cambodia's determination that its territory be respected.[38]

Within a week of the conversations between Ambassador Bowles and Prince Sihanouk, the U.S. government was organizing Operation Vesuvius "to develop hard intelligence on the enemy use of Cambodia, particularly of installations which are accurately located and can be identified on the ground." The information used in Vesuvius came from aerial photo missions over Cambodia, side-looking radar surveillance by aircraft patrolling on the South Vietnamese side of the border, reports from patrols secretly dispatched in Cambodia, and statements by defectors or prisoners of war. After interpretation at the combined intelligence center, jointly operated by the Americans and South Vietnamese, the data was sent to the U.S. Embassy at Saigon before being shipped to Prince Sihanouk. Lt. Col. John J. Rosenow, at the time the project officer at the military assistance command's combined intelligence center, completed the first Vesuvius "package" on January 24. It listed ten "targets" where North Vietnamese or Viet Cong had established bases of operation in the jungles of Cambodia.[39]

Facing Some Hard Decisions

Other Vesuvius packages followed at fairly regular intervals during the year. The areas in Cambodia thus reconnoitered included the Parrot's Beak, which projected to within 35 miles of Saigon and sheltered two hostile bases, and the Nam Lyr Mountains, site of yet another base, about 130 miles north of Saigon. Prince Sihanouk tried to act on the information the Americans gave him, turning first to his generals and then to the International Control Commission. Since the armed forces of Cambodia consisted of about 35,000 indifferently trained men, to attack the bases might trigger a communist counteroffensive that could destroy the nation. Sihanouk asked the International Control Commission to investigate the Nam Lyr region, but the agency did not respond, because of either the persisting ideological stalemate among the members or simply a realization that the group could never enter territory considered sensitive by the North Vietnamese.[40]

Although Cambodia's use of this intelligence proved disappointing, the project yielded benefits to the Americans. Aerial reconnaissance, supplemented by ground probes, revealed extensive activity as supplies and reinforcements passed through eastern Cambodia from Sihanoukville or by way of the roads and trails through southern Laos. The military assistance command became convinced by year's end that communist forces maintained ten major base areas in Cambodia to support operations in South Vietnam.[41]

Since late 1967, the military assistance command's studies and observations group had been sending patrols, made up of nine or ten South Vietnamese and two or three Americans, into easternmost Cambodia. The depth of penetration varied from twenty to thirty kilometers, and the patrols might either land from helicopters or infiltrate on foot through the forest. Although the principal mission of the teams continued to be reconnaissance, they sometimes planted mines and occasionally engaged in combat, either in self-defense or when capturing a prisoner for interrogation across the border in South Vietnam.[42]

By late summer 1968, intelligence indicated that North Vietnamese units in Cambodia were gathering strength for an offensive in South Vietnam. The increasing threat caused General Wheeler to raise the possibility of attacking "the whole range of major bases in the border area of Cambodia ... either entirely ... by air ordnance or by a combination of air-ground operations."[43] Both General Abrams at Saigon and Adm. John S. McCain, Jr. — recently appointed Commander in Chief, Pacific, in Hawaii — expressed interest in Wheeler's proposal which, if it received Presidential approval, would amount to hot pursuit, using brigades supported by the necessary aerial bombardment and artillery fire.[44] When the North Vietnamese autumn offensive came, however, it proved less vigorous than expected, spending its momentum in the western highlands.

Although the enemy struck a comparatively light blow during the fall of 1968, the Cambodian bases remained a source of danger, looming like thunderclouds that might, at any moment, release a deluge, and General Abrams continued to favor hitting them. He now proposed singling out three of the ten — one in the Parrot's Beak and two in the Fishhook, roughly ninety miles to the north — and attacking them with an infantry brigade supported by tactical fighters, artillery, and B–52s.[45]

The Abrams' recommendation encountered a cool reception at Washington. The Department of State and the Central Intelligence Agency did not share his view of the importance of Cambodia in communist strategy, denying — erroneously, as events would prove — that any large volume of cargo moved through Sihanoukville toward the border region. The Central Intelligence Agency seemed convinced that North Vietnam channeled through southern Laos almost all the men and supplies destined for the Cambodian bases. The roads and trails of southern Laos, just coming under systematic attack in the fall of 1968, appeared to be better targets than the Cambodian bases themselves. These lines of communication, after all, could be attacked without extending the conflict into Cambodia, imperiling the improved relations between that kingdom and the United States, and risking worldwide criticism for extending the violence.[46]

Although action against the Cambodian bases lay several months in the future and the Tet offensive had been defeated, the fighting in South Vietnam continued, even as the Johnson administration sought to enter peace negotiations with North Vietnam. May 1968, for instance, saw a series of attacks, mainly on Saigon, that constituted an enemy spring offensive. The initiative did not, however, rest exclusively with the North Vietnamese and Viet Cong, for during the year American and South Vietnamese forces launched more than seventy major operations, some of them lasting several weeks.

Chapter Four

The Air War from Tet to Mini-Tet

The pattern of Air Force activity established in the Tet battles of February 1968 prevailed with minor fluctuations throughout the rest of the year. The share of fixed-wing operational sorties devoted to close combat and logistical support of ground forces did not dip below 75 percent in any month and rose no higher than 84 percent. From February through December, Air Force tactical units used 19 percent of their fixed-wing operational sorties in South Vietnam for reconnaissance, including patrols by forward air controllers. Combat support — the narrow category embracing herbicide, psychological warfare, and battlefield illumination missions — accounted for just 4 percent and airlift for 37 percent. Some 17 percent were attack sorties — either close support strikes on hostile positions on the battlefield, direct support in the vicinity of the front lines but distant enough so that coordination with artillery was not necessary, or interdiction of the supply and communication routes sustaining the enemy.

The total number of attack sorties reached a peak for the year during May. Besides scattered clashes throughout South Vietnam, that month saw the final days of an American thrust into the A Shau Valley, a region firmly in enemy hands for about two years, and enemy attacks on towns and military installations — a kind of mini-Tet — that again involved Air Force security detachments and flying units. Since a majority of aerial operations in the country supported the ground war, the volume of sorties, especially attack sorties, tended to keep pace with the fighting on the ground. November and December, however, may have been exceptions to this due to President Johnson's decision to halt the bombing of the North and release of a large number of tactical fighters to increase the number of missions in the South.

The relationship between the intensity of the ground fighting and the number of Air Force attack sorties persisted even though Marine Corps or Navy squadrons could increase their sorties in time of emergency, and the South Vietnamese air arm was training to assume a greater responsibility for providing air support. The emergence of South Vietnam's air force had barely begun, however, for during 1968 its monthly total of attack sorties exceeded 2,000 just twice, in February and March, at the time of the Tet offensive and immediately afterward. The typical South Vietnamese effort amounted to some 1,800 sorties per month, roughly 9 percent of the monthly average for all the allies.

Two aerial contingents besides the South Vietnamese generated comparatively few attack sorties during the year. The Royal Australian Air Force flew between 230 and 250 attack sorties each month, roughly one percent of the effort. In contrast to the steady contribution by the Australians, the U.S. Navy averaged some 1,500 sorties in South Vietnam during February and March — plus the sorties dispatched against North Vietnam at the time — but operations dropped off to fewer than 200 per month throughout the spring and summer and did not begin to recover until the bombing of the North had ended.

Air Force tactical units therefore set the pace in attack sorties, followed by Marine airmen. The Air Force conducted about 125,000 or 58 percent of the 212,000 attack sorties flown in South Vietnam from February through December 1968. The Marine Corps share was almost 60,000 or 28 percent.[1]

Once the Tet fighting ended, the Seventh Air Force shifted its resources to the relief of Khe Sanh, an operation delayed by the wave of attacks upon towns and military installations. Preparations for a drive to open the road to the encircled Marine combat base had begun late in January, before the Tet offensive. Army Maj. Gen. John Tolson's 1st Cavalry Division (Airmobile) came under the operational control of III Marine Amphibious Force, and the force commander, General Cushman, directed Tolson to devise an operations plan. The Tet battles intervened, however, drawing the air cavalrymen into the fighting around Quang Tri City and Hue, and not until February 29 could General Tolson's staff resume planning for the relief of Khe Sanh.[2]

Tolson's planners realized that an advance to Khe Sanh, where Marines and South Vietnamese rangers remained firmly in control, required a supply base with an airstrip capable of handling Air Force C–123s. Ca Lu on Highway 9, the road leading to the combat base, seemed the perfect choice to support the advance westward. Work began in mid-March, and Marine engineers and Navy Seabees finished the project in time for the attack, Operation Pegasus, to begin on April 1. The name Pegasus, a mythological winged horse, alluded to the air cavalrymen, who in cooperation with Marine units would carry out the U.S. share of a joint undertaking. The South Vietnamese contribution bore the title Operation Lam Son 207 (Lam Son, a frequently used title, referred to the birthplace of Le Loi, a legendary hero who defeated the Chinese in the fifteenth century and established his imperial capital at what became Hanoi).

While completing the Pegasus plan, General Tolson realized how little was known about North Vietnamese strength in an operating area that stretched from Ca Lu along Highway 9 to Khe Sanh and beyond. As a result, he insisted that the 1st Squadron, 9th Cavalry, a helicopter reconnaissance unit, scout the planned battleground for at least six days before the advance began.[3]

Thanks in part to a diversionary attack in eastern Quang Tri Province, the advance to Khe Sanh moved swiftly, even though bad weather had grounded

General Tolson's helicopters at Ca Lu for several hours during the first day, delaying his initial moves. On April 4, Marines stormed out of Khe Sanh to capture an important hill overlooking the bastion and break the encirclement. Two days later, South Vietnamese troops reached the combat base by helicopter, joining the rangers who had formed a part of the defending force. Other South Vietnamese landed west of the base on the following day in an unsuccessful attempt to cut off the retreating enemy. The fight for Khe Sanh ended officially on April 5, when elements of the air cavalry arrived there.[4]

Air power played a critical role in Operation Pegasus, not only during the preliminary reconnaissance, but throughout the advance. As in any operation, General Tolson's headquarters could request two types of tactical air strikes, called preplanned and immediate. Requests for preplanned strikes originated with the battalions, whose lists of proposed targets were consolidated at brigade headquarters and passed on to General Tolson's staff. The division, in turn, had to send its request to the appropriate direct air support center at least twenty hours before the preplanned strikes were to arrive. In contrast, a call for an immediate strike, as the name implied, went by radio to the center in time of emergency. During Pegasus, the air cavalrymen received almost 95 percent of the emergency requests, but only 60 percent of the preplanned strikes.

All too common in the Vietnam war, these statistics were misleading, for the schedule of preplanned strikes sought to achieve a predictably regular flow of aircraft into the operating area so that some could be diverted, whenever necessary, to emergency targets. The diversions, though anticipated in the overall plan, swelled the percentage of immediate strikes conducted, while sharply reducing the other category.

Various factors did, however, affect the timeliness and impact of air support. Fog or low ceilings sometimes forced the cancellation of strikes. Also, at the outset of the operation, planners selected arrival times for preplanned strikes so close together that one flight could not attack before another appeared, causing aerial traffic jams in which fighter-bombers occasionally ran low on fuel and left, sometimes attacking alternate targets en route to refuel.[5]

The air cavalry division also benefitted from extensive support by B–52s, which conducted a dozen strikes during the six-day preattack reconnaissance. By the time Pegasus ended, General Tolson reported a total of fifty-three B–52 raids. His staff, however, could not determine how many of the 1,300 North Vietnamese believed killed during Pegasus lost their lives in strikes by B–52s or other aircraft.[6]

Khe Sanh had dominated General Westmoreland's thinking during the early weeks of 1968, but the base declined in importance after April, as the military assistance command tried to avoid committing large numbers of men to the static defense of outposts like this. In June, the Marines abandoned the plateau on which the struggle had been fought, destroying the very bunkers that had protected the defenders from North Vietnamese shells. Ca Lu now became the

Air War over South Vietnam, 1968–1975

Members of the Army's 1st Cavalry Division (Airmobile)
relieve Marines at Khe Sanh during Operation Pegasus.

westernmost U.S. base in the region, and Khe Sanh did not reappear in the military communiqués until 1971 when it served as springboard for a South Vietnamese advance into Laos.[7]

The relief of Khe Sanh represented just one of several efforts undertaken by General Westmoreland in northern South Vietnam and, like Pegasus, these other operations required Air Force support. Since late 1967, for example, planning had been underway to disrupt the passage of men and cargo through the A Shau Valley, one of the places where the Ho Chi Minh trail, the supply and reinforcement route from North Vietnam by way of southern Laos, entered the South. The assistance command had outlined a series of plans, one of which called for attacking the valley during April 1968. Scarcely had the operation been committed to paper when the Tet offensive demonstrated the importance to the enemy of the valley and the road net passing through it.[8]

Once the Americans and South Vietnamese had beaten back the Tet assaults, the Seventh Air Force considered the problem of interdiction within the A Shau Valley. The airmen proposed dropping mines on the main exit roads, bombing highway choke points with B–52s, and setting up special strike zones where tactical fighters could attack at will. The use of delayed action bombs, set to explode as long as seventy-two hours after impact, received careful scrutiny, but the chemical fuzes fitted to these weapons had a minimum delay of twenty-four hours, giving the enemy adequate time for removal. Aerial mines promised deadlier results, but these could kill or maim the South Vietnamese and U.S.

soldiers that Westmoreland intended to send into the valley. To prevent possible accidents during ground operations, Westmoreland wanted neither minefields nor extensive special strike zones within the valley or along its exit routes.[9]

The task of spearheading the attack into the A Shau fell to General Tolson's air cavalry division, which would land in the valley proper while a brigade of the 101st Airborne Division advanced toward the objective along Route 547A, a recently discovered bypass apparently used by the North Vietnamese to mount their attack on Hue during the Tet holiday. Weather lent a special urgency to General Tolson's activity, for the northeast monsoons were ending and as the prevailing winds shifted, rain clouds would begin appearing from the southwest. Air Force weather specialists at this time could provide five-day forecasts for operations such as this; not until year's end would photographs taken from earth satellites enable forecasters to look further into the future. Whatever the details of the weather predictions available to him, Tolson could be certain that the inevitable tropical downpours would begin in May.[10]

General Tolson's troops, those from the airborne division, and the South Vietnamese forces taking part in the operation needed good weather. Helicopters were to carry most of the men into battle and, since plans called for a raid rather than permanent occupation of the valley, retrieve the units thus deployed. Because only long-range artillery firing from newly established positions near the southeastern exit could reach the heart of the A Shau, air strikes would be vital, and most of the supplies destined for the air cavalry division would have to arrive by way of a dirt airstrip at A Luoi.[11]

Because this airfield, unused for two years and pockmarked by B–52 bombing, loomed so large in his plans, Tolson proposed to seize it first, use it as a main base, while landing troops elsewhere in the valley. Before committing his force to this, he insisted upon three full days of aerial preparation, with Army reconnaissance helicopters skimming the jungle canopy to locate targets for B–52s and tactical fighters. Rain and low-lying clouds intervened, however, creating a curtain over the valley that did not part until April 16. As a result, Tolson postponed the assault from April 17 until the 19th to permit the kind of thorough reconnaissance that had preceded the Pegasus attack.[12]

Although crew members on board the low-flying helicopters could, in the words of an Air Force officer, "locate a gun ... or an enemy position ... by actual eyeball-to-eyeball sighting," the Army squadron did not have the firepower to engage such targets. The reconnaissance craft therefore radioed squadron headquarters, where an Army operations officer conferred with an Air Force liaison officer, who called for tactical fighters if he considered the target worthwhile. As they arrived over the battlefield, the fighter-bombers reported to a forward air controller who directed the actual strikes. Helicopter reconnaissance by the 1st Squadron, 9th Cavalry, also produced area targets suitable for B–52 attack, and the military assistance command requested these strikes, delivered by the 3d Air Division on Guam, through the usual channels.[13]

Air War over South Vietnam, 1968–1975

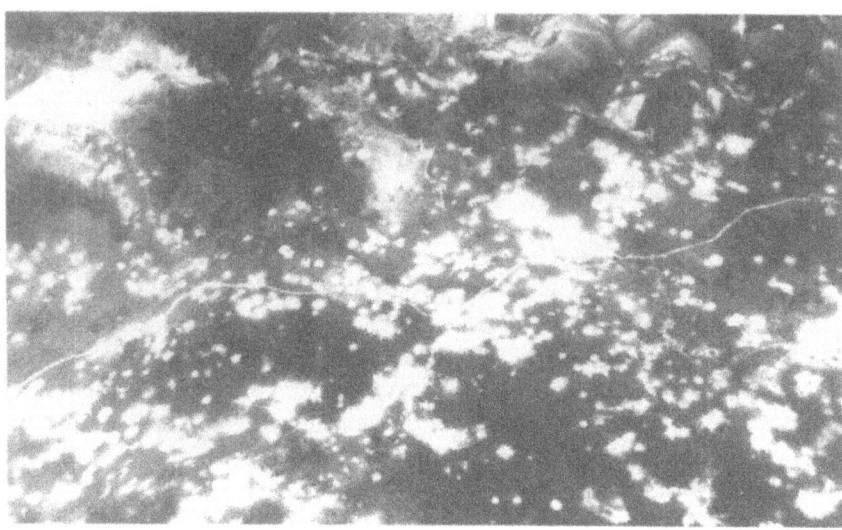

Repeated strikes by B–52 bombers left these craters in the A Shau valley.

Forward air controllers encountered unexpected communications problems in the A Shau region. When they descended to search out targets on the valley floor, towering ridges blocked radio traffic with Camp Evans, the division headquarters, where the air liaison officer coordinating their activity was located. To solve the problem, controllers used a method tried during the relief of Khe Sanh and assigned one O–2A to orbit at 10,000 feet and relay radio calls.[14]

Although the radio relay planes kept out of range of hostile fire, machineguns, 23-mm cannon, and 37-mm guns greeted the forward air controllers over the A Shau Valley. Pilots considered the most dangerous of all to be the 37-mm weapons, carefully camouflaged and apparently scattered at random throughout the operating area.[15] Observation planes flying as high as 10,000 feet above sea level sometimes had to dodge shells from these guns concealed on hillsides, and the same type of weapon, located on the valley floor, occasionally drove off controllers trying to pinpoint targets, including antiaircraft sites, for fighter-bombers. Whenever hostile fire proved too intense, the controllers, according to a controller involved, "would leave and go to another target for a few minutes and then return to the original one when it had cooled down," tactics, born of necessity, that "seemed pretty effective."[16]

Dense forest within the valley hampered efforts to locate targets for air strikes. A key road, for example, that twisted through the region passed beneath lattice work to which the branches of growing trees had been secured. Traffic passing beneath this living canopy would have escaped detection except that bombs directed at some nearby target blasted away portions of the supporting framework and exposed the road below. The highway segments thus revealed appeared to be surfaced with steel planking or corduroyed with logs for use during the rains of the southwest monsoon season. Beside the right of way ran a row of wooden poles carrying what looked like telephone or electric lines. Defoliants might have killed the greenery concealing the road, but the UC–123 spray planes flew too low and slow to survive the intense antiaircraft fire that blanketed much of the valley.[17]

In spite of the enemy's clever use of concealment, aerial observers, especially the helicopter crews of the 1st Squadron, 9th Cavalry, located enough antiaircraft emplacements to persuade General Tolson to modify his plan. Instead of striking first at the heart of the valley, seizing and improving the A Luoi airstrip to serve as both artillery fire base and supply point, he chose to launch the A Shau offensive with an assault at the northwestern end of the valley, landing troop-laden helicopters near the Laotian border and cutting the main road carrying ammunition to the gun crews defending A Luoi.[18]

The descent on April 19 into two landing zones in the northwestern A Shau Valley did not go unopposed. Air strikes to level trees for helicopter landing zones and suppress hostile fire alerted the North Vietnamese to an imminent attack. One veteran Air Force forward air controller paid tribute to the Army helicopter crews who parted the trees in search of antiaircraft positions. However, he pointed out that enemy gunners "just played possum and opened up on the big day," thus nullifying the effect of the daring low-altitude reconnaissance.[19] When that big day arrived on April 19, North Vietnamese forces defending one of the two landing zones correctly anticipated the routes of the Army helicopters and threw up a wall of fire. Before Tolson's headquarters could warn the crews to use alternate approaches, the helicopters bored through the barrage, losing nine of their number. Fortunately, the defenders of the other site reacted less vigorously.[20]

While Tolson's men were getting a grip on the entrance to the valley, elements of the 101st Airborne Division seized the roads exiting from it. Here, too, operations plans underwent last-minute adjustment, for a special forces team reconnoitering a critical landing area stumbled upon a hornets' nest of machine-gun fire, losing three helicopters. Since this unit had received "a pretty good bloody nose," attention shifted a short distance southward to a hilltop that commanded the main road passing through the region.

Dense woodland covered this rise, however, requiring the air liaison officer with the assault brigade to arrange for air strikes to blast a large enough gap to accommodate five helicopters simultaneously. Over two days, tactical fighters, most of then F–4s and Republic F–105s, dropped more than 300 bombs, ranging in weight from 750 to 2,000 pounds, but the larger trees survived. "It's a rude awakening," an Air Force officer acknowledged, "when a 2,000-pound bomb goes off and right next to it you see a tree standing . . . maybe two feet in diameter and 75 feet high."[21]

Weather complicated the blasting of a landing site, for a low ceiling compelled the fast-moving fighters to make shallow dives, causing an elongated bombing pattern in which detonations were separated too widely to reinforce one another. In addition, most of the available bombs simply could not do the job. More 2,000-pounders, fitted with fuse extenders that caused the bombs to explode just above ground, might have snapped off the trees, though without uprooting them.[22] Not until late in the year did the Seventh Air Force acquire a dependable means of blasting out helicopter landing zones — massive bombs weighing five tons or more and extracted by parachute from the cargo compartment of a C–130.[23]

After efforts to clear the hilltop had failed, the Air Force fighter-bombers shifted their effort to a valley nearby. Napalm, along with 750- and 1,000-pound bombs, destroyed the bamboo, brush, and small trees, and a final application of high explosives detonated any mines the defender might have planted. On April 19, the same day that Tolson's men stormed the A Shau's farthest reaches, helicopters began landing the 1st Brigade, 101st Airborne Division, while Air Force forward air controllers directed fighter-bombers against mortars and machineguns firing into the landing zone.[24]

From the southeastern exits of the A Shau, where the airborne brigade had gone into action, the major effort shifted to the central part of the valley. There, on April 25, Tolson's air cavalrymen seized the A Luoi airstrip. Realizing that rain and low ceilings were typical of the fast approaching southwest monsoon season, division planners decided to fly a ground-controlled-approach radar into A Luoi in one of the first helicopters. Somehow the plan miscarried and the equipment failed to arrive as scheduled. Until April 29, Air Force C–130s parachuting supplies onto the airstrip had to rely exclusively on their own airborne radar as they groped through a cloud-choked valley.[25]

When the supply drops began on the morning of April 26, the C–130s had to drop their loads from above a 700-foot ceiling that concealed the A Luoi flying field. To locate the panels marking the drop zone, a pilot had to descend to 500 feet, and align his approach, then raise the nose, increase power, and climb through the clouds to the prescribed altitude. In the cargo compartment behind him, a heavily laden pallet rested on metal rollers built into the floor and leading to an open hatch. As the transport rose into the clouds and crossed the 700-foot level, the loadmaster released the restraints, the pallet slid to the rear, and an extraction chute caught the slipstream, pulling the load clear of the aircraft. A larger parachute then opened and slowed the pallet's earthward descent. At about 2:00 p.m., rain began falling, but the transports kept coming, making some twenty deliveries on that first day.

The crew of the last C–130 to approach the airfield reported that the plane had been hit by 37-mm and .50-caliber fire, then lost radio contact with A Luoi. The handful of airmen at the airstrip, who had laid out the drop zone and organized the retrieval of cargo, saw the transport break through the overcast; holes gaped in its wings and the aircraft trailed a plume of either white smoke or fuel. The roar of the turboprop engines increased and the nose lifted, but as

From Tet to Mini-Tet

Supplies dropped by an Air Force C–130 fall near the airstrip at A Loui.

the extraction chute opened, it seemed to wrap itself around the right horizontal stabilizer, tearing away most of the elevator on that side. Unable to release his cargo, the pilot tried to get out of the valley, but rapidly lost altitude, crashing within a mile of the A Luoi runway. The eight persons on board died in the explosion and fire.[26]

Another crew narrowly escaped the same fate. On the 28th, as Capt. Ross E. Kramer was flying some 30,000 pounds of ammunition toward the drop zone, enemy gunners opened fire through a broken overcast that failed to conceal the transport, even though the ragged clouds helped hide camouflaged antiaircraft sites from the escorting fighter-bombers. During the passage along the valley, the copilot, 1st Lt. Phillip Dibb, and the engineer, SSgt. Charles W. Ellis, kept watch for tracers, clearly visible as they rose from the jungle below, and called out warnings so that Kramer could evade the fire. The navigator, 1st Lt. Gary K. Woods, not only kept the plane on course, but also tried to plot the location of enemy guns for future air strikes. In spite of the pilot's skillful flying, the C–130 took several hits from 37-mm and .50-caliber rounds, but he continued on, fighting a sluggishness in the controls.

Just three miles short of the release point, a 37-mm shell exploded beneath the cockpit. Armor under the floor saved the pilot and copilot from injury or death, but the transport incurred severe damage to the hydraulic and electrical circuits and to the nose-wheel steering mechanism. Since he could still control the plane, Captain Kramer continued on course, determined to drop the badly needed cargo. Another round tore through the left inboard engine, but Sergeant

Air War over South Vietnam, 1968–1975

Ellis shut it down before it could catch fire, and Lieutenant Dibb feathered the propeller, keeping it from windmilling out of control. Moments later, Ellis reported that the inboard engine on the opposite side was losing power, leaving Kramer no choice but to jettison the load. Airman 1st Class Robert Malone and Airman Arthur R. Hagberg had anticipated such an emergency, opening the hatch and lowering the cargo ramp well ahead of time. The transport still had power enough to pull up and rid itself of the cargo pallets, which landed short but directly on line with the drop zone. Retrieval teams gathered up the ammunition as Kramer flew to Da Nang, where he made an emergency landing.[27]

From April 26 until May 3, the big transports dropped more than 2,000 tons of ammunition, food, and gasoline onto the A Luoi drop zone. An estimated 94 percent of this cargo landed safely and was recovered and used by the men on the ground. The parachute drops proved essential because bad weather had delayed the reopening of the airfield for landings and takeoffs.[28]

Plans had called for Army helicopters to fly in bulldozers and similar equipment from Camp Evans, near Quang Tri City, refueling at a point halfway to A Luoi. Unfortunately, clouds blanketed not only the A Shau Valley but the refueling point as well. Lacking the navigational gear carried by the C–130, helicopter crews had to be able to see where they were flying, but the weather refused to cooperate. Almost a week passed before the heavy equipment arrived, delaying the efforts of Army engineers to fill craters blasted by earlier B–52 strikes and to extend the dirt runway. The first de Havilland C–7 twin-engine transports landed and unloaded on May 2, followed two days later by the larger C–123s and C–130s. Air Force planes landing at A Luoi delivered almost 650 tons of cargo.[29]

Weather also hampered the strike pilots and forward air controllers trying to support troops fighting in the valley. Thunderstorms rolled in every afternoon, and one controller insisted that he had been able to set his watch at exactly 2:00 p.m. as the day's curtain of rain descended on the northwestern end of the A Shau. The storm then enveloped the entire valley, forcing the controllers to leave until gaps appeared in the cloud cover, enabling them to lead fighter-bombers beneath the overcast and back into action.[30]

Ironically, weather played no role in the only bombing accident that marred the A Shau operation. An Air Force forward air controller, instructed to lead a flight of F–100s to a free-fire zone where they could jettison their bombs before returning to base, saw several Army helicopters firing into the forest not far from the map coordinates he had been given. He concluded that the Army aircraft were launching their rockets into the same free-fire zone assigned to the F–100s, advised the Army airmen that his fighter-bombers had munitions to drop, and received a response that he interpreted as clearance to do so. He fired a smoke rocket to mark the target only to learn, after one of his aircraft had dropped its bombs, that he had accidentally directed the strike against friendly troops, eighteen of whom were wounded.[31]

From Tet to Mini-Tet

An Air Force C–123 with supplies for the Army's 1st Cavalry Division (Airmobile) touches down at the A Loui airstrip in the A Shau Valley.

General Tolson, among whose troops the bombs had fallen, absolved the Air Force officer of blame, declaring that the pilot "was neither willfully negligent nor had a lack of regard for the responsibility vested in him." All the forward air controllers active in the A Shau Valley, Tolson maintained, had been "fully aware of their responsibility," but "when large volumes of tactical air are used in a fluid situation with ground troops, accidents can and do happen." He paid tribute to the "zest and desire" shown by forward air controllers, adding, "This dedication and enthusiasm should not be dimmed."[32]

The fast-changing situation mentioned by General Tolson also endangered the forward air controllers, two of whom experienced narrow escapes when bombs from unseen B–52s high above them screamed past to explode in the jungle below. One of the controllers who narrowly escaped death, Maj. A. V. P. Anderson, III, conceded that B–52 strikes could have a devastating impact on the enemy, but urged better coordination to ensure that controllers had warning enough to get clear.[33]

The weather, rugged terrain, and intense antiaircraft fire claimed some twenty Army helicopters shot down and incapable of being salvaged, the one Air Force C–130 downed near A Luoi, two Marine Corps attack bombers that collided in mid-air, and one Air Force O–2A. Nine Air Force airmen and one Marine died, but the Army aviators killed in Operation Delaware were included in the service's total — 172 dead or missing and 846 wounded. South Vietnamese troops, who played a comparatively minor role, lost 26 killed and 132 wounded. Enemy casualties reportedly included 900 killed and 8 taken prisoner. More important, the thrust into the A Shau Valley deprived the North Vietnamese of thousands of weapons and thousands of tons of food, munitions, and military equipment.[34]

Although the brigade from the 101st Airborne Division maintained pressure on the exits from the valley, General Tolson's forces departed, as planned, after four weeks. By then, the daily thunderstorms made a quagmire of A Luoi's runway, closing it to Air Force transports and forcing the air cavalrymen to depart by helicopter rather than in C–123s or C–130s. May 17 was the official termination of the A Shau campaign, known as Operation Delaware for the Americans and Lam Son 216 for the South Vietnamese. The thrust into the stoutly defended valley, with its important road net and well-stocked supply depots, represented the boldest stroke delivered by the assistance command in 1968.[35]

The defense and eventual relief of Khe Sanh and the subsequent attack into the A Shau Valley loomed largest in U.S. activities in the spring of 1968, but fighting also occurred elsewhere, as the enemy harassed air bases and other installations before launching a spring offensive of his own. Rockets and mortar shells exploded on airfields used by the Air Force, though less frequently than during the Tet offensive. Tan Son Nhut bore the brunt of the intermittent shelling, though Bien Hoa came under attack, and Cam Ranh Bay, until March 4 spared from bombardment, underwent its baptism of fire.

At Tan Son Nhut, the quest for souvenirs of these occasional shellings sometimes got the better of common sense. Even though rockets or mortar rounds were falling, airmen might dash from their shelters to photograph the action or lay claim to shell fragments. Making off with shell fragments often frustrated the work of Army crater analysis teams, which tried to locate firing positions by examining bursting pattern and crater size in search of clues to the type of weapon, direction of fire, and angle of impact.[36]

The nighttime harassment of Bien Hoa persuaded General Westmoreland to approve an experimental attack against an area believed to shelter the enemy gunners who bombarded the base. On "Napalm Sunday," April 7, 1968, fourteen C–130s flew low over a segment of forest, carefully marked with smoke rockets launched by forward air controllers, and saturated the area with a mixture of jet fuel and diesel oil. Each plane dropped four pallets; once clear of the transport, the bindings fixed to the platform released sixteen fifty-five-gallon drums containing the flammable mixture. The containers burst on contact, and the forward air controllers ignited contents with rockets.[37]

General Westmoreland, whose science adviser, Dr. William McMillan, had devised the scheme, expressed delight with the results achieved here and in later tests. The massive smoke cloud that rose above the burning forest, along with aerial photographs and reports from forward air controllers, convinced Westmoreland it was highly improbable that enemy resources could have survived the heat, flame, smoke, and suffocating environment.[38] Ground troops did not, however, conduct a reconnaissance of the burned-out area to count bodies and damaged equipment.

From Tet to Mini-Tet

With the passage of time and the appointment of Abrams to replace Westmoreland, enthusiasm for this type of fire bombing diminished. Gen. George S. Brown, who took over Seventh Air Force on August 1, 1968, persuaded Abrams that C–130s were too few and too valuable to be exposed to ground fire on bombing missions of dubious value. After seventeen missions, therefore, these tactics were discarded.[39]

The danger to Tan Son Nhut and Bien Hoa, the two air bases nearest the capital, produced yet another defensive measure, an airborne "rocket watch", that embraced Saigon, the two installations, and the surrounding territory. On February 24, after the flames of Tet had turned to embers, Gen. William W. Momyer, Seventh Air Force Commander, approved nightly aerial patrols of the territory within twenty-five kilometers of the bases. Forward air controllers in O–1s or O–2As received authority to direct Douglas AC–47 gunships against any hostile rocket launcher or mortar within the zone that might reveal its position by opening fire. Because of the frequency of such shellings and the danger to air bases and other installations in this area, American airmen could attack without consulting the South Vietnamese province chief.[40]

Since the patrolling AC–47s could direct a torrent of gunfire against a specific rocket or mortar position, Seventh Air Force interpreted the rules of engagement to give gunship crews freedom to attack such weapons with a minimum of delay. Effective March 1, 1968, these aircraft might, in effect, act as their own forward air controller and engage any rocket launcher or mortar within the patrol sector that had opened fire on U.S. or South Vietnamese troops or installations. In addition, the AC–47s could retaliate against fire directed at them from the darkness below, provided that the hostile gunners posed a real threat and the air crew could locate the source. The gunship had to identify the source of fire precisely, for General Momyer and his staff did not want the AC–47s using their multi-barrel machineguns to hose down large areas, endangering friendly troops or South Vietnamese noncombatants.[41]

Even without the distraction of fire from the ground, locating mortar and rocket positions at night proved no easy task. One week after the rocket watch began, a forward air controller assigned to the patrol saw several rockets forming a deep red string of fire. This spectacle vanished within seconds, leaving a "black void" within which the controller tried to fix the exact point where the fiery streak had originated. Since an AC–47 was not near at hand, the pilot reported the estimated grid coordinates, but advised checking with the appropriate ground commander before approving an air strike or firing an artillery concentration, since the location might not be accurate. This word of caution may have saved lives, or at least prevented a waste of ammunition. Ground units had already fixed the location of the rocket battery, some three kilometers from the point reported by the forward air controller, but by the time an infantry patrol arrived, the enemy had pulled out, leaving only his aiming stakes and the shallow trenches dug to accommodate the launchers.[42]

Air War over South Vietnam, 1968–1975

Circling AC–47 gunships fire on Viet Cong targets near Saigon.

To improve chances of destroying the extremely mobile rocket launchers and mortars, General Momyer placed forward air controllers in the right-hand seats of two-place Cessna A–37s. If the controller spotted hostile fire, the pilot could at once bomb or strafe the source. This practice went into effect on April 26.[43]

General Westmoreland soon came to believe that Air Force gunship crews and forward air controllers enjoyed too much freedom within the zone that embraced Bien Hoa, Tan Son Nhut, and Saigon. "I am concerned," he wrote Momyer, that the authority to attack rocket and mortar sites at night without specific clearance "could result in unacceptable casualties to friendly ground forces." He further warned, "In the fluid tactical situation that exists, it would seem extremely difficult to keep FAC [forward air controller] and Spooky [AC–47] crews thoroughly abreast of the exact location of friendly units and personnel." Before Momyer could reply, however, another series of urban attacks had begun.[44]

On May 5, 1968, the North Vietnamese and Viet Cong launched a spring offensive that came to be nicknamed "mini-Tet." In announcing the attacks, the Viet Cong Liberation Radio claimed that the earlier Tet offensive had forced the United States to play a "peace farce," presumably the preliminary talks about to begin at Paris and any substantial negotiations that might follow, and called for "armed revolts...in coordination with the offensive of the liberation troops" to sustain the momentum allegedly gained during February and "smash the ruthless domination of the U.S. puppet clique."[45] In spite of this fanfare, the renewed fighting lacked the surprise, severity, and scope of the January 31 attacks, so that mini-Tet seemed "a pale replica of the earlier offensive."[46]

Lacking the distraction provided by the Tet holiday, with its truce and attendant civilian travel, the enemy's spring offensive failed to achieve surprise. In Quang Nam Province, for instance, intelligence reports indicated that an entire division had moved into place by the end of April and would launch an attack, probably on Da Nang, by mid-May.[47] Around Saigon, the intelligence effort proved even more successful, for an agent obtained plans disclosing the day the capital would come under attack and listing some of the units assigned to the operation.[48]

Early on the morning of May 5, the enemy struck, exerting some effort in the northern provinces and western highlands, but focusing his energy on the capital city. In the north, the anticipated assault against Da Nang failed to materialize, though the enemy showered rockets and mortar shells on the town. The bombardment proved generally ineffectual, except for one round that exploded inside the III Marine Amphibious Force headquarters compound, killing four Marines and wounding eight.[49]

To discourage hit-and-run shelling of this sort, Marine airmen, flying borrowed Army helicopters, patrolled by day within rocket range of Da Nang. Air Force O–2As made a sweep at dusk and then joined AC–47s in keeping watch by night. In spite of an occasional success, the combined surveillance effort did not prove deterrent enough to justify permanent retention. By mid-1969, therefore, the Marines defending Da Nang were relying upon counter-battery fire rather than air power to deal with mortars and rocket launchers.[50]

Nor was Da Nang the only target of enemy gunners in I Corps, for similar attacks took place in all five provinces. At Hue, for instance, rockets and mortar shells damaged several houses, killed as many as twenty-seven South Vietnamese civilians, and wounded eight Americans working at an unloading ramp along the Perfume River. Skirmishes and shelling also occurred in the vicinity of Khe Sanh, where the siege had long since been broken, around Gio Linh, and in Quang Tri City. At Camp Evans a dozen rockets struck the most vulnerable targets — an ammunition dump, the fuel storage area, and helicopters parked beside the airstrip.[51]

The heaviest fighting that erupted in I Corps differed markedly from the shelling of Da Nang, Hue, or Camp Evans. At Kham Duc, a border outpost that Army Special Forces had established, the enemy fought a pitched battle, rather than conducting the kind of hit-and-run raid typical of mini-Tet. Although the struggle ended with the enemy in control of Kham Duc, air power demonstrated its ability to shift troops and mass firepower, reinforcing and then withdrawing the garrison, all the while keeping the enemy at bay.[52]

To the south in mountainous western II Corps, the North Vietnamese shelled Pleiku airfield, causing superficial damage. Engineers promptly filled a hole gouged in a taxiway by a 122-mm rocket, a near miss shook the kennels

Air War over South Vietnam, 1968–1975

and the headquarters of the Air Force sentry dog detachment, and other rockets severed a power line and blew a gap in the perimeter fence. The hits on the outer barrier may have demonstrated the inherent inaccuracy of the rocket rather than a specific plan, since no ground forces tried to exploit the opening.[53]

The heaviest mini-Tet fighting in II Corps began at midmorning on the 5th, when the North Vietnamese or Viet Cong ambushed a U.S. truck convoy bound for Kontum. South Vietnamese tanks and infantry went to the rescue, and both U.S. Army helicopter gunships and Air Force tactical fighters attacked North Vietnamese positions dominating the road. Fighting lasted about four hours, after which the ambush party vanished among the hills. The air strikes contributed to an enemy death toll placed at 120, roughly twice the number of Americans and South Vietnamese killed, wounded, and missing.[54]

Bloody fighting took place around Saigon, though towns and installations farther south experienced no more than the usual violence. The North Vietnamese and Viet Cong assigned to attack the capital encountered alert and aggressive South Vietnamese forces that had gone on the offensive after Tet to uproot the enemy from the five provinces surrounding Saigon. Skirmishes flared at several places around the city, including Tan Son Nhut, but attempts to infiltrate the heart of the city failed, thanks mainly to the efforts of the national police.[55]

Among the early casualties at Saigon was the commander of the national police, Nguyen Ngoc Loan, so severely wounded in the leg that he required medical treatment in the United States. During the Tet offensive, a cameraman had filmed him as he thrust his pistol toward the head of a captured Viet Cong terrorist, fired, and sent the victim toppling lifeless onto the pavement. Shown on American television, the film sequence drove home the brutality of the war, raised questions about the South Vietnamese commitment to the ideal of due process, and dismayed American officials like Secretary of State Dean Rusk, who sensed that the scene would further erode public support for the war.[56]

Although much of the capital emerged unscathed from mini-Tet, the battle for the suburbs lasted a week, as South Vietnamese and American troops fought a stubborn enemy. Wherever the action broke out, U.S. Army helicopter gunships and U.S. and South Vietnamese fighter-bombers pounced on the communists. On May 7, for example, some seventy-nine fighter-bombers based near the capital took off to attack fleeting targets around Saigon. By the end of the month, Air Force F–100s had flown 241 sorties against targets near the capital and South Vietnamese F–5s and A–1s another 185.

As during the Tet fighting, airmen had to attack villages taken over by the Viet Cong or North Vietnamese. In at least one instance, refugees from such a place pointed out for the U.S. commander the exact buildings fortified by the enemy, so that Air Force fighter-bombers could set just these structures on fire with napalm. At other locations, however, communist forces had arrived far enough in advance of the mini-Tet attack to excavate bunkers beneath the concrete floors of new buildings and to burrow tunnels linking these shelters.

Here, air crews had to drop 750-pound bombs to collapse the underground labyrinth, causing severe damage to homes and shops. Before attacking any populated areas, U.S. commanders cleared their action with South Vietnamese authorities and, if the inhabitants had not already fled, made loudspeaker broadcasts or dropped leaflets urging them to do so.[57]

Once again, Tan Son Nhut proved a key objective, coming under attack on the morning of May 6, some thirty hours after mini-Tet began. At 7:22 a.m., Air Force security police manning bunkers on the southern perimeter reported about forty black-clad Viet Cong moving eastward outside the fence. The enemy apparently had chosen a French cemetery outside the base as an assembly area, but fire from the airmen contained him there until South Vietnamese troops arrived. Advancing with the help of a fusillade from the Air Force security detachment, the South Vietnamese drove off the Viet Cong.

As the enemy was falling back from the fringes of Tan Son Nhut, mortar crews lobbed shells among the bunkers guarding the southern perimeter. During this bombardment, a member of the Air Force security unit spotted someone on a nearby roof, steadying a wooden stake apparently being used to aim mortars fired from the street beyond. The airman grazed the roof with a burst of gunfire, killing the observer, and the shells stopped falling. Viet Cong gunners harassed the base later that day and again on the 8th and 10th, but fired fewer than thirty-five rounds in all. No serious shelling occurred until June 12, when rockets destroyed one aircraft and damaged eight. The mini-Tet campaign thus petered out with no further ground attack against Tan Son Nhut.[58]

The enemy shelled Bien Hoa twice on May 5 and again on the 7th, the first attacks on the base since Napalm Sunday, April 7, and the fire-bombing of the forest believed to hide the gunners and their weapons. The May 5 bombardments, about three hours after midnight and again at dawn, wounded eleven airmen, one of them seriously, and damaged thirteen aircraft, five trucks, and three 50,000-gallon rubber bladders used to store fuel. The shelling two days later caused no Air Force casualties and did only minor damage. On neither day did the Viet Cong attempt a ground assault.[59]

Launched by units battered during the Tet fighting and hurriedly reorganized and strengthened, the May offensive accomplished nothing of lasting military value. Ambassador Bunker concluded that Hanoi had launched mini-Tet for diplomatic reasons, timing it to precede by five days the announced opening of preliminary truce negotiations in Paris. Ellsworth Bunker, U.S. Ambassador to South Vietnam, believed that the May 5 attack on Saigon and an effort launched on the 25th, the latter more closely resembling organized vandalism than a military operation, may have had as their objective the capture of some portion of the capital city in order to embarrass the Thieu government and thus strengthen North Vietnam's bargaining position.[60]

Once again, the enemy's losses in manpower outweighed his military gains. Estimates of communist battle deaths between May 1 and 9 totaled some 5,700, about seven times the number of Americans and South Vietnamese killed in action, By mid-May, according to intelligence estimates, the toll of enemy slain had reached 12,500. The greatest impact of the May fighting, as had been true of the Tet battles, fell upon South Vietnamese civilians, 107,000 of whom joined the growing flood of refugees.[61]

Contributing to the refugee problem was the inescapable need to bomb enemy-held villages on the fringes of Saigon and occasionally to attack hostile strongpoints within the capital itself. These strikes, in turn, caused a reorientation of the psychological warfare effort during Tet and mini-Tet. The Air Force and Army transport and liaison planes that normally tried to induce enemy soldiers to defect now had to give first priority to warning noncombatants of impending attack. This important activity did not, however, absorb all their time, for even during the spring offensive, crews continued to drop leaflets and make loudspeaker broadcasts urging civilians and enemy troops to rally behind the Saigon government.

Fighter-bombers and psychological warfare craft were not the aircraft in action around Saigon during this offensive. Reconnaissance planes again photographed possible enemy concentrations threatening the city and completed a photo mosaic to help ground commanders plan for the future security of the capital. As they had during the Tet battles, observation planes carrying forward air controllers, flareships, and AC–47 gunships helped defend Saigon by night. Since Khe Sanh was now secure — and would not be abandoned until June — General Westmoreland began using B–52s against targets within twenty-four miles of the city. From May 5, when the mini-Tet fighting had erupted, until June 21, when the last embers of the spring offensive were extinguished, almost a thousand of the bombers hit targets on the approaches to Saigon.[62]

By late May, with the worst of the springtime fighting ended and Saigon secure, at least temporarily, General Momyer took up General Westmoreland's complaint about the lack of coordination between the airborne rocket watch and ground units patrolling during darkness. Although Westmoreland had specifically mentioned the AC–47s, Momyer limited his response to the A–37s being dispatched with a forward air controller on board, withdrawing permission for them to respond instantly to a rocket or mortar attack. He allowed the AC–47s to operate as before.[63]

This response did not satisfy General Weyand, the U.S. officer responsible for defending the Saigon area. Pointing to the "heavy concentration of ground forces... and the large number of night ambushes, both static and moving," within rocket range of Tan Son Nhut and Bien Hoa, he warned that poorly coordinated air attacks, whether by helicopters or gunships could prove tragic. He therefore asked General Momyer to prohibit the rocket watch from engaging targets without obtaining specific clearance from commanders on the ground.[64]

Westmoreland decided that Weyand's concern for the safety of ground troops was justified, and the rocket watch lost its freedom of action, effective

May 30. General Momyer, however, considered this a temporary restriction and urged Westmoreland to reconsider, pointing out that placing restrictions on the rocket watch exposed "two of the largest bases in Vietnam, with 18,000 people and $500 million of equipment to additional rocket fire."[65]

The decision not only proved permanent, but apparently yielded unforeseen benefits. Captured documents later revealed that during the spring of 1968 the Viet Cong sometimes employed rocket or mortar attacks to provoke air strikes and counterbattery barrages that would cause civilian casualties, destroy property, create new refugees, and generally discredit U.S. and South Vietnamese claims of concern for the welfare of ordinary citizens. Since pinpointing firing positions from the air at night had proved so difficult, the time lost in coordinating with ground forces made little practical difference. Indeed, the restrictions imposed on the rocket watch may have worked to the enemy's disadvantage by preventing the collateral damage he desired.[66]

Subject to the new restrictions, Air Force forward air controllers continued to maintain the rocket watch, exercising sole responsibility for first one and then two of four corridors radiating outward from the capital. Instead of directing immediate attacks on their own authority, they now reported sightings to both an artillery center at Saigon and an airborne controller aloft in an Army helicopter. Moreover, they could not call in either air strikes or artillery without permission from this airborne controller, an Army officer who answered to the call sign Deadly and maintained contact with the duty officer at headquarters of the Capital Military Assistance Command, the individual responsible for coordinating air, artillery, and ground action. The Capital Military Assistance Command, a component of General Weyand's II Field Force, originated during mini-Tet as a headquarters to oversee the defense of Saigon and neighboring Gia Dinh.[67]

The airmen, whether Army or Air Force, who scanned the four corridors around Saigon for rocket or mortar batteries, could take heart from the fact that a series of rocket attacks — a hundred rockets for a hundred days — that enemy propagandists had promised for the summer did not come to pass. The enemy could have been exaggerating, of course, or such factors as ammunition caches destroyed by U.S. forces may have undermined the plan.[68] Indeed, the failure of the Viet Cong to launch the vaunted rocket barrage may have marked the beginning of what came to be interpreted as a North Vietnamese "concession" in the interest of peace negotiations, a "tacit understanding" that the enemy would refrain from attacking South Vietnam's cities while the talks continued.[69]

Although General Weyand had expressed concern that the rocket watch, attacking at night, might hit friendly troops, the most serious accident during the spring offensive occurred in daylight. On June 2, a rocket fired by an Army helicopter exploded in a cluster of South Vietnamese officials watching an attack on a group of Viet Cong who had infiltrated Cholon, the capital's Chinese quarter. Seven persons died, including a brother-in-law of Vice President Ky.

Air War over South Vietnam, 1968–1975

The accident sent tremors through a Department of Defense already concerned — thanks in part to the earlier statement that it was necessary to destroy Ben Tre in order to save it — about the excessive, perhaps careless, use of firepower in urban fighting. Charles Sweet, a member of the U.S. mission at Saigon, studied the attitudes of South Vietnamese civilians and concluded that persons living in the capital and its suburbs resented the destruction caused by their own troops and by the Americans in rooting out enemy infiltrators. Press reports lent credence to Sweet's research, alleging needless property damage in and around the city. Secretary Clifford therefore asked General Wheeler to do something, and this request resulted in a tightening of controls over urban air strikes. The military assistance command stressed the existing rules of engagement, which in general called for clearance from South Vietnamese authorities and warning to civilians of impending attack, and advised the use of precise, direct-fire weapons such as recoilless rifles before resorting to less accurate ordnance, including aerial rockets and bombs.[70]

As part of the campaign to reduce casualties among noncombatants, General Weyand, as commanding general, II Field Force, Vietnam, reserved the responsibility to use air power and artillery in Saigon and its surroundings. In practice, however, he delegated authority to the senior American adviser and the South Vietnamese officer in command of the Military Region of Saigon. At the end of August, the commanding general of the new Capital Military Assistance Command, an American, assumed the mantle of responsibility for defending Saigon that the field force commander had worn. No matter who exercised authority over air and artillery, he obtained clearance from the appropriate South Vietnamese official before unleashing these forms of destruction.[71]

Chapter Five

Above Highlands, Plain, and Delta

After Khe Sanh was secure, but before the A Shau Valley campaign ended, the enemy launched his spring offensive, the so-called mini-Tet attacks. Typical of the Vietnam conflict, the last of the A Shau fighting and repulse of the spring offensive competed with still other actions for the resources available to Generals Westmoreland and Momyer. Throughout 1968, these two officers and their successors, Generals Abrams and Brown, engaged in simultaneous operations along the demilitarized zone, among the mountains in the tri-border area where South Vietnam abuts Laos and Cambodia, on the coastal plain south of Da Nang, and amid the maze of streams and embankments that scarred the rice lands of the Mekong Delta. In each diverse region, the Seventh Air Force used a variety of close combat and logistic support techniques and tactics in performing the ground support function.

The tri-border fighting — a combination of aerial interdiction by tactical fighters, massive bombardment by B–52s, artillery fire, and infantry assault — resulted from intelligence obtained during Operation Vesuvius early in 1968. Forward air controllers played a key role in gathering this information. After detecting one short segment of road winding among the jungle-clad ridges, they searched out the rest, spotting a few trucks, some elephants apparently being used as beasts of burden, and signs of construction. "A couple of us," one of the pilots recalled, "had actually ventured into Cambodia to find out where the road did go." This violation of Cambodian airspace, which occurred before Operation Vesuvius began, revealed that the road discovered in South Vietnam connected with a north-south route beyond the Cambodian border.[1]

The military assistance command became acutely interested in what obviously was an important avenue for the supply and reinforcement of hostile units in South Vietnam. General Westmoreland's headquarters arranged for Air Force planes to photograph the area, sent Army and Air Force observation craft low among the mountains, and dispatched long-range ground patrols into the region. Interrogators questioned prisoners captured in the highlands and discovered that some of them belonged to the North Vietnamese 325th Division, last located in the hills around Khe Sanh.

Air War over South Vietnam, 1968–1975

The surge in road building, along with the presence of this veteran division, raised the possibility of an attack in South Vietnam's central highlands, supplied at least in part by cargo passing through Cambodia. Trucks could sustain such an offensive by carrying men and war material over routes already cut through southern Laos and the northeastern corner of Cambodia. If the North Vietnamese and Viet Cong isolated the town of Kontum and pushed eastward, a vigorous thrust could succeed in reaching the coast, thus isolating the northern provinces from the rest of South Vietnam. To forestall this calamity, General Westmoreland called on air power to interdict enemy traffic on key roads in western Kontum Province, while American ground forces advanced toward the border.[2]

Seventh Air Force tactical fighters, together with B–52s of the Strategic Air Command, received the mission of disrupting traffic on two road systems within South Vietnam that would carry the men and munitions necessary to launch an eastward drive. One network ran roughly parallel to Route 512 toward Ben Het; the other followed the Plei Trap Valley, west of Kontum city and generally parallel to the Cambodian border. Beginning in the first week of April, the aircraft attacked bridges and similar choke points, truck parks, and supply dumps along both road nets, using high-explosive bombs, mines, and, on occasion, tear gas.[3]

In a typical attempt at interdiction, Seventh Air Force planners consulted aerial photographs, reports from forward air controllers, and other intelligence to isolate several choke points along a specific segment of road. One such point began as the route passed between two hills, continued across a bridge, bent around another hill, and passed beside the foot of a towering cliff. Another consisted of a section of highway that crossed a spring-fed marsh where ground water quickly oozed into even shallow craters blasted in the road surface. At one or more places within a choke point, aircraft cut the road with bombs and scattered gravel mines — high-explosive pellets that could inflict painful minor wounds — to discourage repair crews. Once established, the interdiction point required continuing surveillance, so airmen could again cut the road when a break was mended.[4]

The Seventh Air Force twice experimented with tear gas to replace or reinforce the gravel mines. Lockheed C–130 transports dropped 256 drums of gas on one choke point and 192 on another. Almost all the containers plunged through the jungle canopy, burst, and released a non-toxic cloud that clung to the ground. The effects of the gas defied precise measurement, largely because aerial cameras could not penetrate the trees and discover when road repairs began or the pace of construction.[5]

Aerial interdiction of the tri-border region, reinforced at times by fire from 175-mm guns, continued from April 7 until June 22. At the outset, finding targets proved difficult, for the highlands were poorly charted and one ridge line looked like another. To further complicate matters, intelligence officers tried to piece together traces of camouflaged roads by linking segments revealed in aerial photos or glimpsed from the sky through gaps in the jungle. As the forward air controllers became more familiar with the region, their proficiency improved, enabling them to locate an increasing number of targets for strike pilots and to furnish intelligence specialists with a greater quantity of sound information.

Of the three basic interdiction weapons — tactical fighters, B–52s, and artillery, the tactical fighter seemed the deadliest, at least in the judgment of one Air Force forward air controller. This type of plane, if skillfully flown, could destroy a bridge no more than a dozen feet long or blast a crater in a road barely wide enough for a single truck. To score a direct hit on so small a target might require ten or more tries, but it could be done. Not so with the B–52s, whose sprawling bomb pattern had proved excellent for ripping away jungle to reveal potential targets or for battering truck parks, bivouacs, or storage areas. The spread of bombs from even one of these huge aircraft might crater a narrow, twisting road, but to do so required extremely good luck. Artillery, this same airman declared, lacked the accuracy at ranges beyond twenty kilometers to score more than an occasional hit on a road junction or similar target.[6]

Unlike the men on board the high-flying B–52s, forward air controllers and fighter-bomber crews had to run a gantlet of fire from automatic weapons and light antiaircraft guns. An Army officer, paying tribute to the airborne controllers supporting the brigade he commanded, said they "proved tremendous," braving fire from the ground that was "about as intense" as he would "care to fly in, in any aircraft." The North Vietnamese shot down one F–105, but the pilot ejected and was rescued by an Army helicopter carrying the commander of the very battalion he had been supporting.[7]

The interdiction campaign served as prelude to an advance westward from Dak To by a brigade of the 4th Infantry Division, reinforced by elements of the 101st Airborne Division. As the main force surged ahead, one battalion would make a helicopter assault near the border, a move designed to prevent the North Vietnamese from finding refuge in Cambodia. Besides maintaining pressure on the road net during the offensive, air power hammered troop concentrations as the enemy massed his forces to meet the threat.[8]

The infantrymen surged forward on May 27, encountering feeble resistance, a result, said one forward air controller, of the devastating B–52 bombardment that supported the attack. This officer, Maj. Eugene Carnahan, said that the big bombers appeared in such rapid succession that he and his fellow controllers could not assess the results of one strike before they had to get out of the way of the next. He recalled flying over a vast area, ten or more kilometers square, "where the triple canopy jungle had been turned into desert," and bomb craters had "changed the course of small creeks and streams."[9]

Col. Joseph E. Fix, whose reinforced brigade was making the attack, expressed delight with the work of the B–52s. When the enemy chose to fight, the brigade commander arranged for the bombers to attack by day or night, under radar control, as close as 1,500 meters to his own troops. The raids, he believed,

Air War over South Vietnam, 1968–1975

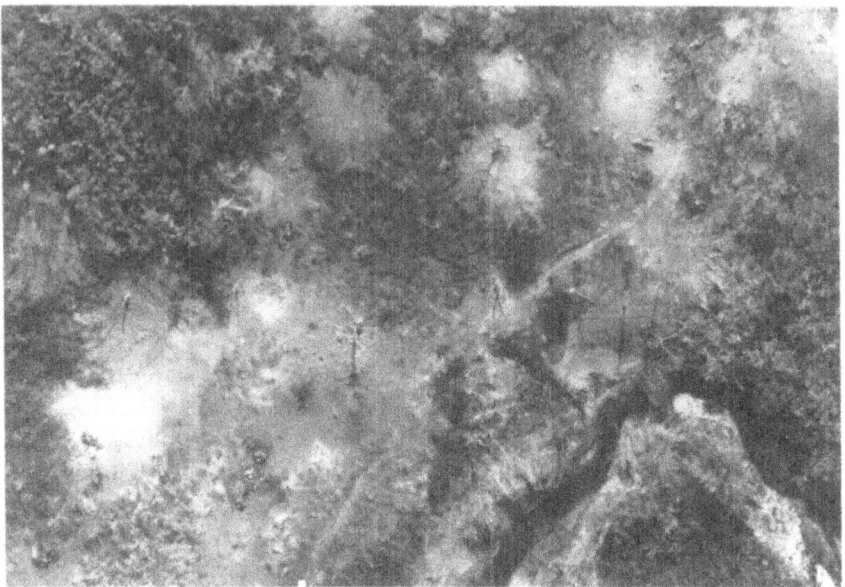

Bombing on this section of the Ho Chi Minh Trail has removed the forest cover and destroyed trucks parked alongside the road.

were a "horrendous psychological weapon," not unlike the nuclear attacks on Hiroshima and Nagasaki. One moment, he recalled, everything was peaceful and serene, "and all of a sudden all hell erupts." Putting himself in the place of a North Vietnamese soldier, Colonel Fix reasoned that "to live under this threat must be a fantastic psychological problem," especially for those who had survived a raid and seen "the destruction wrought by these strikes that come without warning."[10]

To exploit the psychological impact of this bombardment, Air Force and Army planes scattered some two million leaflets and reinforced the printed word with propaganda broadcasts from airborne loudspeakers. While only three of the enemy surrendered, each of them numbered B–52 strikes among the reasons for their defection.[11]

Although Colonel Fix welcomed B–52 bombardment and the psychological impact it apparently had, he realized that thunderous explosions did not always result in gruesome slaughter. All too often he had seen enemy riflemen emerge from shelter and fight to the death after having undergone an earth-shaking artillery barrage comparable to a B–52 strike. He simply did not know how many enemy troops the B–52s had killed or maimed, for no bomb damage assessment was possible after 61 percent of the bombings. In other cases, the reports were limited to events visible from the air, principally explosions and fires. Only once did his advancing troops arrive on the scene in time to obtain first-hand evidence.[12]

Above Highlands, Plain, and Delta

In terms of effort, if not necessarily results, the three-month bombing campaign west of Kontum City marked the second mightiest aerial endeavor of the war to that time, surpassed only by the bombing around Khe Sanh earlier in 1968. Some 1,300 tactical fighter strikes dropped almost two tons of bombs each, and 233 B–52 strikes took place, each involving from one to three of the bombers. In spite of this aerial bombardment, the attacking infantry could not be certain that the 325th Division had not escaped intact into Cambodia. Twice Colonel Fix prepared to fly a battalion westward to establish a blocking position near the border, thus placing a stopper in the open bottle, and twice the enemy attacked at Dak Pek to the north, forcing him to cancel the planned move in case the unit was needed there. As a result, the escape route remained open.[13]

This massive bombardment could not be duplicated in IV Corps, where the potential for disaster from a misdirected bomb or shell was perhaps the greatest in all of South Vietnam. Some eight million people lived within the 16,000-square-mile IV Corps operating area, which extended from the Plain of Reeds to the southernmost tip of the Ca Mau peninsula. This area contained one-fourth of South Vietnam's land mass and about half the nation's total population.

The IV Corps tactical zone included the delta formed as the Bassac and Mekong Rivers emptied into the sea. A huge rice crop grew in the deposited silt, a crop valuable to both the Saigon government and the enemy. Because so much of the delta was irrigated paddy land, the people clustered along rivers, canals, and the area's one hard-surfaced road, further increasing the likelihood of civilian casualties as some 80,000 Viet Cong troops and political agitators sought to merge with the general populace.[14] The large B–52s seldom attacked in the delta "because it was just too crowded."[15]

When 1968 began, a special force of infantry, transported on shallow-draft landing vessels, harried the enemy along the waterways that laced the delta. These soldiers, a brigade of the 9th Infantry Division, lived on Navy landing ships designed to carry tanks, but converted into floating barracks, and embarked in landing craft to storm enemy strongholds. The naval flotilla that conducted these operations had its own ammunition, supply, and repair vessels, as well as artillery barges and a variety of powered fire-support craft. Mobility remained the watchword through the early months of 1968, as this river force, independent insofar as possible from its advance base at Dong Tam, churned the muddy rivers and canals in pursuit of an elusive foe.[16]

The so-called Mobile Riverine Force tried to isolate enemy detachments and destroy them before they could vanish among the peasantry. After one element of the force lured the Viet Cong into battle, another swarmed ashore to cut the enemy's avenues of retreat, while helicopter gunships sought to cover any gaps through which the communists might escape. To make the best possible use of tactical fighters in rapidly moving combat, the brigade relied on air liaison parties that maintained radio contact between units slogging through the delta mud and the forward air controllers assigned to support them.[17]

Air War over South Vietnam, 1968–1975

South Vietnamese troops taking part in an operation in the Mekong Delta.

From four to six forward air controllers directed air strikes, called down artillery, and performed reconnaissance for the amphibious brigade. Various Army officers had contrasting opinions about the contribution made by the airborne controllers. Whereas one stated flatly that the controllers were "damned fine... willing to go out of their way to help you,"[18] another, whose command post had been hit by an errant napalm canister, insisted that the controllers of 1968 and 1969 were less skillful than their predecessors of three years earlier, who "would come in at tree top level and guide the jets in beautifully." The new breed, this Army officer declared, seemed unwilling to "come in below 1,500 feet."[19] He neglected to mention, however, that antiaircraft fire had grown infinitely more dangerous during the intervening time.

A similar lack of unanimity characterized estimates by Army officers of the value of the air strikes, usually few in number, launched in support of each day's operations. One officer complained, for instance, that "we make lots of lakes out there in the paddies,"[20] but one of his colleagues pointed out that this apparently wasteful area bombing served to detonate mines and booby traps. In such areas, he conceded, "it must look as though we are just making holes in the paddies, but if those strikes... save some grunt's leg, then the strike has been worthwhile."[21]

Valuable as such preparatory bombing might be, the soldier wading through knee-deep ooze or treading warily along an embankment needed air power most when the Viet Cong opened fire from the concealment of some tree line. "For on-the-spot, immediate response," declared an Army staff officer, "I'd rather have air than artillery any time. It's much more accurate than artillery, too — if the first round isn't on target, the second one and the following ones are."[22]

Above Highlands, Plain, and Delta

When the riflemen ran into unexpected trouble, their battalion commander had the air liaison party contact the forward air controller, who immediately radioed the direct air support center responsible for assisting the river force — beginning in 1968, IV Direct Air Support Center at Can Tho did this job. The center responded by either launching aircraft, occasionally from Binh Thuy but usually from Bien Hoa, or diverting fighters already aloft. Response time varied from fifteen minutes, if the flight was in the air near the target and could report promptly to the forward air controller; to thirty minutes, if the planes took off from Bien Hoa; or to perhaps forty-five minutes, if the strike originated at some more distant base like Nha Trang.[23]

As during Operation Pegasus in the north, preplanned air strikes scheduled on the previous day served as the principal source of aircraft diverted to meet emergencies in the delta. Instead of grouping most scheduled missions early in the assault, the 9th Infantry Division sought to arrange the preplanned strikes — those requested by brigade headquarters before 11:00 a.m. of the day before the operation — to "get a good time spread on air strikes coming into the area." A target that seemed vital the day before might vanish with the dawn, and if such was the case, the assigned aircraft would be available if a firefight should erupt. Ideally, these flights would arrive on station four times during the day, either attacking the planned target or, if it had disappeared or diminished in importance, remaining available as long as they could. If the fighter-bombers ran low on fuel before the river force needed them, they might hit suspected minefields, storage bunkers, or other targets located by intelligence.[24]

A key element in the intelligence network was the forward air controller, who enjoyed great success in detecting enemy movement by day. Prisoner interrogation, captured documents, and intercepted radio broadcasts revealed information about Viet Cong activity, and the river force could employ a variety of electronic devices to penetrate darkness or other concealment. Army aircraft fitted with infrared equipment, side-looking radar, or light-intensifying night observation devices searched the delta terrain. Army helicopters fitted with "people sniffers" — sensors capable of detecting odors given off by the human body — patrolled the region. Outposts on the ground maintained radar surveillance over segments of the flooded plain, and Army or Navy technicians monitored signals from acoustic and seismic sensors capable of detecting movement on routes the enemy might use.[25]

Although ground fighting sometimes broke out at night, generating calls for emergency air support, Air Force units normally saw little action between dusk and dawn. Forward air controllers occasionally tried, with scant success, to conduct surveillance during darkness. As one pilot conceded, "We've tried it, but we can't see anything."[26] Frequently, AC–47 gunships intervened in the delta by night, usually against Viet Cong gunners firing upon Binh Thuy Air Base. Radar controllers on the ground sometimes directed tactical fighters in nighttime strikes on targets located by piecing together intelligence data.[27]

Air War over South Vietnam, 1968–1975

During 1968, the mission of the river force changed, even as infantry strength increased from three to seven American battalions. Instead of roving the delta as before, the command at mid-year undertook the pacification of Kien Hoa Province, lying between the northernmost and southernmost forks of the Mekong. Concentrating on this single province meant that operations normally started from one of four permanent anchorages, using a limited number of waterways. As a result, the Viet Cong could more easily set up ambushes. Since the landing craft had become more vulnerable, the force made greater use of helicopters, both to suppress hostile fire and, where terrain and vegetation permitted, to land troops.[28]

By year's end, South Vietnamese troops had begun training with the river force, and South Vietnamese airmen were bombing and strafing in support of these units and the American infantry as well. An Air Force liaison officer with the Army division characterized the South Vietnamese pilots as "very accurate bombers," though American forward air controllers had difficulty with them because of the language barrier.[29] Another liaison officer echoed this assessment, acknowledging South Vietnamese skill, but declaring, "I still prefer to call in U.S. fighters for support of troops in contact [with the enemy]. We use the same terms and the FAC is always certain that he and the jocks [fighter pilots] are on the same wavelength."[30]

The river force reached its peak strength as 1968 came to an end. Ahead lay the withdrawal of American forces and the substitution of South Vietnamese. Within the delta, emphasis shifted from pacification to the interdiction of supplies moving by river and canal from the Parrot's Beak into South Vietnam.[31]

Not every operation in IV Corps during 1968 involved air strikes in support of landing craft butting their way along the muddy streams that laced the fertile rice lands. Near the Cambodian border, the terrain rose sharply, and here, in the so-called Seven Mountains of Chau Doc Province, a parachute assault took place. On November 17, 1968, Air Force C–130s dropped South Vietnamese paratroops some six miles southwest of the village of Tri Ton. The drop zone lay at the base of an enemy-held mountain, where B–52s, Air Force fighters, artillery, and army helicopters had pummeled the Viet Cong weapons emplaced there.[32]

The drop proved a trickier operation than anticipated. Clouds settled over Nha Trang Air Base, where the troops were loading, and also concealed navigational checkpoints over much of the route to the target. The change in weather came too late for preparation of an instrument flight plan. As a result, the C–130s took off early and improvised a convoluted course, seeking canyons through the clouds. The transports did not emerge from the overcast until they were approaching a fork of the Mekong, which they followed inland through clear skies until they made their turn for Tri Ton. Because the drop zone was so small and difficult to identify, each transport had to make two passes just to be sure, increasing the risk of enemy fire, which damaged two planes.

As Army helicopters released smoke to blind hostile gunners, the C–130s roared past the mountain, dropping the first troops well away from a tree line at the edge of the zone. Word soon came from the ground, however, that the men were landing in a marsh, where their heavy loads might trap them in pools of water, some deep enough to drown a person. The next group, therefore, dropped near the trees, running the lesser risk that the parachutes would become entangled among the branches.[33]

Besides the parachute troops, South Vietnamese infantry and irregular forces took part in the attack, advancing by land. General Abrams' headquarters reported that the operation, which lasted twelve days, killed more than a hundred of the enemy. In addition, the South Vietnamese got credit for capturing some ninety Viet Cong guerrillas and arresting half-again as many persons suspected of supporting the insurgents.[34]

Throughout South Vietnam, air power played a variety of roles. Depending on the weather, geography, and hostile activity within a certain region, these might include close air support of friendly troops, defoliation, reconnaissance, the delivery of troops and supplies, interdiction of roads and waterways, and the bombing of bases and supply depots. Aircraft, moreover, flew these missions over dense forest, open rice paddies, mountain wilderness, and densely populated regions. Nowhere, however, did aviation do more than in the defense of the isolated outposts established by U.S. Army Special Forces.

Since 1965, Special Forces detachments had operated a series of border outposts from Khe Sanh and Lang Vei in the north, past the tri-border area, the Fishhook and Parrot's Beak, beyond the Plain of Reeds, to the Ca Mau peninsula. At each camp, the Americans trained and organized local inhabitants, whether lowland South Vietnamese, members of one of the mountain tribes, or persons of Cambodian ancestry, to become "hunters of the Viet Cong and North Vietnamese Army," ambushing infiltration groups, raiding bases, and locating enemy concentrations for attack by air or ground forces. Except for an occasional foray into Laos or Cambodia, these hunters seldom ventured far from the villages where their families lived, each protected by a fort that served as an operating base.[35]

Typical of the larger Special Forces camps was Duc Lap, near the Cambodian border southwest of Ban Me Thuot. The garrison built the strongpoint on two small hills, emplacing machineguns and recoilless rifles and encircling the perimeter with barbed wire. Behind the wire entanglement, the defenders dug a trench, constructed bunkers, and set up claymore mines — weapons fired by remote control that spewed lethal fragments to the front. The light infantry companies organized for the defense of Duc Lap also had some 81-mm mortars and one 105-mm howitzer to engage targets screened by the nearby hills. If an attack penetrated the wire and overran the outer defenses, the mountain tribesmen and their U.S. advisers had an inner perimeter of trenches and bunkers or, if necessary, could retreat to a final redoubt on one of the hills.[36]

Air War over South Vietnam, 1968–1975

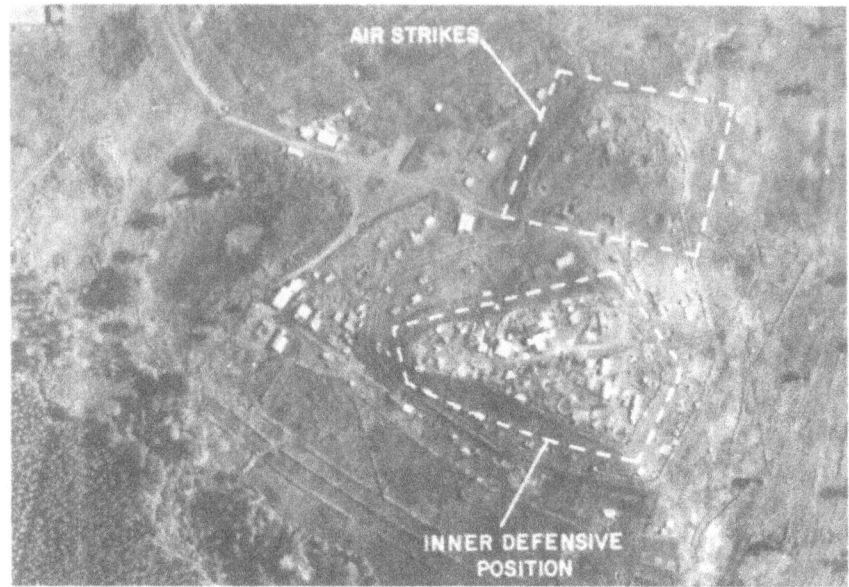

Duc Lap Special Forces camp.

At about 1:15 on the morning of August 23, the North Vietnamese attacked Duc Lap, bypassing or frightening off the ambush parties posted along the approaches to the camp. After some five hours, the Special Forces commander, 1st Lt. William J. Harp, ordered one platoon of mountain tribesmen to counterattack, but this advance did not get beyond the camp's main gate. While shells burst among the defenders, the enemy overran the airstrip and broke through the outer perimeter of the camp itself.[37]

With Duc Lap's survival at stake, an AC–47 gunship, patrolling nearby to deal with just such an emergency, appeared overhead shortly after the fighting began, and Air Force tactical fighters, directed against targets on the ground by forward air controllers, joined the action after daybreak. During the morning, the enemy scored a hit on an attacking F–100C flown by 1st Lt. Julius Thurn, one of the recently mobilized Air National Guard pilots, who ejected safely. His parachute caught the attention of the Duc Lap Special Forces detachment, and eight of its members, plus two tribesmen, piled into a pair of 3/4-ton trucks and roared out of camp, past astonished North Vietnamese soldiers crouching on either side of the road. The rescuers found Lieutenant Thurn, who leveled his pistol at them before he realized they were friends, and brought him back unhurt to camp. Handed an automatic rifle, the pilot shared for three hours the dangers of infantry combat before a helicopter returned him to Tuy Hoa Air Base.[38]

Early attempts to land reinforcements near the besieged outpost ended in failure, and not until August 25 could mountain tribesmen flown by Army helicopter from Nha Trang and Pleiku fight their way from the landing zones into

Above Highlands, Plain, and Delta

An Air Force C–7 landing at Duc Lap Special Forces Camp.

the camp. Until these reinforcements arrived, napalm, aerial bombs, and strafing helped Harp's men hold out, even though the North Vietnamese overran part of the compound. On one occasion, a forward air controller broke up an attack by diving into a barrage of automatic weapons fire to launch marking rockets, tricking the North Vietnamese into seeking cover and keeping them pinned down until fighter-bombers could carry out a strike. Later, aerial attacks against enemy-held bunkers and trenches inside the camp perimeter cleared the way for a final drive that routed the surviving North Vietnamese at dusk on the 25th.[39]

Throughout the struggle for Duc Lap, the irregular forces defending it depended on supplies delivered by air. Army helicopter crews flew 18 missions into the camp, sometimes carrying their cargo in nets slung beneath Boeing CH–47s. Air Force C–7 transports made eight supply drops, parachuting water, ammunition, rations, and medicine to the embattled garrison.[40]

Air power also came to the rescue of Thuong Duc, a similar camp located at the base of the western highlands in Quang Nam Province. This fort came under attack on September 28, about a month after the fight at Duc Lap. Here, too, the North Vietnamese struck in the early morning darkness, overrunning the outposts manned by irregular troops, firing into the camp itself, and seizing the airfield and most of the nearby village. The battle remained deadlocked until 1:00 p.m., when a forward air controller directed four sorties against the captured outposts, in preparation for a successful counterattack. The force that advanced from the main camp found grisly proof of the effectiveness of the air strikes. Scattered about one outpost were parts of eight to ten bodies, while similar remains indicated that about twenty persons died at another. By dusk, some forty fighter-bombers had hit targets in enemy-held territory.[41]

Night found the enemy in control of most of the high ground around the camp. To help keep him at bay, a Marine airborne controller flying an airplane fitted with a radar transponder established an aerial checkpoint over the battlefield. Grumman A–6 Intruders, normally flown by Marines on nighttime armed reconnaissance missions over Laos or southern North Vietnam, homed on this beacon and then followed instructions from Marine radar operators on the ground to bomb the North Vietnamese without endangering friendly forces.[42]

Along with the Marine A–6s, Air Force AC–47 gunships took part in the nighttime defense of Thuong Duc. Because of its long endurance, devastating firepower, and night vision scope, the AC–47, nicknamed Spooky, proved a formidable instrument for defending special forces camps. At Thuong Duc on the night of September 29, for example, the Spooky on station fired 113,000 rounds from its three multi-barrel machineguns.[43]

Air strikes proved essential in expelling the enemy holding out in the village, fighting from new concrete-walled houses, many of them built by the families of Thuong Duc's defenders. On September 28, after the South Vietnamese district chief reported that all noncombatants had departed, a force of irregulars attacked the village but became pinned down in the marketplace because their supporting 106-mm recoilless rifles could not penetrate the sturdy buildings nearby. An Army Special Forces officer called for air strikes that annihilated both the structures and the troops that had fortified them. In the vicinity of the marketplace, the advancing irregulars found 40 to 50 bodies, with other corpses half-buried in collapsed trenches or houses.

Shortly afterward, a forward air controller called in F–4s against a suspected mortar position across a river from the camp. Dust from the first bombs had barely settled when yellow smoke billowed upward, a signal sometimes used to indicate the presence of friendly troops. The ruse failed, however, since the controller had received word that neither Americans nor South Vietnamese had crossed the stream. Again and again, fighter-bombers swept low over the target, and frantic messages crackled over a captured North Vietnamese radio being monitored by members of the Thuong Duc Special Forces detachment. The radio traffic indicated that American bombs had fallen squarely upon a North Vietnamese unit, wounding a high-ranking officer and causing momentary panic.[44]

The struggle for Thuong Duc lasted until the morning of September 30, when a mobile strike force, landed from Army helicopters the previous day, helped drive off the North Vietnamese. The aerial firepower unleashed in close proximity to the camp had proved overwhelming. Besides the nighttime activity of the slowly circling AC–47s and the more modern AC–130A with its side-firing 20-mm guns, the enemy had to contend each night with as many as ten radar-directed A–6 strikes. In addition, B–52s bombed suspected troop concentrations some distance from the battlefield.[45] No wonder that a Special Forces officer declared, "Air saved the camp. There is no doubt about it."[46]

The successful defense of Thuong Duc led to the launching on October 6, of a combined U.S. Marine-South Vietnamese attack that overcame fierce opposition to clear the hills around the base. The drive encountered stubborn resistance from the outset, even though B–52s had battered areas where the enemy was believed to be massing. When the North Vietnamese beat back a Marine battalion, Air Force planes sought to blast a path through the defenses, dropping bombs filled with an explosive gas resembling propane that seeped into foxholes and underground bunkers before detonating. At night, an AC–130 took over, strafing the ridges in the Marine zone. Rather than have an O–2A circling in the dark, the direct air support center responsible for this area added a forward air controller to the gunship crew, enabling him to use the night vision scope and the other sensors on board to direct its fire.[47]

Despite these Air Force contributions, Marines flew and directed most of the air strikes conducted in support of the advance during its first six days. On October 12, however, when the attackers collided with an entrenched North Vietnamese regiment, bad weather had grounded the Marine airborne controllers who normally patrolled overhead. At about noon on that day, the direct air support center handling aerial activity in this portion of I Corps received word from Army officers advising the South Vietnamese forces that the enemy had checked the assault in a narrow valley north of Thuong Duc. Air Force officers at the support center chose an experienced forward air controller, who took off under poor conditions, hoping to find better weather over the battlefield. After a flight of just fifteen minutes, he arrived over the battlefield and found that visibility was adequate for air strikes to aid the Marines and South Vietnamese below.

From the battlefield came a call for a helicopter to evacuate wounded. The controller relayed the request and when the helicopters arrived, he fired his rockets as though marking a target for fighter-bombers. The enemy immediately took cover and could not fire accurately as the wounded were borne away. After helping meet this emergency, the forward air controller helped direct air strikes until dusk, leaving only when necessary to refuel and take on marking rockets. Among the first strike aircraft on the scene were Marine A–4s, highly maneuverable attack planes ideally suited to bombing targets within the confines of the valley. A Marine airborne controller arrived late in the afternoon to help locate the enemy and suspend artillery fire while aerial attacks were taking place.

Handling a flight of South Vietnamese A–1s, whose pilots spoke no English, posed the most difficult problem the Air Force forward air controller faced that day. An Army adviser with the South Vietnamese troops on the ground improvised a solution, however. He repeated messages from the Air Force officer to an English-speaking South Vietnamese, who translated the instructions and radioed them to his countrymen circling above the valley. Bombs from the A–1s helped break North Vietnamese resistance, enabling the advance to proceed.[48]

The AC–130A gunship, the prototype of which saw action over Thuong Duc and the hills nearby, was one of several new weapons used in South Vietnam during 1968, as the Air Force carried out the function of developing equipment, preparing doctrine for its employment, and training men in its operation. To locate targets concealed by darkness, the new plane carried a variety of sensors, including an infrared detector and a night observation scope. While normally firing its 20-mm cannon and 7.62-mm machineguns on trucks traveling the roads of southern Laos, the AC–130A and its even more heavily armed successors could help meet emergencies in South Vietnam.[49]

Another type of gunship, the AC–119G, arrived at Nha Trang during the final days of 1968. Reservists mobilized after the Tet offensive flew this converted Fairchild transport, which was intended as a replacement for the AC–47. Armed with 7.62-mm multi-barrel machineguns and mounting a night observation device, this twin-engine plane lacked the speed, ceiling, firepower, and sensors to attack highway traffic in heavily defended southern Laos. A better-armed variant, the AC–119K, carried an infrared detector and had two pod-mounted jet engines that improved performance, enabling it to patrol the Ho Chi Minh Trail and other target areas.[50]

The Fairchild AC–123, intended for night attacks against the road net of southern Laos, underwent combat testing over the Mekong Delta. Another converted transport like the AC–47, AC–119, and AC–130, this plane featured an ignition detector to pick up electromagnetic impulses from gasoline-powered trucks, along with low-light-level television, infrared gear, and a laser range finder. After locating a target, the AC–123 salvoed fragmentation bombs from dispensers stowed in the cargo compartment. The aircraft arrived in South Vietnam late in 1968 and, as in the case of the AC–119G, testing continued into the next year.[51]

Two other night attack aircraft underwent testing in South Vietnam during 1968. The Tropic Moon I was an A–1E that relied on low-light-level television

Above Highlands, Plain, and Delta

The night observation device on an AC–119.

to locate its targets. Because the camera required straight and level flight, preferably at an altitude of about 2,500 feet, Tropic Moon I could not search areas protected by concentrations of light antiaircraft guns. In spite of its vulnerability, the modified A–1 flew some armed reconnaissance missions near Khe Sanh, during the defense of that base.

The Tropic Moon II was a Martin B–57B that sought out targets using television and an infrared sensor. A laser beam measured the range, and an onboard computer calculated a bomb-release point based on speed, altitude, and type of ordnance. During the tests, which began in December 1967, one of the three planes accidentally bombed a police post in the delta, but Tropic Moon II nevertheless saw emergency use in the vicinity of Khe Sanh and underwent further testing in southern Laos. Over the Ho Chi Minh Trail, however, the aircraft showed no more than marginal value in night attack.[52]

Few of the bombs introduced into Southeast Asia during 1968 yielded immediate benefit within South Vietnam, valuable though they may have been against targets in the North or on the Ho Chi Minh Trail in southern Laos. The bombs filled with explosive gas, known as fuel-air munitions and used in the fighting around Thuong Duc, conferred an advantage against bunkers and other fortifications, and the massive 10,000-pound high-explosive bombs parachuted from C–130s effectively blasted helicopter landing zones amid dense jungle. The laser-guided bomb, which made its debut in 1968 against caves, fords, and bridges in southern Laos, saw only limited use in South Vietnam. Rockeye, used over the North by the Navy and Marine Corps, though not yet adopted by the Air Force, was a cylindrical canister that popped open to scatter 247 bomblets, each carrying a .39-pound shaped charge capable of blasting through some seven inches of armor plate. Rockeye later would prove deadly in suppressing antiaircraft fire during fighter strikes throughout Southeast Asia.[53]

A new observation plane, the twin-turboprop North American Rockwell OV–10 Bronco, promised to have a marked impact on the air war over South Vietnam. The aircraft was designed for visual reconnaissance, especially by forward air controllers, the mission of some 85 percent of the 150,000-odd tactical reconnaissance sorties flown in 1968. To forward air controllers, this two-place aircraft offered a number of advantages. It was faster and featured better visibility than either the O–1 or O–2A, had better radio equipment, mounted four machineguns, and could carry bombs and both target-marking and high-explosive rockets. Armor protection exceeded that in the O–2A, which had been an improvement over the O–1. Of the three, only the OV–10 had self-sealing fuel tanks. Although the best of its type thus far, the new plane lacked the endurance of the O–2A — four hours in the air compared to six — and exhibited other flaws, among them poor cockpit ventilation, a severe drawback in the heat and humidity of South Vietnam.[54]

Support of ground troops, as the statistics on fixed-wing operational sorties clearly indicated, tended at this time to monopolize the energies of the Seventh Air Force. The command, however, also provided fighters for the aerial defense of South Vietnam, maintained radar surveillance to warn of attack, and operated a computerized control center that would direct the interceptors to attack the enemy. During the spring of 1968, even as the mini-Tet offensive was failing, North Vietnam presented a challenge to the air defense system.

American and South Vietnamese observers posted near the southern edge of the demilitarized zone began reporting helicopters dodging by night among the hills and valleys in that region. After dusk on June 15, sightings became so numerous that the Seventh Air Force Tactical Air Control Center at Tan Son Nhut, having made sure that no U.S. air traffic was in the area, sent F–4 fighters from Da Nang to investigate. A confused melee erupted at the eastern shoulder of the demilitarized zone and in adjacent coastal waters: the F–4s reported firing rockets at Soviet-built helicopters, the cruiser USS *Boston* reported a rocket attack by a North Vietnamese fighter, and about an hour later rockets and gunfire, described as from a helicopter, sank a Navy motor patrol boat, though all on board escaped. Certain they had been fired on by North Vietnamese — and were not accidentally in the path of rockets from the F–4s — the naval units involved did not report the incident to the Seventh Air Force control center, which knew only that the F–4 crews had reported attacking helicopters.

After dark on the 16th, word reached Tan Son Nhut that enemy helicopters had returned to the demilitarized zone, and F–4s again intercepted. The Air Force fighter crews reported a successful night's work. One fired a pair of rockets that, according to an observer on the ground, scored a direct hit on a helicopter that sent fiery debris tumbling earthward from the victim. Another Phantom sighted three helicopters on the ground and dropped six 500-pound

Above Highlands, Plain, and Delta

An OV–10 Bronco, with machineguns and rocket pods under the fuselage.

bombs that started three fires. A third F–4 crew encountered an airborne helicopter and fired a missile that, according to witnesses aboard a KC–135 tanker flying nearby, scored an apparently mortal hit.

After this encouraging beginning on the night of June 16, the air battle turned chaotic shortly after midnight. Two missiles launched from an F–4 detonated close to the *Boston*, but caused no casualties and only superficial damage. Less fortunate was the Australian cruiser *Hobart*, struck by a pair of missiles that killed two and wounded seven. Another missile, fired by an F–4 at what the crew thought was a helicopter, exploded harmlessly near an U.S. destroyer. This time, the source of fire could not possibly have been North Vietnamese, and the control center issued a warning that on future patrols, fighter crews should have the helicopter in sight before firing. Relying solely on radar returns had proved too dangerous.[55]

Besides resulting in this emergency restriction, the accidents brought about closer coordination between aerial activity over the eastern part of the demilitarized zone and naval patrols. The misdirected rockets also led to a test of F–4 radar against slow, low-flying targets like helicopters. Following instructions from a radar controller at Da Nang, an F–4 had no trouble intercepting the test helicopter, but the weapon systems officer in the fighter found that on his radar scope the return from the helicopter looked exactly like the image of one of the patrol boats on the water nearby. The Da Nang controller also coached a second aircraft participating in the test, a Cessna A–37, into position to intercept, but the crew lacked airborne radar for engaging a target by night.[56]

As the summer wore on, observers and radar operators continued to detect North Vietnamese helicopter activity in the demilitarized zone at night, but efforts to confirm the presence of these intruders rarely succeeded. Since airborne radar had proved unreliable, the Air Force Weapons Laboratory began a somewhat bizarre effort that was sponsored by the Office of Director, Defense Research and Engineering, in conjunction with Dr. McMillan, science adviser to General Abrams.

A team from the weapons laboratory set up a night observation device, a laser range finder, and video taping equipment near a battery of eight-inch howitzers at Con Thien, a Marine outpost south of the demilitarized zone. After spotting a helicopter with the observation device, Air Force technicians used the laser to determine the range and calculate when the target would pass through the trajectory of shells fired by the battery and timed to explode after traveling 25,000 feet. If the helicopter's projected flight path and the point of explosion seemed likely to coincide, the gunners opened fire. The airmen used low-light-level television to tape the results, and on one occasion, bursting shells appeared to have destroyed a helicopter. A fire glowed afterward in the darkness, and on the next morning a reconnaissance pilot saw an oil slick drifting offshore. This possible kill marked the high point of the short-lived project.[57]

Meanwhile, the Convair F–102 interceptors assigned to defend South Vietnam against air attack were about to depart. The danger from bombers seemed to be diminishing, and this obsolete fighter-interceptor could not fly slow enough to deal with helicopters. First to go was the F–102 detachment at Bien Hoa, which departed in September 1968 for the Philippines. McDonnell Douglas F–4Es Phantoms, with a multi-barrel cannon installed in the air frame instead of mounted in a pod as in the D series, took the place of the older F–102s. Because the F–4Es arrived so slowly, the last F–102 did not leave the country until late 1969. Afterward, responsibility for aerial interception rested on four Air Force F–4Es at Da Nang and a pair of Marine F–4s at Chu Lai.[58]

Such were representative techniques, typical operations, and new equipment of Air Force units fighting in South Vietnam during 1968. The year also saw the approval of an expansion of the authority exercised by the Seventh Air Force commander, who doubled as deputy for air operations on the military assistance command staff. General Momyer gained acceptance of the tenet of Air Force doctrine that held an Air Force officer should exercise control over all tactical aviation, whether Air Force or Marine Corps, to take full advantage of the inherent flexibility and striking power of this form of air power.

Chapter Six

Testing the Single Manager Concept

When North Vietnamese troops were massing around Khe Sanh in early January 1968, the arrangements governing tactical air strikes in I Corps had endured for almost three years. The first contingent of Marines had scarcely established itself at Da Nang in 1965 when General Westmoreland proposed that his deputy for air operations, Lt. Gen. Joseph H. Moore, assume control of the Marine tactical combat squadrons. Such a move would not only reflect Air Force doctrine, which promised greater flexibility and economy through centralized control, but also follow a Korean War precedent. During that conflict, a Marine aircraft wing had functioned, insofar as communications proved reliable, as a task force under the "coordination control" of an Air Force officer, Lt. Gen. Earle E. Partridge, who commanded the Fifth Air Force. The Korean example did not prevail, however. The Commander in Chief, Pacific, Admiral Sharp, denied Westmoreland's request, insisting on coordination between Air Force and Marine Corps rather than subordination of Marines to airmen.

Thanks to Sharp's decision and the composition of forces in the I Corps tactical zone, the Commanding General, III Marine Amphibious Force, could employ Marine Corps aircraft, artillery, and infantry as components of a unified air-ground team. At first, Marines had been the dominant American force in I Corps, with the Army supplying mainly artillery battalions, but this balance began to change late in 1967, when the Army's Task Force Oregon arrived in the region. In mid-January 1968, Marine airmen normally flew strikes for Marine infantry, and Air Force squadrons assisted the task force, now designated the Americal Division. Such an apportionment of the aerial effort remained feasible only as long as the Marine Corps and Army fought in separate portions of I Corps. Additional Army battalions would soon be coming, however, to fight alongside the Marines. This change provided the occasion for General Westmoreland to try once again to obtain Admiral Sharp's approval to place all U.S. fighter-bomber, attack, and tactical reconnaissance squadrons based in South Vietnam, whether Marine or Air Force, under the authority of his deputy for air operations, General Momyer. Other factors influenced Westmoreland, including a lack of confidence in the leadership of III Marine Am-

Air War over South Vietnam, 1968–1975

phibious Force and Momyer's insistent advocacy of the Air Force doctrine of centralized control.[1]

In again recommending that an Air Force officer exercise what amounted to operational control over Vietnam-based Marine aviation, Westmoreland endorsed Air Force doctrine, as presented by Momyer. General Momyer argued the Air Force position that a central authority could best take advantage of the speed and versatility of air power, shifting strike aircraft to critical areas without deferring to the Marine Corps view that, as elements of an integrated air-ground team, Marine airmen should support Marine infantry. Momyer insisted that Air Force doctrine on this point should prevail; indeed, he told General Chaisson, the Marine in charge of General Westmoreland's combat operations center, that he saw no need to have two air arms, Air Force and Marine, fighting the war in South Vietnam. More important, Momyer enjoyed Westmoreland's confidence, deservedly so, since he was, as even those who disagreed with him acknowledged, "a very competent commander... a convincing man [who] knew his stuff and knew how to present his stuff..."[2]

Along with the existence of an Air Force doctrine on the subject and the presence of a forceful spokesman to enunciate it, the changed composition of the American ground forces fighting in I Corps helped convince General Westmoreland that centralization was necessary. During 1967, the entire length of the I Corps tactical zone had separated Marines in the north from soldiers to the south, so that Air Force planes had been able to support Army battalions without running afoul of Marine aircraft assisting Marines on the ground. As 1968 began, Westmoreland could anticipate the introduction of additional Army troops that would cooperate closely with the Marines. By the end of January, a second Army division, General Tolson's air cavalry, would be assigned to I Corps and come under General Cushman's operational control for the projected advance to Khe Sanh. Still another major Army unit, the 101st Airborne Division, was to reach I Corps in February, with the result that soldiers came to outnumber Marines by two to one in this tactical zone. As the U.S. forces inevitably intermingled, the need to use air power efficiently in a constricted space seemed to preclude a division of labor in which Marine aviation supported Marines and soldiers looked to the Air Force for help.[3]

While Momyer cited the shifting balance of I Corps forces in his campaign "to get air responsibilities straightened out as we had them in... Korea,"[4] Westmoreland was losing confidence in the leadership and tactics of the Marines fighting in the northern provinces. Although his dissatisfaction focused on staff work and ground combat, he became convinced that Marine aviation could not meet the needs of the Army battalions coming under Cushman's operational control.[5] To some extent, Westmoreland's attitude reflected the fact that the Marine Corps, on the basis of its experience in World War II and Korea, had not anticipated that one of its commanders would assume responsibility for so large an Army contingent. Tailored to support a comparatively small amphibious force, Maj. Gen. Norman J. Anderson's aircraft wing could not suddenly expand to cope with the Army influx. At best, the wing could make sorties in excess of Marine needs available to the attached Army units and rely on the Air Force to continue its support of these newly arrived battalions.[6]

Lacking full confidence in the leadership of III Marine Amphibious Force, Westmoreland sought to tighten his control over ground activity in I Corps. Since responsibilities elsewhere prevented his personally directing operations in the northern provinces, he decided to set up a headquarters echelon at Phu Bai, southeast of Hue. This so-called "MACV [Military Assistance Command, Vietnam] Forward" came into being on February 3, 1968. On the 12th his principal deputy, General Abrams, left Saigon to take over the new headquarters.[7] The matter of tactical aviation could not be resolved so easily, however, for Admiral Sharp had to approve any change in the policy adopted in 1965.

The effort to persuade Sharp, however difficult it might be, seemed essential. Air Force doctrine, effectively championed by General Momyer, and doubts about the ability of the Marines to support Army forces might not in themselves have resulted in a renewed effort to bring Marine Corps aviation under the Air Force officer's control, but these factors coincided with the threat to Khe Sanh. General Westmoreland was convinced that the enemy intended to storm this base in quest of a victory to rival the triumph over the French at Dien Bien Phu. Determined to crush the North Vietnamese massing in the hills around Khe Sanh, he heeded General Momyer's warning that, "The control of the air is getting so complex that we could fail to apply our air power in a timely manner if the enemy should launch an attack tomorrow."[8]

Such were the arguments for centralization. Before Admiral Sharp confirmed or denied Westmoreland's selection of Momyer to control all tactical combat aviation based in South Vietnam, Sharp would weigh this case against the arguments for retaining the status quo. Opponents could cite the importance of aviation to a Marine air-ground team in which Marine pilots, trained in close support, compensated for a lack of artillery by providing a reliable source of firepower that the ground commander could incorporate in his tactical plans and depend upon in an emergency. This reliance on aviation reflected the realities of amphibious warfare, the unique mission of the Marine Corps, for during the first, critical hours of assault landing, helicopters and landing craft imposed restrictions on the weight and type of weapons that could be brought ashore. To wary Marines, a break-up of the air-ground team not only would blunt their organization's combat edge, but might well imperil the amphibious mission and the future of the Corps itself.[9]

Apparently sensitive to both the tactical needs of the Marine Corps and the organization's concern for its future, Admiral Sharp proved reluctant to endorse Westmoreland's January 1968 proposal for centralization. At Sharp's urging, Generals Momyer, Anderson, and Cushman drew up an agreement that gave Khe Sanh's defenders, most of them Marines, first call on Marine aviation for strikes close to the base. Air Force tactical fighters hit the more distant targets, with any surplus sorties of the 1st Marine Aircraft Wing placed at Momyer's disposal.[10]

Although the arrangement enabled Momyer to position an airborne battlefield command and control center in the skies over Khe Sanh to serve as strike coordinating agency, he did not receive the authority over Marine aviation that both he and Westmoreland wanted. Two separate air wars continued fighting in the northern provinces of South Vietnam: the Marines primarily supporting the Marines on the ground and the Air Force essentially supporting the Army. In the aftermath of the Tet offensive, with Marines and soldiers now fighting side-by-side in the same operations, this duplication of effort seemed intolerable, and Westmoreland tried once again to give Momyer unified control over tactical combat aviation, both Air Force and Marine.[11]

This time Admiral Sharp agreed. "I didn't think the single manager concept was necessary," he later explained, "as long as the Marines were the only troops in I Corps," but with three Army divisions in place, the compromise method of control had not worked to General Westmoreland's satisfaction, and "it got to a point where a single manager got to be a reasonable thing."[12] As a result, on March 8, 1968, General Momyer received "mission direction" over the attack, fighter-bomber, and reconnaissance planes of the 1st Marine Aircraft Wing. Although mission direction had no accepted definition, it seemed at first to possess the main elements of operational control. In approving Westmoreland's proposal to give Momyer de facto operational control, Sharp insisted on two points: first, Marine requests for immediate strikes would not have to be processed by the Seventh Air Force Tactical Air Control Center at Tan Son Nhut; and, second, the Marines could present their complaints and suggestions for improvement not only to General Westmoreland but directly to Sharp himself.[13]

Mission direction seemed merely a euphemism for operational control and embraced several command functions, among them the composition of forces, the assignment of tasks, the designation of objectives, and the authoritative direction necessary to accomplish the mission.[14] Although mission direction dealt mainly with attack sorties, which indicated a functional approach rather than the organizational one generally used in establishing operational control, the internal cohesiveness of the air-ground team could not help but be affected, for the new arrangement imposed outside control over the response by Marine airmen to requests by Marines on the ground.

In spite of the March decision, the 1st Marine Aircraft Wing retained its identity as the aviation component of General Cushman's III Marine Amphibious Force, thus preserving — in General Westmoreland's opinion, at least — the integrity of the Marine air-ground team. However, the functioning of the team changed, for Marine squadrons would not react as before in providing a battalion commander with the air support he requested. This support continued to take the form of preplanned and immediate strikes, terms used by both the

Testing the Single Manager Concept

Marine Corps and Air Force, but the words now took on an Air Force interpretation.

For the Marines, amphibious troops lacking in organic artillery, the preplanned strikes requested in advance of an operation had normally been integrated with available artillery and other supporting weapons into a precisely timed plan. To meet battlefield emergencies, the prescribed purpose of immediate strikes, the Marines kept a number of aircraft on airborne or ground alert, planes flown by men thoroughly familiar with the area of operation. Marines, in short, were used to planning and executing missions precisely as requested by the commander on the ground, and they boasted that their method was "user oriented," designed to meet the needs of the man with the rifle, an orientation forced upon them by their lack of artillery, especially the heavier types.

In contrast, Air Force planners looked upon preplanned strikes both as a means of meeting requirements predicted by the battalion commander a day or more in advance and as a source of aircraft to be diverted for immediate strikes in case of emergency. For these reasons, a day's operations order issued by an Air Force headquarters sought to group strikes according to the timing of actions on the ground, while at the same time ensuring a fairly steady flow of aircraft into an area so that planes would be available throughout the day for immediate strikes. To make certain that fighter-bombers would be on hand as needed, unified management required that preplanned strikes be arranged further in advance — a minimum of about thirty-six hours instead of twenty. As the Pegasus operation in April would demonstrate, the percentage of preplanned strikes actually delivered tended to be somewhat low, since many of these scheduled sorties would be diverted to immediate strikes against new and dangerous targets.

Unlike the Marine Corps, the Air Force preferred to keep as few aircraft as possible on alert, relying instead upon planes diverted from previously assigned targets to conduct immediate strikes. This policy reflected the fact that the volume of air power available throughout South Vietnam was limited; since speed and flexibility compensated for the lack of numbers, aircraft had to be kept active, shifting from lower priority targets to mass at points of greatest danger, and not allowed to remain idle, waiting in one part of the country for a threat that might never arise.

Along with the underlying philosophy, the mechanics of obtaining air support also changed, though the ultimate goal remained the focusing of air power where it most was needed. Formerly the nerve center for Marine aviation, the direct air support center at Da Nang lost its preeminence, becoming an extension of Momyer's Seventh Air Force Tactical Air Control Center. Marines would join the Seventh Air Force organization at Tan Son Nhut to help prepare the daily strike order, while Air Force officers — as well as a few South Vietnamese airmen — received assignments to the Da Nang facility. Within I Corps a second direct air support center, subordinate to the one at Da Nang, assumed responsibility for processing strikes requested by elements of Provisional Corps, Vietnam — the headquarters for all Army units under the operational control of Cushman's amphibious force. In effect, the loss of autonomy by I Direct Air Support Center meant that the schedule of preplanned strikes, but not requests for immediate strikes, would have to pass through another level of review, the Tactical Air Control Center, albeit one where Marines now served.[15]

About three weeks elapsed before every element of the new single manager system established on March 8 began functioning. On March 10, the Seventh Air Force first used its tactical air control system, including the airborne battlefield command and control center, to assist Marine aviators responding to calls for immediate strikes. The Marines assigned to the new V Direct Air Support Center, serving Lt. Gen. William B. Rosson's provisional corps, and to the Tactical Air Control Center at Tan Son Nhut began arriving on March 21. The Tactical Air Control Center produced the fragmentary order or "frag," so named because a rigid format permitted fragmentary content with no sacrifice of meaning. The first frag — the daily operations order specifying aircraft, timing, ordnance, and targets for all of South Vietnam — that embraced Marine aviation covered missions flown on March 22, but the hurriedly formed Marine-Air Force team at Tan Son Nhut could not produce a truly integrated frag order until about April 1.[16] In the meantime, the direct air support center created for Provisional Corps, Vietnam, had encountered similar delays, complicated by the need for exclusive communications circuits linking it to the Army divisions and to General Cushman's headquarters. Enough men and equipment became available, however, to permit a limited operation to begin on March 21.[17]

When Operation Pegasus got underway on April 1, the new procedures for arranging air strikes had gone into effect. To obtain scheduled strikes, a battalion commander or South Vietnamese province chief met a specified deadline in submitting his requests to the brigade or regimental headquarters. There, a tactical operations center or fire support coordination center accepted the lists, assigned a priority to each proposed strike, and forwarded the compilation to division headquarters, where a similar process took place. From division, the proposal went to corps or amphibious force, where officers in the tactical operations center conferred with members of the direct air support center in determining the precedence of the various missions. Next the slate traveled to Saigon for review by Westmoreland's tactical air support element, where Marines also now served. This agency studied lists from all over South Vietnam, singling out areas of emphasis (such as the Pegasus operating zone) before turning the requests over to General Momyer's Tactical Air Control Center for preparation of the day's frag order.

As Admiral Sharp had insisted, the Tactical Air Control Center could not veto immediate strikes; instead it played a purely supportive role, helping to marshal air power to meet emergencies. The tactical air control party of the battalion or other unit that had run into trouble called for an immediate strike by contacting the appropriate direct air support center, sometimes by means of a forward air controller. Since the Marines had, in effect, an extension of this center in the division headquarters, either the 1st or 3d Marine Division or III Marine Amphibious Corps might divert a scheduled strike to deal with the threat. If no aircraft were available in the immediate vicinity, the Marines could call on V Direct Air Support Center and, if that agency could not help, on the Seventh Air Force Tactical Air Control Center, which could divert any aircraft within range of the embattled unit, regardless of corps boundaries. The Tan Son Nhut center might also grant permission for the Marines to launch an aircraft, "scrambling" it to deal with the threat.[18]

Such was the basic form of unified management that took shape during the last three weeks of March. Besides fearing the impact of these procedures on the future of the air-ground team and the Corps itself, Marine leaders considered the new method slower and less responsive than the one it replaced. They charged that centralization had increased by sixteen to thirty hours the time required to process preplannned strikes. Nor did they believe that a plane diverted to an immediate strike was as likely to be carrying suitable munitions as one that had been on airborne or ground alert to attack a specific kind of target. These Marines intended to take full advantage of Westmoreland's promise to review the system in thirty days, and they also planned to argue their case before President Johnson and his defense advisers.[19]

While the Marines honed their arguments for the first of the monthly evaluations Westmoreland had promised, which was scheduled for the end of April, Gen. Leonard F. Chapman, Jr., Commandant of the Marine Corps, launched an offensive in Washington, trying to persuade the Joint Chiefs of Staff to undo what Westmoreland had done. By the end of March, the Joint Chiefs had discussed the selection of a single manager for Vietnam-based tactical combat aviation, but had not reached a decision. According to General Wheeler, the chairman, his colleagues had been unable to find a satisfactory answer to the key question, "What caused General Westmoreland to feel that the arrangement in I Corps needed changing?"[20]

General Momyer, whom Westmoreland sent to Washington to explain unified management, offered an answer to this question, an explanation based on two considerations: the need to use air power efficiently; and the introduction of Army divisions into I Corps, formerly a Marine operating area. After outlining the new procedures and the conditions that had brought them about, Momyer repeated the presentation for the President, who, according to General Chapman, had vowed that nothing would be done to hurt the battlefield Marine. The session with Momyer, Wheeler believed, laid to rest the Chief Executive's fears for the man in the foxhole and dissuaded him from intervening on behalf of the Marine Corps.[21]

Although unable to enlist the President as an active ally, General Chapman continued to campaign within the Joint Chiefs of Staff against single manage-

Air War over South Vietnam, 1968–1975

Gen. William C. Westmoreland, Commander, U.S. Military Assistance Command, Vietnam (left), and Lt. Gen. William W. Momyer, Commander, Seventh Air Force (right).

ment and the threat it seemed to pose to the Marine Corps. The Joint Chiefs, however, could not reach a consensus; they neither sustained Chapman's objections nor formally approved the Westmoreland policy. General Wheeler nevertheless felt confident that the Secretary of Defense — or his deputy secretary, Paul Nitze, who had become executive agent for this matter — ultimately would accept his position, a compromise that combined endorsement of Westmoreland's decision — the legitimate exercise of a senior commander's authority over the resources at his disposal — with assurances that the arrangement did not set a "precedent governing the future assignment of Marine Corps air units or as affecting the Marine concept of the air/ground team."[22] As Wheeler was drawing up a formal recommendation to this effect for the deputy secretary, time came for General Westmoreland's first evaluation of unified management, giving the Marines another opportunity to present their case.

From his III Marine Amphibious Force headquarters, General Cushman sent General Westmoreland two assessments in rapid succession, one covering the period March 22 to April 21 and the other focusing upon the month of April. Both expressed dissatisfaction with the new procedures, charging that they were less responsive than those they replaced. Although the second report conceded that the average reaction time had improved late in April, Cushman insisted that this greater responsiveness resulted from the diversion of aircraft from preplanned strikes, which in Marine Corps tactics formed part of a unified scheme of fire support. Because of the balance in Marine Corps operations among artillery, other supporting weapons, and preplanned air, Cushman warned that additional Marine aircraft sometimes had to take off and replace the ones diverted

Testing the Single Manager Concept

Adm. U. S. Grant Sharp, Commander in Chief, Pacific (left),
and Lt. Gen. Robert E. Cushman, Jr., Commander,
III Marine Amphibious Force (right)

to immediate targets. Admittedly, the Marines had sometimes diverted strikes under their old management system, though they tried to avoid the practice, relying instead on aircraft on airborne or ground alert. When the diversion of preplanned sorties proved unavoidable, General Cushman maintained that his fellow Marines had shown "greater discretion" than did the Seventh Air Force Tactical Air Control Center because they were "completely cognizant of . . . the effect of the divert on the ground action."[23] Besides the diversion of air strikes, the Marines in South Vietnam complained about excessive paperwork and the incompatibility of Air Force and Marine Corps doctrine.[24]

After conferring with Cushman and Momyer about the substance of these two reports, General Westmoreland thought he detected in both parties "a depth of introspection" that boded well for the future of unified management.[25] The Seventh Air Force, for instance, conceded that requests for preplanned strikes were taking too long to process — thirty-six to fifty hours from request by battalion commander to actual execution. Although blaming the delays in part on unrealistic deadlines arbitrarily imposed by ground commanders, Momyer's headquarters agreed to unclog the congested administrative channels. Seventh Air Force offered, for example, to begin providing just the applicable portion of the frag to each corps tactical zone instead of issuing copies of an order that covered the entire country.[26]

Interpreting the Seventh Air Force's offer as a sign of cooperation, General Westmoreland sent a team of six officers to Hawaii to advise Admiral Sharp of accomplishments and problems during the month of April. The group included Maj. Gen. Gordon F. Blood and Col. DeVol Brett of the Seventh Air Force and two Marines, Major General Anderson of the 1st Marine Aircraft Wing and Col. Clement C. Chamberlain. The delegation met with Sharp on May 10 and found him far from satisfied with Seventh Air Force's concessions.[27]

According to Maj. Gen. Walter T. Kerwin, Jr., Westmoreland's chief of staff and the head of the group that flew to Hawaii, Sharp wanted to see the latest Air Force proposals in writing and to have the Marines comment upon them. "Admiral Sharp," Kerwin reported, "indicated that he feels we have not yet come up with the solution to the problem and is not convinced that the corrective measures will be satisfactory." The principal change Sharp suggested was the allocation to General Cushman of a specific number of sorties, which his headquarters could use for preplanned strikes.[28]

The Seventh Air Force staff and Westmoreland's tactical air support element immediately set about drafting procedures designed to satisfy Admiral Sharp's objections.[29] The revisions, endorsed by General Momyer, called for reprogramming the Tactical Air Control Center computer to produce a basic weekly operations order that would be supplemented by a simplified daily frag containing only the data needed by a specific recipient. The new weekly frag served as a vehicle for the key reform inspired by the Hawaii meeting — the allocation of sorties among corps tactical zones, rather than among specific operations. Each week, the Seventh Air Force Tactical Air Control Center would earmark a certain number of sorties for each tactical zone, listing the ordnance load and time of availability. The nature of the ground operations within the corps area, and the requests these operations generated, would determine the actual targets these aircraft would attack.

Momyer also streamlined the administrative procedures for drawing up the weekly or daily strike schedules. One change relieved battalion commanders of the need to obtain formal approval from brigade or regiment when requesting preplanned air strikes; silence at the higher headquarters now implied consent. Another change allowed the tactical air support element at Westmoreland's headquarters to deal directly with Provisional Corps, Vietnam, although the III Marine Amphibious Force retained final authority over the diversion of preplanned sorties to the Army corps, over which Cushman exercised operational control.

Under this modification of unified management, Cushman now received an allocation equalling 70 percent of the preplanned sorties, both Air Force and Marine, normally flown in I Corps in the weekly frag. His headquarters apportioned this total between I and V Direct Air Support Centers, so that Marine and Army commanders both had a definite volume of air power on which they could depend. If a major operation loomed on the horizon, battalion commanders might call for additional preplanned strikes, their requests moving forward through the tactical operations center or fire support coordination center and, if approved at the various levels, to the tactical air support element and tactical air support center for inclusion in a daily frag.[30]

Testing the Single Manager Concept

General Momyer agreed to a further adjustment to the single manager system that resolved another issue raised by Admiral Sharp during the discussions in Hawaii. Sharp pointed out at the May meeting that Army helicopter gunships, not subject to the single manager, did many of the same jobs as Marine Corps fighter-bombers or attack aircraft and asked that this factor influence the apportionment of sorties. Since General Cushman's Marines could not muster the helicopter gunship armada available to General Tolson's air cavalry, a new revision to the management system permitted the 1st Marine Aircraft Wing to reserve up to 10 percent of its available tactical aircraft for escorting troop-carrying or supply helicopters and suppressing fire from enemy gunners.[31]

The changes inspired by Admiral Sharp ensured that mission direction, as yet undefined, meant something less than operational control. Even as he was narrowing the scope of mission direction, he accepted the justification for unified management, the principle that air power had to go wherever it could do the most good, and he agreed that the changes now endorsed by General Momyer would meet the objections raised at the Hawaii meeting and help tactical aviation realize its true flexibility. Sharp, however, did not with a single decision resolve all the details of single management, for the modified system would have to undergo its own thirty-day evaluation during June.[32]

Air Force and Marine Corps commands were nevertheless making progress toward unified control, a point that General Wheeler stressed as the Joint Chiefs of Staff continued their discussion of the subject. In contrast to the chairman, who highlighted the accomplishments, General Chapman emphasized the defects that had appeared during the first month of operation. In the hope of resolving the split between the Marine Corps view, generally supported by the Army and Navy, and Westmoreland's position, which Wheeler accepted and the Air Force heartily endorsed, Wheeler pointed out that the responsible commanders were cooperating to correct the very failings that Chapman had noted.

Although the Joint Chiefs could not agree, Deputy Secretary of Defense Nitze found Wheeler's logic persuasive. On May 15, as the latest modifications to the system were beginning to take shape in South Vietnam, Nitze adopted the course of action Wheeler had been advocating for several weeks. In brief, the deputy secretary upheld Westmoreland's right, as the commander on the scene, to centralize the management of tactical aviation, denied that such a move established a precedent governing the status of Marine aviation in future conflicts, and urged a return to normal as soon as circumstances would permit.[33]

As Momyer's staff was responding to Sharp's call to meet Marine Corps objections to unified management and Chapman was trying unsuccessfully to rally the Joint Chiefs against this practice, a battle that Momyer called "the real test of the validity of the single management system" broke out in South Vietnam's western highlands.[34] The enemy hurled the challenge during an attack at the Kham Duc Special Forces camp. Within seventy-two hours, air power reinforced, helped defend, and finally evacuated this outpost, located southwest of Da Nang, near the border with Laos.

The Kham Duc attack began with an assault on a forward operating base at nearby Ngok Tavak. Early on the morning of May 10, North Vietnamese gunners shelled the outposts scattered along the ridges overlooking the old French fort at the heart of Ngok Tavak's defenses. Out of the darkness came a group of men, shouting that they were friends, causing the defenders to hold their fire. The newcomers suddenly began throwing grenades and firing automatic rifles and used satchel charges to blast a path through the protective barbed wire. By the time an Air Force AC–47 arrived overhead, the mountain tribesmen manning the fort itself had withdrawn to the command bunker, joining their Special Forces advisers, three Australians, and the surviving members of a Marine Corps howitzer detachment posted at Ngok Tavak. The gunship fired into the perimeter, concentrating on a 105-mm howitzer revetment that the attackers had overrun and converted into a strongpoint. Joined in about an hour by a flareship, the AC–47 remained in action until dawn, when helicopter gunships, tactical fighters, and a forward air controller took over.

Although air strikes kept the enemy at bay throughout the morning, the plight of Ngok Tavak's defenders worsened by the hour. Two of four Marine CH–46 helicopters bringing in reinforcements were disabled after landing and abandoned, and when a smaller helicopter took off after picking up wounded, at least two of the irregulars clung to the landing skids, but each lost his hold and from high above the jungle fell to his death. Cut off from further reinforcement and sustained solely by air power, the command fought its way out of the base, found refuge on a hilltop across the Dak Se River from Ngok Tavak, and hacked out a landing zone for rescue helicopters.[35]

As Ngok Tavak was being abandoned, reinforcements began arriving at Kham Duc, some five miles to the northeast. As soon as he realized the threat to the main camp and its forward operating base, General Cushman on his own initiative dispatched four rifle companies, an artillery battery, and a company of engineers, all from the Americal Division, an Army unit under his operational control. At mid-morning on May 10, Air Force C–130s began flying this group, commanded by Lt. Col. Robert B. Nelson, into Kham Duc. When Westmoreland learned that Cushman had decided to reinforce, he counseled caution, suggesting that General Cushman discuss possible alternatives with him or his deputy, General Abrams. If necessary, the Army and Marine Corps leaders might confer to weigh further reinforcement against evacuation and the substitution of massed B–52 strikes for the firepower of infantry and artillery.[36]

With further reinforcement of Nelson's Kham Duc task force a possibility, an Air Force ground control team accompanied the first contingent to land. The team's three members — Maj. John W. Gallagher, TSgt. Morton J. Freedman, and Sgt. James D. Lundie — were to control airlift traffic, making sure that

Testing the Single Manager Concept

planes did not attempt to land unless the runway was clear, that soldiers were at hand to unload cargo, and that any departing passengers were ready to board. Major Gallagher and his men stepped from a C–130 late in the afternoon of the 10th, as the day's airlift was coming to an end.[37]

Since Gallagher's team dealt exclusively with air transport, someone else had to link Nelson's headquarters with the forward air controllers directing strikes in the jungle-covered hills around Kham Duc. Lt. Col. Reece B. Black volunteered for the job, arranging for an O–1 pilot to fly him into the base after dark on May 10, when enemy observers could not see to call down mortar fire. The light plane settled safely on the blacked-out airstrip, and Black emerged to search out Nelson's command post. The battalion staff, Black later reported, was so pleased to have an airman on hand to help coordinate attacks on the mortar sites that one of its members gave him an air mattress — "quite a prized possession" — so he could rest for the battle that seemed sure to come.[38]

Colonel Black, who remained at Kham Duc for twelve hours, and Capt. Willard C. Johnson, his replacement, proved well worth the investment of an air mattress. Until the battle neared its climax, they radioed information to between two and five Air Force forward air controllers on station day and night. On a typical day, a forward air controller arrived before dawn, found an AC–47 finishing its nighttime chores, and checked in with the Air Force officer at the Kham Duc command post, receiving Colonel Nelson's instructions as relayed by Black or Johnson. The controller might direct his first tactical fighter strikes by flare light, until the transport providing the illumination departed with the approach of sunrise. After two hours on station, time enough for perhaps a half-dozen flights of fighter-bombers to make their passes, another forward air controller took over.[39]

Besides the flareships and gunships, the forward air controllers and the tactical fighters they directed, B–52s also came to the aid of Kham Duc's defenders. Following the evacuation of Ngok Tavak, General Westmoreland's staff arranged for III Marine Amphibious Force to select five B–52 target boxes in the enemy-held jungle, including one that embraced the abandoned camp. On May 11, radar controllers on the ground radioed new headings to a total of thirty bombers, diverteing them to boxes at Ngok Tavak and its environs.[40]

Even as Nelson's force was joining the locally recruited irregulars in defending Kham Duc, Westmoreland weighed "the pros and cons of reinforcing Kham Duc or, alternatively, evacuating it." He decided to withdraw, using "tactical air and B–52 firepower in an attempt to punish the enemy massed around the place to the maximum." General Abrams, who also favored evacuation, flew to Da Nang, where he discovered that General Cushman had reached the same decision. The pull-out would begin the following day, May 12.[41]

At 6:05 a.m., Momyer received word to start the evacuation. Radar-directed fighter-bombers had been attacking the approaches to the camp throughout the night, but reports from Major Gallagher, relayed from the airlift control center, indicated that the North Vietnamese had begun closing the vise. To handle tactical air power over Kham Duc, Momyer dispatched an airborne battlefield command and control center, a C–130 fitted out with communications and data processing equipment that enabled the airmen on board to keep track of the available strike aircraft, matching them with targets appropriate to the ordnance they carried, as well as recording the reported results of the attacks. While this converted transport was still en route, the Tactical Air Control Center began shifting fighter-bombers from preplanned targets in Laos, southern North Vietnam, or elsewhere in South Vietnam, directing the planes to check in with the airborne battlefield command and control center, which handed off its first flight to the forward air controllers at about 9:20 a.m.[42]

Until the airborne battlefield command and control center appeared, forward air controllers handled the arriving strike aircraft. At sunrise, fog and low clouds settled over Kham Duc, but one of the controllers, Capt. Herbert J. Spier, who had directed strikes on the previous day, knew the lay of the land. Following instructions from Captain Johnson at the command post beside the airfield, Spier guided fighter-bombers over the invisible targets and told the pilots when to release their bombs. Below, Johnson adjusted the strikes, even though he sometimes could not see the explosions and had to rely on sound alone to determine corrections. The overcast, however, had begun breaking up when the specially equipped C–130 arrived.[43]

In planning the withdrawal, the Marine headquarters at Da Nang had proposed four additional B–52 target boxes located three or more kilometers from the camp. The first of these came under attack at 8:35 a.m., when six of the planes released their bombs. All sixty B–52 sorties scheduled for the day were diverted to the defense of Kham Duc, with some 6,000 bombs dropped and the impact area gradually moved within 500 yards of the runway, as the enemy kept pressure on the shrinking perimeter.[44]

Army helicopters launched the evacuation, but one of the first CH–47s to arrive at Kham Duc was shot down, crashing at the edge of the runway. The airborne battlefield command and control center, which had no direct radio contact with the Army helicopters, remained unaware of the beginnings of the withdrawal. Officers of the Army's 14th Combat Aviation Battalion took charge, orbiting the battlefield throughout the day, relaying instructions to the incoming helicopters from Nelson's headquarters and from the forward air controllers.[45]

The appearance late in the day of Marine helicopters complicated the control problem. Hurriedly briefed on conditions at Kham Duc, the crews arrived low on fuel; indeed, some of them had to leave and refuel before receiving clearance to land at the airstrip. The craft that did pick up troops usually sustained damage from small arms fire or mortar fragments. Marine 1st Lt. S. T. Summerman, at the controls of the fourth helicopter in his flight to land at Kham Duc, had his craft hit by enemy gunners and, in his opinion, might well have been shot down, except that "Air Force F–100s suppressed the fire tremendously with napalm."[46] Another Marine, unable to land because he ran low on fuel, complained that "there was no control between fighters and helicopters," though forward air controllers did provide a communication channel that soon became overcrowded. He also cited a "lack of liaison...between Army [and] Marine Corps," probably alluding to the sketchy information he had received before taking off for Kham Duc.[47]

Ironically, control would have been worse except for the accuracy of North Vietnamese gunners. A shell tore away the right wing tip of an O–2A flown by Capt. Philip R. Smothermon, who made a forced landing and taxied to the edge of the runway to avoid blocking the Air Force transports that had already begun arriving to pick up troops. He found an abandoned Air Force radio, borrowed some months before by the Special Forces contingent to call for strikes on the roads and trails west of Kham Duc. Since the set worked, he radioed the direct air support center, which told him to stay at the camp, by order of General Momyer, and act as air liaison officer, replacing Captain Johnson, who had just departed after spending some twenty-four hours at the command post.

The discovery of the radio enabled Smothermon to contact Americal Division headquarters as well as the direct air support center, the airlift control element at Da Nang, the forward air controllers overhead, and the airborne battlefield command and control center. In addition to helping Nelson select targets to keep the North Vietnamese at bay, he advised him when transports would land so that the designated evacuees would be ready to board. He also relayed messages between Nelson and Maj. Gen. Samuel W. Koster, the division commander, when the Army transmitter at Kham Duc failed.[48]

At about 10:30 a.m., Air Force transports joined the Army and Marine Corps helicopters in evacuating troops and noncombatants, when two C–130s and a C–123, hurriedly diverted from other tasks, began circling high over the besieged camp. First to land was a C–130, piloted by Lt. Col. Daryl D. Cole, which touched down amid bursting mortar shells, blew a tire, and sustained a tear in a wing fuel tank. As soon as Cole's loadmaster lowered the ramp, members of the families of Kham Duc's irregular forces swarmed on board the plane, preventing the crew from unloading cargo intended for the defenders.

Colonel Cole tried to take off, but had to abandon the attempt because the shredded tire prevented the heavily loaded transport from gathering enough speed to become airborne. Taxiing off the runway, he had his crew clear the refugees from the cargo compartment, unload the plane, and try, unsuccessfully, to cut away the ruined tire. With mortar bursts drawing progressively nearer, Cole decided to attempt another takeoff with an almost empty airplane. After two perilous hours on the ground, he headed onto the runway, keeping one engine shut down to prevent its heat from igniting the fuel leaking from the hole in the nearby tank. Before beginning his takeoff run, he started the engine

Air War over South Vietnam, 1968–1975

and watched to see that the wing did not catch fire. An examination after he landed revealed that bullets and shell fragments had torn some eighty-five holes in the metal skin of the aircraft.

On board Cole's plane were just four passengers: Captain Johnson, who had replaced Colonel Black as air liaison officer, and the three members of Major Gallagher's control team. In the confusion of the evacuation, Gallagher, himself a C–130 pilot, heard that all transport missions had been canceled, a report that seemed plausible in view of what had befallen Cole's aircraft. Since most of the team's equipment had been destroyed by a mortar shell and one of the members, Sergeant Lundie, had broken his hand, Gallagher and his men clambered inside for the dangerous takeoff.[49]

While Cole's crew struggled to get rid of the blown tire, the only C–123 to evacuate people landed and picked up forty-four Army engineers and twenty-one dependents of members of the irregular force based at Kham Duc, pushing the number evacuated, mostly by helicopter, beyond 200, but not yet one-eighth of the garrison, its dependents, and its Army reinforcements.[50]

The second C–130, flown by Maj. Bernard L. Bucher, landed at about 3:30 p.m. At least 150 wives and children of the local tribesmen crowded on board the transport, which thundered into the sky only to come under fire from a pair of .50-caliber gun mounted on a hillside nearby. Fatally damaged by the barrage, Major Bucher's transport crashed and exploded about a mile from the end of the runway, killing all on board. A forward air controller had seen muzzle flashes and called in air strikes, though too late to save Bucher, his crew, and his passengers.[51]

Lt. Col. William Boyd, Jr., who was approaching Kham Duc as Bucher's plane exploded, made a steep descent, passing through a torrent of small-arms fire before flaring out to land. The wheels had not yet touched, however, when a mortar shell burst on the runway ahead of the plane, forcing Boyd to pull up and go around a second time, again braving enemy fire as he landed to pick up about a hundred persons. As the C–130 gathered speed for the takeoff, bullets punctured the metal fuselage, but caused no injury to passengers or crew and only minor damage to the aircraft.[52]

Looking down on Kham Duc from the C–130 piloted by Lt. Col. John Delmore, the flight engineer, TSgt. John K. McCall, saw "something out of a John Wayne movie," with helicopters making rocket runs and F–4s bombing. Boyd's transport lunged down the runway, straining to become airborne and clear the way for Delmore's plane, already in its steep descent toward Kham Duc. At an altitude of about 300 feet, McCall heard a sound "like sledgehammers, like someone banging on the aircraft." The loadmaster, SSgt. Dave Chesser, suddenly decided to go aft to the cargo compartment to prepare to open the doors and lower the ramp. "And he no sooner left," the flight engineer recalled, "than right where his head was, there was a six-inch hole in the airplane."

Testing the Single Manager Concept

Both Delmore and his copilot, Capt. Joseph Donohue, struggled to hold the wings level as the plane settled onto an airstrip littered with brass cartridge casings and shell fragments. Tires burst and the cargo craft veered out of control, crashing into a wrecked helicopter. The crew ran from the disabled transport and hid behind some barrels. Drawing their .38-caliber pistols, they waited, feeling, according to McCall, like "little kids going out with the big kids, because of the AK–47s [Soviet-built automatic rifles] all around us going off." Six men came running toward Delmore's crew, and the sight of blond hair under one of the helmets assured the airmen that these were not the enemy. Except for the navigator, Capt. Robert Lake, who found room on one of the last C–130s out of Kham Duc, the members of Delmore's crew departed by helicopter.[53]

Two more C–130s picked up troops at Kham Duc on the afternoon of May 12. Lt. Col. Franklin Montgomery brought his plane in and out of the airstrip without sustaining a single hit and carried away another 150 persons. Last to land was Maj. James L. Wallace, who reversed propellers, dropped the ramp and opened the cargo doors, then turned about to take off in the direction from which he had landed. Irregular troops bolted for the plane, ignoring the now idling propellers, and knocked down a woman and baby trying to board. Luckily one of Wallace's crewmen saw the plight of the two and helped mother and child into the crowded aircraft. Next came the rear guard, some two dozen Americans, including Captain Smothermon, who had been serving as air liaison officer since his crash landing earlier in the day.[54]

As Wallace took off, another C–130 was approaching the abandoned base, its mission to land men rather than evacuate them. On board were the three members of Gallagher's ground control team who had been under the impression that no more transports would land at Kham Duc when they left earlier in the afternoon on Cole's C–130. Discovering that the team had departed, Brig. Gen. Burl W. McLaughlin, the 834th Air Division commander, ordered them to return. They stepped onto the Kham Duc airstrip for the second time that day at about 4:20 p.m. from a C–130 piloted by Maj. Jay Van Cleeff. As it took off, Gallagher and the others went first to the Special Forces camp and then to Colonel Nelson's command post. Both were deserted. Realizing that they were alone and that death or capture could be minutes away, they took a radio from their survival kit and began signalling for help.[55]

Major Van Cleeff's C–130 was climbing away from the outpost when he heard a radio message stating that Kham Duc had been abandoned and granting the circling fighter-bombers permission to attack and destroy the crippled aircraft that littered the runway — Smothermon's O–2A, Delmore's C–130, one large helicopter, and a helicopter gunship. Van Cleeff broke in, warning the control agencies that he had just landed three persons who would have to be picked up. The rescue became the responsibility of Lt. Col. Alfred J. Jeannotte, Jr., whose C–123K was next on call.

109

Air War over South Vietnam, 1968–1975

Jeannotte made the usual steep approach, escorted by fighter-bombers to pin down the North Vietnamese closing in on the runway. The plane touched down safely, but the crew could not see the three men, who had scrambled from a ditch and were waving their arms. Unable to reverse his propellers, for to do so would have automatically shut down the two jet auxiliary engines, the pilot applied maximum power, and the transport leapt into the air again. As he banked, he caught sight of the team on the ground below, but a glance at his fuel gauge revealed that he could not make another fast approach and full-power takeoff. The task of saving the three men devolved upon the next transport in sequence, a C–123K flown by Lt. Col. Joe M. Jackson.[56]

Colonel Jackson had started out that morning on an evaluation flight, a periodic check of proficiency, during which Maj. Jesse W. "Bill" Campbell, in the copilot seat, served as examiner. When orders came to head for Kham Duc and stand by to aid in the evacuation, Campbell declared the evaluation over, congratulated Jackson on passing, and settled in as copilot. Over the base, Jackson again demonstrated his flying skill, beginning with the steepest possible descent to foil enemy gunners.

When Jackson's transport plunged toward them and they realized that a second rescue attempt was underway, Gallagher, Lundie, and Freedman left the protection of a ditch, determined they would not be missed this time. They were on their feet and waving as the plane touched down and began rolling in their direction. About a hundred yards from the men, who were running toward their rescuers, Jackson braked and turned the C–123K. He applied power for the takeoff while his crew hauled the team members on board. A 122-mm rocket struck nearby, but skidded to a stop without exploding. Bunkers on either side of the airstrip spewed small-arms fire, and burning ammunition detonated, showering metal fragments on the airfield, but Colonel Jackson managed to guide the plane safely into the air. The rescue earned him the Medal of Honor; Major Campbell received the Air Force Cross; the flight engineer, TSgt. Edward M. Trejo, and the loadmaster, SSgt. Manson Grubbs, were awarded the Silver Star.[57]

As the adventures of Major Gallagher's control team demonstrated, confusion had abounded at Kham Duc, though perhaps no more so than in most battles. After all, the evacuation had succeeded, with Air Force transports carrying away about 700 persons, with helicopters — Army and Marine Corps combined — removing roughly the same number. Dependents of the irregular soldiers posed a serious problem, since no complete tally of their numbers existed. Several hundred found places on board the Air Force cargo planes, 150 or more died in the crash of Major Bucher's C–130, and perhaps 200 hid in the forest to emerge when the fighting had died away. Many of the irregular soldiers joined their families, and several hundred remained unaccounted for the day after the battle.

American casualties on the ground at Ngok Tavak and Kham Duc totaled twenty-five killed and about four times that number wounded. The toll in aircraft proved high: one C–130 was shot down, with all on board killed; another

Testing the Single Manager Concept

Lt. Col. Joe M. Jackson received the Medal of Honor for his rescue mission at Kham Duc.

crashed on landing, but without loss of life; an O–2A was damaged beyond repair, though the pilot, Captain Smothermon, survived; an Air Force A–1E was downed, but the pilot was rescued; and five helicopters were destroyed, three Marine and two Army.[58]

Many of the difficulties encountered at Kham Duc dealt with the exchange of information among different communications systems. One radio net handled tactical fighters, another Air Force transports, and still others served the helicopters and linked the Army battalion at the base with division headquarters. Equipment failure or heavy traffic at the points where these networks intersected could, at a critical moment, isolate a commander or an entire phase of the operation. Such problems, however, probably proved no more severe at Kham Duc than in similar operations elsewhere. Indeed, breakdowns were few, and the efforts of resourceful individuals — including Captain Smothermon, working with the radio he found — kept communication channels open despite the occasional failure.[59]

Despite the absence of overall centralization of control, two unified management systems functioned as intended throughout the action. The airlift control center marshaled Air Force transports in time to play a key part in the evacuation, and the system controlling tactical fighters succeeded in concentrating air power at the critical point. Indeed, General Momyer's various control echelons launched or diverted to Kham Duc 120 Air Force fighter-bombers based in both South Vietnam and Thailand. Only 16 Marine aircraft, all of them A–4s, appeared over the battlefield, which lay in far southwestern I Corps. The other tactical aircraft that took part, two from the Navy and a half-dozen South Vietnamese, were not subject to unified management. An Air Force C–130 airborne battlefield command and control center, a key element in the new control network, brought all the fighter-bomber activity into focus.[60]

Air War over South Vietnam, 1968–1975

Although General Momyer hailed the Kham Duc evacuation as a vindication of unified control of tactical combat aviation, he apparently was referring more to the principle involved than to the details of the system then in effect and its specific accomplishments. During the action, comparatively few Marine Corps tactical aircraft took part, and the Air Force fighters from Thailand, the South Vietnamese participation, and the pair of Navy sorties would have been as readily available without the March directive. Moreover, single management, as exercised at Kham Duc, was even then undergoing revisions that would limit the authority of the Seventh Air Force commander over Marine Corps tactical aviation. The changes already underway would lead to others and culminate in a narrow interpretation of mission direction as something different from and less sweeping than operational control.

Chapter Seven

Unified Management takes a Final Form

Single management, as tested at Kham Duc, had not yet undergone the changes wanted by Admiral Sharp, the Commander in Chief, Pacific, and fashioned by General Momyer. Not until May 30, a month after the end of the evaluation period that had lead to their adoption, did the modifications go into effect. The Tactical Air Control Center began preparing both daily and weekly frags, specifying the preplanned missions in a degree of detail tailored to the needs of the recipient. Within I Corps, the recipient was, in effect, the commanding general of III Marine Amphibious Force, since his I Direct Air Support Center received all preplanned sorties allocated for the tactical zone and then released an appropriate number to V Direct Air Support Center for Army operations. The revised management system also made available to the Marines a block of sorties for helicopter escort, and the procedure for immediate requests now functioned more swiftly because approval by intermediate headquarters — brigade or regiment — was taken for granted in the absence of a specific statement to the contrary.[1]

Would the new weekly frag and the streamlined administrative procedures prove satisfactory to General Cushman? Would the Marine Corps accept this less rigorous form of unified management in exchange for Deputy Secretary of Defense Nitze's assurances concerning the future of the air-ground team? No, Marine Corps leaders believed that too much was at stake both tactically and in terms of the survival of their organization. Before May had ended, Lt. Gen. Victor H. Krulak, commander of the Fleet Marine Force, Pacific, pointed out what he considered a "loophole" in Nitze's decision to have command arrangements return to normal as quickly as possible. Krulak suggested that because the military situation had returned to normal once the Khe Sanh garrison had prevailed, an immediate revival of the old system of command, with the III Marine Amphibious Force reasserting control of its aircraft wing, though making a certain percentage of the sorties available to Seventh Air Force for missions in the northern provinces, should occur.[2]

General Chapman sought to convert General Krulak's idea into a formal proposal for the Joint Chiefs of Staff. He suggested that the Marines in South

Air War over South Vietnam, 1968–1975

Vietnam receive unrestricted control over 70 percent of their weekly sorties. The Seventh Air Force Tactical Air Control Center no longer would specify times or ordnance for these sorties, and the Marines would, in effect, prepare a weekly operations order of their own. If the Joint Chiefs endorsed General Chapman's idea, the III Marine Amphibious Force would again be able to treat the 1st Marine Aircraft Wing — 70 percent of its sorties, at any rate — like any other organic supporting arm. In presenting his plan, Chapman described the authorization of what amounted to a Marine Corps frag order as a transitional move away from centralization and toward the return to the Marines of operational control over their aircraft. As a concession to Westmoreland's policy of centralized management, he would leave 30 percent of the wing's tactical sorties under the control of the single manager during the period of transition.[3]

At the end of June, in assessing the first month's experience with the procedures as modified to meet Sharp's objections, Cushman recommended the same solution as Chapman. "The modified system," Cushman conceded, "is an improvement, a step forward from the cumbersome system implemented on 20 March," but in his opinion centralization continued to "harbor deficiencies." All too often, he complained, the rapidly changing tactical situation forced Marine battalion commanders to request additional preplanned sorties not listed in the weekly frag; obtaining approval caused no problem, but the change imposed an unanticipated burden on pilots, mechanics, and planners as they changed ordnance loads and otherwise prepared for the new targets.[4]

In spite of the need for adjustments of this type, the 1st Marine Aircraft Wing enjoyed a great measure of autonomy under the modified single manager procedures that went into effect on May 31. Assigned a sortie rate of 1.2 per aircraft, General Anderson's wing held out two F–4s for air defense, leaving 188 planes available for tactical missions. These could fly 225 sorties in a single day, but 48 sorties were earmarked for alert status, reducing the total to 177. The Marines also retained another 18 sorties for helicopter escort or for the general support of ground troops, if not needed in the escort role. Of the 225 sorties normally flown each day, 66 thus remained under Marine control, available for either escort or emergencies, while 111 were allocated in the weekly frag for preplanned strikes to be carried out during that period. The daily frag listed 48 Marine Corps sorties, 16 of them scheduled against targets in Laos or southern North Vietnam. Fighter-bombers assigned to preplanned strikes on a given day could, of course, be diverted to immediate attacks.[5]

Despite the increased number of sorties under Marine control, General Momyer and his Seventh Air Force staff disputed the claim that the recent changes had undermined the principle of unified control or justified further concession to the Marine Corps' point of view. In the critical matter of immediate strikes, rather than the preplanned variety authorized in the weekly operations order, Momyer maintained that the Tactical Air Control Center, which functioned as the executive arm of the single manager, knew "where the flights are

Unified Management takes a Final Form

Gen. Leonard F. Chapman, Jr., Commandant of the Marine Corps, (left) and Lt. Gen. Victor H. Krulak, Commander of the Fleet Marine Force, Pacific (right).

going and when." As a result, the control mechanism, especially the airborne battlefield command and control center, found it comparatively easy to concentrate air power, as at Kham Duc, or to divert tactical fighters into holding patterns to permit B–52 strikes or facilitate the passage of transport planes.[6]

Far from providing a precedent for decentralization, these Air Force officers insisted, the weekly frag, whatever its exact contents, remained an allocation from the central manager to his agent, a distribution that could be varied according to anticipated need. General Cushman's tactical zone was making full use of its weekly slate of sorties — indeed, it absorbed some 50 percent of all tactical sorties flown in South Vietnam — but some new threat might arise elsewhere and the approaches to Saigon or the western highlands become the decisive battlefield. As circumstances changed, the single manager could shift his strength to meet the current threat, something he could not do as easily if the Marines again controlled the bulk of their aviation.[7]

This Air Force insistence on flexibility could not help but clash with the Marine Corps treatment of air power as simply another supporting weapon organic to the air-ground team. According to the findings of a panel appointed by General Westmoreland to examine the controversy, the Marines "will never embrace the single manager concept because of the implicit threat it poses to the Marine air-ground principle." Accordingly, the panel concluded, not even "continued modification of the system" would make centralized control "more palatable to them."

Aware of the incompatibility of Air Force and Marine doctrine, Westmoreland's study group nevertheless concluded that some form of unified management was essential for the Vietnam conflict, in which a limited number of aircraft had to wage war throughout a comparatively large area. On the other hand, the inquiry found some justification in the recurring Marine Corps complaint that the Seventh Air Force system of highly centralized management is "more oriented toward the producer than it is to the customer." The four members of the study group, one an Air Force officer but none a Marine, suggested that over the years the bone and muscle required to exercise centralized control had become layered with fat in the form of "control echelons, increased mission standardization, increased administrative burden." The periodic review and resulting modification of the management system adopted in March seemed, however, to have removed much of that excess, bringing about, according to this panel, procedures that the Marines could endure, though never endorse.[8]

This favorable assessment received General Westmoreland's prompt endorsement. On the verge of departing from South Vietnam to become Army Chief of Staff, he pronounced as successful the arrangement he had championed. The "modified preplanned support procedures now in operation," he declared, formed "the most effective system" of management to satisfy the demands of the Vietnam War.[9]

Admiral Sharp, who would soon retire, did not share General Westmoreland's enthusiasm, and word reached Saigon that he now endorsed the recommendation of Generals Cushman and Chapman that Marine aviation be returned, in almost its entirety, to Marine control. However, General Abrams, the new commander of the military assistance command, accepted Westmoreland's view and declared that the system launched by Westmoreland "was working well and should continue . . . and that he was damned if he would give an inch on this issue."[10]

Meanwhile, Adm. John S. McCain, Jr., had taken over the Pacific Command. Lt. Gen. Henry W. Buse, Jr., the new commander of the Fleet Marine Force, Pacific, urged McCain to endorse the views Admiral Sharp had recently expressed and to discuss the return, on a trial basis, of fixed-wing assets used in I Corps Tactical Zone with General Abrams.[11] When he visited Saigon, however, McCain found that General Abrams bristled at the suggestion of further tinkering with centralized management, and the plan to restore Marine Corps control expired early in August, though Generals Buse, Cushman, and Chapman persisted for several weeks in trying to revive it.[12]

During the first week of September, Admiral McCain confirmed the control arrangements set up by General Westmoreland and modified at Admiral Sharp's insistence. He reviewed the arguments for and against centralization, talking with General Chapman and Adm. Thomas W. Moorer, the Chief of Naval Operations, as well as with General Abrams, concluding that further evaluations, conducted monthly since April, would be fruitless. McCain concluded that the single manager system had so improved that it now was "providing for the best overall use of tactical air." In large measure, he based his decision on reports of

Unified Management takes a Final Form

the effectiveness of air power, not merely in I Corps, but throughout all of South Vietnam. Army commanders, whose combat battalions outnumbered the Marines four-to-one, seemed all but unanimous in declaring that they now received better air support than ever before. Only the Marines claimed to be worse off under single management, and in McCain's opinion, they would never endorse the system, since a mechanism they did not fully control could never be as responsive as one they did.[13]

Between the beginning of June and Admiral McCain's final evaluation, additional minor changes had occurred. A third direct air support center began functioning in I Corps, this one at Camp Horn, the site of III Marine Amphibious Force headquarters. The Horn Direct Air Support Center, commanded by an Air Force officer, began operation on August 10, receiving the weekly and daily slates of preplanned strikes for I Corps and apportioning them between the I and V Direct Air Support Centers. The new agency helped allocate strikes between Cushman's amphibious force and Rosson's provisional corps, a responsibility that Cushman had assumed at the end of May.

In addition, General Brown, as single manager, relaxed his control to permit the Marines to experiment with a daytime airborne alert, provided the wing had aircraft to spare after meeting all its commitments. During the day, beginning on August 5, a Marine fighter-bomber or attack plane went on alert, standing by in its revetment. If not scrambled within a half-hour, the alert aircraft took off, flew to an assigned station, and orbited there for some forty-five minutes, while another aircraft took its place on the tarmac. If not used that time for an immediate strike, the plane on airborne alert attacked some previously selected target. By August 28, these alert aircraft had demonstrated a reaction time of fifteen minutes or less, compared to roughly thirty minutes for most other immediate strikes. This method of alert resulted in attacks on 464 emergency targets, such as enemy artillery or infantry engaging friendly troops, and upon twenty-eight objectives derived from intelligence reports, among them infiltration routes or possible assembly areas. The Marines, however, paid for this prompt response in the coin of increased maintenance, additional fuel burned, and sometimes wasted effort against targets that could have been destroyed almost as promptly by a plane diverted from another mission or launched from ground alert.[14]

The frequent use of helicopters in I Corps, whether by Marines or Army air cavalrymen, created a demand for up-to-date aerial photographs of possible landing zones. These pictures had to be taken, processed, interpreted, and in the hands of helicopter crews within six hours. General Cushman sought to meet the demand by asking permission to launch photo missions as needed, but General Abrams chose to ensure speed by having the amphibious force headquarters telephone his tactical air support element, which would obtain concurrence from the appropriate duty officer at the Tactical Air Control Center and immediately notify the Marine organization.[15]

Air War over South Vietnam, 1968–1975

Gen. Creighton W. Abrams, Commander, U.S. Military Assistance Command, Vietnam (left), and Gen. George S. Brown, Commander, Seventh Air Force (right).

As the method of centralizing control over tactical aviation was thus taking final shape, an operation occurred that seemed to renew Marine Corps hopes of circumventing, if not reversing, this policy. The source of hope for Marines and concern to the Air Force was Operation Thor, a seven-day attack that pitted air power, naval gunfire, and artillery against some 450 artillery and antiaircraft positions within the eastern segment of the demilitarized zone and the adjacent portion of North Vietnam, a total area of roughly thirty-five square miles.

Undertaken in response to a request from the 3d Marine Division to neutralize the enemy guns that raked the unit from within that area, Thor consisted of three phases. During the first, which began on July 1 and lasted two days, the Seventh Air Force commander exercised control, as tactical aircraft and B–52s battered targets selected by intelligence specialists. Taking advantage of the resulting curtain of explosives, Marine and Army artillery units moved into position for the next part of the operation. During the second phase, also lasting two days, General Cushman — through his agent, General Rosson of the provisional corps — exercised operational control over an aerial and artillery bombardment that had as its primary goal the silencing of North Vietnamese antiaircraft batteries and coastal defense guns to permit low-altitude reconnaissance flights and inshore naval bombardment during the next phase. Rosson continued serving as Cushman's agent in the third and final phase, in which air strikes, artillery, and naval gunfire destroyed antiaircraft, surface-to-air missile, and artillery sites, whether occupied or not, throughout the operating area.[16]

In making a transition from the first to the second phase, planners simply moved the forward bomb line — the line beyond which air strikes no longer

Unified Management takes a Final Form

need be coordinated with the ground commander — to the farthest limit of the operating area, so that General Rosson's headquarters had to receive notice of all aerial attacks in phases two and three. An airborne battlefield command and control center, on station during the first phase, continued to serve as the principal coordinating agency, since the overall artillery commander for Operation Thor had agreed to cease fire at its request, unless the guns were delivering counterbattery fire. This temporary arrangement, necessary because the constricted battle area increased the danger that tactical fighters might fly into the path of friendly artillery fire, ended with Operation Thor.[17]

The savage bombardment of Thor targets seemed, at first glance, to have overwhelmed the North Vietnamese artillery, though once again effort was more easily measured than results. Some 8,000 tons of aerial bombs and 41,000 shells, ranging in size from 105-mm artillery projectiles to eight-inch shells from Navy cruisers, shook the earth. Enemy gunners all but ceased their bombardment of Marine outposts and their harassment of the supply line along the Cua Viet River, firing tens of rounds when they formerly had fired hundreds. American warships, moreover, had been able during the final phase to steam within 5,000 yards of shore and blast the silent coastal guns.[18]

Despite this evidence of success, intelligence analysts could not provide specific proof of damage inflicted upon the enemy, a shortcoming typical of the war in Southeast Asia. Air Force photo interpreters, for instance, listed over 1,000 artillery or antiaircraft positions destroyed, but the overwhelming majority must have been unoccupied, since these same specialists could verify the destruction of fewer than a hundred guns. Whatever destruction the bombs and shells actually inflicted, the effect proved transitory, for by the end of September hostile gunners, silent after Thor, had returned to action.[19]

Citing the revived threat, Cushman sought permission "to plan and conduct future Thor-type operations under the ground commander's control and, if necessary, using only his available resources." In these undertakings, he insisted, "fire support planning and coordination must be continuous and responsible to the ground commander." In justifying the supremacy of the commander on the ground, Cushman called attention to the Seventh Air Force intelligence analysis during Operation Thor, arguing that its obvious vagueness proved that the information he received — based on visual sightings by airborne controllers, artillery forward observers, and reconnaissance helicopters — surpassed in accuracy and timeliness the photographic evidence on which the Seventh Air Force commander, General Brown, seemed to rely. For this reason, Cushman argued, he was better able than Brown to inflict real damage on the enemy in the vicinity of the demilitarized zone, a contention buttressed by provisional corps estimates that counterbattery artillery fire and naval gunfire had accounted for two-thirds of the enemy gun positions listed as destroyed during Thor.[20]

Cushman's argument rested, however, on a shaky premise, for the human eye could be just as fallible as the camera. If this weakness in logic were ignored and the plan adopted, General Cushman or his executive agent would have coordinated air with artillery and other supporting weapons through a fire support coordination center similar to that operated by the Khe Sanh garrison. The Cushman proposal relegated the airborne battlefield command and control center to the kind of subsidiary role it had played during much of the fighting around that Marine Corps base. The Marines, in effect, could use as many sorties as they wished from their aircraft wing in the renewed Thor attacks. Once again, there would be two air wars, one fought by Marines in support of Marines and the other waged in support of Rosson's soldiers by the Air Force and whatever aircraft the Marines could spare.[21]

General Brown chose to ignore the contention that Marine sources of information were better than his own as he marshaled a case against this attempt to turn back the clock. He warned that General Cushman's proposed method of control would interfere with the aerial interdiction effort underway in southern North Vietnam. This campaign embraced the proposed Thor area but extended far beyond it; operations included not only tactical air strikes but also aerial refueling, search and rescue, psychological warfare, and electronic countermeasures — elements of air combat not amenable to control from a fire support coordination center at a division headquarters.[22]

In his defense of the current form of unified management, Brown reminded Abrams that Cushman had asked to launch future Thor operations using his own available resources. "If by 'his available resources' is meant artillery," said Brown, "then it would not be appropriate for me to comment. But if [Cushman] intends tac [tactical] air including the 1st Marine Air[craft] Wing, then I can't agree." To employ Marine aviation in this fashion would not only violate the procedures Nitze had ratified for the Vietnam War, but also commit the squadrons to an "inefficient and wasteful effort" that could "result in placing the lives of airmen at needless risk through the lack of adequate and effective control." If there were another Thor — and that seemed to depend upon North Vietnam's reaction to the latest U.S. cease-fire initiative — the Marines could nominate targets for the weekly and daily slates and single out others for immediate strikes, in short, making full use of the existing system instead of trying to circumvent it.

A proposed ban on all air and naval bombardment of North Vietnam overshadowed both Cushman's plan to repeat Operation Thor under his command and Brown's defense of the single manager. President Johnson's advisers had recommended offering such a bombing halt in exchange for three concessions by the North Vietnamese. The Hanoi regime would have to respect the demilitarized zone, thus easing Cushman's concerns and removing the need for other Thor operations; refrain from attacking South Vietnamese cities; and accept the government of South Vietnam as a party to truce negotiations. The Paris talks, begun in May, had become mired in procedural questions, the most important of which seemed to be South Vietnamese participation. A bombing halt ap-

Unified Management takes a Final Form

peared to offer a means of resolving this issue and obtaining the other assurances of North Vietnamese cooperation, assuming, of course, that the communists would agree.[23]

Since May, however, Hanoi's spokesmen had insisted that the United States stop the bombing "unconditionally" and refused even to consider offering formal concessions in return. Now, as 1968 wore on, signs appeared that North Vietnam would agree to negotiate with the South, provided that the bombing came to an end and the reality of Hanoi's making such a concession were somehow camouflaged. President Johnson consulted General Abrams and Ambassador Bunker, who agreed that to halt the bombing would prove militarily and politically acceptable. President Thieu of South Vietnam gave his approval, which he later tried to disavow, provided that the United States stood ready to renew the air attacks if Hanoi intensified the war.

To resolve the question of participation by the Thieu government, the North Vietnamese accepted an "our side, your side" formula. A group representing the Viet Cong, though not formally recognized as a separate party to the negotiations, would accompany the Hanoi delegation, and Saigon's representatives would participate in similar fashion beside the Americans. The other concessions the United States wanted from Hanoi — to spare South Vietnamese cities and to respect the demilitarized zone — remained subjects of fragile, tacit "understandings." For example, the fact that Viet Cong rockets rarely exploded in the cities of the South as the year progressed seemed to reinforce the notion that an unwritten agreement caused the enemy to refrain from attacking.[24]

On November 1, not quite one week before the Presidential election that pitted Republican Richard M. Nixon against incumbent Vice President Hubert H. Humphrey, the bombing halt went into effect. South Vietnamese second thoughts, however, delayed the beginning of the expanded negotiations until the end of the month. In the meantime, the United States took certain military precautions, such as invoking another of the supposed tacit understandings with Hanoi to fly continued aerial reconnaissance missions over parts of North Vietnam. The Joint Chiefs of Staff also discussed the responses appropriate to North Vietnamese violations of the demilitarized zone, reactions that varied from air strikes or shelling to ground combat, depending upon the severity of Hanoi's provocations.[25]

Once the bombing halt took effect, General Abrams and his staff attempted to revise the directive governing the control of tactical air power to reflect the changes that had taken place since the spring of 1965.[26] Marine Corps objections surfaced immediately. General Cushman declared that he could not agree to such an undertaking, since it "would constitute a precedent for centralized control of air resources under any and all combat conditions" and make permanent that which secretary Nitze had recognized as temporary.[27] The effort to bring the 1965 directive up to date languished for another eighteen months.

Revised directive or none, unified management remained in effect, though undergoing subtle refinement by the Marine Corps and Air Force officers responsible for carrying out the underlying concept. These adjustments reflected the changing uses of air power. In April 1968, the first full month in which the Seventh Air Force commander exercised mission direction over the Marines, 55 percent of the 32,000 attack sorties flown in Southeast Asia, including 60 percent of the 18,000 Air Force attack sorties, struck targets in South Vietnam. A comparable ratio prevailed during June of that year — the first full month the modified single manager system functioned — with 64 percent of all attack sorties and 70 percent of the Air Force contribution directed against the enemy in South Vietnam. By June 1970, however, only 48 percent of all attack sorties and 38 percent of those flown by the Air Force had a direct effect on the battle in the South; the remainder hit troop concentrations or supply lines in Cambodia, where the fighting had recently spread, or in Laos.[28]

Although the distribution of strikes between targets had changed, one of the arguments for unified management remained valid after two years. Army and Marine Corps units continued to fight side by side in the I Corps tactical zone. Their total strength had declined, however. The 1st Cavalry Division (Airmobile) moved southward to the vicinity of the capital in the fall of 1968, and by the end of 1969, the 3d Marine Division was gone from South Vietnam. An Army mechanized brigade, dispatched from the United States following the Tet offensive, remained in the northern provinces, its presence serving to justify continuation of centralized control over tactical air strikes.[29]

Since General Momyer became single manager in March 1968, the number of American troops fighting the war had peaked and begun to decline. Beginning about the time of the bombing halt, the tide of violence in South Vietnam had in general ebbed, despite occasional flare-ups, enabling the United States to reduce its authorized strength in the country from a maximum of 549,000 early in 1969 to 434,000 in the spring of 1970. This decline in strength represented one aspect of what President Nixon called Vietnamization — training and equipping the South Vietnamese to take over the war as American ground forces withdrew. During this period of reductions in manpower, Marine Corps strength underwent an even sharper decline, from an authorized 82,000 to a mere 43,000. The Marine Corps reduction of roughly 47 percent affected aviation as well as the ground elements of the amphibious force.[30]

At about this same time, a budget crisis arose, surfacing early in 1970 and threatening to challenge the practices of unified control. As single manager, General Brown faced the task of cutting costs by reducing sorties and saving munitions. The cost-cutting suggestions he received included a proposal to replace some preplanned strikes with fighter-bombers on ground or airborne alert that might engage targets as necessary. This he could not do, except on a limited scale, for, as he pointed out, the ability to divert preplanned sorties to immediate targets provided him the flexibility needed to use air power both economically and effectively.[31]

Unified Management takes a Final Form

As part of its share of the general withdrawal and cost cutting, the Marine Corps slashed the number of aviation squadrons based in South Vietnam and subject to centralized management. By mid-1970, the 1st Marine Aircraft Wing could muster only eighty-nine strike aircraft — three F–4, two A–6, and one A–4 squadrons, compared to five F–4, two A–6 and four A–4 squadrons in late 1968. Because of the persisting lull in the fighting within South Vietnam, the Tactical Air Control Center at Tan Son Nhut no longer expected more than one daily sortie from each Marine aircraft. Of these eighty-nine sorties, the Marines on a typical day retained sixteen for such missions as flak suppression at helicopter landing zones or precision bombing with the aid of radar beacons emplaced on the ground. In apportioning the other seventy-three, the Tactical Air Control Center might send thirteen on missions into Laos, allocate just thirty-six for preplanned strikes in South Vietnam, and return twenty-four to the Marines as alert aircraft to use as they chose. As a result of this typical apportionment, the Marines exercised unrestricted control over forty of the eighty-nine sorties, employed thirty-six for preplanned strikes in I Corps, and could generate additional sorties beyond the required one per day per aircraft — usually between nine and twenty-seven — for other targets of their choosing.

Marine Corps aerial autonomy, which had increased gradually during a time of reinforcement and heavy fighting, accelerated as the number of squadrons dwindled and the battlefield remained comparatively calm. At the beginning of April 1968, for example, the Marines had total control over just those sorties in excess of a ratio per aircraft fixed by the Tactical Air Control Center. An aircraft representing one of these surplus sorties might stand by on alert, but before launching it, the Marines had to consult the Tactical Air Control Center. After two months, however, the Marines gained control of enough sorties to escort helicopter assaults plus any surplus the aircraft wing might generate beyond the requirements in the frag. Now, after more than two years under an Air Force manager, the Marines possessed outright control of roughly 40 percent the daily sorties levied upon them, plus the extra 10 to 30 percent that the wing could launch in addition to the required number. Preplanned sorties, listed by time and bomb load in a weekly frag and turned over to the Marines, declined in volume, reflecting a lack of ground action. In the summer of 1970, these scheduled missions might require less than 40 percent of a day's nominal maximum of sorties.[32] Such was the type of arrangement that, according to Marine Lt. Gen. Keith B. McCutcheon, "evolved over a long period of time . . . a lot of it due to gentlemen's agreements between on-the-scene commanders."[33]

Events sometimes might strain this understanding, for an occasional foul-up was bound to occur among the different air and ground units operating in the northern provinces. In the summer of 1970, for instance, XXIV Corps, commanded at the time by Army Lt. Gen. James W. Sutherland, Jr., relied on the 1st Marine Aircraft Wing to drop bombs and napalm on a ridge near the Thuong Duc Special Forces camp, along which South Vietnamese infantry planned to advance. Within twenty-four hours of the impending attack, General Sutherland's headquarters advised Seventh Air Force of the number of preplanned tactical sorties — 16 by A–6s, 28 by F–4s, and 12 by A–4s — the Marines intended to fly, assuring General Brown that the strikes would not affect the overall weekly schedule, and asking only that the daily frag for June 15, the day of the operation, use Marine Corps planes in the afternoon when the South Vietnamese attacked. Marine helicopters also would figure in the operation, dropping containers of incendiary jelly much as Air Force transports had done two years earlier on "Napalm Sunday," in an attempt to silence the Viet Cong batteries firing on Bien Hoa Air Base.[34]

Postponed until the morning of June 16, the attack proved a spectacular success. South Vietnamese troops advanced swiftly after napalm had burned away the natural concealment, killing ten of the enemy, and high explosive had battered the defenses. Unfortunately, the single manager for tactical aviation knew nothing of the action until it was over. Despite the twelve-hour delay, the initial message from General Sutherland's headquarters, advising of the Marine Corps sorties on the afternoon of the 15th, had not yet reached Brown when the battle came to an end. Since the sorties had come out of the number available to the 1st Marine Aircraft Wing, General Brown merely reminded the corps commander to obtain approval for any adjustment of the aerial effort.[35]

In actual fact, no divergence from plans issued by the Tactical Air Control Center had taken place — which explains why Brown responded with only the gentlest reminder — principally because of the freedom of action now exercised by Maj. Gen. William G. Thrash's 1st Marine Aircraft Wing. On his own initiative, Thrash had revised his air support plan so that it required no adjustment of the operations order issued for that day. Instead of the fifty-six fighter or attack sorties that Sutherland had sought, Thrash used no more than eight, well within the number under his control, and relied on CH–53D helicopters, which were exempt from unified management, to drench the ridge with more than a hundred tons of napalm.[36]

Brown saw no harm in allowing the Marines greater latitude within a managerial set-up that had been functioning to his satisfaction since he took over as Seventh Air Force commander from General Momyer in August 1968. "I sort of looked the other way on a lot of things the Marines did," he conceded, considering it folly to revive the controversy at this time. He was confident that "if things ever got hot anywhere and we needed the resources," the 1st Marine Aircraft Wing would come through, prodded if necessary by General Abrams, a firm believer in unified management. During these comparatively quiet times, Brown showed himself to be more interested in maintaining the precedent established by Momyer than in rigidly enforcing every detail of Air Force doctrine. The existence of a single manager, "ought to be pointed out by every airman down the line," General Brown maintained, though they should not "go out of their way in peacetime to rub someone's nose in it."[37]

Unified Management takes a Final Form

Some Marine leaders realized that a precedent had apparently been set, regardless of the assurances given by Nitze in May 1968. In any event, General McCutcheon, an aviator who had taken command of III Marine Amphibious Force, now tried to clarify the limits of the Vietnam management system, in the event it should be applied in the future. During July 1970, as General Brown's tour of duty drew to an end, McCutcheon sought to capitalize upon the military assistance command's latest attempt to revise the 1965 directive governing the control of tactical aviation to reflect the principle of unified management. Rather than oppose the project as a threat to the future of the air-ground team, General McCutcheon decided to cooperate in order to "establish beyond a doubt that the Marine Corps team remains intact and retains operational control over its air component." Since General Brown seemed "more or less happy with the way things were going and wasn't anxious to change the status quo," the Marines hoped to interpret mission direction, which had escaped definition since its introduction in March 1968, strictly in terms of the centralized management procedures that had evolved in the intervening twenty-eight months.[38]

When completed, the revised directive specified that the III Marine Amphibious Force commander normally exercised operational control over Marine aviation, with the Seventh Air Force commander, as deputy for air on the staff of the military assistance command, serving as coordinating authority for all United States/Free World Military Assistance Forces and South Vietnamese Air Force in the Military Assistance Command, Vietnam area of responsibility. To carry out the duties of single manager, the coordinating authority exercised mission direction over Marine Corps strike and reconnaissance aircraft. The Marines, under this arrangement, released to the single manager "those strike and reconnaissance assets required for mission direction," while exercising control over those aircraft needed for missions peculiar to the Marine Corps, such as landing-zone preparation or helicopter escort, and retaining authority to launch immediate strikes. In the event of a major emergency, such as the fight for Khe Sanh, the Seventh Air Force commander would assume operational control over those Marine Corps aviation units selected by the commander of the military assistance command.[39]

In effect, Generals Brown and McCutcheon had agreed that mission direction referred exclusively to the authority delegated to one commander to assign specific aerial tasks to another in carrying out a previously assigned basic mission. "In other words," said McCutcheon, "COMUSMACV [Commander, U.S. Military Assistance Command, Vietnam] assigned CG III MAF a basic mission to conduct offensive air support and COMUSMACV delegated to his Deputy for Air the authority to task CG III MAF for specific missions on a daily and weekly basis." The directive thus limited mission direction to the assignment of tasks, one of the four elements of operational control, and excluded the other three — composition of subordinate forces, designation of objectives, and the issuance of directives to accomplish the mission.[40]

Air War over South Vietnam, 1968–1975

Looking back on the evolution of the control mechanism for tactical combat aviation in South Vietnam, General McCutcheon acknowledged, "There is no doubt about whether single management was an overall improvement as far as MACV as a whole was concerned. It was." Some form of centralization was essential, he conceded, for "there was no denying that, when three Army divisions were assigned to I Corps, a higher degree of coordination and cooperation was necessary." Through trial and error, evaluation and adjustment, and concessions by the commanders involved, a form of unified control emerged that, in McCutcheon's opinion, satisfied the needs of the Army and Air Force while being acceptable to the Marine Corps.[41]

Even General Cushman, who had fought the appointment of a single manager, eventually took a more benign view of the arrangement, at least in the form agreed on by Generals Brown and McCutcheon. Although still convinced that the system adopted in 1968 had gone too far, giving an Air Force officer authority over Marine Corps aviation that closely approximated operational control, the former commander of III Marine Amphibious Force now acknowledged that centralization had not brought disaster. Because of "some revisions in the system," unified management "gave the Army, I would say, better and more responsive air support than they had and didn't hurt the Marines."

General Cushman further indicated that he could "truthfully say no Marine was ever killed for lack of air support." He again maintained that modifications to the original single manager procedures led to success. Thanks to the weekly allocation of preplanned sorties and the increasing freedom to retain aircraft for immediate strikes, "we still had Marine aircraft supporting Marine forces," and as a result "it came out all right in the end." He considered unified management potentially dangerous, however, both to the future of the Corps and to its immediate tactical effectiveness. He therefore warned that, in view of what he considered a narrow escape from operational control by the Air Force, Marines should continue to oppose "the basic philosophy" of centralized direction.[42]

The single manager issue subsided with the passage of time, not because Air Force and Marine Corps doctrine had somehow merged but for other reasons. New commanders — Generals Abrams, Brown, and McCutcheon — had taken over, and the intensity of the fighting eased. There were no Khe Sanhs in 1969 or 1970 — nor a Tet offensive — to raise the threat of massive losses and sharpen doctrinal differences among the leaders concerning the control of tactical aviation.

In addition, an American withdrawal had begun in earnest. During his last year in office, President Johnson had outlined a strategy that looked to eventual reductions in American strength, fewer American casualties, and greater South Vietnamese participation in the fighting. The timing and degree of disengagement, as well as the means of enlarging South Vietnam's combat role, now became the principal concerns of President Nixon, who launched his administration by attempting to formulate his own policy for Southeast Asia.

Chapter Eight

Secret Bombing and Troop Withdrawals

After taking office in January 1969, President Nixon began setting up a more formal arrangement for determining national security policy. By rejecting President Johnson's less rigid approach — which included a weekly luncheon with selected military and civilian policy makers — Nixon sounded the knell for a number of ad hoc coordinating or planning groups, among them the White House intelligence function presided over by General Ginsburgh at the time of the Tet offensive and the siege of Khe Sanh.[1]

He had scarcely begun his revision of the policy-making machinery, when he encountered a problem requiring a degree of secrecy that led him to circumvent the channels of authority he was creating. What should he do about Cambodia, its supply lines and bases? One day after his inauguration, President Nixon asked General Wheeler for a study on "the feasibility and utility of quarantining Cambodia against the receipt of supplies and equipment for . . . the North Vietnamese forces operating in and from Cambodia against South Vietnam."[2] The Joint Chiefs of Staff, however, showed scant enthusiasm for a blockade of this sort, envisioned by the President as mainly a naval venture. They recommended instead an attempt to persuade Prince Sihanouk to allow air and ground attacks against bases and supply routes in sparsely inhabited parts of Cambodia. These actions, in conjunction with continued strikes against the logistics complex in southern Laos, seemed likely to achieve the purposes of a quarantine, though a supplementary naval blockade might prove necessary.[3]

Soon after he had submitted his contribution to the Chiefs' proposal, General Abrams offered an idea that was less ambitious in scope, but nevertheless fired the imagination of the President. Abrams advocated B–52 strikes against the Central Office for South Vietnam, a communist headquarters believed located in the Fishhook region of Cambodia, which directed enemy activity in South Vietnam. Nixon ordered the suggestion veiled in secrecy and asked Abrams for further details. The President feared that civilian casualties would result from such an attack, but Abrams assured him that few, if any, Cambodians had access to this most sensitive installation or to the nearby bivouac areas and supply dumps.[4]

Air War over South Vietnam, 1968–1975

The suggestion to bomb targets in Cambodia remained in limbo until late February, when enemy gunners fired several rockets into Saigon — a violation of one of those "understandings" that had accompanied the bombing halt — and hit other targets, mostly military bases, throughout Vietnam. President Nixon, then meeting with government leaders in western Europe, apparently interpreted the widespread shelling, though light in comparison to the previous year's Tet attacks, as a deliberate North Vietnamese challenge to test his own courage and the nation's commitment to the struggle. He therefore approved the bombing of bases and headquarters installations in Cambodia, only to cancel the operation almost immediately, when doubt surfaced about the wisdom of extending the war westward. The President chose to delay the bombing until he could consult his most trusted advisers and allay concerns that the bombing of Cambodia might ignite public demonstrations that could disrupt his European tour.[5]

Whatever the political impact, purely military reasons justified prompt retaliation for the shelling of urban targets in South Vietnam, or so Abrams argued. In launching these latest attacks, he insisted, the enemy had again demonstrated "his complete reliance on the exploitation of base areas in Cambodia and Laos from which he supports and projects his military actions." In other words, the rockets that exploded in Saigon and the gunners who fired them had more than likely passed through eastern Cambodia. As a counterblow, Abrams proposed limited air attacks on North Vietnam, as well as thrusts against the supply net in southern Laos and the Cambodian bases, a far more ambitious plan than his earlier call for B–52 strikes on the enemy headquarters in Cambodia.[6]

The President's decision to seek advice imposed a delay that, in effect, overruled both his original decision to bomb the Central Office for South Vietnam and also the expanded plan offered by Abrams. General Wheeler pointed out that the retaliation had to be prompt or the link between provocation and reaction would disappear. By early March, the North Vietnamese might not interpret U.S. bombings or ground attacks as punishment for an attack some two weeks earlier. Wheeler therefore recommended that the United States ignore the February incident and instead respond promptly to the next attack on a major South Vietnamese city.[7]

Moreover, one form of retaliation advocated by General Abrams had been ruled out in advance by Nixon's civilian advisers. As long as their counsel prevailed, there would be no air strikes against the North, however attractive such measures might be from a purely military standpoint. "No one in the administration," said Dr. Henry Kissinger, the President's Special Assistant for National Security Affairs, "could anticipate a resumption of the bombing of the North with anything but distaste.... None of us had the stomach for the domestic outburst we knew the renewed bombing would provoke — even if it were the direct result of North Vietnamese betrayal of the understandings that had led to the bombing halt." With punitive bombing of North Vietnam ruled out because

Secret Bombing and Troop Withdrawals

of its likely impact on American public opinion and an invasion of Laos a violation of longstanding policy, Nixon and his key counselors fixed their attention on the Cambodian bases.[8]

Besides avoiding the public uproar that the renewed bombing of the North seemed sure to provoke, raids on the Cambodian installations afforded unique military and diplomatic advantages. The strikes, according to General Abrams, would hit the very bases that enabled the enemy to wage war in South Vietnam, thus restricting hostile activity and reducing American casualties. Resolute action in Cambodia, moreover, would offer proof of American firmness that might pay dividends at the negotiating table in Paris.[9]

Nor was the bombing at all certain to harm the improving relations between the United States and Cambodia. Prince Sihanouk, after all, seemed to have been hinting, since the Bowles mission of January 1968, that he would not object to the bombing of North Vietnamese bases in his country, provided that Cambodian citizens were not endangered and the aerial attacks were carried out in secrecy.[10]

For almost three weeks the President waited, reviewing arguments for and against the bombing of Cambodia. Secretary of State William P. Rogers reportedly opposed the attacks because he feared a possibly adverse impact on the Paris talks. Secretary of Defense Melvin Laird favored the raids but doubted that they could be conducted in secrecy. Dr. Kissinger believed the strikes would be worthwhile even though North Vietnam might react by increasing the tempo of the war in the South, the Soviet Union or Cambodia might object, and a segment of the American public might protest the action. After receiving reports that on March 14 hostile rockets had again exploded in Saigon, the President launched Operation Menu, the bombing of the Cambodian bases. The first mission, nicknamed Operation Breakfast, took place on March 18, when fifty-nine of sixty scheduled B–52s hit targets near the Fishhook, touching off more than seventy secondary explosions visible high in the night sky.[11]

Strict secrecy concealed every aspect of the Menu bombing. Concerned about possible domestic opposition as well as diplomatic complications overseas, the President confided in only a few advisers, and not all of them knew every detail of the operation. By summer, five members of Congress — Senators John Stennis and Richard Russell and Representatives Mendel Rivers, Gerald Ford, and Leslie Arends — had received information about the raids. All held important positions. Arends and Ford were leaders of the Republican minority; the other three were Democratic members of committees dealing with the armed services or government appropriations. A few other members of these committees learned of the attacks from Secretary Laird.[12]

Throughout the Menu raids, the procedures for requesting, approving, reporting, and assessing strikes remained shrouded in secrecy. When feasible, encoded messages traveled over secure means of transmission, so that only those persons directly involved in the operation and fully aware of its sensitive status received information on the attacks. If the use of routine message traffic proved unavoidable, the true nature and location of the target was concealed.

The first Breakfast mission, carried out by 59 of some 3,800 B–52 sorties flown during the Menu campaign, began like all subsequent attacks with two requests from General Abrams. One request, traveling through normal communications channels, proposed an attack on a target in South Vietnam located near the Cambodian border. After the usual review, this mission was approved and given a time over target and an identifying title. Meanwhile, Abrams was using a special communications link to call for a raid inside Cambodia. After review by Admiral McCain, the Menu request went to the Joint Chiefs of Staff, who gave their approval only after reviewing the accompanying evidence that no Cambodian noncombatants lived near the target. They then referred the request to Secretary Laird, who might consult President Nixon if the timing or location of the attack seemed especially sensitive.

After receiving the Defense Secretary's approval, the Joint Chiefs of Staff alerted Gen. Bruce K. Holloway, Commander in Chief, Strategic Air Command, who used secure communications circuits to contact Lt. Gen. Alvan C. Gillem, II, commander of the 3d Air Division on Guam. General Gillem planned and launched the strike, preserving secrecy by concealing it with the mission identifier and time already assigned the nearby target in South Vietnam. Gillem's planners plotted a course that would bring the bombers near the cover target, which became an alternate that could be struck in case of bad weather or equipment failure, but led to the real one across the border.

Menu missions took place at night, with Combat Skyspot radar directing the release of bombs and surveillance radar monitoring the flight. Therefore, special precautions were necessary to prevent members of aircrews or radar teams from compromising a secret operation. The 3d Air Division (soon to be redesignated Eighth Air Force) briefed the bomber crews as though the attack would occur in South Vietnam. Only the pilot and navigator knew for certain that their plane had crossed the border into Cambodia, and they were trusted to keep silent.

Radar operators on the ground, whether they gave the signal to release the bombs or kept watch over flights near the border, knew that the targets lay inside Cambodia. As a result, a representative from the Strategic Air Command advance echelon visited the Skyspot radar site directing the mission and gave the operator the information necessary to bomb the Menu target. Similarly, an officer from Seventh Air Force headquarters went to the ground control intercept radar site that would track the mission and warned the technicians not to alert the bombers as the planes neared the border, the usual practice to prevent violation of Cambodian airspace.

Reporting Menu activity required similar security measures. Radar surveillance teams on the ground did not record the border violation, and the Combat Skyspot strike controllers destroyed their calculations of the impact point inside Cambodia, submitting instead a summary showing flight patterns the B–52s

Secret Bombing and Troop Withdrawals

Combat Skyspot installation at Da Lat, South Vietnam.

would have followed to hit the cover target. A routine message reported the hours flown, fuel burned, and bombs dropped, while secure channels carried a report of the actual strike, including an initial assessment of damage done, usually in the form of a tally of secondary explosions. This dual reporting maintained secrecy while at the same time providing logistics and personnel specialists the information they needed to replace air crews or aircraft and replenish stocks of fuel and munitions.[13]

As was true of most B–52 strikes against enemy base camps, regardless of location, damage proved difficult to estimate. The presence of cloud cover, for example, not only prevented the bomber crews from seeing secondary explosions, but also might hamper the use of helicopters to land American-led South Vietnamese reconnaissance patrols in the area. Nevertheless, crew reports of detonations touched off by their bombs remained a normal source of intelligence, as did probes by troops, though General Abrams considered the reconnaissance teams more valuable in determining that no Cambodians lived near the target than in evaluating strike results. Ordinary post-strike photographic reconnaissance by RF–4Cs or RF–101s was out of the question because the film passed through too many hands in the processing and interpretation, increasing the likelihood of a leak in security. Throughout most of the Menu bombing, high-altitude photography by U–2s seemed unnecessary, since the destruction amid the concealing jungle did not show up well on the high-resolution film. The most reliable sources of information were pictures and visual sightings by crews of Air Force observation planes dispatched over Cambodia by General Abrams' Studies and Observations Group. The low-flying airmen brought back an estimated 70 percent of the Menu bomb damage assessment, reporting movement by troops or vehicles, abandoned or collapsed bunkers, and the condition of roads or trails.[14]

By the end of April 1969, President Nixon told General Wheeler of his "great satisfaction" with the early Menu strikes against targets near the Fishhook and in the region where the territories of Laos, South Vietnam, and Cambodia converge.[15] The attacks did not, however, deter a North Vietnamese and Viet Cong offensive in May, near the anniversary of the 1968 mini-Tet uprising, which it resembled in its lack of intensity. Nonetheless, General Abrams remained pleased with what the strikes in Cambodia had accomplished. Besides relieving pressure on Special Forces camps located in South Vietnam's western highlands, the raids seemed to have forced the enemy to invest time and manpower in dispersing supplies and constructing blast-resistant storage bunkers.[16]

Just one week after the first Menu attack, Jack Walsh of United Press International reported that General Abrams was seeking permission to bomb the enemy sanctuaries in Cambodia.[17] Surprisingly, this important story languished for more than a month until William Beecher of the *New York Times* reported that raids on "Viet Cong and North Vietnamese supply dumps and base camps in Cambodia" had begun "in recent weeks."[18] Although President Nixon became concerned over these two stories and the threat they posed to the secrecy surrounding Menu activity, he insisted that the attacks continue.[19]

Actually, Nixon need not have worried. Possibly put off the track by the lack of reaction from military leaders and civilian authorities, the press failed to pursue the matter. As it turned out, more than four years elapsed from the first Menu bombing in 1969 until Maj. Hal Knight, a former Air Force officer, told the Senate Armed Services Committee in 1973 that, while serving at a Combat Skyspot radar site, he had destroyed records of strikes in Cambodia and substituted reports of attacks on cover targets in South Vietnam.[20]

Nixon insisted upon secrecy to avoid the kind of crisis that would certainly have arisen if Prince Sihanouk had felt compelled to acknowledge the bombing. Had the Cambodian ruler publicly endorsed Menu, North Vietnam might have decided to punish him by extending its control deep into the kingdom; had he demanded that the raids stop, the gradual accommodation between the United States and Cambodia would have been destroyed, to the benefit of the North Vietnamese. As long as secrecy prevailed, the Prince could maintain the appearance of neutrality, the North Vietnamese need not extend their control deeper into the kingdom, and the United States could continue an apparently successful aerial campaign that endangered few noncombatants. For those officials who had approved the Menu bombing, the most surprising aspect of the entire operation was North Vietnam's silence concerning the attacks. Hanoi did not denounce the raids for propaganda purposes and, according to Kissinger, did not raise the matter during formal or secret truce negotiations. Apparently the enemy preferred Cambodia's nominal neutrality to acknowledging the presence

Secret Bombing and Troop Withdrawals

of North Vietnamese troops in that country and possibly risking a deeper military involvement there.[21]

In terms of American relations with Cambodia, secrecy paid dividends. Prince Sihanouk could dismiss the occasional press report by denying that Cambodian lives or property were being endangered by American air strikes. He was able, therefore, to renew formal contact with the United States declaring that he was responding to American expressions of respect for Cambodian independence, sovereignty, neutrality, and territorial integrity. To celebrate the restoration of diplomatic ties, which occurred on July 2, 1969, with the arrival in Phnom Penh of an American charge' d'affaires, Senator Mike Mansfield visited the Cambodian capital in August. Sihanouk used the occasion to pay tribute to Mansfield and his colleagues who, according to the Prince, had resisted the temptation to use force and thus helped restore friendship between the two nations. The rapprochement begun with the Bowles visit had progressed smoothly despite the bombing.[22]

The Menu bombing continued for fourteen months, as B–52s flew 3,875 sorties against six base areas, each of which bore a code name appropriate to a menu. Once again, strategic bombers designed for intercontinental nuclear retaliation served as aerial artillery, harassing an unseen enemy and impeding his movement. More than 100,000 tons of bombs fell on the six targets — Lunch in the tri-border region; Snack, Dessert, Dinner, and Breakfast in and around the Fishhook; and Supper, about a third of the way from the Fishhook to the tri-border bases. From the first mission in March 1969 until the last in May 1970, Air Force statistical summaries recorded all Menu strikes as being flown against targets in South Vietnam. During this period, roughly one in five of the B–52 sorties listed for the South actually hit a target in Cambodia. The raids ended with the invasion of the border sanctuaries in the spring of 1970, an offensive directed against some of the same bases that the B–52s had been bombing.[23]

Cambodia, however, represented just one aspect of the Nixon administration's attempt to shape a plan for extricating the United States from an unpopular war. Indeed, President Nixon had benefitted during the Presidential campaign from the belief he had a secret plan to end the war. For Kissinger, the ideal method of liquidating the conflict would have been to sever the negotiating tangle by proposing that communist and noncommunist compete peacefully through free elections for control of South Vietnam. If the enemy should reject such an offer, the United States would intensify the war, mining North Vietnamese ports and bombing rail lines to cut off the flow of war materials into the country and force the Hanoi regime to enter negotiations. This ideal solution did not seem feasible, however, for Kissinger acknowledged that public opinion was likely to balk at such drastic actions.[24]

The apparent willingness to rule out bombing of North Vietnam troubled the Air Staff, who feared that the new administration had committed itself to negotiating a settlement, considering resumption of the air war against the North as a form of escalation rather than a means of retaliation. The staff believed that renewed bombing might prove necessary if the enemy should break off the Paris talks or intensify the war in the South. Nor did these Air Force officers share Kissinger's belief that the public had grown weary of the war; from an isolated view in the Pentagon, it appeared that the American people would continue to support the present level of fighting. Only the defeat of the Viet Cong, surely not a contested election, could justify to the public the expenditure thus far of $100 billion and the loss of 30,000 American lives.[25]

After examining courses of action during the transitional period between election and inauguration, Kissinger, before launching the Nixon administration onto Southeast Asia's turbulent currents, asked the agencies waging the war to answer specific questions on the progress made thus far, the problems remaining, and the reliability of the information upon which the judgments were made. Not only did the estimates of success vary from one reporting agency to another, the replies did not agree on such basic data as enemy strength in the south, infiltration routes from North Vietnam, and the importance of Cambodia in Hanoi's plans.[26] "The answers made clear," wrote Kissinger in his memoirs, "that there was no consensus as to facts, much less as to policy."[27]

Nothing in Kissinger's survey changed President Nixon's plan to reduce American participation in combat and negotiate a settlement of the war. With the secret bombing in Cambodia serving as a shield, Nixon hoped to begin withdrawing U.S. forces. Ideally, the rate of reduction would depend on increases in South Vietnamese military might and progress in the Paris talks. The policy of replacing U.S. troops with South Vietnamese had been foreshadowed in President Johnson's address announcing the April 1968 bombing restrictions, and his administration had begun improving South Vietnam's armed forces. President Thieu, whose military establishment had acquired more men and improved equipment since the Johnson speech, now agreed that a large number of Americans could depart during 1969 without jeopardizing South Vietnam's survival. The withdrawal of perhaps 50,000 men, the Nixon administration hoped, would for a time silence domestic criticism without affecting the military balance between North and South.[28]

Shortly after President Thieu indicated that American troop reductions would be acceptable to his government, Secretary Laird visited Saigon and discovered that General Abrams and his staff were basing their plans for 1969 on the assumption that the United States would not withdraw troops from South Vietnam until North Vietnamese units had begun departing.[29] General Brown, Abrams' deputy for air operations, adamantly opposed reductions in American strength, arguing that withdrawals before June 1970 involved "greater risk than advantage." Money saved through troop withdrawals in the near term could, he warned, require the eventual expenditure of American blood.[30]

Arguments like General Brown's did not convince Secretary Laird that the United States, considering its other military commitments, could maintain a

Secret Bombing and Troop Withdrawals

force of 500,000 men in South Vietnam. Even if such a course were feasible, it might prove counterproductive, for the Secretary of Defense doubted that the South Vietnamese would attempt to pacify the countryside while "our own forces constitute so pervasive a presence." As a result, Laird recommended drafting plans to return 50,000 to 70,000 American troops from South Vietnam during 1969.[31]

Designed to "enhance the vital interests of our country (particularly in recognition of our world-wide military requirements), to stimulate increased self-defense awareness and self-reliance by the Government of South Vietnam, and to sustain the support of the American public,"[32] the program of withdrawing U.S. troops and turning the war over to the South Vietnamese at first bore the label "de-Americanization." Secretary Laird, however, objected to the term because it emphasized the American departure without reflecting the increasing importance of better trained and more formidably equipped South Vietnamese combat forces. He therefore proposed "Vietnamization," a scarcely less awkward term, which promptly received Presidential approval.[33]

Faced with three alternatives — escalation of the war, abandonment of South Vietnam, and Vietnamization — the Nixon administration had selected the one that seemed likely to achieve an independent South Vietnam without further alienating public opinion at home. Such a course entailed certain risks, however. "Withdrawal of U.S. troops," Kissinger warned the President, "could become like salted peanuts to the American public: the more U.S. troops come home, the more will be demanded." Besides preventing the administration from linking withdrawals to progress in negotiations at Paris and communist inactivity in South Vietnam, snowballing departures might encourage Hanoi to take advantage of the headlong retreat by attacking and possibly embarrassing the United States.[34]

Because of the attendant dangers, U.S. military leaders sought assurance that Nixon would not allow the withdrawals to become unmanageable. Air Force General McConnell, serving as acting Chairman, Joint Chiefs of Staff, in General Wheeler's absence, proposed three conditions essential to successful Vietnamization. He told the National Security Council that the reductions should not place the remaining American forces at a tactical disadvantage, should not result in abandonment of equipment the South Vietnamese could not use, and should not be completed until South Vietnamese units were able to take over their nation's defense.[35]

The decision made on the basis of views expressed at the Security Council meeting reflected General McConnell's concerns. Although Nixon did not repeat McConnell's three points, they apparently influenced him as he declared that U.S. forces would not reduce pressure on the enemy except as a consequence of a North Vietnamese withdrawal. The departure of U.S. forces and transfer of responsibility to the South Vietnamese would, moreover, be carefully controlled to avoid pulling out completely before Hanoi's troops had done so.[36]

Air War over South Vietnam, 1968–1975

Kissinger then issued a directive that set in motion planning for the first reduction in U.S. strength since 1963, during the advisory years, and for a corresponding transfer to the South Vietnamese of responsibility for combat operations. A large contingent was to depart on July 1, 1969, arming and training South Vietnam's forces would receive the "highest national priority" within the Nixon administration, and the United States might revert to a purely advisory and support role as early as December 31, 1970.[37]

For the Air Force, the initial withdrawals would involve four Air National Guard squadrons mobilized after the capture of the *Pueblo* and sent to South Vietnam in response to the Tet offensive, but now due for release from active service. The replacement of these units had come under discussion even before Kissinger formally launched the planning for Vietnamization. As early as February 1969, the Air Staff had concluded that some reduction of Air Force strength in Southeast Asia was all but inevitable in the near future and formed a study group to address the subject.

The panel suggested the Air Force choose among four courses of action. One possibility was to retain in the United States the four F–4 squadrons that were scheduled to replace the departing Air National Guard F–100Cs when they reverted to inactive service. Two other possibilities involved replacing the National Guard units and either canceling plans to substitute four squadrons of A–37s for two F–100D units that would leave South Vietnam in the spring of 1970 or simply withdrawing three F–105 squadrons from Thailand. Under a fourth option, B–52 sorties might decline from 1,800 to 1,440 per month; the F–4s and A–37s would deploy and the F–105s remain in place, enabling tactical fighters to take up the slack left by the scaling back of B–52 operations.

Generals Brown at Seventh Air Force headquarters and Nazzaro at Pacific Air Forces opposed any reduction of fighter strength in Southeast Asia. They insisted they needed all the scheduled replacements, both F–4s and A–37s, to maintain pressure on the enemy in South Vietnam and Laos while retaining the ability to resume the bombing of North Vietnam, if necessary. Brown rejected claims by Dr. Ivan Selin, acting Assistant Secretary of Defense for Systems Analysis, that only 20 percent of all tactical sorties in South Vietnam — for the most part close air support and battlefield interdiction — benefitted troops in contact with the enemy. Dr. Selin, Brown declared, failed to see the true contribution of tactical aviation, for even strikes in southern Laos helped the man with the rifle by delaying or destroying supplies destined for the battlefield.[38]

General Brown had little patience with the attempts of Dr. Selin and his Department of Defense colleagues to measure the impact of tactical air power solely in terms of strikes upon hostile forces actually exchanging fire with Americans or South Vietnamese. General Abrams, Brown pointed out, used air attacks as a kind of reconnaissance by fire. Troops advanced until they located a confirmed or suspected defensive strongpoint then called for air strikes to flush the enemy from cover. In some cases, the North Vietnamese or Viet Cong

Secret Bombing and Troop Withdrawals

The Cessna A–37 was a greatly modified model of the T–37 basic trainer, with a strengthened fuselage and wings, hard points under the wings, refueling capability, and an internal gun mounted in the nose.

were not present or fled immediately, so that the advancing unit did not make actual contact with the enemy, and the air attack did not meet Dr. Selin's standard, even though it may have kept the advance moving and saved lives by preventing a firefight from erupting.[39]

In fact, Nixon's commitment to troop withdrawals, rather than Selin's analysis, was becoming the principal determinant in establishing American aerial strength in South Vietnam. Conversations with Secretary Laird and his deputy, David Packard, convinced General McConnell that the Seventh Air Force would lose two of twenty-three Vietnam-based tactical fighter squadrons. Faced with the inevitable loss, the Air Force Chief of Staff formally proposed to the Joint Chiefs of Staff that just two F–4 squadrons replace the four Air National Guard units scheduled to return to the United States.

Of the Air Force commanders who commented on the McConnell proposal, only General Momyer, now in charge of the Tactical Air Command, favored it. He based his support on two assumptions: that the ban on the bombing of North Vietnam would remain in effect; and that combat in the South would continue to be relatively light, at least through the rainy season beginning in May. Neither Generals Brown nor Nazzaro, however, retreated from their belief that no squadrons could be spared, and Brown argued that the number of tactical air strikes would actually have to increase during the rainy season because of the effect of cloud cover on bombing accuracy.[40]

General Abrams shared the views of Brown and Nazzaro. When apprised of the McConnell proposal, the Army officer declared that "regardless how we phrase it, the net result ... would be the unilateral reduction ... of those all-important U.S. capabilities on which our allies rely heavily and which give me

Air War over South Vietnam, 1968–1975

Departing troops board a commercial airliner at Da Nang.

the means and flexibility to deal with a constantly shifting threat." Nor did Abrams believe in trading "force improvement" — the acquisition of two squadrons of newer and deadlier aircraft — for "force reduction" — the loss of the four F–100C squadrons. "There are battlefield situations," he warned, "which make the availability of tactical aircraft relatively more important than the capability of the individual aircraft employed."[41]

Although Admiral McCain endorsed the arguments offered by General Abrams, and the Joint Chiefs of Staff agreed that four, rather than two, squadrons of F–4s should replace the four squadrons of F–100Cs, Secretary Laird inclined toward a two-squadron reduction, possibly in Thailand rather than South Vietnam. Any suggestion to reduce the number of Thailand-based tactical fighters alarmed Abrams, who pointed out that war planes based there could concentrate on targets in southern Laos, where the greater weight of the aerial effort was shifting, and still be able to help deal with any tactical emergency that might arise in South Vietnam. Having heard from the commanders involved, the Joint Chiefs of Staff reminded Laird that they considered a reduction in fighter strength militarily unwise, adding however that if the Secretary of Defense insisted on such an action for other than purely military reasons, the reductions should take place in South Vietnam.[42]

While the question of tactical fighter reduction was debated, planning went ahead for the withdrawal from South Vietnam of 25,000 troops — some 15,000 soldiers, almost 8,500 Marines, and the rest sailors. No airmen would leave South Vietnam as part of this group. During a meeting with President Nixon at Midway Island early in June, President Thieu endorsed the policy of Vietnamization, agreeing that South Vietnamese forces could take over from departing

American combat units. Nixon then announced the 25,000-man withdrawal, which was completed as scheduled by the end of August.[43]

The net loss of two Air Force tactical fighter squadrons became a part of a second withdrawal, in the works since late March, when Abrams first addressed the question of returning another 25,000-man contingent. During President Nixon's visit to Saigon late in July, Abrams advised against withdrawing more than 25,000 men in this group, the second that would depart during 1969. The President, however, was coming under pressure to increase that number. As Kissinger later acknowledged, the return of some men tended to demoralize the families of those who remained, and one reduction increased the desire for other larger ones, proof of his "salted peanuts" analogy. When Nixon returned to the United States from Saigon, he rejected the ceiling recommended by Abrams and told Laird to increase the second contingent to 37,000, thus bringing the year's total to 62,000.[44]

Like General Abrams, the Joint Chiefs of Staff insisted that no more than 50,000 men be withdrawn during 1969 — the 25,000 who had departed that summer and an equal number that would leave by the end of December. The President, however, ignored this advice, as he had the views of Abrams, for he was determined that the second reduction would be greater than the first. The number finally decided on for group number two was 40,500 — 31,000 actually withdrawn and 9,500 vacancies left unfilled, reducing authorized strength to 484,000. Although the Joint Chiefs of Staff warned that so bold a move, a total reduction of 65,500 during 1969, was "clearly without justification on military grounds and beyond the threshold of prudent risk," Nixon persisted, and the last elements of the second contingent departed in mid-December.[45]

The Air Force share of the reduction was 2,541 officers and men, about 5 percent of the total, divided among five squadrons either withdrawn from South Vietnam or not sent there as originally scheduled. The major units selected for departure under the approved plan were two special operations squadrons and a light bomber or tactical fighter unit. As anticipated, two squadrons of F–4Es, formerly designated as replacements for two of the four Air National Guard F–100C squadrons already recalled from Vietnam, did not join General Brown's Seventh Air Force.[46] The absence of the Phantoms would, according to Brown, "result in a small decrease in our sortie capability," an acceptable impact given the decline in ground combat within the country.[47]

During the final planning for this reduction of men and aircraft within South Vietnam, a new economy drive heralded further cuts in aerial strength, the full impact of which would not be felt until 1970, and limitations on sorties by the forces that remained. Facing a growing budget deficit, President Nixon in the summer of 1969 directed the various departments and agencies of government to collaborate in reducing federal spending by an additional $3.5 billion during the fiscal year that would begin on July 1, 1969. The share projected for the Department of Defense amounted to $3 billion, a reduction of $1 billion by

Air War over South Vietnam, 1968–1975

each of the three services. This action, called Project 703, would affect Air Force units throughout the world, including those fighting in Southeast Asia.[48]

As he searched for savings, General Brown hoped to concentrate the reductions in three kinds of missions; psychological warfare, defoliation, and the admittedly important area of reconnaissance. He maintained that air power could do infinitely more harm to the enemy by dropping high explosives than by scattering leaflets or spraying herbicide, and he had become convinced that sensor-laden gunships, aerial cameras, communications monitoring, and visual sightings by forward air controllers and other pilots gave him "more reconnaissance that we really needed." His experience in command of the Seventh Air Force had persuaded him that the fighter-bomber and the transport comprised the essential tools of tactical air power in South Vietnam.[49]

In the reductions, consolidations, and redesignations that he recommended during the latter half of 1969, Brown tried with some success to put these views into practice. The second redeployment, completed on December 15, included the 5th Special Operations Squadron, a psychological warfare unit, which used its C–47s and U–10 Helio Couriers to support Thai, South Vietnamese, and South Korean air forces in Southeast Asia. The 4th Special Operations Squadron also became inactive, after turning most of its AC–47 gunships over to Lao and South Vietnamese airmen. To compensate for the loss, General Brown received a squadron of AC–119Ks — the model with auxiliary jet engines — that arrived in South Vietnam by year's end. The 6th Special Operations Squadron passed from the scene, transferring its A–1 Skyraiders to an Air Force wing based at Nakhon Phanom, Thailand. In addition, General Brown accomplished another of his goals, at least in part, by shifting a dozen UC–123s from spraying herbicide to carrying troops and cargo, a mission that he considered more useful.

The manipulation of fighter and bomber resources verged on the Byzantine. The 5th Tactical Bomber Squadron dispatched its Martin B–57s to the United States, took over the A–37s assigned to an attack unit scheduled for movement to South Vietnam, and became the 5th Attack Squadron. Similar legerdemain converted the 90th Tactical Fighter Squadron into the 90th Attack Squadron, also flying A–37s, though its F–100Ds were redistributed in South Vietnam instead of being returned to the United States, as the bombers had been. The 510th Tactical Fighter Squadron was inactivated and its aircraft, too, were divided among the F–100D units remaining in the country.

During 1969, therefore, the Seventh Air Force lost four Air National Guard units, receiving two squadrons of F–4Es in their place, and also surrendered one B–57 squadron with its aircraft and two F–100D units (though retaining the fighter-bombers), while in effect gaining two A–37 squadrons. A psychological warfare squadron disbanded, as did a second special operations unit that had flown Douglas Skyraiders. One gunship squadron replaced another. The number of airmen actually serving in South Vietnam had declined as projected in the reduction plan, with the 2,500-man cut completed at about the end of the year.[50]

Secret Bombing and Troop Withdrawals

In General Brown's key categories of fighter-bomber (or attack) and transport, Air Force strength in South Vietnam now totaled 65 A–37s in the two newly designated attack units and one special operations squadron; 123 F–4s divided among eight squadrons, including two F–4E units; 187 F–100Ds in ten squadrons; 67 C–123 transports, including those recently converted from herbicide spraying; 64 C–130s; and 81 C–7s. Other aircraft not in Brown's enumeration of critical types included 91 O–1s, 231 O–2s — the most numerous type of aircraft in South Vietnam at this time — and 83 OV–10s. During 1969, adjustments resulting from losses, overhaul, replacement, and withdrawal had increased the number of A–37s by 47 and F–4s by 24 but eliminated 66 F–100s. The fleet of C–130s declined by 17, while C–7s increased by one, and the total of cargo-carrying C–123s grew by virtue of the 12 planes converted from herbicide duty. In the observation category, Seventh Air Force ended the year with 56 fewer O–1s, but 120 additional O–2s and 70 more OV–10s. The grand total of the principal kinds of attack planes and fighter-bombers — A–37s, F–4s, and F–100Ds — did not decline, for the number of smaller, less versatile A–37s tripled, offsetting a 26-percent reduction in F–100s. In spite of the departure of 2,500 officers and airmen, the aggregate number of Air Force planes based in South Vietnam actually increased by about 40 during the course of the year.[51]

Not all the changes during 1969 involved flying units. The 555th Civil Engineer Squadron was deactivated at Cam Ranh Bay and its equipment redistributed throughout the country. Also, the security police reserve at Phan Rang, established as a result of the 1968 Tet offensive, began declining in strength. The Air Force reduced that contingent by about 150 persons in December, the first step toward inactivation, which took place early in 1971.[52]

Presidential concern over the war's impact on the federal budget antedated Project 703 and the cost reductions it foreshadowed; indeed, President Nixon had inherited the problem from his predecessor. Even before President Johnson left the White House, a reduction seemed likely in the number of combat sorties flown in South Vietnam. This prospect did not dismay General Brown, who questioned the value of leaflet dropping and other missions and was convinced that "there is more air support of all types being provided U.S. forces in South Vietnam than is needed." He acknowledged, however, that such a view, which implicitly questioned the effectiveness of B–52 attacks, would seem heretical to Abrams, who was determined that the sorties by these bombers remain at 1,800 per month, the level established at the time of Tet and Khe Sanh.[53]

Even though the Tet battles had ended long ago and the encirclement of Khe Sanh been broken, Abrams continued throughout 1968 to echo Westmoreland's enthusiasm for the B–52s, declaring that what he described as "centralized control" over the bombers provided the assistance command with "the punching power of several ground divisions," giving its commander a "means of influencing the battle without a constant shift of troop units."[54] Far from accepting the possibility of fewer B–52 sorties, he stated he could use even

Air War over South Vietnam, 1968–1975

The Cessna O–2 had two engines and hardpoints under the wings.

more, though he would settle for continuation of the existing rate until there was "some major change in the tactical situation which warrants its reduction."[55]

The Strategic Air Command could not share Abram's enthusiasm, particularly in the absence of solid proof that the B–52s were hurting the enemy. The command lacked the bombers, crews, and maintenance men needed to fulfill its commitment to the single integrated operations plan for nuclear war and at the same time fly 1,800 sorties per month in Southeast Asia. Reducing the sortie rate would prove difficult, however, for Abrams would not willingly accept restraints upon a swift and powerful weapon unless convinced that the bombing was not achieving worthwhile results.[56] Before the Strategic Air Command could begin marshaling arguments to challenge the military judgment of so experienced a commander, financial considerations intervened.

The departing Johnson administration, troubled by the cost of B–52 operations in Southeast Asia, addressed the issue in December 1968. Secretary Nitze suggested a variable sortie rate. Instead of requesting an inflexible 1,800 sorties per month, Abrams might vary the number from 1,400 to 1,800, depending on the tactical situation, provided that the annual total did not exceed 19,000, or a monthly average of 1,650.[57] This compromise, however, satisfied neither the Strategic Air Command nor the military assistance command.

The Strategic Air Command staff pointed out that the Air Force would have to retain in the western Pacific enough B–52s to fly the maximum of 1,800 sorties in any month. To effect worthwhile savings, planners would have to divide the year into two segments, flying 1,400 sorties per month during the rainy season from mid-March to mid-September, when the pace usually slowed, and maintaining the higher rate for the rest of the year. Although dividing the year in such a fashion could, to some extent, hamper tactical flexibility, the policy would cut costs by reducing to 1,600 the average monthly sorties, permitting the withdrawal of some men and bombers for half the year.[58]

Whereas the organization that flew the B–52 missions objected to the Nitze proposal because it offered only the illusion of savings, Admiral McCain op-

Secret Bombing and Troop Withdrawals

posed the plan because it would produce fewer than the current 1,800 monthly sorties. Like Abrams, he argued that troops in South Vietnam could use even more B–52 strikes, declaring that commanders there proposed each day roughly three times as many targets as were actually bombed.[59]

The Joint Chiefs of Staff endorsed the views of Abrams and McCain, advising Secretary Laird that to reduce the B–52 sortie rate below 1,800 per month would be "militarily inadvisable." Financial pressure did not abate, however, and after some two months in office, Laird realized that he could not continue the existing rate beyond June 1969. He proposed to fix the monthly number of B–52 sorties at 1,600 for the fiscal year ending on June 30, 1970, even though this level of effort would cost more than had been budgeted.[60]

At this point, when Laird knew he had to act but had not yet done so, the President's call for a $3 billion cut in Department of Defense spending, the so-called Project 703, exerted its effect on all sortie rates, tactical fighter as well as bomber. Facing the necessity of cutting costs by about $1 billion, the Air Force had no choice but to propose further limitations on aerial activity in Southeast Asia, offering to reduce monthly B–52 sorties to 1,500, 100 fewer than Laird had proposed, and tactical sorties by 4,000 to 14,000 each month. After reviewing the Air Force recommendation, the Joint Chiefs of Staff opposed such cuts at a time when Marine aviation squadrons and Navy ships with supporting guns would also be departing from Southeast Asia. General Wheeler, the chairman, raised this objection with Secretary Laird and President Nixon, but to no avail. While accepting the 14,000 tactical sorties, Laird cut the B–52 sorties to 1,400 monthly, twice the reduction offered by the Air Force. On October 2, 1969, the new rates went into effect, and the declining frequency of B–52 operations permitted a reduction in the aggregate number of the bombers based in the western Pacific — on Guam, in Thailand, and on Okinawa — from 104 in January to 88 in December.[61]

During the debate over B–52 sorties, the tactics used by the big bombers underwent revision. The 3d Air Division had adopted a practice of dispatching two cells, each of three aircraft, against most targets in Southeast Asia. By the end of 1968, however, the bombers were attacking relatively compact targets in southern Laos, such as mountain passes or road junctions, where fewer planes could obtain adequate coverage. As a result, General Brown suggested dividing the usual six-plane missions so that each cell of three B–52s could attack a different target. The Strategic Air Command endorsed the idea, and the 3d Air Division began dispatching six bombers to a single initial point, where the two cells separated so that Combat Skyspot radar operators could direct each against one of two nearby targets. At first these so-called tandem tactics saw service only in southern Laos, but during April 1969 the practice was authorized for South Vietnam, as well.[62]

Besides making provision for more economical coverage of relatively compact targets, the 3d Air Division adjusted the relationship of aircraft within the

Air War over South Vietnam, 1968–1975

cell to obtain a better bomb pattern within sprawling targets such as the base camps attacked by the Menu strikes. Instead of following each other in trail, the B–52s within a cell might now form an arrowhead so that the three tracks were 500 yards apart. However, this formation, adopted in January 1969, could never be used where the wider lateral separation might bring bombs dangerously close to friendly troops.[63]

Although tactics and formations changed and aerial activity declined, the American public focused its interest during 1969 on the Nixon administration's withdrawal of ground troops from South Vietnam. This reduction in strength failed to satisfy opponents of the war. Neither the initial 25,000-man withdrawal nor the subsequent decision to reduce the U.S. force by an additional 40,500 men silenced the President's critics in Congress. During September, even as the air war was undergoing sharp reduction, Republican Senator Charles E. Goodell from New York proposed enacting a law that would require the removal of all U.S. forces from South Vietnam by the end of 1970,[64] and Senator Mansfield called for a cease-fire as the first step toward free elections in the South.[65] The President rejected these recommendations, telling a group of Marines back from South Vietnam that "peace . . . will be due to the fact that Americans, when it really counted, did not buckle and run away, but stood fast."[66]

The halls of Congress did not provide the only forum for dissent. In mid-October 1969, foes of the war staged rallies, prayer vigils, and processions throughout the country. Although this so-called Moratorium Day drew crowds varying from a few thousand in some cities to 100,000 in others, it brought no announced change of policy, for Nixon insisted he would continue the gradual withdrawal begun during the past summer, while working toward a negotiated settlement of the conflict. Counterdemonstrations and declarations of support encouraged Nixon to stand fast.[67]

The President and his supporters could not still the voices of protest, however. An estimated quarter-million persons gathered at Washington, D.C., during November in a mobilization against the war. Senator Goodell and other antiwar legislators addressed the throng, which offered vocal and occasionally violent proof that the withdrawal of American forces from South Vietnam was gathering the kind of headlong momentum that Kissinger had feared.[68]

Against this backdrop of opposition to the war, the President had launched B–52 attacks upon enemy bases in Cambodia, thus reducing the likelihood of repetition of the 1968 Tet offensive as the United States reduced its own combat forces and turned responsibility for the fighting over to the South Vietnamese. The secret bombing and the highly publicized troop withdrawals formed elements of the President's plan, a strategy that could not succeed unless South Vietnam became strong enough to sustain itself and help pressure the North into peace negotiations. As the withdrawal got underway, therefore, American airmen continued to wage war in the South, while helping train and equip that nation's armed forces.

Chapter Nine

The Nature of the Air War, 1969

The Air Force throughout 1969 continued to devote most of its efforts within South Vietnam to supporting the ground forces. Aviation, however, also carried out a number of tasks that Air Force doctrine normally catalogued as independent of the Army's war. These functions of air power included the making of maps and aerial charts, which received new emphasis during the conflict. Maps of Southeast Asia tended to become unreliable as the fighting moved farther from the areas charted by the French, whose cartographers had focused on regions along the coast, near towns, or on rivers and main highways. To remedy this failing, RF–4Cs photographed the poorly mapped terrain, using signals from long-range radio aids to navigation (Loran) transmitters on the ground to fix the exact location of checkpoints, such as a mountaintop or the conflux of two streams. Technicians at the Aeronautical Charting and Information Center at St. Louis, Missouri, transferred the control data to mosaics made up of high-altitude photographs, thus recording a series of precise references to be used in locating targets.

By mid-1971, this geographic information was being fed into a computer at Tan Son Nhut Air Base. When asked for the location of a possible target, operators could retrieve from the machine's memory the Loran coordinates of nearby checkpoints and then interpolate the location in question, a task that took no more than forty-five minutes. Although aerial mapping remained a separate function, doctrinally distinct from the support of ground forces, the Loran-controlled photography had immediate benefits for airmen directing strikes to assist troops. Specialists at Tan Son Nhut could print an arbitrary grid on photographs taken by the Loran-equipped RF–4Cs. Forward air controllers then used this grid to locate targets and submitted the coordinates to Tan Son Nhut, where the computer converted the information into Loran data for fighter-bombers fitted out to use that navigation aid.[1]

Operation of the Military Airlift Command, a worldwide airline that carried both passengers and cargo, proved important throughout the war in Southeast Asia. Having flown reinforcements into South Vietnam during the buildup that followed the Tet offensive, the Military Airlift Command then brought

Air War over South Vietnam, 1968–1975

Tactical reconnaissance aircraft used in Southeast Asia, top to bottom: the McDonnell RF–101, the McDonnell Douglas RF–4, and the Grumman OV–1.

home the troops that President Nixon withdrew from the country. During the first reduction in the summer of 1969, the command's Lockheed C–141s flew more than 15,000 men from Bien Hoa to McChord Air Force Base, Washington, by way of Hickam Air Force Base, Hawaii. The second withdrawal, ending in mid-December, required that the command fly some 14,000 troops and thirty tons of cargo to a variety of bases in the United States, using chartered commercial aircraft, regularly scheduled military flights, and special airlift missions.[2]

The Nature of the Air War, 1969

The evacuation of the wounded from South Vietnam for medical treatment elsewhere was another continuing activity of the Military Airlift Command. Some of the planes engaged in this effort flew a polar route by way of Japan and Alaska to bases on the east coast of the United States, while others crossed the Pacific via Hawaii, and still others brought the wounded to hospitals in Japan or the Philippines. The number of flights reached a peak in the summer of 1968, with twenty-six dispatched each week from South Vietnam or Japan to the United States and twenty-three from South Vietnam to Japan, some of the latter stopping en route at Guam or in the Philippines. Each week a special burn flight left Japan, carrying patients via Travis Air Force Base, California, to Kelly Air Force Base, Texas, and the burn treatment center at nearby Wilford Hall Medical Center. Despite the beginning of Vietnamization and the first troop withdrawals, the Military Airlift Command scheduled forty-eight medical evacuation flights each week during 1969, though the number declined afterward to reflect further reductions in American combat strength[3]

In 1969, air power's important contributions to success on the ground in South Vietnam included 174,000 tactical reconnaissance sorties, both aerial photography and radio direction finding, projects that involved Army aviation. In the case of aerial photography, the Army, dissatisfied with Air Force efforts, had developed its own equipment and techniques. The centralization of photo processing and interpretation at Tan Son Nhut Air Base, the Army claimed, slowed the distribution of intelligence to combat units. As early as 1966, General McConnell, Air Force Chief of Staff, attempted to meet these objections by establishing photo processing centers at other bases in South Vietnam.

This measure of decentralization helped, as did the creation of an aerial courier service to speed the processed and annotated photographs to ground combat units, but the fact remained that the McDonnell RF–101C, in 1969 being withdrawn from active service, and the more modern RF–4C were ill-suited to the kind of aerial photography that the Army usually wanted. Air Force jets with their wide-angle cameras covered a vast area quickly, but ground commanders tended to want detailed information on a hill mass or other small objective or repeated coverage of a specific road or hamlet. Only a plane like the Army's Grumman OV–1 Mohawk, flying slowly at low altitude over the target, could provide the desired information.[4]

General Brown, Seventh Air Force Commander, concluded that the attempt to improve responsiveness had come too late. Although courier service and a modicum of decentralization "might have been adequate back in 1947 or 1954," the changes had not come until "the Army had acquired aircraft, equipped them with cameras, and gotten into the business." The Air Force, he conceded, "had neglected the thing for so long" that Army airmen "geared up to handle it themselves, and you couldn't blame them." The Army's tactical reconnaissance force may have contributed to Brown's belief that the Air Force might be placing too much emphasis on this function in the Southeast Asia conflict.[5]

147

Air War over South Vietnam, 1968–1975

A Military Airlift Command C–141 receives wounded.

In radio direction finding missions, the Army and Air Force cooperated smoothly as they tried to locate radio transmitters broadcasting from North Vietnamese or Viet Cong field headquarters. A coordinating committee at assistance command headquarters parceled out requests among the various squadrons, but aircraft characteristics, rather than jointly agreed policy, determined who would fly where. Only the Air Force SC–47Ds, almost sixty in number, had the endurance for long patrols over Laos, western South Vietnam, or the coastal waters off North Vietnam's panhandle. Other missions, where time on station was a lesser consideration, became the responsibility the Army's Beechcraft U–8s or U–21s.[6]

The air war in South Vietnam, of which these reconnaissance missions formed so important a part, continued throughout 1969 to be fought mainly in support of ground operations, with almost 85 percent of all fixed-wing operational sorties by Seventh Air Force planes contributing in one way or another to success on the battlefield. Some 49 percent of these almost 590,000 sorties involved the delivery of men and supplies by tactical airlift units operating inside the country. Combat support, the loosely defined category that included battlefield illumination, herbicide spraying, and psychological warfare, accounted for about 4 percent of the total. Tactical reconnaissance, including sorties by forward air controllers, made up 29 percent and attack sorties 16 percent.[7]

The total number of attack sorties flown in South Vietnam — and the Air Force contribution, as well — had increased in the final months of 1968. This change resulted from the bombing halt that had taken effect throughout North Vietnam on November 1. Once the air strikes ended there, additional sorties became available in South Vietnam and southern Laos. A large number of Air Force planes formerly dispatched against targets in the North now helped intensify the campaign to disrupt the movement of men and cargo over the Ho Chi Minh Trail, the complex of roads, waterways, trails, dumps, and bases that passed through Laos and sustained the enemy in South Vietnam. Indeed, about as many Air Force planes were attacking in southern Laos at year's end as were battering the North Vietnamese and Viet Cong within the South.[8] A similar division of effort persisted into 1969, though the tempo of the air war slowed in Laos when the southwest monsoon rains were falling there, and restrictions on the number of tactical sorties — a result of budgetary considerations and the withdrawal of U.S. forces — reduced the level of aerial activity in South Vietnam. The ever-changing demands of the ground war, as well as weather and policy, affected Air Force operations, for, as General Brown pointed out, the focus of the aerial effort could be "changed by a telephone call" to meet an emergency.[9]

In 1969 the B–52s began attacking with greater frequency outside South Vietnam. Of more than 20,000 sorties flown by the bombers during that year, approximately two-thirds hit targets in the South; the remainder divided their attention between Laos and Cambodia, with roughly two bombers attacking in Laos for every one that took part in the secret raids inside Cambodia. By way of comparison, the previous year's ratio of B–52 sorties in South Vietnam to those in Laos had been four to one, and the Menu strikes had not yet begun. Wherever the B–52s attacked, they functioned in both years as long-range artillery, usually attempting to disrupt the flow of men and material to the battlefield by hitting supply dumps, troop bivouacs, truck parks, and the like.[10]

The budget-based ceiling imposed on tactical sorties during the fall of 1969 applied only to American aerial endeavors. Attack sorties flown by the South Vietnamese air arm increased during the year as the early effects of Vietnamization made themselves felt. The Royal Australian Air Force, meanwhile, sustained its usual level of activity, flying an average of 231 sorties per month.[11]

Although Canberra bombers manned by New Zealanders and Australians hit targets by day and occasionally by night throughout all of South Vietnam, the planes did most of their bombing by daylight in the delta, where a task force from Australia and New Zealand fought among the waterways and paddies. The combination of an optical bombsight and precise navigational gear gave the Canberra, upon which the American B–57 had been based, exceptional accuracy from altitudes between 1,000 and 3,000 feet. Although under operational control of the Seventh Air Force, the Canberra squadron, based at Phan Rang, had as its principal mission the support of troops from Australia and New Zealand.

Usually, as many as ten airmen from Australia or New Zealand served as forward air controllers for the task force, directing strikes by the Canberras, by American fighter-bombers, or by the sixteen helicopter gunships in an Australian squadron at Vung Tau. Whether incorporating air strikes in their operational plan or calling for air strikes to meet an emergency, task force officers proved reluctant, excessively so in the opinion of some American airmen, to call for strafing or bombing in close proximity to their own troops. The Australians, however, made extensive use of aerial reconnaissance, for example using Vung Tau-based helicopters, fitted with a people sniffer, to detect enemy troops at night for attack by artillery or air.

Besides the helicopters and light bombers, the Royal Australian Air Force operated a squadron of a half-dozen de Havilland Caribou transports, essentially the same aircraft as the U.S. Air Force C–7A. Although the Americans had integrated the Caribou unit into a centralized airlift control system, they had promised to give first consideration to the needs of the Australian task force in assigning missions to the squadron. In general, the Australians and New Zealanders flying the Caribou did the same work as their American equivalents, delivering cargo, carrying troops and occasionally dropping South Vietnamese paratroopers, helping move refugee families, dispensing flares, and sometimes bringing out sick or wounded from isolated camps or villages.[12]

Two other nations, Thailand and the Republic of Korea, had substantial ground forces in South Vietnam, but made only minor contributions to the air war. The South Koreans maintained a fleet of about two dozen miscellaneous planes, used mainly on administrative missions. A pair of C–54s, the largest of the group, sometimes flew wounded men back to South Korea.

Like their Australian counterparts, South Korean commanders made little use of tactical aviation in close support of ground troops. Although aware of the value of air strikes in suppressing enemy fire around a helicopter landing zone or similar objective, the South Koreans seemed to distrust the accuracy of fighter-bombers attacking close to their forces. Moreover, these troops maintained security among the villages between Qui Nhon and Phan Rang, a kind of duty in which counterintelligence, the setting of ambushes, and aggressive patrolling proved more effective than aerial attack.[13]

Thai combat leaders shared South Korean misgivings about bombing accuracy and tended to call for immediate strikes only after troops had broken contact and withdrawn some distance from the target. An innovation that helped overcome this lack of confidence was the use, beginning in 1970, of Thai pilots as forward air controllers. Normally, between five and ten officers, each on a one-year tour of duty, flew O–2s provided by one of the Air Force tactical air support squadrons. Instead of merely translating the conversation between an American strike controller and a Thai commander on the ground, the Thai airman now dealt directly with his infantry comrades, obtaining clarification of their situation and advising them of the ordnance available to help them. The men on the ground could be confident that their requests were understood.

The Royal Thai Air Force had begun early in the war to send transport crewmen to serve first with South Vietnamese squadrons and later in American C–123K units. From just sixteen members, the contingent increased to a maximum of forty-five, with a one-year tour of duty remaining the rule. The experienced Thais considered themselves advisers, but to the South Vietnamese these foreigners simply represented a source of replacements. In contrast, the Thai pilots who had joined an American C–123K squadron received more suitable recognition for their skills, becoming aircraft commanders or, if fluent enough in English, pilot instructors.[14]

The types of aerial action undertaken by units from the United States and other nations, the tactics they used, and in some cases the major battlefields remained unchanged from the previous year. In 1969, the enemy again launched a late winter offensive that included the bombardment of Saigon, a shelling that killed twenty-two civilians, wounded twenty-eight, and contributed to President Nixon's decision to bomb the Cambodian bases in the Menu operation. This time, however, the North Vietnamese and Viet Cong conducted raids and shelled objectives, instead of trying to seize towns and military installations as they had attempted at Tet in 1968. Just fourteen major attacks took place in early 1969, the most serious directed against Bien Hoa Air Base and the Army's depot and administrative center at nearby Long Binh.

A barrage that fell upon Bien Hoa in the early hours of February 23 destroyed two Air Force planes on the ground, damaged eight others, and served to signal an abortive ground attack. Air Force security police, reinforced by U.S. Army armored cavalry and aided by forward air controllers and Air Force gunships, pounded the huts where the enemy appeared to be massing, and the anticipated assault did not take place. On the morning of the 26th, however, two North Vietnamese battalions tried to raid the base, but failed to breach the perimeter defenses and instead entrenched themselves in nearby villages. After loudspeaker broadcasts had urged the enemy to surrender and warned any civilians still in their homes to flee, the South Vietnamese corps commander approved the destruction of the two communist-held villages. Air Force F–100s and F–4s, directed by forward air controllers, joined South Vietnamese planes and U.S. Army helicopter gunships in ending this particular threat to the base.

Enemy forces closing in on Long Binh encountered the same sort of resistance that ended the danger to Bien Hoa. On the morning of February 23, local security units blunted a ground attack launched in conjunction with an artillery and rocket barrage. Later that day, tactical fighters helped rout a company of Viet Cong and joined in an attack, successfully completed on the 25th, against the fortified bunkers the enemy had used as an assembly area and supply point. The strong defenses at Long Binh, manned in part by Thai troops, proved a surprise to enemy soldiers, who had been assured that only clerks and typists guarded the base.[15]

Although Bien Hoa, not far from Long Binh, was the only Air Force base subjected to an infantry assault, shells, rockets, or small-arms fire struck Phan Rang, Pleiku, Phu Cat, Da Nang, Cam Ranh Bay, and several lesser airfields used by American airmen from the different services. The February attacks

Air War over South Vietnam, 1968–1975

killed four Americans, one of them a member of the Air Force, and destroyed three Air Force planes — an O–1E at Dau Tieng and an F–100 and a U–10 at Bien Hoa. The greatest loss of aircraft occurred among Army helicopters, nine of which were destroyed on the airfield at Kontum.[16]

The attacks on Bien Hoa, Long Binh, Saigon, and the other towns or installations coincided with a renewal of pressure against the Special Forces camps in the highlands along the western border of South Vietnam. In February 1969, at the time of the late winter offensive, the North Vietnamese directed their fire against the outpost at Ben Het, within howitzer range of Base Area 609 in Cambodia, a hostile staging area soon to become a Menu target. From either side of the Cambodian border, 100-mm guns commenced shelling the camp.

Faced with this threat, General Abrams invoked the rules of engagement that permitted retaliation with tactical aircraft and artillery against hostile gunners firing from Cambodian soil at American or South Vietnamese border garrisons. Fighter-bombers attacked on February 24 and 25, destroying at least one gun but failing to end the danger. Abrams wanted to use B–52s in defense of Ben Het, but at this time, less than a month before the Menu operation began, he could not obtain permission for the bombing, which might have alerted the enemy to the raids that began in March. The shelling of Ben Het continued until early March when the enemy advanced upon the camp, using Soviet-designed amphibious light tanks in an unsuccessful attempt to overwhelm the defenders. Confronted by heavier American armor and subjected to tactical air strikes, the enemy broke off his attack. Essentially a probe of the defenses of the highlands, rather than a serious attempt to overwhelm Ben Het, this North Vietnamese effort served mainly as the prelude to further action later in the year.[17]

While helping the South Vietnamese retain Ben Het as an outpost from which to contest infiltration by way of Cambodia, General Abrams continued the effort to impede the passage of North Vietnamese troops and cargo through the A Shau Valley, relying exclusively on air power to accomplish this objective. In December 1968, some six weeks after the roads in southern Laos had dried following the seasonal rains and traffic toward the A Shau Valley increased, the Seventh Air Force sought to establish three interdiction points on Route 548, over which men and cargo could travel the length of the valley. Planners chose the usual kind of choke points where the road appeared vulnerable to bombing and bypasses seemed difficult to construct. The northernmost interdiction point embraced a stretch of highway that hugged a cliff, the central point encompassed the narrowest part of the valley, and the southern one covered a segment of road that followed the crest of a narrow ridge. Severing the route at these three places marked just the first step, for the planning group intended to harass repair crews and attack any truck convoys moving cargo from one cut to another for transshipment to South Vietnam.

As single manager for tactical combat aviation, General Brown could call upon the Marines to use the Grumman A–6, with airborne radar capable of

The Nature of the Air War, 1969

A Marine Corps Grumman A–6 at Chu Lai Marine Base.

tracking a truck. Army OV–1 Mohawks, though not under Brown's control, scanned the valley with side-looking airborne radar, alerting a patrolling A–6 to any traffic they detected so that the Marine airmen could use their radar to lock onto and attack the target. Air Force forward air controllers and Combat Skyspot radar directed other strikes in the valley.[18]

Although carefully thought out and diligently executed, the aerial interdiction plan could only fail, a victim as much of geography as of enemy resourcefulness. Those who drafted it thought they had chosen the best possible choke points, and initially they had, but within the valley a number of trails or paths could be improved to accept truck traffic, forcing the planners to select new interdiction sites to keep pace with an expanding road net. Despite ridges and cliffs, the A Shau Valley, even at its narrowest, afforded room to maneuver around the increasing number of cuts. In fact, North Vietnamese engineers demonstrated they could construct a bypass overnight and move almost as quickly to close a cut in the main road, working despite aerial harassment, delayed action bombs, tear gas, and even mines.[19] By the end of February, with road traffic reaching a seasonal peak in adjacent parts of Laos, the valley again became "a hot spot of enemy activity" that could be dealt with only on the ground.[20]

The first attempt during 1969 to use ground forces to impede enemy movement through the A Shau began late in January when the 9th Marines, in Operation Dewey Canyon, attacked toward the Laotian border and the entrance to the valley. Whenever the skies above the battleground cleared, Marine airborne controllers directed their fellow aviators against North Vietnamese artillery. Unfortunately, clouds blanketed the northern A Shau about half the time, providing concealment that enabled the enemy to continue using the roads and trails funneling into the valley. Unobserved Marine artillery fire, B–52 sorties directed by Air Force Combat Skyspot radar, and fighter attacks controlled by Marine Corps radar operators with the regiment could do little more than harass the North Vietnamese.

Air War over South Vietnam, 1968–1975

The Air Force contributed in several ways to Dewey Canyon, which ended in mid-March. Four times gunships went to the aid of Marine infantrymen under attack by night, flare ships flew fourteen illumination missions, and the radio relay aircraft linked the 9th Marines with higher headquarters.[21] The B–52s attempted for the most part to disrupt supply lines, but the Marines who later advanced through one of the target boxes found that the enemy was making the best of what must have been a harrowing experience. Lt. Col. George C. Fox, a Marine battalion commander, reported that North Vietnamese engineers were taking advantage of the destruction caused by the bombing, using downed trees to corduroy roads and storing cargo in bomb craters.[22]

During Dewey Canyon, the leader of an element of Air Force F–105s lined up on smoke from a forward air controller's marking rocket and took aim on a target that lay within a free-fire zone inside Laos. Before the two planes could release their bombs, a radio message, relayed by the controller, warned that the troops below were American. Even as he was breaking off the attack by his F–105s, the leader protested that anyone on the ground in this part of Laos had to be an enemy, but in this instance he was wrong. The commanding officer of the 9th Marines, Col. Robert H. Barrow, had sent patrols beyond the border into southern Laos, an action that his superiors approved, but word had not reached the direct air support center or the Air Force squadrons flying missions in the area. If the F–105 pilots were surprised, so, too, were the North Vietnamese, for the probe resulted in the destruction of a large quantity of supplies cached along a road inside Laos and awaiting shipment through the A Shau Valley.[23]

The second part of the ground interdiction effort, Operation Massachusetts Striker, attacked the southern part of the A Shau. Once again, the action took the form of a raid designed to disrupt traffic and destroy supplies rather than an attempt to seal off the valley. On March 1, 1969, reinforced elements of an airborne brigade established the first of a planned series of fire support bases, so that troops leapfrogging by helicopter could enjoy artillery as well as air support as they advanced into the valley. Scarcely had this first outpost been completed when clouds descended upon the A Shau, blinding Air Force forward air controllers, forcing the attackers to rely upon radar controlled air strikes and unobserved artillery fire, and delaying subsequent moves for about ten days. Once the operations plan began unfolding in its successive stages, Air Force C–130s dropped 10,000-pound bombs to blast helicopter landing zones on forested hilltops. Army engineers enlarged two of these zones into artillery fire support bases that functioned throughout the rest of the operation, which ended on May 8, some 250 of the enemy killed, almost six tons of rice captured, and several North Vietnamese trucks and other pieces of equipment destroyed.[24]

During Massachusetts Striker, the Air Force performed much as it had during the previous year's raids into the A Shau. Forward air controllers spent more than 500 hours aloft, two-thirds of that time actually handling strike aircraft. Attacks by some 500 fighters lashed the southern reaches of the valley with three million pounds of munitions — incendiary weapons, high-explosive bombs, and 20-mm shells.[25]

The third raid into the A Shau Valley during 1969, Operation Apache Snow, began two days after Massachusetts Striker ended. The objective this time was the central part of the valley, the area generally west of A Luoi and Ta Bat, where Air Force forward air controllers had been reporting signs of recurring truck traffic. This evidence, backed by statements from a captured North Vietnamese soldier, convinced Army Capt. Robert Fredericks, intelligence officer for the brigade scheduled to attack in this area, that a large supply depot lay concealed on a ridge about five miles northwest of A Luoi, rather than on the valley floor as previously believed. Capt. Albert W. Estes and other forward air controllers working with this unit, the 3d Brigade, 101st Airborne Division, located the dump, nicknamed Warehouse 54. Strikes by tactical fighters and B–52s, followed by a reconnaissance in force by troops landed from helicopters, revealed a series of caches and defensive strongpoints extending from this ridge south toward the border with Laos.[26]

Despite the preliminary fighting around Warehouse 54, the main assault on the central A Shau Valley seemed to catch the enemy off guard, for opposition proved light at the landing zones. Three American and two South Vietnamese battalions touched down in areas cleared of scrub growth by 1,000-pound and 3,000-pound bombs fitted with fuse extenders to detonate just above the ground. As the operation progressed, the fighting became more intense, and American commanders soon realized that Ap Bia, a mountain about three miles southwest of A Luoi, was the key to the North Vietnamese defenses. Not until May 12, however, had the airborne forces secured the approaches and fought their way into position to storm the redoubt.[27]

Ap Bia, which crested 937 meters above sea level, derived its importance not from its height — other nearby peaks towered above it — but from the fact that North Vietnamese troops had turned it into a fortress. When the American commander decided that the enemy force entrenched there was too dangerous to cordon off or somehow neutralize, the objective became the killing of North Vietnamese rather than the capture of the height itself. The defenders had constructed two basic kinds of bunkers, built from logs and covered with sod, that studded Ap Bia's slopes. The smaller kind measured four feet on a side, had eight to sixteen inches of overhead cover, and featured firing ports to the front and two outside foxholes from which riflemen could fight off attacks from the flanks or rear. The larger variety, measuring eight by ten feet with a roof one foot thick, had firing positions at the front and an area at the rear for sleeping. Instead of being cube-shaped, both types resembled pyramids, which made the structures easier to camouflage and gave them greater resistance to explosions.[28]

So formidable were the fortifications of Ap Bia that the attackers had to commit four battalions to a struggle that lasted until May 20. Of an estimated 700 to 800 North Vietnamese defenders, about 600 fought until killed in their

Air War over South Vietnam, 1968–1975

bunkers or foxholes, while only two surrendered. American losses on the hill and its approaches numbered fifty-six killed and 420 wounded, even though air strikes and artillery barrages had pounded the mountain. Because so many soldiers had been killed or wounded in what seemed like a meat-grinder operation, the airborne troops nicknamed the objective Hamburger Hill, a title that caught on with press and public.[29]

"Seldom in . . . . any . . . . battle," concluded a report on the fighting, "had TAC air been employed so massively as in the battle of Dong [Mount] Ap Bia."[30] The assault force had been unable, however, to take advantage of the numbing shock of B–52 strikes. Because preliminary aerial reconnaissance had not revealed this strongpoint, the bombers made no strikes before Apache Snow began, and once the airborne battalions had begun fighting their way to the summit, the safety margin required for B–52 strikes no longer existed. At night, AC–47s dropping flares and AC–119Gs fitted with searchlights illuminated the mountainside and trained their multibarrel guns on the counterattacking North Vietnamese. Besides the gunships, fighter-bombers made some 270 strikes, dropping a million pounds of munitions, including delayed action bombs, which could bury themselves among the timbers of a bunker roof before exploding, and napalm, which burned away camouflage and could consume the oxygen within the shelters. However, of some 600 North Vietnamese killed during the fight for Ap Bia, only forty-seven could be listed as definitely killed by tactical air strikes. In addition to the Air Force planes, Army helicopters took part in the battle, conducting treetop reconnaissance, evacuating wounded, broadcasting surrender appeals, and dropping tear gas among the fortifications.[31]

After the capture of Ap Bia, Operation Apache Snow continued until June 7, when the Americans and South Vietnamese withdrew from the A Shau Valley, never to return, save for an ineffectual probe two years later. Hamburger Hill joined Khe Sanh on the list of battlefields abandoned after a great investment in blood and effort. The A Shau Valley campaign of 1969 proved important not because of any innovations in the use of air power, since there were none, or because of the more than 700 enemy killed and the tons of supplies destroyed. Hamburger Hill had its greatest impact on politics — and ultimately on the conduct of the war — for a flurry of criticism soon erupted in Congress.[32]

When Senator Edward M. Kennedy learned of the struggle for the mountain and the fact that American forces had promptly abandoned it, he condemned the attack as "senseless and irresponsible." To the Massachusetts Democrat, the battle seemed a waste of lives to gain a temporary success that, because of the withdrawal, could have no lasting effect on the course of the war. His Democratic colleague, Mike Mansfield of Montana, added that, though objectives like Ap Bia are gained and lost many times, human lives are lost just once.[33]

Senator J. William Fulbright, an Arkansas Democrat, asked to see the specific directive under which General Abrams was fighting the war, in order to determine whether actions like the Hamburger Hill fighting were indeed authorized. On the Republican side, Dr. Kissinger suggested shifting the military emphasis from sharing in the defense of South Vietnam, which recognized the need for operations like those in the A Shau Valley, to preparing the South Vietnamese to defend themselves, a change that would inevitably reduce American casualties. In short, Kissinger sought to neutralize the critics by stressing the shift of responsibility to the South Vietnamese, a program begun by the Johnson administration and accelerated when Nixon took office.[34]

The controversy stemming from the fight for Hamburger Hill and the decision to redefine the Vietnam commitment in terms of training rather than combat may well have been on President Nixon's mind when he made a brief visit to Saigon in July 1969. While there, he modified the instructions to General Abrams to reflect Dr. Kissinger's reaction to Senator Fulbright's request. Instead of the former goal of preserving South Vietnam from communism, Nixon emphasized handing over to improved South Vietnamese forces a progressively greater role in fighting the war, a policy that President Thieu had already accepted. "Under the new orders," Nixon explained to the American public, "the primary mission of our troops is to enable South Vietnamese forces to assume the full responsibility for the security of South Vietnam."[35]

The battle for Hamburger Hill, which had prompted the President to announce this change in emphasis, represented but a single element in one of three related efforts in the A Shau Valley and its northern approaches — by the 9th Marines in the north; the 2d Brigade, 101st Airborne Division in the south; and the 3d Brigade, 101st Airborne Division at Ap Bia Mountain in the center. As these were drawing to a close, the enemy again demonstrated his annoyance with the Special Forces camps astride other infiltration routes.

During May 1969, coinciding with a spring offensive, North Vietnamese tanks, infantry, and artillery again massed near Ben Het, which lay within ten miles of the meeting point of the borders of South Vietnam, Cambodia, and Laos. The portents of an impending attack on Ben Het lent urgency to the interdiction of roads and trails in the vicinity of the camp. Such a campaign had begun in January with the establishment of an Air Force special interdiction program, which permitted pilots to attack after obtaining clearance from only the commander of the major ground unit in whose sector the target had appeared. Clearance from the province chief was no longer necessary, for all noncombatants were believed to have fled the region around Ben Het. The main concern, therefore, was to avoid strikes on friendly patrols or outposts, and the commander on the ground should know the locations of these.

By the end of June, intelligence indicated that motor traffic in the area had declined some 90 percent, a reduction that Seventh Air Force analysts attributed to air power alone, although seasonal rains probably helped impede movement. This estimate of the impact of aerial interdiction may have been overly optimistic, but the fact remained that enemy armor, now forced to travel over alternate roads hacked through the jungle, did not again test Ben Het's defenses.[36]

Air War over South Vietnam, 1968–1975

Fog persisted around Ben Het during mornings and thunderstorms drenched the region each afternoon, conditions common at that time of year. With the time that forward air controllers could work reduced, tactical strikes depended heavily on radar control, essential for B–52 raids. During the year's second siege of Ben Het, B–52s enjoyed far greater freedom than before, bombing a reported 140 targets on both sides of the Cambodian border. Menu attacks on Base Area 609, Abrams believed, contributed directly to Ben Het's survival.[37]

Targeting around Ben Het, especially for B–52 strikes in South Vietnamese territory, became increasingly difficult as the siege wore on, for friendly outposts and patrols disappeared from the hills around the camp, depriving planners of a useful source of information. In anticipation of the U.S. withdrawals planned for the summer, the region now formed part of the 24th Tactical Zone, commanded by Col. Nguyen Ba Lien. Instead of probing North Vietnamese positions menacing Ben Het and locating targets for air strikes, he pulled his troops back into the camp itself or the nearby headquarters town of Dak To. Because of his reliance on a passive defense, intelligence officers could not find worthwhile targets for all the available B–52 sorties.[38]

By calling in his troops, the colonel yielded control of the ridges that overlooked Ben Het. Hostile antiaircraft crews took advantage of the absence of any threat on the ground and set up their weapons to cover the approaches to the airstrip. At the beginning of June, the C–7As supplying the base could no longer land to unload. Afterward, the transports either parachuted their cargo from medium altitude or roared along the runway at an altitude of a few feet and released an extraction chute that snatched a heavily laden pallet through the rear hatch. Even though they no longer landed, the cargo craft required an escort of fighter-bombers to suppress enemy fire.

For much of the siege, a forward air controller met the approaching cargo planes and shepherded them, spaced fifteen minutes apart, over the camp, while two F–4s stood by to pounce on any antiaircraft battery the controller might spot. In spite of these precautions, North Vietnamese gunners scored hits on six C–7As and wounded three crewmen during the first three weeks of June. To deal with the threat, mission planners increased the number of strike aircraft, made sure that fighters and forward air controllers arrived a few minutes before the transports, and adjusted the tactics used by the C–7As and their escorts.

Beginning on June 27, the direct air support center used the available information — principally visual sightings by air crews, since the South Vietnamese had ceased patrolling — to pinpoint gun positions along the approaches to Ben Het. Forward air controllers marked these for attack by the flak suppression escort of F–4s, and other fighter-bombers placed a smoke screen over part of the valley, blinding some of the gunners without obscuring the camp itself or the road that served as a reference point for incoming pilots. Flying in clusters of three or more, within which the individual aircraft were about one minute apart, the transports headed for Ben Het. Two A–1 Skyraiders and an observation plane carrying a forward air controller accompanied each group to mark and silence any antiaircraft gun that opened fire. The powerfully escorted and irregularly timed clusters seemed to work — even though one-minute separation prevailed within each cluster — for the enemy scored just one hit on the forty-five C–7As sent to the camp after the change went into effect.[39]

The siege of Ben Het ended on July 2, when the North Vietnamese relaxed their pressure after some 1,800 tactical sorties had been flown in defense of the camp, one-third of them radar controlled. The Air Force had been responsible for about 90 percent of these, the South Vietnamese about 8 percent, and the remainder were divided between U.S. Navy and Australian airmen. Although the use of cover targets to conceal Menu strikes complicated the bookkeeping, the number of B–52 sorties in defense of Ben Het totaled about 800, with almost 150 targets attacked. Gunships, AC–47s and AC–119Gs, averaged not quite two sorties each night, firing more than 500,000 rounds into the hills overlooking the camp. Sorties by C–7s averaged four per day; these aircraft delivered more than 200 tons of cargo during the battle.[40]

From Ben Het, the enemy turned his attention to Bu Prang and Duc Lap, Special Forces encampments in southern II Corps, across the border from Base Area 740, another of the Menu targets in Cambodia. The aerial onslaught in defense of the two camps began late in October, and by mid-December, when the enemy broke contact, Air Force tactical fighters had dropped 3,000 tons of bombs and B–52s dropped five times that weight. This explosive deluge did not produce immediate effects, however, so that for a time early in December an even greater aerial effort seemed necessary.[41]

By December 1, General Abrams was seeking permission for the B–52s to hit targets in an area west of Bu Prang that was claimed by both South Vietnam and Cambodia. Although Ambassador Bunker endorsed the strikes, Secretary of State Rogers opposed the plan, apparently out of concern that the bombing would become public knowledge because of press interest in the fate of Bu Prang and, once publicized, be interpreted as an endorsement of South Vietnam's claims to the land. Rogers' view did not prevail, for Secretary of Defense Laird obtained Presidential approval to begin the bombing. In deference to the concerns of the Secretary of State, Laird directed that Menu security procedures conceal the raids. At least two night missions attacked the disputed territory, but reconnaissance photos failed to reveal any damage or casualties.[42]

Although exerting less pressure than against Ben Het or even Bu Prang, hostile forces conducted operations along other parts of South Vietnam's border with Cambodia. The mountains at the southern edge of Chau Doc Province, site of an airborne raid in 1968, served as a dry-season operating base for the Viet Cong and as a place of refuge during the southwest monsoons, when heavy rains inundated the rice lands in the area. In July 1969, as the seasonal rains were falling, General Abrams established two free-fire zones encompassing the mountains. He gave air power the task of demoralizing the troops encamped there and

Air War over South Vietnam, 1968–1975

Bu Prang Special Forces Camp.

forcing them out onto the flooded plain to escape the bombs. There, South Vietnamese ambush parties guarded the earthen dikes upon which the enemy would have to flee across the paddies.

An Air Force command post at the Chui Lang Special Forces camp directed the operation, nicknamed Alpine. An Army intelligence officer suggested targets based on infrared and radar coverage by OV–1 Mohawks, reports from agents, and activations of electronic sensors. The Air Force duty officer at the camp selected the proposed strikes that he considered worthwhile and radioed the IV Direct Air Support Center to arrange the sorties.

During the campaign, Air Force tactical aircraft executed some 300 strikes, more than one-third of them in the first eight days. Rain and low-hanging clouds spawned by the southwest monsoon impeded the efforts of forward air controllers, who directed no more than sixty strikes. Radar operators at Combat Skyspot sites handled the remaining tactical fighter missions plus thirty-six B–52 sorties. The big bombers had rarely hit targets in the densely populated IV Corps, but in this instance the enemy occupied a redoubt isolated from friendly or potentially friendly villages.

Since South Vietnamese troops did not probe the approaches to the Alpine area until the rains abated in first week of August and made no attempt to seize the mountain encampments, the assessment of results depended, as was so often the case, on fragmentary reports by scouts and intelligence agents, who listed some 350 Viet Cong soldiers and laborers killed. A patrol reported finding another forty-one bodies, and interrogations of the few men captured in the vicinity indicated that the aerial bombardment had hurt enemy morale. The southwest monsoon season ended, however, with the base area firmly in Viet Cong hands and its link with the depots in Cambodia still intact.[43]

Chapter Ten

Improving the South Vietnamese Air Force

While conducting combat operations like Alpine, the Air Force helped prepare the South Vietnamese air arm to assume a greater share of responsibility for fighting the war. In imposing restrictions on the bombing of North Vietnam (in effect, placing a ceiling on U.S. participation in the conflict) President Johnson set in motion an effort to strengthen South Vietnam's armed forces. In the spring of 1968, American planners converted the President's policy into a plan for improvement and modernization based on the assumption that the war would continue with the U.S. role basically unchanged, although the South Vietnamese would assume a larger role in the ground fighting as rapidly as possible.

This so-called phase I plan preserved an existing imbalance in the composition of South Vietnam's defense forces. Ground strength remained disproportionately large in comparison to the air and naval establishments, an acceptable arrangement as long as the United States continued to exert its air and naval might on behalf of its ally. Phase I called for the addition of just four UH–1H helicopter squadrons to the twenty-squadron South Vietnamese Air Force. Besides expanding by a total of 124 helicopters, the air arm would undergo a degree of modernization: T–41 trainers replacing some of the older U–17s, four H–34 squadrons converting to UH–1Hs, a C–47 transport squadron reequipping with the AC–47 gunship, and three A–1 squadrons receiving jet-powered A–37s in place of their propeller-driven Skyraiders. These changes increased by some 41 percent the authorized number of aircraft, but after the various increases and substitutions, all but two of the additional aircraft were helicopters, but flown by the U.S. Air Force to lend mobility to the South Vietnamese army.[1]

When the negotiations, to which President Johnson had committed the country, produced a settlement, U.S. forces would withdraw, knocking away the underpinning of the phase I force structure. A new plan was needed, one that would enable South Vietnam to defend itself after a peace treaty, when the opposition would consist of Viet Cong insurgents supplied from the North and strengthened by any North Vietnamese regulars remaining behind after an agreed withdrawal.

161

Air War over South Vietnam, 1968–1975

To deal largely on its own with this type of threat, similar to the conditions that had existed before 1965, South Vietnam would require a better balance among the armed forces. General Abrams therefore proposed enlarging the nation's air arm to forty squadrons — the existing twenty, the four to be added under phase I, and sixteen others — all of which would be in service by July 1974. The latest additions formed the aerial component of a phase II plan aimed at filling those gaps in the overall force structure that would appear as U.S. units withdrew, leaving South Vietnam to cope with an insurrection supported from abroad. Besides an additional five helicopter squadrons — for a total augmentation of nine — phase II called for three new squadrons of A-37s, four of transports (all but one flying C-123s), an AC-119G gunship unit, and three liaison squadrons equipped with planes suitable for use by forward air controllers. The new plan would double the current number of South Vietnamese squadrons, more than double the total number of aircraft, and increase the authorized manning from the present 17,000, beyond the 21,000 authorized for phase I, to a new figure of 32,600.[2]

Abrams believed that these additions, plus the F-5 and A-37 strike aircraft and CH-47 helicopters already scheduled for delivery, would enable the South Vietnamese air arm to conduct operations in the Republic of Vietnam similar to those conducted by the air forces of both the United States and South Vietnam in 1964 and 1965. The AC-47 and AC-119 gunship force were believed sufficient for base defense and the support of ground operations, and by July 1974 the fighter arm would have achieved satisfactory strength and skill, even though the F-5, the first of which had arrived in South Vietnam during 1965, would have to double as strike fighter and interceptor. The planned number of helicopters seemed adequate, moreover, to permit airmobile operations against "insurgency activity." The planned liaison units, which included forward air controllers, and the transport squadrons did not have enough aircraft, however, and General Abrams acknowledged that the proposed reconnaissance force, a half-dozen RF-5s, could not cover an area the size of South Vietnam. The U.S. Air Force would have to compensate somehow for these obvious weaknesses.[3]

Although the stronger air arm would improve the balance among South Vietnam's armed services, phase II could not bring about overall military self-sufficiency, a point that Abrams conceded. In spite of this failing, Deputy Secretary of Defense Paul Nitze approved the plan as suitable for existing conditions, though pointing out that circumstances were certain to change. Indeed, Nitze suggested the possible need for a plan to deal with a postwar insurgency less violent and widespread than the fighting envisioned in phase II. Also, Abrams warned that the President's October 1968 decision to suspend air and naval bombardment throughout the North might result in such rapid progress toward a cease-fire that the phase II effort would have to be accelerated.[4]

After considering the points raised by Nitze and Abrams, the Joint Chiefs of Staff on January 4, 1969, presented the outgoing administration a plan for

Improving the South Vietnamese Air Force

A South Vietnamese A–37.

changing the target date for completion of phase II from July 1974 to July 1972. They next gave incoming President Nixon's newly chosen advisers the kind of plan for a diminished insurgency that former Deputy Secretary Nitze had requested, though they recommended abandoning this proposal in favor of an accelerated phase II, as suggested by General Abrams, for this seemed a more prudent course than preparing exclusively for sporadic guerrilla warfare.[5]

When President Nixon entered the White House, he had Kissinger review the progress being made in South Vietnam. The investigation, which took the form of questions to the agencies responsible for waging the war, included an examination of the status of the South Vietnamese armed forces. As was common during the Vietnam war, the experts disagreed. On the one hand, the Joint Chiefs of Staff, the Pacific Command, the Department of State, and the Military Assistance Command, Vietnam, maintained that South Vietnam's armed services were making "reasonable progress" toward becoming "a self-sufficient force able to hold its own against the VC [Viet Cong] threat." On the other hand, the Central Intelligence Agency and the Office of Secretary of Defense, although acknowledging that the South Vietnamese military establishment had grown in numbers and firepower, insisted that the nation's armed forces had made only "limited progress," leaving many weaknesses uncorrected.[6]

Whatever their present failings, the South Vietnamese forces would have to become more proficient and more aggressive, and do so quickly, if President Nixon were to Vietnamize the war, reducing American casualties while maintaining enough pressure on the enemy to prod him toward a negotiated settlement. Instead of being concerned, as former Deputy Secretary Nitze had been, about a postwar insurgency, Secretary of Defense Laird now emphasized a rapid buildup of South Vietnamese strength so that sizeable American contingents could leave Southeast Asia during 1969. Laird's political experience in the House of Representatives no doubt alerted him to the need for acceleration. Dissension over the Vietnam war had, after all, divided the Democratic party's nominating convention at Chicago, triggered violence in the streets of that city, and, if it had not helped Nixon at the polls, it had certainly handicapped his opponent. Increasing domestic opposition to the war — which had opened gaping cracks in the Democratic party's coalition — served as a warning that a leisurely buildup of South Vietnamese forces to take over the defense of their nation would not be possible. Indeed, South Vietnam might have to accept greater responsibility for waging the war before the North Vietnamese had withdrawn entirely from the country. The United States, Laird believed, would have to act immediately to strengthen the South Vietnamese armed forces so they could begin replacing American combat units during the coming months. The kind of acceleration that General Abrams had mentioned in November 1968 was coming to pass, but the change resulted from political realities at home rather than from progress at the Paris talks.[7]

In April 1969, the Department of Defense issued instructions to accelerate the phase II improvement and modernization plan, as the Joint Chiefs of Staff had proposed three months earlier. Deputy Secretary of Defense David Packard declared that, "Vietnamizing the war should have the highest priority." He warned, however, that the United States, besides providing the needed equipment, would have to make sure that the South Vietnamese knew how to operate, employ, and maintain it.[8]

The government of South Vietnam agreed to reduced American strength on the battlefield in return for more and better weapons and appropriate training. On June 8, 1969, not quite three weeks after the Hamburger Hill fighting, Presidents Nixon and Thieu met on Midway Island and discussed both the withdrawal of American troops and the arming and training of South Vietnamese to take over a greater share of the fighting. Although the controversy surrounding that battle lent immediacy to the topic of Vietnamization, the Nixon plan had been in the works since January and could trace its antecedents back to the Johnson administration.

Although amenable to the idea of Vietnamization, President Thieu had ideas of his own about the kind of weapons his armed forces required. In acceding to an American reduction in strength, he offered a plan of his own for modernizing the military services, asking for what the Joint Chiefs of Staff termed "appreciable quantities of sophisticated and costly equipment," including F–4 fighters and C–130 transports. If South Vietnam received these aircraft and the other weapons he sought, the nation would have the means to play a more nearly decisive role in the struggle against the combined forces of North Vietnam and the Viet Cong. Granted that this was the very objective that Nixon sought, the Joint Chiefs did not believe it could be attained as rapidly or as easily as President Thieu seemed to think, and certainly not by merely handing the South Vietnamese deadlier but far more complex aircraft and other weapons.

To American eyes, Thieu appeared to be trying to move too fast. Compared to their American counterparts, members of South Vietnam's armed forces seemed to lack the technical skills necessary to make effective use of the weaponry the nation's chief executive desired. Nor did the phase II plan, now to be

Improving the South Vietnamese Air Force

President Richard M. Nixon (left) and President Nguyen Van Thieu.

accelerated, envision the South Vietnamese promptly taking on the aggregate strength of North Vietnam and the Viet Cong. However desirable this might be as an ultimate goal, the Joint Chiefs of Staff did not believe that mere weapons could, "in view of such problems as leadership and desertion," enable South Vietnam to "take over major fighting responsibility against the current threat."[9]

A review of the Thieu proposal by General Abrams resulted in a recommendation that the United States turn down almost every request. The South Vietnamese air arm would have to do without F–4s and C–130s, additional VC–47 transports for high-ranking officials, coastal surveillance aircraft, and a search and rescue organization like that operated by the U.S. Air Force. Thieu's ambitious plan did, however, generate an additional $160 million in American military aid to improve logistics support and also produced a decision to speed-up previously authorized recruiting, adding some 4,000 men to the South Vietnamese Air Force by June 1970.[10]

Although Secretary Laird accepted the views of General Abrams and the Joint Chiefs of Staff on the kinds of equipment South Vietnam should receive, he saw acceleration of the phase II effort as signaling a fundamental change of purpose in the modernization project. "Earlier . . . modernization and improvement programs," he wrote, "were designed to provide a balanced and self-sufficient . . . force capable of meeting insurgency requirements and were based on the assumption that U.S., Allied, and North Vietnamese forces would withdraw from South Vietnam. Now the object of Vietnamization is to transfer progressively to the Republic of Vietnam all aspects of the war, assuming current levels of North Vietnamese and Viet Cong forces remain in the Republic of Vietnam and assuming U.S. force deployments [back to the United States] continue."[11]

Air War over South Vietnam, 1968–1975

Throughout the rest of 1969, the United States pushed ahead with accelerated phase II modernization and improvement. The U.S. Air Force Advisory Group, headed by a brigadier general who reported to an Army officer on the staff of the military assistance command, assumed responsibility for Vietnamizing the air war. General Brown, the senior Air Force officer in Southeast Asia, remained outside the formal advisory structure, at least in theory, for he dealt with operations, whether as Seventh Air Force commander or as deputy for air to General Abrams and single manager for tactical combat aviation. He did not, according to the organization charts, serve as principal air adviser to the South Vietnam's armed forces; but in actual practice, he pointed out, "There was never a major decision taken or action on the Vietnamese air force program that I wasn't a party to in my two years under General Abrams." Whatever the organizational diagrams might indicate, the Seventh Air Force commander was "totally responsible, and the advisory group commander works for him." General Brown harbored no doubts that "if there was a problem with the advisory group, I was the guy that was responsible."[12]

As to the mechanics of Vietnamization, General Brown expressed confidence that new squadrons would take shape on time and improved equipment would arrive on schedule. He warned, however, that a modernized and strengthened air arm would differ greatly from the combined American and South Vietnamese air forces currently fighting the war. In the future, South Vietnam's airmen would have to rely on their own leaders and planners in wielding an aerial weapon considerably less devastating than the American armada of strike and support aircraft that had helped fight the battles of 1968 and 1969. If South Vietnam were to survive, the United States, while reducing its own participation in combat, would have to help reduce the communist threat to a level the South Vietnamese could handle. This reduction, General Brown believed, would require more than purely military measures; economic reform and political development were essential, better trained police had to create a climate of security, and the Viet Cong leadership had to be ferreted out and destroyed.[13]

Since he was in overall charge of the entire assistance effort, General Abrams, after consulting with General Brown, established priorities for the South Vietnamese Air Force. Emphasis rested on the activation of helicopter units and the training of pilots and technicians. The air arm was to recruit up to the recently authorized level of 32,600 as rapidly as this increase could be absorbed.[14]

The South Vietnamese tended to follow the American pattern in structuring their armed forces, but the assignment of control over helicopters proved an exception. Even though General Westmoreland had intended the machines primarily for airmobile operations by South Vietnamese army troops, the helicopter squadrons formed a major component of South Vietnam's air force. The reasons for this decision remained unclear, though Brig. Gen. Kendall S. Young, chief of the Air Force advisory group, believed that Vice President Ky,

Improving the South Vietnamese Air Force

a former commander of the air force, had influenced the choice. In any event, U.S. Air Force advisers had to assume responsibility for teaching tactics that their service did not use.[15]

The helicopter program, launched by General Westmoreland early in 1968, had already resulted in the conversion of two squadrons from the old Sikorsky H–34 to the Bell UH–1. Since the U.S. Air Force lacked experience in planning and staging helicopter assault operations, the teams that trained the reequipped units had to include Army airmen. The squadrons, both located in IV Corps, made the transition from the kind of special operations that the U.S. Air Force conducted, such as landing patrols or raiding parties, to airmobile combat, a specialty of the U.S. Army. The change in mission went smoothly and increased the mobility and striking power of South Vietnamese ground forces in that tactical zone. The successful retraining of these two squadrons provided a pattern for the conversion of four more H–34 units during phase I modernization, using UH–1 helicopters shipped to South Vietnam for the U.S. Army, and the addition of one CH–47 and four UH–1 squadrons in phase II.[16]

Coordination between South Vietnamese air and ground elements on the use of helicopters broke down only rarely, but such a failure took place at Binh Thuy on one occasion, when the base commander refused to allow army assault troops onto his installation in time for unhurried and detailed planning of an air assault. In general, Air Force advisory teams, with the help of officers made available by the U.S. Army, succeeded in transferring American air assault concepts and tactics to the South Vietnamese. For each specific operation, South Vietnam's air force made an appropriate number of gunship, transport, and command helicopters available to the corps headquarters that was mounting the attack. The corps tactical operations center, where the South Vietnamese air service had representation, drew up an overall plan and handed it to the direct air support center, which then issued orders to South Vietnamese helicopters and fighter-bombers.[17]

Like General Westmoreland, General Abrams insisted that the primary mission of South Vietnam's new UH–1 helicopters was to carry men and provide firepower for airborne assault. Second priority, according to General Abrams, went to medical evacuation. Any helicopters not needed for these activities might deliver cargo to isolated installations or to tactical units.[18]

All potential mechanics and pilots, whether for helicopters or other aircraft, had to have a basic understanding of English, for most of the operating and technical manuals sent to South Vietnam were written in that language, and most undergraduate pilot training took place in the United States. A technical translation branch, established by the earliest U.S. advisers in 1955, attempted to keep pace with a seemingly endless flood of publications. The hundred or so South Vietnamese civilians employed by the branch became skillful enough to translate a moderate-size manual in twenty-four hours. They eventually turned out translations cheaper, an average of $400 per publication, as well as faster

Air War over South Vietnam, 1968–1975

A new South Vietnamese UH–1 helicopter at Binh Thuy Air Base.

than was possible in the United States, outperforming even a computerized system devised for automated translation.[19]

Because students from all over the world crowded the Defense Language Institute's course in English, offered at Lackland Air Force Base, Texas, the military assistance command arranged for additional language classes at Saigon and Nha Trang. Attending class in their own country spared young South Vietnamese the cultural shock of being flown halfway around the world, deposited in an alien society, and told to learn a difficult subject. By remaining in South Vietnam, U.S. experts believed, the students would need less fluency in conversational English, allowing them to concentrate on technical terms rather than on placing an order at a McDonald's and otherwise getting along in the midst of an English-speaking populace.

Despite the attempt to teach English in South Vietnam, individuals chosen for undergraduate pilot training in the United States often reached their destination without the necessary language skill. Although it avoided a clash of cultures, training in South Vietnam allowed students to escape true immersion in the English language, for they had easy access to friends, family, and even merchants, who spoke only Vietnamese. To make up for this weakness, the language institute at Lackland inaugurated a remedial course designed to help individuals acquire the minimum vocabulary necessary for flight instruction. In addition, the Air Force and Army were trying to reduce the minimum still further, cutting away any linguistic frills that might remain.[20]

Although the corrective program and streamlined curriculum helped, proficiency in English remained an obstacle that barred many candidates from specialized training. During the fiscal year ending in June 1969, some 650 South

Improving the South Vietnamese Air Force

Vietnamese began English language instruction, but roughly 30 percent failed. Some received a second chance; others forfeited the opportunity to learn to fly or to acquire a technical skill.[21]

The language barrier had to be overcome, for acceleration of phase II modernization depended upon intensive training, almost all of it given by American instructors. The South Vietnamese Air Force had no cadre of veterans to pass on what they had learned and guide the service through a period of rapid expansion. Half the enlisted airmen had served a year or less, and more than half had yet to complete basic or specialized training. Three of every four officers were lieutenants, and some 25 percent were themselves undergoing instruction of one sort or another.

The arguments in favor of teaching English in South Vietnam applied to other subjects as well. A training center at Nha Trang Air Base operated six schools with some 2,250 students in subjects that ranged from the duties of the forward air controller to the repair of electronic equipment and included English. Another 1,000 South Vietnamese Air Force trainees were undergoing instruction at operating wings during a typical period of 1969. At those bases where American and South Vietnamese units served side by side, members of the U.S. Air Force did the teaching. If the students had difficulty understanding English, an interpreter translated the lessons, which dealt with such topics as photo processing, civil engineering, base defense, fire fighting, weather forecasting, air traffic control, intelligence, and security.

Undergraduate pilot training did not take place in South Vietnam, though refresher courses and transition instruction were available. Until the nation's security became more stable, combat rather than training received first priority. Since the South Vietnamese armed forces seemed to be gaining the upper hand in the vicinity of Nha Trang, U.S. Air Force advisers were working on a plan to train liaison pilots for O–1 squadrons at that base, beginning in the spring of 1970. At about the same time, helicopter pilots would also begin receiving their initial instruction in South Vietnam, probably at Vung Tau. Rather than agree to interfere with the application of South Vietnamese air power, Seventh Air Force headquarters flatly opposed a suggestion by the Joint Chiefs of Staff that South Vietnam cut back on air operations, thus freeing pilots to serve as instructors. Nothing came of this proposal, which would have exchanged current combat effectiveness for an easing of language problems and the possibility of an increase in the number of aviators at some time in the future.[22]

The transfer to the South Vietnamese of the air bases at Nha Trang, Binh Thuy, and Pleiku had begun when 1969 ended. The shift of Nha Trang enjoyed the highest priority, and by mid-October, all U.S. Air Force flying units had departed, leaving behind some 800 men to operate the base until the formal transfer of authority scheduled for the summer of 1970. The South Vietnamese flying units based there would form the 2d Air Division, supported by its own maintenance and supply wing. At Binh Thuy, the establishment of South Viet-

Air War over South Vietnam, 1968–1975

A South Vietnamese O–1 near Da Nang.

namese liaison squadrons to operate there encountered delays, though the change of status was expected to take place as planned late in 1970. An Air Force A–1 squadron left Pleiku in December 1969, part of a realignment that accompanied the year's reduction in American troop strength, as did the base rescue helicopters, but the airfield would not change hands until 1972, when it was scheduled to become the third air base operated by the South Vietnamese.[23]

Responsibility for these bases included providing protection against both shelling and ground attack. At Nha Trang, an Air Force advisory team chief found the South Vietnamese cooperative and enthusiastic, taking over the defensive perimeter, installing additional floodlights, and laying more barbed wire.[24] In contrast, work lagged on the building of revetments for South Vietnamese planes at Tan Son Nhut, among the last of six air bases that the Americans would yield, apparently because of a belief that construction of these protective structures would be a waste of time, since the United States would replace any aircraft the enemy might destroy. Months of patient persuasion finally got the revetment program moving again.[25]

The conversion of the South Vietnamese air logistics wing into a logistics command capable of serving the needs of a larger, more modern air arm promised to be one of the more important developments during 1969. Besides assuming sole responsibility for base civil engineering, supply, and transportation, the new command would handle the periodic inspection and repair of most aircraft, overhaul jet and piston engines, repair and calibrate precision measuring equipment used by maintenance crews, repair most avionics gear, and overhaul ground equipment such as the power carts used in starting aircraft engines. Once the command came of age, fewer pieces of equipment would have to be entrusted to contractors or shipped back to the United States for repair.[26]

Until the establishment of this command, the South Vietnamese had largely ignored common U.S. Air Force practices. They had, said General Young, chief of the Air Force advisory group, "been concentrating on really fighting as effec-

Improving the South Vietnamese Air Force

tively as they can"; now they would have to "start thinking more in terms of managing those assets for the long pull — not kick the tire, light the fire, and go off into the wild blue." As a first step, General Young suggested, South Vietnam's air force might begin scheduling individual aircraft with an eye toward establishing regular maintenance cycles.[27]

Meanwhile, South Vietnamese fliers were learning to use the airplanes made available to them under the successive improvement and modernization plans. Completed during 1969 were the conversion of four H–34 helicopter squadrons to the UH–1, the reequipping of one C–47 squadron with the AC–47 gunship, and the substitution of the A–37 for the A–1 in three attack units. Of the year's three projects, the transition from transport to gunship proved the most demanding. Crashes that destroyed two planes and killed one crew member marred the changeover. An investigation revealed that changed takeoff characteristics resulting from installation of side-firing guns and related equipment, a modification that increased weight and shifted the center of gravity rearward, probably caused the accidents. The helicopter conversion, during which U.S. Army aviators trained South Vietnamese instructors, who then helped their countrymen make the transition to the UH–1, proved much smoother.[28]

The South Vietnamese also attained greater skill in the use of planes already in the hands of operational squadrons. For example, although the pilots assigned to fly the F–5 found the cockpit uncomfortably humid, and the shorter men had to compensate for their lack of height by using seat cushions and attaching wooden blocks to the control pedals, the plane and its pilots nevertheless performed dependably. More important, perhaps, mechanics of the South Vietnamese Air Logistics Command conducted a successful corrosion control program after cracks appeared in a panel on the upper surface of the wing of an F–5.[29]

South Vietnam's A–1s, three squadrons of which were converting to the A–37, also required structural renovation during 1969. In this instance, however, South Vietnamese did not do the work; instead, members of an Air Force Logistics Command field team and civilian mechanics under contract to maintain these planes repaired the wings of the Skyraiders. South Vietnamese did, however, perform routine work on the A–1, and early in 1970, the outside help ended, leaving them solely responsible for everything from changing tires to periodic inspection and repair.[30]

The Fairchild C–119G, a twin-engine, twin-boom transport delivered to South Vietnam in 1968, proved a headache to the nation's air force. In the first place, flight crews were scarce. Several members of the first operational outfit, trained in the United States, received transfers to AC–47 gunships or even to Air Vietnam commercial transports, and replacements were not readily available. The shortage, said Col. Harrison H. D. Heiberg, a U.S. Air Force adviser, resulted from a "reluctance to qualify sufficient instructor pilots to conduct an upgrade training program" for officers already qualified to fly the C–47. Hei-

Air War over South Vietnam, 1968–1975

The commander of the South Vietnamese Air Force 413th Transportation Squadron accepts an Air Force C–119 at Tan Son Nhut Air Base.

berg attributed this situation to the fact that assignment as an instructor conferred great prestige on the individual, causing South Vietnam's senior airmen to choose carefully, stressing "personal reliability and loyalty in addition to flying skill."[31]

Although the delays annoyed American advisers, the slow process of selection ultimately produced instructors and replacement crews for the C–119G; far more serious were the maintenance problems attendant upon that aircraft. The Wright R–3350 radial engines caused most of the trouble. They had functioned reasonably well until the American advisory team handed the South Vietnamese 33d Wing and the Air Logistics Command full responsibility for operating and maintaining the plane. The number of engine failures promptly soared, but U.S. Air Force advisers correctly placed the blame on lack of experience with a complicated powerplant. The Americans persuaded the South Vietnamese to treat the elderly engines with care, paying particular attention to routine maintenance, careful warmup, protection from dust, and close supervision of mechanics. With these reforms, the average time between engine failures increased from 472 hours early in 1969 to 609 hours, roughly the same as in the U.S. Air Force, by mid-year. When a serious breakdown did occur and the powerplant required overhaul, it had to be sent to the United States where parts and skilled technicians were available, a time-consuming practice that hampered efforts to keep an adequate number of spare engines on hand in Southeast Asia.[32]

During the latter half of 1969, the Air Force began transferring O–1Es to the South Vietnamese as newer O–2s and OV–10s replaced them, just one step

Improving the South Vietnamese Air Force

toward entrusting the entire tactical air control system to the South Vietnamese.[33] Because of the critical importance of air support in the ground war, the United States had established and run a tactical air control system in which the South Vietnamese played a minor role. Thus far, emphasis rested upon the efficient use of tactical aviation rather than upon adapting the control network to the needs and skills of the South Vietnamese. Yet, air power would remain an indispensable weapon despite the American departure, and South Vietnam's air arm would require its own system for requesting, dispatching, and directing air strikes. As a result, Air Force advisers established a control mechanism modeled after the U.S. Air Force system and suitable for Vietnamization.[34]

The direct air request network, as the Vietnamized control system came to be called, had three principal elements: the tactical air control party, the direct air support center, and the Tactical Air Control Center. Grouped together in the tactical air control party were the forward air controllers, various radio operators and maintenance men, and the air liaison officer, who acted as air adviser to the ground commander. Like his American counterpart, the South Vietnamese air liaison officer served as focal point for all matters relating to air activities, from close support to weather reports.

The direct air support center bore responsibility for fulfilling requests from the tactical air control parties for air strikes, tactical reconnaissance, or emergency airlift. Like the tactical air control parties, the centers would continue for a time to be joint operations, with the American role diminishing as South Vietnamese skills improved. Plans called for a direct air support center in conjunction with each South Vietnamese corps headquarters: I Direct Air Support Center at Da Nang, II at Pleiku, III at Bien Hoa, and IV at Binh Thuy Air Base, near the corps command post at Can Tho. Each of these centers would keep in contact by radio, telephone, or teletype with the subordinate tactical air control parties and with the Tactical Air Control Center at Tan Son Nhut.

The Tactical Air Control Center served as nerve center of the Vietnamized system, just as it had with the U.S. prototype. In the tightly centralized American model, this agency functioned as command post for strikes throughout South Vietnam, establishing priorities among competing needs and issuing daily and weekly operations orders in support of the war on the ground. South Vietnamese officers began serving in each component of the center, creating a parallel structure that could sustain the air war after the Americans left.[35]

Whether a tactical air control center of this type could be transplanted and flourish remained open to question, for South Vietnam's armed forces had not yet accepted the concept of centralized control over tactical aviation. The corps commander, though theoretically influenced by an air liaison officer, remained supreme in his fiefdom and could use the direct air support center for his own purposes, regardless of orders issued elsewhere. With these constraints, a single control center that could shift planes across tactical zone boundaries as the overall situation demanded was hard to imagine.

Air War over South Vietnam, 1968–1975

Whatever the fate of the Tactical Air Control Center, the South Vietnamese Air Force would benefit from a control mechanism that would sort out requests, though not necessarily respond to them as the Americans might have. Battalion, regimental, and division commanders, assisted by their air liaison officers, channeled requests into the corps headquarters. The direct air support center would then respond with the aircraft available to it, after obtaining the necessary strike approval from the corps commander (who might have an agenda of his own) and the appropriate province chief.[36]

Progress toward Vietnamizing the tactical air control system proved swifter in the IV Corps Tactical Zone, embracing the Mekong Delta, than elsewhere in the country. The first step consisted of finding and training English-speaking South Vietnamese to work alongside their American counterparts in the parallel tactical air control structures called for in the Vietnamization plan. This went smoothly enough, but the next step, actually transferring authority to these South Vietnamese, proved difficult. Some U.S. Air Force officers refused to yield the ultimate authority for controlling tactical aviation; they believed that placing American airmen under South Vietnamese authority represented too much of a gamble. New Air Force advisers took over in IV Corps in 1969, however, and they forged ahead with Vietnamization. During that year, South Vietnamese forward air controllers began directing strikes by American planes, tactical air control parties and air liaison officers from South Vietnam's air force started handling strike requests for the South Vietnamese divisions that had taken over from the departing American forces, and South Vietnamese airmen commenced operating the local direct air support center, with the Americans serving exclusively as advisers.[37]

The degree of South Vietnamese control over tactical air strikes in each of the corps zones reflected the severity of the combat there. Control was greatest in the comparative calm of IV Corps and least in II Corps, where the enemy was exerting pressure on Special Forces camps in the highlands, and in I Corps along the dangerous northern border. In both I and II Corps, South Vietnamese had begun serving at only one of the two direct air support centers established by the Americans in each of these zones, the scene of recurring savage fighting, leaving the other center in exclusively American hands. The direct air support center for III Corps, the only such organization in that tactical zone, had been integrated by December 1969, so that progress there was faster than in the northern zones but slower than in the delta.[38]

In Vietnamizing the tactical air control system, perhaps the hardest problem facing American advisers proved to be finding suitable air liaison officers. According to General Brown, the Seventh Air Force commander, the trouble stemmed from the fact that South Vietnam's air force enjoyed "an inferior status in the force structure than does our Air Force." If Seventh Air Force were to assign an individual as air liaison to a U.S. Army brigade, he would have suitable rank — that of major or lieutenant colonel — and could, by doing his job well, expect to gain the confidence of the unit commander. Such was not the case in South Vietnam's armed forces.[39] Unlike the U.S. Air Force, the South Vietnamese air arm tended to send junior officers, aerial observers rather than pilots, to advise ground commanders on the employment of tactical aviation. Nor could the air liaison officer expect much support from his superiors within the least prestigious of South Vietnam's armed services. Of four generals in the organization, two were no longer on active duty — Vice President Ky and General Loan, severely wounded during May 1968, while commanding the national police. Also, air force officers assigned to South Vietnam's Joint General Staff remained few and their influence slight.[40]

To remedy the situation, U.S. Air Force advisers worked closely with South Vietnamese air liaison officers, not only to perfect their skills but to persuade ground commanders to listen to them. In an attempt to increase the credibility of air liaison officers, the South Vietnamese Air Force agreed to assign additional pilots to this important job, selecting them from fighter, transport, liaison, and helicopter units until 60 percent were fliers and the rest observers. The new breed of air liaison officer would carry a suitable rank, be able to speak English to communicate with the Americans, and serve a two-year tour in his job — or so the South Vietnamese promised.

Aerial observers had also dominated the ranks of the forward air controllers, directing strikes from the second seat, while a pilot flew the plane. As in the case of air liaison officers, U.S. Air Force advisers urged that pilots take over the controller's duties from the observers, and the South Vietnamese tried to comply. Here, too, progress proved slow. Not only did pilots resent exchanging the comforts of a permanent air base for a more primitive existence in the field, but the chief of the air service, Gen. Tranh Van Minh, was himself an observer rather than a pilot and was used to doing things the old way.

By early 1970, the American-sponsored reforms seemed to be taking hold, with South Vietnamese pilots beginning to serve as forward air controllers and air liaison officers. These men, together with their radio operators, formed the tactical air control parties assigned to the major South Vietnamese ground units, where they received a final indoctrination from American advisers. Commanders in South Vietnam's army were turning to the newly arrived liaison officers to obtain air support, and the South Vietnamese were controlling and delivering much of that support[41].

Besides playing a greater role in controlling tactical aviation, the South Vietnamese were becoming acquainted with methods of electronic surveillance. Early in 1969, a deployable automatic relay terminal, or Dart, arrived at Pleiku, where it was intended to function as a Spartan version of the infiltration surveillance center at Nakhon Phanom, the facility that gathered, analyzed, and stored data from electronic sensor fields emplaced to report nighttime truck traffic on enemy supply routes passing through southern Laos. Initially, plans called for incorporating the Dart into the tactical air control system, using it to keep electronic watch over supply and infiltration routes leading from Cambodia. If necessary, the terminal could be loaded into a cargo plane and flown to Thailand as temporary replacement for the more elaborate surveillance center at Nakhon Phanom.[42]

General Brown, however, had no confidence in an electronic border surveillance scheme based on Dart. Such an undertaking impressed him as "totally impractical." Sensors could sound false alarms, he pointed out, and the aerial verification of signals was "complicated by mountainous terrain... over very heavy jungle foliage." Moreover, in the region where main infiltration routes entered South Vietnam from Cambodia, "haze was prevalent at this time of year [March] and cloud or fog can come in either monsoon period," but were more common during the southwest monsoons, usually lasting from May through September.[43]

Whether for the reasons pointed out by the Seventh Air Force commander or simply because of the great cost, no electronic barrier comparable to the surveillance net across southern Laos took shape along the Cambodian border. Instead of functioning as part of the tactical air control system, the Dart terminal at Pleiku served as nerve center for sensor fields maintained by the U.S. Army units responsible for security along the Cambodian border. Air Force technicians monitoring the Dart equipment took note of likely targets for immediate air attack and alerted III Direct Air Support Center at Bien Hoa, which at night might divert a patrolling AC–47 to investigate. The division commander in charge of this area of operation usually consulted the Dart record of sensor activations in planning artillery fire, and General Abrams' headquarters might occasionally use this information in requesting a B–52 strike.[44]

The sensor array reporting to Dart was far simpler than the Igloo White network that signalled indications of enemy activity to a computer-equipped surveillance center at Nakhon Phanom. For example, signals from the more compact fields guarding access routes from Cambodia could be relayed as well from a hilltop station as from the slowly circling Lockheed EC–121 used with Igloo White. Instead of the computer memory and display panels at the Thailand facility, the Dart van featured equipment that recorded sensor activations on a roll of paper for interpretation by the operator. Because of its simplicity, the deployable automatic relay terminal became a candidate for Vietnamization, whereas Igloo White did not.[45]

Beginning in April 1969, the military assistance command established a school at Vung Tau to train South Vietnamese soldiers, sailors, and marines to use sensor fields for detecting infiltration and providing local security. In October 1969, Air Force advisers began offering similar instruction at Pleiku, teaching a succession of classes, each numbering about twenty students, to operate the Dart equipment. After a year, however, the course for South Vietnamese airmen came to an end, for the assistance command decided to Vietnamize an Army-developed terminal judged less complex than Dart.[46]

Improving the South Vietnamese Air Force

The decision to give the South Vietnamese the simpler of two possible sensor arrays was typical of Vietnamization. In the words of General Young, who headed the Air Force advisory effort during the latter months of 1969, "the simpler we can keep it, the better." He saw two principles governing the arming of South Vietnam's air force: "First, we are trying not to give them sophisticated equipment unless it is absolutely necessary to the mission (and seldom do we find that it is); second, we are trying to minimize the proliferation of equipment," settling upon a few basic types within each category, three kinds of tactical transports, for example, out of five possibilities.[47]

The policy described by General Young did not, in the view of some U.S. officials, reflect a lack of flying skill on the part of the South Vietnamese but stemmed from logistical considerations. "They can fly our best aircraft now," said Curtis W. Tarr, Assistant Secretary of the Air Force (Manpower and Reserve Affairs), but "they will not be able to maintain them for several years; they could not hope to overhaul them for a decade."[48]

In spite of lingering problems of maintenance and logistics, the South Vietnamese air arm had improved during 1969. In the last three months of the year, it flew some 74,000 sorties of all kinds, compared with 55,000 for the first quarter of that year.[49] Indeed, all of the nation's armed forces, and the South Vietnamese economy as well, seemed to be growing stronger. Despite some 300 casualties in an average week's fighting, South Vietnam's military had taken up the slack during the American troop withdrawals of 1969. The reduced participation by the United States in ground combat brought a decline in battle deaths from 225 each week during January to a hundred per week at year's end.[50]

Although the accelerated phase II improvement and modernization plan was moving forward, Secretary Laird realized that continuing American departures would require a further strengthening of South Vietnam's armed forces. In mid-November 1969, he directed the Joint Chiefs of Staff to commence work on a phase III plan designed to increase effectiveness "to the point where the government of Vietnam can maintain current levels of security while the U.S. forces are phased down first to a support force" by July 1, 1971 and then, by continuing towards an advisory assistance group two years later.[51]

Unless carefully executed, any further acceleration of Vietnamization could easily disrupt the South Vietnamese Air Force, already in the midst of an expansion that would double its number of aircraft in two years and leave the organization in charge of its own tactical air control system. During the phase III effort, South Vietnam's airmen would face the same basic problems, though greatly intensified, that they already were trying to solve. According to David Packard, Secretary Laird's principal deputy, the manpower needs of the air arm would have to be measured against those of the other services and of South Vietnamese society as a whole. Simplicity would have to remain a guiding principal in selecting aircraft and other weapons for the country's armed forces, and "new and different approaches to the solution of the training problem" would be necessary, especially when providing on-the-job instruction. "In developing a new force structure . . . ," Packard continued, "it is essential that we focus on what the Vietnamese forces must have rather than [on] what . . . we are doing that they could do."[52]

Throughout phase III, assuming the Laird proposal went into effect, the Air Force would continue to fly combat and support missions even as it prepared the South Vietnamese to shoulder the entire burden of the air war. South Vietnam's rapidly expanding air arm had a number of weaknesses that defied easy correction. The most dangerous, in terms of its impact upon troop withdrawals, was an inability to conduct the kind of systematic interdiction that would disrupt the enemy's attempts to infiltrate men and supplies for attacks on the scale of the 1968 Tet offensive. A blow of comparable violence, delivered in 1970 or 1971 after the American departures were well underway, could create havoc among the forces remaining behind.[53] Until the South Vietnamese Air Force attained a capacity for interdiction, or the North Vietnamese bases in Cambodia and supply lines in southern Laos were somehow neutralized, U.S. air power would have to help General Abrams with firepower to keep losses down.[54]

Like so many of the programs conducted in South Vietnam, the improvement and modernization of the air arm proved difficult to measure. Numbers were increasing, but the South Vietnamese Air Force could not yet conduct sustained, independent action under centralized control. The language barrier thus far remained largely intact, and concern existed that complex technology, introduced too rapidly, might overwhelm the South Vietnamese. In North Vietnam, however, Soviet-trained controllers operated an integrated air defense — including radar, missiles, antiaircraft guns, and jet interceptors — all more complex than any comparable equipment made available to America's ally.

Chapter Eleven

Storming the Cambodian Bases

Operation Menu, the secret bombing of Cambodia, sought to forestall a North Vietnamese offensive timed to take advantage of the American withdrawal from the South; it continued into 1970 without measurable results. Since the Menu B–52s performed the function of long-range heavy artillery, harrying the enemy and trying to disrupt his activity, bomb damage proved difficult to assess on the basis of evidence from aerial photographs and an occasional ground patrol. Whatever loss or inconvenience the North Vietnamese suffered, they maintained a stoic silence; on the other hand, they did not mount the kind of attack in South Vietnam that President Nixon was attempting to discourage.[1]

Nor did Prince Sihanouk protest the secret attacks, apparently because he hoped they would loosen North Vietnam's grip on easternmost Cambodia.[2] Fear that the North Vietnamese would, in effect, annex this part of his country moved Sihanouk, in the spring of 1969, to stop the flow of cargo through the port of Sihanoukville to the base camps near the South Vietnamese border. In September of that year, while in Hanoi attending the funeral of Ho Chi Minh, Sihanouk apparently obtained assurances that the North Vietnamese army would exercise restraint and not extend its authority beyond the base areas it already controlled and from which Cambodian officials, soldiers, and citizens had been excluded. In return for this vague pledge, Cambodia's ruler allowed weapons and other supplies from North Vietnam to move once again through the port that bore his name, but he kept close watch on events along the eastern border.[3]

Besides the threat from North Vietnam, Cambodia faced economic difficulties that forced Sihanouk to broaden his government and include members opposed to his variant of socialism. Gen. Lon Nol became prime minister and minister of defense, and another of the opposition, Sisouth Sirik Matak, accepted the office of deputy prime minister. Although willing to heed the advice of these two men on domestic and narrowly military topics, Sihanouk reserved for himself all matters of foreign relations, including the problem of the North Vietnamese bases.

Unfortunately for Prince Sihanouk, this division of labor proved infeasible. North Vietnamese forces along the border with South Vietnam demanded and got a lion's share of Cambodia's rice crop, which otherwise could have been sold overseas to obtain foreign credits for needed imports. The impact of the base areas upon the domestic economy emboldened Sihanouk's opposition to try to eliminate the North Vietnamese presence, put an end to Cambodian socialism, and restore prosperity to the nation by establishing their own form of capitalism.

Even as the political storm was gathering, Sihanouk and his family left on a journey that included a vacation in France and a visit to the Soviet Union. In his absence, the prince's enemies authorized an expansion of the army, issued orders on March 13, 1970, for the North Vietnamese to leave the country, and five days later deposed Sihanouk, who had led the nation for almost thirty years as either hereditary monarch or constitutional chief of state. Lon Nol promptly took charge of the government, seeking to capitalize on the resentment shared by many Cambodians toward the intruders from North Vietnam, apparently determined to provoke the armed clash that Sihanouk had carefully avoided.[4]

When the North Vietnamese ignored a forty-eight-hour deadline for abandoning their bases, Cambodian officers called on South Vietnamese commanders on the opposite side of the border to help drive out the common foe. The response took the form of an occasional artillery barrage or air strike, though infantry sometimes probed the enemy bases in Cambodia. American forces were prohibited from joining in this South Vietnamese activity, though they had permission to cover gaps in defensive positions caused when South Vietnamese troops abandoned assignments to take a hand in the Cambodian fighting. American advisers, upon learning that a South Vietnamese commander had decided to cooperate with the Cambodians, were to avoid crossing the border and taking part in the action, but instead remain in South Vietnam after warning the officer to avoid endangering noncombatants.[5]

Despite the prohibition against direct American involvement, the right of self-defense, set forth in the rules of engagement, continued to apply if the enemy fired from Cambodian soil at American or South Vietnamese troops within South Vietnam. On March 24, roughly one week after the cross-border skirmishing had started, just such an incident occurred in Kien Tuong Province, south of the Parrot's Beak. The senior American adviser to the South Vietnamese unit under attack called for air strikes, and Seventh Air Force planes silenced North Vietnamese batteries inside Cambodia.[6]

Lon Nol's appeal to Cambodian nationalism, in effect pitting the pride of the Khmer people against North Vietnamese firepower, held out the possibility of either triumph or disaster for the United States. Taking advantage of the uprising against Sihanouk, invading South Vietnamese or American ground forces, supported by air power, might ferret out military stockpiles unscathed by the Menu raids, destroying or capturing food and munitions needed by North Vietnamese and Viet Cong troops in South Vietnam. On the other hand, such an operation, whatever its initial success, could commit the United States to the long-

Storming the Cambodian Bases

Prince Norodom Sihanouk, after his ouster as leader of
Cambodia, visiting North Vietnamese Premier Pham Van Dong.

term support of a Khmer army of dubious competence. To President Nixon, however, opportunity seemed to outweigh danger, for he was confident he could control the degree and duration of American participation. "Nixon," Henry Kissinger recalled, "from the first was for a more active policy."[7]

By the morning of March 26, the President had presented General Wheeler, who would continue until July 2 to serve as Joint Chiefs Chairman, with an urgent requirement for a plan for ground action against the North Vietnamese and Viet Cong logistics sanctuaries along the South Vietnamese/Cambodian border. The plan would offer three options: an attack exclusively by South Vietnamese forces, the course that Nixon favored; a joint undertaking by South Vietnamese and American troops; or an exclusively American effort, the course that the President considered least attractive. No more than two communist base areas would be attacked, and the operation would begin only if the enemy menaced Phnom Penh, threatening the survival of Lon Nol's government.[8]

Sihanouk's overthrow and Lon Nol's defiance of North Vietnam had rekindled General Abrams' interest in neutralizing the Cambodian bases and he was already sketching outline plans for a possible advance across the border. This staff exercise produced objectives for both U.S. and South Vietnamese forces and went forward for consideration by the Joint Chiefs of Staff. The preferred target was Base Area 352, located in the shank of the Fishhook and believed to be the site of the Central Office for South Vietnam. If General Abrams could not obtain permission to attack this jungle depot and the communist headquarters, he hoped to deliver simultaneous blows against three other Base Areas: 367 and 706 in the Parrot's Beak and 704 astride the Mekong and Bassac Rivers.[9]

As he had in considering the Menu bombing, Nixon relied on as few advisers as possible. Not yet admitted to the inner council during discussions of an invasion of Cambodia, Secretary of State Rogers was instructing Ambassador Bunker at Saigon to dissuade President Thieu from sending South Vietnamese units into Cambodia, even as President Nixon pondered military action against the communist bases there. Cooperation between Thieu's troops and those of Lon Nol might, Rogers feared, convince opponents of the Vietnam War that the United States was expanding the conflict and result in renewed antiwar demonstrations.

The instructions from the Secretary of State to the embassy at Saigon reflected the official policy of the moment, based to some degree on the concerns Rogers expressed. Even Dr. Kissinger, who favored intervention, realized that South Vietnamese operations in Cambodia might provoke a North Vietnamese response that would topple Lon Nol. Because the President's interventionist attitude had not yet become administration policy, Ambassador Bunker passed along the concerns expressed by Secretary Rogers, even though Abrams had advised him that preliminary planning was underway for attacks against the bases. In persuading President Thieu to suspend activity in Cambodia, Bunker indicated that the U.S. government was reviewing its policy and might decide to encourage, or even take part in, the kind actions that the South Vietnamese were being asked to abandon.[10]

As Bunker was gently cautioning Thieu, a group met at Abrams' headquarters to work out the details of the basic concept that Nixon had suggested, with its three options involving either American troops, South Vietnamese forces, or a combination of both. During a session on March 27, representatives of General Brown's Seventh Air Force called attention to the lack of information on military conditions in eastern Cambodia. The intelligence that was available came from three main sources: the Vesuvius photography that antedated Operation Menu; the pictures taken by the Studies and Observations Group of the military assistance command in conjunction with the Menu strikes; and the reports of Salem House ground probes of the border region. The troops advancing into Cambodia and the airmen supporting them would need precise and timely intelligence to find and destroy the bases; and roads and trails in the border area had to be pinpointed, if air power were to harry the enemy's attempts at withdrawal or reinforcement.

Planning went ahead, however, without provision for intensive aerial reconnaissance, out of concern that the flights would disclose a sudden American interest in the bases. The sessions at Saigon emphasized ground combat rather than air power, preventing the Seventh Air Force from contributing to an integrated plan that would have called for extensive aerial preparations for assaults by infantry, armored, and airmobile units. Besides avoiding preliminary aerial reconnaissance, planners postponed tactical air strikes until the morning of the invasion, also to avoid alerting the enemy.[11]

The only air activity within Cambodia in preparation for the invasion would consist of Menu bombing. Originally, Secretary of Defense Laird had offered intensified B–52 raids as a substitute for an invasion, which he opposed, but the President incorporated the raids into the invasion plan, endorsing the stepped-up Menu attacks as a means of weakening the defenses of the Fishhook, a logical objective of a cross-border assault. The Fishhook seemed especially attractive not only because of the depots and headquarters installations located there but also because the native populace apparently had fled or been expelled, thus reducing the likelihood of casualties among noncombatants.

The effectiveness of the proposed preparatory bombing by B–52s remained open to question. Coordination was tenuous at best between planners of the Menu raids and those officers who were at work on the ground assault. Moreover, the staff had no body of past results from which to predict the impact of future attacks; intelligence concerning the earlier Menu bombardment proved far too sketchy for that purpose.[12]

The fact that Laird proposed using B–52s rather than assault troops against the Fishhook reflected his desire to limit American involvement in Cambodia. Indeed, the Secretary of Defense and Secretary of State Rogers — who was now participating in formal National Security Council deliberations about Cambodia — seemed so unenthusiastic about invading the sanctuaries that Kissinger characterized the behavior of both men as "bureaucratic foot dragging." This reluctance stemmed from their conviction that the use of American troops in Cambodia was certain to intensify domestic opposition to the war. For the time being, however, their fears proved groundless; the President unexpectedly balked at sending American forces across the border.[13]

Since Nixon would not commit American units at this time, responsibility for diverting pressure from Lon Nol's ill-trained and poorly equipped forces fell on the South Vietnamese. On April 1, Nixon agreed that President Thieu of South Vietnam should resume attacks into enemy-held Cambodia, provided that no American troops crossed the border, except to prevent the slaughter of a South Vietnamese unit, and that precautions were taken to avoid killing or injuring Cambodian civilians. Once unleashed, South Vietnam's Joint General Staff responded to a request from Lon Nol's commanders by launching a three-hour probe of Base Area 706, in the northern part of the Parrot's Beak, using infantry and armor. American advisers left their assigned units just before the attack, and the South Vietnamese furnished their own air and artillery support.[14]

As April wore on, the South Vietnamese continued to do the fighting, with Seventh Air Force remaining on the periphery of both the planning of future combat in Cambodia and the conduct of operations already in progress. South Vietnamese airmen assisted their country's ground forces, with the Americans offering only advice. Moreover, a proposed Seventh Air Force undertaking, an expanded leaflet-dropping campaign to rally the populace behind Lon Nol, met a veto at the hands of Secretary Laird, who feared that the effort would result in his being branded an American puppet.[15] The role of the Seventh Air Force in preparing for a possible attack on the Fishhook remained nominal at best, in part a result of the need to preserve the secrecy of the Menu bombing, now considered an overture for any thrust into Cambodia. "We are walking a tight rope," confessed General Abrams, "to maintain the security of Menu operations while trying to satisfy planners' requirements for aerial photos."[16]

To provide planners with the information necessary for ground operations against the Fishhook, Abrams turned to his Studies and Observations Group, which had been dispatching American-led South Vietnamese patrols, some of which included ethnic Cambodians, on reconnaissance missions within Cambodia. Unfortunately, these Salem House probes, which might travel on foot or in U.S. Air Force or South Vietnamese helicopters, had avoided Base Areas 352 and 353 since October 1969. By that time, American aircraft were scattering antipersonnel mines on the South Vietnamese side of the border, thus impeding movement on foot by both Salem House patrols and communist infiltrators. Moreover, the defenses in the Fishhook had grown so strong as to inflict unacceptable casualties on patrols trying to probe the two sites; indeed, had it not been for the support of artillery and air strikes, the reconnaissance teams could not even have approached the base areas.[17]

While Abrams grappled with the intelligence problem and the other aspects of planning, the Nixon administration was trying to "navigate between giving enough, quickly enough, to the Lon Nol government . . . to contribute to its self-confidence as well as its capabilities, while on the other hand not doing so much as to embolden the Cambodians to take excessively strong military actions."[18] A partial solution to this quandary lay in the thousands of Soviet-designed AK–47 rifles and stocks of ammunition captured over the years and stored in South Vietnam. The North Vietnamese, however, were consolidating their hold over the border provinces of Cambodia, preventing shipment by road or river. During April, therefore, five C–119Gs of the South Vietnamese Air Force, planes ideally suited for the mission because of their convenient loading doors and cavernous interiors, flew 2,500 rifles and 84,000 rounds of ammunition to Phnom Penh.[19] By the end of June, U.S. Air Force C–130s and South Vietnamese C–47s had joined in a greatly expanded supply effort.[20]

Besides providing weapons and ammunition, the United States acceded to a Cambodian request, first made in March, to jam pro-Sihanouk radio broadcasts from Hanoi and Beijing. An Air Force EC–121, fitted out with transmitters whose signals disrupted the communist broadcasts, carried out the mission.[21]

Despite the help received thus far from the Americans and South Vietnamese, Lon Nol's forces could not hold their own against the North Vietnamese, let alone expel the enemy from the border provinces. While President Nixon was visiting Hawaii to congratulate the three Apollo XIII astronauts, who had returned safely despite an explosion on board their spacecraft, communist attacks intensified throughout eastern Cambodia. Only the strongest of Lon Nol's outposts managed to hold out in the border region, and hostile forces were reported within twenty miles of Phnom Penh. During the discussions in Washing-

Storming the Cambodian Bases

Lon Nol, center, speaks to Cambodian troops in the field.

ton of a possible American incursion, Nixon had indicated that a genuine threat to the Cambodian capital would justify such an action.[22]

The nighttime Menu bombing could not prevent the enemy from shifting his forces, isolating garrisons loyal to Lon Nol, and closing in on the capital. The secret raids, after all, were intended as a shield for the U.S. withdrawal from South Vietnam, a purpose achieved by disrupting bivouacs or destroying storage depots rather than by breaking sieges or impeding road traffic. General Abrams therefore sought to supplement the B–52 attacks with strikes by tactical fighters, better able than the huge bombers to hit troop columns or other compact, moving targets. On April 18, he made such a request of the Joint Chiefs of Staff, which promptly approved the tactical air strikes.

The kind of security restrictions that concealed Menu enveloped the newly authorized tactical air campaign, Operation Patio. All message traffic dealing with Patio strikes traveled over secure circuits, and the information went only to those directly involved in the undertaking. To preserve the cloak of secrecy, Patio raids were described as strikes in Laos, just as the Menu attacks had used cover targets in South Vietnam.[23]

Plans called for the Patio strikes to continue for thirty days, until the third week of May, but the onset of a ground campaign in Cambodia caused an early termination on May 4. At first the attacking aircraft hit targets in that portion of northeastern Cambodia extending eight miles west of the border with South Vietnam. On April 25, however, the Patio area was extended to a depth of eighteen miles all along that boundary.[24]

Because of the confused situation along the border, where the enemy rapidly shifted his strength and Lon Nol's troops reacted, General Abrams specified that all Patio attacks be directed by a forward air controller or by a Salem House patrol. On April 24, a forward air controller spotted the first Patio target — a column of 125 North Vietnamese wearing dark green uniforms, carrying packs, and moving southward into the Fishhook — and called in six F–100Ds. The Air Force tactical fighter pilots dropped antipersonnel and general purpose bombs, strafed with 20-mm cannon, and claimed a hundred of the enemy killed.[25]

The original Patio operation, which totaled just 124 sorties, had run its course when Secretary Laird approved a proposal to attack a North Vietnamese truck park on the Kong River, a stream in Cambodia near the border with Laos, well beyond the current limit of thirty kilometers established for American activity in Cambodia. The operation order called for forty-eight fighter-bombers to attack within an interval of twelve hours and for the strike to be listed as a raid in Laos. On May 14, this special Patio bombing mission began, but after thirty-two aircraft had blasted the installation, damage seemed so complete that the remaining sixteen planes were diverted to other targets.[26]

Even as the secret Patio bombing campaign took shape, President Nixon continued to follow his inclination toward decisive action against the communist sanctuaries in Cambodia, even though his advisers were far from unanimous in supporting such a course. "I think we need a bold move in Cambodia . . . ," he told Kissinger, "to show that we stand with Lon Nol." Nixon believed that the United States was entirely too concerned that its help for the new Khmer government might spur the North Vietnamese into action. "Over and over again, we fail to learn that Communists never need an excuse to come in . . . ," he declared, warning that "the only government in Cambodia in the last 25 years that had the guts to take a pro-Western and pro-American stand is ready to fall."[27]

Although determined to aid Lon Nol, Nixon was reluctant to commit American ground forces. As a result, the approved plan called for attacks by South Vietnamese units against Base Areas 706 and 367, both located in the northern jaw of the Parrot's Beak, while U.S. Army battalions took over the border security mission as the assault troops advanced into Cambodia. Nixon wanted this attack to begin about April 27, and the operation, called Toan Thang (Total Victory) 43, got underway on the 29th.[28]

For President Nixon, the South Vietnamese offensive into the Parrot's Beak represented a definite political risk. With good reason, he told Admiral Moorer and General Wheeler that failure would bring the sort of criticism that had befallen John F. Kennedy in 1961 after the Bay of Pigs fiasco, when Castro's communist forces defeated an American-trained invasion army of Cuban exiles. He was determined that there be no repetition of Kennedy's embarrassment of almost a decade before. Consequently, American advisers, even though they could not accompany the South Vietnamese assault troops into Cambodia, had to make sure the South Vietnamese developed an aggressive attitude, instilling determination and boldness in any who might seem too cautious.[29]

Besides making preparations for the impending South Vietnamese advance into Cambodia, American commanders in Southeast Asia conducted the secret Menu and Patio air strikes and drew up contingency plans for an attack into the

Storming the Cambodian Bases

Fishhook, using U.S. troops. A Fishhook operation, Admiral Moorer believed, was becoming increasingly likely despite tenacious opposition on the part of some Presidential advisers. Moorer, now serving as acting chairman of the Joint Chiefs of Staff, acknowledged that "there is much opposition in Washington to introducing even a single U.S. soldier into Cambodia," but he believed that the President might yet overrule these objections. Nixon, after all, had expressed determination that the Cambodian bases be destroyed, using whatever force might be necessary. According to Moorer, Nixon had said, "If we get caught with our hand in the cookie jar, we must be sure we get the cookies." Alluding to a popular motion picture about Gen. George S. Patton, Jr., Nixon had urged that Abrams imitate the aggressive Patton rather than Bernard Law Montgomery, a British field marshal and World War II colleague of Patton with a reputation for caution.[30]

Admiral Moorer's analysis proved correct. When the South Vietnamese hesitated to attack in the vicinity of the Fishhook on the grounds that the bases there posed a lesser threat than those in the Parrot's Beak, President Nixon approved General Abrams' plan for a combined operation involving the 1st Cavalry Division (Airmobile) and South Vietnam's airborne division. B–52 strikes, which ended shortly after midnight on the morning of the assault, and last-minute artillery concentrations helped prepare the way for an advance into the Fishhook on May 1, 1970.[31]

Initially named Operation Shoemaker after the task force commander, Brig. Gen. Robert Shoemaker, the American drive into the Fishhook might well have delighted Patton, with helicopters providing mobility and B–52s, fighter-bombers, and tanks joining in battering the North Vietnamese defenders. "Truly a majestic sight," declared one participant, as eighty-seven helicopters in perfect formation, along with tactical aircraft and gunships, inserted an entire brigade within two hours. So devastating was the onslaught that the brigade from the 1st Cavalry Division (Airmobile) came through the day all but unscathed, suffering twelve wounded but none killed.[32]

As the combined South Vietnamese and American advance surged into the Fishhook, President Nixon, on the evening of April 30, Washington time, appeared on television to explain the need for "cleaning out the major North Vietnamese and Viet Cong occupied territories — those sanctuaries which serve as bases for attacks on both Cambodia . . . and forces in South Vietnam." If Vietnamization of the war and the withdrawal of American combat troops were to continue, the communist bases had to be destroyed. "We take this action," said the President, "not for the purpose of expanding the war into Cambodia but for the purpose of ending the war in South Vietnam." As a result, the attacking U.S. troops would withdraw once the enemy had been driven from the border region and his military stockpiles destroyed. "We will not," Nixon vowed, "allow American men by the thousand to be killed by an enemy from privileged sanctuaries."[33]

Air War over South Vietnam, 1968–1975

Meanwhile, the Thieu government was asking the assistance command to stop using the nickname Operation Shoemaker and adopt the title selected by the South Vietnamese, Toan Thang 43. Since the armed forces of South Vietnam were making an important contribution to the Fishhook offensive, General Abrams readily agreed. Doubt soon arose at Washington whether Toan Thang, translated as Total Victory, reflected the objective of a limited incursion, but no further change took place.[34]

Besides approving this thrust into the Fishhook, Nixon authorized other attacks, to a depth of thirty kilometers, against North Vietnamese and Viet Cong bases elsewhere in Cambodia's border provinces. If possible, South Vietnamese troops were to carry out the raids, with such American support as they might need. Should an objective seem too difficult for the South Vietnamese alone, a combined operation might be planned, though actual execution would require approval by the President or Secretary Laird. Forces of the two nations launched eleven major raids, beginning with Toan Thang 43 on April 29, an undertaking the Americans joined on May 1, and lasting until July 22, when that longest-lived of all the operations came to an end.[35]

The attacks against North Vietnam's Cambodian sanctuaries rendered obsolete the elaborate security measures that had concealed the Menu and Patio air operations. On May 4, the Joint Chiefs of Staff put an end to the secret Patio reporting methods, which had veiled fighter activity in Cambodia since April. The security practices reappeared, however, for the May 14 attack on the Kong River truck park. This target, personally approved by Laird, qualified for strict security because it lay beyond the thirty-kilometer line that Nixon had established as the limit of American operations.[36]

American armored and airmobile units taking part in Toan Thang 43 had scarcely crossed the border on May 1 when the Joint Chiefs began reviewing the practice of creating cover targets for Menu strikes. As ground forces probed the Fishhook and other border redoubts, the need for these security precautions abated. The last of the secret Menu bombings took place on the night of May 26 in Base Area 609, which was not stormed during the 1970 incursion.[37]

The change in Menu security procedures came too slowly to avoid confusion at Bangkok, Thailand, where, about one hour before President Nixon's speech announcing the incursion into Cambodia, the ambassador learned from the local press that B–52s were taking off from U-Tapao Air Base to bomb the Cambodian sanctuaries. These accounts provided the first word that Ambassador Leonard Unger had heard of air operations originating in Thailand against targets in Cambodia. The absence of advance notice from Washington annoyed Unger but not the Thai government, which apparently understood that the desire for secrecy had ruled out prior consultation.[38]

Following the last-minute Menu strikes on May 1 that caught the attention of Ambassador Unger, Seventh Air Force lent its striking power to the assault into the Fishhook. On the first day, General Brown's airmen supported

Storming the Cambodian Bases

American and South Vietnamese units with 192 sorties by fighter-bombers, two by gunships, and one by a flareship patrolling throughout the night. This flurry marked the beginning of a rapidly expanding air campaign.[39]

Indeed, the aerial might and military power unleashed against the Fishhook foreshadowed even more extensive ground action, assisted as always by air power. President Nixon was determined to destroy the border sanctuaries and eliminate the threat they posed to Vietnamization and the accompanying American withdrawal. He had, after all, asked Abrams about the need to attack other bases outside the Parrot's Beak and Fishhook and given Toan Thang 43 a top priority. In calling for a hard-hitting imaginative offensive in Cambodia, he had authorized planning for possible additional attacks, using either American or South Vietnamese forces, singly or in combination. He suggested, moreover, that the advancing columns might ultimately penetrate beyond the thirty-kilometer limit established for Toan Thang 43.[40]

Because of the President's attitude, the ground war expanded in scope and increased in intensity, with aerial combat keeping pace. On May 5, a combined American and South Vietnamese task force entered Base Area 702, west of Kontum, South Vietnam, launching Operation Binh Tay (Tame the West) I. A day later, South Vietnamese forces invaded Base Area 350, northeast of the Fishhook, while American soldiers probed Base Areas 354, north of the Parrot's Beak, and 351, not far from the boundary between the II and III Corps Tactical Zones. These three operations bore the designations Toan Thang 46, 44, and 45, respectively. From the April 29 attack through the expanded fighting on May 6, American and South Vietnamese tactical aircraft flew 1,129 sorties into Cambodia, striking targets within thirty kilometers of the South Vietnamese border. Included among the fighter-bombers, flareships, and gunships were four C–130 transports, each of which dropped a 15,000-pound bomb to clear landing zones for helicopters assaulting the Fishhook and Base Area 354.[41]

Ground and aerial operations in Cambodia continued, and on May 9, a new offensive started when a predominately South Vietnamese task force began clearing the enemy from the banks of the Mekong River in Operation Cuu Long (Mekong River) I. Besides driving communist boat traffic from the river, the operation sought to clear the way for convoys carrying supplies to Phnom Penh. Air operations during this Mekong offensive totaled some 1,900 sorties by mid-May, not quite 6 percent by U.S. or South Vietnamese Air Force gunships and almost all the others by fighter-bombers.[42]

After May 15, aerial activity within the thirty-kilometer zone prescribed by President Nixon began to ebb, even though fighting continued on the ground. Toan Thang 43, 44, 45, and 46 entered new phases, as did Binh Tay I and Cuu Long I. In addition, South Vietnamese units, with a minimum of U.S. participation, launched three new efforts — Binh Tay II and III against Base Areas 701, west of Pleiku, and 740, across the border from Ban Me Thuot, and Cuu Long II, a thrust toward Takeo in Cambodia from Chau Doc Province, South Viet-

Air War over South Vietnam, 1968–1975

Flying through the smoke of previous strikes, an Air Force F–4
hits an enemy bunker complex in the Fishhook region of Cambodia.

nam. Despite a surge in air action late in May — the result of good weather, a flurry of combat within Base Areas 350 and 351, and a South Vietnamese advance toward Kompong Trach in Cuu Long II — the decline continued as the invasion of Cambodia drew to an end.[43]

As early as May 8, President Nixon assured Congress that the Cambodian venture would be short-lived, with American soldiers leaving the country after three to six weeks. At the beginning of June, he became more specific, promising the American people that the last U.S. combat troops would leave Cambodia by the end of that month. Since more than half the force had departed when he made the pledge, the military assistance command had no trouble in carrying out his wishes. All American ground troops, including those serving with Salem House teams, were out of Cambodia on schedule, but South Vietnamese units continued to operate there.[44]

Begun on April 29 by the South Vietnamese, and a joint operation with the Americans after May 1, Operation Toan Thang 43 ended on July 2, the first incursion of the Cambodian campaign and the last completed. During Toan Thang 43, assault troops penetrated Base Areas 354 and 706, overrunning both those objectives, and South Vietnamese troops probed as far as the town of Prey Veng, some fifty kilometers beyond the border, not quite twice the depth approved for American forces. During the three months that embraced the Toan Thang, Binh Tay, and Cuu Long operations, six Seventh Air Force fighter squadrons, with a minimum of reinforcement, flew all tactical missions in the border area. Indeed, the only outside help received by General Brown's half-

Storming the Cambodian Bases

dozen squadrons consisted of three C–130 flareships shifted to Cam Ranh Bay from Ubon, Thailand, and four A–1s moved from Nakhon Phanom, Thailand, to Bien Hoa where they flew cover for rescue helicopters.

The incursion into Cambodia imposed new demands on Air Force fliers, armorers, and maintenance men, but luckily this expansion of the conflict came during a lull in the fighting in South Vietnam. Moreover, the comparative calm in South Vietnam coincided with the approach of the rainy season in southern Laos, which heralded a sharp decline in the volume of truck traffic detected on the Ho Chi Minh Trail and, as a result, fewer targets for air attack. This combination of circumstances enabled General Brown's planners to support the fighting in Cambodia by boosting the daily utilization rate from .75 or .80 sorties per aircraft to one sortie or more, depending upon the needs of the ground forces. From May 6 through 12, for example, F–100s of the 3d Tactical Fighter Wing managed 1.44 sorties per aircraft per day, dropping to .84 the following week. The same organization flew .89 daily sorties with each of its A–37Bs during the week ending April 28, reached a figure of 1.20 the following week, peaked by May 12 at 1.38 sorties per aircraft per day, then declined to .98, still in excess of the pre-incursion average.

This redirection of effort from South Vietnam and southern Laos to easternmost Cambodia complicated the work of planners at the tactical air control center, who were responsible for committing air power when and where it was needed. To accomplish this goal, they assigned Seventh Air Force fighter-bombers to preplanned strikes in South Vietnam that otherwise would have been carried out by South Vietnamese airmen. Whenever an emergency arose in Cambodia, the control center diverted some of these Air Force fighters for immediate strikes across the border. The South Vietnamese air crews thus freed for preplanned strikes in Cambodia made a valuable contribution to the success of the incursion, flying more than 300 sorties in the critical first week.[45]

Air support for the ten individual operations of the Cambodian offensive in 1970 represented an extension of the air war in South Vietnam. The direct air support center at the corps headquarters nearest the scene of the fighting controlled and coordinated aerial activity in that sector of Cambodia. As a result, II Direct Air Support Center handled combat missions for the three Binh Tay operations; III Direct Air Support Center for the four elements of the Toan Thang series; and IV Direct Air Support Center for the three components of the Cuu Long fighting. The basic rules of engagement followed in South Vietnam applied in Cambodia, but interpretation was simpler during the incursion, if not afterward, because the North Vietnamese had expelled the noncombatants from the base areas, and the few Cambodian military units in the border region were easily located.[46]

As in South Vietnam, forward air controllers linked troops on the ground in Cambodia with the fighter-bombers assigned to support them. In this aspect of the air war, Vietnamization paid dividends, for many South Vietnamese controllers had qualified to direct strikes by American airmen and now did so over Cambodia. South Vietnam's aerial resources remained limited, however, and U.S. Air Force forward air controllers and fighter pilots continued to come to the aid of the embattled South Vietnamese throughout the incursion. Across the border from Pleiku, Capt. James C. Weatherbee, an Air Force forward air controller, received word from a tactical air control party that advancing South Vietnamese had collided with a North Vietnamese strongpoint. Once the troops below him had marked their position, Captain Weatherbee directed an F–4 against the enemy entrenchment farthest from the unit that had been pinned down. He assigned a second Phantom to bomb and strafe the likeliest escape route and then fired a series of rockets that marked a succession of impact areas that brought American bombs progressively closer to the South Vietnamese infantrymen. He thus succeeded in clearing the way for the attackers, while at the same time harassing the most probable avenue of retreat open to the defenders. Weatherbee's application of aerial firepower killed eight of the enemy manning the trenches and contributed not only to the capture of the machinegun that had stalled the advance but also to the confiscation of military supplies cached nearby.[47]

Light observation helicopters from the U.S. Army also performed as they normally did in South Vietnam, locating and investigating gaps in the jungle canopy to find targets for Air Force forward air controllers. On May 18, near Se San, Cambodia, the Army scout helicopters alerted Air Force 1st Lt. Joseph Faherty to a cluster of bunkers and huts on the jungle floor. Since no fighters were immediately at hand, Faherty radioed the II Direct Air Support Center, which launched two F–4s and a pair of F–100s. As soon as the fighters arrived, Lieutenant Faherty had the helicopters mark the target, a task that brought them low over the trees and attracted fire from the ground. The F–4s and F–100s then attacked, silencing the guns and destroying the structures they guarded. Army helicopter crews reported the strike had leveled twenty storage bunkers and killed ten North Vietnamese.[48]

Throughout the Cambodian incursion, the enemy tried to conceal his strongholds and supply depots from forward air controllers and the crews of scout helicopters. In addition to regularly scheduled visual reconnaissance, U.S. airmen used whatever devices were available to ferret out stockpiles and fortifications — airborne radio direction finding, infrared equipment, aerial cameras, and even people sniffers. Finding camouflaged bunkers proved no less difficult than determining the damage done them by aerial attack. Unless U.S. or South Vietnamese troops promptly occupied the site of an air strike, or leisurely low-altitude reconnaissance was possible, the only measure of destruction was the number and size of the fires or secondary explosions touched off by the attack.[49]

To be really useful to the ground war in Cambodia, reconnaissance aircraft like the RF–4 had to range beyond the thirty-kilometer limit imposed on the American advance. Initially, these planes flew sixty nautical miles into Cam-

Storming the Cambodian Bases

bodia, reconnoitering the roads and waterways in the northeastern part of Cambodia to gauge enemy reaction to the invasion, but avoiding Phnom Penh and its environs. The rules of engagement governing missions beyond the immediate border region prohibited armed reconnaissance or fighters escorting reconnaissance missions to prevent injury to noncombatants or unnecessary damage to Cambodian property.[50]

Each day the aerial cameras recorded movement along rivers and highways, and supplementary infrared detection missions took place each week. Specially scheduled flights investigated areas of immediate interest, using whatever equipment seemed suitable. The resulting intelligence revealed the general pattern of North Vietnamese reaction to the incursion, disclosing heavy traffic moving southward from Laos by road and water. Indeed, during the four weeks beginning in mid-May, a daily average of 31 trucks and 116 boats or barges was detected — convincing evidence that further aerial action was needed.[51]

Throughout this expanding reconnaissance effort, Air Force C–130s scattered propaganda leaflets over Cambodia. At first the printed messages fell among the border bases, urging the North Vietnamese and Viet Cong defenders to lay down their weapons. Later, as the enemy regrouped to the west and began attacking Khmer outposts, the air war expanded accordingly, and Air Force psychological warfare specialists began using leaflets and loudspeaker broadcasts to warn Cambodian noncombatants of strikes against targets nearby.[52]

Even as General Brown's air crews were joining South Vietnamese airmen in supporting the incursion, some U.S. Air Force planes bombed or strafed highways and storage dumps in southern North Vietnam. Seventh Air Force planners had been making preparations for these raids before receiving orders for the advance into Cambodia, and General Wheeler, in announcing President Nixon's approval of the strikes in the North, issued instructions to coordinate this effort with the Cambodian incursion. As a result, from May 1 through May 4, Air Force and Navy planes struck a variety of targets along the road net that channeled supplies through Mu Gia, Ban Karai, and Barthelemy Passes into Laos, where the cargo might make its way westward to the Laotian plateau or southward to Cambodia and South Vietnam.[53]

In his April 30 speech announcing the incursion into Cambodia, President Nixon declared, "Tonight American and South Vietnamese units will attack the headquarters for the entire Communist military operation in South Vietnam." With these words, the Central Office for South Vietnam, believed located within the Fishhook "in blatant violation of Cambodia's neutrality,"[54] became fixed in the mind of the American public as the key objective of Operation Toan Thang 43, a development that troubled General Wheeler. "As you know," he told Admiral McCain and General Abrams, "this has never been a principal objective, and, indeed, I have been careful to point out to higher authority that it would probably be sheer good luck if we were able to bag it as part of this operation." To avoid the bad publicity that seemed likely to result from failure to seize the headquarters, Wheeler recommended educating the press to the true goal of the invasion, the disruption of the enemy's logistics network, while at the same time following up any leads that might help pinpoint the headquarters.[55]

Frequently on the move, the Central Office for South Vietnam proved an elusive target, evading both aerial bombardment and ground attack. A North Vietnamese headquarters clerk captured in mid-May claimed that the organization received twenty-four-hour warning of B–52 strikes and that, while he served there, it had moved three times to escape approaching troops.[56]

Despite early failure to locate the central office and Wheeler's emphasis on logistical targets, Abrams continued searching for the headquarters that controlled communist activity throughout South Vietnam. Late in May, intelligence reports encouraged him to obtain temporary authority to attack sites as far as ten kilometers beyond the thirty-kilometer operating zone that President Nixon had established. To protect Cambodian civilians, General Wheeler insisted upon a one-kilometer buffer, separating B–52 target boxes from inhabited villages. Moreover, a forward air controller had to direct strikes by tactical fighters to prevent potentially deadly errors.[57]

Even as he pursued the various intelligence leads, General Abrams tried publicly to play down the importance of the Central Office for South Vietnam as an objective of the Cambodian incursion. Still wary of the bad publicity that could result from failure to destroy the headquarters, he continued to insist that statements to the press deal exclusively with the campaign against the supply depots and that reports on the search for the communist command post use secure communications channels.[58]

Another probable headquarters site soon surfaced in the Fishhook, well within the thirty-kilometer area of operations prescribed by the President, and Abrams promptly alerted Brown to send Seventh Air Force fighter-bombers against it. The B–52s battered two target boxes on May 21 and 23, followed by ninety tactical fighters, directed by fourteen tactical air controllers, concentrating on the untouched areas between rows of bomb craters left by the B–52s. A photo reconnaissance plane recorded the damage as best it could, and Seventh Air Force fliers reported touching off ten secondary explosions and destroying or damaging nineteen bunkers. Dense foliage and smoke from fires prevented the kind of visual or photographic reconnaissance that might have verified damage to — or even the presence of — the Central Office for South Vietnam.[59]

The fruitless search for the central office persisted through June. On the 21st, Abrams responded to fresh evidence by arranging to divert thirty-five B–52s against another promising target in the Fishhook. The attack produced thirty-seven secondary explosions, an indication that supplies were stored there, but no proof that a headquarters occupied the site.[60]

Although the communist headquarters apparently survived bombing and ground probes, the frequent moves necessary to survive almost certainly disrupted its activities. As to the main purpose of the attacks into the base areas, dislocation of the enemy logistics system, American and South Vietnamese troops unearthed vast stores of weapons, ammunition, food, and other vital supplies. A year of Menu bombing had not prevented the North Vietnamese from filling their Cambodian depots to overflowing. The booty captured during the invasion included some 25,000 individual and crew-served weapons, almost eighty tons of food, more than fifty-five tons of medical supplies, and at least fifteen million rounds of ammunition, varying from pistol bullets to artillery shells. Some of the war material came from as far away as eastern Europe, arriving by way of the Ho Chi Minh Trail or the port of Sihanoukville.[61]

For U.S. ground forces, the Cambodian campaign ended on June 29, in keeping with President Nixon's promise to have all these troops out of Cambodia on July 1. South Vietnamese elements of the invasion force would remain in Cambodia for another three weeks, however, and they could return if necessary. President Thieu had authorized his principal commanders to advance as far as forty kilometers beyond the border if requested to intervene by Lon Nol's Cambodian forces.[62]

What had the Cambodian invasion accomplished? According to Sir Robert Thompson, a respected veteran of the successful British counterinsurgency effort in Malaya, the military effects were little short of spectacular. The inability to channel cargo through Sihanoukville (renamed Kompong Som by the Lon Nol government) and the destruction or capture of the stockpiles near the border with South Vietnam forced the enemy to divert men and material to improve and defend the supply lines passing through southern Laos and the northeastern corner of Cambodia. Communist forces — whether North Vietnamese, Viet Cong, or Khmer Rouge recruited inside Cambodia — had expended ammunition and sustained casualties in resisting the cross-border attacks and would invest additional men and supplies in an attempt to topple Lon Nol. The incursion, he believed, had reduced to "negligible proportions for at least the next year" the enemy threat in the III and IV Corps Tactical zones of South Vietnam.[63]

The incursion clearly helped facilitate the American withdrawal from the Vietnam conflict, as the British specialist in counterinsurgency maintained. For the Cambodians, however, the attack signaled disaster; the border crossings of April and May 1970 inaugurated more than a decade of foreign conflict or civil war, attended by famine, disease, and mass slaughter. William Shawcross, a British journalist, has blamed the Nixon administration for these years of violence and death. Although he concedes that North Vietnamese troops controlled the border region when the Menu bombing and the invasion took place, he argues that the President and his principal adviser, Henry Kissinger, should have found some other solution to the threat posed by the hostile bases, a course of action that would have enabled Cambodia to remain non-belligerent, it not truly neutral. While condemning U.S. policy, Shawcross admits, "Any ... administration would have faced dreadful decisions from 1969 onward," but insists that alternatives to invasion did exist.

Air War over South Vietnam, 1968-1975

A small part of the vast amount of goods captured in Cambodia: cases of ammunition (top) and 200-pound bags of rice.

Yet, to attribute all Cambodia's suffering solely to decisions made or ratified by President Nixon represents an oversimplification. Sihanouk, after all, was walking a tight-rope, trying to preserve his kingdom by balancing conflicting domestic groups and foreign pressures. He failed, although cleverly playing off the United States against North Vietnam. He nevertheless fell victim to a combination of his own carelessness, Lon Nol's ambition, and the discipline of Cambodian communists, who would embark on their own reign of terror after the American bombs stopped falling.

Shawcross acknowledges that Sihanouk was in an impossible situation. The Prince could not simultaneously accommodate his domestic enemies on the political left and right. Moreover, the United States failed to understand his motives in trying to maintain Cambodia's independence and nominal neutrality or to appreciate that as an active ally, Cambodia would require help that outweighed any military contribution it could make. Fascinated by the willingness of the new Khmer government to defy Hanoi, President Nixon overestimated Lon Nol's competence (to some extent undermined by illness), his political following, and his military strength. The administration, moreover, knew almost nothing of the zeal, discipline, and ruthlessness of the Khmer Rouge.[64]

In the United States, the Cambodian incursion heightened the opposition to the war. News of the attack triggered widespread demonstrations by foes of the war. On May 4, 1970, at Kent State University in Ohio, National Guardsmen sent to maintain order fired into a rock-throwing crowd, killing four students. Two of the dead were women, and one was a cadet in the university's Reserve Officer Training Corps. All were bystanders rather than participants in the disturbance the guardsmen were trying to quell. These deaths inflamed antiwar sentiment among college students, who shut down for varying periods most of the nation's campuses. Nor did the President ease tensions when he referred to the student demonstrators as "bums," contrasting them with the American troops in Vietnam, whom he considered "the greatest."[65]

The reaction, especially among students, to the Kent State killings persuaded the President to maintain tighter surveillance over the activities of persons and groups opposed to the war. Rather than call upon the Federal Bureau of Investigation, which the President blamed for failing to discover the sources of information apparently leaked to the press about the Menu bombing and other matters, Nixon turned to a young aide, Tom Charles Huston, who concocted a patently unconstitutional scheme for domestic intelligence-gathering.[66] According to H. R. Haldeman, one of the President's trusted advisers, adoption of the Huston plan, largely in response to the outbursts that followed the shooting at Kent State, "marked a turning point for Nixon, a beginning of a downhill slide" that led to illegal entries, misuse of campaign funds, impeachment proceedings, and in August 1974, the President's resignation.[67]

Even before the fatal shots rang out at Kent State, a group that had organized two major antiwar demonstrations during 1969 scheduled a protest for Washington, D.C., to be held on May 9. President Nixon sought to reduce the impact of this gathering, appealing for support directly to the public in his first news conference since January. At this session, he emphasized the continuing troop withdrawals from Vietnam, acknowledging that the protesters, too, "want our boys home," but insisting that the invasion of Cambodia would help achieve that very goal by enabling him to bring back another 150,000 men during 1970. He chose this moment to promise that "all Americans of all kinds, including advisers, will be out of Cambodia by the end of June."[68]

The demonstrations against the war scheduled for Washington took place as planned, attracting between 75,000 and 100,000 persons, but producing little in the way of confrontation or violence. In contrast, an antiwar rally held the previous day, May 8, in New York City had triggered an attack on the protesters by construction workers, a clash that resulted in injury to seventy persons, four of them police trying to separate the combatants. The melee in New York City inspired a demonstration in support of President Nixon and his Southeast Asia policy held there on May 20, under sponsorship of the building-trades unions. An estimated 100,000 pro-Nixon demonstrators attended the event.[69]

While crowds protested — or, less frequently, demonstrated approval of — Presidential actions, Congress began considering legislation designed to ensure an American withdrawal from Cambodia by July 1, 1970. Two senators, Republican John Sherman Cooper of Kentucky and Democrat Frank Church of Idaho, offered an amendment to the foreign military sales act that, effective July 1, would have cut off funds not only for the employment of ground forces or advisers in Cambodia but also for the conduct of air operations in support of Cambodian troops. On June 30, the Senate adopted a modified version of the Cooper-Church resolution, but the House of Representatives would not agree. To pass the military sales legislation, Congress shelved the Cooper-Church proviso, though the act in its final form repealed the Tonkin Gulf resolution. Adopted almost without dissent in 1964 in response to reports of attacks by North Vietnamese patrol boats on American destroyers, the resolution had, in effect, given the President a free hand in defining and punishing acts of aggression by North Vietnam.

Far from expiring, the Cooper-Church proposal surfaced again in December and was incorporated in a defense appropriations bill for fiscal 1971. As a result, the amended act barred the introduction of combat troops or military advisers into Cambodia or Laos, while ignoring the air war in both countries. The legislative branch thus curbed Presidential initiative, but did not prevent him from supplying Lon Nol's army, providing it air support, or reacting with air power against any Cambodia-based threat to the American forces not yet withdrawn from South Vietnam.[70]

President Nixon's Southeast Asia policy of Vietnamization and withdrawal weathered the domestic storm caused by the Cambodian incursion. Continuing troop withdrawals and the return from Cambodia of the American invasion force enabled him to wage an air war there. As the tempest of May died away, the burden of campaigning in Cambodia shifted from soldiers, most of them draftees, to airmen serving voluntarily in an organization that sustained far fewer losses than the Army's combat arms. In the Cambodian fighting of 1970, for instance, five Air Force crew members were killed, two others were wounded, and one remained missing when the incursion ended — eight men — roughly one-half of one percent of the total U.S. Army casualties during the period.[71] A comparison of casualties may well have contributed to the decision to embark on the sustained aerial interdiction effort that began as American ground units withdrew from Cambodia.

Chapter Twelve

From Incursion to Interdiction

Searching beyond the immediate area of the incursion into Cambodia, photographic and visual reconnaissance disclosed that the North Vietnamese were shifting their forces to contain the invaders from South Vietnam and at the same time trying to topple Lon Nol's government. Reacting to early reports of hostile movement, the Joint Chiefs of Staff on May 16 suggested an aerial interdiction campaign designed to impede travel by road and river throughout northeastern Cambodia. General Brown's Seventh Air Force staff outlined a plan for attacking traffic in an area bounded by the South Vietnamese border, the Laotian border, a line 200 meters west of the Mekong River, and Cambodian Route 13, a highway leading from Kratie southeastward past the town of Snoul. After coordination with Cambodian authorities, air strikes began on May 30, six days after the Joint Chiefs of Staff issued their formal directive to carry out the Seventh Air Force plan.[1]

As approved by the Joint Chiefs of Staff, the interdiction campaign, officially christened Freedom Deal on June 6,[2] pitted tactical aircraft against "enemy activities" in northeastern Cambodia "as necessary to protect U.S. forces in the Republic of Vietnam." Aerial interdiction, in effect, extended into Cambodia the attempts to disrupt traffic on the Ho Chi Minh Trail in southern Laos. Within northeastern Cambodia, as in southern Laos, B–52 bombers could use their striking power in the interdiction effort, provided that the impact area lay at least one kilometer from inhabited villages or three kilometers from friendly troops. The safety zone for military units was greater because they tended to move about, while villagers were expected to remain close to home.[3]

These safety margins formed one part of a set of rules of engagement designed to prevent bombing accidents in Cambodia. During the drafting of these rules, General Abrams managed to avoid the precedent established in Laos, where the U.S. Ambassador might veto targets because of adverse political consequences. For air attacks in the Freedom Deal area of Cambodia, coordination took place exclusively among military headquarters — the U.S. Military Assistance Command, the South Vietnamese Joint General Staff, and the Cambodian armed forces.[4]

Air War over South Vietnam, 1968–1975

The operational precautions insisted upon in Cambodia differed little from those enforced in South Vietnam. Cambodian authorities had to validate targets, periodically reviewing those roads, areas, or waterways they had already certified as enemy-controlled and cleared of noncombatants. Airmen might attack trucks travelling by night, the time favored by enemy drivers, or motorboats moving at any time, even though the road or stream was known to carry civilian traffic. After all, the peasants of eastern Cambodia rarely, if ever, used trucks or powered boats. Before attempting to disrupt enemy movement on any highway or river used by local civilians, planners relied upon leaflets or loudspeaker broadcasts to warn villagers of the danger, advising them in particular to avoid travel after dark.

As in South Vietnam, a forward air controller directed most strikes, except those by B–52s, for in Cambodia, too, the big bombers dropped their explosive loads on signal from Combat Skyspot radar operators on the ground. Air Force gunships, with their array of on-board sensors, along with F–4s and Marine Corps A–6s fitted out for radar bombing, could also dispense with a forward air controller. Only in special operating areas verified and reviewed by Cambodian officers could tactical aircraft attack solely on the pilot's initiative.

The existence of historic structures like the Angkor Wat, a temple complex dating from the twelfth century, complicated the air war in Cambodia. Planners and air crews exercised care to avoid damaging these buildings, insisting that Cambodian officers approve nearby air attacks. To help protect national shrines, civilian lives, and the safety of friendly troops fighting in Cambodia, English-speaking Cambodian officers joined the Tactical Air Control Center at Tan Son Nhut and the direct air support center at Pleiku. Cambodian airmen fluent in English proved scarce, American pilots who spoke the Khmer language were even fewer, and the Air Force soon was searching out American and South Vietnamese forward air controllers fluent in French, the second language of most educated Cambodians. These bilingual officers formed an essential link in the air control system functioning in Cambodia.[5]

Despite the growing volume of road and river traffic within the Freedom Deal area, profitable targets proved hard to find. The forest, of course, posed a problem, but other handicaps may have resulted from the short tours of duty that Air Force officers served in Southeast Asia. Sometimes changing assignments during their year in the country, even field-grade officers might not learn a job until they were about to leave it. Whatever the reason, Col. Malcolm E. Ryan and Col. James H. Ahmann, two officers who helped plan the interdiction campaign, maintained that some of their colleagues had all but ignored the computerized intelligence available at Tan Son Nhut, apparently not realizing the extent of recent reconnaissance coverage of Cambodia.[6]

Initially, the Cambodian liaison officers did not prove as helpful as expected. After approving eight of the first twenty targets proposed, they returned early in June to suggest designating much of Freedom Deal a special

From Incursion to Interdiction

A C–130 drops leaflets to warn villagers of an impending attack.

operating area to be bombed at will. Colonel Ryan and his fellow planners had to remind the liaison group "that there were people around those areas and that bombs kill people." Afterward, the Cambodians grew "much more conservative in their validation."[7]

Already looking forward to possible extension of the air war west of the Mekong, Seventh Air Force headquarters proposed using Freedom Deal interdiction as the basis for aerial reconnaissance beyond that river. Thus far, visual reconnaissance by F–4s, OV–10s, and A–37s halted at the Mekong, a fact that could not have escaped the enemy's notice. Given the American tendency to respect boundaries, whether geographic or political, the communists might not expect these low-altitude flights to continue on into western Cambodia. Occasional missions beyond the river not only could produce valuable intelligence for future air attacks, but also might confuse the enemy, serving notice that the region did not constitute a sanctuary.[8] The Joint Chiefs of Staff agreed that information was needed on enemy activity west of the Mekong and approved unarmed aerial reconnaissance throughout the remainder of Cambodia. Only the capital city, Phnom Penh, and its environs remained off limits for tactical reconnaissance, ostensibly to prevent civilian casualties, though it is not clear how unarmed aircraft could have caused death or injury among the local populace.[9]

Like reconnaissance, rescue activity expanded to keep pace with the extension of the air war. In mid-June, General Abrams expressed concern about the fate of South Vietnamese air crews who might parachute or crash outside the Freedom Deal area, for South Vietnam's air arm had no organized rescue service. By the end of the month, Air Force rescue units had received permission to range over all of Cambodia to recover downed Americans and any South Vietnamese who could not be reached by their own helicopters or ground patrols. Late in July, moreover, Air Force helicopters began retrieving Cambodian airmen who otherwise might not be saved.[10]

As the Freedom Deal strikes were beginning, a group of Cambodian troops and civilians fled the town of Lomphat and sought refuge from the pursuing enemy at Labansiek, where the South Vietnamese had sent a tactical air control party to handle strikes in support of their own forces engaged in the Binh Tay operations. South Vietnamese forward air controllers and fighter-bomber crews combined to attack ambush sites along the road linking the two towns, but air cover could not prevent the communists from inflicting "serious" losses on the retreating column. For two weeks Labansiek held out, but on June 13 the South Vietnamese withdrew their tactical air control party and called a halt to air activity, since the Binh Tay forces had already departed. Left to fend for themselves were some ten thousand Cambodian soldiers and noncombatants, a total divided between Labansiek and Ba Kev, just to the east.

American airmen replaced the South Vietnamese fliers who had been aiding the embattled Cambodians. Flareships and AC–119K gunships appeared overhead on the evening of the 13th, made radio contact with English-speaking Cambodian officers on the ground, and commenced harrying North Vietnamese concentrations on the outskirts of the two towns. Fighters joined in, attacking visually by day or using Combat Skyspot radar at night, but fatigue and casualties wore away the defenders until an evacuation seemed necessary if the soldiers and civilians were to survive.[11] On June 23, Air Force C–7s and C–123s evacuated some 7,000 persons, most of them members of soldiers' families, and the troops then abandoned Ba Kev and Labansiek, retreating under cover of American aircraft and yielding northeastern Cambodia to the enemy.[12]

As the fighting at Labansiek and Ba Kev drew to an end, the Seventh Air Force embarked upon Freedom Action, an air operation distinct from Freedom Deal. Authorized by the Joint Chiefs of Staff on June 17, Freedom Action empowered General Abrams and his deputy for air, General Brown, to intervene with tactical aviation in any battle, throughout the whole of Cambodia, where a communist victory would pose a serious military or psychological threat to the Lon Nol government. When necessary, B–52s could take part in Freedom Action, just as in Freedom Deal. The principal beneficiaries of the new operation were the defenders of Kompong Thom who, according to Lon Nol, were saved from death or capture thanks to the efforts of American airmen. Freedom Action ended on June 29, a mere ten days after the first strikes were flown. The shortlived endeavor reflected uncertainty within the Nixon administration concerning the nature and scope of aerial operations after American ground troops had withdrawn from Cambodia.[13]

The Nixon administration had difficulty interpreting, in the light of military realities in Cambodia, the President's statement of June 3, which assured the nation that "The only remaining American activity in Cambodia after July 1 will be air missions to interdict the movement of enemy troops and materiel where

From Incursion to Interdiction

I find it necessary to protect the lives and security of our men in South Vietnam."[14] The policy seemed clear at first, for in conversations at his home in San Clemente, California, Nixon told Laird and Abrams that aerial interdiction would be permitted after July 1, but not close air support.[15] The President, however, had scarcely affirmed this policy when he began modifying it.

As Laird reportedly said after the San Clemente talks, "since we are taking all the heat on Cambodia, we might as well use our forces as effectively as possible,"[16] a view the President apparently shared, despite his declaration limiting aerial activity to interdiction. In any event, during conversations with Admiral Moorer, Deputy Secretary of Defense Packard, and other of his advisers, Nixon agreed to a broad interpretation of interdiction, though he insisted he did not want American tactical air control parties accompanying South Vietnamese or Cambodian units operating west of the border. The admiral came away from the meeting convinced that "the President thinks Cambodia can be saved and that it is worth the effort and risks we might run."[17] Indeed, the President's remarks to the acting chairman inspired the Joint Chiefs of Staff to launch Operation Freedom Action.[18]

The President, however, adopted a policy that seemed, at first glance, far less bold than his words, as Moorer understood them. After all, Nixon not only retained the ban on close air support for South Vietnamese forces in Cambodia, at this time finishing the Cuu Long series of operations, but promptly called a halt to Freedom Action, thus forcing General Abrams to evaluate individually each Cambodian request for attacks beyond the Freedom Deal boundary. In practice, though, the restrictions proved more apparent than real. Close support of South Vietnamese troops could be provided by their own airmen instead of Americans, and General Abrams remained free to intervene with air power on behalf of Cambodian troops in any emergency that he interpreted as threatening the survival of the Lon Nol regime.[19]

The announced policy of flying interdiction missions only, within a specified area, proved a matter of appearance rather than substance, affecting bookkeeping instead of tactical employment. In the light of his discussion with President Nixon at San Clemente — and of Moorer's account of his own talks with the Chief Executive — Abrams assumed that he could rely on the Seventh Air Force for close air support, as well as for interdiction, provided only that he did not openly acknowledge any departure from the President's announced policy. As a result, close air support became aerial interdiction in the periodic reports of action in Cambodia, and statistical compilations listed attack sorties, without separating close air support from interdiction, a distinction still being made for air operations in South Vietnam.[20]

As it had in reporting the strike against the Kong River truck park during the incursion, the Seventh Air Force used secure means of communication to report strikes outside the normal operating area, creating for accounting purposes a cover target to be listed in routine reports. Not until February 1971, when the

Air War over South Vietnam, 1968–1975

Refugees from the eastern provinces of Cambodia were airlifted to South Vietnam aboard Air Force C–7s.

same aircraft was reported downed at two different locations, did Department of Defense planners become aware of the cover story. By that time, some 3,600 of the 8,000-odd sorties reported flown in an expanded interdiction zone had hit targets which, at the time of attack, lay beyond the pale.[21]

Events proved Abrams correct in assuming that he could employ air power as the situation required, provided only that he did so discreetly. The American public failed to rally behind those Congressional leaders seeking to exert pressure on the administration to enforce the announced limitations on air strikes in Cambodia. Since Abrams did not face widespread political or public opposition, he enjoyed great discretion in attacking targets. Aerial activity did not arouse the kind of clamor that the recent incursion had, principally because ground action, with larger forces that included many draftees, almost always produced a longer and more demoralizing roster of American dead and wounded.

In January 1971, for example, the Nixon administration aroused little concern, except on Capitol Hill, when it acknowledged an increase in the intensity of the air war in Cambodia. Sixty-four Congressmen co-sponsored legislation to cut off funds for combat support of any kind in that country, but the proposal failed, as did an attempt to fix by law a date for the final American withdrawal from the Vietnam conflict. However futile at the moment, these legislative gestures served to warn of more serious clashes with Congress in the future on the topic of military action in Southeast Asia.

To neutralize the opposition, administration officials quickly pointed out that aerial involvement served a substitute for combat on the ground, not a prelude to another invasion, an assurance that seemed to satisfy Congress and the public. Jerry W. Friedheim, a deputy assistant secretary of defense for public affairs, then declared that the President would apply in Cambodia whatever degree of air power might be necessary to prevent attacks on American troops still serving in South Vietnam, a point repeated late in January by Secretary of State Rogers and reinforced during a February 1971 press conference by Nixon himself. Granted that a South Vietnamese offensive into Laos may have distracted the attention of the American public at the time of the February meeting between the President and reporters, the safety of U.S. soldiers remaining in South Vietnam seemed infinitely more important than the location of targets in Cambodia or the precise nature of the strikes against them.[22]

Despite the President's restrictions, therefore, General Brown, who would serve until the end of August 1970 as the Seventh Air Force commander, as well as deputy for air operations to General Abrams, continued to wage "the most aggressive U.S. and VNAF air campaign in Cambodia which is feasible within the limits of intelligence and control facilities available...." The Americans might routinely employ flareships to meet emergencies anywhere in Cambodia, continue dispatching rescue or reconnaissance missions throughout the entire country, and, provided only that villagers were not endangered, call upon B–52s to hit the enemy anywhere in Freedom Deal.[23] Neither fighters nor bombers could attack, however, until Cambodian authorities had verified the target, for the original Freedom Deal rules of engagement remained in effect. As long as he avoided populated settlements, General Abrams could direct B–52s and tactical fighters into a Freedom Deal Extension — bounded on the north by Route 13, on the west by a line 200 meters beyond the Mekong River, on the south by Route 7, and on the east by the South Vietnamese border. Although the far-reaching Freedom Action authority no longer obtained, the general could also attack beyond the boundary formed by the Mekong and Route 7, if he were satisfied that a critically important town or military position was clearly in jeopardy.[24]

General Abrams promptly invoked his authority to carry the war outside the enlarged Freedom Deal region, approving air strikes in defense of Kompong Thom, roughly seventy-five miles west of the Mekong, even as he attacked Kompong Cham, at the far limit of the newly expanded operating area. Kompong Thom stood astride the route used to bring rice from the Tonle Sap agricultural basin to the capital city, Phnom Penh; Kompong Cham was a transportation hub for road and river traffic. In both instances, intelligence specialists of the military assistance command and the Seventh Air Force confirmed the seriousness of the communist threat, Cambodian officers approved the targets, and Air Force forward air controllers in contact with troops on the ground directed the actual strikes.[25]

The mere presence of hostile forces in an area did not guarantee that American air power would intervene. In July, for instance, Abrams turned down Cambodian requests for aerial attacks around Battambang in the northwestern part of the country and, for the time being, rejected proposed strikes on the Kirirom Plateau, west of Phnom Penh. In contrast, the threat to Siem Riep, a town near the northern shore of Tonle Sap, grew real enough to justify the use of Air Force gunships as well as flareships. The Seventh Air Force also received permission to attack enemy traffic on parts of Route 12, leading southward toward besieged Kompong Thom.[26]

While he used air power to meet emergencies progressively farther from South Vietnam's western border, Abrams succeeded in expanding further the already extended Freedom Deal interdiction zone. On July 21, the Seventh Air Force had requested the further enlargement, citing the results of reconnaissance flights over the proposed addition — south of Route 7, east of the Mekong, north of Route 15, and including the entire Parrot's Beak. Airmen had detected troop movements and supply convoys throughout the region, ample justification, it seemed, to enlarge the interdiction area.[27] The Joint Chiefs of Staff, however, elected to expand Freedom Deal less than half as far as the Seventh Air Force desired. The revised boundary consisted of a combination of highways and one stream — Routes 75, 155, 1543, and the Prek Kompong Spean — that kept the interdiction operation just north of the Parrot's Beak.[28]

This second expansion of Freedom Deal (actually an enlargement of the first extension) could not check the advance of the North Vietnamese and Cambodian Khmer Rouge forces. To deal with the worsening threat, General Brown sought to push the boundary of the interdiction zone westward, almost to Siem Riep, and southwest to the Gulf of Thailand. He also wanted approval to conduct the same intensive air operations in defense of Kompong Speu, Kompong Chhnang, and Kampot that already were being flown at Kompong Thom and Kompong Cham. Although unwilling to go so far, General Abrams, on his own initiative, approved an extension that embraced Kompong Cham, Kompong Thom, and Kompong Chhnang. This change, made on August 20, had the effect of a Band-Aid when a tourniquet clearly was needed, so the Army general immediately turned to the Joint Chiefs of Staff for a more radical adjustment of Freedom Deal.[29]

Intelligence clearly revealed that streams, trails, and highways north of Phnom Penh carried an increasing volume of supplies to communist forces in action at Kompong Thom and elsewhere. Aircrews and Salem House patrols reported seeing porters, bicycles, and ox carts bringing cargo into the country from Laos. At transshipment points in the northern jungle, laborers transferred this material onto trucks, which completed the journey using Route 12 and other roads. Although most of the trucks moved in darkness, forward air controllers used night observation devices to detect them, and infrared film verified the activity. Because of this traffic, moving beyond range of South Vietnamese aircraft based in South Vietnam, the Joint Chiefs of Staff allowed Abrams to push the interdiction zone westward from the Mekong to a line originating where the borders of Cambodia, Laos, and Thailand met and extending southward past

Phum Troun, Phum Ravieng, and Kompong Thom to Kompong Cham. This extension, called Freedom Deal Alpha, excluded the towns of Kompong Speu and Kompong Chhnang.[30]

At the end of July, as Freedom Deal was in the process of expanding, Abrams decided that intervention with American air power was necessary if Lon Nol were to retain a foothold on the Kirirom Plateau. His first move, a five-day air campaign, failed to blunt the communist thrust toward Route 4, linking Phnom Penh and the port of Kompong Som. Following this setback, aerial action continued into September, when communist forces at last drove Lon Nol's defenders from the plateau.[31]

Thus did the American interdiction effort evolve during 1970. At year's end, the normal operating area embraced the original Freedom Deal zone, the two Freedom Deal extensions, and Freedom Deal Alpha; it stretched from Route 7 to the Laotian border and extended some seventy-five miles beyond the Mekong.[32] The expanded interdiction effort included attempts to mine streams used to transport enemy cargo, continuing forays by Salem House teams, strikes on supply lines, and, when necessary, close air support of Cambodian troops.

Early in June, Air Force planes began sowing magnetic mines in the Kong and San Rivers. The planting of more than 1,600 mines, however, did little more than inconvenience the enemy, who substituted wooden boats for metal-hulled, powered craft until he could begin floating rafts made of steel drums downstream in a systematic mine-clearing effort. A similar attempt to mine the Mekong, near its conflux with the Kong, proved no more successful.[33]

The Salem House area of operation expanded throughout 1970, much as had the aerial interdiction zone. By the end of December, teams were patrolling twenty to fifty kilometers into Cambodia from the Laotian border on the north to the Gulf of Thailand. In addition, Abrams' Studies and Observations Group could insert the teams anywhere in the original Freedom Deal area, east of the Mekong, to locate targets for air strikes. Because of President Nixon's decision to withdraw U.S. ground troops from Cambodia, no Americans accompanied these cross-border patrols after July 1, but U.S. Air Force helicopters, escorted by A–1s from Nakhon Phanom, flew some of the teams to their landing zones. On certain roads and trails, the reconnaissance units planted electronic sensors to detect movement and thus locate targets for artillery or air strikes.[34]

The 1970 aerial campaign in Cambodia demonstrated beyond doubt the value of the armed forward air controller, flying the OV–10A Bronco or, less frequently, the F–4 Phantom. The concept of arming the controllers had undergone testing in South Vietnam during 1969, and results there proved so encouraging that General Brown ordered all his Broncos fitted out with machine guns and rocket launchers. Over Cambodia, armed forward air controllers attacked targets, usually traffic on roads or rivers approved as strike zones by Cambodian authorities, that seemed likely to vanish before fighter-bombers could be summoned to the scene.[35]

Air War over South Vietnam, 1968–1975

Americans were not the only airmen flying combat missions over Cambodia during the interdiction campaign. A few Cambodians saw action, along with South Vietnamese. When Lon Nol sought to rally his nation and expel the North Vietnamese, his air force consisted of just ninety-eight planes, with twenty-one operational. Available for combat were nine North American T–28s, trainers modified for counterinsurgency warfare, and a dozen MiG–17s, interceptors that the Soviet Union had given the Sihanouk regime. The Khmer air arm could muster about a hundred pilots, roughly half of them experienced enough to carry out air strikes. Even fewer of these airmen had the combination of experience and fluency in English that would enable them to act as forward air controllers or members of tactical air control parties. Obviously, this force could not in the near future make a major contribution to the air war.[36]

Despite these handicaps, Cambodian fliers did participate to some extent in the fighting. Lack of Soviet-manufactured ammunition grounded the MiGs, but by the end of summer, the few serviceable T–28s, supplemented by five planes of the same type borrowed from the Royal Thai Air Force, enabled Lon Nol's pilots to average a dozen combat sorties per day, occasionally flying half-again that many in an emergency. To circumvent the language barrier, French-speaking U.S. Air Force and Cambodian officers worked together in approving and controlling air strikes.[37]

Like its American counterpart, the South Vietnamese Air Force took part in the attacks on the North Vietnamese sanctuaries and in the air campaign that followed. From the beginning of the incursion until the end of 1970, the South Vietnamese flew some 9,600 attack sorties in Cambodia, compared to 14,600 by American airmen.[38] Besides flying interdiction missions, South Vietnam's air arm delivered close-in strikes for both Cambodian and South Vietnamese troops and provided other assistance.

Examples of participation by South Vietnamese airmen included the relief of Kompong Cham in mid-December 1970. Since summer, Lon Nol's army struggled to hold this town against a determined enemy. During the six weeks beginning on November 1, with the Cambodian defenders barely holding on, U.S. Air Force fighter-bombers flew 78 sorties, AC–119s flew 126, and B–52s three. Throughout this crisis, South Vietnamese tactical aircraft contributed 426 combat sorties. Finally, on December 14, the South Vietnamese mounted an air operation to replace the Khmer garrison with their own troops, using helicopters to bring in an airborne infantry battalion and a battery of artillery.[39]

General Brown, who as commander of the Seventh Air Force had played a key role in the improvement and modernization of South Vietnam's air force, looked upon the Cambodian campaign, especially the airlift to supply the force landed by helicopter at Kompong Cham, as proof that the air arm was achieving balance as well as acquiring skill. The fighter force had already demonstrated its ability in South Vietnam; now, in Cambodia, transport crews had delivered cargo by night, adjusting schedules to meet changing tactical and weather con-

An EC–121D on station over Southeast Asia.

ditions, experience that, in the general's opinion, "was a great thing for them" in terms of increased self-confidence.[40]

When operating in Cambodia, the South Vietnamese Air Force encountered certain handicaps. Strike aircraft based at Da Nang and Nha Trang, for example, consumed too much fuel en route to the interdiction area to remain there for long. Bad weather or darkness impeded aerial combat, with only the AC–47 gunship able to fight effectively at night. Also, any South Vietnamese troops in action received top priority for air strikes, regardless of the peril some Cambodian unit might face. Finally, the shortage of trained South Vietnamese forward air controllers persisted, and the O–1s and U–17s that they used could fly no deeper than eighty miles into Cambodia without an unacceptable sacrifice in time on station.[41]

Despite the impressive record compiled by South Vietnamese airmen, a longstanding hatred at times disrupted cooperation between the governments of Cambodia and South Vietnam. Though he clearly needed its help, Lon Nol feared South Vietnam, for tens of thousands of ethnic Vietnamese living in Cambodia had been objects of contempt and victims of oppression; and a South Vietnamese army might yield to the temptation to redress this wrong. As a result, Cambodian authorities were prompt to blame their allies of the moment for looting and other crimes, not all of which were clearly the fault of South Vietnamese troops.[42]

As the air war spread deeper into Cambodia and came to involve air crews of nations other than the United States, coordination became a problem. An aerial command post had to be found to replace the EC–47D that provided radio relay, and Seventh Air Force headquarters proposed the return to Thailand of four of the Lockheed EC–121s recently withdrawn from that country. The first of the EC–121D radar platforms arrived at Korat Air Base, Thailand, on September 15 and flew its first mission on the following day. Plans called for the planes to serve as airborne battlefield command and control centers until modified C–130s, the type that had performed this role over Khe Sanh in 1968, became available. The airborne command centers, whether EC–121Ds or modified C–130s, would carry French-speaking controllers from the air forces of the United States, Thailand, South Vietnam, and Cambodia, who would apportion the available fighter-bombers among targets in Cambodia. To prevent the enemy from eavesdropping, these officers would use comparatively simple code equipment, not so secret or technologically advanced that the Air Force could not share it with foreign airmen. The concept, however, never became reality. Although the Cambodians agreed to place representatives on board the flying command posts, the South Vietnamese relied on a control center established at Phnom Penh's Pochentong airport, and the Thai air force continued to use its own center located at Battambang.[43]

Plans called for the eventual replacement of the airborne battlefield command and control center by an air operations coordination center at Pochentong airdrome. Unfortunately, American participation in a center there would violate President Nixon's announced policy, soon to be confirmed by Congress, of equipping rather than advising Cambodia's armed forces. At times, however, a fact-finding visit to investigate the use of American-supplied material might become a vehicle for giving military advice, if not for routinely harmonizing operations. On at least one occasion, the U.S. Ambassador at Phnom Penh, Emory S. Swank, allowed an officer from Seventh Air Force headquarters to help the Cambodian Air Force address problems of control and coordination. In the sort of "low key" discussion specified by the diplomat, Lt. Col. Paul D. Wagoner described the layout and functioning of a Pochentong command post, its relationship to intelligence activities, and its communications needs. He came away impressed with the attitude of the Cambodians he met — "They want to fight the war their way, by themselves" — but he confessed that "It will surprise me if the AOCC [air operations coordination center] works effectively without U.S. influence.... I feel we must help them all we can." By year's end, that help had not come, and the coordination center remained unfinished.[44]

Since the spring of 1970, American operations in Cambodia had changed in nature, though the final goal remained the same. Ground attacks upon bases that sustained enemy activity in South Vietnam gave way to an air campaign also designed to save American lives in the South by exerting pressure on the enemy in Cambodia. The aerial effort helped maintain the regime headed by Lon Nol, so that the Cambodian armed forces could absorb the military supplies that the United States was providing and resist the communist opposition. However, the ultimate goal of America's Cambodian intervention remained to contribute to the aerial shield behind which American troops could withdraw as South Vietnamese forces gathered strength to replace them.

Chapter Thirteen

The Continued Growth of South Vietnam's Air Force

The American departures coincided, of course, with South Vietnam's assumption of greater responsibility for fighting the war. By January 1970, Vietnamization of aerial combat was well underway, though some advisers preferred to speak instead of an improvement and modernization program. This choice of words tended to soothe those South Vietnamese who wanted a better and more modern air arm, but feared that the Americans saw Vietnamization as simply a way to rid themselves of responsibility for an unpopular conflict and go home.[1]

Whatever label the process might carry, Gen. Kendall Young's Air Force Advisory Group, Vietnam, was administering an accelerated effort to strengthen South Vietnam's air force. As the advisers forged ahead, Secretary of Defense Laird, his staff, and the Joint Chiefs of Staff debated the merits of speeding the Vietnamization program even more. Under discussion at Washington was the so-called phase III effort, first proposed late the previous year and designed to enable the South Vietnamese armed forces to maintain "current levels of security" as the military assistance command diminished in strength and activity to a mere advisory group. Phase III, however, with its estimated additional cost of $980 million, ran hard aground on fiscal shoals.[2]

The same budget crisis that inspired Project 703 and the resulting manpower cuts had also imposed limits on what the United States could do immediately to improve President Thieu's armed forces. Secretary Laird, a veteran of the House of Representatives, believed that Congress would not vote supplementary defense funds except in a dire emergency. New appropriations for phase III seemed especially unlikely since the program, accelerated though it was, could not dramatically reduce American participation in the Southeast Asia conflict and result in new troop withdrawals. Addressing himself to the question of again speeding up the improvement and modernization effort, the Secretary of Defense warned that "all funding must come from within existing and foreseeable budget ceilings." To step up the pace of Vietnamization would require slowing the tempo of some other program administered by the Department of Defense or the armed services.[3]

Air War over South Vietnam, 1968–1975

The Cambodian invasion, however, gave unexpected impetus to the modernization and improvement of South Vietnam's armed forces. Although the existing budget ceiling remained in effect, Secretary Laird was determined to tap other departmental programs for the money necessary to take advantage of the "new RVNAF [Republic of Vietnam Armed Forces] confidence born in the recent cross-border operations" both to increase South Vietnamese participation in the war and to hasten U.S. withdrawals. "It is abundantly clear...," he declared, "that on completion of our operations [in Cambodia], we must accelerate the RVNAF improvement and modernization program in every possible way."[4]

Secretary Laird thus launched the Consolidated RVNAF Improvement and Modernization Program, which intensified efforts already begun but did not require new appropriations as the phase III scheme would have done. The consolidated program called for a South Vietnamese military establishment totaling 1.1 million in June 1973, with the air arm expanding to 46,998 officers and men. During December 1970, however, the Air Force advisory group became concerned that additional airmen, technicians, and medical professionals would be needed as South Vietnamese replaced U.S. troops at air bases, logistics centers, command posts, and hospital facilities. South Vietnam's Joint General Staff agreed, increasing the projected strength of the air service to 52,171,[5] but even this number could not ensure the self-sufficiency of a Vietnamized air arm. At best, the greater number of South Vietnamese airmen could help the other expanded armed services to deal with the kind of communist threat that existed in the spring of 1970, after the invasion of Cambodia.[6]

Authorized early in June, the consolidated plan imposed an added burden on the Air Force advisory group, which already was carrying out the previous year's accelerated improvement and modernization scheme. General Young complained about the lack of formal directives governing the acceleration that began in 1969, declaring that "the only road map" consisted of "the minutes of several meetings held during the initial development of the program." To maintain control over unit activations, changes in equipment, and transfers of facilities, Young's staff established a system of "milestone dates" that enabled monitors to chart progress, isolate problems, and predict the impact of delays. As hectic in tempo as the plan it supplanted, the consolidated program of 1970 further tested these management procedures.[7]

During 1970, Air Force headquarters gave formal recognition to the role General Brown had been playing in carrying out plans to improve and modernize South Vietnam's air arm, in effect putting him in charge of all service-funded assistance programs. The channel for managing these activities extended from the Pentagon through Pacific Air Forces and Seventh Air Force to General Young's advisory group. General Brown, of course, would continue to coordinate Air Force activity with the work of the other services, operating through General Abrams' headquarters.[8]

Under the consolidated improvement and modernization program, the South

Continued Growth of South Vietnam's Air Force

Vietnamese Air Force expanded from twenty-two squadrons with 486 authorized aircraft in mid-summer 1970 to thirty squadrons with 706 planes at year's end. Two additional A–37 squadrons and one of A–1s (all originally scheduled for activation in the summer of 1971) joined the air arm, as did four new squadrons of UH–1s and, some six months ahead of schedule, the first of two planned CH–47 units.[9] Moreover, the consolidated plan looked beyond these 1970 increases to a force of thirty-seven squadrons by the end of June 1971, forty-five squadrons a year later, and forty-nine by June 30, 1973. The final squadron, eighteen Northrop F–5E interceptors, would arrive at the end of June 1974, raising to 1,299 the authorized total of aircraft.[10]

In terms of squadrons, South Vietnam's air arm expanded by almost 30 percent during 1970, while the number of aircraft increased by not quite 50 percent. Further expansion lay in the future as the consolidated improvement and modernization program surged forward. As a result, throughout 1970 the Air Force advisory group intensified its efforts to fashion the organizational framework capable of sustaining an even bigger force. In doing so, General Young and his fellow advisers struck a compromise between centralization, a key principle of Air Force doctrine, and the diffusion of authority that the South Vietnamese favored.

In two instances, centralization clearly prevailed. An Air Logistics Command began functioning at Bien Hoa, built on the foundation of the logistics wing that had been stationed there, and a training center took shape at Nha Trang. Also, the blueprint now existed for a unified aircraft control and warning system, even though a South Vietnamese interceptor force would not arrive until 1974. The tactical air control system, however, defied centralization, for despite organizational charts to the contrary, the corps or military region commanders, operating through the local direct air support center, exerted control over strikes in their areas.

Five air divisions, one in each military region and one in the Capital Military District, formed the main components of the reorganized South Vietnamese Air Force. The first, located at Da Nang, provided air support throughout Military Region I (formerly called the I Corps Tactical Zone), with fighter-bombers, helicopters, and observation or liaison squadrons assigned to either of two tactical wings. The Second Air Division, its headquarters at Nha Trang, covered Military Region II, operating one wing from Nha Trang and another from Pleiku. Two other tactical wings, grouped at Bien Hoa to form the 3d Air Division, bore responsibility for aerial operations in Military Region III, while the 4th Air Division, its headquarters and one wing at Binh Thuy and a second tactical wing at Soc Trang, used its A–37s, O–1s, U–17s, and UH–1 helicopters throughout Military Region IV.[11]

Different from these four organizations, all of them functioning by September 1970, was the 5th Air Division, activated on New Year's Day, 1971, at Tan Son Nhut Air Base in the Capital Military District. Unlike the other four, this newest air division did not did not support ground forces within a particular region. Instead, it was an outgrowth of the 33d Wing, which flew transports, gunships, and special mission aircraft everywhere in South Vietnam. Since so many of the aircraft flown by this division — the AC–47, VC–47 executive transport, and RC–47 — were variants of the basic Douglas C–47, the South Vietnamese did not balk at centralizing disparate operations in one division.[12]

Despite impressive results in terms of squadrons, manpower, and aircraft, the 1970 reorganization and expansion encountered serious obstacles in the quest for suitable operating facilities and adequate family housing for the expanded South Vietnamese Air Force. General Young's advisory group tackled the housing problem by establishing a pilot program for the construction of model living quarters at each of six bases — Da Nang, Pleiku, Bien Hoa, Nha Trang, Binh Thuy, and Tan Son Nhut. The basic structure was a rectangular cinder-block building with ten family units opening onto a common courtyard that did not exceed $600 per apartment in cost. Although U.S. airmen supervised the work, members of the South Vietnamese air arm mixed concrete, fashioned the blocks, and put up the walls and roof. The models, finished during May, helped persuade South Vietnamese authorities to embark on an ambitious housing plan embracing seven bases (Soc Trang being the addition) and accommodating 2,400 families, a number soon increased to 4,900.[13]

The housing program undertaken by the South Vietnamese Air Force got off to a slow start. Only at Da Nang were sand, lumber, and cement readily available, and this, too, was the only base with adequate manpower for the task. Except at Soc Trang, a former U.S. Army base with no Air Force materials, the Seventh Air Force provided the necessary lumber whenever the South Vietnamese ran short, a contribution that kept the project from losing momentum. At year's end, construction was moving ahead, though slowly.[14]

Progress also occurred in the Vietnamization of base defense. By the end of December 1970, South Vietnamese Air Force security police had assumed full responsibility for protecting Nha Trang, Binh Thuy, and Soc Trang. General Young estimated that 85 percent of the authorized security force was either organized in operational units or undergoing training. Recently assigned sentry dog teams patrolled the perimeter defenses of Binh Thuy and Pleiku. Gradually the South Vietnamese security police would replace their American counterparts at all seven operating bases.[15]

In its plans for transferring facilities to the South Vietnamese, the U.S. Air Force had given top priority to Nha Trang, tentatively scheduled for release during the summer of 1970, with Binh Thuy and Pleiku, Da Nang, Bien Hoa, and ultimately Tan Son Nhut to follow. As it turned out, no base used by the Air Force came under exclusively South Vietnamese control in 1970; the only one that changed hands during the year was Soc Trang, transferred in November by the U.S. Army. The change of responsibility for Soc Trang encountered a number of obstacles, however, for the South Vietnamese lacked many of the skills

Continued Growth of South Vietnam's Air Force

Robert C. Seamans, Secretary of the Air Force, shakes hands with Gen. Cao Van Vien, head of the Vietnamese Joint General Staff, during the transfer of Soc Trang Air Base to Vietnam.

essential for operating an airfield. Telephone service, electrical power, and water pressure failed at times, until the Seventh Air Force, now commanded by Gen. Lucius D. Clay, Jr., sent a team of civil engineers in December to spend ninety days instructing and supervising their South Vietnamese counterparts.[16]

At Nha Trang, the transfer to South Vietnamese control bogged down at mid-year. The 2d Air Division, created in June, could not move immediately into its assigned buildings because the last U.S. Army units did not depart until December. During a six-month transition, South Vietnamese air traffic controllers and meteorologists, recent graduates of the training center located on the base, took over the control tower and weather station. The most serious obstacle to a rapid changeover proved to be the runway, undermined by water and deteriorating badly. Air Force engineers had to remove the disintegrating concrete and resurface before the new tenants could conduct full-scale operations.[17]

Binh Thuy also suffered runway problems, but these were alleviated simply by cutting drainage grooves in the surface to prevent the water from collecting in pools. At this base, four other major construction projects, paid for with U.S. Air Force military construction funds, ended early in 1970. Besides building a headquarters for South Vietnam's 4th Air Division and an operations building, the Air Force invested almost $400,000 in a parking apron and aircraft revetments. On the last day of February, South Vietnamese airmen took over the control tower, and when the year ended, completion of work on the runway seemed the only major obstacle to an orderly transfer of Binh Thuy to South Vietnam's air force.[18]

Pleiku posed fewer problems than either Binh Thuy or Nha Trang. Plans for entrusting the base to the South Vietnamese, completed by the end of March 1970, were being carried out at the close of the year. In contrast to these three, Da Nang, Bien Hoa, and Tan Son Nhut remained, in General Young's phrase, "critical bases."[19]

All three airfields in the critical category were undergoing intensive use by the American squadrons that shared them with South Vietnamese units. Sustained activity by two different air forces posed difficult problems. Col. Roy D. Broadway, an Air Force adviser, pointed out, "There is a resistance on the part of Americans and Vietnamese to share, just as there is a resistance on the part of anyone to share with someone else."[20] The demands of war heightened the effects of this natural friction, forcing American commanders to postpone legitimate needs of the South Vietnamese to avoid disruptions that might interfere with air operations. At Da Nang, for instance, Air Force and Marine commanders could not jeopardize the effectiveness of their units by handing over facilities to the South Vietnamese 1st Air Division. As a result, some 800 South Vietnamese airmen had to sleep in hangars, shops, and offices because American airmen needed the barracks. The situation would not improve until the Marine Corps and Air Force squadrons began leaving for the United States.[21]

To complicate the transition at Bien Hoa, two South Vietnamese organizations — the 3d Air Division and the Air Logistics Command — competed for space. They succeeded, however, in trading some buildings and sharing others until the departure of a U.S. Air Force tactical air support squadron, late in the process of Vietnamization, eased the congestion.[22]

The least progress occurred at Tan Son Nhut, the busiest of the jointly used bases. Facilities there remained "critically short," conceded Lt. Col. Jimmie R. Osborne, an Air Force adviser, because the Americans were "not moving out as fast as expected." Despite the shortage of space, the South Vietnamese showed great resourcefulness in utilizing whatever facilities and equipment became available. Osborne credited them with, among other things, building their own test stands for the AC–47's multibarrel guns and refurbishing the maintenance shops they had recently acquired.[23]

The transfer of facilities at Soc Trang and the other bases revealed a flaw in the improvement and modernization program. South Vietnam's air force did not have trained civil engineers capable of patching taxiways, repairing electrical and water systems, and performing the hundreds of other chores essential to airfield operation. "At the beginning of the Vietnamization program," said General Young, "the primary goal was to turn over increasing combat sortie responsibility" to South Vietnam's Air Force, but while the South Vietnamese were shouldering the weightier burden, their air service remained "highly dependent on USAF support for base maintenance." The advisory group realized

Continued Growth of South Vietnam's Air Force

that "this deficiency was . . . a real hindrance to the future of Vietnamization" and therefore revised training programs and assignment priorities to double the number of civil engineers available by year's end. Although the total rose from roughly 500 to more than 1,000, the South Vietnamese Air Force needed about 1,600 officers and men in this specialty.[24]

To fulfill the need for civil engineers, South Vietnamese airmen underwent English-language training that would enable them to learn the required skills by receiving instruction from and working alongside Americans. To provide actual engineering instruction, whether in the classroom or on the job, the advisory group turned to the civilian contractors — Pacific Architects and Engineers, Philco-Ford, and TransAsia — that helped provide essential services at Nha Trang, Da Nang, Pleiku, and Binh Thuy. These firms organized and supervised courses in which almost 800 South Vietnamese airmen were enrolled.[25]

The need to acquire some fluency in English before starting certain training courses remained an obstacle to many potential South Vietnamese aviators or technicians. Indeed, General Young came to conclude that it had been a mistake to make proficiency in English the key to advanced training. "In retrospect," he suggested, "it would appear wiser to have trained U.S. instructors to speak Vietnamese at the outset." He therefore recommended that in any future advisory effort of this nature, it should be mandatory for all advisers to have learned the language of the host country prior to their assignment.[26]

For the present, however, the Air Force advisory group was committed to a training program that demanded skill in English on the part of the students and required, though to a decreasing extent, instruction in the United States. During the spring of 1970, fifty-five of every hundred men selected to learn English for further training in the United States were failing the language course, almost three times the anticipated failure rate. To ensure that an adequate number of trainees would arrive in an orderly fashion for classes in the United States, the advisory group sought to improve the academic atmosphere by shifting instruction from an armed forces language center to a smaller facility operated at Nha Trang by the South Vietnamese Air Force. Reductions in the required language proficiency helped ensure the arrival of candidates for helicopter training in the United States, where they received additional schooling at the Defense Language Institute before beginning flight instruction.[27]

The advisers tried to obtain full value from the investment in language training. Graduates of language school, whose fluency had deteriorated from lack of use, might take refresher training at Nha Trang that would qualify them for technical training. English-speaking cadets who failed pilot training in the United States now received assignments to courses in air traffic control, air intelligence, civic action, or other subjects taught in that language.[28]

The need to send South Vietnamese airmen outside the country for training complicated efforts to speed the pace of improvement and modernization, and too much time was lost in learning English and traveling. As a result, Young and his staff scrutinized "literally every training requirement," except undergraduate pilot instruction programs in the United States, "to determine if there was any way the requirements could be met by the establishment, either temporarily or permanently, of an in-country training capability."[29]

During 1970, about 20,000 South Vietnamese Air Force students received some kind of instruction inside South Vietnam. Since the Nha Trang training center could not accommodate so many, satellite schools began at Bien Hoa and Tan Son Nhut. In addition, training was available with American units, whether from contractors or from servicemen, including Air Force mobile training teams sent to South Vietnam to provide specific kinds of instruction. The growing emphasis on training opportunities within the country produced more than 12,000 graduates during 1970 in a variety of skills and, in doing so, heralded future reductions of up to 60 percent in annual training costs.[30]

On-the-job training provided by U.S. airmen expanded rapidly during 1970. The number of South Vietnamese undergoing this form of instruction, now called integrated training, increased from 800 in January to 1,500 in June, and the subjects taught included such support specialties as fire protection, communications, and civil engineering. In addition, the South Vietnamese air arm strengthened its on-the-job training program, so that an average of some 700 students per month were receiving instruction in their own language from South Vietnamese technicians trained in the United States.[31]

Because time was lost gathering trainees at instructional centers in South Vietnam, the U.S. Air Force placed strong emphasis on mobile training teams that toured the major bases throughout the country. At first, team members helped polish the skills of South Vietnamese instructors, but afterwards the Americans taught various subjects such as helicopter maintenance and the repair of communications equipment. In carrying out their tasks, the mobile teams introduced simplified job performance aids that employed schematic drawings with step-by-step procedures written in Vietnamese. The eighteen teams that arrived during 1970 made a valuable contribution to improvement and modernization; in fact, only one could be termed unsuccessful — an RF–5 team whose members lacked experience with the camera installed in the plane.[32]

In a further attempt to save time, plans for the training of AC–119G crews underwent modification to avoid long and expensive stays at air bases outside South Vietnam. Tan Son Nhut became the focal point for training in this gunship, as fifty South Vietnamese pilots, half of them experienced in the C–119G transport and the others fresh from flight training in the United States, joined recent graduates of navigator school in forming the nucleus of the AC–119G crews. Flight mechanics and searchlight operators would learn their specialties in the United States before teaming up with the pilots, copilots, and navigators already training at Tan Son Nhut. Once brought together, each crew received a final indoctrination, then reported to the Air Force's 14th Special Operations Wing for the last phase of gunship training — five routine combat missions.[33]

Continued Growth of South Vietnam's Air Force

The South Vietnamese Air Force faced high costs and long delays in obtaining from schools overseas navigators for the reconnaissance, gunship, or transport versions of the C–119G and C–47. To avoid reliance on courses taught in English in the United States, the Air Force advisory group helped establish at Tan Son Nhut a school in which American-trained South Vietnamese instructors taught the basic elements of navigation. The first of seven scheduled classes began in June 1970.[34]

Some six weeks after navigator training commenced at Tan Son Nhut, fifty-five South Vietnamese airmen started transition training from the CH–34 helicopter to the newer, larger CH–47. Maintenance men as well as flight crews received instruction from members of U.S. Army helicopter units at the Phu Loi camp north of Saigon. This training program produced South Vietnam's first CH–47 squadron, which was formally activated on September 30, 1970. Preparations had already begun, moreover, to increase U.S. Air Force participation in the creation of a second squadron.[35]

Certain kinds of training simply could not be given in South Vietnam. Facilities did not yet exist for the 1,900 aviators (1,500 of them helicopter pilots) who completed undergraduate pilot training in the United States during the eighteen months ending in December 1970. Since travel outside South Vietnam was in this case unavoidable, the U.S. Air Force agreed to compress the period of training in fixed-wing aircraft. The duration of the course was reduced from forty-two weeks for all cadets to forty for future fighter pilots and thirty-eight for those destined for transport squadrons. Besides future aviators, some doctors and nurses could receive their specialized training only in the United States. Except for these fledgling pilots, the doctors and nurses, and the communications specialists trained for a time at Clark Air Base in the Philippines, policy called for transplanting courses of instruction to South Vietnam.[36]

Although pilots of helicopters, fighters, or transports and their variants — including gunships — learned to fly in the United States, training for liaison or observation craft went forward in South Vietnam. This curriculum also underwent time-saving revision. Formerly, after 299 hours of training on the ground and 146 hours mastering the U–17 or the recently introduced Cessna T–41, the new liaison pilot had reported to an O–1 unit for 50 hours of additional instruction. Unfortunately, the demands of combat usually forced the veteran fliers in the unit, whose combat missions took precedence over training flights, to spread the required instruction over three to five months. Beginning in September, the same month that the first CH–47 helicopter squadron took shape, the South Vietnamese Air Force demanded 110 hours in the T–41 and 35 to 70 hours in the O–1, all of it acquired before the aspiring forward air controller left Nha Trang. As a result, he arrived at his unit thoroughly familiar with the O–1 and needing only an informal and comparatively brief combat indoctrination.[37]

South Vietnamese assumption of responsibility for tactical air control — a process in which forward air controllers, trained in South Vietnam and flying

Air War over South Vietnam, 1968–1975

South Vietnamese students at Sheppard Air Force Base, Texas.

newly acquired O–1s, played a key part — moved ahead during 1970. At midyear, the South Vietnamese Air Force had ninety O–1 and forty U–17 observation planes organized into five active squadrons and manned by 149 pilots and 135 observers, all of them deemed fully qualified for combat. Of these 284 forward air controllers, 44 pilots and 42 observers had demonstrated sufficient ability to control strikes by U.S. Air Force as well as South Vietnamese aircraft.[38]

Successful control, however, remained limited in most instances to planned strikes conducted in daylight. According to Army Brig. Gen. John H. Cushman, acting commander of the Delta Military Assistance Command, the South Vietnamese forward air controllers in that region did not fly at night or in bad weather, ignored emergency requests to adjust artillery fire or carry out visual reconnaissance, and responded slowly to requests for immediate air strikes, though their work was adequate once they arrived on the scene.[39] In Military Region II, reported Army Lt. Gen. Arthur B. Collins, Jr., the effectiveness of the South Vietnamese forward air controllers was "marginal," primarily due to a limited number of aircraft and crews, dependence for maintenance support on the permanent base at Nha Trang, and reluctance to fly missions in poor weather or during darkness.[40] Similarly, in Military Region III, Lt. Gen. Michael S. Davison, commander of II Field Force, Vietnam, declared that forward air control formed "the weak link in the tactical air control system chain," largely because South Vietnamese pilots lacked the initiative shown by Air Force controllers in conducting visual reconnaissance.[41]

As the South Vietnamese forward air controllers increased in number, though improving less rapidly in skill and dedication, more O–1s were entering service. Consequently, the South Vietnamese Air Force tried to find a useful

Continued Growth of South Vietnam's Air Force

A South Vietnamese cadet pilot at Nha Trang after his first solo flight.

role for the U–17, being supplanted by the Bird Dog as an observation plane and by the T–41 as a trainer. A logical solution seemed to be reassignment of the U–17 to psychological warfare duty, but here the plane proved of little value. Its sixty-watt alternator could not provide power enough for a satisfactory loudspeaker, and a mere handful of hundred-watt replacements were available.[42]

While South Vietnam's inventory of observation craft was changing, American participation in the tactical air control network within Military Region IV came to an end. After a formal ceremony held at Can Tho on August 31, 1970, the South Vietnamese Air Force exercised complete authority, manning the IV Direct Air Support Center and providing air liaison officers, tactical air control parties, and forward air controllers. The only U.S. Air Force officers still assigned to the tactical air control mechanism in this military region were five advisers serving temporarily with the South Vietnamese air liaison officers.[43]

Certain problems persisted after the transfer of responsibility in Military Region IV. South Vietnamese forward air controllers, for example, tended to flock together at Binh Thuy instead of operating from air strips nearer the scene of combat. The forward airfields proved unattractive because they lacked not only revetments for aircraft but also mess facilities and living quarters for the crews that flew them. Nor was the South Vietnamese air arm yet appointing experienced pilots to serve as air liaison officers. The job tended to go to nonfliers, junior in rank, who impressed neither the forward air controllers nor the ground commanders. Equipment as well as attitudes caused difficulty, for the older O–1s still in use over the delta carried obsolete radios with limited range and a restricted choice of channels.[44]

Increased cockpit time, such as South Vietnamese pilots were logging over the delta, seemed to result in safer flying. The accident rate for 1970 throughout all of South Vietnam declined by some 20 percent from the previous year, but the lower ratio of 11.4 accidents per 100,000 flying hours remained roughly two and one-half times the U.S. Air Force figure. The improvement during 1970 represented a sharp decline in accidents involving observation and utility aircraft; fighter and helicopter pilots flew no more safely than they had the year before.[45]

Although South Vietnamese flight proficiency appeared to be improving, if unevenly, some senior U.S. Army officers had reservations about the combat effectiveness of South Vietnam's air arm. General Cushman, for example, acknowledged that the South Vietnamese were "doing a reasonably effective job and slowly getting better" but tempered his endorsement by warning that the organization was "a long way from the standards of motivation, commitment to mission, and dedication to support of the soldier on the ground" characteristic of similar Air Force and Army units.[46] Although Lt. Gen. James W. Sutherland maintained that South Vietnamese airmen had "shown steady improvement" in the northern provinces,[47] General Collins gave South Vietnam's air force an overall rating of "marginal," citing the inadequacies of its forward air controllers, as well as its limited inventory of aircraft and its inability to fight at night.[48]

Air Force advisers rendered more optimistic judgments, however, pointing out that the fighter and attack squadrons had performed well during the Cambodian fighting. Indeed, by year's end, South Vietnamese airmen were flying almost half the combined total of attack sorties in South Vietnam and Cambodia.[49] Progress, moreover, was being made toward early activation of more A-1 and A-37 squadrons, although the A-37 was handicapped by a combat radius of no more than 200 miles. A few F-5 pilots were undergoing training in ground controlled aerial interception, and the air arm was increasing the emphasis on nighttime operations.[50]

Although inability to fight at night or in bad weather remained the gravest weakness of South Vietnamese fliers, training was beginning to produce encouraging results. By the autumn of 1970, some 56 percent of South Vietnam's fighter-bomber pilots had demonstrated the ability to deliver a night attack on a target illuminated by a flareship. Also, the A-37s and A-1s were starting to receive flare dispensers of their own so that nighttime operations were no longer dependent on the few C-47s available to drop flares. Some strike pilots, flying the A-1s or A-37s with the necessary radar transponder, learned to drop bombs on signal from a Combat Skyspot operator on the ground, but this was a stopgap aid to night attack, since the Strategic Air Command was not scheduled to hand over the radar sets to the South Vietnamese.[51]

Despite the growing insistence on night flying, forward air controllers logged fewer nighttime hours than the fighter pilots. This imbalance stemmed at least in part from the fact that the U-17s and older O-1s being flown by the South Vietnamese lacked adequate instrumentation and suitable cockpit lighting

Continued Growth of South Vietnam's Air Force

for operating in darkness. To prepare the South Vietnamese forward air controllers for the better equipped O–1Es and Gs that were becoming available, American pilots were giving nighttime familiarization flights in the right-hand seat of the O–2A.[52]

Strike pilots and forward air controllers were thus beginning to fight in darkness, but the AC–47 remained South Vietnam's most dependable weapon for night combat. The gunship crews used a night-vision scope, but it was handheld, instead of pivoting on a stable mount. Advances had been made, but greater strides were necessary if South Vietnamese airmen were to overcome their reluctance, largely the result of inexperience and gaps in training, to fight after dusk.[53]

Like the fighter squadrons, helicopter units revealed certain weaknesses even as they were meeting the challenge of the 1970 Cambodian fighting. For example, the helicopter force forfeited much of its mobility by relying exclusively on fixed maintenance facilities instead of deploying mechanics to operating locations in the field. Also, the general inability to fly at night handicapped medical evacuation, since casualties sometimes could not be picked up in daylight from units closely engaged with the enemy.[54]

Perhaps the most successful aspect of the year's helicopter program was the rapid creation of a gunship force for assault operations, which usually took place in daylight. A U.S. Air Force mobile training team arrived in South Vietnam on March 31 to begin teaching, in collaboration with Army aviators, the tactical use of the UH–1 fitted out as a gunship. The South Vietnamese apparently proved apt pupils, for on May 29, before the second class of thirty-two students had graduated, South Vietnam's air force mounted its first helicopter assault. Eight troop-carrying UH–1s, another serving as a command post, and three others equipped as gunships successfully landed a small force near Prey Veng, Cambodia.[55]

The unusual status of the helicopter units, elements of the air arm but serving the Army almost exclusively, continued to cause problems. Corps and division commanders had come to expect the kind of support provided by a massive American helicopter fleet, apparently forgetting that U.S. Army aviators had roughly twenty times the number of these aircraft available to South Vietnamese airmen. Even though the Vietnamized helicopter force would eventually exceed 500 craft, this final total would represent little more than one-sixth of the Army's 1970 fleet. Caught between increasing demand, as the republic's ground forces grew more active, and continuing U.S. withdrawals, which had caused a reduction of almost 350 in General Abrams' helicopter strength during 1970, South Vietnamese squadrons pushed their equipment harder, ignoring scheduled maintenance so that as many aircraft as possible would be on the flight line.[56]

Besides revealing strains within the helicopter program, the year's events exerted pressure on South Vietnamese transport units. Pilots of the old but still

Air War over South Vietnam, 1968–1975

South Vietnamese UH–1 helicopters loading troops for an air assault.

useful C–119s began training to fly the gunship version of that plane, and men qualified in the C–47 were about to begin their transition to the newer C–123K, with its auxiliary jet engines. Sparsely manned to begin with, the two existing airlift squadrons had to carry out their usual duties while furnishing trainees for the new gunships and transports. Because of the need for more transports, the advisory group and the air arm's headquarters drew up plans to hasten the activation of two C–123K squadrons, equipped with planes transferred from U.S. Air Force units. The K models would commence operation by mid-1971, six months ahead of schedule. Two squadrons of C–7s, also from U.S. Air Force resources in South Vietnam, would round out the projected airlift force by July 1972.[57]

This planned airlift fleet did not satisfy Vice President Ky, who argued for the addition of a squadron of C–130s. Secretary of the Air Force Robert C. Seamans, Jr., visited South Vietnam in February 1970 and was impressed with Ky's reasoning. The Hercules transport, as Ky pointed out, could carry more cargo than any of the types his nation would receive. A C–130, after all, had five times the cargo capacity of a C–7 or roughly three times that of the C–123K or C–119G. A study by the Air Force advisory group concluded that a combination of C–7s and C–130s could better meet the needs of the South Vietnamese than the planned combination of C–123s and C–7s. The C–123s, however, would soon become surplus to American needs and already were based in South Vietnam. Ease of transfer provided, for the present, a decisive argument in favor of the jet-augmented Fairchilds, and many months would pass before the South Vietnamese Air Force finally received C–130s.[58]

The intelligence and reconnaissance aspects of Vietnamizing the air arm made progress during 1970, but self-sufficiency in these specialties lay far in

Continued Growth of South Vietnam's Air Force

the future. Although plans called for South Vietnamese technicians to establish a photo exploitation center at Tan Son Nhut in April, the persons assigned to train there did not receive security clearances in time. Not until May 2 did the first contingent — thirty-six photo processors and eight photo interpreters — begin training alongside their U.S. Air Force counterparts at the 12th Reconnaissance Intelligence Technical Squadron. By the end of July, South Vietnamese photo exploitation specialists had dispensed with the American instructors and begun operating on their own, and early in September an American-administered proficiency test verified that South Vietnamese airmen could use any piece of equipment found in the U.S. Air Force squadron.[59]

Meanwhile, South Vietnam's air arm had received the first two of six RF–5 reconnaissance planes. In mid-August, South Vietnamese technicians at the exploitation center processed and interpreted film from these aircraft, thus foreshadowing Vietnamization of this form of aerial reconnaissance. The remaining four RF–5s arrived in time for the reconnaissance unit to begin functioning on October 15. At year's end, therefore, South Vietnam's air service possessed the nucleus of a tactical air intelligence operation.[60]

Absent from South Vietnam's aerial intelligence array were certain specialized devices like the infrared sensors mounted on the latest U.S. Air Force gunships or the radio-direction-finding gear in the EC–47. The Joint Chiefs of Staff had suggested the early activation of an EC–47 squadron — handing over four planes by July 1971, six more by July 1972, and the final ten by July 1973 — instead of waiting to assign the entire complement of twenty aircraft during the year ending on June 30, 1973, but nothing came of this plan. For the time being at least, Generals Abrams, Clay, and Nazzaro agreed that to disrupt the current training schedule to obtain EC–47 crews would interfere with the manning of the C–123Ks, C–7s, and AC–119Gs.[61]

Although North Vietnamese airmen had not yet attacked targets in the South, the Air Force advisory group was helping prepare the foundation for a South Vietnamese air defense system. Eventually, F–5 interceptors, armed with missiles and cannon, would take their place in South Vietnam's aerial armada. Until these aircraft arrived and radar operators learned to control them from the ground, the South Vietnamese would practice with surveillance and traffic control radars which could provide warning of an aerial attack but were, at best, marginally useful in directing interceptions.[62]

Even as it trained for air defense and other kinds of aerial warfare, the South Vietnamese Air Force gained skill in maintenance and logistics management. However, whether a member of the Air Force or a civilian employed by a contractor like Lear Sigler, the American instructor teaching maintenance subjects had to avoid becoming a crutch upon which the students could lean. Col. J. R. Lilley urged his advisory team, which specialized in maintenance training, "to show them how, and assist them, but to let them do the actual work themselves."[63]

Air War over South Vietnam, 1968–1975

Americans, however, were not the only persons capable of teaching how to maintain aircraft and related equipment. More than 200 South Vietnamese had returned from schools in the United States fully qualified to teach the servicing and repair of such complex items as jet and piston engines, radios, and aircraft instruments. Unfortunately, in applying the lessons of the instructors, the freshly trained South Vietnamese mechanics faced two handicaps. The first, a shortage of shop space, which would be resolved as U.S. units vacated the air bases in South Vietnam. The second, a tendency to replace rather than repair defective components, could be corrected only through time, patient persuasion on the part of the teachers, and a growing awareness of the importance of the job.[64]

South Vietnamese airmen were performing extensive maintenance on an increasing variety of aircraft, though some work continued to be done outside South Vietnam or by contractors in the country. The South Vietnamese UH–1 helicopters, for instance, underwent periodic inspection and repair in the United States, and C–47s received the same treatment on Taiwan. Also, mechanics employed by Air Vietnam, a commercial carrier, strengthened the wings of some A–1s to correct the ravages of corrosion.[65]

Army mechanics provided on-the-job training for the South Vietnamese airmen responsible for keeping the recently acquired CH–47 helicopters in flying condition, and the U.S. Air Force was training thirty-one of its technicians to take over this instructional responsibility from the soldiers. As a result, an Air Force team would instruct the maintenance specialists for the second CH–47 squadron, which was scheduled to be activated in the spring of 1971.[66]

Although maintenance and maintenance training showed signs of progress, logistics management encountered an unexpected problem, that resulted from the invasion of Cambodia. Early in that fighting, the C–119Gs had to be shifted from logistics courier missions within South Vietnam to carry cargo across the border. As a consequence, South Vietnamese commanders could no longer rely on a one-day response to requests for critically needed parts or supplies, but an Air Force C–123 from the 834th Air Division was available in an extreme emergency to deliver the needed items.[67]

Perhaps the most promising logistics accomplishment of 1970 was the South Vietnam Air Logistics Command's automation of inventory control. In December 1969, Gen. John D. Ryan, Air Force Chief of Staff, decided to make a UNIVAC 1050-II computer available to the South Vietnamese Air Force. By mid-summer, the Logistics Command had established computerized control over its entire inventory and could match requests with existing stocks and determine remaining supply levels. In addition, South Vietnamese computer operators could screen items declared surplus by the Seventh Air Force and identify those needed by the logistics command.[68]

However long the road that lay ahead, the South Vietnamese Air Force had made discernible progress during 1970. The aircrews seemed well trained and eager to carry out the orders of their leaders. Indeed, General Young believed

Continued Growth of South Vietnam's Air Force

Maj. Gen. Tran Van Minh, commander of the South Vietnamese Air Force.

that Maj. Gen. Tran Van Minh, who commanded the air arm, possessed a combination of "wisdom, patience, and leadership" that inspired among his subordinates "a profound respect for his abilities, almost bordering on a god-like reverence." As for the wing and squadron commanders who displayed this attitude of near adoration, Young revised a poor first impression, formed by comparing them to their American counterparts, and now considered them the best officers available to the South Vietnamese Air Force.[69]

Even though they may well have been the best available, these South Vietnamese commanders either lacked faith in their own ability or did not enjoy the complete confidence of their air force's headquarters, perhaps both. Whatever the root cause, wing and squadron leaders tended to shift decision-making to higher levels of command on matters clearly their own responsibility. The situation would not likely be corrected until junior officers gained greater experience and their seniors realized the necessity of delegating authority so the younger men could mature professionally.[70]

In addition, the South Vietnamese had barely begun to appreciate the value of frequent inspections for measuring progress. An officer's periodic submission to another's evaluation, or conducting such a review, seemed alien to a military hierarchy in which performance, status, and self-esteem were tightly intertwined. This attitude seemed to be a manifestation of what Young called "the Oriental mind," a code of behavior that emphasized patience and formal courtesy in personal dealings and contrasted sharply with the "can do" spirit of an American military given to making brusque on-the-spot corrections.[71]

Other handicaps facing the South Vietnamese, and not always understood by American advisers, resulted from diet and physical stature. Lifting loaded boxes or similar work that was simple enough for the average American could prove too much for a comparatively frail South Vietnamese. If called upon to perform such a task, a South Vietnamese might be reluctant to refuse, even though he knew he would fail. His solution to such a dilemma might well be simply to pretend not to understand, a reaction guaranteed to contribute to the myth that all South Vietnamese were either stupid or lazy.[72]

Thus far, financial problems encountered by the government of South Vietnam had not impaired the expansion and re-equipping of the air arm, but the future seemed uncertain. Although the 1970 budget for the air arm increased by 36 percent over 1969, a further increase of 44 percent for 1971 would have to be reduced to 10 percent or less. Funds requested for training in fiscal 1971 would absorb about half the reduction, thus deferring the impact on day-to-day operations until skilled individuals, already in short supply, became desperately needed.

General Young offered several suggestions designed, the South Vietnamese budget permitting, to improve training in their air force. First, if the air arm were to achieve self-sufficiency, it would have to conduct its own undergraduate pilot training. Second, South Vietnamese instructors would have to assume complete responsibility for imparting technical skills, conducting both classroom training and providing broad opportunities to learn on the job. Third, South Vietnam's air force would have to establish and enforce training standards so that an instructor at Nha Trang covered the same points as a person teaching the identical subject at Tan Son Nhut. Once standardization had been achieved, an airman could emerge from school, join an aviation unit, and demonstrate a predictable level of skill.[73]

Although much remained to be done if the South Vietnamese Air Force were to attain self-sufficiency, the organization had increased in size and sharpened its collective skill. Equally important, the officers and men appeared to be showing greater enthusiasm. To American eyes, they seemed more optimistic about South Vietnam's winning the war and surviving as a nation.[74] Yet, the possibility existed that improvement and modernization were proceeding on so broad a front that progress was illusory, not real. The South Vietnamese Air Force might be moving forward in many fields but achieving in too few the mastery that would be needed when the American squadrons completed their withdrawal.

Chapter Fourteen

Further Disengagement

While the consolidated improvement and modernization program took shape, the fighting in South Vietnam continued. The Hanoi government entered 1970 under a leadership coalition that had emerged after the death of Ho Chi Minh in the previous September. The eighty-one-year-old Ton Duc Thang, who had taken over the ceremonial post of chief of state, and the others — Le Duan, Pham Van Dong, and Vo Nguyen Giap — who shared control in the North had not abandoned the ultimate goal of a Vietnam united under communist rule.[1]

As the new year began, supply lines passing through southern Laos and from Sihanoukville through eastern Cambodia sustained communist military activity in South Vietnam. The initiative still lay with the enemy. Although he did not seem strong enough to repeat the Tet offensive of 1968, he could deploy his forces for simultaneous attacks on a few key objectives, possibly in all four military regions.

American intelligence felt that scattered attacks in South Vietnam were all but inevitable, for North Vietnam had to challenge the Vietnamization program and attempt to disrupt the apparently successful pacification of the countryside, and the new rulers at Hanoi could not stand by while South Vietnam gathered strength. On the other hand, it seemed unlikely in January 1970 that they could take advantage of war weariness in the United States, since American forces were pulling out, thus appeasing critics of the nation's involvement in Southeast Asia.[2] Before North Vietnam launched the anticipated attacks, however, President Nixon carried the war into Cambodia, wiping out the logistics base for widespread enemy activity but stirring up renewed antiwar activism.

The attack into Cambodia represented a logical extension of existing U.S. policy. The invasion, after all, exerted additional pressure on a North Vietnamese regime that had thus far resisted every attempt to force it to negotiate, and fruitful bargaining remained Nixon's principal objective. Even as he sought peace through negotiation, the President embarked on Vietnamization, strengthening South Vietnamese forces to take over the war and permit the withdrawal of U.S. troops, thus reducing casualties and depriving critics of their most powerful issue. Initially, Nixon had hoped to adjust the rate of withdrawal to

Air War over South Vietnam, 1968–1975

reflect the level of enemy activity and the increasing competence of the South Vietnamese, but the reduction in strength gathered momentum as the months passed, assuming an existence of its own quite apart from events in South Vietnam or at the conference table in Paris.[3]

In January 1970, however, the Cambodian incursion lay some four months in the future. Authorized American strength in South Vietnam stood at 484,000, the result of a 65,000-man reduction during 1969. To help substitute firepower for the combat troops who had departed, the Seventh Air Force could muster in Southeast Asia a total of 672 fighter-bombers, attack planes, and gunships, while the Navy operated 135 strike aircraft and the Marine Corps, 130. The immediate problem facing President Nixon was how to honor a promise, made in December 1969, to withdraw an additional 50,000 men from South Vietnam by the middle of April. Tentative plans put the Air Force share of this reduction at some 5,600 men, slightly in excess of 10 percent of the projected departures. The possibility of another enemy offensive timed to coincide with the Tet holiday caused postponement of the departures until late February, but once begun, the cuts proceeded swiftly despite the overthrow of Prince Sihanouk in March and Lon Nol's challenge to the North Vietnamese.[4]

The prospect of these Seventh Air Force reductions troubled General Brown, for he stood to lose an entire fighter wing, three squadrons of fairly modern F–4Cs based at Cam Ranh Bay. He maintained that commanders like himself should be able in these circumstances to tailor their own forces, giving up the least essential units, sacrificing numbers but retaining firepower. In the case of the fighter wing, however, its numbers were few — less than 1,000 men in the entire organization — but its firepower was both devastating and versatile.[5]

Brown could not retain the F–4s, but to compensate in part for the sacrifice of firepower, he received an AC–119K gunship unit, which lacked the versatility of the fighter-bombers. In addition, his Seventh Air Force at this time sacrificed a tactical reconnaissance squadron that had flown RF–4Cs from Tan Son Nhut Air Base. Also withdrawn by mid-April were several support units of varying size and importance. The largest and probably the most useful of these were two 400-man civil engineering squadrons, which maintained runways and buildings at air bases, and a field maintenance unit of comparable size that made routine repairs to aircraft. The departures in the spring of 1970, together with routine transfers of individuals whose tours had ended, pared actual Air Force strength in South Vietnam from 57,500 in January to 52,000 at the end of April.[6]

During discussions of yet another withdrawal, a reduction below the April figure of 434,000, two conflicting viewpoints emerged — one advocated by Secretary Laird, the other by General Abrams and the Joint Chiefs of Staff. The Secretary of Defense wanted to continue bringing large numbers of troops home from South Vietnam, aiming for a force level of roughly 260,000 by mid-1971,

Further Disengagement

a reduction of about 174,000 from the April 15 total. In suggesting such a course, he cited political and fiscal reality — a disenchantment with the war that seemed widespread even in the weeks before the Kent State killings, and an acute budget crisis that had already brought on the Project 703 cuts in military expenditures.[7]

The opposing view arose from military considerations — especially Lon Nol's defiance of North Vietnamese power — which, in General Abrams' opinion, "seldom, if ever, more clearly justified the maintenance of the strongest U.S. posture in [South Vietnam]."[8] The Joint Chiefs of Staff agreed with him, insisting that withdrawals follow a "cut and try" principle, with a pause after each reduction to determine the enemy's reaction. The Chiefs warned that the April 15 force level should remain firm for the time being and advised the administration to avoid public commitment to a series of specific cuts stretching far into the future.[9]

The decision rested, however, with President Nixon, who sought a compromise between military and political considerations. On April 20, 1970, he told the nation, "We have now reached a point where we can confidently move from a period of 'cut and try' to a longer range program for the replacement of Americans by South Vietnamese troops." Yet, even as he rejected one piece of advice from his Joint Chiefs, he accepted another, establishing a general goal rather than listing an exact sequence of reductions. "I am ... announcing," Nixon declared ten days before the Cambodian incursion, "plans for the withdrawal of 150,000 American troops to be completed during the spring of next year ....The timing and pace of these new withdrawals ... will be determined by our best judgement of the current military and diplomatic situation."[10]

According to Secretary Laird, the President had chosen to focus on just one aspect of the total military and diplomatic situation — reported progress in Vietnamization. The talks at Paris and enemy activity in South Vietnam might to some degree influence the details of the withdrawal, but regardless of these factors the departures would continue as long as South Vietnamese forces were improving, with as many as 60,000 American troops leaving the country by the end of 1970. Such a plan had obvious drawbacks, however, from the military point of view. Not only did it establish an interim goal in reaching the objective the President had announced, it tended to divorce force levels from conditions on the battlefield and concentrated 90,000 departures into the period from January through May 1971, a time of year when the enemy had mounted Tet attacks and spring offensives. In short, political considerations seemed to have prevailed.[11]

Preoccupation with events in Cambodia apparently delayed the beginning of detailed planning for this fourth withdrawal. Five days after the President's announcement, Admiral McCain was complaining that he had not "received any guidance from Washington on the directed reduction."[12] Finally, late in May, Secretary Laird issued instructions to "hold at the actual manpower levels that existed on April 30, 1970," until a plan could be devised. Because of the timing of individual reassignments, this decision meant that the number of men on duty in South Vietnam would remain slightly below the authorized 434,000.[13]

Even though the Cambodian campaign had already begun, President Nixon remained determined to make the cuts he had promised. On June 3, as he revealed that American ground troops would leave Cambodia at the end of the month, he repeated his pledge to withdraw 150,000 men by the spring of 1971 and added that one-third of the total would depart by October 15. The increment scheduled for the autumn of 1970 became phase IV in the program of troop reductions already under way. At the San Clemente meetings, where he outlined the aerial interdiction campaign that would begin in Cambodia after the U.S. ground units pulled out, the President discussed the 50,000-man intermediate withdrawal with Abrams, and Secretary Laird promptly issued instructions to meet the October deadline. The Secretary of Defense deferred a decision on the timing of the return of the remainder until funding levels had been decided for the fiscal year ending June 30, 1971.[14]

Next came the task of deciding what Air Force units would leave South Vietnam in phase IV. Concerned that he might lose two squadrons of F–4Ds — "the only first-line weapon system we had over there" — General Brown lodged a successful protest with the Air Force Chief of Staff, retaining the thirty-odd fighters and use of the base, Phu Cat, from which they operated.[15] He scarcely had time to savor this victory when he learned, in June, that General Nazzaro, assuming that Phu Cat was about to close, proposed to withdraw a detachment of six F–4Ds recently shifted there from Cam Ranh Bay. Nazarro intended to move the planes to Clark Air Base in the Philippines, where the detachment would form part of the general war emergency force[16], a proposed transfer that Brown found puzzling. It was, he told Nazzaro, "inconceivable ... that any contingency force ... be maintained at the expense of tactical air support of American ground forces in combat."[17] As a result, instead of to Clark, the planes went to Korat in Thailand, from which they could fly missions in Southeast Asia.[18]

General Brown thus retained his F–4Ds, but the phase IV withdrawals sharply reduced his fighter strength, which he considered the cutting edge of the aerial weapon. Among the units to leave South Vietnam were six squadrons of F–100Ds — the 355th, 306th, 307th, 308th, 309th, and 531st.[19] Weighing the comparative value of this plane and the newer F–4, General Brown concluded that sending the F–100s to the United States was "a sensible thing to do."[20]

When the previous reduction had ended — phase III, which reduced aggregate manpower to 434,000 in the spring of 1970 — Seventh Air Force included two A–37 squadrons in its fighter-bomber force. Now, one A–37B unit, the recently redesignated 8th Attack Squadron, was going out of existence, turning its aircraft over to the South Vietnamese. In addition, the 90th Attack Squadron, a fighter outfit before receiving its A–37Bs in 1969, became the 90th Special Operations Squadron and moved from Bien Hoa to Nha Trang. The loss of the

Further Disengagement

Airmen load 500-pound bombs on an F–4 at Phu Cat.

F–100s and transfer of the A–37s, changes that occurred after General Clay had assumed command of Seventh Air Force, cut the number of Air Force tactical fighter squadrons in South Vietnam from seventeen when phase III ended in April 1970 to nine at year's end.[21]

Nor were fighter squadrons the only units to inactivate, depart South Vietnam, or undergo redesignation. During the phase IV withdrawals, which ended in mid-October 1970, the number of reconnaissance squadrons in South Vietnam declined from five to four and transport units from ten to eight, with the number of C–130s dropping from seventy at the time of the incursion, peak strength for the year, to a mere forty-six. All four of the tactical air support squadrons, which furnished observation planes and forward air controllers supporting the ground war, remained in South Vietnam throughout the period, but the number of aircraft was reduced from 380 to 290, a change accomplished by transferring O–2s to the Air National Guard and O–1s to the South Vietnamese. From 1,100 in May 1970, the total number of Air Force planes in South Vietnam, excluding helicopters, declined to 855 in October when phase IV ended, with the number of officers and airmen dropping from 52,000 to 44,000.[22]

In transferring O–2As to the Air National Guard, Seventh Air Force mechanics separated wings from fuselage and loaded these components into the spacious cargo hold of the Douglas C–124 for the flight to the United States. First sent to South Vietnam to ferry in French reinforcements at the time of the Dien Bien Phu fighting, these slow, aging, piston-powered transports were giving way to a massive new jet, the Lockheed C–5A. The new aircraft, called the Galaxy, began service to Southeast Asia in July 1970 and would prove its worth during the buildup of South Vietnamese forces after the 1972 North Vietnamese invasion.[23]

Air War over South Vietnam, 1968–1975

The Air Force units eliminated during the phase IV redeployments included the 12th Special Operations Squadron, which had been spraying herbicide from its UC–123Ks. Since late 1969, enemy gunners had been scoring increasingly frequent hits on the spray planes, preventing them from operating unescorted in defended regions. Moreover, cuts in the Department of Defense budget had raised questions about the value of this program, compared with other aspects of the war effort. Although facing the prospect of a 30-percent fund reduction for buying and spraying herbicide, General Abrams sought to retain a project he considered militarily useful. He believed that spraying deprived the enemy of concealment and food crops and that the most efficient means of application was the UC–123. Without these planes, he would have to rely on helicopters, which lacked the range to destroy crops in distant communist strongholds, or hand-operated sprayers, effective only along roads or on the perimeter of fire support bases and other installations.[24]

General Abrams endorsed spraying and wanted to keep the UC–123s, but a new consideration doomed not only the spray planes but the entire herbicide effort. In the spring of 1970, evidence appeared linking an ingredient of agent orange, the herbicide most widely used in South Vietnam, to birth defects in humans. The results of tests on laboratory animals persuaded Secretary Laird to suspend use of this chemical compound. Still in use were agents white and blue, but neither was as effective as orange against as wide a variety of vegetation. Ironically, agent blue, an arsenic-base compound, had caused misgivings during earlier spraying, but it now proved less dangerous than orange, which had formerly seemed as safe as it was effective. Because white and blue were less versatile than orange, targets for defoliation dwindled rapidly, so that after the ban, the UC–123s flew some 60 percent fewer missions than before.[25]

The slower pace of aerial spraying permitted the inactivation, on July 31, 1970, of the 12th Special Operations Squadron. Only eight of the unit's specially modified spray planes remained in service, assigned to A Flight, 310th Tactical Airlift Squadron, and just six of these could actually fly herbicide missions, mainly the destruction of crops that fed the Viet Cong, while the other two dispensed insecticide as a public health measure. The flight undertook two crop destruction missions during July, encountering intense and accurate fire over both targets and sustaining eighty-nine hits on the spray aircraft that participated. As a result, the UC–123s received a flak suppression escort that reduced the average number of hits to just one on each of the eleven subsequent missions.[26]

In the summer of 1970, some six weeks before he left South Vietnam to take over Air Force Systems Command, General Brown conferred with other staff officers at assistance command headquarters concerning the employment of A Flight and its UC–123s. He came away suspecting that "rather than comply with the instructions of the Deputy Secretary of Defense [David Packard] to the JCS to keep the use of herbicides to an absolute minimum, it is the intention of

Further Disengagement

A flight of UC–123s spraying defoliant over South Vietnam.

the MACV staff to increase herbicide operations." Brown was never really convinced of the military value of herbicide and urged Abrams' chief of staff, Army Maj. Gen. Elias Townsend, to "get those staff officers . . . in hand," especially since agent orange had become so notorious.[27]

Whether or not Brown was correct in accusing them of deviousness, the staff officers he referred to could do no more than prolong the herbicide program into 1971. The prohibition against agent orange remained in effect, reducing the effectiveness of the spraying to the point that no more than five of the fifteen UC–123 missions scheduled each month were actually flown. Consequently, the commander of the 834th Air Division, Brig. Gen. John H. Herring, Jr., called for ending the program so he could remove the tanks and nozzles and use the planes to train crews for the C–123s the South Vietnamese Air Force was about to acquire. His logic proved irresistible. The herbicide mission flown on January 7, 1971, turned out to be the last of its kind; three days later Deputy Secretary Packard called a halt to crop destruction, ending Air Force aerial spraying. The subsequent herbicide activity, which lasted into the spring, consisted of spraying by hand or from helicopters to kill undergrowth and prevent the enemy from finding concealment along roads or near military installations.[28]

The 50,000-man phase IV reduction, which occasioned the reassignment of the UC–123s, had barely begun when Secretary Laird and the Joint Chiefs of Staff tackled the problem of determining how the remainder of the promised 150,000-man adjustment should be handled. President Nixon had intended that no more than 60,000 manpower spaces be eliminated between April and De-

Air War over South Vietnam, 1968–1975

Storage site in Gulfport, Mississippi, for herbicides removed from Vietnam.

cember 1970—phase IV, which ended in mid-October, plus another 10,000 men by year's end, a total acceptable to the Joint Chiefs and General Abrams. Budgetary pressures, however, made it impossible to defer the major portion of the promised 150,000-man cutback until 1971. Only a supplemental appropriation could preserve Nixon's original timetable—60,000 by December 31 and another 90,000 in the following spring—but Laird again made it clear to the military leadership that the administration would not seek the additional money, thus avoiding further Congressional criticism of Southeast Asia policy. As a result, the Joint Chiefs of Staff felt compelled to endorse a plan that reversed the President's earlier schedule, withdrawing 90,000 by the end of 1970 and the remaining 60,000 in the spring of 1971.[29]

The obviously reluctant endorsement of this plan to withdraw an additional 30,000 men by year's end inspired Kissinger, acting perhaps for the record, to protest that the uniformed leaders had allowed budgetary constraints to outweigh strategic considerations.[30] The Chiefs then polled the commanders directing the war and, in effect, acknowledged that they had moved too swiftly. General Abrams described the original plan as "militarily . . . the only prudent redeployment program" and the Joint Chiefs-approved alternative as "a compromise . . . designed to accommodate imposed manpower and budget restraints."[31] Echoing Abrams' words, Admiral McCain warned that "budgetary and manpower limitations currently being experienced by the services" might well sever the relationship between American troop withdrawals and the progress of Vietnamization. Only if the administration were aware of this risk would he recom-

Further Disengagement

mend going ahead with the full reduction, the original 10,000 plus another 30,000 men.[32] Obviously, Nixon was willing to accept the risk, which he considered less dangerous than a renewed policy debate in Congress, so the only real question was which Air Force and other units would leave South Vietnam between October 15 and December 31, as part of a fifth phase.

The Air Force contribution to phase V proved to be small, 600 manpower spaces, including 100 unfilled vacancies. The largest element consisted of 245 members of the 45th Tactical Reconnaissance Squadron. A detachment of this unit, flying RF–101s out of Tan Son Nhut, was inactivated in November 1970, as did the parent organization at Misawa, Japan. Since the squadron headquarters had been in Japan, the total number of reconnaissance squadrons in South Vietnam remained unchanged at four, even though the aircraft declined with the departure of sixteen RF–101s from Tan Son Nhut, the last of their type in Southeast Asia. This change and the continuing transfer of O–1s to the South Vietnamese caused the number of Air Force planes assigned in South Vietnam to decrease by 36 to a year-end total of 819, while actual manpower strength dropped to 43,053.[33]

Secretary of the Air Force Seamans pointed out that the withdrawals of Seventh Air Force units had lacked balance during 1970. The number of fighter-bomber squadrons fell from twenty in January to just nine in December, a 55-percent cut, while the aggregate number of squadrons of all types dropped by about one third. Seamans, however, endorsed the decision to keep a large number of engineers, communications specialists, and other technicians in South Vietnam even though many of the strike units they supported had departed. The "seeming anomaly," he explained, stemmed from the policy of creating South Vietnamese combat squadrons that could quickly take over from Seventh Air Force fighter or attack units, while largely ignoring the necessary support base. Until the emphasis in Vietnamization changed, and support caught up with combat units, South Vietnam's air arm would need U.S. Air Force electronics technicians and base maintenance and operations specialists.[34]

Besides taking up the slack for the departing Seventh Air Force fighter-bombers, the South Vietnamese Air Force had to replace Marine aviation units leaving Military Region I. The number of Marine Corps aircraft, both fixed- and rotary-wing, declined by 50 percent during 1970 to slightly more than 200. The Marine squadrons recalled from South Vietnam included one of CH–46D helicopters, two of F–4B fighter-bombers, and one of A–6A attack planes.[35]

Even as the Air Force units based in South Vietnam were giving up some 250 planes, those in Thailand underwent a similar retrenchment. In both countries, a principal motive for the cuts was to ease the budget crisis that had arisen in 1969, but within a year, reductions become inextricably interwoven with President Nixon's efforts to turn the war over to a strengthened South Vietnam. Although actions tied to Vietnamization and those inspired by the shortage of funds tended to merge, as in the phaseout of the F–100s, the administration's monetary woes were usually manifested in withdrawals from Thailand, rather than from South Vietnam, and in limitations on combat sorties.

The year 1970 had barely begun when Secretary Laird realized that financial pressures would force tactical sortie rates below the level of 14,000 per month established the previous September. Since the Nixon administration had decided against seeking supplemental appropriations, the aerial effort would have to be scaled down. The Secretary of Defense complained that he stood alone in seeking to save money by reducing sorties and, in consequence, the consumption of fuel and munitions. Arrayed against him were General Abrams, Admiral McCain, and the Joint Chiefs of Staff, all of whom advocated continuing the air war at the existing level.[36]

Actually, Secretary Laird had some uniformed allies, especially in the Air Force. By the time senior Air Force leaders met early in 1970 at Ramey Air Force Base, in Puerto Rico, the reality of the budget squeeze had taken hold. If the financial ceiling remained firm, as Laird had vowed, the Air Force could not sustain the air war at current levels without diverting money from needed modernization projects. Gen. John C. Meyer, the Vice Chief of Staff, told Generals Brown and Nazzaro, "obviously, the Chief [General Ryan] is loathe to deny you ... any bedrock requirement for protecting your forces"; yet, in the event of overemphasis on Southeast Asia, "we all know that vital Air Force modernization and improvement programs will go down the drain."[37]

General Brown understood the problem facing the Air Force Chief and offered appropriate suggestions. "Were I in the Chief's position," said Brown, "I would resist mortgaging [Air Force] futures to finance MACV/CINCPAC program requirements, since [Air Force] modernization and force structure are of greater importance to the nation, in my opinion." As for the air war in South Vietnam, Brown felt that his Seventh Air Force was adequate "for today's war," though he could not judge whether it would be "too much for tomorrow — and by how much." At issue was the degree of risk that General Abrams would have to take. "If dollars rule," Brown declared, "then the U.S. must accept a bigger risk."[38]

The level of risk that the Nixon administration was willing to take came to be symbolized by a number — 10,000 — the ceiling that Secretary Laird wanted to impose on monthly sorties by Air Force tactical aircraft. Secretary Seamans agreed that cuts in ammunition expenditure and fuel consumption, and therefore in combat sorties, were essential if the Air Force was to have funds for projects of greater value to national security — like nuclear deterrence — than the ongoing operations in Southeast Asia. Seamans found the reductions acceptable in principle because he believed that improved weapons, such as the AC–130 gunship now attacking enemy road traffic in southern Laos, would enable the Seventh Air Force to achieve the same level of destruction with fewer sorties.[39]

General Meyer went further than Secretary Seamans, declaring that reductions were possible not just in tactical sorties but in other air operations, as well.

Further Disengagement

Tactics adopted during the previous year for B–52s would, he maintained, enable 1,200 sorties to do the work of 1,400, for an expansion of tandem targeting had created several areas within which bombers could be diverted to various targets. Fewer U.S. troops, he further reasoned, would require fewer Air Force airlift sorties, with South Vietnamese fliers taking over air transport just as they were assuming responsibility for fighter-bomber activity. Meyer also argued that aerial interdiction of supply lines within South Vietnam was accomplishing so little that this category of tactical sortie could be cut back. Finally, he resurrected an argument, refuted earlier by General Brown, that strikes against a suspected enemy presence, whether a defensive position or a bivouac, represented a waste of bombs.[40] The Vice Chief of Staff obviously did not share Brown's belief that attacks on suspected positions produced benefits in terms of harassing the enemy or frustrating his plans, thus reducing friendly casualties.

Nor was General Meyer the only person to question once again the value of bombing suspected locations of hostile forces. During discussions of the 10,000-per-month ceiling on tactical sorties, Dr. Kissinger nominated this category of operations as a potential source of reductions,[41] and a study produced within the Air Force Directorate of Plans took a similar position. This document criticized the "big war mentality" that resulted in an excessive use of air power, especially against places the enemy was merely suspected of occupying.[42]

During 1969, General Brown had conceded that air power was being overused in reconnaissance, psychological warfare, and the application of herbicides, even as he successfully defended the need for fighter-bombers capable of attacking both known and suspected enemy concentrations. Facing the near certainty of a reduction in Seventh Air Force tactical sorties to 10,000 per month for all of Southeast Asia, Brown warned against allowing the total number of fighter-bomber squadrons in South Vietnam and Thailand, which had fallen to twenty-nine after the departure of the F–4Cs from Cam Ranh Bay, to decline to the projected low of just twenty-one. He urged the retention in Southeast Asia of twenty-six squadrons, a force that could fly 10,000 sorties per month and have the ability to surge beyond this level in case of emergency. Abrams backed his deputy for air operations, but their arguments could not overcome pressures to save money by withdrawing squadrons from South Vietnam and Thailand.[43]

By the end of 1970, the number of fighter-bomber squadrons had dwindled not to twenty-one, but to eighteen, divided equally between South Vietnam and Thailand. Recalled from the Thai air bases during the year were all the F–105 units except the one that flew the two-place Wild Weasels, aircraft that were configured to detect radars controlling antiaircraft weapons and launch missiles that homed on the source of the electronic transmissions. The eight other units in Thailand operated F–4Ds or Es. Besides these nine, a recently arrived light bomber squadron also operated from Thailand, using specially equipped B–57s to locate and attack trucks traveling the roads of southern Laos.[44]

Although the administration during the spring of 1970 agreed on a monthly

Air War over South Vietnam, 1968–1975

The B–57G, designed for night interdiction, had forward looking radar, low-light TV, infra-red sensors, and a laser range-finder installed in the forward fuselage, but did not perform well in Southeast Asia.

ceiling of 10,000 Air Force tactical sorties in Southeast Asia, Nixon and Kissinger specified that the reductions not take effect until the end of July, one month after U.S. troops had left Cambodia. As that time approached, a consensus emerged that a maximum of 14,000 sorties was possible, taking into account the budget and all the services capable of conducting tactical air strikes.[45] This monthly total was apportioned among the services, with the Air Force, as anticipated, flying 10,000 sorties, down 4,000 from the previous authorization, the Navy 2,700, and the Marine Corps 1,300. Secretary Laird specified that these figures were ceilings, rather than objectives or averages, suggesting that units in Southeast Asia fly fewer sorties in times of bad weather or enemy inactivity and surge to the maximum number only when circumstances demanded. In addition, Seventh Air Force AC–130 gunships would fly no more than 1,000 sorties each month against the Ho Chi Minh Trail; if increased truck traffic on the roads of southern Laos required additional gunship patrols, the necessary sorties could be borrowed from the tactical-fighter authorization.[46]

The President approved this plan on August 12, and almost immediately Admiral McCain, General Abrams, and General Brown (succeeded on September 1 by General Clay), the three American commanders most closely involved, began seeking permission to continue the practice of carrying over for future use any tactical sorties authorized for a given month but not actually flown. In July, the final month during which the Seventh Air Force had been authorized 14,000 tactical sorties, Brown's airmen had flown just 9,000, and in August, under the new rules announced for fiscal year 1971, they totaled just 8,700. These three officers proposed the creation of a sortie bank where the excess — for

Further Disengagement

example, July's 5,000 Air Force tactical sorties and August's 1,300 — could be deposited for subsequent withdrawal in time of emergency.[47]

This attempt to preserve flexibility in sortie allocation failed. The Air Force, Marine Corps, and Navy continued to be authorized a total of 14,000 tactical sorties per month, and, as Admiral Moorer, Chairman of the Joint Chiefs of Staff, acknowledged, "the intent of the decision was to fly at an average as close to 10,000 sorties as the military situation will permit, and not to exceed 14,000 in any one month." In an emergency such as an invasion of Military Region I, however, Moorer had Secretary Laird's promise to cancel all sortie limitations. As for the borrowing of tactical sorties by the gunship force, the Secretary of Defense seemed to doubt that enough of these aircraft would be on hand during fiscal 1971 to fly 1,000 sorties in a given month. The likeliest source of additional aerial striking power would be an improved and expanded South Vietnamese Air Force.[48]

As 1970 drew to a close, Secretary Laird and the Joint Chiefs were looking ahead to a further reduction in tactical sorties during the fiscal year ending on June 30, 1972. Laird proposed 8,325 fighter-bomber and 450 gunship sorties each month, whereas the Chiefs held out for 10,000 by Air Force and Navy tactical aircraft and 450 by Air Force gunships. Two factors complicated any attempt to pare the current authorization — Marine aviation would complete its withdrawal during fiscal 1971 and, as Secretary Seamans pointed out, operational South Vietnamese squadrons could not accelerate sortie rates while at the same time providing cadres and instructors for the planned expansion. In these circumstances, the Secretary of Defense tentatively endorsed a monthly total of 10,200 tactical sorties (7,500 by the Air Force and 2,700 by the Navy) plus 700 by Air Force gunships.[49]

Meanwhile, B–52 activity also underwent curtailment for reasons of economy, despite the greater organizational stature conferred upon the bomber force based in the western Pacific. In April 1970, the 3d Air Division, with headquarters on Guam, had become the Eighth Air Force, a designation transferred from Westover Air Force Base, Massachusetts. In moving from air division commander to commander of an air force, General Gillem faced restrictions beyond those that already had reduced the B–52 sortie rate from a peak of 1,800 per month in 1968 to 1,600 in the summer of 1969 and 1,400 the following autumn. Before further cuts in bomber sorties came to pass, however, Gillem's force had to be tailored to reflect the already reduced commitment.[50]

Since New Year's Day, 1970, the Commander in Chief, Strategic Air Command, Gen. Bruce K. Holloway, had planned to recall twelve of the ninety bombers in the western Pacific, together with some 1,100 men, thus accomplishing three goals. Such a move would reduce General Gillem's force to a level more consistent with an authorization of 1,400 sorties per month, cut costs to help meet the Project 703 objective, and make additional B–52s available for the nuclear war plan. Because repairs to the runway at U-Tapao prevented an increase in operations from that base to take up the slack caused by the projected withdrawal, only ten Guam-based bombers, rather than twelve, departed for the United States. The move was completed on April 15, after the 3d Air Division had become the Eighth Air Force.[51]

Throughout the remainder of the year, B–52 sorties diminished further, yielding to the same budgetary pressures that had slashed Air Force tactical sorties. As he had during the previous year's cuts in bomber activity, Abrams opposed the further reduction, declaring that "not only are further cuts in the sortie rate imprudent . . . the current rate is inadequate." Although conceding that recent tactical innovations, such as substituting three-plane strikes for attacks by formations of six B–52s, had enabled him "to more efficiently spend dwindling resources," he warned that three bombers simply were not "as effective against a given specified target as would be six."[52]

Despite Abram's objections, a B–52 sortie rate of 1,000 per month, or 33 per day, went into effect on August 17, 1970, using a force reduced to sixty-three bombers and seventy-seven crews. Each day, from its refurbished runways, U-Tapao launched 30 sorties, calling upon the thirty-eight bombers and forty-three crews based there. Kadena Air Base on Okinawa, with 10 B–52s and fifteen crews, contributed the other three. Because of the long distance involved and the resulting high fuel consumption, the fifteen bombers then based on Guam no longer flew strikes in Southeast Asia. By the end of August, General Holloway had succeeded in returning another sixteen B–52s to the United States for reassignment to the nuclear strike force. A further transfer of seven bombers became possible because the shorter distances flown from U-Tapao resulted in more frequent sorties. During September, moreover, the last strikes took off from Kadena, and the force based at U-Tapao, now forty-two bombers and fifty-two crews, assumed responsibility for the required 33 sorties per day.[53]

Other economies in B–52 operation went into effect during 1970. Until mid-September, planners had arbitrarily assigned combat air patrol and electronic countermeasures escort on the basis of whether the track of a planned bombing mission passed north of sixteen degrees, thirty minutes, north latitude. Careful study revealed, however, that only some 14 percent of the penetrations of this airspace actually came within range of North Vietnamese interceptors or radar-controlled antiaircraft weapons. As a result, each B–52 route that penetrated the danger zone now underwent an individual threat analysis, and the escort, if needed at all, was tailored to deal with the likely defenses, whether MiG fighters, surface-to-air missiles, or a combination of both. After three weeks using the new method, planners discovered they had reduced by 150 the number of escort sorties actually flown.[54]

The continuing reduction in tactical sorties, along with elimination of the long B–52 flight from Guam to Southeast Asia and back, enabled the Strategic Air Command to recall KC–135 tankers from Southeast Asia. The reductions began in the last six months of 1969, with the stabilization of Air Force activity

Further Disengagement

in Southeast Asia at 1,400 sorties each month by B–52s and 14,000 by tactical fighters. From eighty-five KC–135s in July 1969, the number dropped to sixty-six at the end of the year. After an increase early in 1970 to seventy-one planes and 115 crews, probably the result of the overlap between the arrival of replacement squadrons and the last of the departures, the number diminished rapidly to reflect the new levels of 1,000 B–52 and 10,000 Air Force fighter-bomber sorties. As 1970 drew to a close, forty-eight KC–135s, manned by seventy-seven crews, flew 43 sorties each day, most of them on aerial refueling missions, with a few devoted to radio relay or aerial reconnaissance.[55]

During this period of sortie reduction, the nature of tactical air operations in South Vietnam remained unchanged, with some 83 percent of fixed-wing sorties falling into categories — airlift, aerial attack, tactical reconnaissance, and combat support — identified with the support of ground forces. The tempo of the war within the country had slowed, however, as reflected by the overall decline from the previous year in total sorties, in sorties supporting ground forces, and in the sub-category of attack sorties.[56]

During 1970, a comparative calm descended on South Vietnam. The extension of the war into Cambodia shattered, at least temporarily, the logistics network that sustained enemy operations in southern South Vietnam; and violent weather in late October impeded military activity in the North. Three tropical storms lashed the coast from Cam Ranh Bay northward. The first forced the evacuation of all but the F–4Ds from Phu Cat and seemed headed for Da Nang, when it abruptly changed course. The second, however, passed directly over Da Nang, but did little harm. The third storm came ashore farther south, forcing the evacuation of Cam Ranh Bay and causing wind damage and flooding there and at Phu Cat. In every case, the destruction would have been worse, with probable loss of life, had it not been for an Air Force-operated forecasting service, linked to orbiting weather satellites, that General Westmoreland had established after a violent typhoon struck South Vietnam in the fall of 1965.[57]

Ground combat during 1970 had been sporadic in northern and east central South Vietnam even before the October storms struck. The North Vietnamese improved the depots and bases along the access routes from southern Laos, especially in the A Shau Valley, where they had to endure B–52 strikes and other harassment, but not the combination of aerial interdiction, artillery bombardment, and infantry assault of previous years. Communist troops initiated skirmishes along the demilitarized zone and attacked fire support bases like Ripcord and O'Reilly.[58]

The North Vietnamese lashed out first at Fire Support Base Ripcord. Since its establishment in April 1970 by a battalion from the 101st Airborne Division (Airmobile), this outpost had seen little action. On July 17, however, enemy gunners opened fire, infantry began closing in, and after five days of increasing pressure, the garrison withdrew by helicopter, as fighter-bombers attacked to cover the move.[59]

Air War over South Vietnam, 1968–1975

At Ripcord air power had proved valuable; at Fire Support Base O'Reilly it was decisive. Warning made the difference. A North Vietnamese lieutenant surrendered in mid-August and told of an impending assault against O'Reilly. Documents captured as far away as Da Nang described how Viet Cong throughout the region were mobilizing for this effort, confirming the defector's story.[60]

Alerted to the enemy's plans, General Sutherland, in whose XXIV Corps sector the base was located, obtained overpowering air support. For September 10, when the attack was expected, he received thirty preplanned tactical sorties against suspected troop concentrations and mortar sites, two B–52 strikes, and the promise of as many as twenty sorties by fighter-bombers diverted from other targets to the defense of Fire Support Base O'Reilly. The first day's tactical strikes would, weather permitting, be directed by forward air controllers, but predicted cloud cover seemed likely to force most of the fighter pilots to rely on Combat Skyspot radar.[61]

The aerial onslaught of September 10 served as a preview of the violence to come. Within eight days, B–52s carried out twenty-four strikes, dropping more than 1,550 tons of bombs, while 194 fighter-bombers added almost 550 tons to the deluge. Air power claimed an impressive amount of destruction in the bunkers and weapons' positions the enemy built for his ill-fated attack, but not even a rough estimate of the number killed was possible until late in the fighting. Appropriately, just as a defector had enabled Sutherland to arrange in advance for air strikes, a prisoner of war offered an insight into the results, declaring that air power had killed two-thirds of the soldiers in his 300- to 400-man battalion, and roughly 20 percent of the entire force marshalled for the operation.[62]

As it had become his practice in recent years, the enemy maintained pressure in 1970 on the special forces camps, now manned by South Vietnamese, in the northeastern reaches of Military Region II. In April, North Vietnamese forces threatened Dak Seang and Dak Pek. Almost 3,000 tactical fighter sorties hit targets near these camps, and twenty-three B–52s bombed the enemy around Dak Seang. Elsewhere in South Vietnam, the B–52s continued to serve as flying artillery, hitting enemy concentrations from Tay Ninh Province northwest of Saigon to the remote Seven Mountains redoubt in Military Region IV.[63]

Heavy fighting proved infrequent, but the combat that did erupt on the ground remained confined to the border regions of South Vietnam. The Viet Cong, however, continued to harass Seventh Air Force bases. Tan Son Nhut, a prime target of the 1968 Tet offensive, was unscathed through 1970, whereas three air bases not hit during the Tet battles of 1968 came under attack. These were Phu Cat, shelled four times; Phan Rang, hit eleven times by rockets or grenades; and Cam Ranh Bay, subjected to seven attacks.

The deadliest of the Phu Cat bombardments was the first, on February 1: ten 122-mm rockets killed one airman, wounded fifteen others, and also injured four soldiers. The body of one Viet Cong was discovered after the action. The

Further Disengagement

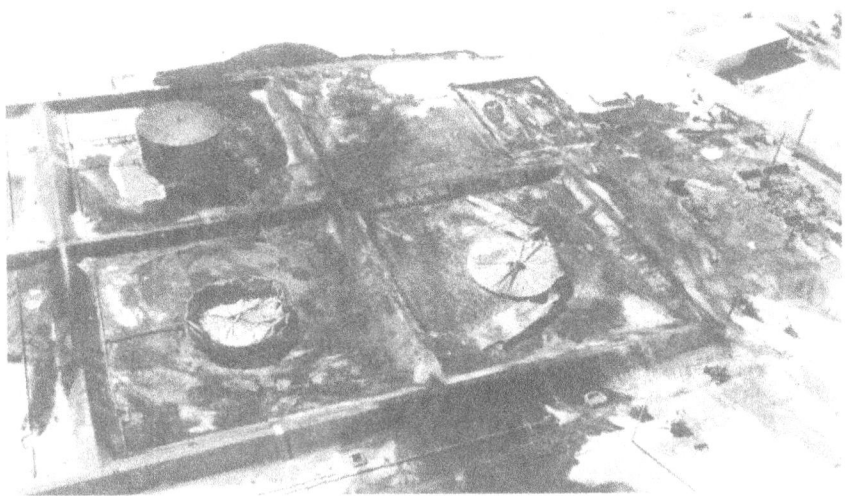

Fuel tanks at Cam Ranh Bay destroyed by rocket attacks in 1970.

subsequent shellings in May, October, and December wounded two men and damaged a C–7, along with other military equipment.

Besides the rocket attacks at Phan Rang— which killed two, wounded nine, and resulted in one injury indirectly related to the bombardment — Viet Cong sappers hit the base twice. On May 3, several teams attacked in conjunction with a mortar and rocket barrage, but the attempted penetration accomplished little, even though shrapnel wounded one airman and caused minor damage to Air Force facilities. Again, on the early morning of September 10, a handful of Viet Cong attacked near the main gate, wounding one South Vietnamese civilian and causing slight damage on the base.[64]

From the enemy's point of view, the most productive of the attacks on air installations occurred a few miles south of Cam Ranh Bay Air Base, when sappers destroyed 460,000 gallons of aviation fuel at an Army storage area.[65] The enemy also directed sapper teams, as well as mortar and rocket barrages, against the airfield itself. A total of nine Air Force men died in these attacks, while ten airmen and two sailors suffered wounds. Ironically, the most determined assault, an attempt on June 1 to break through a Navy-manned section of the base perimeter, resulted in only two Americans wounded, but a comparatively feeble rocket bombardment on December 1 killed three and wounded nine, when one of the missiles exploded in the galley of an officers' mess.[66]

Nha Trang, about fifteen nautical miles north of Cam Ranh Bay, underwent just one attack, but the results proved spectacular. Eleven rockets hit the base, wounding one man and igniting some 10,000 barrels of gasoline in a partially filled tank. Shell fragments punctured another storage tank, but the diesel fuel inside did not catch fire, and the leakage was limited to 3,000 gallons, not quite 10 percent of the contents. To replace the lost storage capacity, Seventh Air

Air War over South Vietnam, 1968–1975

Force delivered and erected a collapsible rubber bladder capable of holding 50,000 gallons of aviation fuel.[67]

Despite its comparatively exposed position, Pleiku airfield underwent only two attacks, both by 122-mm rockets. The first, on May 19, destroyed one EC–47, damaged two others, and an airman sprained his wrist diving for cover. During the second, just one week later, two airmen suffered wounds and two EC–47s, along with other equipment, sustained damage.

In the north, enemy gunners shelled Da Nang airfield five times, beginning on April 8. As at Phu Cat, the first attack was the worst, killing one airman and wounding six, while one Marine died and two were wounded. Four 140-mm rockets leveled a Marine barracks and damaged Air Force communications facilities. Other barrages in September, October, and December inflicted no Air Force casualties.

Bien Hoa, hard hit by the Tet offensive two years earlier, was the target of five attacks that killed two and wounded at least seventy-four. The bombardments also inflicted severe material damage: a shelling on January 21 damaged a C–123, a C–7, and a UH–1; and on February 27, rocket fragments tore into three A–37s, two F–100s, and a C–7.[68]

Despite the recurring hit-and-run raids and the occasional battle, the American disengagement continued, and the armed forces of South Vietnam soon launched their most ambitious offensive of the war. With a minimum of U.S. assistance — mostly from air power, including helicopters, and long-range artillery — an assault force would attack the Ho Chi Minh Trail in southern Laos, testing the success of Vietnamization and the wisdom of the withdrawals.

Chapter Fifteen

The South Vietnamese Invasion of Laos: Operation Lam Son 719

Planning began in November 1970 for Operation Lam Son 719, a campaign that tested not only the skills and tenacity of a particular South Vietnamese task force and its leaders, but the entire concept of Vietnamization. Admiral Moorer, the Chairman of the Joint Chiefs of Staff, started the process when he sought the views of Admiral McCain, the Commander in Chief, Pacific, on major operations in Southeast Asia, including southern Laos, that might take place in the first six months of 1971.[1] McCain responded by suggesting two categories of actions: those that "will probably take place" because they required no real departure from existing policy (in other words, more of the same); and those that "would be desirable but may or may not be attainable within the political and time-limiting constraints." McCain's second category included a major offensive against the Ho Chi Minh Trail that, he believed, would compel Prince Souvanna Phouma, the ruler of Laos, to abandon the guise of neutrality and enter the war openly, renouncing the American-sponsored Geneva Accords which almost a decade earlier had established a nominal truce between the government and the communist insurgents.[2]

The idea of a South Vietnamese offensive sometime during the current dry season, November 1970 to May 1971, appealed to Henry Kissinger, President Nixon's adviser on national security matters, who realized that such an operation could help safeguard the American ground troops still in South Vietnam by forestalling a possible North Vietnamese thrust into the central highlands or across the demilitarized zone. Kissinger believed that a South Vietnamese offensive in Cambodia had better prospects of success than an assault against the more heavily defended Ho Chi Minh Trail and recommended accordingly. Admiral McCain, however, considered any attack in Cambodia subsidiary to a thrust into Laos. Despite McCain's insistence, the formidable defenses of the trail caused Admiral Moorer to suggest the possibility of substituting Cambodia for southern Laos as the main objective. Kissinger sought to resolve the difference of opinion — Cambodia, which he and Moorer favored, versus Laos, recommended by McCain — and sent one of his assistants, Brig. Gen. Alexander

Air War over South Vietnam, 1968–1975

M. Haig, Jr., to sound out General Abrams, the senior American commander in South Vietnam, Ellsworth Bunker, the United States Ambassador to South Vietnam, and Nguyen Van Thieu, the South Vietnamese president. Haig reported that the authorities in Saigon favored the bolder course, a South Vietnamese offensive against the Ho Chi Minh Trail, the enemy's main route for supplies and reinforcements, rather than against the communist forces in Cambodia.[3]

Although an offensive into southern Laos promised immediate benefits by protecting Vietnamization and the withdrawal of American ground forces, the idea of attacking there was not new. It had originated with General Westmoreland, General Abrams' predecessor. Long before Westmoreland left South Vietnam in the summer of 1968 to become Army Chief of Staff — indeed, well before that years's Tet offensive — the Ho Chi Minh Trail had evolved into a major transportation artery. The expansion and extension of the network of roads, paths, waterways, and pipelines presented a target that Westmoreland could not ignore, and he proposed to attack it with American, South Vietnamese, and possibly Thai troops. The alternatives he considered included a thrust westward from Khe Sanh and the nearby village of Lang Vei against the supply complex that since 1959 had grown up in the jungle-covered hills around the abandoned Laotian village of Tchepone. He might also attack the trail from the west, as well as from the east, or use helicopters to establish and maintain strongpoints athwart it. The loss of Lang Vei and the subsequent decision to abandon Khe Sanh, along with the adoption of a policy of Vietnamization and withdrawal, caused Westmoreland and Abrams to shelve the concept, even though Tchepone remained a tempting objective. In the spring of 1970, for example, intelligence estimates indicated that as much as half the supplies destined for the communist forces in South Vietnam passed over roads and through transshipment points near the ruins of that village.

The invasion of Cambodia in April 1970 cut, at least temporarily, the complementary supply line from the port of Sihanoukville to the depots near the South Vietnamese border. By the summer of that year, therefore, the enemy depended even more heavily upon cargo that traveled the Ho Chi Minh Trail past Tchepone and into South Vietnam and Cambodia. American and South Vietnamese leaders alike realized the value of a raid to disrupt traffic on the Ho Chi Minh Trail and destroy the supplies, some of which would formerly have arrived at Sihanoukville, that now filled the bunkers around Tchepone. Besides arousing the interest of Admiral McCain in Hawaii and General Abrams in Saigon, launching such an offensive during the 1970–71 dry season fired the enthusiasm of Lt. Gen. Hoang Xuan Lam, the South Vietnamese commander of I Corps, who once told a Marine Corps adviser, Brig. Gen. Edwin H. Simmons, that he had served in a French column attacking westward along Route 9 in the war against the Viet Minh and hoped to launch the same kind of operation on his own. Similarly, Gen. Cao Van Vien, Chairman of the South Vietnamese Joint General Staff, had for a half-dozen years advocated a strategy that included isolating the enemy in South Vietnam from his sources of supply and reinforcement in the North.[4]

President Thieu accepted the concept of two more or less concurrent operations, a main offensive in southern Laos and a secondary effort in Cambodia. During a conversation on December 7, 1970, he told Bunker and Abrams that the Cambodian operation would serve mainly to relieve communist pressure on the town of Kompong Cham, whereas the thrust into Laos would culminate in the capture of Tchepone, some forty kilometers beyond the border, and the destruction of supplies destined for both South Vietnam and Cambodia. After the assault force had blown up or carried off the cargo stored near the village and begun an orderly retreat, "stay-behinds and guerrillas" would for an unspecified time harry the enemy movement down the Ho Chi Minh Trail.[5]

As President Thieu and Generals Vien and Lam realized, their troops would have to strike before the northeast monsoon season ended in May 1971. Afterward, when the prevailing winds swung around to blow from the southwest, heavy rains would drench southern Laos, inhibiting air support and movement on the ground. Moreover, to obtain the fullest advantage from any disruption of traffic, South Vietnam needed to attack before the enemy further improved the Ho Chi Minh Trail to handle with ease the additional volume of cargo that before the spring of 1970 had passed through Sihanoukville. Finally, an offensive against an objective as formidable as Tchepone required substantial American aid, but the United States was steadily withdrawing its forces. To wait an entire year for the dry season of 1971–72, while American strength continued to ebb, introduced the risk that essential support might no longer be available.[6]

The Americans also favored an offensive during the current dry season — an attack in the spring of 1971 should create supply shortages felt twelve to eighteen months later, when the last American combat troops would be leaving South Vietnam — and they wanted the blow to fall in southern Laos. For them, a raid on Tchepone had obvious advantages over further fighting in Cambodia, since disruption of a key element in the North Vietnamese logistics complex could neutralize any threat to the central highlands and at the same time force the enemy to divert to the defense of the Ho Chi Minh Trail troops that might be massing to attack across the demilitarized zone. Because Thieu had informally endorsed an advance against Tchepone, Kissinger reversed himself and recommended that the United States emphasize the campaign in southern Laos, assigning a lesser priority to any action in Cambodia, an apportionment of effort that President Nixon approved.[7]

In December 1970, with almost six weeks of the present dry season already gone, tactical planning began in South Vietnam for the raid on Tchepone and for the secondary attacks against an enemy entrenched near the Chup plantation in Cambodia. Because of its greater daring and complexity, the invasion of Laos required the more thorough preparations, the earliest of them beginning on the day after Thieu mentioned the possible operations to Bunker and Abrams.[8] The

Air War over South Vietnam, 1968–1975

South Vietnamese chief executive intended to attack toward Tchepone in February, roughly midway through the period of dry weather, which increased the urgency felt by American and South Vietnamese planners.

In conjunction with Vien, who headed South Vietnam's Joint General Staff, Abrams authorized a combined planning effort, but the staff sections of the U.S. Military Assistance Command worked almost independently of the South Vietnamese in producing an operational concept consisting of four distinct phases. During the first phase, American forces would secure and prepare the roads, airfields, and bases in South Vietnam needed to launch and sustain the advance across the border. The next phase encompassed the drive into Laos and the capture of Tchepone. Phase III consisted of the destruction of the supplies stored around the village, and in the fourth and final phase, the assault troops would withdraw, either doubling back on their route of advance or attacking to the southeast through a North Vietnamese base area on the approaches to the A Shau Valley. Guerrillas would remain behind after the task force had withdrawn and continue to disrupt supply lines in the vicinity of Tchepone. A related element called for an advance from the west to threaten the town of Muong Phine and impede North Vietnamese attempts to divert highway traffic around the Tchepone salient.[9]

Because the Cooper-Church amendment prohibited the use of American ground forces in Laos, the United States relied upon air support, plus long-range artillery fire from inside South Vietnam, to provide the foundation upon which the planned South Vietnamese operation rested. Although the South Vietnamese Air Force could play a role in operations within the country or against lightly defended portions of Cambodia, it lacked the numbers and appropriate types of aircraft to overcome the antiaircraft defenses protecting Tchepone. The Vietnamized air arm could not meet the demands of the proposed operation, but General Abrams had Army helicopters and Air Force fighter-bombers and B–52s to batter the defenders when the South Vietnamese task force began its westward assault.[10]

Air Force analysts later complained that the military assistance command had relied too heavily on the Army's helicopter gunships, which lacked the punch of Air Force fighter-bombers, but Army planners had reasons for the choice other than a preference for using aircraft under the direct control of their fellow soldiers. Weather strongly influenced the decision. In February and March, the time chosen for the operation, cloud cover tended to prevail except for a window of perhaps four to six hours at mid-day. Earlier in the morning and later in the afternoon, the ceiling varied from 2,500 feet in the vicinity of Khe Sanh to 1,000 feet in the mountains around Tchepone. The cloud cover would handicap immediate strikes by fighter-bombers, though not the planned variety that utilized radar control. Helicopters, in contrast, normally flew at these low altitudes, hugging the nap of the earth more tightly than was possible for conventional jet aircraft. The Army planners failed to realize that the clouds

South Vietnamese Invasion of Laos

An Air Force C–130 delivers cargo at Khe Sanh, the main
supply center for South Vietnam's Lam Son 719 operation in Laos.

enveloping the mountaintops of southern Laos would force the helicopters into valleys covered by deadly fire from light antiaircraft weapons and machineguns. The over-reliance on helicopters for firepower also reflected the kind of targets, lightly defended by antiaircraft fire, that the planners expected to engage — mainly infantry, artillery, and thin-skinned vehicles. Those who drafted the plan did not foresee either massed antiaircraft fire or heavily armored tanks best destroyed by bombs or large rockets delivered from jet fighters.[11]

Planning moved forward at Saigon, cloaked as completely in secrecy as possible in a city notorious for its disregard of even elementary security practices. To deceive an enemy who seemed to have agents everywhere, planners resurrected a code name, Dewey Canyon, used in the spring of 1969 for a probe of the northern approaches to the A Shau Valley. The Americans at first referred to the entire Operation as Dewey Canyon II, thus suggesting a return to the site of the 1969 fighting. Ultimately, however, the revived code name referred only to Phase I, the preliminary activity by American troops in South Vietnam to provide a launching platform for the attack westward. The South Vietnamese chose Lam Son 719 to designate the thrust along Route 9 from the border to Tchepone.[12]

The staff agencies of the military assistance command emphasized secrecy as they devised the basic concept for Dewey Canyon II-Lam Son 719, often engaging in informal discussions instead of preparing and exchanging written comments that might somehow find their way into North Vietnamese hands. The XXIV Corps, the U.S. Army tactical command in the northern provinces, unveiled its basic plan on January 21, 1971, before a select audience that included a few Air Force officers: General Clay, the Seventh Air Force commander; Brig. Gen. John H. Herring, Jr., the commander of the 834th Air Division and responsible for tactical airlift in South Vietnam; and a handful of their staff officers.

Similar secrecy prevailed when representatives of the U.S. Military Assistance Command and the South Vietnamese Joint General Staff briefed General Lam, who would command the undertaking. Only a few of Lam's staff officers received invitations to the meeting at XXIV Corps headquarters. His chief of operations, Col. Cao Khee Nhat, could not obtain access, even though he had helped write the very plan under discussion.[13]

Because South Vietnamese officials had tended to disregard security during previous operations, resulting in accurate speculation that circulated throughout Saigon, Abrams tried to reach an accommodation with the press. He imposed an embargo on the release of news of the attack, which would last until the South Vietnamese made contact with the enemy, but he sought to take the sting out of this action by arranging a briefing on January 29 to outline the impending operation. The ban proved unenforceable, however, since foreign journalists, who did not feel bound by the prohibition, had access to cable offices outside South Vietnam but within a few flying hours of Saigon. Moreover, a number of American reporters either advised their editors informally without actually filing stories, reported the news embargo itself, or characterized as rumor the talk of an imminent invasion of Laos; they tended, in short, to obey the letter of the order though not its intent. Alerted by these various leaks, journalists in Washington badgered administration officials, mostly without real knowledge of the operation, until Dr. Kissinger saw the futility of the attempt at censorship, which encouraged press speculation instead of suppressing it. Consequently, the embargo lasted only until February 4, four days before the South Vietnamese task force crossed the border.[14]

The commander of the South Vietnamese 1st Infantry Division, Maj. Gen. Nguyen Duy Hinh complained of poor security. In his opinion, the embargo on news, the attempt at compartmentalized planning, and the revival of an old code name, Dewey Canyon, had accomplished nothing. When the attack came, Honh said that the enemy "appeared not to be surprised at all; by contrast, he had been prepared and was waiting for our forces to come in."[15]

Meanwhile, the 834th Air Division stepped up to its assignments in Dewey Canyon II and helped prepare for the launching of Lam Son 719. After receiving 10 additional C–130s, increasing their number to 58 and the total number of transports to 186, the division established a control mechanism for delivering troops and cargo to northernmost South Vietnam. General Herring decided to direct the airlift activity from his control center at Tan Son Nhut Air Base, using satellite control elements at Dong Ha, Quang Tri City, and Da Nang.

Although XXIV Corps, under Lt. Gen. James W. Sutherland, Jr., and Clay's Seventh Air Force produced detailed plans covering ground operations and tac-

South Vietnamese Invasion of Laos

tical air support, airlift planners encountered an unexpected obstacle. To meet an invasion day of February 8, Herring's staff had to complete its work during the Tet holiday, but a number of South Vietnamese officers, kept unaware of the impending attack for security reasons, went on leave and therefore could not submit airlift requirements for mounting Lam Son 719. As a result, U.S. officers decided among themselves the number of troops, the kinds of equipment, and the amount of supplies that the 834th Air Division would deliver.

Despite the hurried and informal drafting of plans, Air Force transports got the required men, weapons, and supplies into place for the attack toward Tchepone. Almost 600 sorties by C–130s and a dozen by C–123s delivered 12,000 troops (including the South Vietnamese 1st Airborne Division, performing as infantry) and 4,600 tons of cargo to airfields in the northern provinces. All did not go smoothly, however. The ground control approach radars at Dong Ha and Quang Tri City broke down, and spare parts proved hard to find.[16]

Since American tactical aviation would play a critical role in Lam Son 719, a centralized control mechanism seemed essential. During Dewey Canyon II, the existing I Direct Air Support Center at Da Nang dealt adequately with requests from tactical air control parties for strikes in support of the Army units establishing control over the northwestern corner of South Vietnam. Once the South Vietnamese forces crossed the border, however, they would rely on a revived V Direct Air Support Center at Quang Tri City. Because of the ban against American troops serving on the ground in Laos, Air Force tactical air control parties could not accompany the advancing South Vietnamese, although forward air controllers would be on station overhead. The Cooper-Church amendment also forbade Army advisers from remaining with units with which they had served.

Since Americans could not enter Laos and carry out their usual duties, Lam decided to establish divisional tactical operations centers near Khe Sanh, where Americans would be on hand to give advice and facilitate air support while remaining on South Vietnamese soil. The decision clearly reflected the dependence of South Vietnamese commanders on American advice, but it provided a poor substitute for an American presence on the battlefield and, because of its detachment from the fighting, complicated the coordination of tactical air support and helicopter operations with the action on the ground.

Except for the distance that the Air Force liaison officers remained from the battlefield, the mechanics of air support during Lam Son 719 resembled those for any comparable operation in South Vietnam. As always, air liaison officers processed requests from ground units for air support and, during Lam Son 719, passed the information to V Direct Air Support Center, which functioned as an advance element of the Seventh Air Force Tactical Air Control Center.

Air Force forward air controllers, accompanied by English-speaking South Vietnamese, did the same work they had in South Vietnam, patrolling an assigned area, searching out targets, and directing air attacks. In an emergency, the forward air controllers bypassed the divisional tactical operations centers and sent requests for immediate strikes straight to V Direct Air Support Center, which diverted or launched the necessary fighter-bombers. The aircraft that responded checked in with Hillsboro, the airborne battlefield command and control center that coordinated the employment of tactical air power over southern Laos. Hillsboro controllers then handed off the fighter-bombers to the appropriate forward air controller.

Once Operation Lam Son 719 encountered fierce resistance, one emergency seemed to follow another, and V Direct Air Support Center tended to entrust responsibility for immediate strikes to the forward air controllers, though it continued to provide general instructions to them, assign them sectors, and fulfill routine requests for planned strikes. The more frenzied the battle became, the more frequently did forward air controllers change targets and divert aircraft, deciding among themselves, or with the assistance of Hillsboro, where a particular flight should attack.[17]

Unless the forward air controllers, aided by the interpreters flying with them, chose to intervene, a South Vietnamese commander inside Laos could not be sure of rapid and reliable communication with the American airmen supporting him. The normal channel for requesting air support passed through the divisional tactical operations center in South Vietnam, miles from the battleground. Gen. Du Quoc Dong, commander of the South Vietnamese airborne division, pointed out this fact during the planning of Lam Son 719 and argued that a commander should have exclusive control over the forward air controllers supporting his unit, thus minimizing any conflict of priorities between airmen and troops on the ground. Although he failed to gain the direct control that he sought, the general did obtain a revision of the original plan that had called for a controller to support both the airborne division and the ranger force. When the airborne troops went into action, their commander did not have to share forward air controllers with another unit, but he could only make requests of them, rather than giving them orders.

Despite this partial success, General Dong remained unhappy with the procedures for getting air support. The South Vietnamese division commander argued that the mechanism functioned too slowly, requiring up to thirty-six hours for planned requests, and made it difficult to coordinate air strikes with the other firepower available to a division commander, though the problem in coordinating firepower resulted not from the forward air controllers but from reliance on a tactical operations center remote from the fighting.[18]

Whereas the South Vietnamese general wanted his fellow division commanders to have greater control over the aircraft supporting their units, General Clay could present a strong case for centralizing control of a complicated air operation. At any time during the advance to Tchepone, a half-dozen forward air controllers would be handling relays of fighter-bombers, while formations of B–52s dropped bombs on or near the battlefield, and Air Force gunships

South Vietnamese Invasion of Laos

A South Vietnamese personnel carrier in Laos during Lam Son 719.

flying nearby attacked North Vietnamese trucks traveling the Ho Chi Minh Trail by night. Swarms of Army helicopters would skim the ground, scouting, strafing, and shifting men, supplies, and artillery from one objective to another. All of this activity increased the danger of accidents, whether mid-air collisions or the bombing of friendly troops, and underscored the importance of centralized control over at least the Air Force aircraft operating in the narrow corridor between Khe Sanh and Tchepone.[19]

The 101st Airborne Division (Airmobile), rather than the XXIV Corps, controlled the Army helicopters in Lam Son 719 and the few South Vietnamese helicopters that participated in the operation. Procedures called for the commander of a division or other major South Vietnamese unit to submit requests for helicopters to the headquarters of the American airborne division, which could respond immediately if aircraft were available. Only when it became necessary to set priorities among competing requests did XXIV Corps intervene. Although responsive to the needs of South Vietnamese commanders, the policy in some cases permitted helicopters to move units without the knowledge of the U.S. corps commander. A South Vietnamese officer, for instance, used U.S. helicopters to shift an entire battalion before advising General Sutherland, who bore the ultimate responsibility for providing long-range artillery fire.[20]

The South Vietnamese I Corps, besides setting up a logistics command to forward the supplies that would sustain Lam Son 719, emplaced long-range artillery to join the American batteries in firing concentrations in support of the attack. The actual assault force consisted of a South Vietnamese Marine divi-

Air War over South Vietnam, 1968–1975

sion, the 1st Ranger Group, the reinforced 1st Infantry Division, the 1st Airborne Division fighting as infantry, and the 1st Armored Brigade, a total of forty-two maneuver battalions, of which thirty-four were to cross the border. While the tanks and armored personnel carriers of the armored brigade advanced along Route 9, American helicopters would leapfrog from one hilltop to another and land troops to establish a succession of fire bases protecting the armored column and the supply-laden trucks following behind it.[21]

The threat from North Vietnamese armored forces influenced the plans for Lam Son 719, though, as events would prove, not to the extent it should have. On the eve of the attack, intelligence reports credited North Vietnam with as many as 200 Soviet-designed tanks, variants of either the T–54, which usually mounted a 100-mm gun, or the PT–76, an amphibious vehicle less than half as heavy as the T–54 and carrying a 76-mm weapon. Planners doubted, however, that the enemy could mass this armor against the attack, a conclusion that ignored the extensive and stoutly defended road net linking North Vietnam with southern Laos. As a result, the South Vietnamese armored brigade relied on light tanks, with 76-mm guns, since these vehicles, along with air strikes and rocket launchers manned by the infantry, seemed adequate to deal with whatever armored threat the enemy might muster.[22]

Besides having to fire rockets at the tanks that might intervene during the planned attack toward Tchepone, the helicopters would face an antiaircraft defense more formidable than any encountered in South Vietnam. Guns defending nearby segments of the Ho Chi Minh Trail could move rapidly — planners did not realize how rapidly — to engage aircraft operating in the Tchepone salient. In fact, by the time Lam Son 719 ended, Air Force fighter-bomber pilots would report destroying more than a hundred antiaircraft weapons where dozens had formerly stood guard. At the outset, Army airmen believed that by skimming the treetops and using the cover of ridge lines or hill masses they could dart about too rapidly for North Vietnamese gunners. At times, reliance on maneuverability and daring might be the only protection for the helicopter crews, who flew below the overcast, attacking in weather that grounded the faster and less vulnerable fighter-bombers which otherwise might have supported them. The North Vietnamese, who had fought against the Army's airmobile units since the Ia Drang Valley campaign of 1965, developed tactics against helicopters; during Lam Son 719, they rarely fired upon the craft in flight but waited in ambush at a likely objective until the troop carriers descended, and then used every available weapon from rifles to 37-mm antiaircraft guns to place a barrier of fire across the landing zone.

While helping plan the attack, representatives of the Seventh Air Force suggested using B–52s to batter by night the chosen landing zones and the terrain around them, following up after dawn with attacks by fighter-bombers and, if the defenses warranted, by transports dropping 15,000-pound bombs improvised to clear landing zones in dense forest. General Lam objected, however, to the

South Vietnamese Invasion of Laos

A Soviet-built PT–76 tank captured during Lam Son 719.

timing of the attacks. He wanted to seize an objective at first light, if possible, so that the troops would have the entire day to prepare for the counterattack certain to come after nightfall, and he willingly traded preparatory bombing for the additional daylight. Not until Lam Son 719 began and helicopters met with deadly fire did preparatory air strikes assume critical importance.

In suppressing the antiaircraft fire designed to isolate the South Vietnamese fire bases, the laser-guided bomb proved the deadliest weapon in the Air Force arsenal. The widely used cluster bomb units released individual bomblets capable of killing or wounding members of gun crews, but they rarely destroyed the weapon itself, as the laser-guided bomb might do. The unguided general purpose high-explosive bomb achieved the poorest results, for it required a direct hit to destroy a gun or kill a crew, accuracy rarely attainable because of camouflage, natural concealment, and enemy fire.[23]

As the operational framework of Lam Son 719 took shape, President Nixon had misgivings about the attack, but, after receiving assurances from General Abrams that the operation would result in only a slight increase in American casualties, on January 29, 1971, he approved it.[24] The next day, Dewey Canyon II got under way, as American troops advanced upon Khe Sanh, designated to become the principal assembly area and supply base for Lam Son 719, and prepared to open Route 9 beyond that base all the way to the border. The reoccupation of the abandoned stronghold encountered little opposition and required only routine air support; once there, however, the soldiers had to fill craters from North Vietnamese shells and remove marine-planted minefields before transports could land on the existing 3,900-foot runway. While they repaired the damage, some of it inflicted during the siege in the spring of 1968, Army engineers built a second runway atop the Khe Sanh plateau. On February 4, the first C–130 touched down on the new 3,200-foot landing strip and promptly became stuck in the mud, the wheels sinking a half-foot, even though the aircraft carried a comparatively light load. To create a satisfactory surface, soldiers laid aluminum matting over the new runway, and on February 15, transports began regular flights into Khe Sanh. The old runway reopened by March 1, in time for the latter part of Lam Son 719. To handle the frequent landings and departures, the Air Force sent air traffic controllers from Clark Air Base in the Philippines to assist the Army men operating the control tower at Khe Sanh.

From the time the South Vietnamese task force went into action on February 8 until March 27 when the operation ended, Air Force transports flew more than 2,000 sorties in support of Lam Son 719, carrying 21,000 tons of cargo and almost 14,000 passengers. More than 1,100 sorties ended at Khe Sanh; others terminated at either Quang Tri City, Dong Ha, Phu Bai, or Da Nang.[25]

The massing of men and supplies for Lam Son 719 imposed demands on strategic as well as tactical airlift. The Military Airlift Command's Douglas C–124s, Lockheed C–141s, and Douglas C–133s delivered bulky cargo across the Pacific, their usual assignment, and sometimes within South Vietnam. To release C–130s for tactical missions to Khe Sanh and elsewhere, some of the larger and longer range transports took over routine cargo runs among airfields like Tan Son Nhut, Cam Ranh Bay, and Da Nang and also flew emergency missions directly related to the invasion of Laos. In fifteen sorties, for instance, the turboprop C–133s delivered four howitzers, two maintenance vans, and nine light tanks needed by the Lam Son 719 task force.[26]

Laotian ruler Souvanna Phouma did not renounce the nation's nominal neutrality as McCain had hoped, but instead protested the invasion, even though the North Vietnamese had for years controlled the area from Tchepone eastward to the border.[27] Except for this diplomatic development and an ominous tactical portent — the appearance of tanks, four attacked unsuccessfully by Army helicopters — all went well on the first day. As some 6,000 South Vietnamese advanced in sullen weather, spearheaded by the airborne division, American artillery fired from positions in South Vietnam, but clouds hung so low over the invasion corridor that some of the fighter-bombers scheduled to deliver planned air strikes could not find their assigned targets.

Weather continued to hamper aerial activity for the next few days. On February 10, for example, a force of rangers spotted three North Vietnamese tanks, along with towed artillery, and requested air attacks, but cloud cover protected the enemy. Air Force fighter-bombers appeared overhead but could not intervene; since the jets attacked at a speed of about 350 knots, they needed a ceiling of at least 3,000 feet above ground level to locate and engage a target, but the overcast hovered too low. Army helicopters could have attacked with a ceiling of only 1,000 feet, but the available craft did not have suitable armament.

South Vietnamese Invasion of Laos

Lam Son 719 moved rapidly forward during the first few days despite the impact of weather on fighter operations. By February 12, the task force had advanced from the border to the intersection of Route 9, leading westward from Khe Sanh to Tchepone, and Route 92, running generally north and south. At the intersection of the two highways, the bombed-out village of Ban Dong, which the Americans called A Luoi, became the site of a major base, and General Lam's troops established seven other large outposts to protect it, four of them north of Route 9 — Ranger North and Ranger South, plus Fire Support Bases 30 and 31 — and three to the south — Hotel, Delta, and Brown.[28]

Strikes by B–52s dug huge craters in the wilderness during the first week of fighting, February 4 through 11, and caused some secondary explosions. The raids, however, could not prevent North Vietnamese resistance from stiffening around the scattered fire support bases, as antiaircraft guns moved into position to challenge American helicopters shuttling troops and cargo within the invasion corridor. South Vietnamese troops succeeded in reconnoitering only about 10 percent of the target boxes the B–52s bombed, and, in those they actually entered, bomb craters and shattered trees impeded movement and prevented accurate damage assessment.

In spite of extensive American air support — which General Hinh of the South Vietnamese 1st Infantry Division placed at "500 to 800 sorties of air cavalry gunships" each day and "approximately 100 sorties of tactical bombers... and a number of missions by B–52 strategic bombers" — the attack lost momentum. As early as February 13, General Abrams became concerned that President Thieu might settle for less than an advance to Tchepone and the destruction of the supplies stored there.[29]

Abrams could think of a number of tactical considerations that might persuade Thieu to curtail Lam Son 719, avoid Tchepone, and move directly to the final phase, the withdrawal through the supply depots at the entrance to the A Shau Valley. Perhaps, Abrams suggested, the South Vietnamese leader would yield to "a sense of caution," possibly inspired by the number of American helicopters already lost to hostile fire, accidents, and mechanical breakdown, even though, as the American general pointed out, more than half of the original helicopter force remained undamaged, with replacements for the others readily available within South Vietnam. Also, the triumvirate of Thieu, Vien, and Lam might simply conclude that the bunkers lining the approaches to the A Shau Valley contained a more valuable hoard of supplies than the region around Tchepone.[30]

Thieu's growing reluctance to push on reflected a combination of military and political factors. Already the North Vietnamese exerted intense pressure against the rangers manning two of the fire support bases northeast of Ban Dong; if the entire screen of four outposts should collapse, the enemy could easily pinch off and destroy any thrust toward Tchepone. By changing direction, the president could preserve as much as possible of the Lam Son 719 task force

Air War over South Vietnam, 1968–1975

Army engineers lay runway matting at Khe Sanh in February 1971.

for future battles, especially the 1st Airborne Division which manned two of the northern bases, and present an acceptably short casualty list to the South Vietnamese people. Just as Nixon had worried about the possibility that American losses in supporting the attack might further erode public acceptance of the war, Thieu realized that massive South Vietnamese casualties could undermine his nation's resolve. According to Kissinger, the idea of shifting the axis of attack southward from Ban Dong reflected Thieu's determination that total casualties should not exceed 3,000.[31]

To prod the South Vietnamese into action, Abrams conferred with Vien, the Chairman of the Joint General Staff, at Saigon and urged that the task force push on to Tchepone as swiftly as possible. On February 16, Vien arrived at the I Corps command post at Dong Ha in South Vietnam, where he talked with Lam and Sutherland. The three generals agreed to establish two landing zones south of the Xepon River, emplace artillery there, and then land elements of the 1st Infantry Division at Tchepone.

President Thieu, however, remained at best ambivalent about pushing farther westward. During a meeting with Lam at Quang Tri City on February 19, the president raised the possibility of changing the main thrust of Operation Lam Son 719, as Abrams had suspected. Thieu suggested that the task force turn away from Tchepone and angle to the south, generally following Route 92, to spend perhaps five days ferreting out supply caches along the main road leading into the A Shau Valley. If the president decided to modify the operation in this way, the weight of Lam Son 719 would fall not on Tchepone but on the entrance to the A Shau Valley. Meanwhile, the North Vietnamese might seize the initiative if the task force hunkered down too long in its fire support bases before either turning south or continuing eastward.[32]

Whether the Lam Son 719 task force continued on to Tchepone as Abrams and Sutherland wanted or turned southward, the American generals considered

South Vietnamese Invasion of Laos

it imperative that the troops keep moving. To pause in the vicinity of Ban Dong gave the enemy a chance to reinforce with men, tanks, and antiaircraft guns and attack the South Vietnamese in their present positions or ambush them when at last they moved. Only a prompt and vigorous advance could keep the enemy off balance. By failing to push on, preferably toward Tchepone, Lam invited defeat.[33]

In spite of the risk, the task force remained in place for almost three weeks, manning its fire support bases and using Route 9 as its main supply route. The offensive spearhead hurled at Tchepone had become a defensive perimeter extending from Ban Dong back to the South Vietnamese border. Although troops fanned out to search for supply dumps in the hills overlooking Routes 9 and 92, they showed little aggressiveness in doing so. The patrols did not stray far from the principal fire support bases and satellite landing zones and relied on air strikes to destroy the supplies in any storage sites found. The bases gradually became friendly islands in a hostile sea, as survival increasingly depended upon air support. The B–52s showered bombs upon supply dumps and troop concentrations, and fighter-bombers joined in attacking the North Vietnamese. Forward air controllers patrolled the salient by day and night, and after dark C–123 flareships and AC–119 and AC–130 gunships came to the aid of the embattled South Vietnamese.[34]

On occasion, air and ground cooperated with spectacular results. On February 24, for instance, two battalions of General Hinh's 1st Infantry Division arranged for a B–52 strike on their positions, then pulled back and allowed the North Vietnamese to occupy them. After the bombs exploded among the enemy, the two battalions counterattacked, encountering only sporadic resistance and finding 159 bodies along with several abandoned weapons.[35]

As this small triumph by Hinh's troops demonstrated, the B–52 could provide devastating firepower in defense of the bases. On February 21, while the North Vietnamese closed in on the outposts northeast of Ban Dong, the Joint Chiefs of Staff approved a surge in daily B–52 sorties from thirty to as many as forty. To sustain this increased activity, the Strategic Air Command transferred a fourteen-plane alert force from Guam to U-Tapao, where it remained through the month of May. Because bombers based in Thailand had a much shorter flight to the Tchepone area, they could carry out missions more frequently than those flying from Guam. By shifting RC–135s, reconnaissance versions of the tanker, to Kadena on Okinawa, the Strategic Air Command made room for the additional B–52s at U-Tapao.[36]

General Abrams sought to direct some of the B–52s against troop concentrations and antiaircraft batteries that had appeared between two Special Arc Light Operating Areas north of Tchepone. Since this target, unlike almost all the others attacked in connection with Operation Lam Son 719, lay outside an area approved for B–52 strikes by the American embassy at Vientiane, Abrams had to consult the ambassador. Reports of prisoner of war camps in the vicinity persuaded Ambassador Godley to veto the proposed bombing. Abrams then asked Admiral Moorer to intercede. Citing recent information acquired by the Central Intelligence Agency indicating that the sites no longer housed captives, Moorer won over Defense Secretary Laird and through him, Secretary of State Rogers. As a result of this end run, Godley withdrew his opposition.[37]

From the beginning of Lam Son 719, B–52s routinely bombed North Vietnamese troops 1,500 yards from friendly positions — close, indeed, but not close enough to frustrate the enemy's "hugging" tactics of infiltrating to within a few hundred yards of the objective. The bombers also attacked bivouac areas and storage sites miles from the nearest South Vietnamese outpost.

Requests for strikes close to friendly troops usually originated with the division commander, while General Lam's corps headquarters nominated the more distant targets, including the helicopter landing zones selected for scheduled airmobile operations. A routine B–52 strike requested by General Lam's headquarters might require advance notice of from thirty-six to sixty hours, but as little as three hours might be time enough to divert approaching B–52s to meet an emergency. The commander who asked for a B–52 strike often did not know the results of the attack; as was true during the first week of the offensive, cloud cover hampered aerial photography and ground forces managed to enter and search only about one target box in ten.

An increase in air strikes as Lam Son 719 continued — for example, 1,100 of some 1,850 B–52 sorties occurred after March 5 — reflected the intensification of North Vietnamese counterattacks. Beginning in mid-February, fighter pilots and forward air controllers reacted to the stiffening resistance with increasingly frequent attacks on tanks menacing the invasion force. During the last week of February, fighter-bombers battered armored vehicles, some of them concealed in huts, south of Ban Dong and along the Route 9 corridor both east and west of the village. Pilots reported destroying fifteen light and medium tanks and damaging two others. Crews of AC–130 gunships claimed that their aircraft, though mounting no weapon larger than a 40-mm gun, had knocked out fourteen tanks. However accurate these claims might be, the increasing frequency of sightings indicated increasing enemy pressure against the salient.[38]

Besides impeding the movement of enemy armor, fighter-bombers also attacked, when weather permitted, those North Vietnamese trying to dislodge South Vietnamese troops from the fire support bases. In defense of Fire Support Base 31, on a hilltop north of Route 9, Air Force A–7s and F–4s took advantage of improved weather to help hold at bay a force of tanks and infantry. On February 25, the airmen reported breaking up one assault by dropping antipersonnel and armor-piercing weapons and stopping another with napalm and general-purpose bombs. At mid-afternoon, however, the aircraft broke off the action, to, among other reasons, engage in a rescue mission; and by midnight the North Vietnamese had overrun the objective, leaving only one of the four northern outposts, Fire Support Base 30, still in South Vietnamese hands.[39]

South Vietnamese Invasion of Laos

In advancing on Ban Dong from the north, the enemy did his best to neutralize American air power. Once he had massed enough armor and infantry, he employed tactics that had served him well on other battlefields. North Vietnamese troops encircled the fire support bases so tightly that B–52s could not attack without endangering the defenders and set up automatic weapons and light antiaircraft guns to place a barrier of fire over the base and thus prevent helicopters from bringing in supplies and reinforcements or evacuating the wounded. To neutralize the deadly fighter-bombers, the attackers waited until weather or darkness prevented accurate bombing from low altitude and then stormed the objective. As the days passed, the North Vietnamese grew stronger and made increasingly proficient use of these tactics, at first against the rangers and then against Fire Support Base 31. Beginning in the final days of February and continuing into March, the enemy, according to an American adviser at the tactical operations center of the South Vietnamese marines, simply "plucked those bases like ripe grapes, one by one."[40]

On at least one occasion, conflicting priorities between air and ground may have contributed to the enemy's plucking of the northern outposts. General Hinh, the commander of the 1st Infantry Division, has attributed the loss of Fire Support Base 31 on the night of February 25 to just such a conflict. According to him, supporting aircraft ignored the danger to the base to go to the rescue of a downed air crew, but weather and darkness, which would themselves have forced a suspension of air strikes, also influenced the decision to let the troops at the base fend for themselves.[41]

Air support of Fire Support Base 31 got off to a bad start on that fatal February 25 when the first of the forward air controllers assigned to direct strikes during daylight somehow received a map with the wrong coordinates for his sector and arrived on station several hours late. As the afternoon wore on and a thunderstorm drew near, the forward air controller then on duty, Capt. Peter J. Ruppert, learned that antiaircraft fire had downed an F–4 nearby. With dusk approaching and the storm threatening to put an end to air operations at Fire Support Base 31, Ruppert finished a strike then in progress and headed for the place where the fighter-bomber went down to help rescue his fellow airmen. When he arrived, five other forward air controllers in OV–10s already circled the site, along with several Air Force fighter-bombers and Army helicopters. For a time, all the forward air controllers flying in the invasion corridor stood by to aid in the rescue. After about half an hour, a flight of A–1s arrived from Nakhon Phanom to coordinate the effort and suppress hostile fire. Ruppert then succeeded in pointing out to the rescue commander the approximate place where the aircraft had gone down, but rain, nightfall, and intense fire from the ground soon put an end to the attempted recovery.

On the morning of February 26, after the North Vietnamese had overwhelmed Fire Support Base 31, the rescue effort resumed, but recurring thunderstorms and persistent antiaircraft fire interfered. When Ruppert again arrived

Air War over South Vietnam, 1968–1975

on station at mid-day, recovery of the two downed airmen had an overriding priority. Once he spotted them, he diverted a flight of napalm-carrying fighter-bombers to silence North Vietnamese fire until an Air Force helicopter could pick them up, some twenty-four hours after they parachuted from their burning F–4.[42]

While this rescue attempt was succeeding north of Route 9, antiaircraft fire struck another F–4 during an air strike south of the highway. Shell fragments severely wounded the pilot, 1st Lt. Robert Eisenbaisz, but another pilot riding in the weapon systems officer's seat, Capt. Maynard Ford, took over and flew the aircraft back to Phu Cat, where he ejected both seats. He survived, but Lieutenant Eisenbaisz had already died of his wounds.[43]

Despite the fighting north of Route 9, which had resulted in the loss of Fire Support Base 31 and a growing threat to Fire Support Base 30, President Thieu had not forgotten Tchepone and the importance that Abrams and Sutherland attached to that way station on the Ho Chi Minh Trail. Certainly as a result of American pressure, though he may also have sought to divert the North Vietnamese from the stalled task force which now clung to only one major fire support base north of Route 9, Thieu told Lam on February 28 to prepare to vault from Ban Dong to the vicinity of Tchepone. The president's instructions called for Lam to relieve the airborne division, which had sustained numerous casualties in the fighting around the northern outposts but remained intact as a fighting unit, with the marines, who would use helicopters for a raid on Tchepone. Reliance on the marines placed Lam in an awkward position. The commander of the South Vietnamese Marine Corps had refused to participate in the planning of Lam Son 719 and then entrusted tactical control to a senior colonel who took orders from him rather than from Lam as corps and task force commander. The marines, moreover, had never fought together as a division but separately as brigades. Lam therefore hurried to Saigon, where he persuaded Thieu to allow him to change the assignments of three of his divisions. Hinh's 1st Infantry Division, still on the defensive around Ban Dong and waiting to begin a possible advance toward the mouth of the A Shau Valley, would provide troops for the descent upon Tchepone, the marines would take its place and constitute a task force reserve, and the airborne troops would keep Route 9 open as the avenue of supply and withdrawal. By now, South Vietnam had committed more than 10,000 troops to the operation, which would reach a climax with the raid on Tchepone, followed by an orderly retreat along Route 9 or across the approaches to the A Shau Valley.

Hinh's soldiers would seize four objectives, each named after an actress popular among Americans, the last of them within striking distance of the objective. Communist propagandists later seized upon this fact, charging that the Americans had chosen the names, thus proving the South Vietnamese to be their puppets. In fact, as General Hinh later explained, a South Vietnamese officer had picked the names for the landing zones — Lolo for Gina Lollobrigida, Liz for Elizabeth Taylor, Sophia for Sophia Loren, and Hope for Hope Lange — because he wanted ones familiar to the Americans and easy for them to pronounce. Although by no means proof that the South Vietnamese served as mere puppets, the selection of names did indicate that they depended on American helicopters, aircraft, and long-range artillery to support the capture of the landing zones and of Tchepone itself. The raid, moreover, clearly represented a concession to the Americans, for Thieu had put aside his concern about casualties and followed the advice of Abrams.[44]

On March 3, the same day that the task force abandoned Fire Support Base 30, the last northern outpost, helicopters from Khe Sanh began depositing troops at Landing Zone Lolo. In spite of preparatory artillery fire and air attacks with napalm and high explosive, the assault force encountered fierce opposition at the objective. Forward air controllers directed a half-dozen F-4s against targets designated by commanders on the ground but could not suppress the hostile fire. Of the first twenty troop-carrying helicopters, North Vietnamese gunners shot down one shortly after it took off from Khe Sanh, destroyed four others at the landing zone, and damaged another eight as they touched down to unload. The senior South Vietnamese officer suspended the operation for about three hours to permit further air strikes by a total of fifty-two fighters or attack aircraft, but when the helicopters reappeared early in the afternoon, enemy artillery destroyed one on the landing zone. After a second pause, the assault resumed; until dusk, helicopters darted into the clearing and out a few at a time, as forward air controllers directed strikes against targets designated by the command post at the landing zone. By nightfall, the South Vietnamese had captured Landing Zone Lolo, but the price of victory included forty-two helicopters damaged by hostile fire and twenty-seven others destroyed, either shot down or hit by mortar or artillery shells while on the ground.

Losses at the other objectives — Landing Zones Liz, Sophia, and Hope — proved less severe; the toll of helicopters destroyed and damaged during these three assaults totaled only a fifth of the number at Landing Zone Lolo. The helicopters fared better during the last three landings because American advisers back in South Vietnam insisted on a more savage aerial bombardment to suppress hostile fire. As a result, at Liz, Sophia, and Hope the helicopters did not attempt to land troops until B-52s had bombed during the night, fighter-bombers had attacked beginning early in the morning, and, if the defenses seemed especially stubborn, at least one 15,000-pound bomb had blasted the objective just before the troops arrived. In short, overwhelming firepower replaced maneuverability as the key to a successful helicopter assault, and firepower enabled the South Vietnamese to complete the move that on March 6 brought them to Landing Zone Hope in the vicinity of Tchepone.[45]

After the South Vietnamese had reached Landing Zone Hope and begun probing the storage sites around Tchepone, Generals Abrams and Sutherland recommended the further reinforcement and exploitation of a salient that now extended all the way to the Ho Chi Minh Trail; indeed, Abrams declared that one more South Vietnamese division and another month of fighting would win a decisive victory. President Thieu rejected this advice, but he did so indirectly by inviting the Americans to send a division of their own into Laos to fight alongside the South Vietnamese, an action prohibited by the Cooper-Church amendment. Even if the amendment had not existed, President Nixon would surely have flinched from combat on the ground, increased American casualties, and the prospect of renewed opposition to the war.

On March 9, the high command of Thieu, Vien, and Lam agreed that the time had come to begin pulling out. They planned to withdraw the task force by the end of the month, abandoning in succession the outposts that the task force still occupied from Landing Zone Hope back to the border, and conducting an orderly retreat along Route 9. The projected raid at the mouth of the A Shau Valley would have to wait until mid-April at the earliest, while the task force rested and regrouped after some two months of heavy fighting. Already, the South Vietnamese had fought in bloody clashes, notably at the fire support bases north of Route 9, that left some battalions too battered for further combat, and the bloodshed might not have ended. Sustained bad weather could, for example, deprive the task force of the air support needed to protect its flanks as it snaked eastward along a single avenue of retreat. Without air strikes, the column, already weakened by casualties, would be hard-pressed to fight its way out of Laos against a reinforced enemy far stronger than it had encountered during the initial advance.[46]

During the retreat, when flank security depended on holding the line of outposts too widely separated for mutual fire support with infantry weapons, air strikes could prove decisive, especially those by B–52s bombing in close proximity to friendly troops. As a result, General Sutherland endorsed Lam's request to change Arc Light tactics — the methods used by B–52s to support the war in the ground — by abandoning the established practice of having the bombers approach in trail when attacking within three kilometers of friendly forces. Lam wanted the B–52s to remain in a three-aircraft cell and drop three parallel strings of bombs when attacking as close as two kilometers to his troops. The broader pattern of detonations, he and Sutherland believed, could kill or wound more of the enemy and do a better job of demoralizing the survivors. The Strategic Air Command considered the risk from friendly bombs too great, however, and insisted that its B–52s attack in trail within the three-kilometer safety zone. That rule remained in force, but in time of grave emergency, at least one South Vietnamese commander called upon B–52s, flying in single file, to drop bombs just 300 yards from his troops. To avoid the friendly bombs that might stray from the predicted trajectory, he did as General Hinh had done on February 24 and ordered his men to fall back shortly before the scheduled time over target. As it turned out, only three misdirected air strikes took place during Lam Son 719, none of them involving B–52s.[47]

South Vietnamese Invasion of Laos

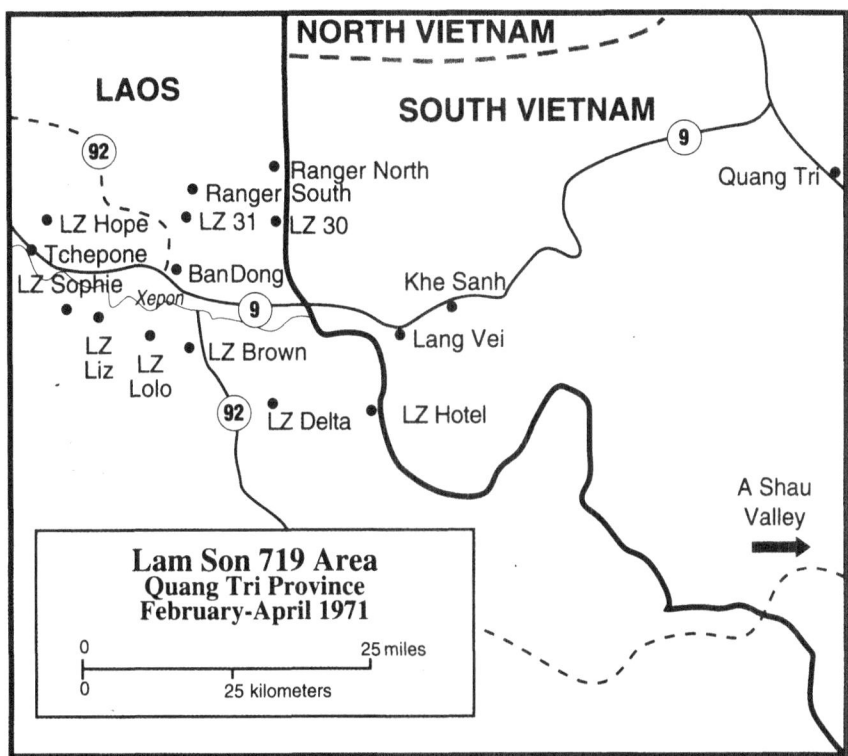

Although the B–52s released their bombs on signal from a Combat Skyspot radar on the ground, most fighter-bombers, especially those diverted to respond to emergencies, needed good weather for the pilot to acquire the target and bomb accurately. Unfortunately, the weather turned bad in mid-March, grounding the fighter-bombers and enabling the North Vietnamese to attack Landing Zone Lolo, which the task force abandoned on the night of March 15-16. Some of the defenders took advantage of radar directed strikes by B–52s delivered within 500 yards of the embattled perimeter, escaped, and found refuge on nearby high ground. Clearing skies after daybreak signaled the arrival of fighter-bombers that pounded the North Vietnamese and enabled helicopters to pick up the survivors of the fight for Landing Zone Lolo.

The capture of Landing Zone Lolo marked the beginning of the systematic elimination of the remaining fire support bases along Route 9. Within three days, from the approaches to Tchepone eastward to Ban Dong, isolated pockets of South Vietnamese were trying to escape encirclement by an enemy using tanks, some of them mounting flame throwers. Intense antiaircraft fire greeted helicopters and fighter-bombers, and darkness or bad weather could interfere with tactical air operations long enough for the North Vietnamese to overwhelm the outnumbered defenders.[48]

Air War over South Vietnam, 1968–1975

At about the time the helicopters were retrieving the soldiers who had escaped from Landing Zone Lolo, General Haig arrived at Quang Tri City to announce, according to Sutherland, that "Washington would like to see the ARVN [Army of the Republic of Vietnam] stay in Laos through April."[49] Although confident that American firepower, especially the B–52s, "had really hurt the enemy in the Tchepone area," Sutherland doubted that the operation could continue that long. To remain in Laos, the task force would require not just individual replacements but also fresh units, and the South Vietnamese army had not planned to send in new brigades or divisions.[50]

By the time his brief visit ended, Haig realized that Washington had lost touch with battlefield reality. Conversations with the key South Vietnamese commanders changed his mind. "He believes," reported Lt. Gen. Michael S. Davison, commander of II Field Force, Vietnam, "that a serious debacle could evolve in the absence of firm ARVN command and control and with the weather's continued neutralization of air support." Instead of urging an extension of Lam Son 719, Haig reached what Davison described as a "tentative conclusion that the time has come for an orderly close-out of the ground operations in Laos."[51]

Unfortunately, Haig's conversion came too late. The enemy had grown so strong that the Lam Son 719 task force could no longer effect an orderly close-out of ground operations, as the American general urged. Since enemy tanks were appearing in increasing numbers, the South Vietnamese armored brigade might well provide the key to a successful withdrawal. On March 19, after abandoning Ban Dong, the brigade formed a column of tanks and armored personnel carriers, some of the latter towing artillery pieces, and started eastward along Route 9, with airborne soldiers assuming responsibility for securing the high ground on either flank. The road-bound formation had barely started when the enemy triggered an ambush that cost the brigade eighteen vehicles destroyed either by hostile fire or by air strikes intended to keep them out of North Vietnamese hands. Two days later, at a point just five miles inside Laos, the North Vietnamese again struck from ambush, knocking out additional tanks and armored personnel carriers and persuading Col. Nguyen Trong Luat, the brigade commander, that it would be suicidal to continue down the vulnerable highway. Abandoning much of its heavy equipment, the battered unit left Route 9 and fled toward the border over a trail that unexpectedly came to a dead end at the steep banks of the Xepon River. While the South Vietnamese struggled to improvise a defense, Soviet-supplied PT–76 light tanks and T–54 mediums closed in for the kill.

On March 22, beneath a ceiling high enough to permit attacks by fighter-bombers, some twenty North Vietnamese tanks drove boldly in daylight along the route the South Vietnamese had taken. Weaving in and out among the abandoned or destroyed light tanks and armored personnel carriers that littered the highway, the armored vehicles turned onto the trail. The first pair of tanks,

South Vietnamese Invasion of Laos

T–54s, closed to within five kilometers of the river before Air Force fighter-bombers appeared overhead, carrying both napalm canisters and high-explosive bombs fitted with brakes to improve accuracy and enable the low-flying aircraft to avoid damage from the detonation. After two F–100s attacked but failed to inflict any damage, a second pair of fighters disabled both tanks, though at the cost of one F–100 shot down and its pilot killed. Subsequent air strikes destroyed two other T–54s, one already disabled by a land mine, and two PT–76s, scattering the remaining tanks and enabling the South Vietnamese to dig in for the night with their backs to the river. On the morning of March 23, the remnants of the column began fording the stream, thanks in part to two bulldozers flown in by Army helicopters to cut away portions of the bank.[52]

Within the collapsing salient, as the armored brigade began the withdrawal that became a rout, North Vietnamese troops surrounded Fire Support Base Delta south of Route 9 and east of Ban Dong. U.S. Army helicopters tried on March 21 to evacuate the marines trapped there. Hoping to take advantage of a fleeting break in weather, the rescuers took off without notifying the direct air support center at Quang Tri City and arranging for fighter-bombers to meet them at the objective. With only their own firepower, the helicopters could not suppress the North Vietnamese weapons covering the outpost; hostile gunners destroyed seven helicopters and damaged fifty others, putting an end to the attempted evacuation.

On the morning of March 22, better weather enabled tactical fighters to hit the North Vietnamese surrounding Fire Support Base Delta with the first of forty sorties flown that day. Despite the air strikes, the enemy attacked, ten flame-throwing tanks leading the way. Mines and infantry missiles disabled three of the tanks and aircraft destroyed another, but the assault cracked the perimeter and seized a portion of the objective. After dark, Air Force flareships and gunships began circling the outpost; they arrived too late, however, for the surviving marines had fled their position and were trying under cover of darkness to make their way to Fire Support Base Hotel, on the south bank of the Xepon River just west of the border, which remained in friendly hands. On the morning of the 23d, a dozen fighters bombed the abandoned strongpoint to harass the victors and destroy ammunition and equipment left behind.[53]

After exchanging fire with North Vietnamese patrols, and at times clashing by accident with fellow marines also fleeing the enemy, many of the men from Fire Support Base Delta succeeded in reaching Fire Support Base Hotel, where army helicopters met them and flew them to an assembly area in South Vietnam. Meanwhile, the commandant of the South Vietnamese Marine Corps, Lt. Gen. Le Nguyen Khang, issued orders to abandon Fire Support Base Hotel before the North Vietnamese could encircle and capture it. As if to underscore the general's concern, hostile armor reached the border south of Route 9, where Air Force fighter-bombers and rocket-firing Army helicopters claimed the destruction of ten tanks.[54]

Air War over South Vietnam, 1968–1975

As stragglers poured across the border, General Khang abandoned Fire Support Base Hotel without consulting General Lam, the task force commander. Next he ignored Lam's orders to place a battalion atop Co Roc, a mountain near Khe Sanh, to help establish a shield behind which the battered invasion force could regroup. Not until two B–52 strikes had shaken the mountain and any North Vietnamese who might have been there, did the marines cooperate, allowing a reconnaissance company rather than an infantry battalion to board helicopters and set up an outpost there.[55]

The raid on the approaches to the A Shau Valley, planned in conjunction with Lam Son 719, no longer seemed feasible in its original form, but the South Vietnamese still hoped to probe the logistics complex in that area, largely as a gesture of defiance directed at the victorious North Vietnamese. Indeed, this final phase of the operation attained a symbolic importance all out of proportion to its military value. South Vietnamese troops had to raid the storage bunkers at the mouth of the valley almost as a point of honor, but General Lam found it difficult to pick an objective his troops could capture. He settled upon Muong Nong, but on March 29, after repeated strikes by B–52s, a last-minute aerial reconnaissance of the landing zone revealed antiaircraft defenses that, in Sutherland's opinion, would have inflicted "unacceptable loses in personnel and equipment." Lam therefore postponed the attack for two days and sought a more realistic objective.[56]

The substitute objective lay on the very fringe of the base area that Lam hoped to attack, some forty kilometers southwest of the intersection of Route 9 and the border. Again B–52s led the way, followed after dawn on March 31 by twenty-two fighter-bombers, but the preparatory bombing failed to suppress North Vietnamese antiaircraft fire, forcing an hour's postponement for additional strikes by tactical aircraft. Army helicopters arrived at 11:30 A.M. and landed a 200-man raiding party that remained in the area until the next afternoon when the helicopters returned. The South Vietnamese discovered that the preliminary air strikes had killed eighty-five enemy soldiers, destroyed a fuel dump, and collapsed a maze of tunnels that housed trucks. During its one night at the objective, the raiding party heard vehicles approaching and alerted a forward air controller who directed a strike credited with destroying five of them.[57]

On April 6, helicopters screened by tactical fighters landed a similar force, 150-strong, at an objective just inside Laos, twenty-two kilometers south of the ruins of the border village of Lang Vei. During the seven hours before the helicopters returned for them, the raiders encountered no opposition but discovered fifteen bodies and twenty discarded weapons. These two raids, mere gestures rather than serious attempts to hurt the enemy, marked the end of Lam Son 719.[58]

Even before the first of the two final raids, Sutherland had begun closing down the supply base at Khe Sanh. Air Force cargo handlers left with their equipment, and engineers took up the recently installed aluminum matting for possible use elsewhere. The last American troops abandoned the base shortly after the second raid.[59] Meanwhile, retrenchment occurred throughout northwestern South Vietnam, as Air Force C–130s flew 195 sorties into Phu Bai and Quang Tri City to retrieve 1,000 tons of cargo and redeploy almost 10,000 troops.[60]

Evaluation of the effect of Lam Son 719 began as the armored brigade was extricating itself from Laos. On March 22, in a nationally televised interview with Howard K. Smith of the American Broadcasting Company, President Nixon declared that the operation had been an unqualified success. Referring to television news broadcasts showing disorganized and demoralized South Vietnamese soldiers, some of them clinging to the landing skids of American helicopters in a desperate attempt to escape from Laos, Nixon insisted that men in just four of the thirty-four battalions had behaved like this; all the other units, he said, had remained steadfast in the face of the enemy. He further claimed that the operation had reduced by 75 percent the volume of North Vietnamese truck traffic on the Ho Chi Minh Trail south of Tchepone. As he had when defending the previous year's invasion of Cambodia, the Chief Executive emphasized the link between Lam Son 719 and the continued withdrawal of American ground forces. He argued that "the thousands of North Vietnamese who were casualties . . . , the hundreds of millions of rounds of ammunition that was destroyed . . . , the time that was bought . . . , all these things" greatly reduced "the risk to American lives" by forestalling an offensive as the last American troops withdrew from South Vietnam. That, he concluded, "is why the operation was worthwhile in my opinion."[61]

Although they insisted that a majority of the South Vietnamese battalions had fought well, some American officers involved in Lam Son 719 conceded that the invasion force had suffered serious losses. General Sutherland, for example, acknowledged that the enemy had all but wiped out the armored brigade, destroying or capturing 60 percent of the unit's tanks and half of its armored personnel carriers. Besides losing these 163 vehicles, the brigade failed to bring back fifty-four 105-mm and twenty-eight 155-mm howitzers.[62] Earlier in the fighting, severe casualties had rendered four battalions — two ranger, one infantry, and one airborne — "combat ineffective," while another airborne battalion possessed "doubtful" effectiveness because of inept leadership and poor morale.[63] Moreover, the Marine division exhibited what General Hinh described as "problems of command and control," inasmuch as the unit cooperated on its own terms with the corps commander, General Lam, and did not necessarily follow his orders. Although the marines fought well and, in Hinh's opinion, "retained unit integrity and cohesiveness," they failed to hold Fire Support Base Delta and yielded Fire Support Base Hotel after a brief fight.[64]

In his public assessment of the condition of the troops who had fought in Lam Son 719, President Nixon obviously erred on the side of optimism; he also

Air War over South Vietnam, 1968–1975

accepted unrealistic reports by the military assistance command concerning the impact of Lam Son 719 on North Vietnamese logistics. General Abrams at first declared that the operation had, in effect, destroyed one entire station on the Ho Chi Minh Trail, forcing the North Vietnamese to divert truck traffic westward and use highways that Thai irregulars briefly threatened. Despite the thrust from the east and pressure from the west, electronic sensors indicated that traffic throughout southern Laos increased immediately after Lam Son 719.[65] Although the greater volume no doubt reflected a need to replace supplies consumed or destroyed in the fighting around Tchepone, it also demonstrated an ability and willingness to make good the loss and continue to prosecute the war in South Vietnam and Cambodia. The invasion of southern Laos had disturbed the logistics flow, surely disrupting any North Vietnamese plans for a major offensive in the immediate future; it had not, however, reduced truck traffic by 75 percent as the President told Howard K. Smith.

After Lam Son 719 had ended, President Nixon declared that "the South Vietnamese had demonstrated that without American advisers they could fight effectively against the best troops North Vietnam could put in the field."[66] General Abrams, too, applauded the fighting ability of the South Vietnamese during Lam Son 719, but he admitted that the Vietnamized armed forces could not carry out so ambitious an undertaking on their own; they still required American advice in both planning and execution, along with air support and artillery fire.[67] General Sutherland underscored the importance of American air power, pointing out that the North Vietnamese suffered as grievously as they had "principally because of TAC air and B–52 strikes."[68]

The Seventh Air Force had conducted a deadly air campaign, though interrupted by bad weather and beset by recurring emergencies. During Lam Son 719, Air Force tactical fighters flew more than 8,000 attack sorties, dropping some 20,000 tons of bombs and napalm on targets within an area of just 550 square miles. To facilitate air strikes, each of the six forward air controllers on duty at any time over the invasion corridor carried a "target bank," a list of known or suspected storage areas or troops concentrations against which the controllers could direct an attack when they had no target with a higher priority. Although the target bank proved of some value while the task force paused around Ban Dong, the clashes on the ground became so furious and widespread, and the threat from armor so dangerous, that forward air controllers seemed to go from one emergency to another and rarely needed the list of stand-by targets. Other aircraft joined the tactical fighters, and the forward air controllers that directed them, in contributing to the aerial onslaught. Hercules transports dropped twenty-five 15,000-pound bombs on proposed landing zones, and Air Force gunships patrolled the roads by night. Thailand-based B–52s, flying more than 1,300 sorties, added some 32,000 tons of bombs.[69]

The South Vietnamese Air Force flew more than 5,500 sorties, most of them by helicopters, essentially a token contribution. In contrast, U.S. Army

South Vietnamese Invasion of Laos

helicopter crews flew more than 160,000 sorties, almost thirty times as many, computed on the same basis as the South Vietnamese tallied theirs. Clearly, Lam Son 719 would have been impossible without U.S. helicopters.[70]

As happened so often in the Vietnam War, the effort in Lam Son 719 proved easier to measure than the results, for the statistics on enemy losses often came from reports by airmen, attacking in poor visibility, and foot soldiers fighting for their lives. Rarely did South Vietnamese troops capture objectives or enter target boxes hit by B–52s to make a more accurate estimate of the carnage. On the basis of the available evidence, the military assistance command claimed almost 20,000 North Vietnamese killed (a total that the South Vietnamese high command reduced to 13,000) and sixty-one captured. The death toll, according the General Abrams' headquarters, included some 3,000 killed by tactical aircraft and 2,600 by B–52s. Of 106 tanks reported destroyed, crews of American tactical fighters claimed seventy-four, but the military assistance command accepted a toll of just 88 and credited the airmen with fifty-nine.[71]

According to General Abrams' headquarters, the U.S. Army lost 215 killed, 1,149 wounded, and thirty missing while capturing and defending the bases in South Vietnam that sustained Lam Son 719 or flying helicopter missions in Laos. Army aviation suffered nineteen killed, fifty-nine wounded, and eleven missing; the other soldiers became casualties during Dewey Canyon II or in sapper attacks and ambushes inside South Vietnam during Lam Son 719. In keeping with the nature of the operation, which pitted a vast fleet of helicopters against dangerous antiaircraft defenses, the Army also had the heaviest losses in aircraft, 100 helicopters destroyed and 600 damaged.

The Seventh Air Force lost six aircraft to enemy fire, three F–4Ds, an A–1H, an O–2A, and an F–100. Of the ten crewmen, two died, two were missing and later declared dead, two suffered wounds but parachuted safely and were recovered, and the three others sustained only minor injuries in ejecting and also were rescued. The Navy lost an A–7 to 23-mm fire; a search and rescue mission failed to locate the pilot.[72]

When the remnants of the South Vietnamese task force straggled back from Laos, the commanders of the various units at first could only estimate their casualties, and the numbers fluctuated as soldiers left behind in the retreat rejoined their units. The final count exceeded 7,600 casualties, some 1,500 of them killed, 5,500 wounded, and the rest missing.[73] Assuming the validity of Kissinger's claim that Thieu intended to keep the total casualties below 3,000, the South Vietnam had suffered more than twice the losses its president believed the public could accept.

As Thieu had feared, the magnitude of the South Vietnamese losses, especially when contrasted to the American casualty list, raised doubts about the willingness of the United States to accept risks on behalf of an ally. The worst of the losses had occurred after the president of South Vietnam yielded to

Abrams and Sutherland and pushed on from Ban Dong to Tchepone, but during that critical period American ground troops had remained in their bases on the South Vietnamese side of the border. Demonstrations broke out in South Vietnam, as students in particular charged that Vietnamization simply meant that the United States would fight to the last South Vietnamese. The protest flared and rapidly subsided, but at least one journalist, Stanley Karnow, believed he could detect a lingering distrust of Americans.[74]

What did Lam Son 719 accomplish? On the one hand, the loss of life suffered by the North Vietnamese, though certainly less than the claim of 20,000 killed, and the destruction of supplies disrupted any plans the enemy might have had for an invasion of South Vietnam during 1971. On the other, the successful counterattack may have encouraged North Vietnam to make good its losses as quickly as possible and again to test the mettle of the South Vietnamese armed forces and the resolve of the United States to help them. Lam Son 719, after all, had ended with the task force reeling in disorder back to its starting point, a result that revealed flaws in the program of Vietnamization. On the ground, General Lam's soldiers had lacked medium tanks and antitank weapons, deficiencies the United States would have to correct even as it replaced the equipment destroyed or abandoned in Laos. In the air, Vietnamization had failed thus far to produce a true striking force: the helicopter fleet did not have the numbers, training, or experience to undertake an operation of the magnitude of Lam Son 719; the transports could not deploy troops and cargo on the scale of Dewey Canyon II; and the tactical aircraft could not overcome the kind of defenses encountered between the border and Tchepone. Under current plans, the South Vietnamese air arm would not receive the OV–10s used by forward air controllers during the operation or the F–4s, A–7s, and F–100s that delivered the actual strikes; nor would the United States make B–52s available to its ally. Of the types of aircraft that bombed and strafed in support of the attack into Laos, South Vietnam would receive only the A–1, which served mainly to suppress hostile fire during aerial rescues, but Vietnamization did not include a rescue service.

Besides revealing failings in equipping the Vietnamized armed forces, Lam Son 719 demonstrated the inability of most South Vietnamese commanders to function without American advisers at their elbow. Suddenly on their own, the leaders had difficulty applying American-taught doctrine in southern Laos. The best of them seemed hesitant and unsure of themselves, while the worst proved incompetent.

The South Vietnamese, however, launched other less ambitious operations during 1971 that proved more successful. The armed forces of South Vietnam may simply have overreached when they challenged the defenses of the Ho Chi Minh Trail, or the weaker opposition in Cambodia and South Vietnam may have masked the flaws in training and equipment so starkly revealed in southern Laos. In either case, Vietnamization required a prompt and thorough overhaul.

Chapter Sixteen

Action in South Vietnam and Cambodia 1971

Although Operation Lam Son 719 in southern Laos assumed critical importance as a test of Vietnamization and a means of facilitating the American withdrawal, fighting also took place in South Vietnam and Cambodia during 1971. Even as the improved armed forces of South Vietnam assumed increasing responsibility for waging war, U.S. air, ground, and naval forces continued to see action from the Mekong River in Cambodia to the demilitarized zone separating the two Vietnams. Indeed, the American activity reflected in part the concern of the Joint Chiefs of Staff that the greater participation by the South Vietnamese in offensive action could actually increase the danger to the American troops still in South Vietnam by relegating them to a purely defensive "guard-type posture" that would make them easy prey for the highly mobile enemy. To reduce the vulnerability of the remaining Americans, the Joint Chiefs, after consultation with General Abrams, proposed, and Secretary of Defense Laird approved, a strategy of "dynamic defense" that called for U.S. battalions to probe beyond the immediate environs of their bases, cooperating with South Vietnamese forces in attacks designed to keep the enemy off balance.

Vietnamization, withdrawal, and the new policy of dynamic defense combined to reduce American casualties. During 1971, 1,380 U.S. soldiers, sailors, marines, and airmen died in combat throughout Southeast Asia, 1,289 of them in South Vietnam. The total number of battle deaths declined by 2,845 from 1970 and by more than 8,000 from 1969, when, in the aftermath of Hamburger Hill, President Nixon had cautioned Abrams about excessive casualties.[1]

The reduction in battle deaths coincided with a decline in American manpower serving in South Vietnam. In January 1971, the aggregate number authorized for duty there stood at 344,000, but a series of withdrawals during the year slashed that number by 205,000 to 139,000. In other words, the departures from South Vietnam snowballed so rapidly in 1971 that more Americans left the country than remained on duty there when the year ended.[2]

Operations in Cambodia also continued throughout 1971, with the United States hoping that the Lon Nol government would retain at least the territory it

Air War over South Vietnam, 1968–1975

held, about half of Cambodia, including the capital of Phnom Penh and its approaches, the rice-producing northwest, and the Mekong River supply line from South Vietnam to Phnom Penh. "Our policy," declared a summary of American relations with Cambodia, "should be to capitalize on Cambodian nationalism, support Cambodian neutrality, and promote ... [the] self-sufficiency" of the government.[3] Unfortunately, Lon Nol had irrevocably forfeited his nation's neutrality in 1970 by sending the ill-equipped and untrained Khmer army against the North Vietnamese in eastern Cambodia. Nor had the United States found it easy to correct the shortcomings of the troops he had impulsively committed and convert them into a reliable instrument of Cambodian self-sufficiency.[4]

Indirectly, the same congressional resolution that prevented American troops from serving on the ground in Laos also affected American participation in the Cambodian fighting. During the invasion of Cambodia in the spring of 1970, Senators John Sherman Cooper and Frank Church introduced an amendment to a foreign military sales bill that would have barred all American soldiers and airmen from fighting there or serving as advisers. This measure failed, largely because the U.S. assault force withdrew as the President had promised. When the Cooper-Church amendment finally passed, attached to different legislation, it ignored Cambodia and aerial warfare and applied only to the introduction of ground forces into Thailand and Laos. Nevertheless, Nixon, wary of needlessly antagonizing the Congress, refrained from establishing in the new Khmer Republic the kind of formal military advisory group that already existed in Thailand and South Vietnam.[5]

Lacking the authorization to establish a full-fledged advisory group at Phnom Penh, the U.S. military had to substitute an attaché office assigned to the embassy and a military equipment distribution team that reported to Abrams in Saigon. Authorized a total of 113 officers and men, the equipment team issued the military gear supplied by the United States and helped train the Cambodians to use it. Of the 60 persons initially assigned to the team, only 16 actually served in Cambodia. By 1971 the organization reached its authorized strength, with 50 persons operating out of Phnom Penh.[6]

Despite his concern over assigning American advisers to Cambodia, President Nixon permitted air strikes in the country. He continued, however, to insist that reports list them as aerial interdiction and not as close air support. He had ruled out this category of air strikes in 1970, perhaps inadvertently, but more likely to avoid the impression that U.S. airmen supported U.S. ground forces still fighting there. During 1971, aircraft of the United States, South Vietnam, and the Khmer Republic operated over Cambodia. The United States sought to combine these efforts under a grandly styled Allied Air Operations Coordinating Center, but the effort failed largely because of Cambodian intransigence. Events demonstrated, moreover, that South Vietnamese airmen would not run risks to help the Cambodians, which left the air war largely in American hands. Lon Nol had little choice but to rely on foreigners for air support, since his own

South Vietnam and Cambodia, 1971

Cambodians training in South Vietnam with South Vietnamese instructors.

army had scant confidence in a Khmer air arm that had barely begun rebuilding after a Khmer Rouge rocket attack in January that destroyed almost the entire inventory of hand-me-down Soviet MiGs and U.S. T–28s at Phnom Penh's Pochentong Airport.

At the urging of the United States, the allies in 1971 created an air coordinating center that underwent a change of name and membership, lingered through the following year, but accomplished little. Because the Americans assigned to the center, unlike the air attaché and his staff or members of the equipment distribution team, could not serve in Cambodia, the coordinating agency set up shop at Tan Son Nhut Air Base in South Vietnam, an obvious handicap since the location reminded the Cambodians of their debt to the hated South Vietnamese. Target nominations went to Tan Son Nhut, where the center granted or withheld endorsement before sending the slate to Phnom Penh for final approval.

When this procedure broke down, more because of Cambodian recalcitrance than the fragile radio link, the Seventh Air Force provided more reliable communications with Phnom Penh and formed a Tripartite Deputies Working Group, also at Tan Son Nhut. Once again, the organization's title proved more impressive than its accomplishments, for the group failed to achieve its objective of allaying hostility among the Asian allies and improving cooperation.[7]

The lack of Cambodian participation in the control agency affected the rules of engagement under which the United States fought the air war. The Americans expected Khmer officers at the appropriate level of command to review all targets — roads, waterways, or tracts of jungle — to determine if the extent of communist use or control justified aerial attack. This kind of review did not always take place, however; and to prevent accidentally bombing or strafing friendly troops or noncombatants in contested areas, the U.S. Air Force command and control agencies insisted that strike aircraft rely on radar or instructions from a forward air controller, preferably an American. U.S. planners, more than the Cambodians, tried to avoid damaging cultural or religious shrines and tried to issue a warning before attacking villages where civilians might suffer injury. In an emergency, however, a pilot might respond immediately to a call for help from a commander on the ground, hesitating only to make sure he had identified the designated target. For air strikes planned in advance, when no Cambodian stood by at the coordinating agency to pass judgment on an individual target, the Americans had to rely on blanket validations embracing a particular area. For example, the Seventh Air Force Tactical Air Control Center routinely approved plans to attack targets throughout communist-controlled northeastern Cambodia and on roads or rivers normally used by the enemy elsewhere in the country. For targets where noncombatants or friendly troops might be endangered, a senior American officer in the military assistance command's directorate of operations reviewed the nomination and passed judgment.[8]

The friction among the Southeast Asian allies, which surfaced during the attempt to establish a coordinating agency for tactical air operations, also prevented the United States from developing close working relationships between the governments of the Khmer Republic, South Vietnam, Thailand, and Laos.[9] The Cambodians tended to hate all Vietnamese, whether from the South or the North; consequently, when Lon Nol in the spring of 1970 stirred up the masses against the northerners in their embassy and jungle enclaves, mobs began slaughtering anticommunist Vietnamese refugees, many of whom had lived in Cambodia since the partition of Vietnam in 1954, in some villages killing every adult male. The bodies of hundreds of Vietnamese bobbing in the Mekong River greeted the South Vietnamese army when it crossed the border to attack the communist bases. Most of the survivors fled Cambodia, increasing by perhaps 200,000 the number of homeless the government of South Vietnam had to assist.[10]

Toward Thailand, Cambodians felt suspicion rather than hatred, for Thai rulers had once controlled the western portions of the Khmer Republic, just as Cambodia formerly exerted authority over parts of Vietnam. Lon Nol and his government experienced the concerns of a weak nation toward a stronger and perhaps covetous neighbor. Cambodia, in short, wanted U.S. help rather than aid from South Vietnam and Thailand, but the United States, as demonstrated by its reluctance to establish a typical military assistance advisory group, remained wary of repeating the sort of commitment it had made to South Vietnam.

For the United States, the fighting in Cambodia represented an extension of the war in the South, another means of gaining time for Vietnamization and withdrawal by easing the pressure on the U.S. forces still in South Vietnam. Moreover, the governments of South Vietnam and Thailand also looked on

South Vietnam and Cambodia, 1971

Cambodia in terms of their own security, seeing the Khmer Republic as an entanglement for North Vietnamese aggressors.[11]

In these circumstances, the United States, Cambodia, and South Vietnam fought their own air wars in Khmer territory. In waging its air war, the United States preserved the appearance of consultation with Cambodian authorities, as it relied increasingly on B–52s to provide firepower capable of stopping the advance of the Khmer Rouge, communist forces recruited from inside Cambodia. Indeed, the bombing became a symbol of U.S. support as well as a weapon of war. The Cambodian air force waged a feeble air campaign that contrasted sharply with the army's battles on the ground, most of which proved savage, if often ineptly planned and fought. South Vietnamese airmen mainly supported their nation's ground forces in action across the border, although they would sometimes respond to American urging and come to the aid of Lon Nol's troops.[12]

By mid-1971, six months after the disastrous rocket attack on Pochentong airdrome, Cambodia had received U.S. T–28s, AC–47 gunships, and O–1s, but it made poor use of the equipment. Admittedly, the O–1s intended for forward air controllers had badly worn engines that increased fuel and oil consumption and reduced range, and the T–28s also tottered at the edge of obsolescence, but these two types and the AC–47 could have proved adequate in the absence of aerial opposition or heavy antiaircraft fire. The fault seemed to lie with officers who still lacked confidence in the airmen and proved reluctant to call upon them. Since front-line Cambodian officers also mistrusted South Vietnamese pilots, U.S. forward air controllers, whose numbers the policy of withdrawal continued to reduce, directed a disproportionate share of close-in strikes. As their number inexorably declined, the ill-equipped, inexperienced, and generally distrusted Cambodian airmen had to assume increasing responsibility for directing air support.[13]

Lon Nol's attack on the North Vietnamese in the spring of 1970 failed to dislodge them from their Cambodian enclaves. His army, although sometimes capable of fierce fighting and vicious atrocities, lacked the leadership, training, and equipment to defeat the North Vietnamese and the Khmer Rouge. The United States simply could not take over a new war as it tried to disengage from an old one in South Vietnam, nor would President Nixon agree to a major advisory effort. Nevertheless, American aid began arriving, administered by the military equipment distribution team, but the new Khmer Republic faced a difficult task in fighting to retain control of Phnom Penh, the surrounding region, and the agricultural west.

The planners of Lam Son 719 gave some thought to an attack into Cambodia, initially as a possible substitute for the foray into Laos and later as a complementary operation. The offensive finally scheduled during the dry season of 1970-71 called for elements of the South Vietnamese III Corps to attack in an area extending from the town of Snoul generally southwestward past Tonle

Air War over South Vietnam, 1968–1975

Bet to the vicinity of Svay Rieng. The overall operation had three components. In the center, troops would advance along Route 22 to the Cambodian border and then seize and hold Route 7 westward to the town of Tonle Bet on the Mekong River, a distance of about forty miles. During this advance, the center force would divert the enemy from Phnom Penh and interfere with infiltration into South Vietnam by seizing the supply caches between Chup on Route 7 and Dambe on Route 75. Meanwhile, the northern force would clear the triangular region north of Route 7 bounded by the towns of Snoul, Mimot, and Kratie. In the south, other South Vietnamese soldiers would conduct a similar sweep of a region defined by Routes 1, 15, and 7, and the border with South Vietnam. The ambitious operation got underway on February 4, just four days before the Lam Son 719 task force started down the road toward Tchepone in Laos.[14]

On the southern flank, the South Vietnamese pushed slowly forward, but despite the sluggish pace, they retained the initiative, forcing the North Vietnamese to channel troops into this area who otherwise might have helped reopen the routes of supply and reinforcement leading from the Ho Chi Minh Trail into South Vietnam's Military Region III. The attack could not, however, dislodge the North Vietnamese from the base areas south of Route 7, and the other elements of the offensive fared only a little better.[15]

By mid-March, the heaviest enemy resistance developed in the center sector, around the Chup Rubber Plantation, probably because of the firmly established North Vietnamese supply depots located there. During the early fighting, B–52s and Air Force fighter-bombers, along with South Vietnamese tactical aircraft, battered the enemy. Indeed, a B–52 attack near Dambe received credit for killing 150 North Vietnamese. During daylight, strike aircraft tried to suppress hostile fire so that helicopters could deliver supplies to the advancing troops; when these attacks failed, the Army helicopters operated under cover of darkness. Unfortunately, air power could not intervene to blast a path into the plantation itself, for Lon Nol persisted in believing that the rubber trees represented a resource his nation needed and objected strenuously to actions that might destroy them. Both President Thieu and General Abrams respected his wishes and spared Chup Plantation. The attack in the center reached Tonle Bet, advanced beyond Dambe all the way to Chhlong, and received credit for killing some 4,000 North Vietnamese or Khmer Rouge while destroying large quantities of ammunition and fuel, but the plantation itself, a major base, remained in communist hands.[16]

While the offensive was bypassing Chup Plantation, leaving in place an unknown quantity of supplies shipped by way of the Ho Chi Minh Trail, the northern prong of the dry season offensive captured Snoul and moved into the countryside. Heavy rains of the southwest monsoon season were approaching when patrols discovered some supply caches near Snoul, destroyed them, and stung the enemy, who reacted late in May by encircling the South Vietnamese at Snoul. Air Force forward air controllers discovered the buildup around the

South Vietnam and Cambodia, 1971

F–100s at Phan Rang prepare for a mission in 1971.

town and along the road that led there, but before air power could intervene, the North Vietnamese attacked. Antiaircraft fire prevented South Vietnamese C–119s from parachuting supplies into Snoul, and the relief column that started up the road ran into an ambush. The result resembled the defeat of the Lam Son 719 task force, though on a lesser scale, since it involved only the one brigade that attempted the rescue. Here, as in southern Laos, air strikes had to destroy equipment abandoned by the fleeing South Vietnamese. A second column succeeded in reaching Snoul, but the perimeter there became a magnet for hostile fire rather than a launching point for attacks on the logistics network.[17]

The main South Vietnamese thrust into Cambodia ended in frustration, and a series of other actions in that country produced results varying from successful to disastrous. For a time, success crowned the effort to keep traffic flowing over Route 4, linking the port of Kompong Som with Phnom Penh, but strikes by the U.S. Air Force, rather than aggressive action by South Vietnamese and Khmer troops, forced the Cambodian communists to abandon blocking positions rather than suffer appalling casualties in trying to hold them. According to American officers attached to the embassy at Phnom Penh, an attack along the shore of the Tonle Toch, a stream forming part of the Mekong watershed, provided Lon Nol's army with its greatest victory yet, and here, too, air power made a critical contribution. Despite the onset of the seasonal rains, Air Force tactical fighters averaged eighty sorties during each of four hard-fought days, and an AC–119 gunship cut down Khmer Rouge soldiers gathering supplies that Cambodian C–47s had parachuted beyond friendly lines.

Disaster awaited, however, when Lon Nol chose the depths of the rainy season to send one of his least competent generals to reopen the highway leading northward from the capital city to the beleaguered town of Kompong Thom. At a time when weather prevented accurate close air support, the North Vietnamese sprung a trap as soon as the head of the column reached the objective; flank security proved nonexistent, and the surprise so overwhelming that most of the troops abandoned their weapons and fled.[18]

Air War over South Vietnam, 1968–1975

As demonstrated at Snoul and again at Kompong Thom, the North Vietnamese had mastered the art of ambush, but even the best laid trap sometimes failed. In September 1971, as a new dry season drew near, North Vietnamese forces attacked the South Vietnamese defenders of Krek in Cambodia in the hope of forcing them, or drawing their reinforcements, into an ambush prepared on Route 22 just inside South Vietnam.[19] While South Vietnamese airborne troops conducted some aggressive patrolling, the garrison at Krek held its ground and relied on artillery and air strikes to kill the enemy. Maj. Gen. Jack J. Wagstaff, the commanding general of the Third Regional Assistance Command, reported that "the greatest number of casualties have been inflicted by our B–52s, Tac Air, and gunships, with the ARVN operations limited to bomb damage assessment after an area has been cleared by our firepower." Without air power, Wagstaff suggested, the South Vietnamese would have "inflicted negligible damage on the enemy," who surely could have driven them from the fire support bases around Krek into the waiting trap.[20]

During the fighting around Krek, which lasted until mid-October, American infantry advisers, assessing the operation from inside South Vietnam, condemned as "100 percent unsatisfactory,"[21] the South Vietnamese CH–47 helicopter units carrying cargo into the besieged town. In contrast, the Air Force advisers who hurried to the airfield at Tay Ninh, South Vietnam, from which the craft operated, decided that the South Vietnamese simply had not understood the U.S. Army's scheduling procedures. Once the working relationship improved between the Army advisers and the crews from the South Vietnamese Air Force, the performance of the helicopters rapidly improved. As a result, supplies delivered by the CH–47s sustained the outpost at Krek until a sufficiently strong relief force had eliminated the threat to the overland route.[22]

Like Operation Lam Son 719 in Laos, the fighting in eastern Cambodia revealed the dependence of the South Vietnamese on American support, especially air power. If forced to rely exclusively on their own resources, the armed forces of the Republic of Vietnam might well have withdrawn from Cambodia, or so General Wagstaff believed. The Vietnamized air arm, for instance, had shown weaknesses that did not appear in routine operations. The fighter-bombers proved successful in strikes just across the border, but lacked the range or the aerial refueling equipment needed for deep penetrations. Moreover, the South Vietnamese Air Force, which operated the helicopter squadrons, did not yet have enough large CH–47s, and it also needed modern transports like the C–130. Finally, South Vietnam's airmen possessed no weapon even remotely comparable to the B–52 in administering massive doses of firepower.[23]

Because the South Vietnamese had no C–130s, the 834th Air Division used its own C–130s, temporarily assigned for duty in Southeast Asia, to drop supplies to isolated South Vietnamese troops inside Cambodia, helping, for example, to supply both Kompong Thom and the ill-fated relief force. Where the

C–130s could not go, either because of a tiny drop zone or murderous antiaircraft defenses, U.S. Army CH–47s supplemented South Vietnamese helicopters of the same kind. The U.S. C–130s also delivered badly needed fuel and munitions to Pochentong Airport at Phnom Penh, taking over in November 1971 from the South Vietnamese who simply lacked the airlift capacity for the task.[24]

The question of the Army's participation in Air Force interdiction efforts arose briefly during January 1971 and promptly disappeared. Army helicopters and helicopter gunships had been inserting and supporting reconnaissance teams in Cambodia in keeping with the prevailing rules of engagement, and this activity continued. General Abrams, however, offered a proposal that seemed to include the helicopter gunships in an interdiction campaign against roads and waterways used by both the North Vietnamese forces in Cambodia and the Khmer Rouge. Lt. Gen. Arthur S. Collins, the senior Army officer in South Vietnam's Military Region II, suggested that tactical fighters, with their greater range and speed, seemed better suited to the mission and opposed the suggestion. Moreover, as Collins pointed out, the Seventh Air Force planned and conducted aerial interdiction, and participation in the Air Force operation implied a diversion of the Army helicopter force from its usual missions.

The arguments advanced by Collins proved unnecessary, once Abrams clarified the reference to interdiction. He did not intend to place Army aircraft under the operational control of the Seventh Air Force. Instead, he had two purposes: first, to avoid accidents by making sure that Army officers in command and control helicopters checked in when bringing their assigned aircraft into a sector where an Air Force forward air controller directed air strikes; and, second, to remind the Air Force to follow President Nixon's wishes and report its air strikes as interdiction, never as close air support.[25]

Checking in with the Air Force forward air controller proved especially important late in January when American aerial firepower went to the aid of the South Vietnamese trying to reopen Route 4 — the road between the port of Kompong Som and the capital city — which the Khmer Rouge had temporarily cut at Pich Nil Pass. Army helicopter light fire teams — each with a command craft, two gunships, and two scout helicopters — took off from USS *Cleveland*, a landing ship operating in Cambodian coastal waters, and joined Air Force fighter-bombers in attacks at and near the pass. Besides supporting the successful attempt to break through the pass, the three light fire teams strafed hostile reinforcements, thus conducting battlefield interdiction despite the short range of the helicopters they flew.[26]

The presence of noncombatants, friendly troops, and hostile forces on the banks of the Mekong River posed special problems for aircraft patrolling the waterway, a vital supply artery for the Lon Nol government. With the enemy harassing traffic on Route 4 between the port of Kompong Som and Phnom Penh, the river carried increasing quantities of fuel, rice, and other bulk cargo not readily transportable by air.

Air War over South Vietnam, 1968–1975

By January 1971, the enemy began firing from the river banks at the convoys plying the stream. South Vietnamese or Khmer troops sometimes combed the banks in search of the enemy, thus exposing themselves to misdirected air strikes, which also might endanger innocent villagers. To protect noncombatants and friendly troops while silencing the fire, modified rules of engagement permitted helicopter gunships and fighter-bombers to attack, provided that a forward air controller directed the strike. If the controller obtained permission by radio from the commander of the convoy under attack, who had a Cambodian officer at his side, and could identify the source of the fire, he could launch an air strike immediately. If unable to contact the convoy commander and his Khmer adviser, the forward air controller had to consult some other Cambodian officer familiar with the location of villages and friendly troops in area. When the air coordinating center functioned at Tan Son Nhut, one of the Cambodian representatives normally reviewed such requests, but with the failure of that agency, the Seventh Air Force for a time included a Cambodian officer in the crew of the airborne battlefield command and control center responsible for the Mekong. By year's end, however, a Cambodian joined the staff of the Tactical Air Control Center expressly to validate such targets. Under this last arrangement, if the forward air controller could not obtain validation by radio from the convoy, he had to treat the banks of the Mekong River like a "no fire" zone and obtain permission from the Tactical Air Control Center before launching an air strike.[27]

Circumstances forced the Americans to take over the task of providing aerial protection for the convoys. The Khmer air arm could not do the job, and the South Vietnamese had the reputation of disregarding the safety of Cambodian noncombatants, possibly in reaction to the earlier killings by Cambodians of ethnic Vietnamese. In the absence of a true coordinating agency, the Seventh Air Force Tactical Air Control Center became the principal means for preventing accidental strikes on villagers or friendly troops by aircraft escorting the Mekong convoys.[28]

After assuming responsibility for escorting the convoys, as formally directed by General Abrams, the Seventh Air Force assigned forward air controllers in O–2s or OV–10s to provide day and night coverage. The controllers could call on any available Air Force fighter-bomber, gunship, or aircraft assigned specifically to escort duty. Beginning in mid-January 1971, a typical escort consisted of an Air Force forward air controller, an Air Force AC–119 gunship, and an Army light fire team. While the Air Force and Army furnished the air cover, the Navy assigned gunboats to travel with the convoy throughout the increasingly dangerous passage from Saigon to Phnom Penh.[29]

The commander of the U.S. naval forces in South Vietnam, since he already provided surface protection for Mekong shipping, sought to take part in the aerial escort, as well. The Seventh Air Force at first opposed bringing Navy aircraft into the operation, but Phnom Penh was growing more dependent on the

Mekong supply route, and the Air Force and Army aviation faced the possibility of becoming overextended, as aerial commitments continued in a time of withdrawal and dwindling resources. Consequently, General Abrams asked the Navy to provide helicopters and OV–10s "within the framework of the established USAF tactical air control system." The naval aircraft, in response to his directive, formed an alert force based in South Vietnam that carried out daily operational orders issued by the Seventh Air Force Tactical Air Control Center at Tan Son Nhut. In an extreme emergency, when an Air Force forward air controller on station over a convoy needed more firepower, he could contact the Navy detachment directly and call for help.[30] When escorting shipping, the naval aviators followed the same rules of engagement as airmen of the other services.[31]

Beginning in February 1971, armed Navy helicopters regularly flew escort missions over the Mekong River, but the Navy OV–10s saw little action until September. During that month, the Seventh Air Force transferred to the South Vietnamese the AC–119G gunships that had helped provide air cover for the convoys. Despite lighter armament, the Navy OV–10s filled the gap until Vietnamized AC–119Gs, with fully trained crews, could take over.[32]

Since the spring of 1970, when Lon Nol toppled Prince Sihanouk and the Americans and South Vietnamese invaded the North Vietnamese bases in eastern Cambodia, the territory under the nominal control of the Khmer Republic had shrunk steadily. Even as the fortunes of his government declined, Lon Nol suffered a stroke in February 1971 that diminished his powers of concentration and decision, even though he would survive for another fourteen years.

When Lon Nol first made war on the North Vietnamese in Cambodia, his armed forces numbered perhaps 36,000. A surge of enthusiasm to punish the traditional enemy swelled the ranks to about 150,000 by the end of 1970 although some of the soldiers almost certainly existed only on payrolls submitted by commanders who then pocketed the money. Whatever the actual size of the force, training and equipment could not keep pace. By December 1971, this army exerted only intermittent control of Route 4, increasing the nation's dependence on the Mekong for the delivery of supplies. The occasional military success, indeed the survival of the republic itself, depended upon U.S. air power and the South Vietnamese troops fighting the communists inside Cambodia. The Khmer Rouge in the meantime had grown stronger, receiving the endorsement of Prince Sihanouk, whose popularity increased as Cambodians realized that, whatever his faults, he had kept the nation out of war.[33]

In short, U.S. aid to Cambodia had wrought no miracles. Nevertheless, the Joint Chiefs of Staff recommended expanding the armed forces of the Khmer Republic during the year ending in June 1972 to 220,000, backed by a 143,000-man paramilitary organization, at a cost to the United States of $325 to $350 million. So ambitious a program would require expansion of the Military Equipment Delivery Team by an additional 629 officers and enlisted men; about 20 percent of the enlarged team would serve in Cambodia and the remainder in

Air War over South Vietnam, 1968–1975

South Vietnam, where the Cambodians would undergo most of their training. David Packard, Secretary Laird's principal deputy, suggested reworking the proposal, since Congress seemed unlikely to approve more than the $200 million for military assistance to Cambodia that the Department of Defense had tentatively proposed for the year. Revisions followed, but Congress proved less accommodating than Packard expected, voting only $180 million to aid Lon Nol's armed forces.[34]

The South Vietnamese offensives in southern Laos and Cambodia did not prevent the enemy from launching attacks of his own in South Vietnam. In Military Region I, embracing the northernmost provinces of South Vietnam, not even Dewey Canyon II, the prelude to the attack toward Tchepone and the most ambitious operation launched anywhere in South Vietnam during 1971, could wrest the initiative from the North Vietnamese. Besides delivering rocket attacks against Khe Sanh, while it served as the main base for Lam Son 719, the enemy conducted a nighttime raid against another outpost in Quang Tri Province, Fire Support Base Mary Ann. A 200-round mortar barrage, which included tear gas as well as high explosive, pinned down the defenders, and a team of sappers worked their way into the perimeter. They attacked the bunkers and artillery positions with explosive charges and small-arms fire, killing 22 and wounding 70 of some 200 U.S. defenders and destroying the command post. The skillfully delivered attack cost the North Vietnamese at least 10 killed.[35]

Mortar and rocket attacks recurred throughout the year in Military Region I, and the enemy sometimes followed up with infantry. Rocket barrages struck Da Nang on six occasions during 1971, and in May, eleven 122-mm rockets killed twenty-nine Americans and wounded thirty-three at Fire Support Base Charlie-2 in Quang Tri Province. About one month after the bombardment of Charlie-2, the enemy battered Fire Support Base Fuller, also in Quang Tri Province, with a 1,500-round bombardment, attacked with infantry, and routed the South Vietnamese who had taken over the outpost from U.S. Marines. In sharp contrast to the defeat at Fire Support Base Fuller, local South Vietnamese defense forces at Dai Loc in Quang Nam Province beat off a North Vietnamese attack launched on the night of May 3 under cover of a tropical downpour that prevented close air support.[36]

Although the enemy struck frequently and sometimes successfully in the northern provinces, the South Vietnamese forces there did not remain exclusively on the defensive. Twice they mounted probes of the A Shau Valley, Lam Son 720 and Lam Son 810. Both operations produced impressive claims of North Vietnamese killed in comparatively light fighting.

The first of the two, Lam Son 720, took place from April to mid-June, involved six American and twenty South Vietnamese battalions, and gave rise to complaints of inadequate American air support. Generals Lam and Phu, veterans of the recent foray into southern Laos, complained that the Seventh Air Force did not respond as readily during the first of the year's A Shau Valley campaigns as it had in the attack toward Tchepone and the subsequent retreat. Statistics for planned sorties tended to substantiate their complaint, for throughout Military Region I American aircraft responded with planned strikes fewer times than the major ground commands requested. During the first three weeks of June, for example, XXIV Corps requested 344 sorties and received 212, and the South Vietnamese I Corps had to settle for 148 out of the 166 it sought. Although bad flying weather contributed to the disparity between planned sorties requested and those flown, the root cause lay in the departure of American aviation units. For example, the Marine Corps withdrew the last of its forces, including the aircraft wing, by the end of June, creating a gap for the South Vietnamese Air Force to fill.

To compensate for the transfers and the resulting decline in planned strikes, the Seventh Air Force set up a quick reaction force at Da Nang; in case of emergency, the Tactical Air Control Center could either launch aircraft standing alert on the ground or divert those already in the air. In either case, the average response time from request to air strike did not exceed forty minutes. According to Lt. Gen. Welborn G. Dolvin, who had taken over XXIV Corps from General Sutherland, the South Vietnamese complaints about air support during Lam Son 720 arose because Lam Son 719 had enjoyed an overriding priority whereas the subsequent undertaking did not. When comparing air support for the two operations, Generals Lam and Phu erred in charging that American air power was inexcusably slighting Lam Son 720, for that essentially routine undertaking rightfully had a lesser priority than the earlier and far more ambitious advance toward Tchepone.[37]

Air support for Lam Son 810, the second sweep of the A Shau region in 1971, aroused no complaints from South Vietnamese commanders. During September, some 16,000 South Vietnamese troops, assisted by fighter-bombers and B–52s, discovered a few supply caches and some recent road construction but encountered comparatively light resistance. In a typical skirmish, North Vietnamese 122-mm artillery fired on the landing zone where Army helicopters were disembarking a reconnaissance unit; strikes by helicopter gunships and B–52s silenced the three guns responsible for the bombardment.[38]

In neighboring Military Region II, encompassing the north central part of the country, action flared from the seacoast to the western highlands. During January 1971, rockets detonated a quantity of ammunition stored at Qui Nhon, and shortly afterward, when a truce marking the Tet holiday came to an end, similar weapons firing from extreme range hit the air bases at Cam Ranh Bay, Nha Trang, Phu Cat, and Tuy Hoa.[39]

The greatest threat to the security of Military Region II arose not at Cam Ranh Bay or elsewhere along the coast, but in the mountains far to the west where the North Vietnamese stored, for future distribution, cargo that had traveled down the Ho Chi Minh Trail. On February 11, a South Vietnamese task force built around the 42d Regiment embarked on a reconnaissance in force to locate and destroy supplies stockpiled in the Plei Trap Valley. Unfortunately, neither the regiment nor the headquarters of the 22d Infantry Division, which provided a command element for the task force, proved at all aggressive, and the attack slowed to a halt early in March.[40] A shortage of air power, which otherwise might have helped compensate for the sluggishness of the troops, contributed to the disappointing results. As Lam Son 719 was still underway, Military Region II competed with it for air support, and the advance toward Tchepone enjoyed the higher priority. As the Plei Trap probe stumbled to its conclusion, Maj. Gen. Charles P. Brown, who commanded I Field Force, Vietnam, conceded that "we are fast running out of air assets" in north central South Vietnam after "pushing all available assets (Army and Air Force aviation) hard for several days."[41]

On March 16, after the Plei Trap operation had ended, North Vietnamese troops attacked the district headquarters at Phu Nhon in Pleiku Province, cracking the defensive perimeter and forcing the defenders of the village to call for help. Reinforcements started up the road but, as happened so often, ran into an ambush, and the relief column stalled short of its objective for four days. Meanwhile, the enemy surrounding Phu Nhon sustained a severe pummelling from the air, as Air Force fighter-bombers flew 36 sorties and South Vietnamese aircraft 120. When the reinforcements at last arrived, the attackers grudgingly pulled back after the village had suffered widespread destruction. Far worse damage occurred, however, to the confidence of the villagers in a government pacification program that had clearly failed to bring them peace and security.[42]

The North Vietnamese, on the last day of March 1971, combined guerrilla and conventional tactics to overrun an outpost in the western portion of Military Region II. Shortly after midnight, bands of guerrillas attacked the airfields at Pleiku and Dak To, damaging thirteen aircraft used by Air Force forward air controllers, and a few hours later North Vietnamese troops stormed Fire Support Base 6, southwest of Dak To. Because of the earlier attacks on the airfields, none of the locally based forward air controllers could take off, and the Seventh Air Force could not divert replacements until mid-day. During the critical early morning hours, South Vietnamese airmen both controlled and conducted the air strikes in defense of the base. Scarcely had American aircraft appeared when the weather changed; by about 3:00 p.m. cloud cover prevented further visual attacks. Radar-controlled aircraft could intervene, however, and after dark eight B–52s, diverted from other targets, dropped their bombs around the base.

These air strikes did not save Fire Support Base 6; when the skies cleared on the morning of April 1, forward air controllers could see enemy gunners firing artillery pieces left behind when the garrison withdrew. A South Vietnamese regiment, supported by air power and artillery fire, counterattacked later in the day, regained the base, and held it, thanks in large measure to air strikes credited with killing most of the 150 or more corpses in two mass graves that patrols discovered among the nearby hills.[43]

South Vietnam and Cambodia, 1971

A frequent target of rockets or hit-and-run raids, the fuel and ammunition storage areas at Cam Ranh Bay presented tempting targets. Attackers could mingle with local civilians, many of them employed somewhere on the base, and obtain information on the timing and composition of mobile patrols as well as the nature of the static defenses. Indeed, a half dozen prostitutes with easy access to the base turned out to be agents of the Viet Cong, and reports from these women may have provided further help in avoiding detection.

Strong defenses protected the fuel tanks and ammunition bunkers at Cam Ranh Bay. Offshore, junks and motorcraft searched for Viet Cong boats or swimmers. At the storage area, Air Force security police used trained dogs and motorized patrols to check the perimeter, while longer range probes looked for signs of hostile activity within rocket range, about 11,000 yards. Tips from local informants, substantiated by the discovery of aiming stakes some distance from the perimeter, convinced agents of the Air Force Office of Special Investigations that the Viet Cong could again attack Cam Ranh Bay sometime between August and October 1971. Twice previously, the enemy had struck damaging blows; in the summer of 1970, an attack had set Air Force fuel storage tanks ablaze, and in May 1971, the Viet Cong had destroyed stocks of fuel belonging to the Army.

Although the security force at Cam Ranh Bay realized the danger to the logistics complex and reacted with increased vigilance, a communist demolitions team took advantage of waning moonlight to slip past the security force and enter the perimeter. The first sign of danger came at about 2:00 p.m. on August 25, when Air Force security police heard a shuffling noise in the vicinity of the ammunition dump. A dog and its handler discovered footprints shortly afterward, but before anyone could follow them, the stored munitions began exploding. The blasts hurled bombs into the air, the concussion armed them, and they fell to earth to spread the destruction, as storage revetments exploded in succession.[44]

The destruction of the ammunition did not affect the course of the war, but it demonstrated once again the ability of the Viet Cong to penetrate even a carefully planned security screen. The handful of demolitions men had produced an effect wildly out of proportion to their numbers; this success contrasted sharply with the South Vietnamese task force that had recently attacked the logistics complex around Tchepone without achieving decisive results.

After the war, a North Vietnamese general asked a Marine Corps veteran of the fighting in Southeast Asia, "If you were our commander and were told to attack . . . [an] air base and destroy the planes there, how many troops would you need? Several divisions, right?" Yet, a few men had penetrated a strongly defended installation located at Cam Ranh Bay, in territory supposedly controlled by the South Vietnamese. The North Vietnamese and the Viet Cong could strike sudden, sharp blows like this, not because of their trained battalions or regiments, but because of what the communist general described as "tens of thou-

Air War over South Vietnam, 1968–1975

An Air Force sentry and his dog watch an F–4 land at Cam Ranh Bay.

sands of . . . scouts, minelayers, spies, political cadres."[45] Thanks to his network of sympathizers and part-time soldiers, the enemy enjoyed a mobility that not even aircraft could confer.

To the south, in Military Region III, which embraced the provinces around Saigon, the enemy remained fairly quiet during 1971, probably because the main battleground for that area now lay across the border in eastern Cambodia. Battalions or regiments rarely clashed in this area, as the war in south central South Vietnam became a struggle between Viet Cong irregulars and local government security forces. Besides attacking security detachments to capture weapons and demoralize the members, the Viet Cong staged a half-dozen ineffectual mortar or rocket attacks on Bien Hoa airfield, the heaviest consisting of only five rounds.

In southernmost South Vietnam, Military Region IV, the Viet Cong conducted a series of attacks on local outposts that undermined the morale of the security forces manning them. The South Vietnamese army, however, claimed victories in two communist strongholds, the U Minh Forest and the Seven Mountains region. In this military region as in the adjacent one, the deadliest fighting had moved to Cambodia where South Vietnamese troops from IV Corps tried to keep open the highway from Kompong Som to Phnom Penh.[46]

South Vietnam and Cambodia, 1971

During 1971, the nature of the air war in the four military regions of South Vietnam remained essentially unchanged from the previous year, with the overwhelming proportion of sorties supporting the war on the ground. The overall American aerial effort declined, however, reflecting withdrawal and progress in Vietnamization. Air Force strength in South Vietnam and Thailand dropped during the year from fifty-five squadrons with 1,267 aircraft on hand to thirty-nine squadrons with 906 aircraft. Marine Corps aviators flew their last missions in May and left the country. The Navy made only a minor contribution to the war in South Vietnam, concentrating instead on southern Laos. Air Force activity in South Vietnam dwindled from 35,000 sorties in January to 15,000 in December, although weather and the tactical situation ensured an uneven progression, marred by an occasional spike as one month's total might exceed that of the previous month, until a steady decline began in September. Meanwhile, the number of sorties that South Vietnamese airmen flew within the country grew rapidly and erratically from 34,000 in January to 67,000 in December.

Aerial activity continued throughout the year in neighboring Laos and Cambodia. The number of sorties in Laos fluctuated, reflecting the weather, which affected both flying conditions and the volume of truck traffic moving down the Ho Chi Minh Trail to South Vietnam and Cambodia. At year's end, when dry weather prevailed, American aircraft were flying more sorties throughout Laos than in South Vietnam. The Air Force also flew between 2,100 and 4,800 sorties in Cambodia during each month of 1971. In Cambodia as in South Vietnam, though not in Laos, the South Vietnamese Air Force took up the slack as American squadrons departed.[47]

As the year drew to an end, evidence mounted that North Vietnam was preparing for an invasion of the South. The indications of an imminent attack included increased truck traffic in the North Vietnamese panhandle and the strengthening of the antiaircraft defenses around the passes through which men and supplies bound for South Vietnam entered southern Laos. The enemy's extension of radar coverage into southern Laos raised the possibility that radar-controlled interceptors might join surface-to-air missiles in North Vietnam and Laos to attack B–52s bombing the roads, trails, depots, bivouac areas, and waterways that made up the Ho Chi Minh Trail.

During December, a MiG interceptor fired a heat-seeking missile at a cell of three B–52s but missed. Later that month a surface-to-air missile downed an F–105 near Mu Gia Pass, and an F–4 escorting a gunship along the trail went out of control and crashed while trying to avoid a pair of the missiles; rescue helicopters, however, picked up three of the four crewmen in the two fighter-bombers. Surface-to-air missiles and MiGs contributed to the loss of two F–4s that ran low on fuel while taking violent evasive action and could not reach an aerial tanker; both crews ejected, but only one of the four men survived.[48]

To deal with a North Vietnamese buildup in preparation for an invasion, the headquarters of the Commander in Chief, Pacific, had prepared two contingency plans, one concentrating on the airfields in North Vietnam from which MiGs threatened the B–52s, the other on the logistics network needed to mount an all-out offensive. Suppression of the antiaircraft weapons defending the targets formed a part of both plans. The Joint Chiefs of Staff directed Admiral McCain to combine the two, Fracture Deep and Proud Bunch, into a single document with options to meet a variety of situations. Coordinating sessions at Tan Son Nhut Air Base produced Proud Deep Alpha, a plan that called for attacks on MiG bases, elements of the logistics infrastructure in southern North Vietnam, and the antiaircraft defenses of both.

Despite bad weather, Air Force and Navy aircraft flew 935 sorties from December 26 to December 30, 1971, encountering determined opposition from missiles and antiaircraft fire. United States losses totaled one Air Force fighter-bomber and two naval aircraft, as the strikes succeeded in cratering runways, did impressive damage at truck parks, but had a lesser effect against buried fuel storage tanks. Only one of the crewmen in the downed airplanes was rescued; the others remained missing in action.[49]

The fighting during 1971 failed to wrest the initiative from the North Vietnamese, whose stoutly defended supply lines enabled them to control the tempo of the war throughout Southeast Asia. Indeed, the unsuccessful Operation Lam Son 719 in southern Laos, the weather-troubled Proud Deep Alpha bombing of North Vietnam, and the inconclusive fighting in Cambodia reflected a growing concern that the enemy would launch an offensive aimed at inflicting severe casualties on the U.S. ground forces as their withdrawal neared completion, thus demoralizing the people of the United States and obtaining a free hand to overrun South Vietnam.

At best, the battles of 1971 bought time, temporarily easing the pressure on the Americans still in South Vietnam, but the United States faced the formidable task of using the respite to prepare the South Vietnamese to repel an impending invasion. North Vietnam's abiding strength might well raise questions about the success of Vietnamization and the wisdom of headlong withdrawal, but once begun, the two closely related programs developed overpowering momentum. Despite the threat of attack, President Nixon realized that domestic political and economic considerations prevented him from reversing the policy of withdrawal or risking increased casualties by making more intensive use of the American combat troops who had not yet departed. Vietnamization held the key. While the danger of invasion loomed ahead, the armed forces of South Vietnam had to train recruits and absorb additional equipment as the Americans pulled out. Throughout this process, which dominated the events of 1971, air power continued to protect Vietnamization and withdrawal, even though it had progressively fewer resources for this vital mission.

Chapter Seventeen

Further Vietnamization and Accelerated Withdrawal

The defeat of Operation Lam Son 719 and, to a lesser extent, the inconclusive fighting in eastern Cambodia aroused concern about the ability of the Vietnamized armed forces to wage war as equipped, especially to interdict the passage of men and cargo down the Ho Chi Minh Trail. To address the problem of interdiction, agencies and individuals within the Department of Defense had for some time been trying to come up with an "Asianizable" means of disrupting infiltration through southern Laos, and later through Cambodia as well, something cheaper and less technologically ambitious than the computerized network of electronic sensors the Air Force operated from Nakhon Phanom Air Base in Thailand. Until the spring of 1971, the usual response to the problem of Vietnamizing interdiction had been to propose some form of ground action that would either disrupt the passage of men and supplies — the basic purpose of Lam Son 719 — or establish a permanent salient, perhaps by an international force.[1] In the aftermath of Lam Son 719 came the realization that South Vietnam could not mount the necessary ground campaign without extensive U.S. participation, which would become increasingly unlikely as Vietnamization proceeded and the United States withdrew its forces.

Moreover, the South Vietnamese Air Force did not have and would never receive the equipment or training to take over the succession of aerial interdiction campaigns, the Commando Hunt operations, that the Americans had been conducting against the Ho Chi Minh Trail since 1968. Regardless of the capacity of South Vietnam's air arm to conduct interdiction, disrupting the infiltration of men and material remained essential to national survival. Maj. Gen. Ernest C. Hardin, Jr., Vice Commander of the Seventh Air Force, conceded that if South Vietnam could not attack the infiltration route by land or air, the United States would have to do so by air, since Congress had prohibited the use of U.S. ground forces in Laos. Indeed, if the United States did not hammer the trail, it would have to intensify the air war in South Vietnam as enemy pressure intensified and the process of Vietnamization and withdrawal continued. "It is hard to resist blabbing the truth," he observed, "which is, if the North Vietnamese continue to use Laos to resupply their forces in the South, we'd better keep substantial U.S. air nearby."[2]

Leonard Sullivan, the Deputy Director of Defense Research and Engineering for Southeast Asia Matters, calculated that South Vietnam's air arm, in the state that existed when Lam Son 719 began, would be roughly one-tenth as effective as the Americans in attacking the Ho Chi Minh Trail. He thereupon proposed supplying weapons that would make up the difference — not electronic sensors reporting to a computer-equipped control center, B–52s or F–4s, nor AC–130 gunships with their infrared scanners and other devices for penetrating the darkness — but simple devices, with only one not in the existing inventory of weapons. Sullivan proposed tapping current Air Force stocks to give the South Vietnam the CBU–55, a so-called fuel-air bomb that released a cloud of vapor, similar to propane gas, that seeped into low places like foxholes or underground bunkers before detonating. He believed that a single-engine A–1, which South Vietnamese airmen already flew, could generate explosive power comparable to that carried on an eight-engine B–52 by dropping several of these bombs. The only new weapon he proposed took the form of a standard light aircraft, inexpensive and easily maintained, fitted with a side-firing multibarrel cannon to serve as a "minigunship." Sullivan envisioned a fleet of minigunships swarming over the segments of the Ho Chi Minh Trail nearest South Vietnam.[3]

Because Lam Son 719 failed to cause lasting damage to the transportation network in southern Laos, Sullivan's ideas seemed singularly attractive. Dr. Kissinger, President Nixon's adviser on national security matters, approved the development of "aerial interdiction options" as part of the overall scheme of Vietnamization.[4] Secretary of Defense Laird therefore launched a review of the subject of Vietnamizing interdiction, directing Secretary of the Air Force Robert C. Seamans, Jr., to investigate the feasibility of arming the South Vietnamese with CBU–55s for their A–1 aircraft and providing them with several squadrons of minigunships that could operate in conjunction with a simple array of electronic sensors.[5]

The defense establishment could not address the topic of interdiction without involving the American commanders responsible for operations in Southeast Asia. Although the U.S. Navy had begun entrusting the South Vietnamese with responsibility for intercepting the movement of supplies and reinforcements in coastal waters or rivers, the Air Force had thus far excluded them from sharing in aerial interdiction. General Abrams had Vietnamized the clandestine patrols that probed southern Laos and eastern Cambodia in search of enemy supply caches, but his headquarters had not incorporated all the various interdiction efforts into a single campaign. Separate air, land, and naval interdiction plans — two of them undergoing Vietnamization while air operations did not — persisted into the summer of 1971. At that point, reacting to Laird's interest in the subject, both Admiral McCain and General Abrams addressed the topic of Vietnamizing interdiction.

Further Vietnamization and Accelerated Withdrawal

A conference at Admiral McCain's headquarters drew up an operations plan, issued on August 5, to integrate U.S. and South Vietnamese interdiction in eastern Cambodia, in southern Laos, and along the waterways and coastline of South Vietnam. The plan, named Island Tree, called for South Vietnamese airmen to participate in the interdiction campaign, beginning on a limited scale with Commando Hunt VII in the fall of 1971. As the U.S. Air Force continued to withdraw, the air force of South Vietnam would assume increasing responsibility for planning and conducting aerial reconnaissance and air strikes over the Ho Chi Minh Trail. Island Tree served as the basis for a combined interdiction plan prepared by the Joint Staff at the Pentagon, reviewed informally by the Joint Chiefs of Staff and the Secretary of Defense, and designed to encourage the South Vietnamese to shoulder more of the burden.[6]

During August 1971, General Abrams set about taking concrete measures to attain the objective of Admiral McCain's Island Tree plan. He established a Combined Interdiction Coordinating Committee that met at least monthly, while South Vietnamese and U.S. planners incorporated an interdiction annex into the annual revision of the Combined Campaign Plan, adopted on the last day of October. The campaign plan envisioned coordinated air, ground, and sea attacks on North Vietnamese lines of supply and reinforcement and would coincide with the destruction of the enemy's depots in South Vietnam, Laos, and Cambodia. Ambitious though it was in scope, the version completed in 1971 did not address the need for major land offensives in South Vietnam and Cambodia to inflict casualties and force the consumption of supplies, thus multiplying the effect of interdiction.[7]

Meanwhile, the Seventh Air Force drafted Operations Plan 732, "designed to enable the VNAF [South Vietnamese Air Force] to plan and conduct limited interdiction missions during the current Laotian dry season [October 1971 to May 1972]." The aerial activity would begin in South Vietnam, where the Ho Chi Minh Trail debouched into the country, and move across the border to the least defended parts of the enemy's logistics complex. Various limitations, however, would hamper the operation, among them the reliance of the South Vietnamese on U.S. photo reconnaissance, electronic surveillance, and signal intelligence.[8]

The Combined Interdiction Coordinating Committee, during its October 1971 meeting, heard a disturbing message. Leonard Sullivan, who had argued throughout the year for the Vietnamization of aerial interdiction, confessed that the Department of Defense had not yet decided how to attain this goal. To Vietnamize the existing network of sensors and relay aircraft, the command center to which they reported, and the high performance aircraft needed to deal with the improving defenses of the trail seemed out of the question. Commando Hunt alone cost the United States some $2 billion annually, far more than South Vietnam could afford. As a substitute for high technology, he suggested ground patrols, essentially expanded versions of those that General Abrams had Viet-

Air War over South Vietnam, 1968–1975

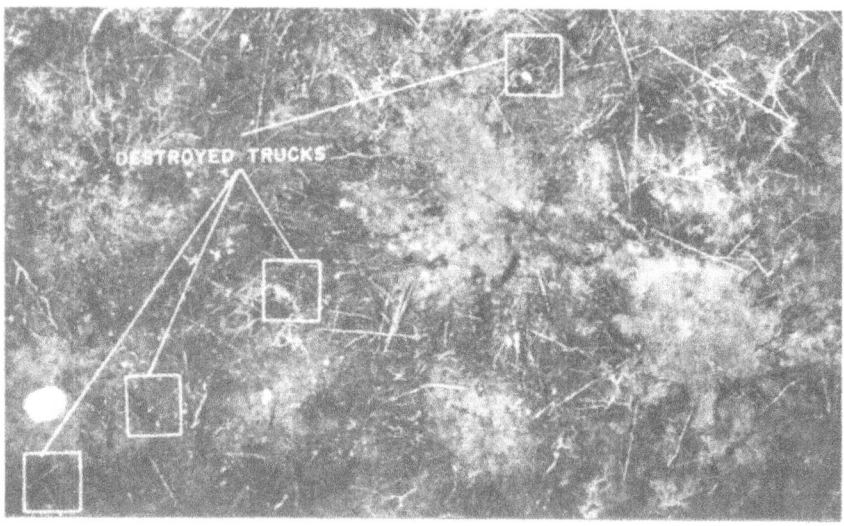

Air Force aircraft destroyed these trucks on the Ho Chi Minh Trail.

namized, and the minigunships currently under development. Since the minigunships lacked the firepower, the endurance, and the extensive sensor arrays necessary to pinpoint and attack truck convoys and supply dumps, the South Vietnamese would need a different target. Infiltrating troops afforded the only alternative, for, as Sullivan pointed out, "the only thing the North Vietnamese are paying for themselves are their people."[9] Unlike the destruction of trucks and supplies provided by other nations, the death of their sons could drive home to the North Vietnamese populace and leadership the true cost of continuing the war in South Vietnam.

Worse news soon followed, for even Sullivan's simplified program of interdiction seemed increasingly unlikely. Tests in the United States revealed the inability of the minigunship to attack as formidable a target as the Ho Chi Minh Trail. The two aircraft chosen for the project, the Fairchild Turboporter and Helio Stallion, performed marginally at best with a heavy, side-firing, multibarrel cannon installed in the cabin behind the pilot. Thus burdened, the minigunships, already cursed with the comparatively feeble destructiveness of the 20-mm shell, lacked the endurance to search out targets.

Instead of minigunships, the South Vietnamese received a few AC–119Ks. The Air Force Advisory Group removed the radar used to track road traffic instead of training the South Vietnamese to operate and maintain it. The advisers insisted, however, on retaining the infrared sensor, which could detect heat sources ranging from campfires to operating internal combustion engines, even though they did not teach the required maintenance. Instead, a U.S. firm received a contract to keep the infrared equipment in working condition. Although an improvement over South Vietnam's AC–47 and AC–119G gunships because

Further Vietnamization and Accelerated Withdrawal

of its auxiliary jet engines, the AC–119K had already proved vulnerable to the rapidly improving antiaircraft defenses along the Ho Chi Minh Trail.[10]

Sullivan's other scheme, besides the minigunship — using the A–1 to carry CBU–55s in order to deliver an explosive punch comparable to that of the B–52 — also failed. Due in part to confusion over the usefulness of the weapon, South Vietnam received very few CBU–55s. Sullivan had championed Vietnamizing interdiction to kill or maim infiltrating troops and make North Vietnam suffer, but proponents of the program within the Air Force tended to think in terms of destroying trucks and the cargo they carried, as the series of Commando Hunt operations had done. Although deadly as an antipersonnel weapon, especially against shelters in bivouac areas, the CBU–55 rarely destroyed trucks. As a result, the Department of Defense curtailed production and assigned a low priority to supplying the bombs to the South Vietnamese for use against the trail.[11]

Even though the minigunship failed to pass its tests and production of the CBU–55 came to an end, a few South Vietnamese airmen did participate in Commando Hunt VII, which proved to be the last of the seasonal interdiction campaigns. During December 1971, A–1s and A–37s from Da Nang, Pleiku, and Nha Trang carried out forty-nine sorties against enemy supply routes in western South Vietnam and thirty-four against segments of the Ho Chi Minh Trail just across the Laotian border.[12] The attacks came to an abrupt halt, however, because the government of South Vietnam had failed to ask permission from Souvanna Phouma for the aerial forays across the border. The Prime Minister of Laos had objected to Lam Son 719, largely to preserve his nation's facade of neutrality and avoid seeming too cooperative with Hanoi's enemies. Since the interdiction strikes appeared insignificant in comparison to the recent attack toward Tchepone and remained largely undetectable amid the American Commando Hunt attacks, Seventh Air Force planners had included the South Vietnamese, assuming that North Vietnamese retaliation against the Laotian government was a remote possibility at most. Souvanna apparently shared this viewpoint. After a delay of three weeks to assuage Laotian honor, bruised because no one had sought his permission to Vietnamize the attacks in Laos, and also make sure that North Vietnam did not react, Souvanna agreed to the resumption of the South Vietnamese air attacks, provided only that they did not become public knowledge.[13]

The failure to begin in 1971 to give South Vietnam an effective means of aerial interdiction reflected an abiding belief within the Air Force that American aircraft, the B–52s in particular, would continue bombing the Ho Chi Minh Trail until mid-1974 and possibly beyond. Secretary Laird thought he knew better, however. Congress, he had concluded, was responding to public opinion and moving toward legislating a deadline for the termination of all American combat activity in Southeast Asia. Assuming that the military situation remained stable, he predicted that Congress would end the war late in 1972. Clearly, the failure to provide South Vietnam with a satisfactory replacement for the B–52 as a weapon of both interdiction and battlefield support constituted a glaring weakness in Vietnamization. The Department of Defense actively considered only the A–1 armed with the CBU–55, and discussions of the overwhelming importance of the B–52 tended to trail off amid suggestions that Air Force advisers encourage the South Vietnamese to make better use of those aircraft they were scheduled to receive.[14]

In the absence of vigorous action on the related topics of furnishing a substitute for the B–52 and providing an effective means of interdicting traffic on the Ho Chi Minh Trail, the Vietnamized air arm remained capable throughout 1971 of supporting small-scale ground operations of the kind the South Vietnamese army might undertake after a truce had removed the major communist units from the South and reduced the war to the status of an insurgency. The immediate objectives that American advisers established for South Vietnam's air force included increased manpower, a greater concentration of forces in the vulnerable provinces north of Saigon, and stronger South Vietnamese leadership as the air service expanded. During its springtime review of Vietnamization, the Joint Chiefs of Staff agreed with General Abrams that the expansion of the South Vietnamese army and air arm should accelerate to achieve in mid-1972 the manpower levels projected for the middle of 1973. The South Vietnamese air force would therefore absorb an additional 2,286 officers and enlisted persons by July 1, 1972, reaching an authorized strength of 46,998.[15]

This acceleration compounded a "dilution of experience" problem already affecting South Vietnam's air arm, especially in maintenance and management, that resulted from the rapid expansion of the previous few years. According to the Air Force advisory group, another two years would pass before South Vietnamese airmen could acquire the needed experience in these fields.[16] Similarly, some Air Force advisers with operational units considered Vietnamization to be about two years short of accomplishing its current objective of self-sufficiency for routine post-truce operations other than interdiction of the Ho Chi Minh Trail. Unless prodded by the Air Force officers, South Vietnamese commanders still tended to ignore maintenance schedules, to fly only when it was convenient, and to avoid pressing home attacks against heavily defended targets. Adding more personnel, though comparatively easy, could accomplish nothing without increased competence and the creation of a fighting spirit.[17]

The tendency of some South Vietnamese to disregard their assigned missions angered the Air Force advisers, who on occasion took over the commander's responsibilities and imposed strict standards of competence and aggressiveness. Over-supervision presented a danger, however. As one Air Force officer observed, "the big-hearted, do-good American is doing the same disservice to these people that we do to our own children when, instead of showing them how, we fix the bicycle for them."[18] The issue, unfortunately, was far more important than repairing a bicycle, and the South Vietnamese were not children.

Further Vietnamization and Accelerated Withdrawal

No wonder that trained Air Force pilots or technicians, when overseeing critically important activities, found it difficult to stand aside and let those who were still learning make their own mistakes. Yet, until the Americans learned to do just that, the South Vietnamese could let the advisers and instructors do the actual work, avoiding responsibility and learning very little.[19]

Equipment for the growing South Vietnamese Air Force continued to arrive throughout 1971. The first squadron of C–123s, organized in April, received its aircraft in May. The delay reflected the extensive maintenance the transports required after heavy usage flying men and cargo to staging areas for Dewey Canyon II and Lam Son 719. A second squadron commenced operation in July, and the third, scheduled for December, took shape in January 1972. The last of two dozen AC–119Gs joined the South Vietnamese air arm in September 1971, and in December, Gen. John D. Ryan, the Air Force Chief of Staff, authorized the transfer of modified AC–119Ks to replace a squadron of AC–47s. At year's end, the South Vietnamese had 1,041 aircraft on hand, 762 of them (roughly 70 percent) ready for combat. Organized into forty-one squadrons, the air arm included three squadrons of A–1s, five of A–37s, one of F–5s, one of AC–47s (which the AC–119Ks would eventually replace), one of AC–119Gs, sixteen of helicopters (mostly UH–1s), and seven squadrons of liaison craft for forward air controllers. It also had one reconnaissance squadron with a mix of U–6s, RF–5s, and variants of the C–47. The transports units totaled one squadron of C–47s, one of C–119s, and two (soon to be three) of C–123s. A special air mission squadron that carried high-ranking passengers and a school squadron to conduct training rounded out the force.[20]

The tactical air control system underwent Vietnamization in 1971, but the original American mechanism continued to function alongside the one operated by the South Vietnamese. In June, the South Vietnamese assumed complete responsibility for assigning targets to their aircraft, selecting ordnance, and scheduling strikes. The U.S. presence at the Vietnamized command and control center now consisted of a two-man liaison party and a few instructors who trained the persons assigned there. The South Vietnamese command and control function did not issue orders to components of the Seventh Air Force, which continued to maintain a separate tactical air control center for its own aircraft. By August, the South Vietnamese Air Force had also taken over the four direct air support centers, one in each corps (or military region), but the parallel structure prevailed there also, for the Seventh Air Force supplied detachments to handle strikes by its aircraft.[21]

As retention by the Seventh Air Force of control over its aircraft indicated, the South Vietnamese had trouble mastering the tactical air control system, but the difficulties went beyond the mechanics of operating the various centers. Ground commanders, for example, frequently ignored the lower ranking air liaison officers assigned to help them make effective use of the aerial weapon. Forward air controllers, who directed the actual strikes, seldom remained with a

Air War over South Vietnam, 1968–1975

Gunships used in Southeast Asia included the AC–47 (top), the AC–119 (above), and the AC–130 (below). The armament and sensors carried by these aircraft progressively improved, with the last AC–130 carrying 20-mm and 40-mm guns and a 105-mm howitzer. The South Vietnamese received models of the AC–47 and the AC–119, but not the AC–130.

Further Vietnamization and Accelerated Withdrawal

particular ground unit long enough to learn its special requirements, the characteristics of the operating area, or the patterns of enemy behavior. Moreover, forward air controllers received, at most, a smattering of night training, and some of them avoided daylight missions over heavily defended areas, on occasion falsifying reports or logs to conceal their dereliction of duty.[22]

By the end of 1971, Vietnamization of the air war formed a mosaic of progress and disappointment. One flaw stemmed from the computerized supply system installed by the Air Force advisory group. The South Vietnamese logistics command, reluctant to accept computerization, could not make the new method work as well as the manual one it was supposed to replace and persisted in using the old style of inventory control.[23]

In addition, differences in emphasis between the South Vietnamese army and air force interfered with aerial reconnaissance. Although competent in the techniques of aerial photography and photo interpretation, the air force had to fly most of its reconnaissance sorties to generate the intelligence that senior army officers demanded to support operations by the ground forces. Until airmen had a stronger influence within the South Vietnamese Joint General Staff, they would be unable to divert enough reconnaissance craft away from missions for the army to locate targets exclusively for air operations.[24]

Aside from aerial interdiction of the Ho Chi Minh Trail, and possibly the overall effectiveness of forward air controllers, the worst weakness of the Vietnamized air arm lay in operating the air bases it had taken over from the United States. Although the Air Force turned over to its South Vietnamese counterpart some $28 million in communications gear needed to operate the airfields — everything from completely equipped control towers to teletype machines — not enough people had received the necessary instruction to maintain and use it. To plug this gap, the Air Force turned once again to civilian contractors. American firms like Philco Ford set up training programs to graduate 1,300 electronics specialists by the end of 1972.[25]

Vietnamization, whatever its flaws, permitted the continuing withdrawal of U.S. forces from Southeast Asia. When 1971 began, the Department of Defense was withdrawing the sixth increment since President Nixon announced the program of reductions in June 1969. The 60,000 manpower spaces of this latest increment included 373 officers and enlisted men of the Air Force, all of them members of service rather than combat units. The sixth in the series of reductions fulfilled the President's pledge to withdraw another 150,000 servicemen by the end of April 1971 and stabilized the authorized strength at 284,000, down from the peak authorization of 549,500.[26]

Even before the last elements of the sixth increment had withdrawn, pressure mounted for further reductions. The Nixon administration had undertaken the series of withdrawals on a "cut and try basis," and thus far the tailoring seemed to have worked, for the North Vietnamese and Viet Cong had not taken advantage of the declining American strength. Air power and spoiling attacks in Cambodia and southern Laos apparently held them at bay. Nixon, however, could not translate success in pulling out of Southeast Asia into political support in the United States. Economic problems —simmering inflation, increasing joblessness, and a growing threat of recession — made cutting the federal budget seem attractive, even essential, and promised to accelerate the pace of withdrawal.

When 1971 began, the Office of Secretary of Defense, the Joint Chiefs of Staff, and the U.S. Military Assistance Command, Vietnam, were working on troop reductions beyond the sixth increment. Unless North Vietnam suddenly and dramatically intensified the war, the related processes of Vietnamization and withdrawal would continue. The only real questions dealt with pace and timing, as the United States tried to avoid demoralizing the South Vietnamese or encouraging the enemy to bolder action.

Secretary of Defense Laird, a knowledgeable politician, called attention to the relationship of troop withdrawals to the federal budget, the health of the nation's economy, and the popularity of the President among voters. In February 1971, he approved a tentative objective of reducing authorized U.S. manpower in South Vietnam to 153,000 by mid 1972. Achieving this goal required a decrease of 131,000 between April 30, 1971, and June 30, 1972.

So drastic a reduction aroused concern within the Joint Chiefs, who assessed the withdrawals in purely military terms, excluding considerations of economics and domestic politics. With the exception of General Westmoreland, the Army Chief of Staff, the Joint Chiefs called for a manpower authorization of 255,000 by July 1971, a reduction of just 29,000 since April, declining to 200,000 a year later, for an aggregate withdrawal of 84,000, a schedule that both Admiral McCain and General Abrams endorsed. Westmoreland based his reservations on the likelihood that economic woes would result in cuts in defense spending that would force the Army to slash its strength in Europe to sustain the force levels in South Vietnam that the other chiefs favored. He believed that Europe contributed more than Southeast Asia to the country's security. Regardless of the views of a majority of the Chiefs, Laird's objective of 153,000 by mid-1972 served as the basis for further planning.

The Secretary of Defense insisted, moreover, that planners look beyond the coming year and think about two possible developments: a peace settlement that reduced the violence in South Vietnam from war to insurgency or a decision by Congress to order the unilateral withdrawal of the remaining combat troops. Given the economic and political conditions in the United States, he considered a negotiated truce less likely than some form of congressional interference that, at the least, would accelerate the pace of Vietnamization and withdrawal. After all, Congress had already repealed the Tonkin Gulf resolution and prohibited the use of American ground forces in Laos or their introduction into Thailand. Consequently, during January 1971, Laird directed General Abrams to begin a planning cycle based on the assumption that American strength in South Vietnam

Further Vietnamization and Accelerated Withdrawal

would decline to 60,000 by the end of September 1972. Abrams complied by shaping a tentative proposal, formally presented to the Secretary of Defense in mid-March, that reduced manpower to 255,000 by June 30, 1971 — the milestone that he, McCain, and all the Joint Chiefs but Westmoreland had previously endorsed — after which the total would decline to 233,000 by October, 95,000 in June 1972 — 58,000 fewer than Laird's earlier planning objective — and finally to 60,000 on September 30.

The Joint Chiefs, except for Westmoreland, favored the plan that would cut the force level no lower than 255,000 at the end of June 1971 and to 200,000 a year later. The sharper decline suggested by Abrams — 233,000 on September 30, 1971, 95,000 on June 30, 1972, to a plateau of 60,000 — represented a reaction to a possible congressional directive to speed the withdrawal, if not to liquidate the war. The possibility also existed that a negotiated settlement could reduce the U.S. presence to an advisory contingent of perhaps 43,000 once the cease-fire went into effect. Taking into account all these alternatives, along with Laird's earlier planning objective of 153,000 on June 30, 1972, the Joint Chiefs on March 26, 1971, warned against cutting too deeply or planning too far ahead. American strength should not decline below 199,000 on December 31, 1971, nor should the Nixon administration venture too far into the unknown and commit itself to troop withdrawals beyond that date. In effect, the Chiefs, Westmoreland included, advocated a reduction of 85,000 during the remaining eight months of 1971, a significant retreat from the former position that the elimination of 85,000 authorized spaces would require fourteen months.

Instead of acting upon this recommendation, Laird on March 29, 1971, presented the Joint Chiefs of Staff with two alternatives of his own: a reduction of 100,000 during the balance of the year or the withdrawal of 150,000 by the end of June 1972. The resulting force levels would be either 184,000 on December 31, 15,000 below the level in the latest proposal by the Joint Chiefs, or 134,000 on June 30, some 19,000 fewer troops than in Laird's earlier planning guidance. After their review of the proposals, Abrams, McCain, and the Joint Chiefs objected, pointing out that to reduce American strength by 100,000 during the balance of 1971 represented a deeper cut than Abrams had envisioned for the same period when he addressed the possibility of congressional acceleration of Vietnamization and withdrawal.[27]

The final decision on the timing of troop withdrawals and the numbers involved rested with President Nixon, like Laird, a person attuned to domestic politics. On April 7, some two weeks after the televised interview that claimed victory for the South Vietnamese in Operation Lam Son 719, the President, by announcing further reductions in American manpower, sought to neutralize press reports and television footage indicating that the operation had ended in a chaotic retreat. After declaring that "Vietnamization has succeeded," he stated that between May 1 and December 1, 1971, 100,000 more U.S. troops would be brought home. The total reduction since the withdrawals began in 1969 thus exceeded 350,000.[28] For purposes of planning, the Office of Secretary of Defense established as milestones a manpower level of 255,000 by July 1; 205,000 by November 1; and 184,000 on December 1.[29]

The withdrawals that actually took place during the balance of 1971 consisted of three increments. The first, between May 1 and June 30, eliminated 29,300 manpower spaces, reducing the authorized strength to 254,700. The second lowered the American strength by 28,700 to 226,000 on August 31. The third, completed on November 30, reached the objective of 184,000, a cut of 42,000.[30]

The first increment of the 1971 program, the seventh withdrawn since July 1969, had little impact on the Seventh Air Force, but eliminated Marine Corps aviation from South Vietnam. The Air Force gave up just 985 spaces, most of them occupied by officers and airmen already scheduled to leave the country in the near future or actually in the process of normal rotation. The Marine Corps, however, closed out two attack squadrons by June 30, removing the last elements of the 1st Marine Aircraft Wing, so that the single manager for tactical aviation in South Vietnam no longer had any Marine Corps aviators over whom to exercise even nominal control. Nevertheless, the concept of centralized control under an Air Force officer would surface in the future and continue to inspire lively debate.

The eighth withdrawal, between June 30 and August 31, cut more deeply into Air Force strength. Besides headquarters elements and support units, it eliminated a tactical reconnaissance squadron, two tactical airlift squadrons, four tactical fighter squadrons, and one special operations squadron, for a total of 5,700 officers and airmen.[31] Admiral McCain hoped to use air bases in Thailand to diminish the effect on air power in Southeast Asia caused by this and the impending ninth increments. He intended to shift the 480th Tactical Fighter Squadron from South Vietnam to Thailand and to retain in Thailand a squadron of B–57Gs that had been attacking the Ho Chi Minh Trail, but stood ready to cease operation and return to the United States. McCain also proposed that certain other aircraft already in Thailand — AC–130 gunships, electronic warfare and radar suppression types, and those engaged in gathering electronic intelligence — intensify their activity, requiring additional crews and support specialists. Unfortunately, the manpower ceiling the Thai government had approved for Thailand threatened McCain's plans to take advantage of Thai airfields.

The Air Force Chief of Staff, General Ryan, pointed out that the limitations on the manpower assigned to Thailand prevented reinforcement or transfers from South Vietnam into the country. Unless the Secretary of Defense could arrange to ease the restrictions, the Air Force would have to return the 480th Tactical Fighter Squadron to the United States instead of shifting it to Thailand, recall the B–57Gs from Thailand early in 1972, and cut back rather than increase the operations of the Thailand-based electronic reconnaissance craft. As the eighth increment left South Vietnam, the future of the 480th Tactical Fighter

Further Vietnamization and Accelerated Withdrawal

Squadron remained unresolved, with Air Force headquarters postponing a decision on its redeployment until Defense Secretary Laird had dealt with the question of force levels in Thailand. After Laird decided not to reopen negotiations with Thai authorities, the 480th Tactical Fighter Squadron joined the ninth increment, withdrawn between September 1 and November 30. This final element in the 100,000-man reduction that Nixon had announced on April 7 included 5,600 Air Force manpower spaces, two tactical fighter squadrons besides the 480th, two tactical airlift squadrons, a tactical electronic warfare squadron, and a special operations squadron.[32]

Between January 1 and November 30, 1971, U.S. armed forces reduced by 160,000 their aggregate manpower authorization for South Vietnam. Because of fluctuations in scheduling the arrival of replacements in the normal course of rotation, actual strength and authorized strength did not coincide. In April 1971, for instance, some 272,000 Americans occupied the 284,000 approved manpower spaces, and the number in South Vietnam declined to about 178,000 at the end of November, 6,000 fewer than the authorized 184,000.

In the first eleven months of 1971, the Seventh Air Force in South Vietnam gave up sixteen operating squadrons: six of fighter-bombers; one each of reconnaissance and tactical electronic warfare aircraft; four of tactical transports; two of special operations, with gunships and attack planes; plus two of observation craft used by forward air controllers. As 1972 began, squadron strength in these categories stood at three fighter-bomber, four special operations, four tactical airlift, two tactical reconnaissance, and two tactical air support. The scaled-down Seventh Air Force in South Vietnam now operated from just four major bases — Bien Hoa, Cam Ranh Bay, Da Nang, and Tan Son Nhut.[33]

Scarcely had the President announced the series of reductions completed during November 1971, when planning started for yet another sequence of withdrawals to begin in December. Secretary Laird initially established objectives of 100,000 Americans in South Vietnam by July 1, 1972 — 84,000 fewer that the authorized strength on November 30, and 43,400 in July 1973, at which time a cease-fire could be in effect. During the discussions that followed, Laird modified his proposal, calling for a manpower level of 60,000 in mid-1972. Although General Abrams objected to reducing strength so rapidly, preferring instead to postpone the goal of 60,000 until September, he nevertheless hewed to the guidance of the Secretary of Defense and produced a plan, which Admiral McCain characterized as realistic but risky. The Joint Chiefs of Staff sided with Abrams in favoring postponement of the 60,000-man level from June to September and warned that the Nixon administration, if it chose the earlier date, would have to accept the risks involved, such as a loss of leverage with which to force North Vietnam to end infiltration by way of the Ho Chi Minh Trail and release the American servicemen it held prisoner.[34]

Although negotiations continued with the North Vietnamese, by December 1971 it seemed unlikely that the publicized sessions at Paris would result in

Air War over South Vietnam, 1968–1975

North Vietnam's voluntary acceptance of a settlement ensuring the survival of the South. Secret diplomacy, conducted since 1969 by Dr. Kissinger for the United States and Xuan Thuy and Le Duc Tho representing the Hanoi government, raised hopes from time to time but thus far had produced no concrete agreement. In short, the North Vietnamese saw no need to make concessions. Their tactics of negotiating while fighting seemed on the verge of success, for the United States was Vietnamizing its way out of the war. Indeed, Congress, as Laird seemed to expect, might yield to public opinion and establish an arbitrary deadline for liquidating an increasingly unpopular commitment to fight for the preservation of South Vietnam.

Two events occurred during 1971 that further eroded popular support of the American war effort. A military court convicted Army 1st Lt. William F. Calley for his part in the killing, three years earlier, of 100 or more unarmed civilians at a village called My Lai; and Daniel Ellsberg, a veteran of the Vietnam War, defied the law and made public the *Pentagon Papers*, the name the press bestowed on a classified documentary history of American policy-making in the early years of the conflict.

Although many Americans viewed Calley as a scapegoat and applauded President Nixon's decision to reduce his sentence from life imprisonment to ten years and afterward grant him parole, the killings in which he participated called into question one of the announced goals of the war — helping the South Vietnamese defend themselves against a communist enemy they feared and hated. Clearly, Calley had seen no difference between the South Vietnamese men, women, and children that he killed or caused to be killed and the armed soldiers of North Vietnam. The reduced sentence seemed to endorse his evaluation of the villagers as enemies to be shot rather than friends, real or potential, to be nurtured and protected. Although less shocking than the massacre at My Lai, the *Pentagon Papers* revealed a dismaying order of priorities among those who had taken the United States into the war. Avoiding a loss of American prestige seemed to have been a stronger motive for involvement than any strategic or moral imperative to save South Vietnam. Now, after six years of large-scale U.S. involvement, the fate of South Vietnam receded further in importance, as the Nixon administration shifted the nation's objective from South Vietnamese survival to obtaining the release of the U.S. servicemen held prisoner in North Vietnam.[35]

Despite the failure of diplomacy, secret or public, to stop the fighting, President Nixon elected to continue the withdrawals into 1972. Given the mood of Congress and the American people, he could not do otherwise. On November 12, 1971, he announced a reduction of 25,000 manpower spaces in December and another 20,000 in January 1972. The abrupt decline from 184,000 to an authorized strength of 139,000 would, he acknowledged, force the remaining Americans to remain purely on the defensive, the culmination of a trend that actually began after the fight for Hamburger Hill in May 1969 and accelerated

Further Vietnamization and Accelerated Withdrawal

to keep pace with the withdrawals that commenced during July of the same year. The President's definition of the defensive, however, included continued aerial interdiction of the Ho Chi Minh Trail and, in the event of provocation, retaliatory strikes against North Vietnam. Nixon promised to make another public announcement before the completion of this latest reduction; the size of this next withdrawal and those to follow would depend upon the actions of the North Vietnamese.[36]

Other nations besides the United States were withdrawing their forces from South Vietnam. In August 1971, Thailand began pulling out its troops; the forty-five-man aviation element left in November and December, and by the spring of 1972 the ground forces had gone. In February 1971, New Zealand recalled its air detachment, other units followed, and by the end of the year fewer than thirty men remained in the country training the South Vietnamese. The Australian contingent — which at once time had included transports, light bombers, and helicopters, as well as ground troops — declined steadily in numbers throughout 1971 until only a training team and a headquarters element, fewer than 200 soldiers, still served in South Vietnam when the year ended. In December 1971, South Korea withdrew the first of its 10,000 combat troops, none of them airmen, and within four months, all had departed.[37]

The pressure that a faltering economy exerted on the defense budget and the withdrawals that diminished the number of combat aircraft available for operations in Southeast Asia threatened to reduce the number of sorties authorized for South Vietnam during the fiscal year ending on June 30, 1972. The Air Force and Navy could no longer sustain the 16,000 sorties per month — 14,000 by tactical aircraft, 1,000 by gunships, and 1,000 by B–52s — flown during fiscal 1971. Midway through fiscal 1971, in January, the Air Force had 399 tactical aircraft — fighter-bombers like the F–4 or attack aircraft like the A–7 — in South Vietnam and Thailand, the Marine Corps had 51 in South Vietnam, and the Navy had 103 on carriers off the coast. When fiscal 1971 ended in June 1971, the Air Force could muster just 313 tactical aircraft and the 1st Marine Aircraft Wing had departed. Although the Navy had three more aircraft available in June 1971 than in January, the net deficit amounted to 134.

Thanks to Vietnamization, the South Vietnamese Air Force had increased during fiscal 1971 from 586 to 1,069 aircraft of all types, but the principal additions had been 231 helicopters, 163 observation craft, and 48 C–123 transports. Excluding two dozen recently acquired AC–119G gunships, the number of attack aircraft actually available declined from 190 to 177, apparently the result of both attrition and scheduled maintenance. Without F–4s, B–52s, or AC–130 gunships, South Vietnam could not wage the kind of air war that the United States had been fighting.[38]

The Air Force continued into fiscal 1972 to provide a shield for Vietnamization and withdrawal despite the dwindling number of tactical aircraft. The Joint Chiefs of Staff believed that protecting continued Vietnamization and

Air War over South Vietnam, 1968–1975

A South Vietnamese gunner trains in a UH–1 helicopter.

further withdrawals would require a minimum of 10,000 sorties per month by tactical aircraft until July 1, 1972, along with 1,000 sorties by B–52s and 700 by gunships. The Chairman, Adm. Thomas H. Moorer, recommended as much to Secretary Laird on January 21, 1971. Laird doubted, however, that Congress would appropriate the money necessary to carry out the program that the Joint Chiefs favored. Consequently, the administration's tentative planning guidance for fiscal 1972, issued by Deputy Secretary Packard in February 1971, agreed to 1,000 B–52 and 700 gunship sorties, but proposed averaging the scale of tactical air activity during the fiscal year, so that in June 1972, when bad weather normally prevailed and the enemy tended to remain inactive, the monthly total might decline to a mere 6,800 sorties.

Establishing an average number of sorties for the year rather than adhering to a rigid maximum for each month would permit more than 10,000 sorties, so long as the monthly average did not exceed 10,000. In brief, Secretary Laird proposed that the Seventh Air Force, insofar as enemy activity permitted, make every effort to hold down sorties, especially in the rainy season when the North Vietnamese tended to be quiescent, so that additional strikes would be available in good weather when the enemy became active and air power could achieve deadlier results. Invoking the shibboleth of doing more with less, he argued that sortie averaging, plus the consolidation of aircraft at fewer bases and the more intensive use of resources, might well increase the effectiveness of air power throughout Southeast Asia.

Further Vietnamization and Accelerated Withdrawal

Initially, the concept of banking sorties in slack periods for use in emergencies appealed to the Joint Chiefs, but further consideration resulted in its rejection on the grounds that squadrons already husbanded their sorties carefully and could not safely make reductions below 10,000 sorties to create an account against which to draw in the future. As a result, the Joint Chiefs continued to call for 10,000 tactical sorties per month during fiscal 1972, with the authorization declining to 8,000 as Vietnamization progressed.

Air Force headquarters found itself trapped between the demand for more sorties, based on military reality as perceived by the Joint Chiefs, and the declining number of squadrons available, as budgetary considerations and weakening support for the war led to further withdrawals from South Vietnam. Admiral McCain's attempt to retain the B–57Gs and shift a South Vietnam-based fighter squadron to Thailand failed, as did a recommendation by Secretary of the Air Force Seamans that the administration seek funds for additional air crews and mechanics to get more sorties from the tactical aircraft that remained in South Vietnam. The Air Force did succeed in transferring a half-dozen gunships from Phan Rang, an air base the South Vietnamese were taking over, to Nakhon Phanom in Thailand, thus reducing the flying time to the segments of the Ho Chi Minh Trail that these aircraft patrolled. Moreover, the increased use of laser-guided bombs to attack truck traffic on the trail promised more first-round hits, possibly reducing munitions costs despite the investment in laser guidance.

On April 28, 1971, Dr. Kissinger called for a study of various aspects of the sortie rates established by the President. The wording of Kissinger's directive made it appear that the President, speaking through his national security adviser, had decided in favor of the Joint Chiefs of Staff and against his Secretary of Defense. Laird insisted, however, that the numbers did not represent a Presidential decision but only a means of generating further discussion. The ensuing debate, he maintained, would produce information on costs and manpower requirements that would provide the basis for Nixon's decision on the sortie rate, and the Chiefs took him at his word.

Ignoring Laird's earlier warning that Congress would not vote funds for so ambitious an air campaign, the Joint Chiefs on June 28, 1971, two days before the end of the fiscal year, resubmitted the recommendation for 10,000 tactical sorties each month during fiscal 1972 and 8,000 per month throughout fiscal 1973. The services, if Congress should refuse to vote the money, proposed to share in making up the deficit by dipping into their appropriations and reprogramming the necessary amounts. In addition to the recommended course of action — 10,000 tactical sorties per month in fiscal 1972 and 8,000 the following year — the Joint Chiefs offered six alternatives, each of which asked the administration to weigh, assuming slightly different circumstances, the danger it would encounter in South Vietnam, as sortie rates declined, against the risks faced elsewhere if it diverted manpower and money into Southeast Asia.

Air War over South Vietnam, 1968–1975

The tactic of forcing the administration to choose between Southeast Asia and other potential battlegrounds worked as the Joint Chiefs intended. President Nixon could neither curtail the withdrawal of ground forces from South Vietnam nor risk the collapse of the Vietnamized armed forces and had to agree to the sortie levels that the Joint Chiefs considered essential, though he did so grudgingly. On July 1, the first day of fiscal 1972, Secretary Laird issued tentative guidance based on one of the six alternatives that, in effect, authorized 10,000 tactical sorties for the immediate future. Not until August 12, 1971, could he announce that the President had approved 10,000 tactical sorties per month during the current fiscal year and 8,000 per month in fiscal 1973. To maintain this level of activity, the services faced some reprogramming of funds, especially during fiscal 1972, and General Abrams would be "authorized and encouraged to keep all combat sorties...as low as the tactical situation permits." The Joint Chiefs of Staff also obtained approval for 1,000 B–52 sorties per month and 750 by gunships. The second figure was fifty more than the Joint Chiefs would have accepted, possibly reflecting growing concern about South Vietnamese inability to participate in the interdiction of traffic on the Ho Chi Minh Trail.

Although the monthly authorization of tactical sorties declined from 10,000 in fiscal 1972 to 8,000 during the following year, the Navy's share would remain at 3,000 throughout the period. To fly 30 percent of the tactical sorties during the current fiscal year and 37 percent in fiscal 1973 would require a third aircraft carrier on station in the Gulf of Tonkin. The proportionate increases in the contribution by naval aviation coincided with the reduction in Air Force squadrons in Thailand and the transfer of air bases to the South Vietnamese.[39]

The Air Force reduced its strength throughout 1971, while committing itself to fly 7,000 tactical sorties each month through June 1972. To meet this objective, the Seventh Air Force would have to overcome the effects of rampant drug abuse and deteriorating race relations and make efficient use of the declining manpower available for duty. By 1971, drugs and racial strife threatened to undermine discipline and impede the effective use of air power, unless the new programs designed to combat them achieved success.

Chapter Eighteen

Discipline, Drug Abuse, and Racial Unrest

Despite the sense of purpose and spirit of professionalism that prevailed earlier in the war, by the end of 1969, two problems — drug abuse and racial violence — had begun to erode discipline and morale at Air Force bases, not only in South Vietnam, but throughout the world. The use of marijuana proved so disruptive by the spring of 1968 that Lt. Gen. Joseph H. Moore, the Inspector General of the Air Force and a former commander of the Seventh Air Force, branded it a menace to the Air Force.[1] Although obviously concerned about marijuana use as being "conduct prejudicial to good order and discipline," Moore did not yet believe it presented a true emergency; as late as September of that year, he maintained that education and the normal functioning of the military justice system could deal with the situation. At this point, when he could still equate drug abuse with marijuana use, he saw no need for special programs.[2]

The Air Force had seemed scarcely affected by a rapidly changing drug culture that went beyond marijuana use and was becoming a symbol of youthful alienation in the United States and elsewhere. The service, in the eyes of its leadership, also appeared to enjoy an immunity from the racial friction that had brought flurries of violence to many American cities. The comparatively few "racial incidents" that did erupt on Air Force bases in the mid-1960s gave the impression of being isolated outbursts, purely local reactions by African-American enlisted men to real or imagined grievances. Racial tensions mounted within the ranks, however; the cumulative number of clashes that occurred after the April 1968 assassination of civil rights leader Dr. Martin Luther King, increased from four by the autumn of that year to a dozen by February 1969. Nevertheless, the service undertook no special effort to correct a racial problem that had not yet surfaced at its bases in South Vietnam, despite incidents in Japan and the Philippines.[3]

The Air Force, apparently confident of both the success of earlier efforts to eradicate racial discrimination and the quality of its men and women, tended to disregard the racial turmoil in the nation's cities and in the other military services. The murder of Dr. King by a white assassin ignited the resentment that had been building in American society and rioting erupted in the black ghettoes of most major cities. Besides embodying the civil rights movement, and receiving a Nobel prize for his work, King had denounced the war in Vietnam, and his assassination unleashed conflicting emotions: on the part of blacks, pride in his accomplishments and indignation at the circumstances of his death; on the part of whites, resentment that the progress he demanded seemed to come at their expense; and in the armed forces, anger at his opposition to the war. Racial incidents erupted at bases all over the world, including naval installations like those at Cua Viet and Cam Ranh Bay in South Vietnam.

Although the leadership of the Air Force might understandably ignore clashes in the Army, which relied heavily on draftees, the Navy, like the Air Force, filled its ranks with volunteers, perceived as educated, stable, and more receptive than draftees to leadership and discipline, even on racial matters. The Navy's experience indicated, however, that many of the young volunteers brought with them into the service the same racial attitudes that were rending the fabric of civil society.[4]

The myth of Air Force immunity soon vanished as both drug abuse and racial tension increased, even in South Vietnam. Smoking marijuana became a recurring subject of disciplinary action in Southeast Asia during 1969, joined the following year by the widespread use of heroin. Indeed, by 1971 drug abuse had replaced venereal disease as the most serious medical problem facing the Air Force in Southeast Asia.[5]

Besides being a medical problem, drug abuse spawned related crimes; some individuals resorted to theft to obtain cash for buying drugs, especially heroin, and others succumbed to the lure of easy money and engaged in smuggling and distribution. As the drug crisis escalated, the struggle to eliminate the use and trafficking of narcotics and other dangerous substances took precedence over efforts to shore up rapidly disintegrating racial amity within the Air Force. Col. Earl M. Chu, former Seventh Air Force Deputy Chief of Staff, Personnel, explained, "When the drug problem became a major issue, it was necessary to realign available manpower to this new effort, and the EOT [Equal Opportunity and Treatment] program was a 'back burner' project for several months."[6]

Why did drug abuse emerge so suddenly as a medical and disciplinary crisis in Southeast Asia? Various persons, ranging from senior commanders to young users of heroin and marijuana, offered interpretations of their own. Some saw the phenomenon as a particularly dangerous manifestation of a lethargy into which the Air Force had sunk, a condition that left officers and men numb to the prodding of duty or discipline and gave rise to racial discord, indifference to personal appearance, and breaches of traditional military courtesy. Those who offered this interpretation might point to colonels living in air-conditioned comfort at Tan Son Nhut and complaining because they had to fetch their own free coffee at the officers' club instead of being waited on. Self-centered officers like these, or so the explanation went, had abdicated their authority, refusing to enforce discipline and by default creating a climate of permissiveness in which drug abuse and other disruptive behavior flourished and morale declined.[7]

At Air Force installations in South Vietnam, permissiveness defied definition. One senior officer, for instance, might allow his juniors to speak freely at informal "rap sessions," even questioning service policies. Another, however, might interpret this kind of free-wheeling discussion of grievances as an ill-considered attempt to cultivate a "nice-guy" image. Those who objected to such group conversations claimed that the practice led unfailingly to a surrender of disciplinary responsibility to committees of officers or even to noncommissioned officers.[8]

Permissiveness, according to a former judge advocate of the Seventh Air Force, included a reluctance by some commanders to deal with minor infractions, either suspending punishment or taking no action at all. This specialist in military law firmly believed that swift and appropriate punishment tended to discourage further offenses. Withholding punishment until something serious occurred might give the impression that the commander did not care what was going on and might actually encourage airmen to test the limits of his tolerance.

The absence of close supervision and swift punishment suited to the particular offense may have resulted in part from a policy of consolidating small units, especially those that supported combat operations, into larger ones that could make economical use of motor pools, mess halls, and equipment for keeping records. In these consolidated organizations, the individual airman seemed a numbered part in an impersonal machine. Moreover, command tended to become diluted, with many young noncommissioned officers supervising airmen of similar age and background and — ominously in Southeast Asia — a similar tolerance toward the use of marijuana and more dangerous drugs. Col. Archie L. Henson, on the basis of his experience as a judge advocate, suggested that smaller units, though more expensive to operate, "would in the long run be far less costly in solving the problems of social and racial unrest."[9]

Weak or indifferent leadership within the Air Force, its effect possibly intensified by the size of many non-flying units, may have helped subvert discipline and dissolve cohesion, but some officers cited other contributing causes. "The single most destructive element...," said one, "was the fact that public figures, under the guise of freedom of speech, maligned the efforts of the [Nixon] administration for an honorable withdrawal from Vietnam, a withdrawal that would also ensure a reasonable opportunity for the survival of a free South Vietnam."[10]

The impact upon the Air Force of public opposition to the war, whether reflected in speeches by public officials or demonstrations by antiwar groups, proved difficult to gauge. A Concerned Officers Movement emerged at some Air Force bases in the United States, though not in Southeast Asia, and sought to focus public attention on two points — the need to end the Vietnam War and what the few adherents described as unnecessary restrictions on the constitutional rights, such as free speech, of men and women in uniform. One member of this group, while in uniform, attended an antiwar rally and sounded a drum roll during a reading of the names of Americans killed in Southeast Asia. Three others joined war protesters in picketing an appearance by Vice President Spiro T. Agnew.[11] On the other hand, opposition to the war sometimes failed to appear where geography indicated it might. The commander of Travis Air Force Base at Fairfield, California, reported that his installation remained unaffected by antiwar sentiment even though the University of California at Berkeley, a short drive to the southwest, seethed with agitation.[12]

The attitude of the individual airman, often shaped before he enlisted, determined how he would respond even to conscientious leaders administering firm but impartial discipline. When asked why he began using drugs in South Vietnam, an Air Force sergeant replied that he was a "peacetime soldier," unused to undergoing hardship or being separated from his family.[13] Everyone experienced a sense of separation, whether from family or from familiar surroundings, but the actual hardship varied from one base to another. An airman stationed at Cam Ranh Bay in early 1971 lived at an airfield earmarked for the South Vietnamese, in quarters rapidly falling apart because of humidity, hard use, and termites. Squalor of this sort, however, did not necessarily result in drug abuse, then judged no worse at Cam Ranh Bay than in the better maintained dormitories at Tan Son Nhut.[14]

Alert leadership could to some extent ease the physical hardship at a base, if not the feeling of separation. For example, turning over parts of Bien Hoa Air Base to the South Vietnamese deprived Americans of facilities built for their use earlier in the war. Col. Robert N. Slane, in command of the combat support group located there, campaigned successfully for a new swimming pool and improvements to enlisted and noncommissioned officers clubs.[15]

Any list of the least desirable air bases in South Vietnam would have included Phan Rang, far from any large city, a location where airmen had to rely for amusement and recreation on the facilities at the installation. At Phan Rang, however, the drug problem either proved comparatively minor in early 1970 or largely escaped detection.[16] The apparent absence of any link between hardship and drug abuse underscored an observation made by agents of the Office of Special Investigations when they probed narcotics use at Tan Son Nhut: what a young airman described as hardship often reflected his feeling of being picked on by those in authority rather than physical discomfort.[17]

Days of boredom, punctuated by moments of terror, also contributed to experimentation with drugs. A pall of tedium might settle over a base for weeks before a salvo of rockets or mortar shells shattered the quiet and sent the airmen diving for cover. Statistics demonstrated that the greatest incidence of drug abuse occurred in those specialties that required long periods of monotonously

Discipline, Drug Abuse, and Racial Unrest

repetitive work; the occasionally recurring danger merely introduced a factor of tense expectation. Security police proved especially susceptible for they operated alone or in small groups, spending long shifts, frequently of twelve hours, routinely manning guard posts or walking the perimeter, all the while exposed to possible attack by the Viet Cong.[18]

An airman's peers might also exert pressure to become involved with drugs, especially on younger persons entering service from a segment of society that experimented with, or at least tolerated, the use of marijuana and other substances. One newly arrived airman recalled that he had moved into a "hootch" or hut with thirteen others, twelve of whom habitually smoked marijuana. Although "a little scared" at first, he discovered that "these guys were old pros," who "had been around a long time in the drug scene." Lonely and unsure of himself, the newcomer soon became a regular user of marijuana (and later of heroin) and found acceptance within an informal but clearly defined group. Drug use, he said, conferred on him a sense of belonging "that I had never seen before, and I liked it."[19]

The availability of drugs for those who considered themselves either beset by hardship or picked on by superiors or those who simply followed the example of their peers helped create an escalating number of users. The cannabis plant flourished in South Vietnam, and marijuana soon became an important cash crop. Poppy fields in Laos, Thailand, and as far away as Burma yielded opium that could be refined into heroin, but transportation of the raw material into South Vietnam at first proved difficult. The traffickers dared not send porters across the Ho Chi Minh Trail, defended by North Vietnamese troops and Lao auxiliaries and harried by American air power. Until 1970, moreover, smugglers could not move easily through Prince Sihanouk's Cambodia without risk of encountering the government's customs officials and several heavily defended North Vietnamese bases. After Lon Nol's revolution, eastern Cambodia became a battleground, even less conducive to nonmilitary travel, whether afoot or in trucks. Because movement overland faced such difficulties, the airplane became the preferred method of carrying opium, usually from distributors in Bangkok, Thailand, to refiners in Saigon.[20]

For airborne smugglers, the cash rewards could be dazzling. In the spring of 1970, Air Force investigators searching a transport that had arrived at Tan Son Nhut from Bangkok discovered packages of opium valued at $75,000 in its existing state but worth some $16 million if refined into heroin and cut with non-narcotic additives. The pilot, an Air Force major with fifteen years of service, was convicted of smuggling 900 pounds of opium and some $5,000 in currency and sentenced to twelve years in prison and a dishonorable discharge. The copilot, though acquitted of criminal charges, received an administrative separation under honorable conditions.[21]

The overthrow of Prince Sihanouk, though it intensified the hazards of land travel through eastern Cambodia, soon eased the task of the drug smuggler.

Air War over South Vietnam, 1968–1975

Living quarters ("hootches") at Tan Son Nhut Air Base.

Aircraft began regular flights between Phnom Penh and Saigon, and ships plied the Mekong waterway. Like the Air Force officer caught flying opium in from Bangkok, some South Vietnamese yielded to the temptation of sharing in a cash windfall estimated at $88 million annually and took part in or protected smuggling, though American officials insisted that corruption remained confined to the lower echelons of the Saigon government. Whatever the extent of official connivance, heroin became as common by mid-1970 as marijuana had been a few months before. Airmen could buy vials of the drug from roadside soft-drink stands, from children in the street, and from the maids who cleaned their quarters. Further contributing to the availability of drugs, many South Vietnamese pharmacists ignored the law and sold amphetamines and barbiturates without requiring a doctor's prescription.

The heroin epidemic engulfed South Vietnam at a time when Air Force law enforcement agents seemed to be making some headway against the marijuana plague. Several factors contributed to their success against marijuana, not the least of them the easily detectable activity of smoking. Besides being bulky and therefore difficult to conceal, cannabis gave off a distinctive odor as it burned. Heroin users could buy that drug as cheaply as marijuana, and they had less trouble concealing it. Whether injected, inhaled, or mixed with cannabis and smoked, heroin soon rivaled marijuana in popularity.[22]

In dealing with drug abuse, the Air Force took a traditional approach, seeking to educate its members about the consequences of using drugs, to discover those who used them, and to punish the offenders. The policy of

Discipline, Drug Abuse, and Racial Unrest

treating drug abuse like any other offense failed, however, to solve a rapidly worsening problem that threatened to spread as airmen dependent on drugs returned to the United States from Southeast Asia. Since all the armed forces faced this crisis, the Department of Defense set up a task force to look for an approach that would work throughout the world, and the U.S. Military Assistance Command, Vietnam, conducted a similar search narrowly focused on drug abuse in Southeast Asia. The departmental task force convened late in July 1970, roughly three weeks before General Abrams' command began its survey of the problem. The two investigations produced similar recommendations, the most important of which called for offering an opportunity for rehabilitation, an especially attractive option for those seeking to break the chains of dependency before returning to the United States. Education, detection, and punishment would continue, but the revised program extended amnesty to anyone who voluntarily entered a treatment program.

The work of the Department of Defense task force inspired the Air Force to adopt in Southeast Asia and elsewhere the Limited Privileged Communication Program, which held out the assurance of medical assistance and psychological counseling to anyone who, "prior to being apprehended, detected, or under investigation," voluntarily requested such aid. Information that a person volunteering for treatment might give could not be used as evidence by a court martial, but his statements might result in administrative actions, including reassignment, loss of a security clearance, or discharge under honorable conditions. The Air Force justified limiting the amnesty program to those who asked for treatment prior to detection by citing the wide range of assignments, from pilot to engine mechanic, that required unimpaired judgment; in any of these, the drug abuser's gambling that he would escape discovery could result in disaster. By the end of July 1971, five months after the privileged communication program began, some 270 persons in Southeast Asia, about one-half of one percent of the total Air Force strength in the theater, took advantage of the limited amnesty.[23]

The Air Force established a program of mandatory urinalysis, required after July 1971 of officers and airmen transferring from Southeast Asia or helping administer the drug treatment program there. Since the test reliably detected the likeliest forms of drug use, it presented abusers a choice of either volunteering for treatment or being found out and therefore ruled ineligible for amnesty and rehabilitation. In the fall of 1971, the categories of officers and airmen in Southeast Asia who underwent the test expanded to include those leaving Southeast Asia after periods of temporary duty, extending their tours or reenlisting, going on leave or rest and recuperation, suspected of drug abuse, or simply selected at random. The widespread employment of urinalysis revealed that Phan Rang, where drug use had once seemed minimal, now had the second most serious problem of any air base, ranking behind Cam Ranh Bay in the ratio of drug users detected. The number of drug users at each base revealed no useful pattern to those trying to eliminate the problem, for the ratios at these two bases abruptly declined while that at Pleiku inexplicably doubled.[24]

Meanwhile, the effort to educate the Air Force in the dangers of drug abuse continued at the bases in Southeast Asia. Some experts, sent to the theater to share the fruits of their experience, antagonized those in charge of the local program, bored the persons being educated, or both, although a few did prove helpful, even inspirational. A better response greeted the drug education field teams dispatched by the Military Assistance Command, Vietnam. Each of these groups consisted of a young officer, a young noncommissioned officer, two former drug users, and one South Vietnamese. One of the rehabilitated drug users and the officer sought to educate the junior officers, while the noncommissioned officer and the other former drug abuser tried to influence the enlisted men. The South Vietnamese member of the team warned local inhabitants who worked on the base of the consequences of dealing in drugs.[25]

A shortage of posters and printed materials delayed the formal drug education program that the Air Force planned for its bases in Southeast Asia and shifted the burden to the teams sent out by the assistance command. In the meantime, the local commander could try to supplement the work of the teams, as at Cam Ranh Bay, where Col. Arden B. Curfman encouraged informal discussions of the drug problem and appointed unofficial counsellors to steer newcomers away from drugs.[26] Later, at the same base, a coffee shop served as the site of larger rap sessions that discussed alcoholism as well as drug abuse.[27]

Stricter law enforcement accompanied the programs of rehabilitation and education and included a tightening of security at aerial ports. Even so, as late as June 1971, representatives of the U.S. Bureau of Customs found that inspection procedures in South Vietnam did not meet the standards established for air terminals in the United States. Later in the year, dogs trained to react to the scent of certain illegal substances helped overcome the weaknesses in security at South Vietnamese airports, as did increased surveillance, closer inspection of passengers and cargo, and a requirement for more complete documentation of containers shipped by air. The vials of heroin and packets of marijuana abandoned by passengers in airport waiting rooms indicated the effectiveness of these measures. Nevertheless, drugs still got through, including one package that reached Williams Air Force Base, Arizona, where the unusually pure heroin it contained killed the 17-year-old wife of the sergeant who had smuggled it out of South Vietnam.[28]

The campaign against drug abuse imposed a staggering burden on the Air Force Office of Special Investigations and the Security Police in Southeast Asia, both of which had difficulty finding the manpower and equipment to follow leads, gather evidence, and lay the groundwork for criminal prosecution.[29] Hard-pressed though they were, agents of the Office of Special Investigations succeeded during the summer of 1971 in surveying the use of drugs at Tan Son Nhut, Bien Hoa, Nha Trang, Da Nang, Cam Ranh Bay, Binh Thuy, Pleiku, and

Discipline, Drug Abuse, and Racial Unrest

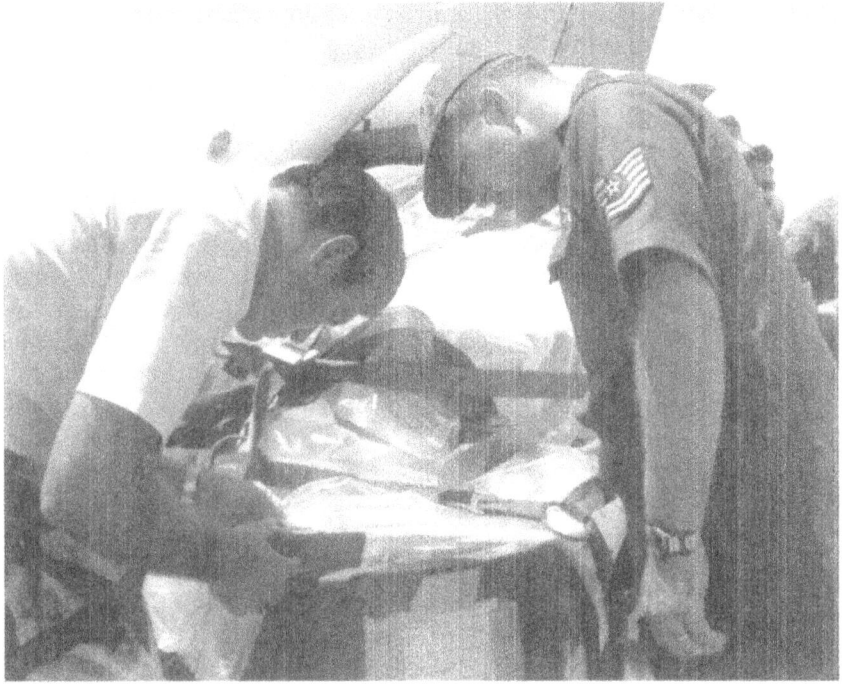

Inspection of cargo bound for the United States from Southeast Asia.

Phu Cat — all the bases where large numbers of Air Force personnel still served. The survey verified the importance of boredom, the feeling of being unjustly "hassled" by authorities, and the persuasiveness of friends in convincing lonely young airmen to engage in potentially self-destructive activity.[30]

The impressions thus gathered also demonstrated the ease with which visitors from nearby Army installations, South Vietnamese civilians, or South Vietnamese servicemen could gain access to an air base and sell drugs.[31] By restricting the airmen to their base, a commander could to some extent neutralize the ubiquitous suppliers, but restriction gave rise to tensions, with the older noncommissioned officers, who tended to prefer alcohol to drugs, blaming the younger men for dealing in drugs and causing the denial of passes to nearby towns. One base commander eased the ill-feeling by arranging cook-outs that featured rap sessions involving both groups and non-contact athletic competition between the two.[32]

The investigative surveys produced no agreement on the number of persons addicted to or experimenting with drugs. Estimates varied among bases and individual observers, with a doctor at Binh Thuy stating that half the airmen in the lower pay grades used heroin or some other drug on a regular basis.[33] At Bien Hoa, estimates of drug use varied from 20–40 percent of the airmen twenty-two years of age or younger.[34] The surveys of air bases thus tended to reinforce the belief that drug abuse most affected young airmen, though the chief nurse at the Bien Hoa dispensary dissented, insisting that roughly half the drug users were older than twenty-two.[35] The members of air crews seemed to have fewer problems with drugs, possibly because of the frequency of physical examinations and the likelihood that drug-induced behavior would attract the attention of fellow crewmen.[36]

Despite the efforts at education, detection, and rehabilitation, drug addiction and experimentation persisted in the Air Force as long as its units served in South Vietnam and for some time afterward. By the summer of 1972, doubts had arisen about the success of the campaign against drug abuse. The most obvious flaw in the Limited Privileged Communication Program proved to be the practice of requiring those who volunteered for rehabilitation to undergo detoxification in Southeast Asia before sending them out of the country, if necessary, for further treatment. To keep a drug user in the very surroundings that had contributed to his problem, said one Air Force officer, made no more sense than "attempting to reform an alcoholic by confining him to a bar."[37]

Moreover, requiring so many persons to undergo urinalysis proved self-defeating, for the increased volume of samples overwhelmed the Army laboratories that did the testing in Southeast Asia. Since the Air Force applied different standards, air base dispensaries sometimes had to confirm the results of tests done by the Army. The resulting workload required scheduling routine urinalysis well in advance, which gave the subject time to abstain from drugs, however painful that might be, so that no detectable trace remained in his system, to arrange for a substitute specimen from a person he knew was drug-free, or to persuade someone to falsify the record. Drug users still feared the unannounced tests administered at random or required of persons suspected of using narcotics, amphetamines, or barbiturates. As demonstrated by the failings in the program of urinalysis, the net the Air Force cast for drug users had such gaping holes that statistical summaries based on detection or apprehension could not reveal the magnitude of the epidemic.[38]

Besides damaging the health and judgment of the individual, and undermining his value to the Air Force, drug abuse contributed to theft at air bases in South Vietnam. A base commander at Bien Hoa declared that the high theft rate at the installation, averaging $33,000 per month at the base exchange alone early in 1971, "was directly related to the existence of an organized drug culture," which aided "in the theft and disposal of property that could be converted into cash for drug purchases." Additional guards and improved lighting sharply reduced the amount of stolen merchandise, the average monthly losses at the exchange stabilizing at $1,000, a decline that the base commander attributed to an assault on the drug culture, through law enforcement and the amnesty program, and also to routine transfers as tours of duty ended. Much of the theft, however, may have been the handiwork not of drug users or even black market operators but of opportunists — visiting soldiers, other exchange customers, and

Discipline, Drug Abuse, and Racial Unrest

Gates to Tan Son Nhut, showing proximity of base to city.

South Vietnamese clerks who saw the chance to take, with a minimum of risk, articles readily converted to cash. This interpretation would explain why simple security measures and closer supervision had such a dramatic effect.[39]

Some of the money obtained from stolen goods assuredly found its way to drug dealers, but full-time thieves also played a part. The latter category included an Air Force officer commanding a transport plane that routinely delivered disassembled helicopters for use by the South Vietnamese. En route from Travis Air Force Base, he regularly removed electronic equipment items from the helicopters and sold them by mail order to unsuspecting owners of private aircraft in the United States. Investigators found stolen items worth $150,000 stored in a warehouse in San Francisco, California, that he had rented in his daughter's name.[40]

As if thievery and drug abuse were not trouble enough, racial harmony deteriorated at Air Force bases in Southeast Asia, indeed, throughout the world, after the murder of Dr. King in 1968. The air bases in South Vietnam escaped outbursts of violence comparable to that year's rioting at the Army-run stockade at Long Binh, which involved only a few imprisoned airmen. Nor did the Air Force experience recurring interracial clashes like those that flared at Marine Corps installations in the northern part of the country or outbursts like those during 1972 on board the aircraft carrier *Kitty Hawk* and the oiler *Hassayampa* in the Philippines or the carrier *Constellation*, training off the California coast for service in Southeast Asia.[41] The worst single disturbance at an air base in South Vietnam occurred at Bien Hoa on November 27, 1969, when whites and blacks brawled over the kind of music played at an airman's club.[42]

Air War over South Vietnam, 1968–1975

Although Seventh Air Force installations seemed calm in comparison to those of the Army and Marine Corps in South Vietnam, racial tensions lurked beneath the placid surface, awaiting the opportunity to erupt. An Air Force-wide study completed in 1970 revealed that, of those questioned, only 16 percent of black officers and 6 percent of enlisted men believed that the service accorded them equal treatment all the time. Moreover, fully 30 percent of the officers and over half of the enlisted men concluded that they could expect equal opportunity rarely, if at all.[43]

The widely held perception of injustice coincided with a growing awareness among African-Americans in the Air Force of their unique cultural heritage, a movement that began in civil society and spread to the military. Informal study groups examined this culture and its current applications, producing a belief summed up and greatly simplified in the slogan "Black is Beautiful." Although not forbidden by Air Force regulations, the groups aroused uneasiness among some whites, for black awareness tended to manifest itself in hairstyles, off-duty dress, and even ritual handshakes. Many whites tended to associate all of these with militant organizations, active in civilian life, that advocated black power and urged African-Americans to rise up against their white oppressors. An Air Force study of the phenomenon of black awareness sought to reassure white commanders by predicting, correctly as events would prove, that the study groups could provide a valuable means of interracial communication, assuming they avoided calling for black power and, in effect, demanding resegregation.[44]

Another phenomenon, known in journalistic shorthand as white backlash, also spread to the military from civilian life. Characterized by a conviction that recent economic and political progress by blacks had come at the expense of whites, those who shared this attitude struggled to hold the line against what they perceived as further erosion of their rights. Urban rioting by blacks, especially after the murder of Dr. King, who had relied on non-violent means in his campaign for equal rights, and the recurring demand for black power reinforced this backlash and contributed to a polarization of the races in both civilian and military society.[45]

Racial enmity worsened throughout 1970 and early 1971, as demands for white power rivaled those for black power, but the air bases in South Vietnam seemed less affected than installations of the other services in Southeast Asia or Air Force bases elsewhere in the world. The atmosphere of wartime Vietnam that caused some individuals to seek companionship in groups using drugs, led others to gather in racially exclusive cliques. Since both blacks and whites tended to consider themselves victimized by reason of race, they drew apart except to inflict violence on each other, which both races instinctively justified as retaliation for perceived offenses. Black power and white power clashed, triggering a series of small-scale outbursts in South Vietnam, but no major riots. During the spring of 1971, for example, Air Force commanders reported some thirty racial incidents, one a cross-burning in the fashion of the Ku Klux Klan.

Discipline, Drug Abuse, and Racial Unrest

The others were assaults of varying severity, mainly fistfights that included a few drunken brawls in which racial antagonism may scarcely have figured.

The agents of the Air Force Office of Special Investigations who looked into the incidents in Southeast Asia considered all of them minor. Since the official inquiry by that office tended to shrug off the increasing friction between the races, it contributed to the belief that the existing machinery for promoting racial harmony had passed the test. The human relations councils at Air Force installations apparently provided a forum for blacks and whites to present their differences, and commanders seemed sensitive to the grievances their men expressed and willing to resolve them insofar as possible.[46]

In South Vietnam, moreover, some commanders used their ingenuity to promote racial harmony. Besides relying on the human relations machinery, they might create informal panels, ad hoc committees, and black awareness groups to discover what troubled their men. One officer, though he deplored the exercise of command by committee, conceded that in his organization a "black committee" ensured "adequate communication between the commander and the black airmen" and served as "a responsible grievance forum that has helped to solve some of our racial problems."[47]

Other officers reported similar experience, one of them declaring that he could not "overemphasize the importance of Airmen's Councils, Rap Sessions, EOT Seminars, Afro-American Associations, and Human Relations Councils" in absorbing "a good deal of the energy that otherwise might have been expended in more violent protests." Even though meetings sometimes degenerated into gripe sessions and served "to give every malcontent a prominent platform," he believed that the various groups represented a worthwhile investment of a commander's time.[48]

While wing and base commanders in South Vietnam tried through the formal organizational structure, supplemented by a variety of informal bodies, to maintain racial amity, a serious riot erupted at an Air Force installation where calm had thus far prevailed, not an airfield in Southeast Asia but a base in California. At Travis Air Force Base, a succession of events, escalating from misunderstandings and insults to rock-throwing and assaults, culminated in a violent outburst during May 1971, when rampaging black airmen burned a building to the ground. This riot, which claimed the life of a civilian fireman who suffered a heart attack, convinced the Department of Defense that the existing mechanisms for easing racial tension did not work. As a result, the department launched a program to train instructors who would educate members of all the services, and civilian employees as well, to understand and cooperate with persons of other races, religions, or cultures. A task force headed by Air Force Col. Lucius Theus, an African-American, had laid plans for this undertaking even before the racial clash at Travis Air Force Base.[49]

The Air Force launched its program of education with volunteers until the Defense Race Relations Institute, which convened its first class at Patrick Air

Air War over South Vietnam, 1968–1975

Force Base, Florida, in January 1972, could begin turning out trained instructors. Although personally dedicated to equal treatment and opportunity, the volunteers tended to substitute confrontation for conciliation and, in spreading the message of racial tolerance throughout the service, sometimes antagonized their audience. At a time when tempers readily flared, only a trained individual could persuade the members of an audience to face their prejudices without arousing defensiveness, even hostility. By January 1973, officers, enlisted men, and civilian employees of the Air Force throughout the world were receiving mandatory training in race relations from graduates of the Defense Race Relations Institute.[50]

Racial tension in South Vietnam, like the use of drugs, persisted until the last Air Force unit left South Vietnam. Mechanisms functioned, however, to deal with both problems: the Limited Privileged Communication Program, backed by education and law enforcement, for drug abuse; and the program of education, supported by a network of councils and committees, for racial conflict. Officers serving with the Seventh Air Force insisted that neither drug abuse nor racial turmoil, although dangerous to the institutional fabric, had diminished the combat effectiveness of the organization. Events in 1972 tended to support this judgment, for neither drug abuse nor racial strife interfered with the response to a North Vietnamese invasion of the South during the spring of that year. The North Vietnamese invasion intensified the workload for officers and airmen, replaced boredom with a sense of urgency, and required uncompromising teamwork on the part of everyone from cooks to security police to pilots. In this hectic time, the Seventh Air Force expanded greatly in size, resumed sustained attacks on the North, and continued to support South Vietnamese troops.[51]

Chapter Nineteen

Invasion

Trying in the summer of 1971 to predict the course of the war in the coming year, the Joint Chiefs of Staff reviewed the available intelligence and concluded that North Vietnam retained the initiative and would try to win "at least one dramatic tactical victory" in either South Vietnam or Cambodia. If the North Vietnamese chose to invade the northern provinces of South Vietnam and seek their symbolic victory there, they could do so as early as the fall of 1971.[1] The attack did not come during that autumn, but an ominous buildup in southernmost North Vietnam triggered the Proud Deep Alpha bombing there as 1971 ended.

Even though North Vietnam held the initiative, the South Vietnamese could land stinging blows to prevent the enemy from setting himself to throw a knockout punch. Consequently, Secretary of Defense Laird called on the Joint Chiefs in June 1971 for a list of major cross-border operations that the Vietnamized armed forces could successfully undertake. Of three possibilities, the Joint Chiefs preferred a course of action that combined thrusts into eastern Cambodia with ambushes and large-scale raids in southern Laos. Unfortunately, the South Vietnamese, as Lam Son 719 had demonstrated, could not execute so ambitious a plan, given the existing restrictions on the employment of the rapidly departing American ground forces. The Joint Chiefs therefore recommended instead the second concept, which eliminated a major offensive in northeastern Cambodia but continued to call for less ambitious attacks elsewhere in that country and in southern Laos. The third alternative, mere probes confined to the border areas of South Vietnam, Cambodia, and Laos, found no favor with the Chiefs, who believed it could not enhance South Vietnamese security.[2]

As 1972 began, South Vietnamese troops undertook a limited offensive in eastern Cambodia, overrunning a bunker complex in the vicinity of the so-called Dog's Head, southwest of Krek, and capturing rice, salt, and weapons. Less ambitious raids took place elsewhere in Cambodia — across the border from Ben Soi, South Vietnam, for instance, and near Neak Luong — and produced correspondingly less impressive results. Meanwhile, southern Laos remained immune to attack on the ground, although South Vietnamese forces east of the border followed up B–52 strikes in and near the A Shau Valley, an exit from the Ho

Air War over South Vietnam, 1968–1975

Chi Minh Trail, assessing the damage done by the bombing and engaging in firefights. Skirmishing also broke out in Tay Ninh and Kontum Provinces of South Vietnam in response to pressure from the North Vietnamese army.[3]

Besides defeating Lam Son 719 and containing the threat in eastern Cambodia, the enemy had waged a protracted struggle throughout 1971, fighting a succession of small battles to maintain pressure on the Americans as they withdrew and to frustrate South Vietnamese efforts to control the countryside. Directives issued by the communist Central Office for South Vietnam endorsed this strategy, but a new statement, appearing in December 1971, suggested that a general offensive and popular uprising loomed on the horizon, the same terminology the enemy had used in describing the Tet offensive of 1968. General Abrams and his staff at first dismissed the declaration as merely an attempt to improve morale, for they believed that the communist infrastructure in the South, apparently uprooted after the Tet fighting in 1968, could not support so ambitious an attack. However, the enemy, to some extent, had repaired the damage inflicted that year and compounded by subsequent American and South Vietnamese efforts to eliminate his local leadership. Whatever the assessment of Viet Cong resiliency, Abrams remembered the impact of the Tet attacks on American policy and advised Admiral Moorer, the Chairman of the Joint Chiefs of Staff, that the enemy might try to duplicate the political effect of the 1968 offensive, perhaps by a limited operation aimed less at inflicting defeat on the battlefield than at influencing American public opinion.[4]

A series of articles in the North Vietnamese press seemed to underscore the December resolution of the Central Office for South Vietnam. The author, who used the name Chien Than — the Victor — clearly spoke for the military leadership of the North Vietnamese. Indeed, some U.S. observers believed he was Vo Nguyen Giap when he declared that the time had come for a campaign of annihilation as the Americans withdrew. The resolution itself and the accompanying official commentary reminded Abrams and his staff of similar statements on the eve of the Tet offensive of 1968. The assistance command's intelligence estimates for 1972, however, indicated an intensification of enemy activity prior to Tet, a lull from February 14 to 20, and, after the Tet holidays, renewed fighting timed to coincide with President Nixon's planned visit to China.[5]

An offensive of some sort was probable, but timing and extent were uncertain. As early as April 1971, the Central Intelligence Agency had predicted an attack during 1972 designed to convince the American public, in a Presidential election year, that the country could not prevail. However, the casualties inflicted on the North Vietnamese and Viet Cong during the Tet battles of 1968, continuing interdiction of the Ho Chi Minh Trail, and efforts to eradicate the Viet Cong command structure combined to create an impression that the enemy could not mount an operation rivalling the 1968 attacks in scope and intensity. As late as February 1972, Secretary Laird expressed doubt that the North Vietnamese could again strike on the scale of the 1968 Tet offensive.[6]

Invasion

During February, the signs of impending attack included almost daily reports by South Vietnamese forward air controllers that they had sighted and sometimes helped destroy hostile tanks in Military Region II, near the border with Laos. Since the array of electronic sensors on the Ho Chi Minh Trail had not reported the passage of armored vehicles to the infiltration surveillance center at Nakhon Phanom Air Base, Thailand, Air Force forward air controllers checked the veracity of the sightings and on at least one occasion found the carcass of a tank at the location of a reported attack.[7]

In Military Region I, enemy infiltration through the A Shau Valley slowed as Tet approached but intensified afterward. Sensor activations in the valley and throughout western Quang Tri Province declined sharply until about February 20, when truck traffic suddenly increased on both sides of the border with Laos. The spate of activity on the Ho Chi Minh Trail and in the A Shau Valley, along with the continued presence of armor just north of the demilitarized zone, suggested a buildup for a spring-summer campaign beginning in May.[8]

Of the two possible objectives—the provinces of Military Region I or Kontum and Pleiku in Military Region II—the latter seemed the more likely. The western highlands abounded in concealment and lay conveniently close to the Ho Chi Minh Trail. Moreover, the defenses there were weaker than along the demilitarized zone and the administrative machinery of the Saigon government less efficient. Assuming that North Vietnamese logistics could not support more than one attack, the western reaches of Military Region II seemed most probable. Although the fighting might spread from the highlands northward into Military Region I, Abrams and his staff believed that the South Vietnamese would ultimately prevail, thanks to Vietnamization and American air support.[9]

Since air power provided the shield to keep the North Vietnamese at bay, the signs of preparations for an attack generated requests for additional aerial support. Lt. Gen. Welborn G. Dolvin, who commanded the XXIV Corps in the northern provinces, conceded that the enemy had made "considerable progress toward preparing the battlefield for an offensive, especially in Quang Tri and Thua Thien Provinces," where forward air controllers already reported "more lucrative targets than there are tac air sorties." Consequently, Dolvin asked for more sorties by tactical fighters in Military Region I.[10]

John Paul Vann, the retired Army officer directing the assistance group in Military Region II, asked specifically for additional help from B–52s. During January, the big bombers conducted sixty strikes along the western boundary of Vann's military region, and tactical fighters flew an average of twenty sorties each day. This level of effort produced no measurable results; in December and January, for example, South Vietnamese soldiers succeeded in entering just seven of the B–52 target boxes and reported "almost negative BDA [bomb damage assessment]." Vann, however, believed he had no choice but to intensify the aerial firepower in the hope of delaying or disrupting the North Vietnamese offensive.[11]

Air War over South Vietnam, 1968–1975

In Military Region III, U.S. air power and South Vietnamese troops probed the Hobo Woods, an area along the Saigon River that the Viet Cong and North Vietnamese had controlled for years. Beginning on February 25, Air Force fighters joined Army artillery and helicopter fire teams in a three-day battering of a group of bunkers that might support a future attack toward the capital city. Air Force fighters flew thirty-two sorties, six of which dropped CBU–55s, and a dozen South Vietnamese A–1Es joined in the final day's bombing. While the high explosives rained down, South Vietnamese cordoned off the cluster of bunkers to prevent the escape of the troops operating the supply complex. The attacking airmen reported the destruction of thirty-nine bunkers and the collapse of three tunnels, but only about fifteen of the enemy killed.[12]

As Dolvin and Vann called for more sorties and bombs exploded in the Hobo Woods, additional Air Force tactical fighters arrived in the western Pacific. To deal with the increasingly likely North Vietnamese attack, the Pacific Air Forces had a plan, Commando Flash, for shifting all or part of an eighteen-aircraft tactical fighter squadron from Clark to airfields in Southeast Asia. With a minimum of publicity, as many as six F–4s would reinforce the fighter units at each of three bases — Da Nang in South Vietnam and Ubon and Udorn in Thailand. By the end of December 1971, during the threat that prompted Operation Proud Deep Alpha, two F–4s had moved from Clark to each of the bases, and when the signs of invasion did not abate, Gen. John D. Lavelle, the new commander of the Seventh Air Force, asked for the additional aircraft. Early in February, General Clay, the Commander in Chief, Pacific Air Forces, sent the rest of the 523d Tactical Fighter Squadron, as planned. Lt. Gen. Marvin L. McNickle, in command of the Thirteenth Air Force, hoped to establish a regular rotation, bringing back some of the F–4s to the Philippines where they would resume training and later relieve other aircraft still in South Vietnam and Thailand, enabling them to undergo maintenance and reenter the training cycle at Clark Air Base. The threat of imminent combat prevented the fighters' rotation, and by mid-February the entire squadron had begun flying combat missions in Southeast Asia. Meanwhile, the Navy adjusted its scheduled ship movements to maintain three carriers off the coast of North Vietnam and the Pacific Air Forces prepared for another deployment to Southeast Asia, Commando Fly, by shifting eighteen F–4s fitted with electronic countermeasures pods from South Korea to Clark Air Base.[13]

The movement of tactical aircraft coincided with an augmentation of the B–52 bomber force in Thailand and on Guam. In January 1972, the Commander in Chief, Pacific, Admiral McCain, alerted the Strategic Air Command to be ready to increase the authorized number of B–52 sorties beyond 1,000 per month as early as mid-February. The command could raise the monthly rate to 1,200 sorties simply by shifting its aircraft within the western Pacific; eight B–52Ds and fourteen crews would go from Andersen to U-Tapao, although at the cost of eliminating six B–52Ds from the nuclear alert force. To sustain

1,200 sorties per month for more than thirty days, however, would require additional B–52s from the United States. Having given the Strategic Air Command the chance to review its options, McCain formally requested the establishment of a force capable of 1,200 sorties per month on February 5. The Joint Chiefs of Staff immediately approved the request, and by February 8, the last of the required eight aircraft and fourteen crews had arrived at U-Tapao.

Depending on the severity of the expected North Vietnamese offensive, still heavier bombing might prove necessary. The Joint Chiefs authorized the Strategic Air Command to prepare to sustain 1,500 sorties per month from U-Tapao and Guam. In response, on February 8 the command launched Bullet Shot, a four-day operation that deployed twenty-nine B–52Ds, with thirty-six crews, to Guam and ten KC–135s, with seventeen crews, to Kadena Air Base, Okinawa.[14]

As all this aerial activity indicated, defeating a "possible enemy-initiated offensive designed to impair Vietnamization or impede U.S. redeployments" depended on U.S. air power. The basic defensive plan called for "maximum support for RVNAF with TACAIR, Arc Light, naval gunfire, and troop lift." The Army helicopters still in the country would serve mainly to shift South Vietnamese reserves to meet the threat, a task that might require additional Air Force C–130s or even larger C–141s. The remaining American ground forces would "maintain the present defensive posture."[15] In public statements during January, President Nixon acknowledged the defensive mission, declaring that U.S. strength would decline to 69,000 by May 1972 as the Army's involvement in the ground war drew to a close.[16]

While the Air Force and Navy strengthened U.S. air power to meet an attack, the North Vietnamese continued their preparations to invade. Despite frequent strikes by B–52s, the enemy gathered strength in Quang Tri, Thua Thien, and Quang Ngai Provinces of Military Region I, as North Vietnamese 130-mm artillery pieces moved into position north of the demilitarized zone to shell South Vietnamese outposts.[17] Moreover, surface-to-air missiles located in North Vietnam could engage targets from four to twenty-four miles beyond the border in an L-shaped region extending from Mu Gia Pass southward to the demilitarized zone, then eastward the length of that zone to the seacoast.[18]

Electronic sensors that monitored the demilitarized zone frequently reported hostile movement, but the South Vietnamese troops in northernmost Military Region I contented themselves with a routine response, depending on the weapons available and the location and probable nature of the target: two rounds of 175-mm artillery fire, six rounds of 155-mm, or ten rounds of 105-mm directed at the place where the sensors indicated the enemy should be. Rarely did South Vietnamese forward air controllers stray from their assigned areas to investigate. In an effort to discover what was happening in the demilitarized zone, Air Force advisers urged, with only limited success, that commanders have each forward air controller check for activity around one or more of the sensor strings over which he flew en route to patrol his sector.[19]

Air War over South Vietnam, 1968–1975

Farther south, near Kontum in Military Region II, the South Vietnamese also proved reluctant to challenge an enemy buildup. Vann reported that senior officers balked when he suggested vigorous patrolling or spoiling attacks. They remained content, he complained, to fight the war with air strikes and artillery.[20]

On March 23, 1972, as hostile activity intensified, the Air Force Chief of Staff, General Ryan, summoned Lavelle to Washington to answer allegations that he had violated the rules of engagement governing strikes against North Vietnam and submitted false reports to conceal his actions. Convinced that the general had interpreted the rules too broadly and then falsified the official record, Ryan spurred him to retire in the grade of lieutenant general, rather than four-star general, a punishment that did not affect Lavelle's retirement pay. The armed services committees of both the House of Representatives and the Senate conducted hearings, during which Lavelle indicated that he believed his superiors knew full well how he interpreted the rules. The Senate committee expressed its displeasure with Lavelle by not recommending his advancement from his permanent grade of major general to lieutenant general on the retired list, but the House committee endorsed the strikes as essential and proper, although avoiding the issue of false reporting. In effect, the congressional actions upheld the decision of the Air Force. Lt. Gen. John W. Vogt, the Director of the Joint Staff, replaced Lavelle in command of the Seventh Air Force, but by April 6, when Laird announced Vogt's assignment, the nature of the Vietnam War had changed.[21]

On the morning of March 30, Maj. David A. Brookbank, an air liaison adviser with the recently organized South Vietnamese 3d Infantry Division, accompanied a forward air controller on a mission to adjust naval gunfire and artillery in the eastern part of the demilitarized zone. As the observation plane flew below an 800-foot overcast, he saw a squad of infantrymen moving southward. Recognizing them as North Vietnamese, Brookbank opened fire with the rifle he was carrying, and the troops below cut loose with their AK–47s, forcing the aircraft to seek concealment in the clouds.[22] The expected attack had begun.

In the next few days, 125,000 North Vietnamese troops supported by artillery and hundreds of tanks launched three major offensives and one diversionary attack across the borders. When the enemy invaded Military Region I on March 30, two divisions and three independent regiments attacked across the demilitarized zone toward Quang Tri City, while another division advanced on Hue from the vicinity of the A Shau Valley. On April 2, another offensive began some 600 kilometers south of the northernmost battlefield, as three divisions and their supporting troops advanced from base areas in Cambodia toward Loc Ninh, An Loc, and the highway leading to Saigon, about 100 kilometers to the south. The North Vietnamese also invaded the western highlands, not quite halfway from the demilitarized zone to An Loc, advancing from the triborder region — where the territories of Cambodia, Laos, and South Vietnam met — toward Kontum and Pleiku. The attacking force of two divisions began probing

Invasion

Gen. John D. Lavelle (left) and Lt. Gen. John W. Vogt (right), who replaced Lavelle as Commander of the Seventh Air Force.

the local defenses of the highlands as early as April 2, but the fighting did not attain full fury until April 14. Meanwhile, a single North Vietnamese division advanced into the rice-growing area of the Mekong Delta, both to seize food and to pin down South Vietnamese troops in the region.[23]

The Easter offensive, so called because the holiday fell on April 2, came as a surprise to those who expected a comparatively feeble reprise of the Tet offensive of four years earlier. Once again, the North Vietnamese leadership had adjusted its tactics to reflect recent experience, a recurring process throughout the war. Until 1965, General Giap and his colleagues at Hanoi may have assumed that the war would follow an ideologically sound progression from guerrilla actions, through more ambitious attacks designed to drive a wedge between the Saigon regime and the people dependent upon it for protection, to an orthodox conventional war toppling the government of South Vietnam. The introduction in 1965 of closely coordinated U.S. firepower, including artillery and air strikes, and the strategic mobility provided by the helicopter, disrupted the expected progression toward victory, forcing the North Vietnamese to revise their tactics.

Although North Vietnam's field commanders could not shuttle reinforcements throughout the country as the Americans could or call down vast destruction almost at will, they nonetheless enjoyed unmatched mobility before a battle began. As long as the Viet Cong provided intelligence, food, additional manpower, and other support, the enemy could join undetected in the normal movement of the populace. Consequently, the communists materialized suddenly, struck swiftly, and vanished. Giap proposed to capitalize on this mobility, jabbing repeatedly at the stronger forces, causing embarrassment, annoyance, and

Air War over South Vietnam, 1968–1975

pain. From time to time, a clever feint might cause the Americans to lower their guard so he could land a truly damaging blow. He tested this concept in the winter and spring of 1967 and 1968, drawing attention to the border areas, then attacking the ill-defended cities during the Tet holidays, but he failed to hold Hue or storm Khe Sanh, if he actually considered either a major objective. Moreover, U.S. firepower inflicted staggering casualties when the Americans and South Vietnamese recovered from their initial surprise. Hanoi multiplied its losses by attempting a second wave of urban attacks in May. Stubborn attachment to a particular tactical concept resulted in crippling losses that compelled the survivors to recoil and regroup in the distant base camps, leaving a military vacuum in the countryside for the Saigon regime to fill.

Although a failure in a purely military sense, the Tet offensive of 1968 achieved spectacular political results, and every North Vietnamese military action had a political purpose. The sudden and unexpected fury that the communist enemy unleashed during the Tet fighting shocked the U.S. public and demoralized the nation's political leaders who imposed a ceiling on American participation in the fighting and, with the coming of the Nixon administration, formally substituted Vietnamization and withdrawal for continued escalation.

The change in U.S. policy toward the war eased the pressure on the North Vietnamese and Viet Cong, who could refuse to give battle while they rebuilt their strength in preparation for future action. Between the fall of 1968 and the end of 1971, Giap contented himself with hit and run strikes like the raid on the ammunition dump at Cam Ranh Bay, while parrying thrusts in Cambodia and southern Laos and resisting attempts to eradicate the local Viet Cong leadership throughout South Vietnam. He seemed to be waiting patiently, as American strength declined, for the decisive moment to strike again.

Because the Tet offensive had such a devastating political effect in 1968, the American leadership in South Vietnam expected something similar in 1972, possibly during Tet. Giap, however, had different tactics in mind. Instead of swarming over the defenses of South Vietnam as he had in 1968, landing flurries of stinging blows, none in itself decisive, he decided to try for a knockout, landing three blows that, in combination, would at least cripple South Vietnam's military forces or possibly topple its government. Since the Lam Son 719 task force had proved vulnerable to armor, Giap obtained hundreds of T–54 and T–55 tanks from the Soviet Union, along with 130-mm artillery and shoulder-fired, heat-seeking antiaircraft missiles. In 1968, the enemy achieved surprise when lightly armed troops attacked throughout all of South Vietnam. Four years later, the surprise stemmed from the application of overpowering force, the large-scale use of entire combat divisions armed with modern weapons that matched or surpassed in quantity and quality those available to the South Vietnamese.[24]

Chapter Twenty

Reinforcement, Continuing Withdrawal, and Further Vietnamization

When North Vietnam invaded, the South Vietnamese armed forces numbered about 1.06 million, some 50,000 of them in military aviation, while U.S. strength in the South stood at 95,541, of whom 20,605 served in the Air Force. In terms of both manpower or machines, South Vietnam's air arm outnumbered the American air power based in that country. The South Vietnamese Air Force had on hand 1,285 aircraft organized into forty-four squadrons. Nine squadrons flew A–1s, A–37s, or F–5s — a total of 119 aircraft classified as combat-ready fighter-bombers; two squadrons operated AC–47 or AC–119G gunships, 28 of the aircraft ready for action; seventeen squadrons had helicopters, 367 of them combat-ready out of a total of 620; seven forward air controller squadrons flew O–1 or U–17 light aircraft, 247 operationally ready out of 303, and the remaining units carried out training, transport, and reconnaissance duties.

In contrast, the Air Force had just fifteen squadrons with 339 aircraft in South Vietnam, among them three squadrons of F–4D and F–4E fighters (60 aircraft including the pair deployed to Da Nang in Commando Flash) and one squadron of 23 A–37s. Other aircraft included 126 OV–10s and O–2s for forward air controllers, 22 helicopters and modified C–130s for rescue, 48 tactical transports, and 48 C–47s modified for various kinds of reconnaissance.

A larger Air Force contingent, twenty squadrons with 30,680 officers and enlisted persons, served in Thailand. The 473 aircraft available there included nine squadrons of tactical fighters that had 177 F–4s and F–105s, two squadrons of gunships with 34 AC–130s and AC–119Ks, plus 52 B–52s and 38 KC–135 tankers. Another 31 B–52s, along with a pair of aerial tankers, flew from Andersen Air Base, Guam, and 37 additional KC–135s operated out of Kadena Air Base on Okinawa.[1]

As the North Vietnamese surged forward, President Nixon and his assistant for national security affairs, Henry Kissinger, realized the danger not only to the survival of South Vietnam but to American diplomatic efforts to exploit the differences between the Soviet Union and China and ease the tensions between the United States and those two communist nations. The negotiations to end the

Air War over South Vietnam, 1968–1975

Vietnam War — both the publicized sessions at Paris and the formerly secret meetings there between Kissinger and representatives of North Vietnam, which the President had revealed in January 1972 — depended upon the outcome of the current fighting, as might the reception accorded Nixon when he went to Moscow in May. The President had made a successful visit to Beijing in February and hoped for similar results when he conferred with Leonid I. Brezhnev and the other Soviet leaders. If South Vietnam stumbled toward defeat, as Kissinger would later write, "Our negotiating position in the eyes of the cold calculators of power in the Kremlin would be pathetically weak [and] China might reconsider the value of American ties."[2] Nixon agreed, warning that if the invasion ended in a North Vietnamese victory, "The foreign policy of the United States will have been destroyed."[3]

Although Nixon and Kissinger tended to interpret the invasion as a desperate gamble to destroy South Vietnam before the completion of Vietnamization, indeed, as a reaction to the success thus far in Vietnamizing Saigon's armed forces, the leadership in Hanoi may have been willing to settle for less than an immediate and overwhelming victory. By mid-May, Pacific Air Forces' intelligence raised the possibility that North Vietnam might be content to seize liberated zones inside South Vietnam as bases for further military action and political pressure. In the process of carving out these zones, the People's Army of Vietnam would destroy certain of the Vietnamized divisions, discrediting the process and demoralizing both the government of Nguyen Van Thieu in Saigon and its backers in Washington. As American support withered and Thieu collapsed, the continuing peace negotiations would result in the withdrawal of the last American forces and the establishment of a communist-dominated coalition government in South Vietnam.[4]

Giap later suggested that a sudden collapse of South Vietnamese resistance would have come as a bonus; it had not, he said, served as the primary goal. If the invasion — nicknamed Operation Nguyen Hue after an eighteenth-century military leader who surprised and defeated the Chinese on the outskirts of Hanoi — actually knocked Saigon out of the war, Giap would have been delighted, but even a partial victory served to strengthen North Vietnam's military and diplomatic positions while undercutting those of the United States and South Vietnam.[5]

Whatever the immediate objective of Giap and his colleagues, the United States had to immediately intensify its support of South Vietnam. The President refused to consider sending ground troops, but not because of the time required to introduce them. He simply did not believe that the country would support a war on the ground, with the resulting increase in U.S. casualties, even in response to a potentially decisive attack. Consequently, the withdrawal of U.S. troops continued. Not only did Nixon insist on cutting back the authorized strength to 69,000, as he proposed in January 1972, on April 26 he announced a further reduction of 20,000 spaces by July 1, with further cuts to follow.[6]

Reinforcement and Continuing Withdrawal

The decision to continue withdrawing American ground forces meant that the armed services of the Republic of Vietnam and U.S. air power would have to contain the onslaught and hurl back the invaders. The Nixon administration faced four simultaneous tasks: expanding the scope of the air war as necessary to deal with the invasion; reinforcing aerial strength in Southeast Asia without shattering the manpower ceilings that the President established for South Vietnam, even though some of the newly arrived squadrons would operate from that country; continuing the withdrawals from South Vietnam; and strengthening the South Vietnamese armed forces to repel the invaders and defend the country after the signing of a peace treaty.

According to Kissinger, Nixon, on April 1, approved strikes up to twenty-five nautical miles above the demilitarized zone. On the next day, the Joint Chiefs of Staff formally authorized the use of tactical air strikes, artillery, and naval gunfire in that region. B–52s could not bomb north of the demilitarized zone, but that lasted only until April 9, when they struck Vinh. Gradually, the region subject to routine bombing by tactical aircraft extended northward until, on April 25, it embraced the entire panhandle of North Vietnam, with attacks occasionally beyond that area. On April 16, for example, fighter-bombers joined eighteen B–52Ds from Thailand in raiding fuel storage tanks and other targets at Hanoi and Haiphong (with the B–52s restricted to Haiphong).[7]

Besides the attack on the railroad yard and petroleum tank farm at Vinh by a dozen bombers on April 9 and the raid on the petroleum storage area at Haiphong one week later, Thailand-based B–52Ds made three other strikes against North Vietnam in the weeks following the invasion of the South. On April 12, the Bai Thuong airfield, northwest of the town of Thanh Hoa, served as target for eighteen of the aircraft, and on April 21 and 23, a force of eighteen B–52s struck Thanh Hoa and its environs, bombing warehouses, rail facilities, and a thermal power plant. During all five raids, the attacking bombers relied on chaff corridors and escorting fighters armed with anti-radiation weapons to deal with the radar that acquired targets for surface-to-air missiles, and the missiles launched against the B–52s caused no damage.[8]

As the pattern of B–52 bombing demonstrated, the air war rapidly shifted northward during April. The systematic air attacks on the Ho Chi Minh Trail in southern Laos came to an end, and the focus of aerial interdiction moved to North Vietnam. When Kissinger, returning from Moscow where he had helped prepare for the imminent visit by President Nixon, talked briefly in Paris with Le Dúc Tho and Xuan Thuy, the North Vietnamese principals in the recently revealed secret negotiations, he came away convinced that further discussion would prove fruitless unless the Hanoi government suffered a military reverse. To help choke off the North Vietnamese advance, Nixon decided to mine the harbors of North Vietnam, a decision quietly communicated to the Soviet leaders, who nevertheless chose to go ahead with the meeting at Moscow despite the possible danger to Soviet ships discharging cargo in North Vietnam.

Air War over South Vietnam, 1968–1975

Warehouse and transshipment areas of Haiphong under attack in May 1972.

Navy aircraft had already begun dropping mines in Haiphong harbor when the President on May 8, Washington time, publicly announced both the mine barrage and the intensification of the bombing campaign. He pointed out that the mines would not become armed for seventy-two hours, a delay that gave shipping an opportunity to escape to the open sea. The mine barrage went into place at Haiphong on May 9, local time, and two days later aircraft began sealing the lesser ports like Vinh and Thanh Hoa.[9]

The intensified air campaign, which called for strikes throughout North Vietnam except for a buffer zone along the border with China, began as Operation Rolling Thunder Alpha but almost immediately became Operation Linebacker. During the first strike, laser-guided bombs severed the Paul Doumer Bridge at Hanoi, while conventional high explosives churned up a nearby rail yard.[10] A systematic attack on North Vietnam's transportation and logistics networks at first focused on petroleum storage, the railroad linking China with the Hanoi-Haiphong logistics hub, and the supply lines leading away from Hanoi and Haiphong that sustained the offensive in the South.[11]

The cancellation of plans to continue aerial interdiction of the Ho Chi Minh Trail beyond the dry season of 1972 did not release enough aircraft based in Southeast Asia to attack targets on the battlefields of South Vietnam and at the same time carry the war to the North. To reinforce the B–52s in Thailand and on Guam, the Strategic Air Command continued the Bullet Shot deployments, the first of which had dispatched twenty-nine B–52Ds to Andersen during February and enabled Abrams to increase the total of monthly bomber sorties from 1,200 to 1,500 when North Vietnam invaded. On April 3, with the invasion underway, Abrams asked the Joint Chiefs of Staff for the resources to fly 1,800

Reinforcement and Continuing Withdrawal

B–52 sorties per month. The Joint Chiefs approved the request on the following day, and the Strategic Air Command responded with Bullet Shot II, sending twenty B–52s and thirty-six crews to Guam and nine KC–135s, with fifteen crews, to Kadena.

On April 8, one day before the last of the Bullet Shot II aircraft reached its destination, the Joint Chiefs directed the Strategic Air Command to deploy to Guam all the B–52Ds modified for high-explosive bombing that remained in the United States, except those needed to train crews. This decision produced Bullet Shot IIA. Between April 8 and 11, six B–52Ds, with ten crews, landed at Guam, while three KC–135s and four crews arrived at Kadena. Bullet Shot IIA had barely begun when the Joint Chiefs approved Bullet Shot III. By April 11, twenty-eight B–52Gs, modified to drop conventional weapons, and forty-five crews converged on Guam from ten different bases in the United States, while three KC–135s and their crews flew to Kadena. The number of B–52Ds in the western Pacific swelled as a result of Bullet Shot II and IIA from fifty at U-Tapao and twenty-nine on Guam to fifty at U-Tapao and fifty-five at Andersen, with another twenty-eight newly arrived G models also at Guam following Bullet Shot III. Meanwhile, these deployments increased the number of tankers on Okinawa to twenty-one.[12]

As these deployments ended, the series of five B–52 strikes against North Vietnam began. The town of An Loc, the gateway to Saigon, remained in peril, however, despite the intensification of the air war against the North. Because of the danger, General Abrams obtained two more deployments of B–52s. Bullet Shot IV and V, completed on May 21 and 24, added 70 B–52Gs and 88 crews, bringing the number of the big bombers to 200 — 50 D models at U-Tapao and 52 at Andersen, with 98 B–52Gs at Andersen. Two additional KC–135s, with their crews, touched down at Kadena during Bullet Shot V, and two other tankers flew to Guam to provide an alert force.[13] The vastly enlarged bomber force could fly 105 sorties per day, but the Commander in Chief, Strategic Air Command, Gen. John C. Meyer, preferred a more easily sustained daily rate of 99 sorties.[14]

Like the heavy bomber force, tactical aviation expanded to meet the North Vietnamese threat. A deployment of Navy and Air Force tactical aircraft, underway before the invasion, accelerated after North Vietnam launched its offensive, and Marine Corps aviation immediately joined in. To provide a fourth aircraft carrier in the Gulf of Tonkin, Admiral Moorer, the Chairman of the Joint Chiefs of Staff, obtained Secretary Laird's approval to retain USS *Constellation* on station there instead of bringing the ship back to the United States by way of Japan. A fifth carrier, USS *Midway*, arrived on April 30, and USS *Saratoga*, summoned from Mayport, Florida, launched its first strikes on May 18, bringing the total in the western Pacific to six. By maintaining this many aircraft carriers in the region, the Navy kept at least four on station throughout the critical early months of the offensive, while at the same time

Air War over South Vietnam, 1968–1975

B–52s cover Andersen's flightlines after the Bullet Shot deployments.

rotating among them the opportunity to grant liberty and take on supplies at Subic Bay in the Philippines.[15]

The first step taken after the invasion to shore up Air Force tactical fighter strength in Southeast Asia consisted of retaining in place the Commando Flash F–4s temporarily deployed as the preinvasion crisis worsened. Admiral Moorer asked for a thirty-day extension on March 30, the day of the North Vietnamese attack, and Secretary Laird gave formal approval on April 1. Besides keeping the Commando Flash aircraft in place at Udorn, Ubon, and Da Nang, the Secretary of Defense at the same time approved deployment to Southeast Asia of the Commando Fly contingent, eighteen F–4s dispatched to the Philippines and kept in readiness there in the event North Vietnam should invade the South.[16] The Commando Fly fighter-bombers reached their destinations on April 3, nine reinforcing the aircraft at Da Nang and the other nine augmenting the fighter strength at Ubon.

The Commander in Chief, Pacific Air Forces, General Clay, decided within three days after the arrival of Commando Fly to pull together the recently deployed aircraft, establish the necessary headquarters, and reconstitute them as squadrons. Nine Commando Fly F–4s flew from Ubon to Da Nang and, with the nine already there, formed the 35th Tactical Fighter Squadron to augment the 366th Tactical Fighter Wing. Similarly, all eighteen Commando Flash fighter-bombers gathered at Udorn and became the 523d Tactical Fighter Squadron.[17]

On April 5, Washington time, Laird authorized and Moorer directed the deployment of three Air Force tactical units from the United States, a squadron of twelve F–105Gs and two squadrons of F–4s, with eighteen fighter-bombers

Reinforcement and Continuing Withdrawal

each. A waiver of the existing manpower ceiling for American units in Thailand permitted the aircraft to operate from bases there for as long as ninety days. In general, the Secretary of Defense preferred to exceed the levels established for Thailand, while respecting the ceilings the President had announced for South Vietnam.

In this instance, however, the Joint Chiefs also directed the Commander in Chief, Pacific, Admiral McCain, to execute a plan suggested immediately after the invasion by Lt. Gen. William K. Jones at Fleet Marine Force, Pacific, and deploy a squadron of twelve Marine Corps F–4Bs and another of fifteen F–4Js from Iwakuni Air Base, Japan. Although originally earmarked to operate from Cam Ranh Bay, the fighters began landing late on April 6, local time, at Da Nang, located closer to the battlefields of northern South Vietnam and the routes of supply and reinforcement in the panhandle of North Vietnam. A third squadron, with twelve F–4Js, arrived at Da Nang from Hawaii on April 14, to be joined two days later by five two-place TA–4F attack planes from Japan.[18]

The initial Marine Corps contingent, organized as Marine Aircraft Group 15 (Forward), served, in effect, as reinforcements for General Vogt's Seventh Air Force, as did the Marine airmen who followed. They became cogs in the partly Vietnamized mechanism that responded to requests for air support from liaison parties with South Vietnamese ground forces. In carrying out this task, the Marines advised the Seventh Air Force Tactical Air Control Center of the number of available sorties and received assignments in the daily operations order that specified times, targets, and munitions. The forward air controllers who actually directed the Marine Corps strikes might be Air Force pilots of the 20th Tactical Air Support Squadron, South Vietnamese airmen, or members of Marine air-naval gunfire companies riding as observers in two-place TA–4s, until those aircraft returned to Japan in June.[19]

The Marine airmen who deployed to South Vietnam required a supporting establishment that included specialties ranging from clerk to jet-engine mechanic. Marine Aircraft Group 15 (Forward) brought from Japan almost 1,000 Marines and more than 1,000 tons of cargo. The personnel and the material, which totaled 187,000 cubic feet, traveled by a combination of airlift and sealift, with the Military Airlift Command and Marine Air Refueler Transport Squadron 152 supplying the transport aircraft.[20]

General Lavelle, before he was summoned to Washington to answer for the unauthorized bombing and the attendant cover-up, drew up a list of recommended deployments that included two already in the process of being approved — the Commando Fly F–4s and a squadron of Wild Weasel F–105Gs to silence the radars at surface-to-air missile sites. Lavelle also requested additional EB–66s for stand-off radar jamming and KC–135 tankers for his tactical fighters. Defense Secretary Laird endorsed the moves and also agreed with General Lavelle that the squadron of B–57Gs, fitted with various electronic sensors and used exclusively against truck traffic on the Ho Chi Minh Trail, no longer served a

Air War over South Vietnam, 1968–1975

EB–66s at Takhli Air Base, Thailand.

useful purpose in Southeast Asia. Laird did not, however, order the squadron to leave Thailand immediately, an oversight that complicated the deployments to Ubon, where the bombers remained.[21]

The post-invasion reinforcement of Air Force tactical aircraft in Southeast Asia, called Constant Guard, began with one of the actions that Laird had approved and Moorer directed on April 5 — the deployment of one squadron of Wild Weasel F–105Gs and two of F–4s — and continued through six increments that involved aerial tankers and included C–130 transports as well as tactical fighters. Constant Guard I saw the movement of the 561st Tactical Fighter Squadron, with twelve F–105Gs, from McConnell Air Force Base, Kansas, to Korat in Thailand. The Thai government granted its approval in time for the support personnel and their equipment to board transports of the Military Airlift Command and take off on April 6. On the following day, the first three Wild Weasels headed west, and by April 12 the entire squadron had arrived in Thailand.

Constant Guard I also included the movement of two squadrons of F–4Es, the other major deployment Laird authorized on April 5. The 334th and 336th Tactical Fighter Squadrons at Seymour Johnson Air Force Base, North Carolina, received orders to depart for Korat. The 334th Tactical Fighter Squadron began taking off on April 8, while the 336th prepared to follow. Once again, transports carrying personnel and equipment led the way. Six C–141s carrying 197 passengers and some sixty tons of cargo arrived at Korat on April 8, providing the host organization, the 388th Tactical Fighter Wing, its first hint that the two squadrons were supposed to appear.

Meanwhile, the Tactical Air Command, responsible for deploying the units, amended the orders so that only the 334th Tactical Fighter Squadron would touch down at Korat. The 336th and the Military Airlift Command transports carrying its support personnel and equipment were directed instead to Udorn,

Reinforcement and Continuing Withdrawal

An F–105F Wild Weasel at Korat. The Wild Weasel's mission
was to find and destroy radars that controlled surface-to-air missiles.

a destination changed almost immediately to Ubon. Ubon could have accommodated both units except for the presence of the squadron of B–57Gs, which Secretary Laird had earmarked for transfer to the Philippines, though he had not formally approved the move. Approval came swiftly, and the departure of the bombers on April 11 made room for both squadrons. As a result, Military Airlift Command transports reloaded the men and equipment of the 334th so recently deposited at Korat and delivered them to Ubon. Despite the confusion, the combat elements of the 334th arrived at Ubon on April 11 and commenced operations three days later. The 336th reached the base on April 12 and flew its first sorties on the 15th.[22]

The overall deployment proved confusing as destinations changed and host units were caught off guard: a decision to treat Constant Guard as top secret restricted the distribution of message traffic, and the 388th Tactical Fighter Wing at Korat received no advance notice of the move that, if carried out, would have forced it to absorb two squadrons. Uncertainty about which airfields the two squadrons would use in Thailand forced planners at the Tactical Air Command headquarters to rely on standard deployment packages instead of tailoring support equipment to a particular base. Because of the use of these packages, the 334th and 336th Tactical Fighter Squadrons inundated Ubon with unneeded maintenance gear, and the 8th Tactical Fighter Wing, the host at Ubon, released some ninety-five tons for redistribution.[23]

The EB–66s that General Lavelle asked for deployed independently of Constant Guard I. The first increment of electronic warfare aircraft, a pair of EB–66Es, had already received orders when the North Vietnamese invaded.

Air War over South Vietnam, 1968–1975

They, along with another E model and an EB–66C, both alerted on April 4, took off on the 7th as part of a routine move to replace damaged or downed aircraft and bring the Korat-based 42d Tactical Electronic Warfare Squadron to its authorized strength of seventeen aircraft. Another four EB–66Es, which jammed radar more effectively than the C models, began departing for Southeast Asia on April 10 in specific response to the need for additional jamming capacity. By the 16th, all four had reached Korat, bringing the strength of the squadron to twenty-one aircraft.

Korat also provided accommodations for recent arrivals other than the four EB–66s. The 39th Air Rescue and Recovery Squadron moved seven HC–130s from Cam Ranh Bay to Korat in March, and the 7th Airborne Command and Control Squadron, with its dozen C–130 airborne battlefield command and control centers, began arriving in mid-April from Udorn, where space was needed for future Constant Guard deployments.[24]

Constant Guard II consisted of the movement of the 58th and 308th Tactical Fighter Squadrons to Udorn, where the 432d Tactical Reconnaissance Wing served as host. The Joint Chiefs of Staff issued the directive on April 26, and on the following day, the 308th Tactical Fighter Squadron, with eighteen F–4Es, launched its first cell of three aircraft from Homestead Air Force Base, Florida. By May 1, seventeen of the fighters had arrived at Udorn; the other one, delayed by a mechanical problem, arrived on May 2. Three days later, the squadron flew its first mission from Udorn. The 58th Tactical Fighter Squadron, at Eglin Air Force Base, Florida, launched its eighteen aircraft on April 28 and 29; all of them reached Udorn in time to go into action on May 5. As it had in Constant Guard I, the Military Airlift Command delivered the cargo earmarked for the two squadrons and more than 1,100 passengers.

The fact that two wings at different bases in the United States had provided support for the 58th and 308th Tactical Fighter Squadrons resulted in the duplication of maintenance equipment when both squadrons arrived at the same destination in Thailand. Neither, however, had brought office furniture, nontactical vehicles, bedding, or even foot lockers. The squadrons obtained these locally, usually by scrounging from the host unit, which in turn tapped stocks on Taiwan. Luckily, the 432d Tactical Reconnaissance Wing had been preparing for a possible reinforcement even before the Easter invasion, and the Commando Flash detachments had already assembled at Udorn to form a squadron, thus providing a limited rehearsal. Consequently, late notice of Constant Guard II, a result of security considerations in the previous deployment, did not prove especially disruptive.

When the Joint Chiefs began considering Constant Guard III, they thought in terms of sending as many as four squadrons of F–4s either to Takhli, from which Air Force units had withdrawn prior to turning the base over to the Thai air arm in March 1971, or to Nam Phong, a partially developed and rarely used Thai base. On May 3, the Joint Chiefs settled on Takhli, directing that the Air

Reinforcement and Continuing Withdrawal

Force reopen it to accommodate the 49th Tactical Fighter Wing, with four squadrons of F–4D fighter-bombers, which would take off from Holloman Air Force Base, New Mexico. The movement had two related elements: the deployment itself, Constant Guard III; and the preparation of Takhli, being used by the Royal Thai Air Force for training, to serve as an operational base for an entire wing of seventy-two tactical fighters.

The return to Takhli got off to a shaky start, when advance elements of the 800-man Air Force site preparation team arrived on May 5, the first day of a four-day national holiday, and surprised the Thai base commander who had heard nothing about the impending deployment. To save cargo space in the Military Airlift Command transports, the team left its trucks behind and planned to use Thai vehicles already in place when reopening and operating the base. Takhli, however, proved short of trucks, forcing the Americans to rent them locally. Fortunately, a squadron of sixteen KC–135s, the 11th Air Refueling Squadron, also bound for Takhli, learned of the shortage and brought its own vehicles from Altus Air Force Base, Oklahoma. Despite catching the Thai base commander off guard, the site preparation team had Takhli ready for operation when the wing's fighters arrived. The squadrons left Holloman between May 7 and May 10 and landed between May 10 and 14. The first unit to touch down launched its first strike on May 11. Equipment and some 4,000 supporting personnel for Constant Guard III deployed to Takhli from various bases in a mixed force of C–5s and C–141s.[25]

The emphasis now shifted from tactical fighters to C–130 transports. Constant Guard IV, completed between May 13 and 23, increased to 110 the number of C–130s available in the western Pacific for possible temporary duty in South Vietnam. Sixteen C–130Es deployed from Langley Air Force Base, Virginia, to Ching Chuan Kang Air Base on Taiwan. Another twelve arrived there from Little Rock Air Force Base, Arkansas, and four from Pope Air Force Base, North Carolina.[26]

The increase in tactical fighter sorties made possible by the first three Constant Guard deployments required the support of additional aerial tankers, but finding suitable bases posed a problem. On April 15, the Strategic Air Command, the manager of the refueling fleet, ordered 16 KC–135s to U-Tapao, which brought the total there to 46, with 87 crews, all the base could accommodate. Because U-Tapao had reached capacity and both Kadena and Guam were too far from the aerial battlefield, Clark Air Base in the Philippines became the temporary home of the tankers that had refueled the 308th Tactical Fighter Squadron during its deployment. These KC–135s operated from Clark until relieved by those that refueled the other Constant Guard II unit, the 58th Tactical Fighter Squadron. The 16 KC–135s of the 11th Air Refueling Squadron at Altus and 28 crews, most of them from that squadron, accompanied the 49th Tactical Fighter Wing, which deployed to Takhli in Constant Guard III. Other tankers augmented the existing force, including detachments at Don Muang Airport in

Air War over South Vietnam, 1968–1975

Bangkok and at Korat. By the end of June, the Young Tiger Task Force, which refueled tactical fighters operating in Southeast Asia, totaled 114 aerial tankers and 196 crews, enabling it to fly 130 sorties per day from U-Tapao, Clark, Don Muang, Takhli, and Korat. When heavy rains and settling earth damaged the runways at Clark and caused a leak in a fuel pipeline, operations by the heavily laden tankers shifted to Ching Chuan Kang. The slower pace of air operations during the fall of 1972 resulted in a reduction in tanker activity. The detachments at Don Muang and Ching Chuan Kang returned to the United States, and the tankers at Korat moved to U-Tapao. When the air war against the North intensified later in the year, a force of tankers returned to Clark.[27]

During April 1972, when the Constant Guard deployments began, the invading North Vietnamese threatened to overwhelm An Loc and launch a drive toward Saigon. At the time, tactical air support for the defenders of An Loc depended heavily on a squadron of Air Force A–37s flying from Bien Hoa. Even as Constant Guard rushed aircraft to Southeast Asia, the Commanding General, III Marine Amphibious Force, Lt. Gen. Louis Metzger, alerted Maj. Gen. Leslie E. Brown, the commander of the 1st Marine Aircraft Wing, to stand by to send two squadrons of A–4 Skyhawk attack planes to Bien Hoa, in case the Joint Chiefs decided to reinforce the Air Force unit there. On May 16, the Commander in Chief, Pacific, relayed the decision to deploy, and on the next day, General Brown dispatched twenty-two Skyhawks from Iwakuni and ten others that had been training at Cubi Point in the Philippines. The two squadrons constituted Marine Aircraft Group 12 (Forward). To transfer the group's support elements, 870 Marines, plus cargo, the Military Airlift Command summoned C–141s and C–130s from around the world to Iwakuni in what the Marine wing commander considered "an absolutely superior performance."[28]

The arrival at Bien Hoa of the Marines and their A–4s posed problems for a base from which the United States planned to withdraw as a part of Vietnamization. Regardless of its impending change of status, Bien Hoa had already found accommodations for a detachment of six AC–119K gunships and 150 officers and men from Nakhon Phanom, plus an F–4 turnaround team of 300 that serviced and armed fighter-bombers, saving the time that would have been lost returning to an airfield in Thailand. Despite the crowding, the air base squadron that operated the American portion of Bien Hoa allocated the Marines a suitable share of offices, barracks, aircraft revetments, and maintenance space.

The spirit of cooperation extended to operations. Air Force pilots of the 8th Special Operations Squadron held briefings for the Marines, took them along as copilots on orientation strikes in the two-place A–37s, and led the way in an A–37 on the first combat mission flown by each pair of A–4s. This effort paid off, inasmuch as Marine Aircraft Group 12 (Forward) lost neither pilots nor aircraft during its first hundred days of fighting.[29]

Da Nang Air Base, where Marine Aircraft Group 15 (Forward) had arrived early in April, experienced worse overcrowding than Bien Hoa. To make room

Reinforcement and Continuing Withdrawal

for the Marines, the Seventh Air Force headquarters shifted some OV–10s and O–2s to airfields elsewhere in South Vietnam and sent twelve EC–47s to Nakhon Phanom in Thailand. Now an exodus from Da Nang began, perhaps in belated acknowledgment of its vulnerability as revealed by the earlier North Vietnamese victories in northernmost South Vietnam. At Iwakuni on May 24, Marine Brig. Gen. Andrew W. O'Donnell took command of Task Force Delta, which would open and operate the air base at Nam Phong in east-central Thailand. On that same day, a Marine KC–130 flew the advance party, numbering thirty-nine, to Nam Phong, which consisted of a new 10,000-foot concrete runway, but little else. Subsequently, the Military Airlift Command flew in some 500 passengers and almost 1,400 tons of cargo. An Air Force aerial port detachment unloaded construction materials as a crew of 3,200 Navy Seabees and Marine Corps engineers embarked on a massive project that included 310 huts, 128 larger structures for offices and maintenance facilities, a bomb dump, and a storage site for 360,000 gallons of fuel complete with a dispensing system.

By June 16, enough work had been finished to permit a squadron of Marine Corps F–4s to take off from Da Nang, bomb its assigned target, and land at Nam Phong to begin operations there. Within the next four days, two more Marine Corps squadrons arrived; an all-weather attack unit, flying A–6s, came from Iwakuni, and another fighter outfit came from Da Nang. They were followed by four air-refueling transports and four rescue helicopters. The fighter squadron left behind at Da Nang returned to Hawaii, and the detachment of TA–4s went back to Japan.[30]

The Air Force Chief of Staff, General Ryan, intended as early as January 1972 to pull his tactical fighters out of Da Nang and concentrate them in Thailand. Had the invasion not intervened, he would have preferred that General Lavelle, in the time before Vogt replaced him, move one squadron of the 366th Tactical Fighter Wing from Da Nang to a base in Thailand, divide the aircraft of another squadron among three sites in Thailand, six aircraft to each, and send the third, the 390th Tactical Fighter Squadron, back to the United States. The emergency caused by the Easter invasion postponed further action on the plan until May 27, when the Commanding General, Pacific Air Forces, proposed a modified version to the Commander in Chief, Pacific.

The plan, which Admiral McCain approved, called for moving the 336th Tactical Fighter Wing, less the 390th Tactical Fighter Squadron, from Da Nang to Takhli in Thailand, where it would take over the base support function from the 49th Tactical Fighter Wing, enabling that unit to concentrate on combat operations. The 390th Tactical Fighter Squadron would return to the United States without its personnel or equipment, sending half its eighteen aircraft to Udorn and half to Ubon. The 35th Tactical Fighter Squadron, formed at Da Nang from the Commando Fly contingent that deployed from South Korea by way of the Philippines, would transfer to Udorn, remain there until the crisis abated, and then leave the country.[31]

Air War over South Vietnam, 1968–1975

Dividing the resources shifted from Da Nang among Udorn, Ubon, and Takhli left room in Thailand for the introduction of two squadrons of F–111A fighter-bombers, each with twenty-four aircraft. The deployment of these airplanes, Constant Guard V, began on September 27 from Nellis Air Force Base, Nevada. Twelve of the F–111s departing that day conducted an experiment in rapid deployment; relief aircrews and support personnel flew ahead to Andersen Air Force Base, the only stop en route, then to Takhli and waited for the aircraft. Thanks to these preparations, supplemented by aerial refueling, the advance increment of F–111s landed at Takhli after just twenty-eight hours and flew their first mission on September 28. The balance of this squadron and the second one reached Takhli by October 5. The arrival of the F–111s permitted the return to the United States of the F–4Ds deployed in Constant Guard III, aircraft judged less effective than the F–4Es that had reached Thailand earlier. Although the F–111 flew occasional missions in South Vietnam, it performed its most valuable service in delivering nighttime attacks against heavily defended targets in North Vietnam, such as surface-to-air missile sites.

The last of the Constant Guard deployments, Constant Guard VI, took place between October 10 and 16 when the 354th Tactical Fighter Wing dispatched its three squadrons, totaling seventy-two A–7Ds, from Myrtle Beach Air Force Base, South Carolina, to Korat. The wing, in effect, replaced the thirty-six F–4Es of the 58th and 308th Tactical Fighter Squadrons, deployed in Constant Guard II, which returned to the United States. The A–7Ds flew a variety of missions throughout Southeast Asia: escorting convoys on the Mekong River in Cambodia, for example; bombing by daylight in North Vietnam and South Vietnam; escorting gunships at night; and replacing the A–1s in escorting rescue helicopters.[32]

The Constant Guard deployments to Southeast Asia, five of which consisted of fighter-bombers, increased Seventh Air Force strength in that category from 237, 60 in South Vietnam and 177 in Thailand, when North Vietnam invaded to a peak of 396, all but two aircraft in Thailand, at the end of September. At that point, departures made themselves felt, as the total declined by the end of October to 290 tactical fighters, all in Thailand. At the end of the Constant Guard cycle in October, the overall proportion of aircraft between Thailand and South Vietnam stood at three-to-one, compared to four-to-three when the deployments began. The changed ratio clearly indicates that the United States withdrew aircraft as well as men from South Vietnam, remaining within the announced force levels there, simultaneously with a buildup in Thailand.[33]

By channeling Air Force tactical fighter units into Thailand and increasing the use of B–52s based in Thailand or on Guam and carrier aircraft, the Nixon administration managed to continue the withdrawal of American forces from South Vietnam while helping the Saigon government resist the North Vietnamese invasion. On April 26, when the very survival of South Vietnam seemed at risk, President Nixon announced that authorized American strength

Reinforcement and Continuing Withdrawal

F–111s and F–4s at Takhli (top); A–7s and F–4s at Korat (bottom).

there, established at 69,000 by the end of that month, would decline by 20,000 during May and June. He insisted, moreover, that General Abrams meet this goal. Consequently, the Military Assistance Command further trimmed Army and to a lesser extent Navy forces in compensating for the arrival in South Vietnam of 2,889 officers and enlisted men from the Air Force and Marine Corps aviation. Because of the careful juggling of service strengths, the twelfth reduction since 1969 brought the total authorization to a mere 49,000 on June 30, with the actual strength perhaps 1,000 fewer.

Air War over South Vietnam, 1968–1975

At this point, both Abrams and Admiral McCain, the Commander in Chief, Pacific, warned that further cuts might jeopardize the American troops still in the country and impair their ability to support the South Vietnamese. Abrams agreed, however, that a further reduction of 10,000 by September might be feasible; whereas McCain recommended a summer-long moratorium on troop reductions. In mid-June, the Joint Chiefs of Staff forwarded these differing recommendations to Secretary of Defense Laird, along with a reminder of the critical nature of the military situation, and in doing so, endorsed a 10,000-space reduction, if "overriding considerations at the national level" so dictated. Once the Joint Chiefs had lobbed the ball into his court, Nixon slammed it back, announcing on June 28 the thirteenth reduction in the series, which would cut the authorized strength to 39,000 on September 1.

The pattern of brushing aside military objections, which the Joint Chiefs did not assert vigorously, and announcing the next withdrawal as the current one ended persisted into late summer. A new Commander, U.S. Military Assistance Command, Vietnam, Gen. Frederick C. Weyand, and a new Commander in Chief, Pacific, Adm. Noel A. M. Gayler, in effect repeated the advice given by their predecessors before the previous reduction. Although the Joint Chiefs recommended maintaining a force of about 30,000 through the end of the year, the Nixon administration on August 29 announced an objective of 27,000 by November 30.

The series of sequential reductions and announcements of further cuts ended in August, for during October peace negotiations stalled. The leadership at Hanoi seemed hopeful that the November election would return a Congress willing to cut off funding for the war and thus legislate a North Vietnamese victory. Instead of setting a further goal as the fourteenth increment ended, the newly reelected President intensified the air war against the North in an attempt to force the negotiation of a settlement. Meanwhile, unpublicized withdrawals continued. Actual U.S. strength in South Vietnam declined to 24,069 at the end of December, after B–52s and other aircraft had conducted eleven days of bombing against targets in Hanoi and Haiphong, and to 23,156 at the signing of a cease-fire agreement on January 27, 1973.[34]

The withdrawals, which continued despite the invasion, reassured the American people of President Nixon's intention to liquidate the war and prevented the intense reaction during 1972 that the invasion of Cambodia had triggered two years earlier, but some opposition did surface. The air offensive launched against North Vietnam in April, though limited in scope and clearly a reaction to the invasion, spurred congressional opponents of the war to call for cutting off funds to continue the fighting and for establishing a date to end U.S. involvement. Protests erupted on some college campuses, and major cities again served as the sites for antiwar demonstrations. The intensification of the air war in May, accompanied by the mining of North Vietnam's harbors, triggered new congressional agitation along with antiwar demonstrations that for a time shut

Reinforcement and Continuing Withdrawal

down the Capitol building and resulted in the detonation of a bomb in the Pentagon. Passions subsided, however, for U.S. casualties remained few as the President not only avoided reintroducing ground forces but continued reducing the number still in South Vietnam.[35]

Moreover, the Selective Service System no longer served as a catalyst for youthful dissent, since the threat of being drafted to fight in Vietnam had all but disappeared. As the Army began its conversion to an all-volunteer service, draft calls declined to a mere 50,000 in 1972, compared to 299,000 in 1968, before the beginning of Vietnamization and withdrawal.[36] Not even the heavy bombing near Hanoi and Haiphong during the eleven days surrounding Christmas 1972, denounced as an atrocity by North Vietnamese propaganda, provoked much of a reaction in the United States, other than on the editorial pages of some newspapers. The absence of demonstrations resulted in part from the fact that colleges had suspended classes for the holidays and that Congress was not in session, muting dissent on Capitol Hill.[37]

Besides rebuilding aerial strength in Southeast Asia to blunt the North Vietnamese offensive and continuing the reduction of American numbers in South Vietnam, the Nixon administration increased military aid to the government at Saigon. Planning for an acceleration of military assistance began during 1971 with a force structure review that, among other things, sought to improve coastal surveillance, to strengthen both the army and the local defense forces, and, of most direct concern to the Air Force, to enable the South Vietnamese to conduct aerial interdiction of North Vietnamese supply and infiltration routes. The review included a program, approved by Secretary Laird, that increased the authorized strength of the South Vietnamese Air Force by some 4,100 to operate and maintain the proposed five squadrons of minigunships.[38]

However, the minigunship program, nicknamed Credible Chase, failed to survive initial tests in the United States. Two aircraft underwent modification and entered a competition at Eglin Air Force Base in 1972, but neither had the endurance, structural strength, or aerodynamic stability to function as a gunship. The unsuccessful test came to an abrupt conclusion shortly after North Vietnam invaded the South.[39]

Before the minigunship program fizzled out, the Joint Chiefs in February 1972 endorsed the latest force structure review, thus increasing the authorized strength of the South Vietnamese Air Force to 61,000 at mid-1973. As approved by Secretary Laird, the plan called for the addition of 16,905 spaces to the air arm, including the 4,100 for the minigunship squadrons. To maintain overall South Vietnamese strength at the 1.1 million programmed in the budget for fiscal 1973, while at the same time increasing the air force, the South Vietnamese Joint General Staff suggested making a corresponding reduction in the irregular forces. Abrams agreed, as did the Joint Chiefs of Staff and Secretary Laird. By the time Laird approved the plan in July 1972, Credible Chase had failed to produce a credible weapon. As a result, the 4,100 spaces set aside for that project became a manpower pool for the South Vietnamese Air Force as it expanded toward a projected 64,507 by June 30, 1973.[40]

The North Vietnamese invasion at the end of March 1972 underscored the concerns of Nixon and Laird that the program of military aid then being devised might accomplish too little too late. The early battles required a vast expenditure of ammunition by the South Vietnamese, and the defeats they suffered cost them equipment, supplies, and casualties. Ahead lay the daunting prospect of reestablishing military stockpiles while training, equipping, and organizing replacements — interrelated tasks that would require massive aid from the United States. This assistance came to be known as Project Enhance.

In shaping Project Enhance, the Joint Chiefs persuaded Laird to resist any impulse to embark on new programs that the South Vietnamese, still reeling from the recent onslaught, might not be able to absorb. The immediate purpose, the Chiefs argued, should be to restore the armed forces of South Vietnam to their pre-invasion strength and effectiveness, while attempting modest improvements. As a result, Project Enhance consisted of a series of layered building blocks that restored the authorized 1.1-million-man structure and introduced only such new, or more numerous, equipment as the South Vietnamese could readily operate and maintain. The building blocks would be in place by August 1. President Nixon approved the concept, despite a possible cost of $730 million. On May 24, while he was in Moscow conferring with Brezhnev, the Secretary General of the Soviet Union's ruling Communist Party, Nixon informed President Thieu of South Vietnam that Project Enhance would begin.[41]

In carrying out its share of Project Enhance, the Air Force first tried to identify and deliver what South Vietnamese airmen needed to blunt the invasion. The initial layer of building blocks, intended to restore effectiveness, included 32 UH–1 helicopters, 5 F–5A fighter-bombers, and 48 A–37 attack aircraft. The delivery of 30 minigunships, projected as the first increment, never took place because of the collapse of the Credible Chase program.

The subsequent layers of building blocks, which did not have the initial deadline of August 1, looked to the improvement of the South Vietnamese Air Force. The U.S. Army, for example, would provide enough CH–47 helicopters to equip two squadrons, but this could not take place until September. At the same time, the Air Force would accelerate the delivery of 14 RC–47s, 23 AC–119K gunships, 23 EC–47s, 28 C–7 transports, and 14 C–119Gs modified for coastal fire support and maritime patrol. The lack of urgency in putting these later blocks into place reflected problems in training crews and maintenance specialists. For example, in the spring of 1972, the South Vietnamese Air Force formally acquired two squadrons of C–7s that U.S. Air Force crews had flown out of Cam Ranh Bay, but the airplanes could not go into action immediately. Since no South Vietnamese could fly the C–7, the crews delivered the aircraft to Phu Cat where American instructors had to train the necessary replacements. Project Enhance, confirmed by a new force structure review in the summer of

Reinforcement and Continuing Withdrawal

1972, brought prompt results, though largely in terms of numbers. By the end of October, the South Vietnamese Air Force activated all but 7 of the 58 squadrons planned for June 30 of the following year, and actual strength stood at 52,400.[42]

In October, as Project Enhance neared completion, the Nixon administration approved another infusion of equipment, Project Enhance Plus. The new undertaking served two purposes: to rush war material to South Vietnam before a cease-fire imposed restrictions on military assistance and to reconcile President Thieu to the fact that the United States, without having consulted him, now stood ready to accept a settlement that would permit North Vietnamese troops to remain on South Vietnamese soil, thus legitimizing the results of the Easter offensive. Although heavily weighted toward equipment for the South Vietnamese army, Project Enhance Plus did not ignore the air arm, for it included 19 A–1s (replaced as rescue escorts by the recently arrived A–7s), 90 A–37Bs, 32 C–130s, 126 F–5s, 177 UH–1s, together with the AC–119Ks and some other types not yet delivered in Project Enhance. The plan originally called for completing Enhance Plus by November 20, but later changes moved the deadline to November 10 and added 35 O–2 observation craft, already in South Vietnam, as replacements for the older O–1s and U–17s. The collapse of truce negotiations, which did not resume until after the Christmas bombing, caused the possible signing of a peace settlement to recede beyond January 1, 1973, and eased the pressure for prompt completion. Reflecting the changing circumstances, the last items in Project Enhance Plus did not arrive until December 10.

Urgency had prevailed, however, when the project began, and the American armed forces moved swiftly to carry out President Nixon's intentions. By November 10, an estimated 100,000 tons of equipment and cargo for Project Enhance Plus had arrived in South Vietnam or had begun the journey there. To make aircraft available, the Air Force diverted shipments intended for other nations or arranged the recall of airplanes already delivered outside South Vietnam. When necessary, Enhance Plus tapped the resources of Air Force Reserve and Air National Guard units. The Air Force dispatched a total of 256 aircraft that arrived in South Vietnam either under their own power or partially disassembled in the cavernous hulls of C–5A or C–141 transports. Another 61 airplanes and 307 helicopters came from Air Force and Army inventories in South Vietnam. The Military Airlift Command delivered 4,998 tons of cargo, not quite 5 percent of the total, including all the A–37s shipped during Enhance Plus.[43]

Project Enhance Plus increased the inventory of the South Vietnamese Air Force by some 595 aircraft, excluding about 30 of the helicopters intended for a postwar truce surveillance agency. To absorb this influx, the air arm by mid-1973 organized eight additional fighter or attack squadrons, two transport squadrons, fourteen squadrons or flights of helicopters, and one training squadron. Besides accomplishing all of this, the project reequipped some tactical air support squadrons with O–2s, increased each UH–1 squadron from

Air War over South Vietnam, 1968–1975

F–5s sent to South Vietnam as part of Enhance Plus wait to be assembled.

33 helicopters to 38, and began organizing the squadron of armed C–119Gs for coastal and maritime patrol. When the South Vietnamese Air Force absorbed all the Enhance Plus aircraft — and eliminated the recently organized C–123 squadrons in 1973, as scheduled — it would total sixty-six squadrons with more than 61,000 officers and men. This rapid augmentation, however, imposed strains on the supporting establishment and failed to generate the kind of air power that the United States had exercised over the years.[44]

The training of pilots and crews to fly the aircraft provided by Project Enhance Plus proceeded on the principle that instruction in the United States soon would merely supplement that administered in South Vietnam. To cope with the additional aircraft, the South Vietnamese Air Force no longer waited for trainees to emerge from the pipeline, but tried instead, with American collaboration, to teach persons already familiar with one kind of aircraft to make the transition to a more advanced type. Assignments vacated by those who retrained would go to officers that had recently learned to fly. Pilots of A–37s retrained for F–5s; O–1 pilots for the O–2 and the A–37; crews of AC–119Gs for AC–119Ks; crews of C–119s and C–123s for the C–130s; and those of C–123s for the armed C–119s. Since the C–123 squadrons would disband during 1973, they seemed a valuable source of pilots and crew members for transition training. The Air Force Advisory Group, using teams of instructors dispatched from the United States, planned to teach a number of the South Vietnamese to take over the postwar training programs for the various types of aircraft, assisted as necessary by American civilians working under contract. In contrast to the fixed-wing aircraft, the vast increase in helicopters during Enhance and Enhance Plus required, at least for the near future, pilots trained exclusively for this type of aircraft by Army instructors in the United States.[45] Despite the emphasis on training, in February 1973, two weeks after the cease-fire took effect, the South Vietnamese Air Force projected a shortage of some 800 pilots or copilots, 300 for fixed-wing aircraft and the rest for helicopters.

The South Vietnamese Air Force also needed additional navigators for the gunships, transports, and especially the coastal and maritime patrol aircraft it was acquiring. Unfortunately, the air arm gave a low priority to the aerial navigation school operated in South Vietnam, reducing the course from twenty weeks to twelve, and finally closing the course entirely when Project Enhance created a critical need for pilots. By the time the cease-fire went into effect, the South Vietnamese had not yet accepted U.S. advice to reopen the navigation school; indeed, only twenty-three trainees, all of them eliminated from pilot training, were undergoing instruction in the United States.[46]

Although logistics had caused problems over the years, the Air Force Advisory Group seemed generally confident that the South Vietnamese Air Force could maintain the aircraft provided by Projects Enhance and Enhance Plus. Although the absence of a common language remained a barrier to the transfer of maintenance skills, the translation of manuals and technical orders into Vietnamese helped, as did accelerated programs for teaching English to the South Vietnamese. Moreover, the average airman entering the South Vietnamese Air Force, though he might be a farmer or laborer unfamiliar with machinery, demonstrated an ability to master fairly complex technical skills. Patience and motivation seemed the keys to success, for American instructors had to expect the inevitable errors, correct them again and again, and above all, avoid giving up and simply doing the job for the persons they were supposed to teach.[47]

Plans called for the South Vietnamese to operate a computer-assisted logistics system patterned on the Air Force model, but oriented toward the specific aircraft in their inventory. Under this arrangement, a computer at the Air Logistics Command kept track of spare parts and other material to insure the presence of adequate stocks at base and depot. Maintenance and repair began at the base, moving to the depot if the nature of the work proved too demanding.

As a general rule, the more complex the task, the greater the dependence on American help. When Project Enhance Plus came to an end, the South Vietnamese Air Force bore full responsibility for maintaining the A–1, a technologically straightforward airplane, and all its components and for repairing battle damage to most other of its aircraft. South Vietnamese technicians could not, however, repair all kinds of electronic gear, for in some instances the succession of modernization and improvement programs had not given them the necessary test equipment or training. Once the cease-fire took effect, American contractors would have to deal with this category of electronic devices and also perform depot, though not base-level, maintenance on the J–85 jet engines that powered the F–5 and A–37. The C–130, new to the inventory, presented a special postwar challenge, but the Air Force Logistics Command expected South Vietnamese mechanics to learn to perform all base-level procedures, while Lockheed, the manufacturer, did the more technologically demanding work at depots outside South Vietnam. A similar division of labor would also apply to the helicopter fleet, as the South Vietnamese assumed postwar responsibility for the engines, air frames, and rotors, with the U.S. contractors repairing the more complex components, like the fuel control system of the Bell UH–1. The computer and the various terminals used by the South Vietnamese Air Logistics Command depended exclusively on American technicians for repair and maintenance.[48]

Although the postwar South Vietnamese Air Force would continue to require outside help for computer services and aircraft maintenance, its logistics system seemed, to American eyes, adequate for the support of the aerial armada that Projects Enhance and Enhance Plus had completed. Later, some of the Vietnamese assigned to the Air Logistics Command provided a different assessment, one affected, no doubt, by the collapse of the South Vietnamese armed forces and government and their own escape to the United States. One of them, Gen. Tu Van Be, pointed out that the expansion of the South Vietnamese Air Force brought in a vast number of recruits at the very time when American reductions in funding and the cost of intensified aerial combat put an end to the technical training of lower-ranking airmen in the United States. In spite of help from on-the-job training by Air Force technicians, replaced after the cease-fire by American civilians under contract, South Vietnamese noncommissioned officers, themselves needed by operational units, had to impart some degree of technical skill to unwieldy groups of twenty or twenty-five recruits, whereas they formerly had taught only six or seven persons at a time. He believed, moreover, that many of the American civilians, who provided technical training immediately after the cease-fire, did not meet the high standards established by the Air Force instructors they replaced. Until the contractors weeded out their unfit employees, the task of training lay heavily on the already overburdened South Vietnamese noncommissioned officers.[49]

Brigadier General Dang Dinh Linh, the South Vietnamese Air Force's Deputy Chief of Staff for Materiel, praised the Air Logistics Command's data processing network, which consisted of a main computer at Bien Hoa and terminals at the other bases. Data automation, he believed, successfully matched stocks with the needs of the operational units and helped with logistics planning.[50] One of the officers in Linh's staff section argued, however, that the computer should have been located at South Vietnamese Air Force headquarters at Tan Son Nhut, thus enabling the logistics command to mass supplies in anticipation of planned operations instead of reacting, as it consistently had done, to requisitions and reported shortages.[51]

The same officer who had criticized the location of the main computer, also complained that Enhance Plus had inundated South Vietnam's army and air

Reinforcement and Continuing Withdrawal

force with more equipment than they could handle. To support this view, he cited the example of the C–130s, more complicated than the C–123 already in the inventory, old and in need of maintenance when the South Vietnamese took them over, and a source of recurring mechanical problems until the fall of Saigon in April 1975. The two helicopters made available in sizeable numbers during 1972, the CH–47 and the UH–1, also proved difficult to keep in operating condition.[52] In terms of logistics, the decision to replace some F–5As with F–5Es also seemed a mistake, for, as General Linh himself pointed out, a different and more complex fighter took the place of a familiar one.[53]

Besides being difficult for the South Vietnamese Air Force to maintain, the aircraft that arrived during the 1972 augmentation failed to correct glaring weaknesses in the organization's ability to wage aerial warfare. The inability of the minigunship to survive testing in Florida left the South Vietnamese with no aircraft capable of attacking the Ho Chi Minh Trail or comparably defended lines of supply and communication. The most modern gunship, the lumbering AC–119K, could not survive conventional antiaircraft fire, let alone radar-directed guns or heat-seeking missiles. The A–1, though sturdy and able to carry up to four tons of bombs, lacked speed, but the fast jets like the A–37 or F–5, which might survive antiaircraft defenses, had neither the endurance nor the bomb capacity for armed reconnaissance and, because of the failure to equip and train the South Vietnamese for aerial refueling, could not attack targets deep within southern Laos or North Vietnam. Moreover, only the F–5E provided an effective weapon for air defense, should North Vietnam break with tradition and launch an air campaign against the South.[54]

As it coped with these weaknesses in tactical aviation and air defense, the South Vietnamese Air Force faced the formidable task of finding an aerial weapon with the versatility and firepower of the B–52, a high-altitude bomber that could drop as many thirty tons of bombs on targets varying from troops massing for an assault to docks and warehouses hundreds of miles from the battlefield. The Nixon administration sought to substitute a powerful bomb for a mighty bomber, providing a fuel-air weapon, containing a volatile gas-like propane, which the A–1 or A–37 could deliver by parachute, and the pallet-load of high explosive, and sometimes oil or gasoline, parachuted from a transport like the C–130.[55] The South Vietnamese Air Force received some of the CBU–55 fuel-air devices in time to try them against the enemy-held citadel at Quang Tri City, where the sturdy masonry walls proved impervious to 500-pound bombs dropped by A–37s. In this instance, the cloud of gas exploded ineffectually in the opening along the base of the wall instead of first seeping into a confined space, like a cellar or bunker, for maximum destructive effect. After the CBU–55 failed, Air Force F–4s breached the barrier with laser-guided bombs, which the South Vietnamese did not have.[56]

The South Vietnamese airmen, lacking laser-guided bombs, had to achieve the necessary accuracy with ordinary munitions, which required attacks at low altitude. However, the North Vietnamese introduction of a shoulder-launched, heat-seeking antiaircraft missile, the SA–7, forced a change in tactics. Although flares might fool the infrared homing device or shields screen the heat source, the surest protection against the SA–7, until flare dispensers and heat shielding became commonplace, consisted of staying out of range and bombing from 9,000 or 10,000 feet. At that altitude, even a skilled pilot found it difficult to hit a compact target with a conventional bomb.[57]

Despite its use of EC–47s to intercept radio signals and locate transmitters in the field, the South Vietnamese Air Force depended heavily on photo reconnaissance for discovering and pinpointing targets. A Vietnamized photo interpretation center functioned at Tan Son Nhut, but neither of the available camera-equipped aircraft, the RF–5A and the RC–47D, could supply it with satisfactory pictures of the battlefield. The RF–5A, though fast enough to penetrate defended areas, carried a camera that photographed too narrow a swath to be of much value in finding targets. The RC–47D, flying low and slow, provided more panoramic coverage but presented an easy target for hostile antiaircraft gunners.[58]

In another form of reconnaissance, visual searches by forward air controllers, the South Vietnamese also suffered from second-line equipment. They did not have the OV–10, the newest aircraft that American forward air controllers used; indeed, the old and extremely vulnerable O–1 and U–17 remained in service, along with the O–2A, better performing but by no means the equal of the OV–10. In general, South Vietnamese forward air controllers seemed competent in the procedures for actually directing strikes, but they had done much of their flying in what American analysts called "a benign environment."[59] Moreover, as some of the South Vietnamese controllers had demonstrated over the eastern part of the demilitarized zone in the weeks before the Easter invasion, they tended, perhaps because of a lack of confidence that they could operate in heavily defended areas, to show very little initiative as they adhered strictly to their prescribed routes.[60]

American air power had protected the withdrawal, principally of ground forces, that began in 1969 and continued after the Easter invasion of 1972. Despite three years of Vietnamization, the South Vietnamese Air Force could not yet take over the air war when the North Vietnamese attacked, though they did enjoy limited success against poorly defended targets. South Vietnam's air arm, moreover, could not absorb and make use of the material provided by Projects Enhance and Enhance Plus quickly enough to meet the current emergency; indeed, it seemed unlikely that South Vietnamese military aviation could deal, unaided, with a future assault of comparable scope. Whatever the future might bring, the task of responding to the North Vietnamese offensive of 1972 fell to rapidly reinforced U.S. air power wielded by the Air Force, Navy, and Marine Corps.

Chapter Twenty-One

Military Region I
Quang Tri City Lost and Regained

After announcing that General Vogt would replace General Lavelle, President Nixon summoned the new commander of the Seventh Air Force to the White House for what turned out to be a pep talk. As Vogt remembered the conversation, the President complained that Lavelle had shown a lack of aggressiveness, even though he actually was being replaced because he had broken the rules of engagement governing the air war.[1] Consequently, Vogt was to "use whatever air you need to turn this thing around."[2] In carrying out the Presidential mandate, Vogt wanted a free hand; as he told Nixon, "I can't have people telling me what targets to hit ... I've got to be able to run the war." Nixon agreed, "You've got all that authority," he replied, though he never reinforced his oral assurance with a formal directive.

As it turned out, Vogt's concern lest he fail to "get command arrangements squared away" proved largely groundless. The practice of approving at Washington each individual target in North Vietnam, normal for the earlier Rolling Thunder air campaign, was not sustained during Operation Linebacker, although certain areas, like the buffer zone along the Chinese border, and some targets, principally hydroelectric dams (but not the related generators) and irrigation dikes, remained exempt from attack.

Vogt's operational control of Marine Corps aircraft did not cause tension because the Marine airmen returned to Southeast Asia as reinforcements for the Seventh Air Force, and no combat Marines — except for the limited number of advisers with the South Vietnamese — served on the ground in South Vietnam where they would have an emotional as well as doctrinal claim to sorties by Marine Corps aviation. Finally, as Seventh Air Force commander, Vogt became more than a deputy for air operations like his predecessors; at the end of June, he replaced Gen. Frederick C. Weyand as deputy commander of the Military Assistance Command when Weyand took over as commander from Abrams. In effect, the headquarters of the Seventh Air Force and assistance command merged, thus reflecting the dominant U.S. role in the air war as participation in the fighting on the ground continued to decline.

Air War over South Vietnam, 1968–1975

In spite of some disharmony at the start, Vogt got along well with Abrams and with Weyand, after Abrams left South Vietnam to become Army Chief of Staff. He moved into an office next to Weyand and saw to it that the staffs of the Seventh Air Force and the military assistance command collaborated on operational planning. Convinced that duty required him to present Abrams with the facts as he saw them, Vogt challenged an intelligence report that justified turning down a request from Maj. Gen. James F. Hollingsworth, the senior U.S. adviser in Military Region III, to concentrate B–52 strikes against an expected attack on the town of An Loc. At a staff meeting where Abrams considered Hollingsworth's request, Vogt boldly warned that the fall of An Loc could undercut the American bargaining position on the eve of Nixon's meeting with Brezhnev. Abrams, embarrassed by Vogt's bluntness in the presence of other officers, angrily overruled the airman. However, the evidence that Vogt immediately mustered, including reports from forward air controllers, caused Abrams to reconsider, change his mind, contact the Strategic Air Command's planning group in South Vietnam, and arrange for diversion of the bombers. This willingness on the part of Abrams to ignore bruised feelings and let Vogt "walk in" and renew the argument "from a professional standpoint" impressed Vogt as being to Abram's "everlasting credit."[3]

When Vogt arrived at Seventh Air Force headquarters on April 7, bad weather, dominant since the offensive began, screened the assault troops in northern South Vietnam from systematic air attack. At times, according to Maj. David A. Brookbank, the Air Force adviser with the South Vietnamese 3d Division, only B–52s using Combat Skyspot or fighter-bombers aided by radar or Loran could harry the North Vietnamese invaders of Quang Tri Province.[4] Indeed, cloud cover also persisted in North Vietnam during the summer months, as the prevailing monsoon winds brought moisture-laden air from the Indian Ocean. Dr. Kissinger recalled that during these frustrating days he pressed Admiral Moorer for news of successful strikes against the North, but "his answer for the first forty-eight hours was negative." The subject of the weather became "nearly an obsession" with Kissinger and the occasion for "sarcasm and badgering" directed at the Chairman of the Joint Chiefs of Staff. "It seemed to me," Kissinger recalled several years later, "that our entire Air Force consisted of delicate machines capable of flying only in a war in the desert in July. I suggested that if they could not fly maybe they could taxi north for twenty-five miles." Not until the arrival of Marine A–6s in June and Air Force F–111s in September and October did Vogt acquire genuine all-weather fighter-bombers. According to statistics compiled for Admiral Moorer, by mid-August, bad weather had forced the cancellation or diversion to secondary targets of 42 percent of the strikes scheduled against targets in North Vietnam.[5]

Unfavorable weather, the confusion of war, and clashing priorities undermined the Vietnamized air control system as the South Vietnamese 3d Division struggled to defend Quang Tri Province. When the North Vietnamese stormed

Quang Tri City Lost and Regained

across the demilitarized zone, catching the recently organized division in the process of rotating its components among defensive positions inherited from the Americans, Major Brookbank tried to function as an air adviser, but his counterpart, the South Vietnamese air liaison officer, proved reluctant to accept responsibility for marshaling air power in support of the division. While cloud cover and the South Vietnamese officer's hesitancy handicapped Brookbank's efforts to employ aircraft, the hard-pressed division fell back from its northern and western outposts and organized a line south of the Cua Viet and Mieu Giang Rivers. At Camp Carroll, the position turned sharply southward, extending to the border with neighboring Thua Thien Province. On April 2, however, the commander at Camp Carroll surrendered his 1,500 troops, opening a gap that the division commander, Brig. Gen. Vu Van Giai, could close only by retreating some ten miles toward Quang Tri City.[6]

On the day that the defenses of Camp Carroll collapsed, April 2, two EB–66s, with radio call signs Bat 21 and Bat 22, were providing electronic jamming for B–52s using Combat Skyspot to bomb through the overcast near the demilitarized zone, from which enemy troops now pushed southward. Despite the jamming signal, two radar-guided SA–2 surface-to-air missiles roared through the clouds, one of them scoring a direct hit on Bat 21. Of the six crewmen, only the navigator, Lt. Col. Iceal E. Hambleton, escaped from the shattered airplane. He suffered minor injuries as he parachuted to earth near a major highway in the vicinity of Cam Lo. Using the hand-held radio that formed a part of his escape equipment, he contacted would-be rescuers who planned to pick him up by helicopter on the next day.

To protect the downed airman and the aircrews trying to recover him, the Seventh Air Force established restrictions on air strikes and artillery barrages throughout a so-called no-fire zone, 27 kilometers in radius, encompassing much of the 3d Division's area of operation, including the North Vietnamese route of advance from Camp Carroll toward Quang Tri City. The I Direct Air Support Center was to control the use of firepower within that area, giving an absolute priority to activity directly related to the rescue. After antiaircraft fire downed three of the aircraft participating in the planned rescue, along with two Army helicopters that tried on their own to pick up Hambleton, an officer at his wing headquarters coached the downed airman by radio to a point on the Cua Viet River, disguising the instructions by referring to the layout from tee to green of various holes on golf courses familiar to both men. As Hambleton golfed his way to safety, starting off in the direction of the tee shot then taking a dog-leg to the right, Seventh Air Force headquarters tracked his location and reduced the radius of the safety zone surrounding him to 5,000 and then 2,700 meters. Two other airmen, 1st Lieutenants Mark Clark and Bruce Walker, whose aircraft were shot down while protecting Hambleton, also received instructions by radio, though without the references to golf courses, a story that has become one of the legends of the Vietnam conflict.

Air War over South Vietnam, 1968–1975

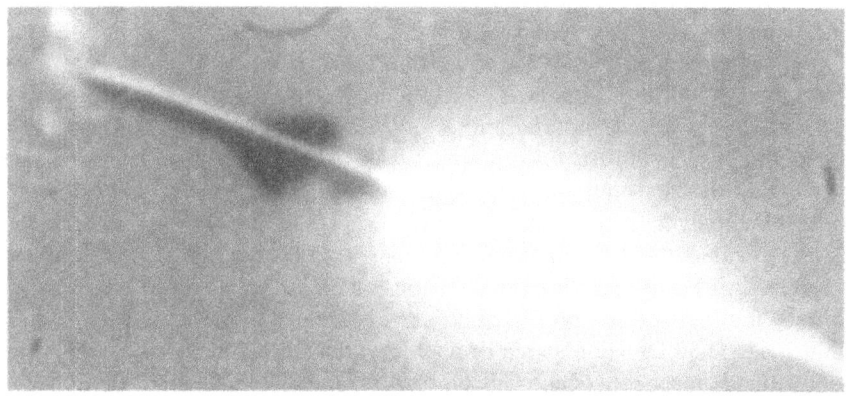

SA–2 launcher (top) and an SA–2 flashing past a reconnaissance aircraft.

Marine Lt. Col. Andrew E. Andersen, a member of the assistance command's Studies and Observations Group who specialized in the recovery of Americans captured by the North Vietnamese or Viet Cong, dispatched a team of South Vietnamese led by U.S. Navy Lt. Thomas R. Norris to infiltrate hostile territory and effect a rescue. Norris and one of the South Vietnamese disguised themselves as fishermen, took a boat up the Cua Viet, and plucked Hambleton from the river bank. The exploit earned Norris the Medal of Honor. Thus ended, after eleven days, a rescue effort that had resulted in the destruction of two OV–10s, an HH–53, two Army UH–1s, and the loss of eleven American lives.[7]

The establishment of the no-fire zone to facilitate Hambleton's rescue occurred when an estimated three North Vietnamese divisions, with tanks and artillery, were advancing from the northwest toward the river defenses and from

Quang Tri City Lost and Regained

the northwest toward Quang Tri City. The enemy moved at will through the zone, safe for the most part from artillery fire, but impeded to some extent by air strikes on road traffic, troop concentrations, or antiaircraft sites that threatened the rescue. Even intelligence collection, especially visual reconnaissance by low-flying forward air controllers, sought primarily to aid the recovery effort. Brookbank, the Air Force adviser in Giai's headquarters, believed that the Bat 21 no-fire zone "cost the 3d ARVN Division dearly" by giving the North Vietnamese an immunity to attack "unprecedented in the annals of warfare." Despite Brookbank's somber critique, South Vietnamese artillery did not fall silent, but continued to fire against carefully chosen targets, largely on the initiative of its officers.[8]

The interruption of the air war caused by the rescue of Hambleton raised a number of issues. An account of Air Force search and rescue activity in Southeast Asia, for example, compares rescuing Hambleton against the U.S. lives lost, "How much was the one life worth?" The question had not arisen before the rescue attempt and no formal answer appeared afterward. Air Force rescue and recovery units avoided throwing away lives on suicidal missions against the most heavily defended portions of North Vietnam and the Ho Chi Minh Trail in Laos, but prior to the Easter offensive, operations in South Vietnam had usually encountered only automatic weapons and optically aimed, light antiaircraft guns, the kind of opposition that a fighter escort could readily suppress. The rescue attempt on April 3 began with every expectation of success, but ended in failure after North Vietnamese missiles and antiaircraft guns, deadlier because of radar control, proved too powerful for the rescue force. Once the enemy demonstrated the actual strength of his battlefield aerial defenses, the Seventh Air Force launched no further recovery attempts but instead maintained surveillance while Lieutenant Colonel Andersen's organization assumed responsibility for the pickup. No formal evaluation proved necessary, balancing the number of lives risked against those that might be saved. The area around Cam Lo simply joined the list of regions, like Hanoi and Haiphong in the north or Tchepone in southern Laos, where rescue helicopters dared not venture.[9]

A popular history, John Morrocco's *Rain of Fire*, makes much of the fact that Brookbank, who criticized suspending air support for the 3d Division to avoid endangering Hambleton (and later Clark and Walker), cried out "Thank God for the U.S. Air Force" when HH–53 helicopters extricated the unit's American advisers as the enemy overran Quang Tri City.[10] The attempt at irony misses the point, which is not that rescues took place, often involving loss of life among the rescuers and always inspiring gratitude in the individual saved, but that American authorities were willing to risk the destruction of an entire division in setting up the recovery of one officer, Hambleton. Upon learning that the no-fire zone had gone into effect for a lone airman — only Hambleton had been shot down at that time — a South Vietnamese officer asked one of the division's American advisers, "Just one?"[11]

361

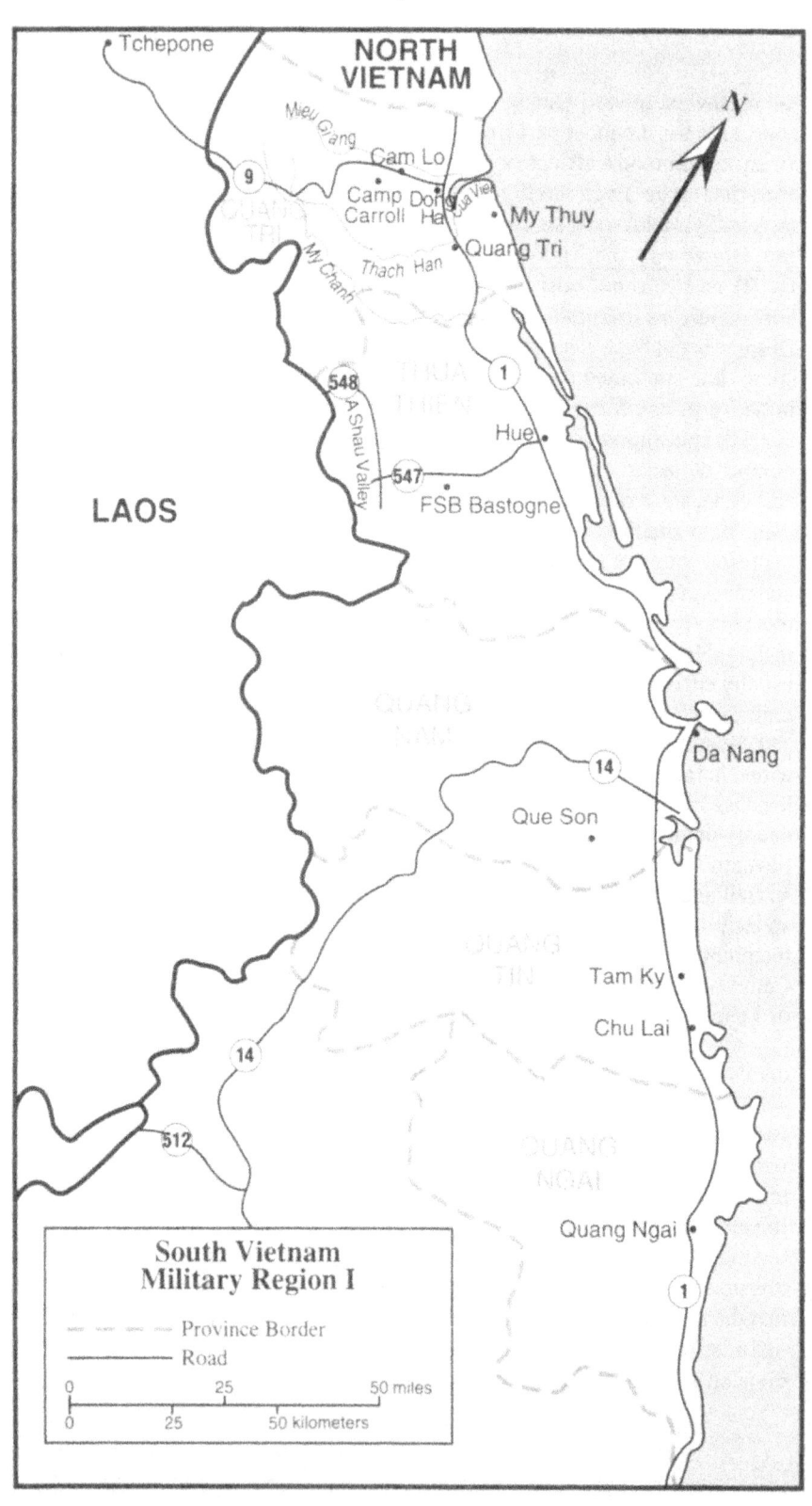

Quang Tri City Lost and Regained

Nor is it pertinent that a subsequent rescue saved Brookbank, together with more than a hundred others, from death or capture at Quang Tri City. Brookbank carried out his duties to the bitter end. Marine Lt. Col. Gerald H. Turley, serving as an adviser to the 3d Division, described Brookbank's "personal efforts to get TAC [tactical aircraft] on targets" as "instrumental in slowing the enemy's advance." Moreover, in Turley's opinion, Brookbank had "demonstrated that he possessed the stamina and those special qualities of which heroes are made."[12]

In spite of his respect for Brookbank, with whom he worked in the division's tactical operations center, Turley criticized a decision that, in his words, "the U.S. Air Force would control all air strikes and artillery fire" through the I Direct Air Support Center. In actual practice, however, South Vietnamese artillery continued firing, although the U.S. advisers monitored the fire control network and tried to veto any concentrations within 1,000 meters of the reported positions of Hambleton, Clark, or Walker. Only air support remained under the strict control of the I Direct Air Support Center throughout the recovery operation, though the forward air controllers could put in strikes as required, provided they did not violate overall instructions.[13] The policy on air strikes relaxed only gradually, keeping pace with the progress of the rescue. According to Maj. Gen. Frederick J. Kroesen, the senior U.S. adviser in Military Region I, "No commander in MR I could change it and no command authority in Saigon could be convinced of the need to change it."[14]

The emphasis on saving downed American fliers, if at all possible, had become a tradition by 1972. The rescue of Hambleton differed from the norm only in the willingness of the U.S. leadership to risk the already battered South Vietnamese 3d Division. This attitude may conceivably have reflected the impatience, perhaps the disdain, that some Americans tended to show South Vietnamese units, which seemed as dependent on American advice and support after Vietnamization as before. Had the 3d Division been American, either Army or Marine Corps, the commanders and command authorities might well have struck a different balance between the survival of the individual and the military effectiveness of a major unit. Indeed, Earl H. Tilford, Jr., the author of the Air Force's history of rescue operations in Southeast Asia suggests that "the Americans were vastly more concerned with saving the life of one of their own and, conversely, held the lives of their Asian allies in lower regard."[15]

Restrictions on air strikes and fire support other than those related to the Bat 21 rescue also handicapped the South Vietnamese 3d Division. Another search and rescue near Route 1, some eight miles north of the Cua Viet River, permitted North Vietnamese armor for a time to pass unchallenged by air strikes. Suspected short rounds from air or artillery resulted in a temporary cease-fire while friendly gunners or airmen checked their data. In the confused fighting of early April, South Vietnamese artillery, American aircraft, and American naval gunfire, sometimes directed by Marine Corps spotters in TA–4s or other aircraft, blasted targets along Giai's front. At the same time, North Vietnamese long-range 130-mm guns fired into the division's defensive positions. Troops on the ground could mistake hostile shelling for friendly fire and report a short round, as apparently happened on April 4 near the mouth of the Cua Viet. On that occasion, a forward air controller had directed naval gunfire against seven tanks crossing the river and destroyed three of them, when an erroneous report of a short round, forwarded by the I Direct Air Support Center, forced him to halt the firing and enabled three to escape.[16]

Outside the no-fire zones, air power killed many tanks. A forward air controller from Da Nang spotted a column of armored vehicles moving down Route 1, called on a forward air controller from Nakhon Phanom to confirm the location, and discovered that the enemy would pass from one planned Arc Light target to another. The forward air controller from Nakhon Phanom used his secure radio link to advise the infiltration surveillance center at the Thai air base, which contacted the Seventh Air Force command and control center and arranged to divert an approaching cell of B–52s to the box the enemy was about to enter. Half an hour later, high explosives began churning the road, destroying an estimated thirty-five tanks and, according to unconfirmed reports, a division command post as well.[17]

Despite the surrender of Camp Carroll, the cloud cover that hindered air support, and the no-fire zones, General Giai succeeded in clinging to a shrunken perimeter, anchored by the Cua Viet River and a strongpoint at Dong Ha, that included Quang Tri City. The commander of South Vietnam's I Corps, Lt. Gen. Hoang Xuan Lam, rarely stirred from his headquarters throughout the crisis in Military Region I, coterminous with the area of tactical responsibility assigned to his corps. He remained content to pass along orders from Saigon, including a call for a counterattack.[18]

Preparations for this counterthrust led to the final collapse of the division's air liaison machinery. Brookbank sought to arrange continuous daytime coverage of the operation using American forward air controllers and just three South Vietnamese missions each day, but even this proved too much for his counterpart. The South Vietnamese air liaison officer responded with what Brookbank described as "an adamant 'can't do'," and refused even to pass the request to the air division responsible for implementation. As a result, Brookbank took over as air liaison officer for the 3d Division, relying on U.S. forward air controllers to conduct reconnaissance and direct air strikes, except in lightly defended areas, which became increasingly fewer as the enemy introduced the SA–7 shoulder-fired, heat-seeking antiaircraft missile and moved both antiaircraft guns and radar-guided SA–2 missiles into position to cover the battlefield. Brookbank also sorted out the requests for Loran and Combat Skyspot strikes, which exceeded by far the capacity of those systems, trying to limit the attacks to genuinely rewarding targets and eliminate the "suspected enemy troop locations" that all too often reflected a South Vietnamese reluctance to invite counterbattery fire by using mortars or artillery for harassment and interdiction missions.[19]

The attempted counterattack regained no ground and merely resulted in casualties that further weakened the bloodied division. On April 23, the Cua Viet line collapsed, but Giai managed to halt the retreat at the Thach Han River and form a ragged perimeter around Quang Tri City, the site of his headquarters and a depot by now largely empty of supplies.

In a final effort to sustain the embattled 3d Division, South Vietnamese C–123s attempted an emergency delivery of ammunition on April 30. Escorted by American forward air controllers who directed Air Force fighter-bombers against antiaircraft sites, two of the transports flew north along Route 1, released their cargo by parachute, and exited safely over the sea. The North Vietnamese fire proved so violent that Giai's assistant division commander concluded that further efforts would proved suicidal and canceled the supply mission. Another pair of C–123s did not receive word of this decision and bored through antiaircraft fire that had grown even more intense in the absence of coordinated flak suppression strikes by forward air controllers and fighter-bombers. One of the transports got away, but the other sustained mortal damage and crashed offshore. This display of courage accomplished nothing, however, for all the cargo dropped that day landed behind North Vietnamese lines.

Cut off from supplies, his division in the last throes of disintegration, Giai prepared to break out of the encirclement. He tried at last to eliminate a longstanding obstacle to emergency air support. Throughout the fighting thus far, I Corps headquarters had shown reluctance to approve diverting air strikes from other targets to help the division, probably for fear of hitting retreating troops or noncombatant refugees. On one occasion, the I Direct Air Support Center waited seven hours before approving an attack on a captured bunker believed to house a North Vietnamese command post. Now Giai, without consulting corps headquarters, granted blanket authority for any target Brookbank might consider worth attacking. This one show of initiative did not redeem the overall failure of the Vietnamized command and control network; already the Seventh Air Force had ignored Vietnamization and reestablished a parallel system to control its aircraft.[20]

Instead of fighting its way out as Giai intended, the 3d Division fell apart under attack from armor, artillery, and infantry, although the fleeing survivors regrouped around attached Marine and ranger units that remained intact south of Quang Tri City. The final collapse trapped eighty U.S. advisers, Brookbank among them, and some fifty South Vietnamese in the citadel at Quang Tri City, the site of Giai's headquarters. At mid-afternoon on May 1, the I Direct Air Support Center told Brookbank that rescue helicopters would pick up the group at a large clearing about 1,000 yards from the command post. The advisers realized, however, that the enemy had cut them off from that landing zone and arranged for the HH–53s to use a small helicopter pad at the citadel itself. Three

Air War over South Vietnam, 1968–1975

forward air controllers, each directing four teams of fighters, some two dozen in all, covered the approaches. Brookbank briefed them, speaking to two of the airborne controllers by secure radio but relying on circumlocution in talking with the third, whose voice scrambler did not work. When North Vietnamese artillery knocked out the generator and silenced Brookbank, he advised the I Direct Air Support Center by telephone to turn the operation over to the airborne battlefield command and control center. While A–1s bombed and strafed to isolate the landing zone and its approaches, three helicopters arrived, flying at treetop height to avoid radar but accepting the increased risk of small arms and light antiaircraft guns. The HH–53s landed in succession, loaded, and roared off again, while a fourth helicopter lagged behind in case it was needed. A radio message from the citadel alerted Capt. Donald A. Sutton, the pilot of this fourth rescue craft, that Americans remained at the landing zone, and he swooped down to save them. Scarcely had the landing gear settled to earth when hostile riflemen opened fire. When no Americans sprinted toward the lowered ramp, Sutton realized the North Vietnamese had lured him into a trap. While his gunner sprayed the area with fire from a multibarrel cannon, he poured on the power and escaped.[21]

The fall of Quang Tri City brought changes in the command structure within Military Region I. Although Giai got as much from his troops as anyone could have, given the ferocity of the attack and the impact of weather on air operations, a court-martial sentenced him to prison where he remained until the spring of 1975 when South Vietnam collapsed. (The triumphant North Vietnamese thereupon jailed him for reeducation in the ways of communism.) On May 3, Lt. Gen. Ngo Quang Truong moved from command of IV Corps in southernmost South Vietnam to take over I Corps from General Lam who had demonstrated in Lam Son 719 and again during the Easter invasion his inability to handle a large and complex military organization. Lam, however, escaped further punishment for his role in the collapse of the defenses of Quang Tri Province. Giai alone served as a scapegoat in defeat.[22]

Truong set up an advance headquarters at Hue, where he had formerly served and still enjoyed numerous military and civilian contacts. As part of his command post, he established a fire support coordination center to meld artillery, naval gunfire, and air strikes. To ease the task of combining all the firepower available for the defense of the city, he urged that the Seventh Air Force move the I Direct Air Support Center from Da Nang to Hue, but Vogt at first resisted, arguing that the facility would function better at the air base. Truong insisted, however, and Vogt finally agreed to a transfer that required what the American later described as "superhuman efforts." Rather than entrust the region's tactical air control machinery entirely to the dubious security of Hue, Vogt retained a rear echelon at Da Nang.[23]

General Truong inherited a potential disaster. Abrams advised Laird on May 1 that South Vietnamese "military leadership has begun to bend and in

Quang Tri City Lost and Regained

some instances break.... There is no basis for confidence that Hue or Kontum will be held."[24] Indeed, the city of Hue stood balanced precariously at the edge of panic, as disorderly groups of soldiers, defeated in battle elsewhere, prowled the streets. Truong moved swiftly, however, to restore order and incorporate the stragglers into combat formations. While shattered units like the 3d Division and its attached components regrouped, Truong launched what he called Loi Phong, Thunder Hurricane, a series of offensives involving bombardment by B–52s, tactical aviation, naval gunfire, and artillery. Loi Phong sought to kill, wound, or demoralize North Vietnamese reinforcements before they could add their momentum to the attack on Hue. To take advantage of this deluge of firepower, Truong authorized the commanders of the divisions and brigades deployed around Hue to launch limited attacks as they saw fit.[25]

During the capture of Quang Tri City and again in the advance upon Hue, North Vietnamese 130-mm guns demonstrated each day their deadly accuracy and their ability to outrange the 155-mm howitzers the United States had supplied South Vietnam. The 130-mm weapon not only inflicted casualties but also undermined morale. Indeed, in General Vogt's opinion, North Vietnamese artillery had won the battle for Quang Tri City, forcing the defenders to flee "because they didn't want to take the artillery rounds being fired at them," an oversimplification, to be sure, but nevertheless containing some truth.[26]

In the hope of locating the cleverly camouflaged 130-mm batteries, the Seventh Air Force modified a technique developed by the Rome Air Development Center and used unsuccessfully to locate surface-to-air missile sites that protected the Ho Chi Minh Trail in southern Laos. Acoustic sensors, activated on command from the infiltration surveillance center at Nakhon Phanom, Thailand, had listened during the spring of 1972 for the sound of the portable generators that provided electrical power for the radar at the launch site. In theory, if three sensors not in a line reported the sound, analysts at the surveillance center could locate the source by simple triangulation. The engineers, however, had not taken into account the realities of the Ho Chi Minh Trail. Success required the precise emplacement of sensors, no easy task in an area bristling with antiaircraft guns. The electronic devices, moreover, proved easily fooled by other sounds, like the idling of diesel-powered trucks, and by the fact that noise did not radiate uniformly in all directions from the generator but was strongest along a direct line from the exhaust port. The aerial interdiction of the Ho Chi Minh Trail ended before Air Force technicians could make the locating system work satisfactorily.

In spite of this failure, the 130-mm guns proved so dangerous that the Rome Air Development Center tried to apply the same principle to the detection of artillery positions. The proposed gun locating system used the sensors to listen for the sound of firing rather than for the roar of a generator. A pattern of sensors deployed around a suspected artillery position should, proponents of the method believed, produce directional lines that would intersect at the source and reveal the position of the weapon. The technique failed, however, to detect even one of the 130-mm guns. The background noise of the battlefield to obscure the firing of a particular gun, and the weapons frequently fired barrages of several rounds from a number of weapons, which temporarily deafened the sensors. Even if the equipment had succeeded in pinpointing one of the guns, a truck or tractor might well shift the highly mobile weapon to a new firing site before aircraft could attack. In fact, forward air controllers, assigned to search visually for the guns in specific areas, had the most success in locating the artillery positions and directing strikes against them. This success resulted from having the forward air controllers monitor the frequency on which ground commanders reported artillery fire; upon hearing such a report, they would begin searching for muzzle flashes.[27]

Although artillery remained a persistent threat to the defenders of Military Region I, North Vietnamese armor repeatedly fell victim to American air power. Seventh Air Force headquarters boasted that "nobody has a better feel for tank movements in the I Corps area than we have." As the skies cleared, Vogt's airmen maintained surveillance over all the roads that armor might use to approach Hue. On the morning of May 6, forward air controllers located three tanks moving south, paralleling Route 1 and threatening the defensive line that Truong had established along the My Chanh River. Several F–4s, armed with laser-guided bombs for attacking bridges, responded to the emergency, joined by other aircraft as additional tanks appeared. Air Force pilots claimed, by mid-afternoon, the destruction of eleven tanks and damage to twelve others. "They reported," said a Seventh Air Force account of the action, "it had been a turkey shoot, with the tanks breaking wildly, some running into the sides of huts to hide under their roofs . . . "[28]

Thanks to improving weather — the cloud cover lifted for a week immediately after Truong took command at Hue — tactical aircraft visited destruction on all road traffic, trucks as well as tanks. In addition, the laser-guided weapons carried by some F–4s proved deadly against bridges. On one occasion, air strikes destroyed two cranes brought from North Vietnam to help repair the bomb-shattered spans.

Meanwhile, B–52s attacked targets in Military Region I as far distant as the A Shau Valley, the principal conduit for supplies to sustain the attack toward Hue from the west. On that front, near Fire Support Base Bastogne, recaptured by the South Vietnamese in mid-May, a patrol swept through a B–52 target box on May 9 and found forty bodies, plus a large store of ammunition of various types and a cache of explosives.[29] The explosives may have been intended for Viet Cong irregulars like those who, in early May, blew up a large bridge between Da Nang and Hue and temporarily severed the highway linking them.[30]

While air power pounded the roads that funneled men and material to the battlefields around Hue, Truong went ahead with a series of limited attacks. Besides recapturing Fire Support Base Bastogne, his troops beat back an

Quang Tri City Lost and Regained

A U.S. Army helicopter gunship escorts U.S. Marine Corps helicopters carrying South Vietnamese on an airborne assault near Hue in May 1972.

advance across the My Chanh River, and South Vietnamese marines conducted an amphibious raid at My Thuy, north of the river line. The South Vietnamese Airborne Division reinforced Truong's corps during May, and in June the 3d Division absorbed equipment provided by Operation Enhance and incorporated replacements for casualties sustained in the earlier fighting. The strengthened I Corps, assisted by air attack, fought the North Vietnamese offensive in Military Region I to a halt by the end of June.[31]

Throughout their advance, the North Vietnamese had used antiaircraft weapons, including SA–7 heat-seeking missiles, to protect the advancing troops, and they also moved radar-directed SA–2s south of the demilitarized zone. The intense defensive fire over the battlefield forced South Vietnamese airmen to attack from higher altitudes and claimed most of the forty-one aircraft destroyed throughout South Vietnam between the end of March and the end of June, though sappers or rocket attacks accounted for a few. During the same period, after losing no aircraft in the northern provinces of South Vietnam in the first three months of 1972, the Seventh Air Force lost twenty fighter-bombers, observation craft, and helicopters while defending Military Region I. The SA–7 downed six of them, the older SA–2 destroyed seven, and more conventional antiaircraft weapons claimed the rest. An SA–7 hit the OV–10 flown by Air Force Capt. Steven L. Bennett, jamming the ejection seat of the Marine flying as his observer. Bennett died attempting to ditch in the Gulf of Tonkin, but the observer survived. The victims of the SA–7 also included the first AC–130 shot down over South Vietnam, destroyed when a heat-seeking missile homed on one of its engines while the gunship patrolled the A Shau Valley.[32]

As these losses suggest, tactical aviation helped mightily in stopping the offensive in Military Region I. Indeed, despite bad weather at the outset, the tactical effort from April through June totaled 18,000 sorties, 45 percent flown by the Air Force, 30 percent by the Navy and Marine Corps, and 25 percent by

Air War over South Vietnam, 1968–1975

Capt. Steven L. Bennett, awarded the Medal of Honor for his actions as pilot of an OV–10.

the South Vietnamese. In addition, B–52s flew 2,700 sorties against targets in the northern provinces and dropped 57,000 tons of bombs.[33]

This aerial battering did severe damage to an enemy who had chosen to mount a conventional attack requiring fuel for tanks and trucks and vast quantities of artillery ammunition. The number of troops involved could not cut loose from supply depots and live off local sympathizers, as a smaller force of lightly armed guerrillas might have done. Giap's choice of tactics, whatever his motivation, enhanced the effect of aerial attack on his army. Giap also erred in assigning essentially the same priority to three offensive thrusts — into Military Region I, from Kontum toward the coast, and from An Loc toward Saigon. Only the operations in Military Region IV had a clearly subsidiary importance. Although Giap invested enough manpower and other resources in each of the main attacks to permit sustained fighting against determined resistance — as demonstrated by the push across the My Chanh River in June — his division of effort weakened all three. The overwhelming success of any one might well have won the war. Better, surely, to have landed one crushing blow than three that could not help but be less damaging.[34]

Giap might have triumphed despite his mistakes if the South Vietnamese defenders of Military Region I had not regrouped, dug in, and forced the enemy to mass his forces and present targets for air power, especially the B–52s. Abrams believed from the onset of the offensive that South Vietnam's soldiers would fight if properly led, but as he told Spiro T. Agnew during a visit to South Vietnam by the Vice President, only about ten generals really earned their pay. Troubled by what he perceived as unwillingness on the part of senior South Vietnamese officers to fight, Abrams issued orders early in May that no American helicopter or airplane could evacuate any South Vietnamese commander

Quang Tri City Lost and Regained

without a corps commander's approval.[35] Clearly the cadre of generals willing to fight included Truong, whose troops, having stopped the North Vietnamese, stood ready to counterattack toward Quang Tri City.

Upon taking command at Hue, Truong considered the successful defense of the city as the first phase of an operation that would regain Quang Tri City and restore Saigon's authority over coastal Quang Tri Province south of the Cua Viet and Thach Han Rivers. He had difficulty, however, in convincing both the Saigon government and Abrams' headquarters of the feasibility of so ambitious an undertaking. At last, President Thieu reluctantly agreed, realizing perhaps the political benefits that the recapture of Quang Tri City would bring him.[36]

Truong launched his counterattack on June 28, and his troops advanced swiftly against an enemy battered over the months by aerial bombardment, artillery, and naval gunfire. Indeed, enemy documents captured on the eve of the South Vietnamese advance revealed that "the violent sacrifices of recent weeks" had cut some tactical units "to ribbons" and were eroding the morale of North Vietnam's civilian populace.[37] Within ten days, the leading elements of I Corps reached the outskirts of Quang Tri City, where the rapidly reinforced defenses blunted the South Vietnamese spearhead. "The offensive then took on a new concept," Truong later wrote, although the objective remained the same. "I concluded," he said, "that if the enemy indeed chose to defend Quang Tri City and concentrate his forces there, he would give me the opportunity to accomplish my mission" — the destruction of the hostile forces — "employing the superior firepower of our American ally."[38] On September 8, after two months of sustained hammering, Truong realized that the defenses of Quang Tri City were about to crack and launched a final assault that recaptured the citadel on the 16th. The advance continued beyond the city to the Thach Han River on the left of the corps sector but ground to a halt short of the Cua Viet.[39]

Elsewhere in Military Region I, the North Vietnamese tried unsuccessfully to divert Truong's attention from regaining Quang Tri City. In August, for example, an attack down the Que Son Valley penetrated to within twenty-five miles of Da Nang Air Base, but elements of the advancing division suffered grievously from B–52 strikes — and later from malaria — and the threat to the airfield receded. Meanwhile, southwest of Hue, the South Vietnamese succeeded in consolidating their gains in the vicinity of Fire Support Base Bastogne and beyond. Finally, on October 1, South Vietnamese Rangers reopened Route 1 in Quang Ngai Province, linking Military Regions I and II.[40]

By November, as the pace of the fighting slowed in the northern provinces, Truong could take heart from the fact that his corps controlled a coastal strip that embraced the major cities of Quang Tri, Hue, Tam Ky, and Quang Ngai along with Route 1, the highway that linked them. In spite of this success, the North Vietnamese had made strategically important gains as a result of the Easter offensive, rendering the Ho Chi Minh Trail and the A Shau Valley immune to ground attack as they absorbed the entire demilitarized zone, the succession of strongpoints just to the south, and the territory southward to the Cua Viet River and beyond. The conquests during 1972 reduced the width of Military Region I by as much as one-half, thus placing secure assembly areas for future attacks that much closer to the likely objectives.

The South Vietnamese defenders of Military Region I could not have held or recaptured even as much territory as they did without U.S. assistance. In spite of Vietnamization, neither the air force nor the navy of South Vietnam had more than a "marginal" impact on the fighting in Military Region I, even though both organizations, as General Truong conceded, fought "to the maximum of their limited capabilities." To compensate for the naval deficiencies, the Seventh Fleet employed as many as thirty-eight destroyers and three cruisers to bombard targets along the shores of both Vietnams. In support of operations in Military Region I, these warships fired as many as 7,000 rounds in a single day. The Seventh Air Force, in the meantime, took over the air support system for I Corps, in effect Americanizing the previously Vietnamized control network. Truong, however, maintained a fire support coordination center at Hue designed "to integrate and make the most effective use of all U.S. and RVN fire support available." The I Direct Air Support Center dispatched the bulk of its resources to Hue to facilitate the work of the center, which Truong believed, "contributed significantly to the ultimate success in I Corps."

American B–52s gave Truong powerful aid as he successfully defended Hue and recaptured Quang Tri City. The bombers flew thirty or more missions each day during the time when bad weather hampered tactical air strikes in Military Region I. The B–52s, Truong declared, "caused the most damage and the greatest losses to enemy support activities" and also provided "close support to ARVN ground forces on several occasions."

Tactical aircraft, which rarely flew more than ten sorties per day in Military Region I during the months immediately preceding the invasion, attained a peak of 300 sorties in a single day, though not during the critical month of April, when a lack of aircraft, the need to engage in rescue efforts, and cloud cover impeded the air support of ground forces. In spite of the early shortcomings on the part of tactical aviation, Truong seemed pleased with its accomplishments. In general, he maintained that U.S. fire support — whether by tactical air, B–52s, or naval gunfire — "was effective and met all I Corps requirements."[41]

In Military Region I, a skilled and vigorous corps commander took charge at the decisive moment, restoring discipline and effectiveness to an organization that faced total defeat. Elsewhere in the country, South Vietnamese leadership of similar caliber did not emerge. When facing disaster, senior officers tended to entrust the conduct of the defense to their American advisers: in Military Region II, John Paul Vann, a retired Army officer with long service in South Vietnam, and General Hollingsworth in Military Region III. Here, and also in Military Region IV, U.S. aerial firepower, especially from B–52s, stiffened the South Vietnamese defense.

Chapter Twenty-Two

Kontum City, An Loc, and the Delta

In Military Region II, which embraced the dozen provinces of north-central South Vietnam, Lt. Gen. Ngo Dzu served as II Corps commander. His adviser, John Paul Vann, bore the title of Director, rather than Commanding General, Second Regional Assistance Group, a reflection of Vann's civilian status. A retired lieutenant colonel with long experience in South Vietnam as an Army officer and a civilian consultant, Vann directed rather than commanded the advisory effort in the region. He acknowledged that Dzu tended to be insecure, even panicky, and to value American advice over the recommendations of his staff, but nevertheless considered him capable and hardworking.[1] With Vann at his side to provide advice and reassurance, Dzu seemed adequate to meet the challenge of the invasion. Indeed, as early as February, in the expectation that a forward deployment would disrupt the imminent attack, he and Vann had reinforced the exposed outposts north of Kontum City and the villages of Dak To I, Dak To II, and Tan Canh.[2]

Vann had no illusions about the ability of South Vietnamese soldiers to launch spoiling attacks to deflect the blow that North Vietnam would soon deliver. "I'm enough of a realist," he was quoted as saying, "that I'm not going to ask the ARVN to do what they won't do." Dzu's troops, thinly spread and handicapped by a road net vulnerable to ambush, seemed unlikely to leave their fortified positions to seize the initiative. By staying put, however, they could force the enemy to mass, increasing his vulnerability to aerial attack and artillery concentrations. A static but stubborn defense, along with overwhelming support from aircraft and artillery, formed the basis of Vann's defensive plan.[3]

Although Base Area 609 — located in the triborder area where the territories of South Vietnam, Laos, and Cambodia converged — provided a springboard, the attack in Military Region II gathered momentum slowly, unlike the sudden plunge into Quang Tri Province to the north. Vann believed that the B–52's bombing of suspected troop concentrations and supply dumps caused the delay, but the North Vietnamese may simply have needed more time to pull together the soldiers and tanks hidden among the folds of the rugged, heavily forested highlands and prepare to move systematically against the main objective,

Air War over South Vietnam, 1968–1975

Kontum City, its nearby towns, and its outlying fortified bases. Given the difficult terrain and lack of good roads, the enemy must have been hard-pressed to commit two divisions, supported by tanks, in the highlands, while another division infiltrated eastward to join the local Viet Cong in attacks along the coast in the Bong Son region.[4]

During the first two days of April 1972, North Vietnamese troops probed the chain of fire support bases along Route 14 north of Kontum City and directed artillery fire against the airfields at Dak To II and Pleiku. Beginning on April 2, the pressure focused on Rocket Ridge, a frequently shelled escarpment that guarded both Route 512, the most direct route from Base Area 609 to Route 14, and the segment of Route 14 linking Kontum City with the two Dak To villages and Tan Canh. Early the next morning, Brig. Gen. George E. Wear, Vann's deputy, reported that "The enemy has apparently launched his offensive in the highlands."[5]

South Vietnamese airborne troops dug in on Rocket Ridge fought stubbornly, however, and for a time events seemed to justify Vann's belief that the defenders could force the enemy to mass and thus create profitable targets for air strikes and artillery. For example, a reconnaissance patrol northwest of Kontum City reported discovering 192 bodies and 100 shattered bunkers in a B-52 target box and, in another location, the bodies of eighty North Vietnamese apparently killed by tactical air strikes and artillery.[6] The enemy suffered severe losses but nevertheless succeeded by April 21 in capturing the northern and southern anchors of the line of outposts along Rocket Ridge. The battle-weary airborne troops went into reserve, handing over to others the defense of the fire support bases along the ridge line that remained in friendly hands.[7]

Meanwhile, pressure mounted against the Dak To villages and Tan Canh. The North Vietnamese seized the high ground that dominated Tan Canh and Dak To I and II, forcing the commander of the South Vietnamese division responsible for their defense to pull back into his fortifications and await an attack. Directed by observers on the heights, North Vietnamese gunners fired as many as 1,000 shells per day into the Tan Canh-Dak To defensive complex.

On the morning of April 23, the enemy attacked Tan Canh using wire-guided antitank missiles, a weapon new to the North Vietnamese. The deadly accurate rockets destroyed partially dug-in tanks and shattered bunkers, knocking out the division's tactical operations center and for a time cutting off communication with aircraft and other ground units. The U.S. advisers jury-rigged a new operations center at an undamaged bunker, but the division commander refused to leave the ruins of the old one and, in effect, abdicated his command responsibilities. When daylight faded, a demoralized group of South Vietnamese still clung to Tan Canh, though isolated from Kontum City by a roadblock south of Dak To. Another enemy strongpoint blocked Route 14 between Kontum City and Pleiku, further disrupting the movement of men and supplies.

Kontum City, An Loc, and the Delta

At dusk, outposts on the highway north of Tan Canh began reporting the approach of vehicles, which subsequent sightings revealed to be tanks. A howitzer-equipped AC–130 gunship, commanded by Capt. Russell T. Olson, arrived to support the defenders in the event of a night attack and promptly opened fire on the enemy. The approaching force of perhaps twenty vehicles included eight or more T–54 tanks mounting 100-mm guns and at least two ZSU–57–2 antiaircraft weapons, modified T–54 tanks, each with a turret containing two visually aimed 57-mm guns. The 105-mm howitzer carried by the AC–130 enabled Olson to orbit beyond reach of the 57-mm weapons and immobilize as many as seven of the armored vehicles. Fighter-bombers also attempted to come to the aid of Tan Canh's defenders, but haze and low-lying cloud cover frustrated the effort. The approach of the tanks caused panic among the South Vietnamese, already shaken by the earlier wire-guided missile attack. Responding to a call for help from the U.S. advisers at Tan Canh, Vann boarded a helicopter and helped extricate them. The AC–130 that had engaged the tanks remained overhead and North Vietnamese antiaircraft gunners, apparently impressed by the carnage Olson and his crew had inflicted on the armored vehicles, ignored the rescue helicopters and tried unsuccessfully to down the gunship.

After overwhelming Tan Canh and nearby Dak To I, the North Vietnamese took advantage of cloud cover and an umbrella of antiaircraft fire to attack Dak To II and its airfield, located southwest of the captured villages, on the opposite side of Route 14. The garrison at Ben Het, a border outpost the enemy had bypassed, sent tanks and infantry eastward on Route 512, but halfway to Dak To II, the North Vietnamese triggered an ambush that destroyed every vehicle and scattered the surviving soldiers. The defenses of Dak To II promptly collapsed, and the troops still in place on Rocket Ridge pulled out to avoid being trapped. By April 26, Kontum City lay open to attack from the north.[8]

While two North Vietnamese divisions overran Tan Canh and Dak To I and II and prepared to move against Kontum City, another division joined forces with local Viet Cong units in Binh Dinh Province to sever Route 1, the coastal highway, at Bong Son Pass, attack nearby towns, and exert pressure on military bases in the A Lao Valley. After hostile fire damaged South Vietnamese Caribou transports landing cargo at the largest of the bases, Landing Zone English, Air Force C–130s parachuted supplies in an attempt to sustain the defenders, who seemed on the verge of panic. Rumors reached Vann that a few South Vietnamese pilots were charging 20,000 Vietnamese dollars and more to fly passengers out of the besieged landing zone. Neither AC–119 and AC–130 gunships by night nor Air Force F–4s by day could prevent the North Vietnamese from forcing the South Vietnamese troops to abandon Landing Zone English on May 2. Accompanied by a large number of dependents and other refugees, the garrison fled to a nearby beach for evacuation by sea. Air Force fighter-bombers thereupon attacked the abandoned base, using laser-

Air War over South Vietnam, 1968–1975

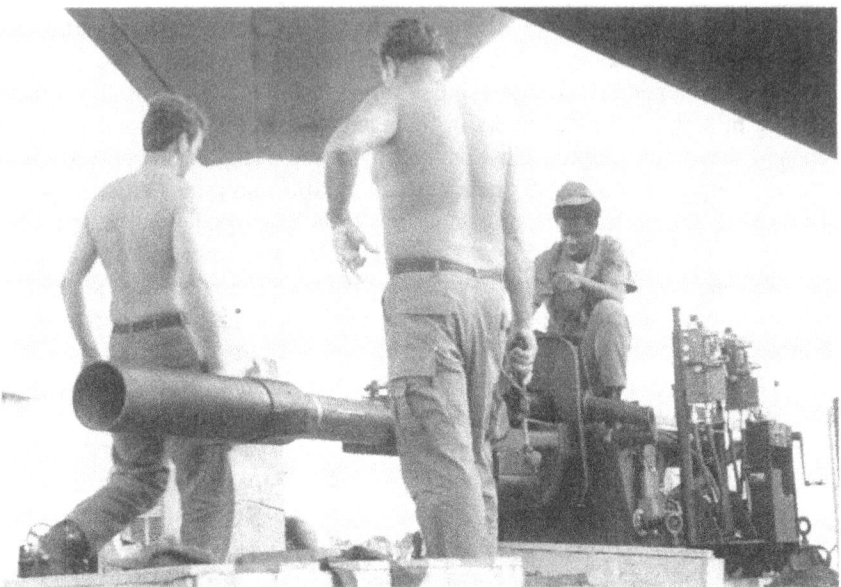

Armament personnel at Ubon Air Base, Thailand, inspect a 105-mm howitzer before installing it on an AC–130 gunship.

guided bombs to destroy artillery and armored personnel carriers left behind in the retreat.[9]

The gravest danger lay not along the coast, but in the highlands, where the North Vietnamese cut the Pleiku-Kontum City highway in the vicinity of a quarry known as the Rockpile and kept it closed through the month of June. After being separated from the supply depots at Pleiku, Col. Ly Tong Ba, in charge of defending Kontum City, tried to establish a new defensive line anchored at the Polei Kleng ranger camp in the west and the village of Vo Dinh to the north. The defenders of the outpost at Vo Dinh withdrew into Kontum City at the first hint of an attack, thus frustrating Vann's intention to delay the enemy there and force him to present targets for aerial attack. At Kontum City, the American advisers used fresh troops from Colonel Ba's division to replace the soldiers, survivors of Tan Canh and Dak To II, who had bolted from Vo Dinh.

Despite the abandonment of Vo Dinh, the rangers at Polei Kleng held out long enough for air power to inflict casualties on the enemy. A dozen fighter-bombers responded when Polei Kleng called for help on the afternoon of May 5, attacking North Vietnamese tanks with laser-guided weapons, armor-piercing bomblets, and general purpose bombs. A hurriedly launched AC–130, mounting the 105-mm howitzer, arrived over Polei Kleng after dark on May 6 to fend off the enemy while a helicopter carried away the American advisers, a sure indication that Vann's headquarters expected the attackers to overrun the outpost. The gunship pilot, Lt. Col. Loyd J. King, listened to the radio traffic as a South

Vietnamese helicopter crew refused to land and retrieve the advisory team, but an American craft soon did so. Once the advisers abandoned Polei Kleng, no one remained who could speak English and communicate directly with King. Requests for fire support, regardless of urgency, had to undergo translation by an interpreter at the II Direct Air Support Center, who knew little or nothing about the gunship, its sensors, and its weapons.

This cumbersome control mechanism sent King's AC–130E on a fruitless 30-minute search for North Vietnamese 130-mm guns, which the sensors could locate only if the gunship happened to be overhead when the weapon fired. King then returned to Polei Kleng, where the II Direct Air Support Center instructed him to hose down the area outside the perimeter, from which the attackers delivered withering fire against the outpost. "I told the sensor [operator] ... to just pick out the flashes on the ground and hold the flash positions," King recalled, "and we could put a 105 [-mm shell] down on each one until we ran out." Firing in succession at the clusters of hostile muzzle flashes, the gunship exhausted its entire supply of ninety-six 105-mm rounds and silenced the North Vietnamese riflemen and machinegunners. The II Direct Air Support Center then forwarded a request to lay down a ring of fire around the camp, using the gunship's lighter weapons. Circling so that the torrent of gunfire would fall outside the defenses, the gunship exhausted all its 40-mm and most of its 20-mm ammunition. A single gunship saved Polei Kleng, but only temporarily. On May 9, less than sixty hours later, the enemy took advantage of poor weather that prevented fighter-bombers from attacking to launch an attack that quickly overwhelmed the camp.[10]

The withdrawal of the American advisers from Polei Kleng — which Brig. Gen. John G. Hill, who had replaced Wear as Vann's deputy, directed from a helicopter circling overhead — caused a demoralized General Dzu to lose faith in Vann's assurances that the South Vietnamese, by a combination of air power and determined action on the ground, could save Kontum City. To encourage Dzu and his senior commanders in II Corps, Vann promised that a "hard corps of advisers ... would stay with them to the last in the defense of Kontum City and this hard corps would not leave." Special circumstances, he explained, had prompted the withdrawal of the advisers from Polei Kleng. That outpost, though it did hold out for two and one-half days after the Americans departed, seemed on the verge of collapse when they left. Prior to leaving, Vann continued, they had become separated from Dzu, who had been stunned by shells exploding against his bunker and could no longer influence the conduct of the battle.[11]

According to General Truong, the commander of neighboring I Corps, Dzu despaired of being able to hold Kontum City or even Pleiku, the site of II Corps headquarters. On May 10, Maj. Gen. Nguyen Van Toan, Truong's operations officer, replaced Dzu.[12] Control of the defense, however, remained in the hands of Vann, who orchestrated air power as he prodded the South Vietnamese to greater efforts. Because of Vann's critical role, Maj. Gary H. Gerlitz, a fighter pilot assigned to the II Direct Air Support Center, declared that the B–52 was "no longer an Air Force weapon." Explaining, in an oversimplified way, the relationship of the services in defending Kontum City, he claimed, "We fly the airplane, but the Army" — including the civilian Vann — "puts in the target request; they handle the clearing; the only thing we do is hand out the air strike warning to our own aircraft, so they won't have bombs dumped on them."[13]

As Gerlitz suggested, Vann's use of air power contributed powerfully to the defense of Kontum City. On May 14, for example, after an intercepted North Vietnamese message revealed an attack scheduled for shortly after dawn, missile-firing Army helicopters, Air Force and South Vietnamese fighter-bombers, and artillery fire broke up the assault by tanks and infantry. Another thrust later that day succeeded in penetrating South Vietnamese lines in a battle fought at grenade-throwing range, far too close to permit the use of air strikes. Vann gambled that the defenders could break contact after dark and fall back far enough to permit B–52 strikes to do their deadly work. His gamble paid off in the early hours of May 15, when the bombers rained high explosive upon tanks and troops advancing from north and northwest of the city. A subsequent examination of one target box revealed at least 200 bodies. Again on the 18th, when the North Vietnamese surged forward, B–52s bombed target boxes as close as one kilometer to defensive positions, causing casualties among the attackers that panicked the demoralized survivors into fleeing for the refuge of their own lines, thus exposing themselves to fire from South Vietnamese mortars and artillery.[14]

While B–52s, Air Force fighter-bombers and gunships, South Vietnamese aircraft, and armed Army helicopters — some of these last firing wire-guided antitank missiles — combined to blunt a succession of North Vietnamese attacks, air transport took over the delivery of supplies to besieged Kontum City and the border camps, like Ben Het, that the enemy had bypassed. The routine airlift to Kontum City accelerated after Vann on April 16 reported that he had only enough supplies for three days. Even so, the supply situation worsened on April 24 when North Vietnamese troops captured Dak To II and its airstrip and blocked the road leading from Pleiku to Kontum City. Afterward, aircraft using the Kontum City airfield provided the only means of delivering supplies.

Although shelling occasionally disrupted operations at Kontum City's airfield, activity there intensified even before the severing of Route 14, as Air Force transports responded to Vann's report of a supply shortfall, with the highest priority going to the delivery of jet fuel and gasoline in C–130s specially modified for the purpose. On April 21, hostile gunners demonstrated the vulnerability of aircraft on the ground at Kontum City when they scored hits on an Air Vietnam transport, killing a flight attendant and wounding some of the passengers. Three days later, long-range rockets disabled an Air Force C–130, piloted by Lt. Col. Reed C. Mulkey, after it had delivered a cargo of fuel. Mechanics flew in from Pleiku, but before they could fix all the damage,

Kontum City, An Loc, and the Delta

another rocket set fire to a South Vietnamese C–123 parked next to the Air Force transport. American soldiers and airmen extinguished the blaze before it could spread, and the repaired C–130, despite new but superficial damage from rocket fragments, took off on May 1.

Airlift operations settled into a routine between April 26 and May 3, averaging seven C–130s landing each day to unload ammunition and rice, as well as fuel, while one or two South Vietnamese C–123s also delivered cargo. Rocket fire continued, however, damaging one C–130, and a collision with a helicopter in the crowded sky over Kontum City tore a piece of wing from a C–130, but it limped safely to Pleiku. The combination of crowded skies by daylight and increasing enemy fire caused the C–130s to shift to night landings.

During the nighttime operations at Kontum City, which began after dark on May 3, sensor-equipped AC–130 gunships suppressed antiaircraft fire as the C–130s spiraled down to an altitude of about 3,000 feet and then lunged for the airstrip below. Faintly shining portable lights outlined the rectangle of the runway, and the approaching pilot did not turn on his landing lights until a few seconds from touchdown. The aircraft remained on the ground as briefly as possible, unloading rapidly and usually taking refugees on board before roaring down the runway and into the darkened sky. Because of the inherent danger of crashing in night operations, the C–130s twice tried to resume daytime landings, but each time hostile fire proved too formidable. On May 17, for example, rocket fragments ripped into a C–130 as it gathered speed for a daylight takeoff; the aircraft crashed and exploded, killing all but one of the crew.

Even at night, North Vietnamese gunners firing from the hills north of the city disrupted airlift activity. They ignited stored fuel, littered the runway with shell fragments, and disabled two South Vietnamese C–123s in addition to the one set afire earlier. The incoming flights, however, had to land regardless of the peril, first to replenish the ammunition the defenders had expended in repelling the attacks on May 14 and 15 and then to sustain the garrison. Bulldozers made room for unloading by pushing the wrecked C–123s out of the way. Sweepers tried to keep the surface free of shell fragments and other debris, but a flat tire immobilized a C–130 in the early morning hours of May 23, and hostile fire destroyed the aircraft before the tire could be replaced. Another C–130 succeeded in taking off despite a flat tire and landed safely at Da Nang. After a final flurry of airlift activity, thirty-eight C–130s landed and unloaded between the evening of May 23 and the early morning of May 25, when the airfield at Kontum City became too dangerous to use.[15]

Despite savage aerial attack and a stout defense by troops using recently arrived wire-guided antitank missiles, North Vietnamese infiltrators reached the eastern edge of the runway in one prong of an attack designed to capture the city. General Hill, who had ordered the advisers out of Polei Kleng, circled overhead in a helicopter and kept track of the battle as it developed below. North Vietnamese troop movements tended to confirm intercepted radio traffic indicating that the enemy was closing in for the kill. Since counterbattery fire had all but silenced the South Vietnamese artillery defending Kontum City, Hill turned for help to air power.

Once again, air power rose to the occasion. B–52s and gunships pounded the enemy by night, while fighter-bombers and Army helicopters ranged the daytime skies despite bad weather. At a critical moment near dawn on May 26, the clouds parted, enabling Army helicopters to attack North Vietnamese armor with wire-guided missiles, destroying seven tanks, including one that an AC–130 had damaged a short time before, and a water tower used as an observation post for the enemy's artillery. U.S. fighter-bombers also took advantage of the break in the weather to attack North Vietnamese artillery batteries. Some South Vietnamese soldiers fought stubbornly, especially those trained to use wire-guided missiles or light antitank rockets, and the appearance of tanks no longer caused panic, as had happened at Tan Canh. The attackers managed to penetrate Kontum City from the north, northwest, and south, but the offensive bogged down, in part because B–52 strikes forced the enemy to establish supply points in the distant hills and increased the time that food and ammunition had to travel to reach the front lines and, as a result, the exposure to aerial attack. The North Vietnamese could advance no further, and the defenders could not dislodge them. The stalemate lasted until May 31, when the enemy began withdrawing, almost imperceptibly at first, from the ruins of the city.[16]

Kontum City remained in South Vietnamese hands essentially because the U.S. advisers solved the problem of resupplying the defenders, whereas the enemy failed to reinforce his assault force and replenish its supplies. Immediately following the closing of the airfield on May 25, U.S. Army and South Vietnamese Air Force helicopters, with cargo suspended in nets slung beneath them, began depositing supplies at a soccer field. The aircraft touched down just long enough to pick up casualties. The defenders relied on this shuttle until the afternoon of May 27, when Air Force C–130s began parachuting cargo onto a drop zone near the Dak Bla River in the southwest corner of the city, using equipment and techniques already tested at An Loc in Military Region III.[17]

The so-called ground radar air delivery system required the installation of a radar transponder in the C–130, enabling Combat Skyspot or a mobile radar to track the aircraft and direct it to a precisely calculated release point beyond reach of light and medium antiaircraft guns. Further to increase accuracy, the drop employed the high-altitude, low-opening technique, in which a pyrotechnic timer, after a certain number of seconds, triggered an explosive squib that severed a retaining line and allowed a partially furled parachute to open fully. The parachute deployed at an altitude low enough to minimize wind-drift as it deposited the attached cargo container on the drop zone.[18]

Before the fighting died away at Kontum City, the adverse-weather aerial delivery system also saw action, mainly to supplement the ground-radar drops. The C–130s using the adverse-weather system carried station-keeping equipment to maintain formation in bad weather or at night, a forward-looking radar, and a computer that used the radar image to calculate a release point. A radar transponder on the ground could provide an offset aiming point in the absence of terrain features or man-made objects with a distinctive radar return. This delivery system normally employed a high-velocity drop with a fifteen-foot slotted parachute that minimized the effect of wind by lowering the load at 100 feet per second, roughly four times the rate of descent with a conventional parachute. Riggers prepared for the high-velocity method by packing a half-ton of cargo in a container reinforced with several layers of honeycombed cardboard. The addition of a second parachute could double the load to one ton, but delicate equipment, barrels of liquids, and some medical supplies could not withstand the shock of a high-velocity drop.[19]

A test mission at Kontum City, flown on June 3, and fifteen other drops between June 7 and 15, used the high-velocity method of delivery. On one occasion, the navigator of a C–130 equipped with the adverse-weather system did the aiming for two other transports flying in line behind him and directed them to release their loads when each aircraft reached the proper point.[20]

Because the enemy controlled much of the Kontum City, the C–130s relied heavily on ground-control radar and high-altitude, low-opening drops to achieve the necessary accuracy. From May 28 to 31, Air Force transports flew nineteen missions using a mobile radar at Pleiku. As the North Vietnamese grip on Kontum City relaxed, the defenders enlarged their area of control and on June 2 established a larger drop zone in the northwestern part of town. The South Vietnamese progress on the ground enabled the C–130s to resume landing at the airfield on the night of June 8 and early morning of June 9. Due to the danger from heat-seeking antiaircraft missiles, as the transports descended sharply toward the faintly marked runway, South Vietnamese artillery shelled likely SA–7 sites and launched flares to divert the infrared seekers from the heat of the turboprop engines. Only one C–130 crew spotted an approaching SA–7 missile, and the pilot avoided it. Since the first highway convoy since April did not get past the Rockpile until June 30, Kontum City continued to rely on airlift throughout that month; drops using the ground radar air delivery system ended on June 14, but nighttime landings continued.[21]

On June 9, as the last North Vietnamese soldiers withdrew from Kontum City, John Paul Vann died in the crash of a helicopter. His ability to inspire South Vietnamese leaders like Colonel Ba clearly helped repulse the enemy, as did the aerial resources at his call. Strikes by B–52s, bombing within 1,000 meters of friendly troops, and by tactical fighters disrupted and demoralized the attackers, as did attacks by armed Army helicopters and Air Force gunships, especially AC–130s with 105-mm howitzers. Behind the curtain of aerial firepower that Vann manipulated, the defenders learned to make deadly use of antitank weapons that blunted armored thrusts or sealed off and eliminated the tanks that did penetrate the city.

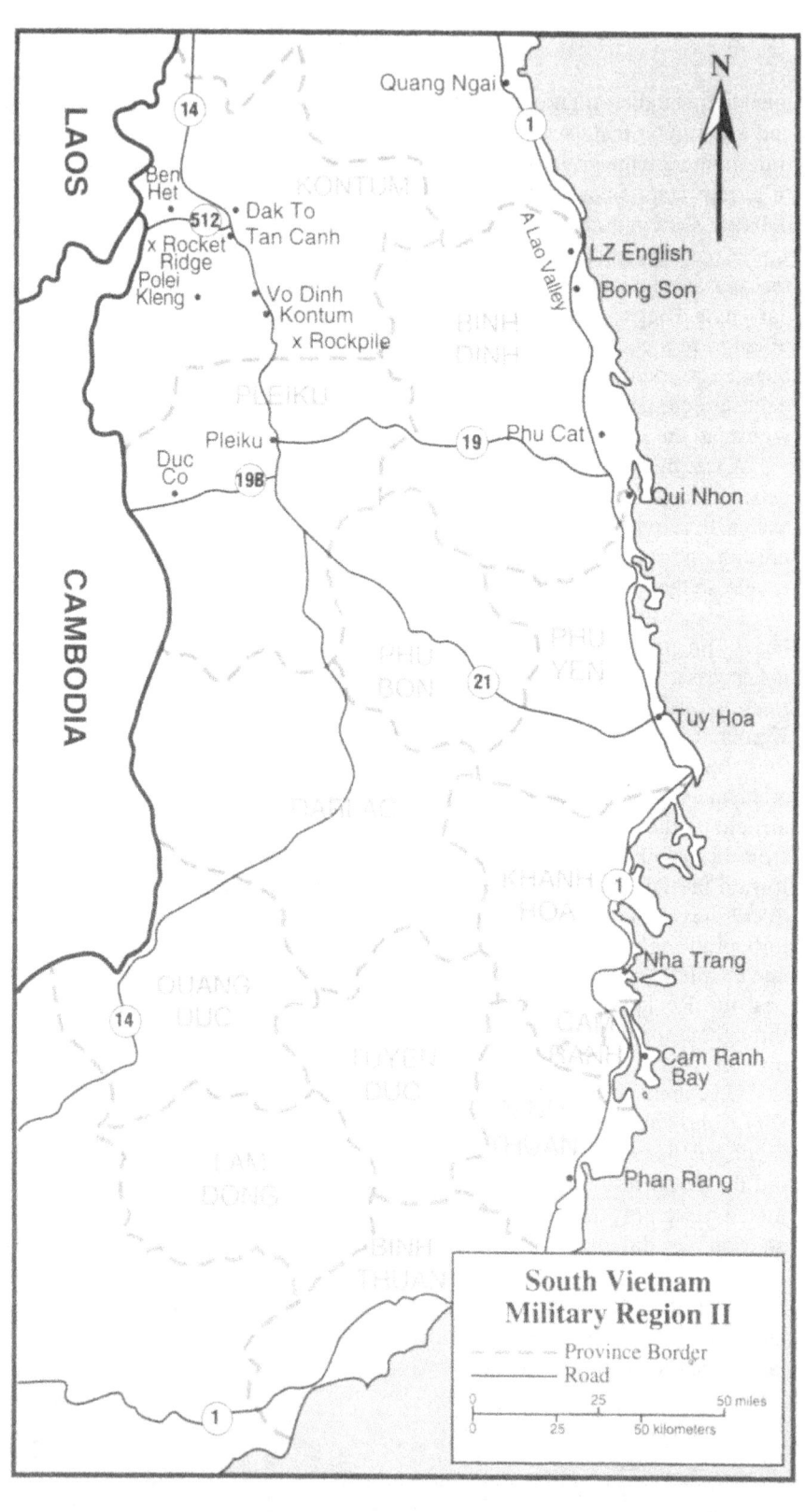

Kontum City, An Loc, and the Delta

Fighting continued in the highlands of Kontum Province until the signing of a cease-fire on January 27, 1973, but the skirmishes lacked the intensity of the battle for Kontum City. In spite of South Vietnamese patrols and limited offensives, the enemy occasionally challenged road convoys to Kontum City from the south, though those with armed escorts usually got through. The North Vietnamese also retained control of the Dak To-Tan Canh area, and exerted pressure on the outposts bypassed during the Easter offensive. North of the Dak To villages, the enemy forced the abandonment of Ben Het, and west of Pleiku they gained control of Duc Co. Along the coast, the South Vietnamese reopened Route 1, probed the A Lao Valley, and regained Landing Zone English and the towns lost during the Easter offensive.[22]

The fighting in Military Region II followed a pattern that resembled the struggle to the north, inasmuch as resistance on the ground forced the enemy to mass his troops and maintain them in place for several weeks, presenting targets for air power. Here, as in neighboring Military Region I, U.S. aircraft provided most of the air support, with the South Vietnamese Air Force participating as best it could. If Giap and his fellow North Vietnamese generals planned to cut South Vietnam in half, they failed to do so, but they strengthened their grip on the highlands, increased the security of the Ho Chi Minh Trail, and rendered all but invulnerable their bases in the triborder area. As in Military Region I, the gains made here in the spring and summer of 1972 greatly diminished the ability of South Vietnam to resist a future offensive after a cease-fire took effect.

South of the battlefields of the western highlands and the Bong Son area lay Military Region III, which encompassed the northern approaches to Saigon, with its various nearby bases and headquarters installations. The capital city and its immediate environs shared a boundary with the region but formed a separate district. Until the third prong of the Easter offensive penetrated Military Region III in April 1972, it seemed an unlikely place for a major attack. The South Vietnamese invasion of Cambodia in the spring of 1970 had overrun the enemy's potentially dangerous base areas on the border of Tay Ninh and Binh Long Provinces, and afterward South Vietnamese troops conducted sporadic operations in eastern Cambodia. The North Vietnamese, however, established new depots deeper inside Cambodia where they armed and trained. When the attack came in 1972, it consisted of a feint toward Tay Ninh City to divert attention from the attacks on Loc Ninh and An Loc, two cities in Binh Long Province on Route 13, the highway to Saigon.

North Vietnam struck its first blow in Military Region III on April 2 — sixty-odd hours after the attack in the north toward Quang Tri City and Hue but at roughly the same time that the enemy began probing the defenses of Kontum Province — when a column of tanks overwhelmed a fire support base in Tay Ninh Province. The commander of III Corps, Lt. Gen. Nguyen Van Minh, reacted to this attack by pulling back all but one of the border outposts to form a new line in the vicinity of Tay Ninh City, thus giving the North Vietnamese troops in Cambodia unimpeded access to the province. Minh left in place the garrison at Tong Le Chon because the commander there protested that a retreat would invite a North Vietnamese ambush. As it turned out, that outpost remained in South Vietnamese hands until the cease-fire of January 1973. In contrast, the defenders of Thien Ngon followed orders to withdraw and fell into a trap that destroyed most of their vehicles and artillery. Once the North Vietnamese had caught Minh's attention, they abruptly broke off the action, leaving the South Vietnamese equipment abandoned at the ambush site still littering the roadway. An Loc, rather than Tay Ninh City, proved to be the main objective; for, as captured documents and the interrogation of prisoners soon revealed, the North Vietnamese intended that the captured city would become the capital of a liberated zone. Only after the establishment of this puppet government would the enemy exploit his hold on An Loc and advance southwestward into Tay Ninh Province or southward down Route 13 toward Saigon.[23]

The battle for An Loc began in the early morning darkness of April 5, when shells burst in the town and a hostile patrol probed the Quan Loi airstrip, some seven kilometers to the northeast. The South Vietnamese rangers stationed at the airfield withdrew, along with their U.S. advisers. The soldiers who remained behind held the runway only until April 6, when the enemy overran the airfield and established a roadblock on Route 13 south of An Loc, forcing the defenders to rely on supplies delivered by helicopter or parachute.[24]

While isolating An Loc, the North Vietnamese eliminated the outpost at Loc Ninh, a dozen miles to the north on Route 13. The first attack, on the morning of April 5, pinned the defenders in two compounds separated by the length of an airstrip, but resistance continued. Shortly before midnight, the situation became so desperate that the senior adviser, Army Capt. Mark A. Smith, called for an Air Force gunship to fire into the compound where he had his headquarters. Smith reasoned correctly that the defenders, who had overhead cover, would be safer from 20-mm and 40-mm fire than the North Vietnamese trying to break into the bunkers. The torrent of fire from the gunship saved Loc Ninh until daybreak when other aircraft could come to its defense.

During an afternoon attack on April 5, fighter-bombers dropped cluster bombs with antipersonnel munitions, and thousands of fragments cut into the assault troops as they tried to cross the runway and again storm the bunkers. Maj. Gen. James F. Hollingsworth, the Commanding General, Third Regional Assistance Command, credited Army helicopter gunships with inflicting similar slaughter during a second attack later in the day. The Loc Ninh garrison held on throughout the night of April 6, but when daylight came, the North Vietnamese intensified the volume of fire and sent tanks to help the infantry. Captain Smith called for air strikes on his compound, but this desperate measure could not prevent the attackers from overrunning the position at about 8:00 a.m. The second compound, at the opposite end of the runway, held out until dusk before North Vietnamese numbers and firepower overwhelmed it.

Kontum City, An Loc, and the Delta

Although Hollingsworth estimated that Loc Ninh would have fallen in a few hours except for air strikes, air support might have done more, except for poor coordination during the night of April 6. Some of the forward air controllers knew very little about the array of weapons and sensors carried by the AC–130 gunships. On one occasion, a gunship pilot, after reporting that his flare dispenser did not work, had to remind the controller that this problem would not affect his mission, since low-light-level television and infrared equipment still enabled him to attack targets on the ground. At other times, a controller might prevent a gunship from engaging a profitable target because another aircraft, also capable of attacking though perhaps with less deadly effect, had run low on fuel. A series of formal and informal meetings apprised the forward air controllers of the value of the gunship, and gunship crews of the compromises necessary when working with large numbers of other aircraft.[25]

When the North Vietnamese attacked Loc Ninh, a two-battalion South Vietnamese task force reoccupied two abandoned fire support bases near the junction of Routes 13 and 17, about halfway from An Loc to Loc Ninh. On April 6, the second day of the fight for Loc Ninh, one of the battalions, engaged in patrolling Route 17, received orders to relieve the embattled Loc Ninh garrison. At the road junction, the battalion collided with a North Vietnamese strongpoint, which it could not reduce because the available tactical aircraft were bombing and strafing at Loc Ninh.

Unable to push northward and running short of supplies, the task force received new orders to retreat to An Loc, but the movement had barely begun on the morning of April 7 when an attack from ambush sent the survivors reeling back to the fire support bases they had just left. Air strikes, which became available as the fighting tapered off at Loc Ninh, destroyed three howitzers left at the ambush site. The task force disabled its vehicles and other equipment and started for An Loc on foot, only to run into a succession of roadblocks. While the bulk of troops ran this gantlet, the wounded, three Americans and fifteen South Vietnamese, who could not keep up, took cover, and awaited rescue. After the North Vietnamese shot down one helicopter and damaged two others, Army Brig. Gen. John McGiffert, Hollingsworth's deputy, called off the rescue attempt until additional aircraft became available. An AC–130 gunship circled over the wounded men, keeping the enemy at bay throughout the night. On the morning of April 8, armed helicopters and tactical aircraft pinned down the North Vietnamese so that scout helicopters could dart in and retrieve the three Americans and nine surviving South Vietnamese.[26]

The fall of Loc Ninh, the defeat of the task force, the capture of the Quan Loi airstrip, and the closing of Route 13 to the south isolated An Loc. A siege began that taxed the abilities of the South Vietnamese commanders and the patience of their U.S. advisers. Indeed, in the opinion of these advisers, Minh proved "wanting" as a corps commander, and Brig. Gen. Le Van Hung, whose division defended An Loc, "didn't do a damn thing."[27] Consequently, Hollingsworth, a flamboyant leader who patterned himself after George S. Patton, Jr., of World War II fame, took over the defense of An Loc, much as Vann had done at Kontum City. "You hold," he reportedly told the South Vietnamese, "and I'll do the killing,"[28] and the principal instrument of slaughter proved to be the B–52. Like the legendary Patton, moreover, Hollingsworth demanded compliance with uniform regulations, announcing as the siege of An Loc began that he intended "to restore the image of dignity and discipline among American troops in MR III."[29]

Forward air controllers reported tanks and antiaircraft guns converging on An Loc, as the North Vietnamese sought to take advantage of the city's isolation. In recognition of the danger, the province chief, Saigon's principal civilian official in Binh Long, removed himself from the process of selecting targets for air strikes; during the fight for An Loc, military officers could designate targets without obtaining his approval. This simplification of procedures may have helped tactical aircraft kill an estimated 200 of the enemy in strikes southwest of An Loc on April 12. Although targets could be approved more quickly, a problem in communications arose on April 8, when North Vietnamese soldiers overran a radio relay station atop Black Virgin Mountain that served forward air controllers throughout Military Region III. The airborne battlefield command and control center had to take up the slack.[30]

Aware of the threat the loss of An Loc could pose for the capital, the Saigon regime moved swiftly to provide reinforcements, and President Thieu visited the city to demonstrate the importance he attached to its defense. Army helicopters flew more than two battalions of South Vietnamese soldiers into An Loc, delivered supplies, and evacuated wounded and noncombatants. Hollingsworth, who reconnoitered the area each day by helicopter, met with McGiffert, his deputy, and planned B–52 target boxes for the impending battle, as the defense tried to make every hour count.

The struggle for An Loc began on the morning of April 13, shortly after midnight, when an AC–130 responded to reports from the ground by firing on tanks and trucks approaching the defensive perimeter from the southwest. The gunship crew claimed the destruction of four trucks and, even though the largest weapon on board was a 40-mm cannon, one tank. At dawn, other tanks appeared east of town, but the main thrust came from the north, an ill-coordinated attack in which the armor outdistanced its protecting infantry and presented easy targets to defenders armed with antitank weapons. The North Vietnamese infantry, McGiffert believed, had failed to advance in conjunction with the tanks because of the disruption and confusion caused by B–52 strikes on bivouac areas and approach routes.[31]

Later in the morning, the enemy attacked again, this time from the northwest. The assault force was moving through one of the B–52 target boxes that Hollingsworth and McGiffert had chosen, when a cell of the big bombers released its bombs; the resulting explosions destroyed three or four tanks and killed an estimated 100 infantrymen. Despite the impact of this air strike, the North Vietnamese by day's end controlled the northern half of An Loc. Meanwhile, a South Vietnamese attempt to advance up Route 13 ended in failure. Although the enemy had gained a lodgment in the encircled city and strengthened his grip on the southern approaches, Hollingsworth rejected a proposal to pull out the American advisers. Like Vann at Kontum City, he insisted that they remain in An Loc until the very end.[32]

For two more days, April 14 and 15, the North Vietnamese persisted in attacking the An Loc perimeter, but the defenders eliminated every penetration by infantry and armor. The enemy failed to extend his control within the city. To the south, however, he continued to block Route 13, despite some minor gains by the South Vietnamese relief force.[33]

When An Loc survived this series of attacks, the North Vietnamese dug in the artillery pieces and mortars and ringed the city with antiaircraft guns. The enemy seemed to be settling in, relying on a continuing bombardment — along with the shortages of food, medicines and ammunition caused by the encirclement — to weaken the garrison before the next assault. In furtherance of this design, artillery fire destroyed An Loc's main ammunition dump on April 16.

During the initial three-day onslaught against An Loc, from April 13 to 15, the control mechanism for air strikes underwent hurried revision to cope with the large number of American and South Vietnamese tactical aircraft swarming in the skies over the city. As if to demonstrate the need for on-the-scene coordination, an AC–130 was firing away by daylight on April 13 when a flight of South Vietnamese A–1s dived through the gunship's orbit. A new arrangement took effect on the following day that divided airspace over An Loc into two sectors. Within one, South Vietnamese forward air controllers directed strikes by South Vietnamese aircraft; in the other, Air Force forward air controllers, operating in shifts so that three were always on duty, directed U.S. tactical aircraft. One of the Air Force controllers functioned as "King," informing the other two of the situation as described by advisers on the ground and passing along instructions from the II Direct Air Support Center.[34]

The division of responsibility for directing strikes between the U.S. and South Vietnamese air forces and the designation of a King forward air controller within the American sector, improved coordination. Despite these arrangements, complaints persisted about the reliability of South Vietnamese forward air controllers. As late as May 13, Hollingsworth protested their tendency to withdraw at any hint of bad weather and their inability, along with the fighter-bomber pilots they controlled, to operate at night.[35]

As was true elsewhere, the contributions of South Vietnamese airmen to the defense of An Loc depended on training and equipment. When the North Vietnamese isolated the city, the tasks of delivering supplies and evacuating the wounded devolved upon the South Vietnamese. Since the enemy controlled the airstrip, cargo aircraft had to parachute food and ammunition into the city, while

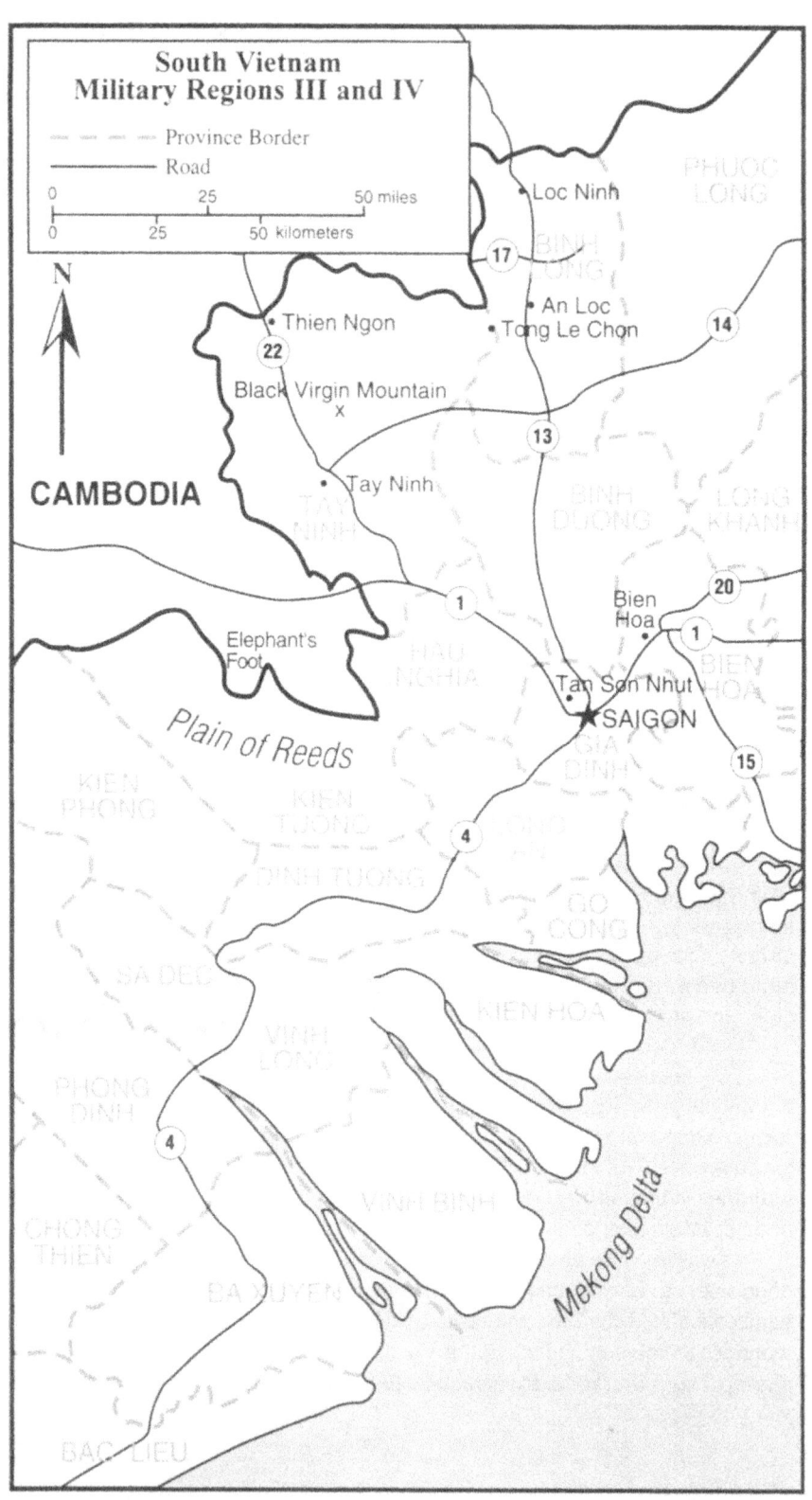

helicopters delivered additional supplies and picked up the wounded. Unfortunately, events soon demonstrated that South Vietnamese transport and helicopter crews lacked the skill, equipment, and sometimes the motivation to sustain the An Loc garrison.

South Vietnamese attempts to deal with casualties, both military and civilian, in an artillery-battered city choked with refugees proved dismaying, especially after April 13, when shelling destroyed the city's hospital. The aerial evacuation system broke down completely; helicopters arrived sporadically, and the walking wounded, or even the able-bodied, pushed their way past stretcher cases to find room on the craft. At the request of General Minh, commander of III Corps, Hollingsworth directed his aviation officer, Army Col. John Richardson, to undertake a demonstration mission. Richardson not only planned the flight, but on May 4 personally led four South Vietnamese helicopters, flying at treetop height, that brought in thirty-nine replacements and evacuated forty-two wounded men, sustaining only minor damage to the aircraft.[36] Richardson's success encouraged a flurry of South Vietnamese evacuation missions, but Hollingsworth still found fault with the attitude, if not the flying skill of the helicopter crews. He believed that the loss of life since the Easter offensive began had undermined "the desire to fly missions in a hostile environment."[37] Not until June, as the battle waned, did the South Vietnamese overcome their reluctance to risk helicopters by challenging the gunners around An Loc, establish discipline at the landing zone, and undertake systematic medical evacuation from the embattled city.[38]

In contrast, a lack of aircraft and suitable delivery technique, rather than any failure of discipline or determination, prevented the South Vietnamese from parachuting into An Loc the volume of cargo needed to sustain its defenders. Between April 7 and 19, a combination of U.S. and South Vietnamese helicopters and South Vietnamese C–123 transports delivered 337 tons of supplies; but the operation, dangerous to begin with, rapidly became almost suicidal. North Vietnamese fire damaged three U.S. Army helicopters as they unloaded and on April 12 destroyed a South Vietnamese CH–47, thus putting an end to supply by helicopter one day before the first major assault on An Loc.

South Vietnamese AC–123s and a few C–119s, aiming their cargo without the aid of radar, braved intense antiaircraft fire and attempted to drop cargo from altitudes of 700 to 5,000 feet but lost one transport on April 15 and another on the 19th. The C–123, the best tactical transport South Vietnam's airmen had, could not survive at low altitude over heavily defended An Loc, and the missions there came to an end, except for one improvised higher altitude drop at night. On April 27, directed by radar on the ground, the South Vietnamese got through to An Loc, but only 5 percent of the bundles actually reached the troops for whom they were intended. In June, a program began to train South Vietnamese crews for high-altitude drops using radar beacons as aiming points. It did not produce results until September, long after the siege of An Loc had ended.[39]

Air War over South Vietnam, 1968–1975

On April 15, four-engine Air Force C–130s, with greater speed and carrying capacity than the smaller South Vietnamese C–123s, parachuted supplies into An Loc for the first time since the siege began. American participation increased until the downing of a second C–123 on April 19, when the Air Force took over the aerial supply line, using C–130s exclusively. The initial mission flown on April 15, however, boded ill for the Air Force and its Hercules transports. Two C–130s approached An Loc that afternoon, planning to descend sharply and level off at an altitude of 600 feet roughly two minutes from a prescribed release point that would place the containers of cargo within the drop zone. Antiaircraft fire greeted the first of the transports, damaging the rudder, but the crew nevertheless parachuted the load. The second C–130 chose a different heading but encountered an antiaircraft barrage that killed one crewman and wounded two others. Shell fragments severed a hot-air line, raising the temperature of the cargo of artillery and mortar ammunition almost to the flash point and forcing the loadmaster, SSgt. Charles L. Shaub, to jettison the containers in order to save the airplane, which the pilot, Capt. William R. Caldwell, landed safely at Tan Son Nhut. The two aircraft had carried twenty-six tons of cargo, none of which reached the South Vietnamese defenders of An Loc.

The first day's experience caused the commander of the 374th Tactical Airlift Wing, Col. Andrew P. Iosue, to change the profile of the mission. The C–130s would approach at treetop height to present a fleeting target to antiaircraft gunners then climb to 600 feet over the release point. A pair of transports, Iosue in the cockpit of one of them, tested the new tactics on April 16; both sustained some damage from antiaircraft fire, but dropped their loads at the computed release point. Unfortunately, that point was based on an incorrect set of grid coordinates and all twenty-six tons of cargo landed on the wrong side of Route 13 in territory controlled by the North Vietnamese.

On April 18, after a day's delay, Capt. Don B. Jensen piloted another C–130 toward the soccer field that served as drop zone. When the aircraft reached the prescribed altitude of 600 feet, antiaircraft fire tore into it, setting ablaze the right wing and one engine and knocking out a second engine. The crew jettisoned the load and headed north toward Pleiku, but had to come down in a swamp short of their destination. Everyone survived the crash, and an Army helicopter soon picked them up. Hostile gunners at An Loc thus claimed their first C–130 one day before they downed the second South Vietnamese C–123 and caused the Air Force to take over the airlift operation.

To avoid the savage low-altitude antiaircraft fire, much of it from visually aimed machineguns, Iosue's airlift wing turned to the ground air delivery system, using it in conjunction with the high-altitude, low-opening parachute technique. A radar at Bien Hoa guided the transport onto position to drop its load at an altitude beyond reach of the weapons around An Loc. On the night of April 19, two C–130s returned unscathed after successfully releasing their loads from 8,000 feet; unfortunately, only two tons out of twenty-six actually reached the An Loc garrison. Six more drops, directed by the Bien Hoa radar, took place during the next four days, and the Hercules aircraft sustained no damage whether flying by night or in daylight.

Accuracy remained a problem, however, largely because of a flaw in the equipment that delayed the opening of the parachute for a specified number of seconds as the load descended to the desired altitude. The pyrotechnic timing device proved erratic in triggering the charge that cut the bonds keeping the parachute partially furled. When the timer released the restraints too soon, the parachute might drift hundreds of yards from the drop zone; if full deployment of the parachute came too late or not at all, a hard landing short of the drop zone could destroy the attached cargo and possibly maim or kill friendly troops or some of the noncombatants who had sought refuge at An Loc.

Until Army parachute riggers could make the delayed-opening equipment work properly, the airlift force went back to a nighttime variant of the tactics used earlier. A blacked-out C–130 might approach the An Loc soccer field at 1,000 feet and descend abruptly to 600 feet for the drop or, if the moonlight permitted, skim the treetops and climb to 600 feet to release the load. With AC–130 gunships attempting to suppress antiaircraft fires during the final approach and drop, nighttime missions succeeded on April 23 and 24; the aircraft suffered no damage, and the troops at An Loc retrieved about 70 percent of the cargo parachuted to them. The North Vietnamese persisted, however, in trying to create a curtain of fire across the drop zone approaches and managed to shoot down another C–130 on April 25, the last of four to drop supplies that night.

Despite the loss of this aircraft and its crew, problems with the high-altitude, low-opening timing device compelled the Air Force to continue dropping from 600 feet, even flying a mission in daylight on April 27. The two C–130s that flew the missiom had a powerful flak-suppression escort, but even so both returned with battle damage. In preparation for the ordeal, mechanics reinstalled seat armor removed earlier to save weight, and crewmen donned flack jackets and steel helmets and even brought on board metal trash containers, draping them with chains to provide the lucky few who could climb inside with additional protection when the antiaircraft guns began to fire.

Except for the one daytime mission, the drops from 600 feet continued through the early morning of May 4 to take place in darkness. Various expedients helped mark the drop zone, but they all had disadvantages that could prove deadly to the aircrews involved. Fires and lights on the ground provided little help because they tended to blend in with the flames and explosions caused by the fighting. The light from aerial flares reflected off clouds and off the aircraft, sometimes silhouetting the transport against an overcast. The AC–130s and AC–119Ks might pinpoint the drop zone with low-light-level television or with the night vision scope, then use their searchlights, with the infrared filter removed, to illuminate it until the approaching transport was barely seconds from entering the cone of light. Merely turning on the searchlight could trick the antiaircraft gunners into thinking a supply mission was approaching, but the use of illumination also revealed the position of the gunship.

Although the airlift units, because of the inability to rig loads for high-altitude release, had no choice but to persist in dropping from 600 feet, the supplies parachuted from that height seldom reached the troops at An Loc. The failure stemmed in part from an unwillingness to try to retrieve the bundles in the face of the artillery fire that raked the drop zone after each delivery and the lack of procedures for systematically distributing the contents. Since many of the containers held food, soldiers engaged in a free-for-all to open them, keeping what they wanted instead of dividing the goods among all the units.

Although a lack of discipline contributed to the loss of supplies dropped at great risk, the fact remained that the containers all too often missed the mark. The tiny size of the drop zone, the difficulty in locating it through smoke or in darkness, and the savage antiaircraft fire vastly complicated the task of finding the exact point in the sky that would place a load of cargo in the hands of the soldiers below. The infuriating sight of drifting parachutes carrying supplies into hostile territory became commonplace, as illustrated by the story, perhaps apocryphal but nevertheless frequently told, of the captured North Vietnamese officer who asked for more of the canned fruit salad that he had obtained in recent days from misdirected bundles and found delicious.[40]

In short, parachuting cargo from 600 feet, even by night, entailed risks out of proportion to the results achieved. On the night of May 3, North Vietnamese antiaircraft gunners shot down another C–130, the third such aircraft lost at An Loc; an additional thirty-eight Hercules transports had by this time sustained varying degrees of damage. Clearly, transports using low-altitude tactics could rarely emerge unscathed by hostile fire.[41]

Avoiding aircraft damage or destruction required finding remedies for the failings of the high-altitude, low-opening method of delivery. The search began on April 24 with the arrival at Tan Son Nhut Air Base of additional Army and Air Force parachute riggers thoroughly familiar with the equipment involved. Success proved elusive, but by May 4, modified equipment that featured, among other things, heavier reefing lines to contain the partially furled parachute, enabled a C–130 to hit a drop zone from 10,000 feet in a test conducted near Tan Son Nhut. By flying at 10,000 feet, beyond reach of antiaircraft fire, a C–130 could make more than one drop, using the first to confirm the accuracy of the release point and the effect of the wind before dropping the additional bundles. The C–130s tested these procedures at An Loc from May 4 through May 7, but achieved mixed results. The high-altitude, low-opening technique delivered 185 tons of supplies, some of the items salvaged from shattered containers, since roughly half the parachutes failed to open.

Further trial and error adjustments of the rigging resulted in more extensive changes. Longer reefing lines furled the parachute more loosely; a sling increased the separation between parachute and load, enabling a greater volume

Kontum City, An Loc, and the Delta

of air to rush into the canopy; and the use of a second or back-up timer and cutter ensured that the reefing line would break cleanly at the proper moment. The number of failures became negligible, but a shortage of the fifty-second and sixty-second timers used to drop from 10,000 feet threatened to put an end to this successful technique. Riggers had plenty of the thirty-second variety, which required releasing the load at a lower altitude, but the appearance at An Loc of the SA–7 heat-seeking antiaircraft missile placed a premium on high-altitude operation by the C–130s.

Altitude did not provide the sole protection against the SA–7, which proved susceptible to various countermeasures, but for transports dropping supplies it proved the best. Screening materials, for example, reduced the plume of heat generated by the engines of certain aircraft and flares decoyed the infrared sensor, especially when released as the aircraft turned toward the ascending missile and placed a large mass of cooler metal between the engine exhaust and the heat seeker. However, when parachuting cargo from a transport with four turboprop engines generating heat, a task that did not lend itself to turns, altitude afforded the best defense. As the supply of fifty-second and sixty-second timers dwindled, continuation of the airlift to An Loc again seemed in jeopardy.

Fortunately, the Air Force had a substitute for the scarce timer, a barometric device that fired the cutter at a pressure setting corresponding to a specific altitude. The device proved generally satisfactory, although malfunctions did occur. Premature openings caused cargo to stray far from the drop zone and on at least two occasions, failures to unfurl turned loads of ammunition into potentially deadly bombs.

In addition, an alternative to the high-altitude, low-opening method proved readily available. Although normally an element of the adverse weather air delivery system that employed a radar in the aircraft, the high-velocity drop, using a slotted parachute and a reinforced container, replaced the delayed-opening release as part of the ground radar air delivery system. The first high-velocity drops took place on May 8, and during three days, 139 of 140 bundles dropped with this technique landed safely in the intended area. The 1,000-pound load suspended from the slotted parachute landed with an earth-shaking jolt, as demonstrated when a half-ton of canned peaches crushed a parked jeep. The complete adverse weather air delivery system, with airborne radar and the high-velocity drop technique, went into action at An Loc in June but merely supplemented ground radar air delivery.[42]

Although statistics on the tonnage actually delivered to An Loc defy consensus, the resupply effort clearly enabled the garrison to keep on fighting. Hollingsworth, in fact, worried that the airlift removed the incentive to reopen the highway to An Loc and suggested cutting back on the airlift to encourage a breakthrough from the south. Abrams, however, did not heed his advice, and the South Vietnamese never regained the uncontested use of Route 13.[43]

Air War over South Vietnam, 1968–1975

The airlift of supplies to An Loc triumphed over many obstacles, some of them resulting only indirectly from enemy action. Parachutes, for example, proved difficult to recover; hostile artillery fire in the drop zone shredded some canopies and discouraged attempts at retrieval, whereas others simply drifted with their loads into North Vietnamese hands, and still others became makeshift shelters to protect An Loc's defenders from the sun and rain. The sustained use of the C–130 fleet, reinforced by Constant Guard IV, imposed severe demands on maintenance specialists, who met the challenge and actually increased the in-commission rate of the transports from 63 to 71 percent, even though years of hard use had produced an epidemic of leaking fuel cells in the older models.[44]

During the transition from low-altitude to high-altitude supply drops, Hollingsworth lost the daytime use of one aerial weapon he had come to value and became concerned that he might lose another. On May 2, during a daylight mission, 37-mm antiaircraft fire tore into the right wing of an AC–119K Stinger, ripping off the pod-mounted jet engine and knocking out the piston engine. Seven crewmen parachuted safely from the doomed airplane, but the other three died. A forward air controller followed the AC–119K in its final descent and plotted where each parachute came down, enabling two Air Force HH–53 helicopters and an Army UH–1 to pick up the survivors. Antiaircraft fire thus banished the slow-moving AC–119K, with its short-range 20-mm guns, from the daytime skies over An Loc.[45]

General Hollingsworth protested the decision not to risk the AC–119Ks by daylight in part because he apparently assumed that the same restriction would apply to the AC–130s. He objected to forfeiting the ability of the Spectre, its sensors working in conjunction with 40-mm guns or even a 105-mm howitzer, to "pick up, lock onto, and destroy enemy mortar positions which are employed using 'hugging' tactics too close to friendly units to be vulnerable to tac air and B–52 fires."[46] His concerns proved groundless, however, for the AC–130 gunships remained in action over An Loc by day and night. Ironically, the only Spectre to sustain severe damage there did so at night rather than in the more dangerous daylight hours. On May 12, a heat-seeking SA–7 missile tracked the infrared beam from one of the gunships and struck the aircraft near the lowered cargo ramp at the rear, where an observer secured by a safety line hung over the lip and warned the pilot of antiaircraft fire. The weapon grazed the crew member's helmet, laying it open, and inflicted cuts to his head that required several stitches. Continuing on, the missile damaged a beam in the upper fuselage but exited without exploding. The gunship landed safely at Tan Son Nhut, its tail section canted slightly sideways because of the structural damage. Until decoy flares became generally available, the AC–130Es had to remain beyond range of the SA–7 and operate from 10,000 feet or above, too high for effective use of the 20-mm cannon.[47]

During the supply effort from mid-April through mid-May, air power also helped the defenders of An Loc break up another assault and then launch a

Kontum City, An Loc, and the Delta

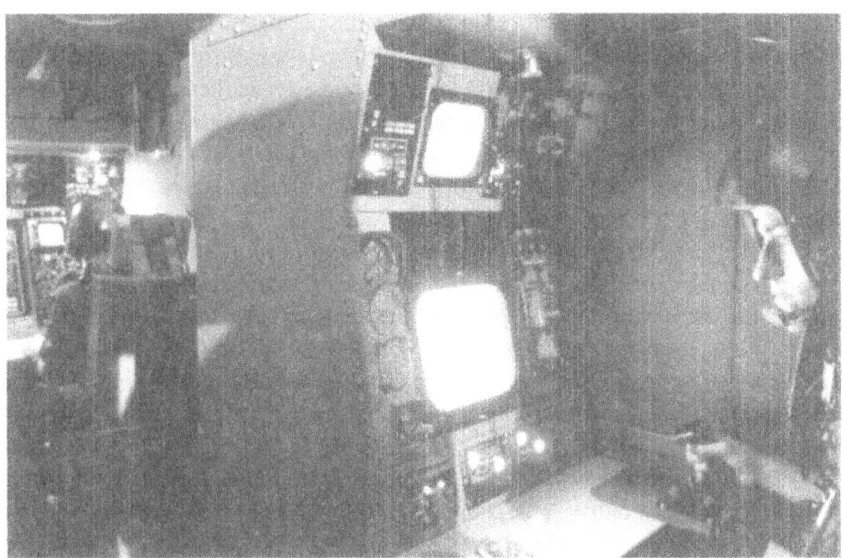

AC–130 crewmembers at consoles inside the aircraft. The sensors of the most advanced AC–130 deployed in Southeast Asia included radar, low-light television, infrared, and a device that detected truck engines.

limited counterattack that strengthened the South Vietnamese grip on the shattered city. Beginning in the first week of May, North Vietnamese patrols probed the defenses, artillery fire became increasingly intense, and statements by prisoners revealed an abiding determination to seize An Loc. On May 11, amid mounting evidence of an impending attack, Hollingsworth conferred with Abrams and requested B–52 strikes against eighteen previously selected target boxes and 200 sorties by tactical aircraft.

The priorities of the two generals clashed. Hollingsworth wanted the full weight of the available air power during the period of gravest danger to An Loc. Abrams also faced important, though not necessarily decisive, battles in Military Regions I and II and hoped to rotate the B–52s among the three endangered areas, concentrating for one day on each region in turn and striking blows from which the enemy could not recover in the two days before the bombers returned. At this point, General Vogt argued in a staff meeting for supporting An Loc to the fullest, expressing his opinion with a bluntness that annoyed Abrams and served only to strengthen his resolve. Vogt gathered evidence that substantiated Hollingsworth's views, presented it privately to Abrams, and convinced him to give the highest priority to An Loc on the predicted day of the attack. As a result, B–52s hit one of the eighteen target boxes every fifty-five minutes for twenty-five hours, beginning at 5:30 a.m. on May 11.[48]

A preparatory artillery barrage, which began at thirty-five minutes after midnight on the morning of May 11, signaled the onset of the attack that

Air War over South Vietnam, 1968–1975

Hollingsworth expected; before the bombardment ended, an estimated 8,300 shells had exploded within a defensive perimeter measuring about 1,000 by 1,500 meters. As the morning passed, two armored spearheads penetrated the defenses from the north and west, but the South Vietnamese troops did not panic. Antitank weapons fired by infantrymen and air strikes destroyed or disabled all of the forty tanks or armored personnel carriers that led the morning's thrusts, causing the assault to lose momentum.

As the North Vietnamese bogged down in the ruins of An Loc, tactical aviation pounced on the attackers, even though they had SA–7 missiles for their protection. Almost 300 sorties struck the enemy on May 11, and roughly 260 on each of the next four days. South Vietnamese A–1s and Air Force AC–130s helped the American fighter-bombers pound the western salient, but only the Spectre gunships could blast the North Vietnamese in the narrow northern salient, where friendly and enemy troops fought at ranges too close to permit ordinary bombing and strafing. In the north, accurate fire from the Air Force gunships drove the North Vietnamese from the cover of the bunkers they had overrun, forcing them into the open where the defenders of An Loc slaughtered them with infantry weapons, including claymore mines placed on standards, aimed into the salient, and detonated by remote control.[49]

By mid-day on May 11, the combination of air power and determined resistance on the ground had stopped the North Vietnamese attack. In An Loc, a few tank crews actually abandoned their vehicles when they encountered antitank weapons. Outside the city, panic-stricken survivors of bombing by B–52s came under fighter-bomber attack and artillery fire as they fled. The North Vietnamese regrouped, however, and renewed the attack on the night of May 12, taking advantage of bad weather that impeded the fighter-bombers. The AC–130s, however, could use their sensors regardless of the weather, and the B–52s bombed through the cloud cover; consequently, the assault troops failed to crack the defenses. Two days later, when the North Vietnamese seemed to be preparing for yet another attack to exploit what remained of the gains already made, three Arc Light strikes thwarted the enemy, who, in Hollingsworth's opinion, no longer seemed capable of offensive action against An Loc. Another month of skirmishing remained, as South Vietnamese forces regained the heights dominating the city and a relief column, supported by B–52 strikes, fought its way into An Loc from the south, ending the siege.[50]

During the critical days of May, B–52s disrupted several attacks as the enemy massed to launch them, and AC–130 gunships, especially those mounting the 105-mm howitzer, remained out of range of antiaircraft guns and heat-seeking missiles while shattering individual buildings within An Loc that the North Vietnamese had fortified. Navy fighter-bombers, refueling and rearming at Bien Hoa, joined the Air Force and Marine Corps aircraft based there in providing sustained support, attacking targets designated by forward air controllers. Airmen paid a price in conducting these operations, however, for antiaircraft fire downed three Air Force planes from mid-morning of May 11 to mid-morning of the 12th.

The loss on May 11 of the first of two A–37s caused all the forward air controllers around An Loc to converge on the place where the aircraft went down and search, unsuccessfully it turned out, for the missing pilot. (Except on indoctrination flights for newly arrived Marines, the right-hand seat remained empty in the A–37.) At the time of this diversion, the King forward air controller called off a strike by a cell of B–52s diverted to An Loc. Besides being deprived of the B–52 strike, the town's defenders lost fighter-bomber support for an hour and twenty minutes, but the North Vietnamese failed to take advantage of the break in aerial coverage, possibly because earlier air attacks had scourged them so cruelly.[51] When the enemy shot down an O–2A later on May 11, "it was edifying to note," Hollingsworth told Abrams, that "the remaining FACs [forward air controllers] continued on station."[52]

Because of its proximity to An Loc, the airfield at Bien Hoa and the Air Force A–37s based there made an important contribution to saving the city. General Vogt pronounced the work of the A–37s to be "absolutely spectacular,"[53] as demonstrated by Lt. Col. Gordon H. Weed during the May 11 fighting. After he dropped one of his two 250-pound bombs squarely on a North Vietnamese tank, only to have the weapon fail to explode, he braved the antiaircraft fire to make a dangerous second pass and score another hit with the second bomb, this time destroying the tank.[54] When the Marine Corps A–4s arrived at Bien Hoa on May 16 and 17, the A–37 pilots introduced the newcomers, few of whom had any combat experience, to the aerial battlefield over An Loc. The airmen who operated Bien Hoa also played host to an Air Force turnaround team that refueled and rearmed F–4 fighter-bombers based in Thailand, thus eliminating the use of an aerial tanker, saving the time required to return to a Thai air base, and doubling or tripling the number of sorties one of these aircraft could fly in a day. Finally, Bien Hoa sometimes provided the fuel, bombs, and ammunition that enabled carrier-based aircraft to return swiftly to action.[55]

As they had at Kontum City, the South Vietnamese prevailed at An Loc, inflicting grievous losses on the enemy. The defenders of An Loc, however, had also depended on U.S. leadership — McGiffert and Hollingsworth — and on U.S. aerial firepower, especially that of the B–52, which South Vietnam's air force would never have. The siege ended, moreover, with the South Vietnamese controlling less territory than when the offensive began. Here, as in Military Regions I and II, the enemy's gains enhanced the security of his bases and supply lines and brought him closer to the likely objectives of future operations.

The offensive in Military Region IV, clearly a subsidiary attack, differed in some respects from the fighting in the other military regions. The struggle began, for example, in Cambodia; no major battle ensued, as at An Loc, Kontum City, and Quang Tri City; and no clear-cut strategic objective emerged. In southernmost South Vietnam, the Easter offensive seemed designed to protect the North Vietnamese bases in Cambodia, which South Vietnamese troops had been harassing; to capture foodstuffs in a rice-growing region; and to prevent Saigon from shifting troops to defend more important objectives elsewhere. Nor did the American officer who commanded the Delta Regional Assistance Command, Maj. Gen. Thomas M. Tarpley, assume de facto command, as Vann and Hollingsworth had. Vigorous intervention in the South Vietnamese command structure proved unnecessary, in part because of the lack of a decisive battle, but also because of the competence of the IV Corps commanders — General Truong, who went to I Corps and directed the recapture of Quang Tri City, and his successor, Maj. Gen. Nguyen Van Nghi.

Despite the unique aspects of the action in Military Region IV — which embraced the Mekong Delta — air power proved as important here as it had elsewhere in halting the Easter offensive. The airplane provided a far-ranging and versatile kind of firepower capable of influencing the fighting on the ground or along waterways from Cambodia to the South Vietnamese coast. The North Vietnamese forces in Military Region IV did not mass for a major battle, however, so that aerial bombing could not shatter entire regiments as it had at An Loc, Kontum City, or Quang Tri City.[56]

The nearest approach to an all-out land battle occurred in Cambodia. During the first week of April, a division of the People's Army of North Vietnam attempted to overrun a series of South Vietnamese outposts in the vicinity of Kompong Trach, some fifteen kilometers beyond the Cambodian border. The attackers sought to isolate that town and destroy the garrison, thus playing out on a much smaller scale the scenario for An Loc and Kontum City. After the North Vietnamese surrounded Kompong Trach, the South Vietnamese lost forty-six armored personnel carriers and tanks in unsuccessful attempts to break through, and supplies dropped by parachute sustained the garrison when antiaircraft fire became too deadly for helicopters. South Vietnamese mechanized troops finally broke the siege on April 28, after B–52s had blasted the supply caches that sustained the enemy force blocking access to Kompong Trach. Fighter-bombers joined in the strikes, which seemed highly effective, even though aerial reconnaissance of a typical target revealed only five North Vietnamese soldiers, three of them dead, among the shattered bunkers.[57]

While air power helped frustrate the attack on Kompong Trach, scattered fighting erupted in nearby Cambodia and across the border in Military Region IV, as Viet Cong units and North Vietnamese regulars emerged from their various base areas. Besides harassing several towns defended by IV Corps, the enemy tried, after his failure to overrun An Loc, to infiltrate southward from Cambodia into the rice growing provinces of the delta. General Nghi reacted by attacking in northern Kien Tuong Province and the so-called Elephant's Foot, a portion of Cambodia jutting into that corner of Military Region IV. His troops advanced behind strikes by B–52s and fighter-bombers, and here the tactical aircraft encountered the SA–7 missile that had proved so effective at An Loc

Kontum City, An Loc, and the Delta

and elsewhere. A series of clashes followed in Kien Tuong, Kien Phong, and Dinh Tuong Provinces, focusing on the Plain of Reeds, a Viet Cong stronghold near the center of this area, as the enemy tried to disrupt the delivery of rice to Saigon. The fighting in Military Region IV subsided by September and did not resume until late October, when the enemy again became active, perhaps in the hope of improving his position before a cease-fire went into effect.[58]

General Truong, having commanded both IV Corps and I Corps during the fighting triggered by the North Vietnamese invasion, expressed satisfaction with what he and General Nghi had done. The enemy failed to tie down the troops defending Military Region IV, and the high command at Saigon tapped the area for reinforcements needed to the north. The North Vietnamese failed to capture a single town, confiscate the rice crop, stop the flow of rice to the capital (though they did disrupt this vital traffic for a time), or impede South Vietnamese movement throughout the delta. In claiming victory, Truong acknowledged that American air power had helped maintain what he described as "tactical balance"; indeed, he doubted that the Army of the Republic of Vietnam, without this support, "would have been able to defeat so decisively the large enemy forces" at Kompong Trach, the Elephant's Foot, and in Kien Tuong, Kien Phong, and Dinh Tuong Provinces.[59]

The Easter offensive of 1972 failed to accomplish the most ambitious objective attributed to it, the conquest of South Vietnam. Stubborn resistance at decisive points, massive aerial attack, and aerial resupply that frustrated North Vietnamese roadblocks combined to stop an enemy who fought to exhaustion for towns he might conceivably have bypassed. Handicapped by poor communications and dependent on roads because of his choice of conventional tactics, the enemy clung to a plan that increased his vulnerability to aerial attack. Vehicles, along with the bridges and to some extent the roads over which they travelled, afforded profitable targets for bombs, howitzers in gunships, and rockets fired from helicopters. Moreover, the supply of fuel for tanks and trucks, and also the movement of replacement vehicles to sustain the attack, came under aerial attack all along the routes between the ports where they arrived and the using unit on the battlefield.

The leadership at Hanoi gambled that the three major thrusts could generate enough momentum to overcome the cumulative impact of air power, but lost the bet. Despite battle damage and attacks by rockets or demolition teams on air bases and fuel supplies in South Vietnam, the United States reinforced and supplied its air forces more swiftly and efficiently than the North could sustain the offensive. Those who interpreted the Easter offensive as a bid for immediate victory concluded that South Vietnam, aided by U.S. leadership and air power, had won. For example, Gen. Phillip B. Davidson, the former intelligence officer for Generals Westmoreland and Abrams, concluded that Giap had gone whole hog, *totus porcus*, and failed in an attempt to defeat South Vietnam on the battlefield and demoralize the Saigon government's American supporters.[60]

Air War over South Vietnam, 1968–1975

Davidson conceded, however, that from the outset the North Vietnamese invaders might have willingly settled for less than a complete and immediate victory.[61] If so, North Vietnam emerged as the clear victor. The Easter offensive made inroads into South Vietnam that Saigon's armed forces could not eliminate. The captured territory brought the People's Army of North Vietnam closer to future objectives, enhanced the security of the Ho Chi Minh Trail and permitted its improvement to handle a greater volume of traffic more efficiently, and provided a buffer to protect the enemy's bases in southern Laos and Cambodia and on the northern and western fringes of what had been South Vietnam. Difficult to defend when the offensive began in March 1972, South Vietnam became even more so as a consequence of fighting that left the enemy dominant in the far north, firmly in control of the western highlands and the triborder area, and still strong in the southernmost provinces.

The United States, in the meantime, stopped insisting that North Vietnam withdraw its troops from the South as a condition of any settlement. Instead, the Nixon administration indicated a willingness to agree to a cease-fire in place, followed by the release of the Americans being held as prisoners of war and the departure of the last Americans from South Vietnam. The North Vietnamese negotiators also offered a major concession, backing away from their demand that a coalition, including communists, replace the Thieu government as part of any agreement to end the hostilities. To persuade Hanoi to formally ratify the negotiated arrangement, President Nixon on October 27 suspended the bombing of North Vietnam north of the 20th parallel.

Although the North Vietnamese leadership seemed agreeable to ending the war under these terms, a storm of opposition burst in Saigon where Thieu, even though assured of remaining in office after the cease-fire, balked at accepting the continued presence of North Vietnamese forces in postwar South Vietnam.[62] Aware of the threat these troops posed to the survival of his country, Thieu agreed to a cease-fire in place only after President Nixon, early in November, extended "absolute assurance that if Hanoi fails to live up to the terms of this agreement it is my intention to take swift and severe retaliatory action."[63] Nixon in effect pledged that the United States would respond to another North Vietnamese invasion, launched from the territory captured in 1972, with the kind of rapid deployment of aircraft and unrelenting aerial attack that had halted the Easter offensive.

Although ultimately Thieu agreed to accept a settlement that legitimized North Vietnam's recent conquests, he did so reluctantly and continued to look for something better. Meanwhile, Hanoi's negotiating team began quibbling over details in the hope of getting truce terms more generous than those already accepted in principle, perhaps actually accomplishing the removal of Thieu and the replacement of his regime by a communist-dominated coalition. While Nixon won re-election on November 7, 1972, amassing 520 of 538 electoral votes, the leaders at Hanoi may have felt that the new Congress, reflecting the mood of the American people, would decide that the United States had already done enough for South Vietnam and eliminate or sharply reduce assistance to the government at Saigon. Nixon acted before Congress convened, however, demanding on December 14 that Hanoi resume negotiations or face a renewal of the bombing north of the 20th parallel. The resulting aerial campaign, Operation Linebacker II, persuaded North Vietnam to negotiate an end to the fighting, and a blunt warning from the White House that the United States stood ready to negotiate a truce that reflected only its own interests cut the ground from under the South Vietnamese president.

The peace agreement, finally signed at Paris on January 27, 1973, represented a truce rather than a true settlement, for it left North Vietnamese forces in control of territory within South Vietnam from which they could renew the war. The survival of South Vietnam depended on the attitudes of two foreign powers: North Vietnam's willingness to abide by the treaty and the determination of the United States to honor President Nixon's pledge to intervene swiftly and decisively if Hanoi attacked.[64]

Whatever Thieu may have believed, or Nixon when he made the promise, General Vogt doubted that the United States would react to a future invasion with the overwhelming aerial firepower unleashed in 1972. He recalled that General Haig, still a member of Kissinger's staff, and others urged him to use his influence with various South Vietnamese generals to assure them they could depend on the American commitment. This he refused to do.[65]

The war, Americanized and then Vietnamized, ended for the United States in January 1973. Air power, supplemented by ground offensives of varying success in Cambodia and southern Laos, had provided a shield for Vietnamization and the withdrawal of American troops. As the United States reduced its ground forces, the nature and purpose of the fighting changed. The South Vietnamese, at best, had the numbers, equipment, training, firepower, and mobility to fight a defensive war — in short, to fix an attacking enemy so that overwhelming U.S. firepower, increasingly delivered by aircraft, could finish him. The initiative lay with the North Vietnamese, who, during the Easter offensive, massed their forces, forfeited their mobility and besieged towns, and suffered grievously from aerial bombardment.

The battlefield strategy in effect during 1972, as described in the U.S. Army's history of the advisory effort, called for South Vietnam "to fight a defensive war of attrition similar to that which had been waged by the withdrawing American forces, with local deficiencies being made up by U.S. air and sea power." This arrangement had bled the North Vietnamese invaders to a standstill during 1972, and the Saigon government remained "confident that American firepower would be made available when necessary" in any future emergency.[66] The goal of training and equipping the South Vietnamese armed forces to ensure the nation's independence no longer existed. Instead of an essentially self-sufficient force capable of decisive action, South Vietnam's

Air War over South Vietnam, 1968–1975

military establishment could do little more than serve as a trip wire to trigger aerial intervention by the United States.

The composition of the South Vietnamese Air Force reflected the changed role of the nation's armed forces. Large though it was, the air arm lacked some essential tools. South Vietnam did not have fighter-bombers capable of attacking the Ho Chi Minh Trail, the most modern aircraft for its forward air controllers, enough transports to duplicate the supply drops of 1972, enough helicopters for the airmobile tactics pioneered by the Americans, nor any means of approximating the firepower of the B–52. Instead of emerging as an independent organization capable of obliterating targets in North Vietnam, Cambodia, or Laos, the post-truce South Vietnamese Air Force remained tied to the corps commanders and their tactical zones.

South Vietnam's survival required that future Presidents honor Nixon's personal commitment to intervene with air power in the event of another North Vietnamese invasion. Until the promised help arrived, the South Vietnamese armed forces would have to hold in check an enemy who had already carved out deep salients that could serve as secure bases for renewing the war. If it were to function as a trip wire, South Vietnam's military establishment would require continuous training and planning, lavish stockpiles of fuel and ammunition, and better leadership than displayed during the 1972 fighting. If Hanoi attacked, the defense of South Vietnam would surely depend on materials the United States had supplied before hostilities resumed, and the survival of South Vietnam would depend on the willingness of the United States to renew a war that had generated among the American people apathy, if not outright contempt, toward the South Vietnamese.

Chapter Twenty-Three

After the Truce

The cease-fire agreement of January 1973 enabled the United States to obtain the release from communist prisons of almost 600 Americans, most of them fliers, carry out their repatriation, and withdraw the last of its forces from South Vietnam. The settlement, however, did not put an end to skirmishing between the Saigon government and the communist opposition. Despite the nominal cease-fire in place, communist forces sought to extend their area of control through limited attacks, engaging in what Cao Van Vien, Chairman of the South Vietnamese Joint General Staff, described as land grabbing and population nibbling. The Saigon government retaliated, and during 1973, in the absence of major battles, some 2,900 skirmishes erupted.[1]

As a consequence of the pact negotiated at Paris, the U.S. Military Assistance Command, Vietnam passed into history on March 29, 1973. The major American headquarters in Southeast Asia became the U.S. Support Activities Group — also known as the U.S. Support Activities Group/Seventh Air Force — a joint command established at Nakhon Phanom, Thailand, under General Vogt of the Air Force. The new organization took over the complex from which Task Force Alpha had maintained surveillance of traffic on the Ho Chi Minh Trail, including the computer the task force had used for data storage and targeting.[2]

Besides directing the air war in Cambodia from the buildings it had inherited at Nakhon Phanom, the U.S. Support Activities Group conducted liaison and planning activity. As a liaison center, it linked the South Vietnamese Air Force and the U.S. Air Force units based in Thailand and the western Pacific. The Support Activities Group's planning function included preparations for air power intervention should the United States have to honor President Nixon's pledge to respond to another North Vietnamese invasion.

During the spring of 1973, General Vogt's headquarters received a directive from the Commander in Chief, Pacific, to plan for two possible responses to a North Vietnamese invasion. In the event of such an attack, Vogt might launch the available U.S. air power — Air Force, Navy, and Marine Corps — against the Hanoi-Haiphong area or the panhandle of North Vietnam. The support group's planners proposed two ten-day bombing campaigns, neither of them a

Air War over South Vietnam, 1968–1975

Jubliant ex-prisoners of war aboard a C–141 on their way home.

rigid progression of strikes but rather ten daily slates of targets that might be attacked in any sequence, as circumstances required, not necessarily proceeding from the first day to the tenth. The Strategic Air Command did not participate in the planning but committed itself to one day of bombing as part of each ten-day effort.[3]

To execute either plan and carry out subsequent operations to defeat a North Vietnamese invasion would require a reintroduction of tactical air power into South Vietnam. A tentative concept, not yet approved by the Department of Defense, called for the Air Force to send turn-around teams to Bien Hoa and Da Nang, where they would service, arm, and launch fighter-bombers shuttling there from airfields in Thailand. A renewal of large-unit fighting in South Vietnam would require additional U.S. forward air controllers at Da Nang and at Nakhon Phanom. In addition, the Air Force would again assign officers to the South Vietnamese Tactical Air Control Center, the direct air support centers, and the combat reporting posts. The deployment would total 268 officers, 2,535 airmen, and 177 civilians.[4]

While planning to respond to future North Vietnamese aggression, General Vogt's support activities group fought the air war in Cambodia. Requests for air strikes from elements of the army of the Khmer Republic underwent one review by Cambodian authorities in a Khmer Direct Air Support Center and another at the U.S. Embassy in Phnom Penh, where the office of the Defense Attaché and the ambassador granted or withheld approval.

Attacks within the previously defined Freedom Deal area in eastern Cambodia, whether by B–52s or tactical fighters, received automatic validation

After the Truce

by the embassy. For targets elsewhere in the country, the embassy had to decide each one individually, determining, for example, that it lay on a road, trail, or waterway used by the enemy, and that an attack would not unnecessarily endanger noncombatants.[5]

By the end of April 1973, however, the validation procedure became too cumbersome for a Khmer army that seemed, in the opinion of Air Force Col. Frederick W, Fowler, "as hapless and helpless as could be imagined."[6] The embassy at Phnom Penh therefore adopted the practice of issuing blanket validations for gunship and fighter-bomber strikes in broad areas, but continued to deal with B–52 strikes on a target-by-target basis. Since the support group had access to the latest aerial photographs and other current intelligence, it assumed responsibility in the summer of 1973 for the actual targeting of each day's tactical air strikes, operating within the validations issued by the ambassador and sometimes denying requests from the Khmer army because of danger to noncombatants. Normally, requests from the Khmer ground forces for strikes by aircraft other than B–52s or F–111s using offset aiming points went initially to a forward air controller. He obtained approval from the Khmer Direct Air Support Center and the director of airborne battlefield command and control center, who functioned as the executive agent of General Vogt's headquarters.[7]

In the revised scheme of targeting, the airborne battlefield command and control center approved scheduled strikes by tactical aircraft within previously validated areas of Cambodia and authorized forward air controllers to direct the attacks. According to the chief of General Vogt's Command and Control Division, Col. Russell F. Crutchlow, "the final result has been an airborne command and control element with full authority for air strikes, full control of fragged TACAIR listed in the day's fragmentary operations order, and full . . . authority for assuring that the ROE [rules of engagement] is complied with in the target selection/validation process."[8]

While the U.S. Support Activities Group maintained liaison, conducted operations in Cambodia, and prepared to resume operations in South Vietnam, another organization, also located in hand-me-down quarters, provided nonoperational support of Saigon's armed forces. From a part of Pentagon East — formerly the headquarters of the Military Assistance Command at Tan Son Nhut Air Base — the fifty-man Defense Attaché Office, under Army Maj. Gen. John E. Murray, monitored the activity of the South Vietnamese armed forces and supervised the U.S. contractors who conducted training and provided technical support. Murray's group could not, however, give tactical advice or operational assistance.

Assisted by officers from all the services, many of them specialists in logistics, Murray followed the guidance of the U.S. Ambassador to South Vietnam, Graham Martin, who functioned as the overall chief of mission. A U.S. delegation, drawn from the armed forces, joined representatives of South Vietnam, North Vietnam, and the Viet Cong in the Four-Party Joint Military Team,

405

which, as one of its duties, sought to discover the fate of known or suspected prisoners who had not been repatriated when the fighting ended.[9]

Although Air Force advisers had tried for more than a decade to shape the South Vietnamese Air Force in an American image, the effort had not succeeded. The goal of having an airman command air forces remained as elusive after the truce as it had been during the war. The commanders of South Vietnam's military regions, always soldiers, exercised authority over all the forces, air and ground, within their territory. The airman who headed the direct air support center that provided air support within the region, usually a colonel or lieutenant colonel, reported to the corps operations officer, who was an army officer, and maintained informal contact with the generals in command of the divisions operating in the region. South Vietnam lacked any major aerial command, like the recently departed Seventh Air Force, nor did it have a nominally joint command comparable to the U.S. Military Assistance Command, Vietnam, or its successor, the U.S. Support Activities Group in Thailand. Moreover, South Vietnamese army officers dominated Saigon's Joint General Staff.[10]

The South Vietnamese Air Force also lacked the operational flexibility of the U.S. Air Force. Most missions were planned strikes; rarely could a direct air support center divert air strikes, or launch them, to meet a battlefield emergency. The rigid application of air power reflected, to some extent, the status of the air liaison officers assigned to ground units and the forward air controllers overhead. The air liaison parties served at headquarters higher than the battalion level and tended to consist of junior air force officers, hurriedly trained, who might not be pilots and, even if they were, could exert scant influence within the headquarters. Army officers, recent graduates of a thirty-day familiarization course in air operations, handled liaison chores in the battalions. The forward air controllers, who worked in conjunction with the liaison officers, varied markedly in skill and dedication. Unfortunately, Americans no longer could advise, guide, and encourage them because of the truce.[11]

By the time the cease-fire went into effect, the South Vietnamese Air Force had received the benefits of Project Enhance Plus, a final American push to strengthen the armed forces before the peace settlement restricted the flow of equipment to replacing, on a one-for-one basis, items already in the inventory. South Vietnamese airmen were in the process of absorbing C–130 transports, RC–119G maritime patrol craft, F–5 fighters, A–37 attack planes, as well as UH–1 and CH–47 helicopters provided by the U.S. Army. Imperfect though it proved to be, the cease-fire of January 1973 afforded a badly needed respite from major operations for the air arm to train the pilots, aircrews, mechanics, staff officers, clerks, and administrators necessary for effective operation.[12] This period of comparative stability, plus continued training and logistics support from American firms under contract to the Air Force, seemed likely to ensure progress toward self-sufficiency. Such, at least, was the opinion of the last officer to head the Air Force Advisory Group, Maj. Gen. Jimmy J. Jumper.[13]

Unfortunately, the aircraft recently incorporated into the South Vietnamese Air Force brought with them problems that impeded progress toward General Jumper's announced goal of self-sufficiency. The war-weary C–130s, for example, required 199 civilian technicians, supplied under contract by Lear Sigler Incorporated, plus two technical representatives from Lockheed, the manufacturer of the transport.[14] The RC–119G, moreover, seemed unlikely to succeed as a coastal patrol craft. Although crews who flew the C–119 or C–47 could readily transition to the patrol plane, navigators remained in short supply, and the modification of just thirteen AC–119Gs proved expensive, costing more than $4 million. Once the aircraft were fitted out and manned, tactical problems would arise. The enemy trawlers and junks, for which the modified gunships would search, could carry the same antiaircraft guns and shoulder-fired surface-to-air missiles that earlier had driven the planes from vigorously defended portions of the Ho Chi Minh Trail.[15] An even more serious obstacle to self-sufficiency resulted from the short range of the F–5 and A–37, which could not carry the war much beyond South Vietnam's borders.[16]

The A–1, which Leonard Sullivan had hoped to employ with fuel-air munitions — sometimes described as propane bombs — as a substitute for the B–52, suffered from decades of hard usage. The Skyraider could no longer dive more steeply than thirty degrees or exceed four Gs — four times the force of gravity — in pulling out. These limitations increased the vulnerability of the airplane to fire from the ground, but against weak antiaircraft defenses the A–1 could accurately deliver a heavy load of bombs.[17]

The C–47, an airplane dating from the mid-1930s, also remained a useful weapon. Indeed, when faced with the prospect of losing the C–47 flareships slated for conversion to intercept the enemy's radio traffic, General Vien, Chief of the Joint General Staff, protested to General Weyand, at the time in charge of the military assistance command. The U.S. officer decided, however, that the electronic reconnaissance mission took precedence over flare-dropping, which could be done by AC–119s.[18]

Despite the emphasis on using the converted C–47s for intercepting radio traffic, the Defense Attaché Office looked at the status of military intelligence and reported a "decided drop in total usable information since the demise of MACV." The most notable decline occurred in electronic intelligence. The ancient EC–47s that located the enemy's radio transmitters carried equipment that had become difficult to maintain after years of hard use, first by American airmen and more recently by the South Vietnamese. Ground-based intercept stations supplemented the EC–47s, but the operators lacked the experience to make timely evaluations, so that interpretations lagged an average of five days behind the message traffic with which they dealt. Photo interpretation also proved tardy at a time when the South Vietnamese were exposing more film than ever before. Indeed, the attaché office brought in U.S. photo interpreters to keep General Murray informed of the military situation in the South.[19]

Air War over South Vietnam, 1968–1975

South Vietnamese airmen perform maintenance on an A–37.

Whatever its failings, the intelligence collection effort could not help but confirm that the North Vietnamese and Viet Cong dominated increasingly vast tracts of rural South Vietnam, isolating the Saigon government's political and military outposts. By November 1973, twenty-six of these outlying sites depended for survival on supplies delivered by air. The South Vietnamese Air Force was flying an average of 628 sorties per month to sustain an estimated 100,000 soldiers and civilians.

Not even helicopters could land at one of the outposts, the ranger camp at Tonle Cham in Military Region III, which depended exclusively on supplies dropped by parachute onto a clearing measuring roughly 150 by 130 meters. Since hostile antiaircraft guns ringed Tonle Cham, transports had to release their loads from an altitude of 10,000 feet. Despite radar guidance from the ground, the early missions delivered only 18 percent of the cargo into the hands of the rangers. By July, the success rate had reached 50 percent, but during that month, a shift from the C–123 to the C–130 disrupted the learning curve and cut the proportion of cargo delivered to 35 percent. Increasing familiarity with the C–130, however, improved the accuracy of air drops at Tonle Cham.[20]

The Defense Attaché Office had scarcely taken over its portion of the assistance command's duties, when serious problems surfaced within South Vietnam's air arm, mostly because of the frenzied expansion. The South Vietnamese Air Force now totaled 65,000 officers and enlisted men, but half of them were undergoing some form of training to qualify them for new assignments. Nevertheless, the air service flew over 81,000 sorties by individual aircraft during September 1973; helicopters accounted for 62,000 of these and training craft for 1,100. Fighter-bombers or attack planes flew most of the others, but all too often they attacked from 10,000 feet or higher out of respect for antiaircraft weapons. Strikes from this altitude, in the opinion of the chief of the attaché office, General Murray, not only "failed to contribute to productive destruction" but caused inaccuracy that actually harmed "interservice relationships."[21]

The South Vietnamese could not yet maintain the mixed fleet of aircraft, many of them cast-offs, they had inherited. For example, maintenance on the force of UH–1s fell behind schedule throughout 1973, even though Air Vietnam, the national airline, lent its civilian mechanics to help with inspections. Similar delays affected maintenance of the EC–47, largely because crews failed to report equipment failures, and of the C–7, handicapped by a shortage of spare parts and trained mechanics. Almost every aircraft suffered from corrosion, the inevitable result of service in a tropical climate.[22]

During 1973, Lear Sigler launched an ambitious program of maintenance training. The instructors concentrated on the lagging UH–1 program, but teams of specialists also taught the South Vietnamese to repair corrosion and battle damage to the F–5 and A–37. Unfortunately, a shortage of spare parts hampered the training effort.[23]

The inability of South Vietnam's Air Logistics Command to keep track of inventories contributed to the shortage of spare parts. By October 1973, the command enjoyed a manning level of 92 percent, but its top managers lacked experience, and too many other officers, as well as noncommissioned officers, either had not yet completed training or were awaiting assignment. The headquarters computer that processed data from the depots in the military regions frequently broke down during the spring and summer. Indeed, in one thirty-day period of 1973, the logistics computer at Tan Son Nhut remained out of service 65 percent of the time. A mobile computer from Clark Air Base in the Philippines took over in July and, by early September, had conducted more than 400,000 transactions. Meanwhile, new parts, along with emergency maintenance and closer supervision of the operators, had put the idled computer back in action. Even so, clogged warehouses continued to impede supply flow.[24]

The Air Training Command, with headquarters at Nha Trang Air Base, assumed responsibility for flying training and for instruction in most career fields. The command operated six schools: flying, technical training, communications and electronics, military training, general service, and English language. General Murray and his staff believed that South Vietnamese instructors had, or could acquire, the skills to lay a foundation of basic knowledge upon which Lear Sigler Incorporated or schools outside South Vietnam might build. The effectiveness of the Air Training Command suffered, however, from a fragmentation of training courses among the military regions, lax supervision, and erratic logistics support. Moreover, power struggles for control of the various instructional functions pitted the training command against the headquarters of the South Vietnamese Air Force, as well as the military regions.

Because of these weaknesses in the fundamental courses of instruction conducted in South Vietnam, subjects taught outside the country remained essential to the operation of an expanded air arm. Plans for fiscal 1974 called for more than 1,200 South Vietnamese to train overseas, most of them in the United States, at a cost in excess of $30 million. The program would produce instructor pilots for fighters, trainers, and helicopters, who would teach students in South Vietnam, and it also turned out maintenance specialists, administrators, doctors, and other professionals.

The abiding emphasis on training in the United States underscored the importance of the Air Training Command's English Language School. Unfortunately, quotas for the course sometimes remained unfilled. Since combat continued despite the cease-fire, commanders proved reluctant to release key individuals, especially pilots, for the language training that served as the first step toward becoming a pilot instructor or other specialist. Consequently, classes might be postponed or canceled, thus disrupting the overall training plan.[25]

While the South Vietnamese Air Force participated throughout 1973 in a succession of local clashes, the air war in Cambodia flared and came to an end. When the cease-fire took effect in South Vietnam, the United States backed Lon Nol's efforts to extend the truce to Cambodia, urging him to suspend offensive operations but reserve the right of self defense, in the hope that the Khmer Rouge would accept the invitation and negotiate a settlement. Under the unflinching leadership of Pol Pot, however, the communist faction refused to relax the pressure on the Khmer Republic.[26]

Faced with a relentless enemy, the Khmer Republic seemed leaderless. The effects of his recent stroke had left Lon Nol, in the words of Brig. Gen. John R. D. Cleland, Jr., "a chief of state who is no longer in touch with his people." Cleland, who headed the Military Equipment Delivery Team, Cambodia, acknowledged, "For the first time in the 13 months I have been here, I am gravely concerned over the future of the GKR [Government of the Khmer Republic]."[27]

The Khmer army depended on U.S. air power for success, indeed for survival. When the troops gained ground, they followed behind a deluge of aerial bombs. As an Air Force officer declared in retrospect, Lon Nol's army "did not fight its way into the positions it held at the end of the air campaign, it walked to them."[28]

Because American bombs exploded so close to the advancing Khmer forces, accuracy was essential, especially for the B–52s with their large bombing pattern. Unfortunately, the ground-based Combat Skyspot radars, which directed the bombers before the cease-fire, left South Vietnam as part of the final U.S. withdrawal. To replace Combat Skyspot, Loran-equipped F–4s or F–111s led B–52 cells, unless the bombers carried this precise navigation system. In addition, radar transponders set up in friendly territory served as offset aiming points for some strikes by B–52s or F–111s.[29]

In spite of these precautions, concern mounted that B–52 strikes in particular killed or wounded noncombatants, forced survivors to flee to Phnom Penh — already crowded with refugees — disrupted agriculture in the vicinity of the capital, and interfered with supply flights into Pochentong airport. The U.S. Ambassador to the Khmer Republic, Emory Swank, decided by May 10 to validate only nighttime strikes by B–52s in southern and southwestern Cambodia to avoid interference with farming and essential air traffic. These restrictions, however, did not affect the number of B–52 sorties, fifty-four each day during May, but instead concentrated much of the bombing at a time when thunderstorms frequently appeared, disrupting Loran signals. The use of alternate targets enabled the bombers to make worthwhile attacks when weather interfered with the primary mission. In addition, General Vogt could employ the F–111 — using its own radar, sometimes in conjunction with a transponder on the ground — to hit targets protected by weather or lead B–52s against them.[30]

In Vogt's opinion, Swank seemed likely to impose further restrictions after a subcommittee of the Senate Foreign Relations Committee paid a visit to Phnom Penh and discussed with him the flood of refugees trying to escape the bombing. General Vogt warned that Swank might well recommend halting the B–52 strikes throughout Cambodia and advised the Joint Chiefs of Staff to marshal their arguments against such a decision, which, he believed, might jeopardize the survival of the Khmer Republic.[31]

Congress, however, acted before Swank made a formal recommendation. The House of Representatives, its attitude shaped by public disenchantment with the war in Southeast Asia, voted on May 10, 1973, to reject the supplemental appropriations needed to continue the air war in Cambodia. The Nixon administration campaigned for the restoration of this money, but the President had already begun stumbling toward impeachment, which he would avoid in August 1974 by resigning. Beset by revelations of his role in Watergate — the web of felonies surrounding a break-in at the headquarters of the Democratic National Committee in the Watergate office complex at Washington, D.C., and the subsequent cover-up — Nixon could no longer rally public opinion to impose his will on the Congress. The administration succeeded only in persuading the House and Senate conferees to allow the bombing to continue until August 15, 1973. The President on June 29 signed into law the supplemental appropriations bill that extended the air war for another two weeks.[32]

On August 6, as a bombing drew to an end, a cell of B–52s approached a beacon set up in Neak Luong, a town on the Mekong downstream from Phnom Penh. Instead of using the transponder as an offset aiming point for a target some eight nautical miles to the northwest — and checking the radar return from a terrain feature designated as a checkpoint — the three bombers mistakenly dropped their bombs on the beacon itself, located near the center of the town. The resulting explosions destroyed much of Neak Luong and killed or wounded an estimated 400 persons.[33]

In commenting on the tragedy at Neak Luong, the result of a failure to throw the proper switch, General Vogt conceded that it was the worst bombing error of the Cambodian fighting. A momentary human lapse had undone all the safeguards — validation by the embassy, review by the support group of the latest intelligence, and the use of navigation aids — designed to prevent this kind of accident. Because of Neak Luong, bombers no longer used beacons as offset aiming points.[34]

As August 15 approached, a hurried airlift built up the Khmer army's stocks of ammunition. The Air Force flew as many as twenty-five daily sorties, landing cargo at Pochentong or parachuting it to various outposts.[35] This effort helped the army hold the Khmer Rouge at bay during the fall of 1973.

In his assessment of the fighting during 1973, General Cleland pointed out that the officers and men of the Khmer army had not collapsed as soon as the bombing ended but instead had "demonstrated that, if given the manpower and equipment, they can resist the enemy offensives." Manpower, however, proved a critical shortcoming; units that did most of the recent fighting remained at about half-strength, and the Khmer government seemed unable to marshal the nation's human resources and obtain replacements. Moreover, military leadership grew weak and discipline lax; the martial spirit that surfaced when the war began had long since dissipated. In strategic terms, the government at Phnom Penh had been on the defensive since 1971 and could not regain the initiative.[36]

Although the bombing of Cambodia ended on August 15, Air Force C-130s continued for another year to deliver supplies to Phnom Penh and other locations, either landing to unload or dropping the cargo by parachute. As the Khmer Rouge grew stronger, American authorities became concerned that an Air Force transport might be shot down and the crew taken prisoner by the communists. Rather than risk that Air Force crewmen become hostages, the United States government chose a civilian contractor to operate the airlift. On August 28, 1974, Birdair took over the supply mission, using former members of the Air Force to fly between five and ten sorties each day.[37]

The Khmer air force contributed little to the fight against the communists. With eight C-123s and a few C-47s, the air arm could deliver a small amount of cargo to airstrips within the country. Some AU-24s, unsuccessfully modified as minigunships for the South Vietnamese, arrived in Cambodia but saw limited service, mainly as liaison planes or light transports. The forty AT-28Ds, trainers converted to fighter-bombers, could fly perhaps 160 sorties per day in an all-out effort but lacked the firepower to take over the air war the Americans had halted.[38]

The flaws in the government's military structure, the American bombing halt, and the determination of the Khmer Rouge sealed the doom of the Khmer Republic. By late 1974, the communist faction had isolated the government forces in a few large cities, including Phnom Penh. The fall of the Cambodian capital seemed inevitable, and planning began for Operation Eagle Pull, the withdrawal of the Americans still serving there.

On April 1, 1975, after the Khmer Rouge captured Neak Luong, Lon Nol left the country. Within five days, only fifty members of the embassy staff remained at Phnom Penh; the others had departed on cargo planes returning to Thailand or on the few commercial flights still using Pochentong airport. Meanwhile, Air Force and Marine units made their final preparations to carry out the evacuation. On April 3, at the request of Ambassador John Gunther Deane, an Air Force HH–53 flew the command element of a Marine security force to the grounds of the embassy at Phnom Penh. Enemy troops had already entered the suburbs of Phnom Penh when Ambassador Deane, on April 10, requested that the operation begin two days later.

On the 12th, an HH–53 landed an Air Force control team, and Marine CH–53s brought in the remainder of the security force and carried out 276 passengers, including Ambassador Deane. When the Marine fliers had completed their job, a pair of HH–53s picked up the combat control team and the last of the 360–man security detachment. Rockets began exploding at the soccer field that served as landing zone as the last two Air Force helicopters were taking off. Both HH–53s sustained damage from Khmer Rouge machine guns, and the one that carried the Marines was vibrating badly throughout the flight to Ubon, Thailand, where the two helicopters landed safely. The 7th Airborne Command and Control Squadron at Udorn, Thailand, provided the C–130 airborne battlefield command and control center for overall direction of Operation Eagle Pull. One HC–130 from the 3d Aerospace Rescue and Recovery Group controlled the helicopter traffic, a second refueled the helicopters and stood ready to control the rescue effort in the event the Khmer Rouge shot down any aircraft, and a third served as back-up. Because the number of Air Force HH–53s in Thailand had declined since the cease-fire, the operation included Marine Corps CH–53s. Air Force A–7 attack planes, directed by forward air controllers in OV–10s, and AC–130 gunships had the mission of suppressing hostile fire during the evacuation.[39]

The citizens of Phnom Penh did not interfere with the escape of the Americans or attempt to force their way on board the helicopters. That might not have been so if the bystanders could have glimpsed the horrors that lay ahead. Under Pol Pot, the communist government sought to eradicate western influence through a campaign of terror. His zealots slaughtered tens of thousands outright, and additional tens of thousands starved or died of disease, some of them while confined at re-education camps, where the death rate in the spring of 1977 approached 100 per day.[40]

The end of the bombing in Cambodia, which accelerated the plunge of the Khmer Republic into oblivion, intensified the threat to South Vietnam. Although he could not predict when, General Murray believed that the communist high command at Hanoi would eventually decide to attack the South. He predicted that for two or three months after the air war stopped, the Khmer Rouge would be badly shaken from the previous bombing and concerned that the attacks might resume. As the Cambodian communists recovered and extended their control over the port of Kompong Som and the road net that originated

Air War over South Vietnam, 1968–1975

The assembly area for the evacuation of Phnom Penh in April 1975.

there, the movement of men and cargo through eastern Cambodia into South Vietnam would become progressively easier. The cease-fire in South Vietnam would serve mainly to gain time for the North Vietnamese and Viet Cong, weakened by casualties during the fighting in 1972, to absorb replacements, re-equip, and become seasoned by small-scale combat.[41]

In the summer of 1974, Air Force headquarters, Pacific Air Forces, and the Air Force Logistics Command examined the structure of the South Vietnamese Air Force and offered specific recommendations to help it repulse an invasion like the Easter offensive of 1972. Even though public and Congressional support for South Vietnam was diminishing, the study reflected a tacit assumption that American air power would intervene on behalf of the Saigon government.

Some of the findings dealt with the problem of gathering intelligence on enemy activity. The panel concluded that the authorized reconnaissance force of twelve RC–47s, thirty-two EC–47s, and seven RF–5s was adequate, but proposed that the RF–5s be divided between Da Nang and Bien Hoa, instead of concentrating at Bien Hoa, thus expanding the area covered by these short-range aircraft. Also, the South Vietnamese should devise tactics and countermeasures — fighter escort, for example, and flares to decoy heat-seeking antiaircraft missiles — to enable the RC–47 and EC–47 to operate in more areas strongly defended.

Similarly, the review expressed confidence that the 200 authorized aircraft would meet the needs of South Vietnamese forward air controllers. The U–17, judged at best a light transport and liaison plane, seemed too vulnerable for the forward air controllers to use. The threat posed by the heat-seeking SA–7 missile inspired two recommendations: the training of forward air control parties to direct strikes from the ground; and the use of the F–5 as a vehicle for forward air controllers facing powerful antiaircraft defenses.

After the Truce

The interceptor variant of the F–5, the E model, impressed the panel as a match for the North Vietnamese MiG–21. They believed that a squadron at Da Nang should meet the threat of MiG incursions over South Vietnam, if necessary launching as many as twenty air defense sorties within two hours.

Turning to airlift, the study declared that the fleet of transports, though adequate for routine operations, could not sustain a maximum effort for an extended time. Better management, however, could to some extent make up the deficiency in the number of aircraft, estimated at 10 percent.

The helicopter armada seemed "more than adequate to meet the projected requirement." The number of UH–1s, used by the Americans for assault operations, could safely be reduced from 842 to 640, since the South Vietnamese would not be employing airmobile tactics. The fleet of larger CH–47s could supplement cargo-carrying, fixed-wing transports in an emergency and therefore should remain at the authorized total of sixty-four.

Fighters and attack aircraft, according to the study, fell "127 aircraft short of the computed requirement," although AC–47 and AC–119K gunships might help make up the difference. Moreover, careful scheduling of maintenance and the massing of available aircraft could ensure an adequate number of F–5s, A–1s, and A–37s to deal with the threatened invasion.[42]

Although the mid-1974 assessment of the force structure generally approved of the composition of South Vietnam's air arm, General Murray warned in October of serious failings that could erode the ability of the South Vietnamese to control the air. At times, Murray said, pilots crossed "the narrow line between the brave and the foolhardy." They flew with an almost suicidal disregard of basic safety procedures, even though they respected the heat-seeking SA–7 missile and remained reluctant to venture below 10,000 feet to attack targets defended by that missile or radar-directed antiaircraft guns. Joyriding or careless taxiing, sometimes by drunken pilots, and failure to make preflight inspections cost the South Vietnamese Air Force, by Murray's reckoning, "the equivalent of an entire squadron of jet aircraft."

While pilots were thus squandering aircraft, communist air defenses took a steady toll. By June 1974, the enemy had launched 136 SA–7s, costing an estimated $680,000, and downed twenty-three aircraft worth perhaps $12 million. Antiaircraft weapons proved so deadly that they, in effect, gained control of the air over a large expanse of South Vietnamese territory, especially in the west, on the border with Laos and Cambodia. In Military Region I, for example, the air arm could operate freely over only a narrow strip of land along the seacoast. Accidents and hostile fire claimed 237 South Vietnamese aircraft in the twenty-three months following the cease-fire.

The losses, especially the toll from preventable accidents, raised the price of equipping and training the air arm and consequently discouraged the United States from spending money to replace aircraft, as the treaty permitted. Support for the South Vietnamese Air Force cost $382 million in fiscal 1974, excluding the cost of munitions, more than the combined cost for the army and navy. The air arm also required the services of 1,540 employees of contractors like Lear Sigler Incorporated, compared with 723 for the Army and 61 for the Navy. Of 466 civilian employees of the United States government assigned to aid the South Vietnamese armed forces, 202 worked with the Air Force. No wonder that Murray characterized the South Vietnamese Air Force as "costly, careless, and conceding air space."

The chief of the Defense Attaché Office suggested some basic remedies to correct the failings he described. Besides an emphasis on flight safety, he proposed reducing costs by consolidating the South Vietnamese inventory of aircraft, perhaps eliminating the T-37 and T-41 trainers and using just one type for forward air controllers. He also would encourage commanders to choose the cheaper-to-operate A-37 over the F-5 whenever such a choice was possible. To reduce combat losses, he suggested fitting some A-37s and F-5s with radar homing and warning gear to alert pilots that they were being tracked by radar-controlled antiaircraft weapons.[43]

Even as he offered this evaluation and proposed changes for the immediate future, General Murray pointed out that the South Vietnamese Air Force still packed a punch. Despite the current weaknesses of the air service, North Vietnam had invested heavily in SA-7s and other antiaircraft weapons, thus acknowledging the threat from the skies.[44] Apparently, Murray's insistence on safety paid immediate dividends, for as early as October 1974, the Defense Intelligence Agency listed "a reduction of accidents" as one of the reasons that the air arm, in the present tactical situation, could render "sustained and effective support to the army."[45] Should the communists launch what Murray described as a "super offensive," however, the United States would have to intervene, as it had in 1972, with "the only ultimate counterforce."[46]

During 1974, the South Vietnamese Air Force did take part in some operations that General Murray considered successful. Tactical fighters and gunships displayed "mobility, aggressiveness, and initiative" during an armored thrust into Hau Nghia Province to protect the approaches to Saigon. Also, some 400 sorties, flown during ten days of fighting, helped repulse an attack from the enemy's Cambodian bases that made use of armored personnel carriers captured from the South Vietnamese.

The North Vietnamese and Viet Cong in the meantime increased the intensity of their offensive operations in all four military regions. Tonle Cham, the isolated ranger camp supplied by airlift since the cease-fire, fell at last, and the enemy shelled Phu Cat Air Base and overran four nearby outposts. Elsewhere, regiments and even divisions clashed, but neither Saigon nor Hanoi won a decisive victory.[47]

A captured resolution of the communist Central Office for South Vietnam called for a nation-wide offensive in 1975, but to American eyes, this operation seemed likely to be the overture to a final assault sometime the following year.

After the Truce

Attacks in 1975 would therefore be less ambitious than the 1968 Tet operation or the 1972 Easter offensive. According to Leonard Sullivan, Jr., now the Assistant Secretary of Defense (Program Analysis and Evaluation), the South Vietnamese could prevent "decisive communist gains" in 1975, assuming that the United States made available an additional $130 million to $170 million for ammunition. Such an outlay would enable Saigon's forces to restrict communist progress to northern South Vietnam, the central highlands, and the northern fringes of Military Regions III and IV.

Sullivan believed that without the ammunition Quang Tri City and Kontum might fall, bringing a communist victory that much closer, though South Vietnam would survive at least until the dry season extending from the fall of 1975 to the spring of 1976. What happened then would depend on the ability and willingness of the South Vietnamese to fight and the determination of the United States to support them.[48]

Events taking place as far from Saigon as the Middle East and Washington, D.C., conspired against the survival of South Vietnam. On October 6, 1973, Egyptian and Syrian forces invaded territory controlled by Israel. Within three weeks, the Israeli armed forces repulsed the attackers; a truce ensued that led ultimately to peaceful relations between Egypt and Israel. Unfortunately, the war also resulted in a refusal by Arab oil producers to sell petroleum to nations that supported Israel and, more important, a longer-lasting sense of solidarity within the Arab-dominated Organization of Petroleum Exporting Countries, which succeeded for a time in controlling production, driving up oil prices, and touching off world-wide inflation. The dollars the Saigon government received during the period of rampant inflation could not buy as much fuel, ammunition, or other tools of war as in previous years.[49]

Another blow struck the Saigon government on August 9, 1974, when President Richard M. Nixon resigned rather than face impeachment and trial. His successor, Gerald R. Ford, assured President Thieu that "our support will be adequate." Shortly before Ford extended this promise, which was less specific than his predecessor's personal vow to unleash U.S. air power in the event of a North Vietnamese invasion, the term "adequate" lost some of its meaning. In one of his last acts before resigning, Nixon had signed legislation that authorized $1 billion in military assistance for South Vietnam, instead of the $1.6 billion he had sought, a reduction of almost 40 percent from his original request for fiscal 1975. Congressional dissatisfaction with the Thieu government — and public eagerness to exorcise the ghost of the Vietnam War — fed by perceptions of rampant corruption throughout South Vietnam and a belief that the Saigon government had misused much of the aid it already had received.[50] Saigon's armed forces were unlikely to get the quantity of ammunition that Assistant Secretary of Defense Sullivan had recommended.

After the summer of 1974, South Vietnam began receiving progressively less support to fight an increasing number of battles throughout the nation. As the fighting became more severe and deliveries dwindled, stocks of ammunition declined by early 1975 from the desired sixty-day supply to a thirty-to-forty-day level. Moreover, the reserve of gasoline dropped by almost one-third between 1973 and 1975.

General Vien of the South Vietnamese Joint General Staff also complained that a shortage of spare parts had disabled some 4,000 trucks provided by the Americans.[51] The root cause, however, may have been an indifference to routine maintenance rather than a lack of parts. South Vietnamese abuse of vehicles had been a source of frequent complaints by U.S. advisers like Air Force Col. David B. Ballou, who had seen many trucks driven to destruction with no thought even for oil changes. "As long as a vehicle will run," he said, "they will use it."[52]

The decline in U.S. aid tended to inspire dissatisfaction with President Thieu among those South Vietnamese who realized the nation's dependence on the United States. The cease-fire left the North Vietnamese in control of much of the South; only American aid and the promise of American firepower could offset this advantage. Thieu, however, obtained military assistance in a diminishing volume, and the loss of aid could well be a manifestation of U.S. indifference to the fate of South Vietnam.

Along with Thieu's failure to maintain the flow of aid, widespread corruption threatened his popularity among the South Vietnamese. Indeed, graft grew worse as inflation soared, forcing civilian officials and military officers to scramble to supplement their declining income with bribes and kickbacks. In the armed forces, so-called "flower soldiers" wilted away when the shooting began, having paid their superiors for blanket permission to take leave as desired. Thieu might replace blatantly corrupt senior officers, as he occasionally did, but he could do nothing to lower the price of oil, which fueled inflation and contributed to corruption. Nevertheless, the common wisdom held that the house leaks from the roof, and Thieu stood at the top of the governmental structure.

As if to demonstrate the growing disenchantment with both Thieu and his American sponsors, a new book about the overthrow and assassination of Ngo Dinh Diem in 1963 got an enthusiastic reception among the South Vietnamese. *How the Americans Killed a Vietnamese President* ignored the repressive measures Diem had carried out, his arbitrary rule, the failure of his armed forces to maintain security and suppress a comparatively small-scale insurgency, and the widespread celebration when he was overthrown. Instead, the account reshaped history to make it appear that the United States, by collaborating in the overthrow and death of Diem, had put an end to a golden age and, under his American-supported successors, begun an era of death and suffering. The populace, however, was not yet willing to turn against Thieu and the Americans, as the communist leadership at Hanoi realized.[53]

Whereas U.S. aid to South Vietnam declined, the Hanoi regime could deliver military cargo to the battlefield in greater volume than ever before. Once the threat of aerial attack ended, the North Vietnamese began extending the Ho

After the Truce

Chi Minh Trail all the way to the Mekong Delta and converting the maze of roads, trails, and waterways into an all-weather highway, over which truck convoys, sometimes numbering 200 vehicles, rolled by day and night.[54]

Emboldened by the buildup that the expanded trail made possible, Gen. Tran Van Tra, who had commanded Viet Cong forces attacking Saigon during the Tet offensive of 1968, argued for launching the final onslaught immediately. The conservatism of the communist high command prevailed for the moment, though he received permission for a limited offensive in Phuoc Long Province. He attacked on December 13, 1974, and the fighting that ensued revealed the failings of the South Vietnamese Air Force. North Vietnamese antiaircraft weapons gained control of the skies over the battlefield, and rockets and artillery fire shut down the forward airstrips and harassed Bien Hoa, the main air base serving the III Corps tactical zone. When the enemy cut the main roads that reinforcements might use, CH–47 helicopter and C–130 transports could not take the place of the truck convoys. Indeed, to mount an all-out airlift for even ten days would have stripped the other military regions of transports and risked crippling losses of cargo planes and helicopters to antiaircraft weapons in the threatened province. At most, the high command at Saigon could commit the few reserves available within III Corps. Helicopters flew some 250 reinforcements to the town of Phuoc Binh, despite vicious antiaircraft fire, but this force proved too small to seize the initiative. By mid-January 1975, Tran Van Tra had overrun the province, thus demonstrating that the time had come for the final offensive.[55]

Gen. Van Tieng Dung, a member of the ruling politburo in Hanoi, assumed responsibility for delivering the next blow, a four-division thrust from the highlands to the coast that would cut South Vietnam in half. On March 1, he feinted toward Pleiku in Military Region II, only to surround nearby Ban Me Thuot and isolate the central highlands. By March 10, the defenders of Ban Me Thuot and their dependents were fleeing toward the coast.[56]

Conversations earlier in the year with American officials visiting Saigon had convinced President Thieu that his nation could not expect a dramatic infusion of material aid from the United States. Unable to defend all of South Vietnam with the resources at his disposal, he began thinking of tailoring the war to fit the nation's ability to fight. Salvation, he believed, might well lie in abandoning those portions of the northern provinces still under Saigon's control. The defeat at Ban Me Thuot and the headlong flight it triggered persuaded Thieu to execute this concept — actually a succession of phase lines and shaded areas drawn on a standard map of the country — which was far too vague to function as an operations plan. Instead of launching an orderly withdrawal, Thieu succeeded only in sowing doubt and then panic, as troops and civilians alike sought the dubious safety of the southernmost provinces.[57]

As prospects for South Vietnam's survival grew bleaker, the United States began rushing badly needed military equipment, especially ammunition, to the embattled country. Rather than allow the Air Force C–5As delivering the cargo

Air War over South Vietnam, 1968–1975

to return empty, the Defense Attaché Office arranged for the planes to participate in the evacuation. Civilian employees of the office, judged nonessential and ordered back to the United States, volunteered to look after some 250 infants removed from orphanages and loaded on board one of the Galaxy transports. This flight was a part of Operation Babylift, designed to spare the infants the horrors of an apparently inevitable blood bath that would attend the battle for Saigon. The aircraft took off on April 4, crossing the coast near Vung Tau. At 23,000 feet above the ocean, an explosive decompression tore away doors at the rear of the cargo compartment, damaging the tail surfaces. The pilot, Capt. Dennis Traynor, tried to return to Tan Son Nhut and make an emergency landing, but a short distance from the airfield, the crippled transport glanced off an earthen embankment, skipped across a river, and crashed in a swamp. The flying skill of Traynor and his crew members saved 175 lives, but 172 of the passengers, most of them infants, died.[58]

By the time the Babylift C–5A crashed, the enemy had overwhelmed the northern provinces of South Vietnam, and the government at Saigon careened toward defeat. On April 8, as if to foreshadow the approaching disaster, a rogue F–5 pilot of the South Vietnamese Air Force bombed the presidential palace, though without inflicting casualties. On April 21, Thieu bowed to the inevitable and stepped down from the presidency in the hope that someone else could bring the fighting to an end.[59]

Throughout these discouraging weeks, individuals in the Ford administration, like General Weyand, the Army Chief of Staff, sought to drum up support for South Vietnam. Indeed, Weyand visited Saigon late in March to confer with President Thieu and General Vien. On April 10, President Ford asked Congress to grant $922 million in emergency aid to South Vietnam. Of this total, $722 million would provide military assistance to help South Vietnam save itself, and the balance would afford economic and humanitarian help to facilitate the evacuation of Americans and those South Vietnamese whose lives might be endangered by a communist victory. He also asked that Congress agree to the deployment of as many U.S. troops as might be needed to protect the final withdrawal.

By April 23, however, Ford had given up. On that day, during a speech at New Orleans, Louisiana, he wrote off South Vietnam. "Today," he said, "Americans can regain the sense of pride that existed before Vietnam. But it cannot be achieved by reflecting on a war that is finished as far as America is concerned." Although the United States was "saddened indeed by the events in Indochina," Ford consoled the nation with his belief that "These events, tragic as they are, portend neither the end of the world nor of America's leadership." Congress was still debating the request of April 10, when Dung's troops overran Saigon.[60]

As time ran out, Air Force and Marine Corps helicopters prepared to join the cargo planes pressed into service to evacuate by air the Americans still in Saigon and as many as possible of their South Vietnamese associates. Air America, a firm controlled by the Central Intelligence Agency, was readying its

After the Truce

UH–1 helicopters, and the Marine Corps and Air Force marshalled CH–53s, HH–53s and CH–46s, some of which had carried out the evacuation from Phnom Penh on April 17. At Saigon, work parties cleared landing zones and marked rooftops for the final evacuation.[61]

The evacuation of Saigon, Operation Frequent Wind, used both transports and helicopters in conjunction with ships. The aerial portion began on April 20, the day of Thieu's resignation, when Air Force C–141s, after bringing supplies to Tan Son Nhut, flew off with passengers and small amounts of unneeded cargo. On the next day, Philippines-based C–130s joined in the around-the-clock operation. A processing center at the airfield checked identification papers and directed the evacuees to the appropriate aircraft. Some of the departing South Vietnamese and Americans arrived at the air base in vans used to distribute *Pacific Stars and Stripes*, the semi-official newspaper of the American armed forces. Meanwhile, roughly twenty enemy divisions were converging on Saigon, cutting the road to Vung Tau, where evacuation ships rode at anchor, and began on April 27 to fire rockets into the capital city.

As the danger mounted, Air Force officers operating the evacuation center jammed more than 300 persons into C–141s that normally carried 94 passengers. After the shelling on the 27th, the risk became too great to continue flying these valuable aircraft into Tan Son Nhut. The C–130s took over the airlift, operating by day and night. A Hercules transport departing from Tan Son Nhut might carry 240 persons or more, instead of the usual 75.

Tan Son Nhut came under air attack on April 28, when three A–37s, either captured by the North Vietnamese or flown by defectors, bombed the flight line and operations building. North Vietnamese antiaircraft gunners in the vicinity of the airfield opened fire on departing transports, and the combination of bombing and fire from the ground forced a suspension of transport flights until the following morning.

Early on April 29, three C–130s ferrying bombs landed at Tan Son Nhut and unloaded their cargo at an ammunition dump. They then headed to the flight line where evacuees gathered to board them. As the transports approached the waiting passengers, a barrage of 122-mm rockets struck the base, one of them setting on fire the last C–130 in line. While it burned, the crew escaped and ran to another of the transports, both of which took off immediately, without taking on board the assigned passengers. The barrage of rockets and artillery shells that destroyed the aircraft, and also killed two Marines manning a guard post, put an end to the use of fixed-wing transports in Operation Frequent Wind. While the attacking North Vietnamese were thus cutting the lifeline that the C–130s provided to Clark Air Base in the Philippines, UH–1 helicopters flown by Air America went into action, plucking Americans from rooftops and bringing them to the processing center at Tan Son Nhut, to the Embassy, or to one of the ships at sea.[62]

Although a few South Vietnamese pilots and crews braved antiaircraft guns

Air War over South Vietnam, 1968–1975

and heat-seeking missiles in an attempt to hold Dung's troops at bay, the downing of an A–1 and an AC–119 heightened feelings of desperation. Pilots commandeered four Air America helicopters and began scrambling into their own aircraft, but to flee rather than to fight. In addition, some ground troops started to show their resentment at being abandoned, shutting down the Air America operations center at Tan Son Nhut and occasionally shooting in the direction of Americans or their aircraft.[63]

Air Force Lt. Gen. John J. Burns, who had replaced Vogt in command of the U.S. Support Activities Group, anticipated the actions of Ambassador Graham Martin and ordered the evacuees to begin moving to the helicopter landing sites before the embassy issued a formal order. The helicopter phase of Operation Frequent Wind got underway on the afternoon of April 29 with the arrival at Tan Son Nhut of the first Air Force and Marine Corps helicopters. In the confusion of launching the operation, an 840-man Marine security force reached Tan Son Nhut a full hour after its commander, Brig. Gen. Richard E. Carey, stepped onto the tarmac. An airborne battlefield command and control center directed the operation, as at Phnom Penh. For the much larger and more complex evacuation from Saigon, the Strategic Air Command provided radio-relay aircraft and aerial tankers, while Air Force and Navy fighter-bombers, Air Force AC–130 gunships, and Marine Corps helicopter gunships escorted the Air Force and Marine helicopters that would carry away the Americans and South Vietnamese.

The first wave of evacuation helicopters — ten Marine Corps CH–53s and CH–46s, plus two Air Force HH–53s that would not only retrieve any downed airmen but also carry evacuees — took off from the aircraft carrier *Midway* and landed at Tan Son Nhut during the afternoon. Random fire from artillery, rockets, and small-arms challenged the evacuation, though without much effect. As the last three helicopters in the first wave started toward shore — two of them Air Force HH–53s — the radar homing and warning gear in the HH–53 flown by Maj. John F. Guilmartin began buzzing, emitting the rattlesnake's sound indicating that hostile radar had locked onto the craft. Since Guilmartin was not yet within range of radar-controlled surface-to-air missiles, the warning device was obviously malfunctioning, so he shut it down. Luckily, an escorting fighter-bomber had warning equipment that worked, for the aircraft detected the signal from a missile-control radar near Tan Son Nhut and fired an antiradiation missile, designed to home on the radar transmitter, that forced the set to shut down.[64]

Helicopters shuttled throughout the night between the aircraft carrier and the air base. Besides the threat from radar-directed weapons, neutralized by antiradiation missiles, and scattered small-arms fire from the ground, the rescue helicopters had to contend with crowds of panicky South Vietnamese trying to flee the doomed city. When a young woman waiting in line to board pushed her

After the Truce

Civilians evacuated from Saigon on April 29, 1975, arrived on the USS *Blue Ridge* aboard the Marine helicopter in the background.

way onto an HH–53 helicopter, a crew member shoved her backward. As she fell, she stumbled against the multibarrel, rearward-firing cannon, turning the weapon toward the waiting people. In struggling to regain her feet, she accidentally tripped the trigger. One round seated itself in the chamber, but instead of blazing away into the crowd at the rate of 2,000 rounds per minute, the weapon jammed without firing a single shot.

The loading continued until the helicopter staggered into the sky with ninety-seven passengers on board, twice the normal load. As the craft headed for the coast, a heat-seeking SA–7 missile streaked toward it. A mechanic on board saw the exhaust trail and fired a flare to confuse the infrared sensor. The missile veered toward the burning flare, missing the heavily laden helicopter by some sixty feet. The activity of Air Force rescue helicopters in Operation Frequent Wind ended with the their final departure from Tan Son Nhut; in all, they carried some 400 persons to safety.[65]

Late on the night of April 29, General Carey ordered the remaining Americans out of Tan Son Nhut. The Marine security force and two Air Force communications specialists remained until the end, setting fires that destroyed Pentagon East. At a few minutes after midnight, the members of this rear guard boarded Marine helicopters, and all attention focused on the embassy, where thousands of South Vietnamese grappled for a place in the evacuation.[66]

The operation continued until 7:53 a.m. from the roof and grounds of the embassy, despite breakdowns in communications that followed the destruction of the radio equipment at Tan Son Nhut. Since the helicopter phase began on April 29, these craft evacuated some 7,800 persons including Ambassador

Air War over South Vietnam, 1968–1975

Vietnamese refugees crowd the decks of the USS *Pioneer Contender*.

Martin, the Marine security detachment, and Maj. Gen. Homer D. Smith, who had replaced General Murray as defense attaché. Even so, a number of South Korean diplomats remained behind and had to arrange their eventual release. Some South Vietnamese employees of the embassy, still waiting as the last Americans bolted for the final helicopter, fell into the hands of the victors. Another half-dozen sorties could have picked them up, but the radio link failed at that critical time, leaving the impression in Washington that a mob was on the verge of overrunning the embassy. As a result, President Ford stopped Operation Frequent Wind.[67]

The South Vietnamese continued to flee the doomed country by air, however. Even before Gen. Duong Van Minh, the last president of South Vietnam, at mid-morning on April 30 directed his forces to lay down their weapons, the air arm was melting away. Some airmen attacked the enemy before departing, like the A–37 pilots who tried to bomb North Vietnamese tanks, landed to refuel, learned of the surrender, and flew to Thailand. Others cared only for survival. A number of helicopter and transport crews loaded their families on board before fleeing. Fighters, attack planes, and transports generally escaped to airfields in Thailand; some helicopters did likewise, though others, joined by at least one O–1 observation plane, landed on ships off the coast, including the aircraft carrier *Midway*.[68]

Thus ended U.S. involvement with South Vietnam, although one minor operation remained — the rescue of the container ship *Mayaguez*, seized on May 12 by gunboats from communist Cambodia. The nature and purpose of the commitment to the Saigon government — and the role of air power in achieving American goals — had changed since 1968. The Tet offensive of that year shook the confidence of the Johnson administration in its ability to force the Hanoi government to call off the attempt to conquer the South. As a result, the United States sought to return responsibility for fighting the war to the South Vietnamese. President Nixon launched a highly publicized program of Vietnamization — training and equipping the South Vietnamese to defend their nation — and U.S. withdrawal. Ideally, the new strategy would have linked progress in Vietnamization with the pace of withdrawal, with increases in South Vietnamese strength determining the frequency of the American departures and the numbers involved.

As Henry Kissinger warned when he compared making troop withdrawals to snacking on salted peanuts, the American people, weary of the war, quickly developed a greater appetite for reductions in troop strength than a balanced schedule linked to improvement in South Vietnam's armed forces could satisfy. Congress and the Nixon administration realized that support for the war was at best half-hearted. Indeed, the executive and legislative branches seemed at times to be competing to liquidate the American involvement. Whereas Congress made symbolic gestures like rescinding the Tonkin Gulf resolution or requiring consultation by the President before any future commitment of U.S. troops, only the administration could fulfill the public's craving for a succession of U.S. withdrawals that would rapidly reduce U.S. casualties, put an end to the need to send draftees into combat, and eliminate the draft except in some future emergency.

In two of her monographs for the Air Force history program,[69] Elizabeth Hartsook has described how air power became a shield for Vietnamization and withdrawal. Charged with forestalling an offensive that would drive the dwindling number of U.S. troops into the sea, the Air Force attacked the Ho Chi Minh Trail in Laos, carried the war into Cambodia — at first bombing secretly, but in the spring of 1970 supporting an invasion by U.S. ground forces — aided South Vietnamese troops in Laos and Cambodia, and occasionally struck targets in the North. These operations may well have delayed, but did not prevent, the North Vietnamese invasion of March 1972.

When the North Vietnamese attacked, Nixon realized that the public would not support the reintroduction of American ground forces; indeed, the withdrawals continued despite the fighting. He again turned to air power, and the Air Force, Navy, and Marine Corps responded promptly and with deadly effect. This time the Marines raised no objection to serving under Air Force command. The single manager system, a source of bitter contention during 1968, went unchallenged in 1972, for no Marine units fought on the ground where they would have had an emotional and doctrinal claim on Marine aviation.

Aerial attacks throughout South Vietnam — even more effective because the invader massed his troops to seize certain key objectives and thus presented targets ideally suited to bombing and strafing — and strikes against the North led to a peace settlement. The cease-fire, however, left North Vietnamese troops in control of the South Vietnamese territory they held when the fighting ended. The enemy's supply line through Laos and Cambodia remained secure; in fact, engineers would soon extend the Ho Chi Minh Trail and convert it into an all-weather highway. The Saigon government accepted these bleak prospects under

Air War over South Vietnam, 1968–1975

pressure from the United States. President Nixon's personal pledge to react decisively to any future invasion by the North Vietnamese afforded assurance to South Vietnamese leaders, who assumed that a repetition of the Easter invasion of 1972 would trigger a comparably devastating aerial response.

The process of Vietnamization, which the Air Force had helped shield, produced size rather than skill. The South Vietnamese air arm, for example, had too few trained men to operate and maintain all its equipment, despite its vast expansion. Moreover, the post-cease-fire training effort could not make up for the deficiencies left by the wartime program. In addition, the inventory of aircraft had huge gaps: the fighter-bombers and attack planes lacked the range to hit targets outside South Vietnam; the transports and helicopters could not support extended operations on the ground; and no bomber could approach the B–52 in destructiveness. Finally, stocks of fuel and munitions declined as American military assistance diminished.

When Hanoi launched its final offensive in March 1975, South Vietnamese resistance collapsed, and after six weeks Saigon capitulated. President Nixon had by this time resigned, and President Ford waited beyond the eleventh hour before requesting emergency military aid. His proposal to help South Vietnam defend itself, not offered until April 10, accepted the likelihood of a final withdrawal.

In analyzing the causes of his nation's defeat, Cao Van Vien, the last chairman of the Joint General Staff, blamed the U.S. Congress for cutting military assistance and President Ford for not honoring Nixon's promise to intervene with air power if North Vietnam invaded. Both Congress and the President, however, accurately reflected the mood of the American people. In fact, the South Vietnamese general concedes in his analysis that there were grounds for this disillusionment. Pervasive corruption throughout South Vietnam's armed forces and governmental structure aroused opposition to sending Americans to risk their lives to uphold a regime that seemed ethically, militarily, and politically bankrupt.[70]

The collapse of South Vietnam might be interpreted as the result of U.S. domestic politics, which required concessions to antiwar sentiment among the populace. The key concession may well have been the Nixon administration's decision to separate the withdrawal of American troops from improvements in the South Vietnamese armed forces. Liquidating the U.S. involvement became the overriding objective of the United States; the survival of an independent South Vietnam faded into the shadows. Since public opinion did not rally behind South Vietnam, the independence of that country remained a secondary consideration, desirable, perhaps, but not essential to the power and prestige of the United States. President Nixon's establishment of peaceful relations with China and his easing of Cold War tensions with the Soviet Union — not to mention President Ford's vow to whip inflation — supplanted South Vietnam's survival on the list of U.S. priorities.

Chapter Twenty-Four

Recapturing *Mayaguez*: An Epilogue

On the afternoon of May 12, 1975, not quite two weeks after the collapse of the Republic of Vietnam, the SS *Mayaguez*, an American-registered container ship, was steaming off the coast of communist Cambodia en route from Hong Kong to Sattahip in Thailand. Suddenly, the ship's radio operator sent an SOS, reporting that a Cambodian boarding party was seizing the ship. In the initial response to the SOS, a Navy P–3 patrol plane on temporary duty at U-Tapao airfield in Thailand took off shortly after 9:00 p.m. Not long afterward, a P–3 from Cubi Point Air Station in the Philippines joined the first patrol plane off Cambodia, and a third patrol craft soon arrived to help locate the ship.

During the early hours of May 13, a .50-caliber round fired from the darkness below punched a hole in the vertical stabilizer of one of the patrol planes, but the radar search continued until, when the skies brightened, one of the aircrews verified *Mayaguez* as the source of a radar return detected earlier.

The ship weighed anchor, steamed briefly toward Kompong Som, then halted near Koh Tang island, where it lay when Air Force F–111As arrived at mid-day from Thailand to escort the P–3s. Once the Air Force fighter-bombers arrived on the scene, the patrol planes expanded their activity and monitored the movement of all the small craft in the vicinity. The escorting fighters — F–111As and A–7s — kept watch over *Mayaguez* by day and AC–130 gunships took over at night, assisted by P–3s that dropped flares to illuminate the captured ship.[1]

While these aircraft found *Mayaguez* and kept it under surveillance, President Ford and his advisers were deciding the nation's reaction to the ship's capture. Within six hours after the SOS went out, the President learned of the incident. In another three hours, at 12:05 p.m. Washington time, he convened the National Security Council, which included Henry Kissinger, now Secretary of State; Lt. Gen. Brent Scowcroft, an Air Force officer serving as Deputy Assistant to the President for National Security Affairs; William Colby, representing the Central Intelligence Agency; Secretary of Defense James R. Schlesinger; and Air Force Gen. David C. Jones, Acting Chairman, Joint Chiefs of Staff, in place of Gen. George S. Brown, also of the Air Force, who was in

Air War over South Vietnam, 1968–1975

Europe. President Ford and his advisers remembered all too clearly the fate of USS *Pueblo*, an intelligence-gathering ship operated by the Navy, seized by North Korea in January 1968. At the time, the United States, caught by surprise and heavily engaged in the Southeast Asia fighting, could not intervene; as a result, the crew of *Pueblo* remained imprisoned for a year, during which their captors extorted propaganda statements, and North Korea kept the ship after freeing the crewmen.

Although uncertain whether Pol Pot and the Khmer Rouge might use the crew of *Mayaguez* for propaganda purposes or as hostages to obtain concessions of some sort from the United States, President Ford and the Security Council interpreted the capture of the ship and its thirty-nine crewmen as a challenge. Swift reaction seemed essential to punish those responsible for the deliberate affront and to restore American prestige, in decline because of the recent communist victories in Cambodia and Vietnam.

The Ford administration insisted that the War Powers Act, adopted by Congress to prevent another involvement like the Vietnam War, did not apply to the recapture of *Mayaguez*. On November 7, 1973, Congress overrode President Nixon's veto to impose restrictions on the war-making powers of the Commander in Chief, who could commit American forces only in response to a declaration of war, a specific statutory authorization, or an attack on the United States, its overseas territory, or its armed forces.

In the opinion of President Ford and his advisers, the seizure of a ship flying the American flag and steaming in international waters fit comfortably within the third category. Except in these broadly defined circumstances, the law required that the President consult with Congress, if at all possible, before committing or substantially reinforcing combat troops and, within forty-eight hours after any deployment, issue a report justifying the action. If Congress did not give after-the-fact approval, the commitment would end after sixty days, though the President might obtain an additional thirty days, presumably to ensure an orderly withdrawal.

In responding to the capture of *Mayaguez*, the President decided to consult with certain members of Congress before any military action, either advising them through his Congressional liaison machinery or conferring with them at the White House. He also proposed to submit a brief after-action report to both houses of Congress, as called for by the War Powers Act, though he continued to insist that the law did not apply.

The President had another reason for freeing the crew and recapturing the ship as quickly as possible. He hoped to avoid an extended campaign and a possible clash with Congress, which had recently refused emergency aid to South Vietnam and clearly would not approve another long-term entanglement in Southeast Asia. General Jones understood the President's emphasis on speed but nevertheless tried to persuade the National Security Council to delay the response and invest more time in planning. Ford decided, however, to strike immediately with the forces available in Southeast Asia.

Despite his insistence on speed, the President intended to respond with a degree of force proportionate to the provocation. The boarding of *Mayaguez* might have been a free-lance operation by some irresponsible local commander rather than an action ordered by the authorities at Phnom Penh. If a subordinate commander had launched the operation, area bombing of the capital city — or indeed of other targets — might kill noncombatants without punishing those who had actually committed the act of piracy. President Ford finally decided, therefore, against using B–52s, not because he did not expect the Khmer Rouge to fight but because he was trying to avoid unnecessary killing.[2]

In shaping a response to the capture of *Mayaguez*, President Ford and his principal advisers could rely on geosynchronous communications satellites to keep in touch with the major commands and use computer programs that instantly encrypted or decoded message traffic. The President, acting through Secretary of Defense Schlesinger and the National Military Command Center, maintained contact with Air Force Lt. Gen. John J. Burns, who exercised operational control as Commander, U.S. Support Activities Group/Seventh Air Force. As commander of the support activities group, Burns was responsible to the Commander in Chief, Pacific, Adm. Noel Gayler, but because he also functioned as commander of the Seventh Air Force, he looked to the Pacific Air Forces in Hawaii and Air Force headquarters in the Pentagon for administrative support. Since Gayler happened to be in Washington when the crisis erupted, he met frequently with the Joint Chiefs of Staff and thus advised Schlesinger and Ford and helped carry out their decisions.

Air War over South Vietnam, 1968–1975

Operating through an airborne battlefield command and control center, Burns would exercise operational control over Air Force units and also issue instructions and assign tasks to the naval forces and Marines. Relying on a pair of modified U–2 reconnaissance planes that provided a radio-relay link, Burns decided to remain at Nakhon Phanom and make use of its computer and communications facilities. He chose Brig. Gen. Walter H. Baxter, III, who commanded the 13th Air Force Advance Echelon, an administrative headquarters at Udorn, to serve as senior planner at U-Tapao. Baxter's assistant, Col. R. B. Janca, joined him at U-Tapao and took over the combat support group there. Burns sent Col. Robert R. Reed, his Deputy Chief, Operations Division, from Nakhon Phanom to U-Tapao to act as his troubleshooter. Col. Lloyd J. Anders reported to U-Tapao and assumed command of helicopter operations, while Col. William P. Pannell became his operations officer, essentially the same duties Anders and Pannell had performed on the aircraft carrier *Midway* during the evacuation of Saigon.[3]

The evacuations from the Cambodian and South Vietnamese capitals imposed wear and tear on the warships that had helped carry out the operations, limiting the resources available for the liberation of *Mayaguez* and its crew. The assault carrier *Okinawa* could not steam faster than eighteen knots because of a broken-down boiler and would be unable to move its Marine helicopters — which could not refuel in mid-air — to within operating range of the captured ship. A failed valve had temporarily disabled *Hancock*, an attack carrier that had operated helicopters at Saigon. Fortunately, another attack carrier, *Coral Sea*, was steaming toward Australia to commemorate the anniversary of the battle for which it was named, an action fought in May 1942 that ended the threat of a Japanese invasion.

Coral Sea had not yet cleared Indonesian waters and could quickly steam into position to launch aircraft in support of a rescue attempt. Besides *Coral Sea* and her escorts, the destroyer escort *Harold E. Holt* (subsequently redesignated a frigate), the guided missile destroyer *Henry B. Wilson*, and the stores ship *Vega* converged on the scene.

Coral Sea carried only two unarmed SH–3 helicopters used as lifeguards when the ship launched or recovered aircraft. Neither *Okinawa* nor *Hancock* could participate, which eliminated Marine Corps helicopters from the rescue operation. By default, the task of landing the assault troops devolved upon two Air Force helicopter outfits, the 21st Special Operations Squadron, assigned ten CH–53Cs, and the 40th Aerospace Rescue and Recovery Squadron, with a maximum of nine HH–53Cs. Unlike most Marine Corps and Army helicopter units, the Air Force squadrons had not trained to land infantrymen in assault operations; instead, they had conducted rescues, if necessary braving deadly fire, or inserted agents and patrols in lightly defended areas.

The 40th Aerospace Rescue and Recovery Squadron had saved downed airmen throughout Southeast Asia, cooperating with escorting fighters and

Recapturing *Mayaguez*

HC–130P aerial tankers. The 21st Special Operations Squadron had landed reconnaissance or combat patrols, often cooperating more closely with the Central Intelligence Agency than with Air Force organizations. The Jolly Greens of the 40th — so called because the squadron had borrowed as its symbol the Jolly Green Giant, adapted from the advertising of a company that marketed canned and frozen vegetables — differed in experience and training from the 21st Special Operations Squadron, which used the call sign Knife. Whereas the Knives employed stealth in their operations, stalking and thrusting rather than overpowering, the 40th Aerospace Rescue and Recovery Squadron refueled in the air to fly long missions and, with the help of escorting fighters, sometimes overcame strong defenses. Moreover, the HH–53, flown by the Jolly Greens, had better communications than the CH–53, along with explosion-retardant foam in its 450-gallon external auxiliary fuel tanks and a third multibarrel gun that fired rearward over the open loading ramp. The CH–53 operated by the Knives had just two side-firing multibarrel guns and 650-gallon external fuel tanks that lacked protection against explosion.[4]

Besides the nineteen helicopters, not all of them operational, the Air Force had a strong force of other aircraft based in Thailand. Udorn served as the base for 24 RF–4C reconnaissance planes, along with 36 F–4E and 36 F–4D fighters. Korat housed 18 F–111As, 18 F–4Es, 24 A–7Ds, 17 AC–130 gunships, and 5 HC–130Ps. Besides the CH–53 and HH–53 helicopters, Nakhon Phanom provided accommodations for 40 OV–10 observation craft, used by forward air controllers. In liberating the ship and crew, these aircraft could stage as necessary through U-Tapao, the Thai airfield closest to the scene.[5]

Because of the Cooper-Church Amendment, the United States could not maintain ground forces in Thailand to complement the aerial armada. The troops to free the ship and crew would have to come from Marine units on Okinawa and in the Philippines. A reinforced rifle company from the 1st Battalion, 4th Marines — five officers and 115 enlisted men — boarded an Air Force C–141 on the morning of May 14 and flew from Cubi Point in the Philippines to U-Tapao, landing before 5:00 a.m. On Okinawa, a battalion landing team, led by Lt. Col. Randall Austin and drawn from the 2d Battalion, 9th Marines, started boarding Air Force transports during the morning of the 14th. By 8:30 p.m., the landing team had reached U-Tapao, where it reported to Marine Col. John M. Johnson, Jr., the ground forces commander. In the meantime, the Air Force helicopters had deployed from Nakhon Phanom to U-Tapao. Seven CH–53s of the 21st Special Operations Squadron arrived there, as did three Jolly Green HH–53s.

Before the helicopters left Nakhon Phanom, the U.S. Support Activities Group/Seventh Air Force decided to have them deploy seventy-five volunteers from the 656th Security Police Squadron to U-Tapao. If the Marines were delayed, the airmen, though ill-prepared for offensive operations, could attempt on the morning of May 14 to liberate the container ship and any merchant sailors on board. One of the Knife helicopters crashed en route to U-Tapao, killing eighteen security police and the crew of five. The accident forced the headquarters at Nakhon Phanom to abandon the idea of using airmen to effect the rescue. Fortunately, the special operations squadron managed to make emergency repairs to another CH–53 and replace the one that had been destroyed.[6]

The detachment of Marines from Cubi Point in the Philippines, under Maj. Raymond E. Porter, boarded their assigned Air Force helicopters at noon on May 14, waited two hours for orders to attack *Mayaguez* that never came, then disembarked. Authorities at Washington, perhaps President Ford himself, decided against an essentially improvised assault on a ship that might prove heavily defended. When General Burns' planners learned that the room-sized containers covering most of the deck of *Mayaguez* could not support the weight of a helicopter, they ruled out an attack from the air. The ship would have to be recovered in the same way it had been captured — by a boarding party.[7]

Late in the afternoon of May 13, before the Marines reached U-Tapao and while the helicopters were still arriving, aerial surveillance revealed two small craft alongside the container ship. One of them, a fishing boat, cast off and headed for Koh Tang island with some forty persons on board, seated on deck, their heads on their knees. Other sightings indicated that the men — described as Caucasian, whereas many of the captured crew members were Oriental — had landed at Koh Tang and moved inland.

If these were the captives, the next logical step seemed to be to prevent the Khmer Rouge from taking the prisoners to the mainland, where they might disappear into prison camps. The White House issued orders, passed along by General Scowcroft, to "sink anything coming off Koh Tang." On the early morning of May 14, fire from an AC–130 gunship forced a Cambodian patrol boat to run aground on an islet near Koh Tang. Later, at dawn, a fishing boat escorted by patrol craft set out from the island for the port of Kompong Som on the mainland. Air Force A–7s sank the patrol boats and sprayed tear gas on the other craft. Secretary of Defense Schlesinger refused, however, to approve sinking the fishing boat; he stalled for time to make sure the prisoners were not on board. When a Navy pilot reported seeing Caucasians on the fishing craft, Schlesinger persuaded the President to suspend the sink-on-sight order and allow the boat to proceed.

Schlesinger's reluctance to sink every boat leaving Koh Tang almost certainly saved the lives of the captives, who were indeed on board this particular craft. When the cloud of tear gas enveloped the deck, captors and prisoners suffered alike. Blinded by gas and struggling for breath, the men of *Mayaguez* could not seize control. Whenever the Thai helmsman tried to change course for the open sea, one of the guards, who somehow fought off the effects of the gas, leveled his weapon until the bow of the fishing boat again pointed toward the mainland.[8]

Recapturing *Mayaguez*

Cambodian patrol boat resting on the bottom east of Koh Tang Island.

Consultation between Burns and his superiors in Hawaii and at Washington resulted in a revised plan for recovering *Mayaguez* and the captured crew. A Marine boarding party would seize the container ship at the same time that other Marines stormed Koh Tang island, where at least some of the sailors might still be held. The two operations were scheduled for precisely 5:42 a.m., an hour specified by the Joint Chiefs of Staff. The time did not coincide with either sunrise or the beginning of morning nautical twilight — the earliest that a rifleman could see to fire an aimed shot or a pilot to deliver an air strike — and raised questions about the wisdom of trying to issue minutely detailed orders from the other side of the globe.

A third element rounded out the operations plan. While the Marine landing team attacked Koh Tang and the smaller detachment boarded *Mayaguez*, the carrier *Coral Sea* would launch air strikes against military sites on the mainland to punish the communist authorities responsible for the incident. The timetable called for hitting Kompong Som and the other targets after the recapture of the ship and the landing at Koh Tang. Once they began, the attacks on the mainland went ahead independently of the fighting on Koh Tang and continued after the capture of the container ship and recovery of its crew.[9]

The planners could not be sure whether the Khmer Rouge had moved all the prisoners to Kompong Som or left some of them on Koh Tang. Even if all the captives had been carried off to the mainland, seizing the island seemed important as a demonstration of U.S. resolve. The conquest of Koh Tang might well persuade the Cambodian communists to release the crew members, wherever they were held.

The attacking Marines, moreover, did not have up-to-the-minute details on the island's defenses. Although Lt. Col. David Metz, commander of one of the AC–130 gunships that maintained surveillance by night, reported being fired upon by a 40-mm antiaircraft gun, intelligence specialists believed that nothing

433

Air War over South Vietnam, 1968–1975

larger than heavy machineguns protected Koh Tang. The Defense Intelligence Agency in Washington, D.C., and the Pacific Command's intelligence section in Hawaii estimated the strength of the island garrison at between 90 and 200 soldiers armed with recoilless rifles, mortars, and machineguns. These estimates failed somehow — perhaps because of restrictions on access to certain categories of information — to reach the Marines, who believed when they prepared to set out for Koh Tang that the island's garrison consisted of 20 or 30 guerrillas. Not until the first wave was boarding its helicopters did the Marines see aerial photos that revealed bunkers overlooking the invasion beaches.

Even if the larger estimates of enemy strength proved true, a savage preliminary aerial bombardment could silence the deadliest weapons or discourage the gunners, enabling the helicopters to disgorge the landing force, but planners ruled out the preparatory strikes because of the danger to any prisoners who might be on the island. For this reason, a proposal to use Air Force C–130 transports to drop 15,000-pound bombs and blast landing zones in the jungle met prompt rejection, a decision which meant that the helicopters would have to land the Marines on the exposed beach. Because so few helicopters were available, the same aircraft would have to participate in successive waves, and losses could reduce the overall landing force until it was dangerously close to the strength of the defenders.[10]

After an Army U–21 liaison plane flew some of the senior Marine officers on a final reconnaissance of Koh Tang — a mission that revealed very little about the defenses because the aircraft had no sensors capable of penetrating the jungle — Colonel Johnson issued orders for the detachment from the 1st Battalion, 4th Marines, to board and seize *Mayaguez*, while the 2d Battalion, 9th Marines, attacked Koh Tang island. The force assaulting the island had to leave its 4.2-inch mortars at U-Tapao because the cumbersome weapons and heavy ammunition would displace too many infantrymen from the few available helicopters. Once the battle began, air power would have to make up for the absent heavy mortars.

Two tactical fighter wings, the 432d at Udorn and the 347th at Korat, had the mission of providing air support, carrying weapons specified in the daily operations order from the Support Activities Group/Seventh Air Force. An airborne battlefield command and control center was to coordinate the aerial activity through a fighter pilot serving as on-scene commander, while forward air controllers directed the strikes. Both the forward air controllers and on-scene commanders would fly the A–7, the only tactical fighter that had a radio compatible with the type of set used by the Marines. Since the A–7s could maintain contact with the assault force, General Burns decided against using the OV–10s and the skilled forward air controllers that flew them because he did not want to "clog up" the already crowded facilities at U-Tapao.

The recovery of *Mayaguez* and the liberation of the crew began on the morning of May 15, but fell behind schedule. Three Air Force HH–53s delivered the boarding party to USS *Holt*. The force assigned to capture the container ship consisted of fifty-nine Marines, six volunteer seaman from the Military Sealift Command, two Air Force specialists in disarming explosives, and an Army interpreter. The transfer from helicopter to the compact landing pad on the warship proved time-consuming. Because the broad ramp at the rear of the huge helicopter opened over the water, each Jolly Green had to hover in succession, while the passengers disembarked in single file through the crew's access door near the front.

Not until 6:30 a.m. did the destroyer escort take the last Marine on board and started toward *Mayaguez*. Some forty-five minutes later, a flight of A–7s doused the container ship with tear gas released from under-wing dispensers. *Holt* came alongside, and the boarding party found no one on board the merchant ship, which the destroyer escort promptly took in tow.[11]

While the boarding party was retaking *Mayaguez*, USS *Henry B. Wilson*, a guided missile destroyer, arrived on the scene after steaming for forty-eight hours, sustaining a speed of thirty-one knots. The skipper, Comdr. J. Michael Rodgers, checked in with the airborne battlefield command and control center, which assumed he was a naval aviator, rather than a ship's captain, and assigned him an altitude of 10,000 feet. Once the misconception had been corrected, Wilson closed with the island. A lookout spotted men in the water, and the destroyer rescued the survivors of Knife 31, a CH–53 shot down off the eastern beach.

At 9:30 a.m., the pilot of a P–3 patrol plane advised Rodgers of a boat approaching his ship. *Wilson* picked up the intruder on radar, closed the range, and stood ready to open fire, when the telescopic lens of the fire-control television revealed that the boat carried what might be the crew of *Mayaguez*. Over his ship's loudspeaker, Rodgers asked "Are you the crew of *Mayaguez*?" The seamen answered that they were and that all hands were on board the fishing craft. "Lay alongside," the skipper directed, "You are safe now." The prisoners had been released and the ship recovered, but the bitter fight for Koh Tang had barely begun.[12]

The hurriedly drafted plan for seizing Koh Tang entrusted the operation to the 2d Battalion, 9th Marines — organized as a battalion landing team — which would attack in three waves. Company G, under Capt. James H. Davis, was to lead the way, landing at the neck of a diamond-shaped headland at the northern tip of the island. A reinforced platoon, accompanied by Captain Davis, had the mission of attacking from the west and blocking access from the southern part of the island. The rest of the company, along with the battalion commander, Colonel Austin, would land from the east. The entire company then faced the task of clearing the headland to the north and seizing Hill 440 to the south, the dominant terrain feature in this part of the island. Meanwhile, the helicopters that landed these Marines would return to U-Tapao for the second wave, made up of Company E. After landing this unit to reinforce Company G, the

Air War over South Vietnam, 1968–1975

U.S. Marines, wearing gasmasks, board the *Mayaguez*.

helicopters were to pick up the rest of the battalion, organized as a third wave, and fly it to the Koh Tang beachhead.

Eleven helicopters stood ready to launch the day's operations, but three of them were committed to delivering the boarding party to the destroyer escort *Holt*. Because of the shortage of Knife and Jolly Green aircraft, the ground force commander, Colonel Johnson, chose to keep his command element at U-Tapao and direct the operation from there, instead of deploying with the landing team. This decision emphasized the role of the airborne battlefield command and control center in linking Johnson with his Marines. Nevertheless, during the formal briefing at 1:00 a.m. on the morning of May 15, no representatives of the airborne control center participated, nor did an intelligence specialist, who might have presented the latest estimates of enemy strength that had arrived from Washington and Hawaii and caused a radical change of plan, such as conducting extensive preliminary air strikes.[13]

The three HH–53s bound for USS *Holt* took off at 4:14 a.m., and within eleven minutes, the four HH–53s and four CH–53s carrying the first wave set out for Koh Tang. Tracers fired from boats occasionally arced into the darkened sky, but the helicopters sustained no damage en route to the objective. At approximately 6:00 a.m., eighteen minutes after the prescribed time — and at about the same time the boarding party began transferring from the helicopters to the deck of *Holt* — Knife 22 and 21 approached the western beach while Knife 23 and 31 prepared to land Marines on the opposite shore.

Lt. Col. John H. Denham, at the controls of Knife 21, encountered no fire from inland of the western beach as he touched down on the sand, nose pointed seaward, and lowered the ramp so the Marines could run from the aircraft. When the Marines began emerging, the defenders cut loose with rifles, machineguns, and mortars, knocking out one of the helicopter's jet engines. Denham and his copilot, 1st Lt. Karl W. Poulsen, dropped the external fuel tanks and jettisoned additional fuel, lightening the aircraft and enabling Knife 21 to stagger out to sea.

To cover the escape of Denham's helicopter, Capt. Terry Ohlemeier, whose Knife 22 had begun hovering over the landing site, made two passes along the beach and unleashed a hail of fire inland. On board the aircraft, Captain Davis, the company commander, was hit in the face by a spent round, and another bullet, which fortunately had also lost velocity, lodged in the safety harness worn by one of Ohlemeier's door gunners. Knife 22 gushed fuel from its punctured external tanks as the pilot broke off the action and followed Denham, whose helicopter crashed some 300 yards from shore. Although barely able to control his damaged helicopter, which still had its Marines on board, Ohlemeier orbited the wreckage until another CH–53 arrived, lowered its hoist, and plucked Denham, Poulsen, and one of the other crew members from the sea.[14]

The Cambodian gunners peering across the eastern beach, who may have been alerted by the sound of firing behind them, blazed away at 1st Lt. John Schramm's Knife 23 when it landed. The fusillade knocked out an engine and shattered the tail pylon. Miraculously, all on board survived. Twenty Marines, led by 2d Lt. Michael Cicere, ran from the wrecked aircraft toward the tree line, while Schramm and his crew remained for a few minutes in the shattered fuselage and struggled unsuccessfully to establish radio contact with the airborne battlefield command and control center. When the crew members abandoned the wreckage and ran toward the Marines, fire from the tree line wounded one of them, SSgt. Ronald Gross. After linking up with the Marines, 1st Lt. John P. Lucas, Schramm's copilot, used an emergency radio, normally for contacting rescuers, and summoned air support.

Just short of the eastern beach, Knife 31, flown by Maj. Richard Corson, with 2d Lt. Richard Vandegeer as copilot, ran into a wall of fire that killed Vandegeer, ripped open an external fuel tank, and ignited the fuel spilling out. Although wounded, Corson succeeded in crash landing the burning CH–53 in about four feet of water, a short distance offshore. One of the crew, SSgt. Jon Harston, directed some Marines trapped inside Knife 31 to an open hatch. One Marine, who had waded clear of the downed aircraft, returned and tried unsuccessfully to free the copilot from his harness, not realizing the flier was already dead. Of the twenty-six on board the helicopter, eighteen survived the crash, but several of these had suffered burns or wounds. Five more died in the shallow water off Koh Tang before the guided missile destroyer *Wilson* picked up the thirteen survivors.

Marine air controller 1st Lt. Terry Tonkin lived through the crash of Knife 31 and for roughly two hours, until the battery gave out, made use of an Air Force emergency radio to call in air strikes against targets he could see from the surf. For a time he directed the strikes while swimming on his back. Meanwhile,

Air War over South Vietnam, 1968–1975

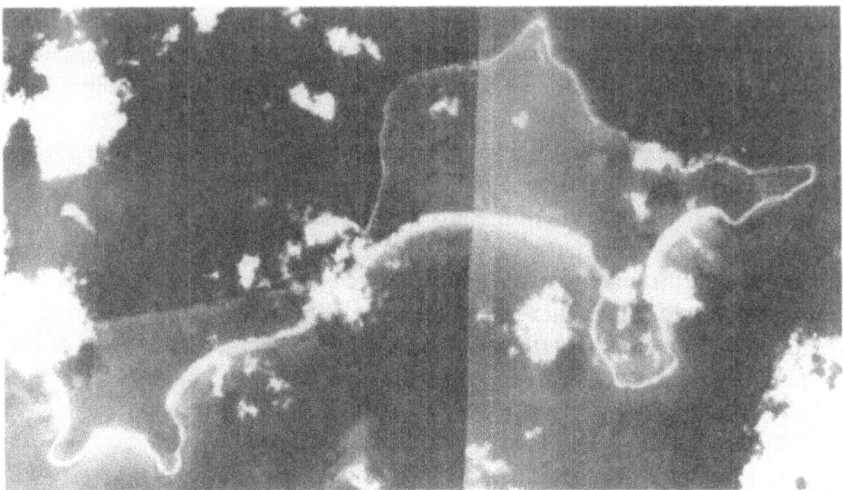

Koh Tang Island, with north to the right. The eastern beach landing area is the curved white area on the far right portion of the island. The western landing area is the small white area just above the eastern beach.

the copilot of the downed Knife 23, Lieutenant Lucas, was using his own emergency transmitter to arrange air support for the men on the eastern beach.

The violent reaction to the appearance of the first four helicopters caused the second four to hold off. Knife 32, flown by 1st Lt. Michael Lackey and his copilot, 2d Lt. Calvin O. Wachs, changed course from the eastern beach, rescued three members of the crew of Denham's Knife 21, which had crashed off the western beach, and spent half an hour searching unsuccessfully for the fourth man. Jolly Green 41 stood by as backup for Lackey's craft, and two other HH–53s, Jolly Green 42 and 43, orbited north of the island awaiting clarification of the situation on the island.[15]

Word of what was happening on Koh Tang came from a platoon leader, 2d Lt. James McDaniel, who, shortly after landing, managed to contact the airborne battlefield command and control center on the Marine tactical radio net. He reported that his men had succeeded in carving out a small beachhead extending perhaps fifty yards inland from the western shoreline. His message arrived just after the control center cleared the three orbiting helicopters — Knife 32, Jolly Green 42, and Jolly Green 43 — to land as planned on the eastern beach. Since two helicopters had already been shot down there — Knife 23 on the beach and Knife 31 offshore — Lackey asked the airborne controllers whether they really wanted him to use that same fiercely defended stretch of beach and was told to land from the west instead.

When 1st Lt. Philip Pacini in Jolly Green 42 heard this transmission, he asked if his aircraft and Jolly Green 43 were to continue their approach to the eastern beach. The controller promptly diverted them to the western beach, where they would land along with Lackey's CH–53, Knife 32. The change of plan surprised the pilots of the A–7s circling overhead, who advised the airborne battlefield command and control center that the helicopters were headed in the wrong direction.

The direction was correct, despite the concerns of the A–7 pilots, but Pacini quickly realized that he had chosen the wrong landing zone — an area south of the perimeter — and turned away for another try. With Colonel Austin and the 2d Battalion's command group on board, Jolly Green 43, flown by Capt. Roland W. Purser and his copilot, 1st Lt. Robert P. Gradle, headed for the proper landing zone, only to be beaten back by Cambodian fire. Of the three helicopters, only Knife 32 reached McDaniel's perimeter on the first try, landing thirteen Marines, but in doing so, the CH–53 sustained severe damage. Although Lackey nursed the craft safely back to U-Tapao, it could no longer take part in the operation.

About three minutes after Lackey had turned out to sea, Pacini succeeded in bringing in his Marines, among them 1st Lt. James D. Keith, the executive officer of Company G, thus increasing the force on Koh Tang to about sixty. Purser's Jolly Green 43 touched down a few minutes later on the landing zone that Pacini had rejected. Austin, his command element, and a mortar section — a total of twenty-nine Marines — sprinted down the ramp, advanced inland, and formed a perimeter about three-quarters of a mile from Keith's men.[16]

Another helicopter carrying part of the first wave, Jolly Green 41, tried to land its Marines on the western beach, only to be repulsed. The pilot and copilot, 1st Lt. Thomas D. Cooper and 1st Lt. David W. Keith, refueled Jolly Green 41 from an aerial tanker and made two more unsuccessful attempts to land. Cooper and Keith made a fourth attempt at about 10:00 a.m., landing twenty Marines before hostile fire inflicted further damage on the helicopter and forced it to take off with five members of the first wave still on board.

Over the years, a command structure had evolved for rescue operations that depended on an HC–130 functioning as an airborne battlefield command and control center specifically for the rescue. The airborne controller used the radio call sign King while coordinating the work of helicopters and escorting fighters. The flaming crash of Knife 31 earlier in the morning alerted the pilot of the HC–130 circling overhead that the assault on the eastern beach had run into trouble. He set up a rescue operation, relying on an A–7 pilot trained in such activity to take command. As part of the hastily organized rescue effort, Jolly Green 13, which had flown part of the *Mayaguez* boarding party to USS *Holt*, landed on the eastern beach, not to reinforce the few Marines there but to evacuate them along with the surviving crew members of Knife 23.

Neither the pilot of Jolly Green 13, 1st Lt. Charles Greer, nor his copilot, 1st Lt. Charles Brown, had been under fire before. As their helicopter waited with lowered ramp, they assumed that the thud of enemy rounds striking the aircraft was the sound of Marine boots pounding against the cabin floor. When bullets passing over the ramp began tearing into the cabin and shattering the glass enclosing some of the instruments, they realized their error and took off empty. By that time, enemy rounds had ignited a flare container, which SSgt. Steven Lemmin threw overboard, and punctured a fuel tank that fortunately contained an explosion-retardant chemical.[17]

The first wave had seized a precarious foothold on the island. Instead of facing a few irregulars, the Marines and the airmen who flew them into combat had collided with two companies of trained soldiers, supported by heavy weapons and protected by log bunkers. The assault struck the island's strongest defenses. Instead of rapidly pinching off the headland and easily destroying the garrison, the attackers were fighting for their lives.[18]

As early as 6:20 a.m., Air Force A–7s, possibly responding to a message over the emergency radio that Marine Lieutenant Tonkin had borrowed, strafed positions inland of the eastern beach. The pilots, however, had great difficulty locating the hostile weapons the Marines wanted them to attack. Moreover, at about 7:00 a.m., the first of the A–7s refueled from KC–135 tankers for the return flight to Korat, and the pilot of an F–4, which did not have a radio that could tie into the Marine tactical net, briefly took command.

By mid-morning, air support had improved. An AC–130 opened fire on bunkers pointed out by the Marines, knocking out the strongpoints with 105-mm rounds that penetrated roofs, exploded inside, and scattered the logs of the walls like a child's building blocks. Fourteen 105-mm shells, along with a deluge of 20-mm and 40-mm fire, bought time for the Marines to consolidate the western beachhead. In addition, the pilot of one of the A–7s now on station functioned as a forward air controller, directing F–4s against other strongholds.[19]

Although exercising command from U-Tapao and in only sporadic contact with the Marines on Koh Tang, Colonel Johnson, the Marine ground force commander, realized that the survival of the assault troops depended on their immediate reinforcement. He had the rest of the 2d Battalion, 9th Marines, at his disposal, but too many helicopters had either failed to return or come back with damage that grounded them. Only five helicopters stood ready to carry a second wave to the island. Captain Purser's Jolly Green 43 remained flyable after returning from delivering a portion of the first wave to a landing zone south of the western beachhead. Jolly Green 11 and 12 had returned directly to U-Tapao from USS *Holt*. Knife 52 had undergone needed maintenance and now was ready, as was Knife 51, which had been loaded with Marines, dispatched to Koh Tang and then recalled.[20]

Knife 52 — with 1st Lt. Robert E. Rakitis and his copilot, 2d Lt. David J. Lykens, at the controls — took off by 9:30 a.m., along with Purser's Jolly Green 43. Within half an hour, Jolly Green 11, 1st Lt. Donald W. Backlund and 1st Lt. Gary L. Weikel, set out for the island, together with Jolly Green 12, flown by Capt. Paul L. Jacobs, pilot, and Capt. Martin A. Nickerson, copilot. At about

10:10 a.m., Knife 51, with 1st Lt. Richard C. Brims the pilot and 2d Lt. Dennis L. Danielson his copilot, joined the second wave after refueling.[21]

The reinforcements had barely taken off when word arrived "to immediately cease all offensive operations" against the Cambodians and to "disengage and withdraw all forces from the operating area as soon as possible."[22] These instructions, subsequently confirmed by a formal message, originated with President Ford and his advisers and traveled over the satellite communications network. Indeed, the satellite system beamed a torrent of messages — advice, instructions, and requests for information — that tended to distract senior commanders from the perilous situation on Koh Tang and thus blunted Colonel Johnson's arguments for rapid reinforcement. The embattled Marines clinging to the western beachhead, for example, received a message from the support activities group asking if they had a bullhorn and a translator, presumably to parley with the enemy. Questions like this underscored the failure of some higher headquarters to understand the tactical situation and their insatiable desire for nonessential detail.[23]

The order to disengage infuriated Colonel Johnson, who realized that the Marines on Koh Tang did not control the landing zones necessary for a successful withdrawal. "We don't even own the beach yet!" he reportedly shouted. "Let's see us get off a piece of property we don't even own."[24] The order also triggered vehement protests from those pilots of the second wave who best understood the situation on the island. General Burns paid attention to the complaints of his helicopter pilots, and the Commanding General, Fleet Marine Force, Pacific, added his voice to the chorus of protest. As a result, the second wave continued toward Koh Tang.[25]

While the second wave was drawing near the island, Colonel Austin tried to link up with the main perimeter on the western beach, but a strongpoint blocked the way. Austin's force included a mortar section, commanded by 2d Lt. Joseph J. McMenamin, which cooperated with attacking fighters in neutralizing the Cambodian forces that stood between the two groups of Marines. Acting on instructions from Lieutenant Keith in the main perimeter and Capt. Barry Cassidy, Austin's Marine air liaison officer, the Air Force fighters attacked with 500-pound bombs and 20-mm cannon. After each pass by the aircraft, the mortar section cut loose. The combination enabled a platoon from the larger group to reach Austin and his men and bring them into the perimeter.

Shortly before noon, as the two contingents of Marines were joining forces and beating back a Cambodian attack, Jolly Green 11 and 12 arrived off the western beach. Each, in turn, fired inland to suppress the defenses while the other landed its men. Jolly Green 12, commanded by Captain Jacobs, waited on the sands until the Marines had loaded four of their wounded, whom the helicopter flew to U-Tapao.

In spite of the fierce resistance encountered at the eastern beach, the airborne battlefield command and control center directed the other three helicopters to land there. Lieutenant Rakitis led the way in Knife 52, but enemy fire tore into the craft and prevented it from touching down. The CH–53 lurched across the neck of the island, fuel gushing from its ruptured tanks, but the crew managed to fly the damaged helicopter to Thailand, with the Marines still on board. After Knife 52 had been driven off, Knife 51 and Jolly Green 43 diverted to the western beach, where they landed their Marines, increasing the force there to roughly 200. Knife 51 then evacuated five wounded men.[26]

After landing the reinforcements, Jolly Green 43, flown by Purser and Gradle, and Jolly Green 11, Backlund and Weikel, stood by near Koh Tang to rescue the twenty-odd Marines and the survivors of Knife 23 from the eastern beach. Purser's HH–53 went first, attempting to take advantage of a screen of riot-control gas dispensed from A–7s, the kind of chemical agent used against the abandoned *Mayaguez*. The helicopter crew donned gas masks, but the A–7s placed the screen across the approach path of Jolly Green 43. As a result, the helicopter passed almost instantly through the cloud and was silhouetted against it for gunners unaffected by the tear gas.

Fire from heavy machineguns severed the fuel line that fed the left engine. Fuel gushed into the passenger compartment, vaporized, and spewed out over the lowered ramp forming a plume that extended 150 yards behind the struggling aircraft. Luckily, *Coral Sea* had steamed to within seventy miles of the island, and Purser had just enough fuel to land on board. The rapid approach of the aircraft carrier not only saved Jolly Green 43 and its crew but would enable other helicopters to avoid the time-consuming flight all the way to U-Tapao.

Naval gunfire may have helped Jolly Green 43 escape destruction. At about 1:00 p.m., before the failed rescue attempt, *Henry B. Wilson* contacted the airborne battlefield command and control center and volunteered to provide fire support from the waters off the eastern beach. While *Harold E. Holt*, with *Mayaguez* still in tow, remained off the western shore, *Wilson* began its bombardment, using a rock jutting from the sea as a reference point. The ship fired a round that exploded near that rock; A–7 pilots saw the splash and adjusted the gunfire by radioing successive changes that walked the shells onto a target ashore.

During the afternoon of May 15, two additional Jolly Greens landed at U-Tapao along with four OV–10A Broncos, the turboprop aircraft used so effectively by forward air controllers during the fighting in South Vietnam, Laos, and Cambodia. Two of the Broncos, flown by Maj. Robert W. Undorf and Capt. Robert Roehrkasse, both trained forward air controllers, arrived over Koh Tang before 4:30 p.m., made contact with the Marines, and began firing smoke rockets to mark targets for fighter-bombers. The work of the OV–10s, along with continued fire from *Wilson's* five-inch guns, set the stage for another attempt to retrieve the men on the eastern beach.[27]

The previous tries had encountered deadly fire from a patrol boat aground off the beach, its decks awash. The Cambodian gunners on board took cover when fighter-bombers appeared, but emerged to fire a pair of heavy machineguns whenever a helicopter started toward shore. *Wilson* eliminated this danger at 4:33 p.m. with twenty-two five-inch shells that ripped the grounded boat to shreds. Meanwhile, Major Undorf, flying one of the OV–10s, directed strikes along the eastern beach, and *Wilson's* gig cruised off the island, firing a .50-caliber machinegun at targets ashore. After a final barrage that included fire from an Air Force gunship, Undorf cleared Backlund to dart in and pick up the men. Undorf and Roehrkasse strafed the Cambodian defenders, silencing a machinegun just north of the beach as Backlund touched down at 6:20 p.m. The Marines fired as they fell back, holding off the advancing enemy long enough for all twenty-five survivors to scramble up the ramp to safety. Backlund raced the jet engines, and the craft roared out to sea, bullets fired from shore churning the sea behind it.[28]

As Jolly Green 11 got away, an Air Force C–130 dropped a 15,000-pound bomb near the center of the island, 1,000 yards south of the western perimeter. Stacked on a pallet, the explosives separated from the extraction parachute and harness, drifted earthward under the main parachute, and exploded with a violence that jolted the Marines, who had no idea that such a weapon would be used. The harness and extraction chute had not yet settled to earth when the bomb exploded, and the Marines who saw the second parachute assumed it meant that another bomb was drifting toward them. Men dug with tools or even finger nails, as the chute and harness flopped to earth some forty yards from the perimeter.

Intended to demoralize the enemy, the bomb had a similar effect on some of the Marines; indeed, at least one officer worried that a huge bomb lay nearby waiting to be detonated by friendly or enemy fire. No wonder the Marine battalion insisted in its after-action report that the commander on the ground be advised of plans to use any aerial ordnance like the 15,000-pound bomb. Whatever the impact on Marine morale, the huge bomb may have disrupted a Cambodian attempt to move reinforcements northward and attack the perimeter in overwhelming numbers.[29]

Once Backlund's Jolly Green 11 had plucked the Marines and airmen from the eastern beach, Jolly Green 12 — now flown by Capt. Barry R. Walls and 1st Lt. Richard L. Comer — got word to rescue someone believed to have taken refuge in the wreckage of Knife 23, off the beach where Backlund had effected the rescue. While Knife 51 laid down covering fire, Walls hovered over the crashed helicopter, and Sgt. Jesus P. DeJesus lowered the hoist, but no one was awaiting rescue in the shattered aircraft. The enemy, who had been shooting at Backlund's aircraft now concentrated on Walls' hovering helicopter, wounding DeJesus and badly damaging the aircraft, which limped to an emergency landing on *Coral Sea*.[30]

In keeping with President Ford's earlier decision, General Burns had decided to immediately pull out the Marines, taking advantage of the approach of

Air War over South Vietnam, 1968–1975

During the rescue of the Marines and airmen trapped on the eastern beach, Jolly Green 11 hovers over the beach, its ramp down in the rocks and surf.

Coral Sea, which would speed the withdrawal by eliminating the need to fly all the way to Thailand before unloading the troops removed from the island. His decision, however, failed to reach Colonel Johnson at U-Tapao or Colonel Austin on the island. Undorf recalled that, at this critical moment, he could not make radio contact with the airborne battlefield command and control center and advised Austin that, though he could use the helicopters already on the scene to evacuate the Marines, he could not be sure that aircraft would be available to fly in additional reinforcements. According to Burns, the battalion commander on the beachhead faced the choice of withdrawing immediately or holding out overnight, probably without further reinforcement, and decided to withdraw. Clearly, Austin expected to withdraw, for the Marines began shortening their lines and collecting the wounded as evening approached, but the commander of the Marine landing team remained unsure of the exact timing until the first of the evacuation helicopters started toward the beach.[31]

Holding off the Cambodians, difficult to begin with, would be all the more dangerous because the few available helicopters would have to return to the island for additional men, thus prolonging the operation as the number of Marines dwindled. One of the two HH–53s that had arrived at U-Tapao during the afternoon — designated Jolly Green 44 and flown by a crew commanded by 1st Lt. Robert D. Blough — could participate along with Jolly Green 43, which had undergone emergency repairs on *Coral Sea*, and Knife 51. Two unarmed SH–3s from *Coral Sea*, their only firepower provided by the M–16 rifles of a few Marines on board, served as backup for the Air Force craft. The gig from *Wilson* had sailed around to the western beach, and *Holt*, no longer towing the container ship, could lower two boats if some Marines had to be rescued by sea.

An AC–130 gunship, with low-light-level television capable of penetrating the deepening twilight, might provide the firepower that would keep the enemy at bay. Although the gunship could fire at night with deadly effect, darkness posed a handicap for the helicopter crews. Since there would be no moon and few stars visible during the withdrawal, pilots would have to rely exclusively on their flight instruments to avoid becoming disoriented.[32]

At about 6:40 p.m., some twenty minutes after sunset, Knife 51 headed for the beach to pick up the first of the Marines, who had no warning that the helicopter was about to land. Although caught by surprise, the Marines reacted instantly. The battalion surgeon got the wounded on board, and Brims and his crew carried a total of forty-one Marines out to *Coral Sea*.

The enemy also reacted to the arrival of Knife 51, hurling grenades into the perimeter, where the Marines threw some of them back, illuminating the beach with flares, and firing high-explosive mortar shells. Circling in his OV–10 above the western beach, Undorf spotted the mortar position, but the A–7 pilots could not see the smoke from the rocket he fired to mark it.

The crew of Purser's Jolly Green 43, which landed seven minutes after Brims touched down, loaded fifty-four Marines, including Lieutenant Keith, the executive officer of Company G, who had landed from one of the second echelon of helicopters in the morning's first wave. Keith later recalled hearing mortar rounds exploding on the sand as his men boarded Purser's helicopter.

While the blacked-out Jolly Green 43 was loading, Jolly Green 44 approached the landing zone. Radio traffic alerted Purser's copilot, Lieutenant Gradle, that the incoming aircraft could not see his helicopter, increasing the likelihood of a collision. Gradle flashed Jolly Green 43's searchlight, and the pilot of the approaching aircraft, Lieutenant Blough, turned away, allowing the other helicopter to take off safely and head for *Coral Sea*. Blough then made a second approach, only to be driven away by fire from the ground, but the pilot and crew persisted, landing at 6:54 p.m. Machinegun fire from *Wilson's* gig and Undorf's OV–10 suppressed the deadliest Cambodian weapons during the three minutes Jolly Green 44 needed to load forty Marines and take off.[33]

Only seventy-odd Marines remained on the island after Blough's departure. For effective fire support, they had to depend on the AC–130 and its cannon, *Wilson's* gig and the OV–10s with their machineguns, and the evacuation helicopters with their multibarrel weapons. Because the Marines faced overwhelming odds that would grow worse as time passed, Blough decided against flying all the way to *Coral Sea* and instead headed for USS *Holt*. His descent onto the destroyer escort's tiny helicopter pad was made even more difficult by the failure of his damaged searchlight and landing lights. He might have been forced to continue seaward to the aircraft carrier, if SSgt. Bobby Bounds, who had the night vision of a cat, had not leaned out of the aircraft to coach Blough onto the landing pad. After unloading, Jolly Green 44 headed back to Koh Tang to pick up another load of Marines.

445

Air War over South Vietnam, 1968–1975

Two OV–10s flown by Capt. Seth Wilson and 1st Lt. Will Carroll arrived to take over for Undorf and his wingman, Captain Roehrkasse. The gunship on station for much of the day ran low on fuel and had to depart while its replacement was ten minutes from Koh Tang. The arriving AC–130 would need an additional ten minutes to zero in its sensors and weapons. During this critical period, *Wilson's* gig, with only 1,000 rounds of ammunition remaining, the newly arrived OV–10s, and Blough's helicopter would have to reinforce the fire of the Marines.

Blough's Jolly Green 44 reappeared, guiding on a flashing strobe light that Captain Davis, the commander of Company G, had hurled from the shrunken perimeter onto the beach. Despite this aid, Blough and his copilot, 1st Lt. Henry Mason, became disoriented, but Sergeant Bounds again made use of his exceptionally keen night vision and guided the craft onto the landing zone, where it settled at 7:15 p.m. While Jolly Green 44 loaded twenty-nine Marines, the AC–130 that had just arrived knocked out a Cambodian mortar and, as Blough took off, silenced an automatic weapon firing at the helicopter. Since seawater ingested during the approach had killed one of the engines, Jolly Green 44 did not have power enough to maneuver onto the deck of *Holt* and had to fly out to the spacious deck of *Coral Sea*.[34]

Knife 51, the CH–53 flown by Brims and Danielson, took off from *Coral Sea* shortly before 8:00 p.m. The AC–130 dropped flares to reduce the danger of vertigo as the helicopter pilot touched down, but the parachute flares swayed as they descended, casting shadows that danced and changed shape with each movement. Wilson, in his OV–10, tried to guide the helicopter, correcting his own position with reference to a direction-finding radio beacon and flashing his landing lights to keep Knife 51 on its approach path. Whenever Wilson turned on his lights, the enemy opened fire, and the AC–130 cut loose at the muzzle flashes. As the incoming helicopter hovered over the beach, vertigo overcame the pilot and copilot, who had no choice but to abandon the attempt to land.

The crew of Knife 51 tried a second time, again became disoriented, and barely avoided crashing in the surf. For their third attempt, they turned on their lights, realizing they would have to risk drawing fire if they were to land and make the rescue. The multibarrel weapons of the helicopter and the orbiting gunship held off the Cambodians as Brims landed. After ten minutes — during which the Marines boarded and one member of the crew, TSgt. Wayne L. Fisk, left the aircraft to make a final check that no one remained behind — Knife 51 took off with twenty-nine Marines on board, the last of the assault force.

While Knife 51 loaded, the ramp, open but unlocked, rested on the beach to provide easy access for the Marines. As Brims increased power and the aircraft rose, the ramp dropped several inches, and the forward movement of the aircraft sent Sergeant Fisk sliding down the sloping ramp toward the opening. One of the Marines grabbed Fisk, and both of them were slipping toward the darkness when Captain Davis grabbed hold and slowed them so other Marines could form a human chain and pull them far enough forward for Fisk to reach the control lever and raise the ramp into the locked position.[35]

The departure of Knife 51 marked the end of the fighting on Koh Tang. The response to the seizure of *Mayaguez* cost the lives of thirty-eight U.S. military personnel — including three Marines who disappeared during the battle for Koh Tang and the Air Force security police and crewmen killed when a helicopter crashed en route to U-Tapao. Another forty-nine suffered wounds of varying severity. Despite the cost in lives, suffering, and the expenditure of an estimated $9.5 million in munitions and equipment, Congress in general backed the President. A few members complained about the hurried and selective process of consultation, but the legislators did not mount an effective challenge to the administration's view that the War Powers Act did not apply.[36]

A student of the conduct of the air war in Southeast Asia, Air Force Maj. Earl H. Tilford, Jr., has described the recovery of *Mayaguez* and the fighting on Koh Tang as "a microcosm of America's larger, recently concluded involvement in Indochina." No one can quarrel with his assertion that the United States underestimated the Cambodian enemy, committed "too limited a force" to the assault on Koh Tang, and had to risk landing reinforcements to permit a successful withdrawal. Indeed, Tilford argues that the assault on the island proved unnecessary because the Cambodians, on their own initiative, released the crew; but the fate of the thirty-nine men did not become known until *Wilson* picked them up at about 9:30 a.m., some three hours after the fighting began. To retrieve the landing force at this point could have been even more difficult than recovering the reinforced Marines later in the day.[37]

Besides underestimating the strength and discipline of Koh Tang's defenders — or failing to disseminate a reasonably accurate assessment — U.S. intelligence failed to pinpoint the location of the crew of *Mayaguez*. Had it not been for misgivings on the part of Secretary of Defense Schlesinger, American aircraft might have sunk the boat carrying the captives to Kompong Som. Indeed, when the Cambodians released them, the crewmen had another brush with death, but *Wilson's* trained and disciplined fire control team took precautions before firing, identified the merchant sailors, and saved their lives.

The hectic nature of the U.S. response created other problems. The Marines flown to U-Tapao from Okinawa and the Philippines had no time to rest before they attacked, let alone to train or rehearse with the helicopters that would carry them into battle. Moreover, those manning the airborne battlefield command and control center lacked the opportunity to familiarize themselves with the plans and capabilities of the Marines.

Besides emphasizing speed at the expense of preparation, the Americans failed to make the most effective use of the forces readily at hand. The OV–10s, for example, played a key role in the withdrawal but contributed nothing to the earlier fighting. The task of controlling air strikes fell initially to the Air Force A–7 pilots who, though they could talk with the Marine Corps tactical radio network, had scant experience in controlling air strikes and none at all in working with Marines. At one time, moreover, senior commanders, rather than calling upon the OV–10s, considered shifting *Coral Sea's* A–6s and A–7s from attacks on the mainland to supporting the Marines fighting on Koh Tang. The idea was abandoned, however, because the radios in the naval aircraft were incompatible with those the Marines used.

Communications caused problems throughout the brief operation. Although Washington could bombard all echelons of command with message traffic, at critical times the airborne battlefield command and control center lost contact with the helicopters, the Marines, or both simultaneously and at other times misinterpreted their reports. Isolated at U-Tapao, Colonel Johnson, the ground forces commander, had to rely on his experience and sharply honed tactical instincts rather than on a steady flow of detailed information from the island.[38]

Brigadier General Richard E. Carey, whose Marines had provided security for the final evacuation of Saigon, complained that at Koh Tang the machinery of command and control left out those commanders closest to the fighting. In his opinion, "coordination was conducted by an isolated commander (USSAG) without the proper input from the field commander. To undertake this type of mission from 195 miles away and with inadequate resources is naive and foolhardy. The results reinforce my statement."[39]

The decision to attack promptly with the mismatched forces readily available, proceeding on the basis of intelligence that was imperfect or inadequately disseminated, might well have resulted in disaster. The courage of the helicopter crews, the tenacity of the Marines, and the ingenuity of both prevented a defeat like that experienced almost a hundred years earlier by another command, contemptuous of the enemy and acting boldly on the basis of poor intelligence—the 7th Cavalry of George Armstrong Custer on the bluffs overlooking the Little Big Horn River in Montana.

Notes

Introduction

1. Robert F. Futrell, with the assistance of Martin Blumenson, *The United States Air Force in Southeast Asia: The Advisory Years to 1965* (Washington, 1981), pp 81–84, 93–102, 133–38; Joseph Buttinger, *Vietnam: A Dragon Embattled*, vol II: *Vietnam at War* (New York, 1967), p 991; *USAF Management Summary, Vietnam*, Feb 1, 1965, p 5; Adm U.S. Grant Sharp and Gen William C. Westmoreland, *Report on the War in Vietnam* (Washington, 1968), p 95.

2. Department of Defense, *The Pentagon Papers: United States-Vietnamese Relations, 1945–1967* (Washington, 1971), bk 4, pt C, p 3:1; Sharp and Westmoreland, *Report*, p 156; Dir/Mgt Analysis, USAF Mgt Summary, SEA, Dec 29, 1967, p 16.

3. AFM 1–1, *Functions and Basic Doctrine of the United States Air Force*, Feb 14, 1979, pp 2:1–2.

4. Mark Clodfelter, *The Limits of Air Power: The American Bombing of North Vietnam* (New York, 1989), pp 91, 109; George Herring, *America's Longest War: The United States and Vietnam, 1950–1975*, 2d ed. (New York, 1986), pp 170–75.

5. Stanley Karnow, *Vietnam: A History* (New York, 1983), pp 505–6.

6. Excerpts from memo, Robert W. Komer to President Johnson, Feb 28, 1967, *The Pentagon Papers as Published by the New York Times* (New York, 1971), p 555.

7. Ellsworth Bunker, "Report on Vietnam," address to the Overseas Press Club at New York City, Nov 17, 1967, *Department of State Bulletin*, Dec 11, 1967, pp 781–84.

8. Gen William C. Westmoreland, "Progress Report on the War in Vietnam," an address made before the National Press Club, Washington, Nov 21, 1967, *Department of State Bulletin*, Dec 11, 1967, pp 785–88.

9. Public Papers of the Presidents of the United States (Washington, 1970), *Lyndon B. Johnson, 1968–1969*, bk 2, pp 1045, 1049, 1053–54.

10. Chester L. Cooper, *The Lost Crusade: America in Vietnam* (New York, 1970), pp 389–92.

Chapter 1

1. Hist, 12th TRSq, atch to hist, 460th TRWg, Jan–Mar 1968.

2. Hist, 7AF, Jan–Jun 1968, vol I, pt 2, pp 480–83.

3. Hist, USMACV, 1968, vol II, p 897.

4. Hist, 12th TRSq, atch to hist, 460th TRWg, Jun–Mar 1968, pp 5–6.

5. Hist, 7AF, Jan–Jun 1968, vol I, pt 2, pp 483–84.

6. Combat After Action Rprt, Tan Son Nhut AB, Jan 31, 1968; Mar 9, 1968, pp 9–12.

7. Don Oberdorfer, *Tet!* (Garden City, New York, 1971), pp 32–33, 40.

8. Hist, 7AF, Jan–Jun 1968, vol I, pt 2, pp 489–90.

9. Ltr, III DASC Hist Rprt, Jan–Jun 1968; Aug 1, 1968.

10. Hist, 7AF, Jan–Jun 1968. vol I, pt 2, pp 490–92.

11. Combat After Action Rprt, Bien Hoa AB, RVN, Jan 31, 1968; nd, pp 4–5.

12. Intvw, Maj A. W. Thompson with Maj James Grant, FAC based at Bien Hoa, 1968, Mar 9, 1968.

13. Hist, USMACV, Jan–Jun 68, vol I, p 882; hist, *The JCS and the War in Vietnam, 1960–1968*, pt III, p 4:12.

14. Hq PACAF, Summary, Air Operations, Southeast Asia, Jan 1968, pp 3:4–5.

15. Hist, 7AF, Jan–Jun 1968, vol I, pt 2, pp 493–95.

16. Maj Miles Waldron, USA, and Sp 5 Cl Richard Beavers, Hq, V Prov Corps Hist

Notes to pages 13–23

Study 2068, *Operation Hue City*, Aug 1968, pp 1–2; Brig Gen Edwin H. Simmons, USMC, "Marine Corps Operations in Vietnam," *U.S. Naval Institute Proceedings*, May 1970, pp 299–300.

17. Simmons, "Marine Corps Operations," p. 299; Maj A. W. Thompson and C. William Thorndale, *Air Response to the Tet Offensive, 30 Jan–29 Feb 68* (Hq PACAF, Proj CHECO, Jul 12, 1968), pp 17–18.

18. Thompson and Thorndale, *Tet Offensive*, p 2; Maj A. W. Thompson, *The Defense of Saigon* (Hq PACAF, Proj CHECO, Dec 14, 1968,), pp 1–2.

19. Intvw, Col John E. Van Duyn and Maj Richard B. Clement with Maj Gen Robert N. Ginsburgh, senior member, NSC staff, 1968, May 26, 1971.

20. Hq PACAF, Dep Dir/OSI, Counterintelligence Digest, Jun 10, 1968, pp 53–55.

21. Msg, CG II FForceV to COMUSMACV, 081155Z Jan 68, subj: Visit of COMUSMACV, Jan 7, 1968; *Warning of Tet Offensive*, Rprt of President's Foreign Intelligence on Tet, 1968, nd.

22. *Warning of the Tet Offensive*; Dave Richard Palmer, *Summons of the Trumpet: U.S.-Vietnam Conflict in Perspective* (San Rafael, Calif, 1978), p 184.

23. Hq PACAF, Dep Dir/OSI, Counterintelligence Digest, Jun 10, 1968, pp 56–58.

24. Ofc of Asst SecDef (Systems Analysis), Response to Question: What information did Washington have on coordinated attacks on cities?, nd [spring 1968].

25. Msg, Westmoreland to Gen Momyer, Comdr 7AF, Lt Gen Palmer, CG USARV, et al, 280153Z Jan 68, subj: Tet Cease-fire; hist, *The JCS and the War in Vietnam, 1960–1968*, pt III, pp 48:4, 6–7.

26. Tab A to memo, Ofc, DCS/Mil Ops, for CSA, Apr 9, 1970, subj: Information, reference Tet '68; msg, COMUSMACV to MACV, 300325Z Jan 68, subj: Cancellation of Tet Cease-fire; Thompson, *Saigon*, p 2; Oberdorfer, *Tet!*, pp 122–24.

27. Hq USMACV, Study of the Comparisons between the Battle of Dien Bien Phu and the Analogous Khe Sanh Situation, Mar 1968.

28. *Armed Forces Journal*, Feb 24, 1968, p 8.

29. Warren A. Trest, *Khe Sanh (Operation Niagara), 22 January–31 March 68* (Hq PACAF, Proj CHECO, Sep 13, 1968), p 26.

30. Capt Moyers S. Shore, USMC, *The Battle for Khe San* (Washington, 1969), pp 72, 74; TSgt Bruce Pollica and TSgt Joe R. Rickey, *834th Air Division Tactical Air Support for Khe Sanh, 21 Jan–8 Apr 1968*, p 5.

31. Translation, Tet Greetings of Chairman Ho Chi Minh, CDEC Bulletin no. 9318.

32. Oberdorfer, *Tet!*, pp 48–49; Buttinger, *Vietnam at War*, pp 751–52.

33. Victoria Pohle, *The Viet Cong in Saigon: Tactics and Objectives during the Tet Offensive*, RAND Memo 5799, ISA/ARPA, Jan 1969, pp 32–35.

34. Oberdorfer, *Tet!*, pp 201, 206–7, 214–15.

Chapter 2

1. PACAF Summary of Air Operations, Feb 1968, pp 3:A:1, 15, 17.

2. Hist, 7AF, vol I, pt 1, pp 116–18.

3. Thompson, *Saigon*, pp 5–8; hist, USMACV, 1968, vol II, pp 896–99.

4. Intvw, Maj A. W. Thompson with Lt Col Thomas P. Garvin, ALO, 25th Inf Div, 1968, Mar 12, 1968.

5. Maj John F. Schlight, *Rules of Engagement, 1 Jan 66–1 Nov 69* (Hq PACAF, Proj CHECO, Aug 31, 1969 [sic]), pp 37–38; Thompson and Thorndale, *Tet Offensive*, p 28.

6. Thompson and Thorndale, *Tet Offensive*, pp 39–40; Intvw, Maj A. W. Thompson with Maj James Gibson, FAC, 9th Inf Div, 1968, Mar 9, 1968.

7. Oberdorfer, *Tet!*, pp 184–85; Peter Braestrup, *Big Story: How the American Press and Television Reported and Interpreted the Crisis of Tet in 1968 in Vietnam and Washington* (Boulder, 1977), vol I, pp 253–62.

8. Combat after Action Rprt, Maj Evans E. Warne, ALO, Phuoc Thuy province, 4:55 a.m.–7:30 p.m., Feb 1, 1968, nd; Intvw, Maj A. W. Thompson with Lt Col Robert C. Mason, ALO, 18th ARVN Div, 1968, nd

[Mar 1968].

9. Thompson and Thorndale, *Tet Offensive*, pp 36–38; Palmer, *Summons of the Trumpet*, pp 195–98.

10. Simmons, "Marine Operations in Vietnam," pp 300–301; Waldron and Beavers, *Hue City*, pp 51–53.

11. Thompson and Thorndale, *Tet Offensive*, pp 32–34, 85–86.

12. Waldron and Beavers, *Hue City*, pp 25–26; Thompson and Thorndale, *Tet Offensive*, p 33, fig 7.

13. Braestrup, Big Story, vol II, app 26; Oberdorfer, *Tet!*, pp 246–51.

14. Schlight, *Rules of Engagement*, 66–69, pp 41–42; 7AF Regulation 55–49, Nov 14, 1968.

15. PACAF Summary of Air Operations, Feb 1968, pp 2, 3:9–10.

16. Intvw, R. R. Kritt, PhD, with Lt Gen J. R. Chaisson, USMC, Dir/MACV COC, 1967–1968, Aug 12, 1971; hist, SAC, Jan–Jun 1968, vol I, pp 75–76; hist, USMACV, 1968, vol I, p 419; Dir/Mgt Analysis, USAF Mgt Summary, SEA, Feb 16, 1968, p 20.

17. Intvw, Maj Richard Clement and Charles Hildreth, PhD, with Gen John P. McConnell, CSAF, 1965–1969, Nov 4, 1970, p 26; SAC Command and Control in the SEA Contingency, Nov 12, 1968, atch to ltr, SAC to Hq USAF, Dec 5, 1968, subj: Trends, Indicators, and Analyses (TIA) (Your ltr, 10 Sep 68); Gen William W. Momyer, *Air Power in Three Wars* (Washington, 1978), pp 101–3.

18. Chaisson intvw [Kritt], pp 29–30; Gen William C. Westmoreland, Historical Summary, Feb 1–29, 1968, p 5.

19. DOD Rprt, Selected Air and Ground Operations in Cambodia and Laos, Sep 10, 1973, pp 8–10, 13.

20. SAC Bugle Note Bombing Concept, Nov 21, 1968, atch to ltr, SAC to Hq USAF, Dec 5, 1968, subj: Trends, Indicators, Analyses (TIA) (Your ltr, 10 Sep 68); USMACV 1968, vol I, pp 419–20.

21. Ofc of Hist, Hq SAC, SAC Historical Study 115, The Search for B–52 Effectiveness, Dec 16, 1969, pp 24–24; Garvin intvw.

22. Donzel E. Betts, Hiram Wolfe, III, Raymond P. Schmidt, and Thomas N. Thompson, *Deadly Transmissions (COMSEC Monitoring and Analysis)*, Dec 1970, pp 85–91; COMUSMACV to CINCPAC and CINCSAC, 290415Z Sep 70, subj: CINCPAC Operations Security (OPSEC) Report on Arc Light (B–52) Operations in Southeast Asia; Intvw, Lt Col Arthur W. McCants and James Hasdorf, PhD, with Gen John W. Vogt, 7AF Comdr, Apr–Sep 1972, Aug 8–9, 1978.

23. Thompson, *Saigon*, p 17; hist, 7AF, Jan–Jun 1968, vol I, pt 1, pp 136, 161.

24. Thompson and Thorndale, *Tet Offensive*, p 71.

25. Notes on intvw, Col Ray Bowers with Lt Col Billy G. Gibson, C–130 pilot in South Vietnam, 1968, Apr 21, 1972.

26. Notes of intvw, Col Ray Bowers with Capt Lloyd J. Probst, C–130 pilot in South Vietnam, 1968, May 8, 1972.

27. Thompson and Thorndale, *Tet Offensive*, pp 42, 48, 51.

28. Ibid, pp. 42–43, 47–49.

29. Ibid, pp 44–45; hist, 834th Air Div, Jul 67–Jun 68, pp 33–34; 315th Air Div Chronology of Korean Contingency Support Actions, Feb 1–29, 68, nd, p 3.

30. Thompson and Thorndale, *Tet Offensive*, pp 10, 55–56.

31. Ibid, pp 57–58; ltr, Dir/Ops, AF Advisory Gp, MACV, to 7AF, Apr 22, 68, subj: VNAF Operations, 30 Jan–29 Feb 68; PACAF Summary of Air Operations, Feb 68, pp 3:A:5, 8.

32. Dir/Mgt Analysis, USAF Mgt Summary, SEA, Jan 5, 68; PACAF Summary of Air Operations, Jan 68, p 3:A:4.

33. End of Tour Rprt, Brig Gen Donavon Smith, Chief, USAF Advisory Gp (MACV), Oct 66–Mar 68, nd [Mar 68], p 3:42.

34. Thompson and Thorndale, *Tet Offensive*, p 59; Dir/Mgt Analysis, USAF Mgt Summary, SEA, Feb 2, 68, p 64.

35. Thompson and Thorndale, *Tet Offensive*, p 71; Dir/Mgt Analysis, USAF Mgt Summary, SEA, Feb 2, 68, p 1; Feb 23, 68, p 1; Mar 68, p 1.

36. Dir/Mgt Analysis, USAF Mgt Summary, SEA, Mar 1, 68, p 1.

37. Hist, USMACV, 1968, vol II, pp 906–7.

38. Ibid, p 906.

39. COSVN Resolution of March 1968, in

7AF Weekly Intelligence Summary, 68–25, Jun 8–14, 68.

40. Hq PACAF, Proj Corona Harvest Input, In-Country and Out-Country Strike Operations in Southeast Asia, vol IV, Support: Air Base Defense, p 14; Roger P. Fox, *Air Base Defense in the Republic of Vietnam, 1961–1973* (Washington, 1979), pp 70–71.

41. Proj Corona Harvest, Air Base Defense, pp 16–17; Thompson and Thorndale, *Tet Offensive*, pp 22–23.

42. Fox, *Base Defense*, pp 67–68, 71.

43. Ibid, pp 140–42; ltr, Lt Col Ray S. Humiston, OSI District 50, to Dir/Ops, OSI District 50, Apr 17, 70, subj: Request for Visual Reconnaissance (VR).

44. Lee Bonetti, *USAF Civic Action in Republic of Vietnam* (Hq PACAF, Proj CHECO, Apr 1, 1968), pp 24, 36; Maj A. W. Thompson, *USAF Civic Action in Republic of Vietnam* (Hq PACAF, Proj CHECO, Mar 17, 1969). pp 22–24.

45. Thompson, *Civic Action*, pp 4–5; comments, Capt Paul Boulanger, base civic action officer, Tan Son Nhut AB, Effects of Tet on Civic Action, nd [Mar 1968].

Chapter 3

1. Hist, JCS, *The JCS and the War in Vietnam, 1960–1968*, pt III, p 49:2.

2. Charles H. Hildreth, Anne B. Moscolino, et al, *The Air Force Response to the Pueblo Crisis, 1968* (Ofc/AF Hist, Jan 69), pp 20–21, 24–25, 37.

3. Hist, JCS, *The JCS and the War in Vietnam, 1960–1968*, pt III. p 49:3.

4. Msg, Gen Wheeler to Gen Westmoreland, JCS 01590, 080448Z Feb 68, subj: none.

5. Msg, Gen Westmoreland to Gen Wheeler and Adm Sharp, 081440Z Feb 68, subj: none.

6. Hist, JCS, *The JCS and the Vietnam War, 1960–1968*, pt III, p 49:4; msg, Gen Westmoreland to Gen Wheeler, 081557Z Feb 68, subj: Additional MACV Requirements.

7. Msg, Gen Wheeler for Gen Westmoreland, JCS 01590, 090021Z Feb 68, subj: none.

8. Hist, JCS, *The JCS and the War in Vietnam, 1960–1968*, pt III, p 49:4.

9. Msg, Gen Westmoreland to Gen Wheeler and Adm Sharp, 091633Z Feb 68, subj: none.

10. Msg, Gen Wheeler to Gen Westmoreland, JCS 01695, 120108Z Feb 68, subj: none.

11. Hist, Gen Westmoreland to Adm Sharp and Gen Wheeler, 120612Z Feb 68, subj: Assessment of Situation and Requirements.

12. Hist, JCS, *The JCS and the War in Vietnam, 1960–1968, pt III, p 49:8;* Journal of the Armed Forces, Feb 24, 1968, pp 8–9.

13. Msg, Gen Westmoreland to Gen Wheeler, 121823Z Feb 68, subj: none.

14. Msg, Gen Wheeler to Gen Westmoreland, 172017Z Feb 68, subj: none.

15. Gen Westmoreland's marginal notations on copy, msg, Gen Wheeler to Gen Westmoreland, JCS 02847, 122014Z Mar 68, subj: none.

16. Msgs, Gen Westmoreland to Gen Wheeler, 111150Z Mar 68 and 171247Z Mar 68, subj: none; Excerpts from memo, Gen Wheeler to President Johnson, Rprt of the JCS on Situation in Vietnam and MACV Recommendations, Feb 27, 68, in *The Pentagon Papers as Published by the New York Times* (New York, 1971), pp 615–21.

17. *Department of Defense (The Pentagon Papers), United States-Vietnam Relations, 1945–1967* (Washington, 1971), bk 6, pt IV:c:7, vol II, pp 149–51.

18. Msg, Gen Wheeler to Gen Westmoreland, JCS 02590, 051558Z Mar 68, subj: none; Senator Gravel Edition, *The Pentagon Papers* (Boston, 1971), vol IV, pp 575–76; Karnow, *Vietnam*, pp 555–56.

19. Msg, Gen Wheeler to Gen Westmoreland, JCS 02767, 090130 Mar 68, subj: none.

20. Msg, Gen Wheeler to Gen Westmoreland, JCS 02848, 122014Z Mar 68, subj: none; *New York Times*, Mar 10, 68, p 1; *Washington Post*, Mar 10, 68, p 1.

21. Msg, Gen Wheeler to Gen Westmoreland, JCS 03024, 162045Z Mar 68, subj: none; Karnow, *Vietnam*, p 556.

22. Msgs, Gen Westmoreland to Gen

Wheeler, 111150Z Mar 68, subj: none; Gen Wheeler for Gen Westmoreland, JCS 0295, 141514Z Mar 68, subj: none; Adm Sharp to Gen Wheeler, 270356Z Mar 68, subj: Deployment of F–84 Aircraft to SEAsia.

23. Gravel, *Pentagon Papers*, vol IV, pp 586–87, 591–92; Ofc Asst Sec Def (Systems Analysis), paper, Alternative Strategies, Feb 29, 1968; David M. Barrett, *Uncertain Warriors: Lyndon Johnson and His Vietnam Advisers* (Lawrence, Kan, 1993), pp 134–59.

24. Msgs, Gen Wheeler to Gen Westmoreland, JCS 03449, 280152Z Mar 68, subj: none; Gen Westmoreland to Gen Wheeler and Adm Sharp, 271333Z Mar 68, subj: none; Gen Westmoreland to Gen Wheeler, 281206Z Mar 68, subj: none; hist, USMACV, 1968, vol I, pp 227–28.

25. Hists, CINCPAC, 1968, vol III, p 40; and 7AF, Jan–Jun 68, vol I, pt 1, pp 234–35; Dep for Reserve Affairs and Education, Ofc of Asst SAF for Manpower and Reserve Affairs, Data Base on the ANG and AFRES, Oct 21, 74, pp 42–45; Dir/Mgt Analysis, USAF Mgt Summary, SEA, Apr 26, 68, p i; May 10, 68, p i; May 17, 68, p i, May 24, p i; Jun 7, 68, p i; Jun 14, 68, pp i, 18–19.

26. Gravel, *Pentagon Papers*, vol IV, pp 593–94; Data Base on the ANG and AFRES, cited above, pp 153–54.

27. Gravel, *Pentagon Papers*, vol IV, pp 594–602; Jacob Van Staaveren, *The Air Force in Southeast Asia: Toward a Bombing Halt* (Ofc/AF Hist, Sep 70), p 37.

28. Msg, Saigon to SecState, 44567 (originally 45436), 170645Z Jul 68, subj: none.

29. Background to CINCPAC Military Assistance Sales Plan for South Vietnam (Country Plan), FY 74–78, Jul 1, 72, pp 8–9.

30. Public Papers of the Presidents, *Lyndon B. Johnson, 1968–1969*, bk 1, p 471.

31. Hist, USMACV, 1968, vol I, pp 421–23; SEA Impact on SAC SIOP Forces, Nov 12, 68, atch to ltr, SAC to USAF, Dec 5, 68, subj: Trends, Indicators, and Analyses (TIA) (Your ltr, 10 Sep 68); Dir/Mgt Analysis, USAF Mgt Summary, SEA, Jan 5, 69, p 22.

32. Ltr, Maj Gen Richard H. Ellis, Dir/Plans. Hq USAF, to Col [Howard M.] Fish, Apr 2, 68, subj: Concepts of Operations for SEA with Increased Emphasis on Air Operations, with attached study; Van Staaveren, *Bombing Halt*, pp 27–29.

33. Msgs, Gen Westmoreland to Gen Wheeler and Adm Sharp, 071227Z Jan 68, subj: Arms and Ammunition from Cambodia; COMNAVFORV to DIA, 240902Z Feb 68, subj: none.

34. Msg, SecState to CINCPAC, State 99756, 170408Z Jan 68, subj: Bowles Meeting, quoting New Delhi to State 8396, Jan 12, 68.

35. Msg, SecState to CINCPAC, State 99895/1, 170528Z Jan 68, subj: Meeting with Prince Sihanouk, repeating Bangkok to State, Jan 10, 68.

36. Ibid; msg, SecState to CINCPAC, State 99897/1 subj: 170532Z Jan 68, Meeting with Prince Sihanouk, repeating New Delhi to State 8395, Jan 12, 68.

37. Msg, SecState to CINCPAC, 170530Z Jan 68, subj: Third Working Session, repeating Bangkok to State 8625, Jan 11, 68.

38. Msg, SecState to CINCPAC, State 9886, 170412Z Jan 68, subj: Bowles Mission Joint Communique, quoting Bangkok to State, 8659, Jan 12, 68.

39. Ltr, Col Alfred G. Hutchens to Dir/Intelligence, 7AF, Feb 28, 68, subj: Operation Vesuvius.

40. Hist, USMACV, 1968, vol II, p 586; Dept of State, memo of conversation, Eugene Black, William P. Bundy, et al, Sep 30, 68, subj: Mr Black's Visit to Cambodia and Asian Tour.

41. Msgs, Gen Wheeler to Adm McCain and Gen Abrams, JCS 11266, 031415Z Oct 68, subj: Base Area 740; Gen Abrams to Gen Wheeler, 260843Z Oct 68, subj: none.

42. Hist, USMACV, 1968, Annex F, pp F:IV:1–5, 7–9.

43. Msg, Adm McCain to Gen Abrams, JCS 02945, 151527Z Aug 68, subj: Military Actions in Cambodia.

44. Msgs, Adm McCain to Gen Abrams, 180448Z Aug 68, subj: Military Action in Cambodia; Gen Abrams to Gen Wheeler and Adm McCain, 010833Z Sep 68, subj: Military Actions in Cambodia.

45. Msg, Gen Abrams to Gen Wheeler and Adm McCain, 271114Z Oct 68, subj: Military Actions in Cambodia.

Notes to pages 52–64

46. Msgs, Gen Wheeler to Adm McCain, 072223Z Nov 68, subj: Actions Against Cambodia; Adm McCain to Gen Wheeler, 210012Z Nov 68, subj: none.

Chapter 4

1. PACAF Summaries of Air Operations, Feb–Dec 68, passim.
2. Shore, *Khe Sanh*, pp 132–33; intvw, Capt J. W. A. Whitehorne, USA, with Maj Gen John Tolson, CG, 1st Cav Div (Airmobile), Jun 17, 68.
3. Palmer, *Summons of the Trumpet*; Tolson intvw, Jun 17, 68; 31st Military Hist Det, Hq, ProvCorpsV, Hist Study 3–68, *Operation Pegasus*, Mar 31–Apr 15, 68, np, nd.
4. Shore, *Khe Sanh*, pp 134–44; Lt Gen John J. Tolson, *Vietnam Studies: Airmobility, 1961–197* (Washington, 1973), pp 173–77; Lt Col John K. Galvin, USA, "The Relief of Khe Sanh," *Military Review*, Jan 70, pp 90–93.
5. 1st ind to ltr, Hq, 1st Cav Div (Airmobile), to Dir, DASC Victor, May 5, 68, subj: Pegasus After Action Rprt, 30 Apr 68; ltr, ALO, 1st Cav Div (Airmobile), to Corps ALO, Dir, I DASC, et al, Apr 30, 68, subj: Pegasus After Action Rprt.
6. Tolson intvw, Jun 17, 68; Tolson, *Air Mobility*, pp 172, 179.
7. Shore, *Khe Sanh*, pp 149–51; Tolson, *Air Mobility*, p 238.
8. Intvw, Whitehorne with Tolson, Jun 24, 68.
9. Ltr, Gen William W. Momyer, 7AF Comdr, to COMUSMACV, subj: Employment of Mk 36 Ordnance; 7AF Air Staff summary Sheet, Current Plans Div, 7AF Tactical Air Control Center, nd [Mar 68], subj: Interdiction of Route 548, nd [Mar 68]; msgs, 7AF Tactical Air Control Center to I DASC, DASC Victor, et al, 230821Z Mar 68, subj: Interdiction in SVN; 7AF to COMUSMACV, CG III MAF, 060506Z Apr 68, subj: 7th Air Force Interdiction of Enemy LOCs.
10. Intvw, Whitehorne with Tolson, May 27, 68; ProvCorpsV OPlan Delaware/Lam Son 216, para 3, Apr 16, 68; 1st Weather Gp, Long Range Forecast Requirement of the U.S. Army, Vietnam (USARV), for the Republic of Vietnam (RVN), nd [Dec 69], atch to hist, 1st Weather Gp, Oct–Dec 69.
11. Tolson intvw, May 27, 68; rprt, 1st Bde, 101st Abn Div, to CG, 101st Abn Div, Apr 29, 68, subj: After Action Rprt, Operation Carentan II.
12. Tolson intvw, May 27, 68; Tolson, *Air Mobility*, p 184.
13. Intvw, C. William Thorndale with Capt Wayne Gayler, ALO, 1st Squadron, 9th Cavalry (Airmobile), 68, May 24, 68.
14. Intvw, Thorndale with Capt Donald L. Abbott, FAC, 1st Cav Div (Airmobile), 68, May 24, 68.
15. Intvw, Thorndale with Maj A. V. P. Anderson, III, ALO, 1st Bde, 1st Cav Div (Airmobile), 68, May 25, 68.
16. Abbott intvw.
17. Anderson intvw.
18. Tolson intvw, May 27, 68.
19. Anderson intvw.
20. Intvw, Thorndale with Capt William R. Bradshaw, FAC, 1st Cav Div (Airmobile), 68, May 25, 68; C. William Thorndale, *Operation Delaware, 19 April–17 May 1968* (Hq PACAF, Proj CHECO, Sep 2, 68), p 22.
21. Intvw, Thorndale with Maj Anthony C. Zielinski, ALO, 1st Bde, 101st Abn Div, 68, May 23, 68.
22. Ibid.
23. Ltr, Maj Robert G. Archer to Lt Col Woods, Feb 2, 69, subj: Aircraft Commander's Report on "Combat Trap"; msg, AFWL to AFSC, 131643Z Mar 69, subj: Combat Trap Jungle Clearing Device.
24. Zielinski intvw.
25. Intvw, Thorndale with Capt Robert F. Miller, ALO, 1st Cav Div (Airmobile), 68, May 24, 68; msg, ProvCorpsV Tactical Ops Center to COMUSMACV, 290315Z Apr 68, subj: Northern I CTZ Special Report, 280900H to 290900H 68.
26. Miller intvw.
27. Rprt, 834th Air Div to Gen Momyer, May 3, 68, subj: none.
28. Miller intvw.
29. Ibid; Thorndale, *Operation Delaware*, p 38.
30. Abbott intvw.

31. Statement by FAC, May 3, 68; 7AF Tactical Air Control Center, Staff Summary Sheet, Jun 2, 68, subj: Short Round Report, 3 May 68.
32. Memo for the Record, Maj Gen John Tolson, CG, 1st Cav Div (Airmobile), May 7, 68, subj: Firing Incident, 03 May 68.
33. Anderson intvw.
34. Thorndale, *Operation Delaware*, pp 38–40, 50–52.
35. Tolson intvw, May 27, 68.
36. PACAF Summary of Air Operations, Mar 68, p 3:5; hist, 7AF, Jan–Jun 68, vol I, pt 2, pp 484–86.
37. Intvw, Col Ray Bowers with Maj Alan L. Gropman, navigator, 463d TAWg, 68, Apr 13, 72.
38. Msg, COMUSMACV to CINCPAC, 150257Z May 68, subj: Operation Inferno.
39. Atch to 7AF Tactical Air Control Center Staff Summary Sheet, Nov 24, 68, subj: Banish Beach; Gen George S. Brown, 7AF Comdr, memo for record, Sep 4, 68, subj: Banish Beach.
40. Fox, *Base Defense*, p 132; 7AF Staff Summary Sheet, May 20, 68, subj: Rules of Engagement for Attacks on Enemy Rocket Positions.
41. Thompson, *Defense of Saigon*, pp 57–58.
42. Garvin intvw.
43. 7AF Staff Summary Sheet, cited in FN 40.
44. Ltr, Gen Westmoreland to 7AF Comdr, May 2, 68, subj: Air Attack on Enemy Rocket Positions.
45. Msg, Foreign Broadcast Information Service, Saigon, to 7th PsyOps, Okinawa, PACAF, et al, 050815Z May 68, subj: none.
46. Hist, USMACV, 1968, vol I, p 132.
47. Msgs, DOD/PRO to CINCPAC, CINCPACFLT, et al, Apr 28, 68, and 301226Z Apr 68, subj: Principal Objectives and Forces to be Used in Enemy Attack against Quang Nam Province.
48. Thompson, *Defense of Saigon*, p 20.
49. Msg, DOD/PRO to CINCPAC, CINCPACFLT, et al, 050945Z May 68, subj: CAS Field Information Rprt.
50. C. William Thorndale, *Defense of Da Nang* (Hq PACAF, Proj CHECO, Aug 31, 69), pp 17–22.

51. Msgs, COMUSMACV to NMCC and CINCPAC, 050830Z May 68, subj: Special Telecon; DOD/PRO to CINCPAC, CINCPACFLT, et al, 050945Z May 68, subj: CAS Field Information Rprt; Simmons "Marine Operations in Vietnam," p 306.
52. Hist, USMACV, 1968, vol I, pp 159–60; Kenneth Sams, Lt Col John Schlight, et al, *The Air War in Vietnam, 1968–1969* (Hq PACAF, Proj CHECO, Apr 1, 70), p 34.
53. Msg, 633d Combat Support Gp, Pleiku, to NMCC, PACAF, et al, 050807Z May 68, subj: none.
54. Msg, COMUSMACV to NMCC and CINCPAC, 052200Z May 68, subj: Morning Telecon.
55. Msgs, Saigon to State, Saigon 26481, 051700Z May 68, subj: none; COMUSMACV to NMCC and CINCPAC, 052200Z May 68, subj: Morning Telecon; Thompson, *Defense of Saigon*, pp 7–9.
56. Msg, DOD/PRO to CINCPAC, CINCPACFLT, et al, 101549Z May 68, subj: Medical Report on General Loan; Oberdorfer, *Tet!*, pp 165–71.
57. Thompson, *Defense of Saigon*, pp 20–29, 36–37.
58. Hist, 7AF, vol I, pt 2, pp 486–88.
59. Ibid, p 493.
60. Hists, JCS, *The JCS and the War in Vietnam, 1960–1968*, pt III, p 52:8; USMACV, 1968, vol I, pp 132–33.
61. Hist, JCS, *The JCS and the War in Vietnam, 1960–1968*, pt III, pp 5:8–9.
62. Ibid, pp 28–32.
63. Ltr, William W, Momyer, 7AF Comdr, to COMUSMACV, May 20, 68, subj: Air Attacks on Enemy Rocket Positions.
64. Msg, II FForceV to 7AF, 260325Z May 68, subj: Rules of Engagement for Armed Helicopters and Air Attacks on Enemy Rocket Positions.
65. Ltr, William W. Momyer, 7AF Comdr, to COMUSMACV, May 31, 68, subj: Rules of Engagement of Air Attacks on Enemy Rocket Positions.
66. Fox, *Base Defense*, p 134.
67. Thompson, *Defense of Saigon*, pp. 47–48, 50–51; hist, USMACV, 1968, vol I, pp 219–20.
68. Thompson, *Defense of Saigon*, pp

Notes to pages 73–86

52–53.

69. Memo for Record, Phil Odeen, Ofc of Asst SecDef (Systems Analysis), Regional Programs, Mar 20, 70, subj: Vietnamization Meeting with Secretary Laird.

70. Hist, JCS, *The JCS and the War in Vietnam, 1960–1968*, pt III, pp 52:12–13; msg, Gen Wheeler to Gen Abrams, JCS 6117, 042315Z Jun 68, subj: none.

71. Thompson, *Defense of Saigon*, p 64.

Chapter 5

1. Intvw, Lt Col R. A. MacDonough with Maj Eugene Carnahan, FAC, 21st TASSq, 68, nd [summer 1968].

2. Lt Col R. A. MacDonough, *Truscott White* (Hq PACAF, Proj CHECO, Dec 1, 68), pp 2–4.

3. Ibid, p 6.

4. Intvw, Macdonough with Maj Michael Burke, ALO, 1st Bde, 4th Inf Div, 68, nd [summer 68].

5. MacDonough, *Truscott White*, pp 17–18.

6. Burke intvw.

7. Intvw, MacDonough with Col Joseph E. Fix, Comdr, 1st Bde, 4th Inf Div, 68, nd [summer 68].

8. Ibid.

9. Carnahan intvw.

10. Fix intvw.

11. MacDonough, *Truscott White*, pp 19–20.

12. Ibid, pp 9–10; Fix intvw.

13. MacDonough, Truscott White, pp 9–17; Fix intvw.

14. Maj Gen William B. Fulton, USA, *Vietnam Studies: Riverine Operations, 1966–1969* (Washington, 1973), p 21.

15. Intvw, Capt Dorrell T. Hanks, Jr., with Maj Donald Frank Kansfield, ALO. 2d Bde, 9th Inf Div, Jan 2–Jun 30, 69, Jul 2, 69.

16. Fulton, *Riverine Operations*, pp 31–32, 56–58.

17. Ibid, pp 31–94.

18. Intvw, Hanks with Maj Dennis Flint, G–3 (Air), 9th Inf Div, 69, Jun 30, 69.

19. Intvw, Hanks with Capt Joseph DiEduardo, S–3 (Ops and Training) 2d Bde, 9th Inf Div, 69, Jul 1, 69.

20. Ibid.

21. Flint intvw.

22. Ibid.

23. Hanks, *Riverine Operations in the Delta* (Hq PACAF, Proj CHECO, Aug 31, 69), p 31.

24. Flint intvw.

25. Intvws, Hanks with Capt Frederick E. Brayee, S–2, 2d Bde, 9th Inf Div, 69, Jun 30, 69; and Lt Comdr James M. Carr, Jr., N2 (Intelligence), TF–117, 69, Jun 30, 69.

26. Intvw, Hanks with Maj Thomas P. Laffey, Asst ALO, 9th Inf Div, 68–69, Jul 1, 69.

27. Kansfield intvw; Flint intvw.

28. Fulton, *Riverine Operations*, pp 170–71; Kansfield intvw; Intvw, Hanks with Lt Col M. E. White, USMC, Dep G–3 (Riverine War), 9th Inf Div, 69, Jul 6, 69.

29. Kansfield intvw.

30. Laffey intvw.

31. Fulton, *Riverine Operations*, pp 179–80; Intvw, Hanks with Comdr James C. Froid, MRF N–4 (Logistics) and comdr, 9th River Assault Squadron, 68–69, Jun 30, 69.

32. Hist, USMACV, 1968, vol I, p 401.

33. Intvw, Col Ray Bowers with Maj Alan L. Gropman, navigator, 463d TAWg, 68, Apr 13, 68.

34. Hist, USMACV, 1968, vol I, p 401.

35. Col Francis J. Kelley, USA, *Vietnam Studies: U.S. Army Special Forces, 1961–1971* (Washington, 1973), pp 78–80.

36. Capt Joseph P. Meissner, USA, and SSgt Leland J. Larson, Battle of Duc Lap: After Action Rprt, Nov 27, 68.

37. Rprt, 1st Lt William J. Harp, USA, through Det B–23 to CO, 5th Special Forces Gp (A Bn), Nov 29, 68, subj: After Action Rprt.

38. Ibid; MACV after action intvw with MSgt Thomas T Boody, nd, incl to Duc Lap After Action Rprt; hist, 31st TFWg, Jul–Sep 68, vol I, pp 27–28.

39. Harp After Action Rprt.

40. Rprt, Logistical Support of Duc Lap, nd, incl to Duc Lap After Action Rprt.

41. Msg, Horn DASC, Da Nang, to 7AF, 301830Z Sep 68, subj: Quang Nam Sector Situation Rprt.

Notes to pages 86–96

42. Ibid; intvws Kenneth Sams with Lt Col Donald J. Parsons, Dir/Ops, Horn DASC, 1968, Oct 14 and 30, 68.

43. Quang Nam Sector Situation Rprt.

44. Intvw, Sams with 1st Lt Richard McDonald, 5th Special Forces Gp, 68, Oct 8, 68.

45. Quang Nam Sector Situation Rprt; Parsons intvws.

46. Statement by Lt Col Connelly in intvw, Sams with Lt Cols Daniel Connelly and Maurice Williams, USA, 5th Special Forces Gp, 68, Lt Col Ralph Albright, ALO, Co C, 5th Special Forces Gp, 68, and Maj Hugh D. Walker, FAC, 5th Special Forces Gp, 68, Oct 16, 68.

47. Parsons intvws; Simmons, "Marine Operations in Vietnam," pp 316–17.

48. Parsons intvws.

49. Lt Col Jack S. Ballard, *The U.S. Air Force in Southeast Asia: Development and Deployment of Fixed-Wing Gunships, 1962–1972* (Washington, 1982), pp 82–89.

50. Ibid, pp 176–89.

51. Maj Victor B. Anthony, *The Air Force in Southeast Asia: Tactics and Techniques of Night Operations, 1961–1970* (Ofc/AF Hist, 1973), pp 172–76; hist data record, Weapons and Force Plans Br, Plans Div, 7AF Tactical Air Control Center, Oct 1–Dec 4, 1968.

52. Anthony, *Night Operations*, pp 121–22, 127–28; ltr, Gen William W. Momyer to Gen James Ferguson, AFSC Comdr, Mar 14, 68, subj: none.

53. Melvin F. Porter, *Second Generation Weaponry in SEA* (Hq PACAF, Proj CHECO, Sept 10, 70), pp 4, 15–17, 21–24, 71–72.

54. Lt Col Ralph A. Rowley, *The Air Force in Southeast Asia: FAC Operations, 1965–1970* (Ofc/Af Hist, May 75), pp 37–39; Weapons and Force Plans Br, Plans Div, 7AF Tactical Air Control Center, Oct 1–Dec 31, 68; PACAF Summary of Air Operations, Jan–Dec 68, passim.

55. Hist, 7AF, Jan–Jun 68, vol I, pt I, pp 114–15; hist data record, Op Div, 7AF Tactical Air Control Center, Apr–Jun 68; C. William Thorndale, *Air War in the DMZ* (Hq PACAF, Proj CHECO, Aug 1, 69), pp 44–45; msg, Gen Abrams to Gen Wheeler and Adm Sharp, 170447Z Jun 68, subj: Enemy Air Activity in the DMZ Area.

56. Hist data record, Current Ops Div, 7AF Tactical Air Control Center, Jul–Sep 68.

57. Msg, 7AF to CINCPACAF, 310505Z Aug 68, subj: Videotape of Helicopter Shoot Down.

58. Sams, Schlight, et al, *The Air War in Vietnam, 1968–1969*, p 64; hist data record, Current Ops Div, 7AF Tactical Air Control Center, Jul–Sep 68; Lt Col Guyman Penix and Maj Paul T. Ringenbach, *Air Defense in Southeast Asia, 1945–1971* (Hq PACAF, Proj CHECO, Jan 17, 73). pp 40–42.

Chapter 6

1. Robert Frank Futrell, *The United States Air Force in Korea*, 1950–1953 (Washington, 1983), pp 114–15, 213–14; msg, CINCPAC to COMUSMACV, 242345Z Apr 65, subj: Control of Close Air Support Operations; Warren A. Trest, *Single Manager for Air in SVN* (Hq PACAF, Proj CHECO, Jul 1, 68), pp 14–17.

2. Intvw, Lt Col Ralph F. Moody, USMC, with Maj Gen John R. Chaisson, USMC, Dir/MACV Combat Ops Center, 67–68, Mar 19, 69.

3. Hist, USMACV, 1968, vol I, pp 376, 381; Trest, *Single Manager*, pp 4–5.

4. Memo for record, William W. Momyer, 7AF Comdr, Jan 21, 68, subj: Air Support in I Corps.

5. Msg, Gen Westmoreland to Gen Wheeler, 220052Z Jan 68, subj: Visit to Washington by Richard E Cabezas, LTC, Inf, USA; Westmoreland hist notes, Dec 28, 67–Jan 31, 68.

6. Chaisson intvw (Moody).

7. Gen Westmoreland hist notes, Dec 28, 67–Jan 31, 68.

8. Memo for record, Gen William W. Momyer, 7AF Comdr, nd [Jan 16, 68], subj: Ops Control of 1st MAW.

9. FMFPAC, Operations of Marine Forces Vietnam, Mar 68, pp 67–68, 71–73; msg, III MAF to COMUSMACV, 18 [illegible] Jan 68, subj: none.

10. Msg, Gen Westmoreland to Adm Sharp, 210945Z Jan 68, subj: none.

457

Notes to pages 96–106

11. Lt Col Robert M. Burch, *Single Manager for Air in SVN* (Hq PACAF, Proj CHECO, Mar 18, 69); msg, Gen Westmoreland for Adm Sharp, 271148Z Feb 68, subj: none.

12. Intvw, Robert W. Kritt with Adm U.S. Grant Sharp, CINCPAC, 64–68, Feb 19, 71.

13. Msg, Gen Westmoreland to Gen Abrams, 081231Z Mar 68, subj: none; ltr, Gen William C. Westmoreland to CG III MAF, Mar 7, 68, subj: Single Management of Strike and Reconnaissance Assets.

14. JCS Dictionary of United Sates Military Terms for Joint Usage, JCS Pub 1, Nov 1, 60; Aug 1, 68.

15. Burch, *Single Manager*, pp 9–12; FMFPAC, Operations of Marine Forces Vietnam, Mar 68, pp 67–68.

16. Trest, *Single Manager*, pp 34–35.

17. Memo, Brig Gen Jones E. Bolt, Dep Dir/Tactical Air Control Center, for Gen Momyer and Gen Blood, Mar 18, 68, subj: Preplanned Sorties from I Corps.

18. Trest, *Single Manager*, pp 23–25.

19. FMFPAC, Operations of Marine Forces Vietnam, Mar 68, p 64; msg, Gen Westmoreland to Gen Abrams, 081231Z Mar 68, subj: none.

20. Msg, Gen Wheeler to Gen Westmoreland, JCS 3562, 310239 Mar 68, subj: none.

21. Msg, Gen Wheeler to Gen Westmoreland, JCS 3665, 031930Z Apr 68, subj: none; Intvw Benis M. Frank, Jack Shulimson, et al with Gen Leonard F. Chapman, Jr., CMC, 68–71, Mar 28, 79.

22. Msg, Gen Wheeler to Gen Westmoreland, 271722Z Apr 68, subj: Operational Control of III MAF Aviation Assets.

23. Msg, CG III MAF to COMUSMACV, 040902Z May 68, subj: Single Management of Strike and Reconnaissance Assets.

24. Burch, *Single Manager*, pp 15–16.

25. Msg, Gen Westmoreland to Adm Sharp, 091025Z May 68, subj: Review of Single Management System for Tactical Fighter Bomber Assets.

26. Burch, *Single Manager*, pp 16–17.

27. Msg, COMUSMACV to CINCPAC, 090003Z May 68, subj: Single Management Presentation; Gen Westmoreland hist notes, May 1–31, 68.

28. Msg, Maj Gen Kerwin to Gen Westmoreland, Gen Abrams, and Gen Momyer, 110346Z May 68, subj: Single Managership.

29. Msg, Gen Westmoreland to Adm Sharp, 151235Z May 68, subj: Single Management of Strike and Reconnaissance Assets.

30. Atch to memo, Gen William W. Momyer for Gen Westmoreland, May 18, 68, subj: Single Management—Preplanned System Modification Test.

31. Ibid; msg, Maj Gen Kerwin to Gen Westmoreland, Gen Abrams, and Gen Momyer, 110346Z May 68, subj: Single Managership.

32. Memo for record, Gen William W, Momyer, May 19, 68, subj: Single Manager of Air Assets.

33. Ibid; msg, Gen Wheeler to Adm Sharp and Gen Westmoreland, 171353Z May 68, subj: Operational Control of III MAF Aviation Assets; Chapman intvw.

34. Ltr, Gen William W. Momyer to COMUSMACV, May 15, 68, subj: Single Management of Strike and Reconnaissance Assets.

35. Rprt, Co C, 5th Special Forces Gp (Abn), May 31, 68, subj: After Action Report, Battle of Kham Duc; rprt, Mobile Strike Forces, Co C, 5th Special Forces Gp (Abn), to CO, Co C, May 16, 68, subj: After Action Report, Ngok Tavak FOB; Statement, Capt Eugene E. Makowski, 5th Special Forces Gp, Ngok Tavak, atch to Kham Duc after action rprt.

36. Gen Westmoreland hist notes, May 1–31, 68; Statement by Capt Robert Henderson, III, USA, nd, atch to Kham Duc after action rprt; Kenneth Sams and Maj A. W. Thompson, *Kham Duc* (Hq PACAF, Proj CHECO, Jul 8, 68), p. 5.

37. Statement, Maj John W. Gallagher, Chief, Kham Duc Ground Control Team, May 68, May 17, 68.

38. Statement, Lt Col Reece B. Black, I Corps ALO, 68, May 16, 68.

39. Ibid; statement, Capt Herbert Spier, FAC, Americal Div, 68, May 29, 68.

40. Sams and Thompson, *Kham Duc*, p 32.

41. Gen Westmoreland hist notes, May 1–31, 68.

42. Atch to ltr, Gen Momyer to COMUSMACV, May 15, 68, subj: Single Manage-

ment of Strike and Reconnaissance Assets.
  43. Spier statement.
  44. Atch, to ltr, Gen Momyer to COMUSMACV, May 15, 68, subj: Single Management of Strike and Reconnaissance Assets.
  45. Statements, Maj Ernest M. Wood, USA, CO, 178th Assault Helicopter Co, 68, May 29, 68; W O James L. Busby, USA, 178th Assault Helicopter Co, 68, May 28, 68.
  46. Statement, 1st Lt S. T. Summerman, USMC, HMM–265, MAG–16, 68, May 28, 68.
  47. Statement, 1st Lt Paul H. Moody, USMC, HMM-265, MAG–16, 68, May 28, 68.
  48. Statements, Capt Philip Smothermon, FAC, Americal Div, 68, May 18, 68; Maj James C. Gibler, FAC, Americal Div, 68, May 18, 68; Lt Col Robert Andrus, FAC, 2d ARVN Div, 68, May 28, 68.
  49. Lt Col Alan L. Gropman, *Airpower and the Airlift Evacuation of Kham Duc* (Maxwell AFB, Ala, 79), pp 37–49, 56; Gallagher statement.
  50. Gropman, *Kham Duc*, pp 4, 49; ltr, 834th Air Div Airlift Control Element to 834th Air Div, May 13, 68, subj: Evacuation of Kham Duc.
  51. Gropman, *Kham Duc*, p 50.
  52. Ibid, pp 51–52.
  53. Intvw, Col Ray Bowers with TSgt John K. McCall, C–130 flight mechanic, 374th TAWg, 68, Apr 7, 72; ltr, 834th Air Div Airlift Control Element to 834th Air Div, May 13, 68, subj: Evacuation of Kham Duc.
  54. Intvw, Col Ray Bowers with Lt Col James L. Wallace, aircraft comdr, 68, Apr 3, 72.
  55. Gallagher statement; Gropman, *Kham Duc*, pp 54, 58.
  56. Gropman, *Kham Duc*, pp 59–60,
  57. Ibid; Statement, Col Joe M. Jackson, Det Comdr, 311th ACSq, 68, May 3, 72; notes of intvw, Col Ray Bowers with Lt Col Emmett A. Niblack, Chief, Standardization and Evaluation, 311th ACSq, 68, May 3, 72.
  58. Msg, COMUSMACV to NMCC and CINCPAC, 131000Z May 68, subj: Evening Telecon; Kham Duc after action rprt.
  59. Statement, Maj Jack Anderson, Asst ALO, Americal Div, 68, May 29, 68.
  60. Gropman, *Kham Duc*, p 25.

Chapter 7

  1. Burch, *Single Manager*, pp 19–22.
  2. Msgs, CG FMFPAC, to CG III MAF, 160911Z May 68, subj: none; to CG III MAF and CG 1st MAW, 182000Z May 68, subj: none.
  3. Memo, CMC for JCS, Jun 14, 68, subj: Operational Control of III MAF, quoted in msg, JCS to CINCPAC, 191952Z Jun 68, subj: same.
  4. Msg, CG III MAF to COMUSMACV, 300636Z Jun 68, subj: III MAF Evaluation of Single Management/Strike Support.
  5. Msg, 7AF Tactical Air Control Center to 1st MAW, 060219Z Jun 68, subj: 1st MAW Sortie Allocation.
  6. Memo, Gen William W. Momyer to 7AF Dir/Ops, Jun 20, 68, subj: none.
  7. Msg, 7AF to PACAF, 270015Z Jun 68, subj: Operational Control of III MAF Aviation.
  8. MACV J–3 Evaluation of Single Management, May 30–Jun 27, 68, nd [Jun 68].
  9. Msg, COMUSMACV to CINCPAC, 061130Z Jul 68, subj: Evaluation of Single Management, 30 May–27 Jun 68.
  10. Msg, 7AF AFSSO to CSAF AFSSO and CINCPACAF AFSSO, 051115Z Aug 68, subj: Single Management of Strike and Reconnaissance Assets.
  11. Msg, CG FMFPAC to CG III MAF, 042313Z Sep 68, subj: none.
  12. Ibid; Chapman intvw; msg, 7AF AFSSO to CSAF AFSSO and CINCPACAF AFSSO, 051115Z Aug 68, subj: Single Management of Strike and Reconnaissance Assets.
  13. Msg, CINCPAC to JCS, 041118Z Sep 68, subj: Single Management.
  14. 7AF rprts, Single Management of Strike and Reconnaissance Assets, Jun 27–Jul 27, 68, nd; Single Management of Strike and Reconnaissance Assets, Jul 28–Aug 28, 68, nd; Ofc of Asst SecDef (Systems Analysis), study, Tactical Air Operations in South Vietnam, nd [Aug 69].
  15. Msg, COMUSMACV to CINCPAC,

459

071218Z Aug 68, subj: Single Management.

16. Msg, CG, ProvCorpsV to CG III MAF, 141538Z Jul 68, subj: Preliminary Rprt, Operation Thor.

17. 7AF Dir/Plans, Staff Summary Sheet, Jun 29, 68, subj: Thor Planning Conference; Maj Robert M. Burch, *The ABCCC in SEA* (Hq PACAF, Proj CHECO, Jan 15, 69), p 16.

18. Msg, CG ProvCorpsV to CG III MAF, 141538Z Jul 68, subj: Preliminary Report, Operation Thor; Notes of briefing by Lt Col T. J. Stevens, USMC, Thor critique, Udorn, Thailand, Jul 13, 68.

19. Msgs, CG ProvCorpsV to CG III MAF, 141538Z Jul 68, subj: Preliminary Report, Operation Thor; Lt Col J. S. Stoer, Rprt, Single Management, Mar 8–Dec 31, 68, Jan 8, 69.

20. Msg, CG III MAF to COMUSMACV, 210932Z Oct 68, subj: Evaluation of Thor.

21. Stoer, Single Mgt Rprt, pp 43–45; msg, CG III MAF to COMUSMACV, 200229Z Oct 68, subj: Relocation of Fwd Bomb Line (FBL).

22. Msg, 7AF to COMUSMACV, 310550Z Oct 68, subj: Relocation of Forward Bomb Line (FBL).

23. Msgs, Gen Wheeler to Adm McCain and Gen Abrams, JCS 10964, 252252Z Sep 68, subj: none.

24. Hist, JCS, *The JCS and the War in Vietnam, 1960–1968*, pt III, pp 54:6–8; Cooper, *The Lost Crusade*, pp 403–4.

25. Msgs, JCS to CINCPAC, CINCSAC, et al, 010150Z Nov 68, subj: Air Reconnaissance Operations; JCS to CINCPAC and COMUSMACV, 242400Z Nov 68, subj: Air Reconnaissance Operations; JCS to AIG 7077, 010100Z Nov 68, subj: Operations against NVN.

26. Proposed MACV Directive 95–4, Dec 68.

27. Msg, CG III MAF to COMUSMACV, 120608Z Jan 69, subj: none.

28. PACAF Summary of Air Operations, Apr 68, Jun 68, Jun 70, passim.

29. Tolson, *Air Mobility*, pp 209–12; hist, USMACV, 1969, vol I, pp IV:20–24. V:40.

30. Hist, USMACV, 1969, vol I, pp IV:12–20; 1970, vol I, pp IV:10–23.

31. Msgs, CINCPAC to CINCPACAF, CINCPACFLT, and COMUSMACV, 200120Z Mar 70, subj: Southeast Asia Air Munitions Expenditures; 7AF to PACAF, 250555Z Mar 70, subj: Southeast Asia Air Munitions Expenditure.

32. Hist, USMACV, 1968, vol III, p 154; ltr, Lt Gen Keith B. McCutcheon, USMC, to Maj Gen Homer S. Hill, DCS/Air, Hq USMC.

33. Lt Gen Keith B, McCutcheon, "Marine Aviation in Vietnam," *U.S. Naval Institute Proceedings*, May 1971, p 137.

34. Msg, XXIV Corps SSO and 7AF SSO, 140300Z Jun 70, subj: Planned Operation.

35. Msgs, 7AF to CG XXIV Corps, 161130Z Jun 70, subj: none; Lt Gen Sutherland to Gen Abrams, 230300Z Jun 70, subj: "Thrash Light" Results.

36. 1st MAW Command Chronology, Jun 70, p 8; msg, CG 1st MAW to AIG–19, 170130Z Jun 70, subj: FMAW SITREP 1777, 160001H–162400H.

37. Intvw, Maj R. B. Clement and Capt R. G. Swenston with Gen George S. Brown, 7AF Comdr, 68–70, Oct 19–20, 70, pp 17–19.

38. Ltr, Lt Gen Keith B. McCutcheon, USMC, to Gen Leonard F. Chapman, Jr., CMC, Aug 16, 70.

39. MACV Directive 95–4, Aug 15, 70.

40. McCutcheon ltr.

41. McCutcheon, "Marine Aviation," p 137.

42. Intvw, R. R. Kritt, ph D, with Lt Gen Robert E. Cushman, Jr., CG III MAF, 67–68, Aug 13, 71.

Chapter 8

1. Hist, JCS, *The JCS and the War in Vietnam, 1969–1970*, pp 5–7.

2. Msg, Dir/Joint Staff to Gen Nazzaro, Acting CINCPAC, and Gen Abrams, JCS 00936, 230107Z Jan 69, subj: Cambodia.

3. Hist, JCS, *The JCS and the War in Vietnam, 1969–1970*, pp 218–19.

4. Msgs, Gen McConnell, Acting CJCS, to Gen Abrams, JCS 01836, 120010Z Feb 69, subj: none; Gen Abrams to Gen McConnell, 130230Z Feb 69, subj: none.

5. Henry Kissinger, *White House Years*

(Boston, 1979), pp 243–44.

6. 7. Msg, Gen Abrams to Gen Wheeler and Adm McCain, 051012Z Mar 69, subj: Retaliatory Actions.

7. Msg, Paul Kearney to Adm McCain and Gen Abrams, JCS 13184, subj: none, retransmitting memo, CJCS to SecDef, Mar 12, 69, subj: Observations and Recommendations Concerning the Military Situation in Southeast Asia.

8. Kissinger, *White House Years*, pp 239–40.

9. Richard M. Nixon, *RN: The Memoirs of Richard Nixon* (New York, 1978), pp 380–81.

10. Msg, CJCS to COMUSMACV, 201917Z Mar 69, subj: Cambodia, retransmitting Bangkok to State 4992, 191145Z Mar 68.

11. Kissinger, *White House Years*, pp 245–47; msgs 3d Air Div SSO (Gillem) to MACV SSO (Abrams), 180420Z Mar 69 and 180750Z Mar 69, subj: none.

12. Kissinger, *White House Years*, p 253.

13. DOD Rprt, Selected Air and Ground Operations in Cambodia and Laos, Sep 10, 73, pp 5–11.

14. Msgs, Gen Abrams to Adm McCain, 100831Z Sep 69, subj: Salem House Evaluation; to Adms Moorer and McCain, Gen Holloway, and Lt Gen Gillem, 110811Z Jun 69, subj: Summary of Operation Dinner Alfa; Gen Wheeler to Adm McCain, Gen Holloway, and Gen Abrams, 121546Z Jul 69, subj: Operation Menu; to Gen Holloway, JCS 04146, 251829Z Mar 70, subj: Operation Menu.

15. Msg, Gen Wheeler to Adm McCain, Gen Abrams, and Lt Gen Gillem, JCS 05292, 302253Z Apr 69, subj: Operations Breakfast and Lunch.

16. Msgs, Gen Abrams to Gen Wheeler, 120535Z May 69, subj: none; to Gen Wheeler and Adm McCain, 311022Z Jan 70, subj: Operation Menu.

17. *Washington Star*, Mar 25, 69, p 1.

18. *New York Times*, May 9, 69, p 1.

19. Msgs, Gen Andrew J. Goodpaster, USA, to Gen Abrams, JCS 03692, 262115Z Mar 69, subj: none; Lt Gen John C. Meyer, USA, J–3, OJCS, to Gen Abrams, Adm McCain, Lt Gen Keith K. Compton, Vice CINCSAC, and Lt Gen Gillem, JCS/J–3, 05706, 091745Z May 69, subj: Operations Breakfast and Lunch.

20. *New York Times*, Jul 15, 73, p 1.

21. Kissinger, *White House Years*, pp 249–52.

22. Ibid, p. 251; msgs, State to Rangoon, Aug 15, 69, subj: Senator Mansfield's Visit to Cambodia, August 21–23, 1969; Phnom Penh to State, Sep 8, 69, subj: Mansfield Visit, August 21 through 23, 1969.

23. PACAF Summary of Air Operations, Mar 69–Apr 70, passim; hist, JCS, *The JCS and the War in Vietnam, 1969–19*, p 221. The Department of Defense "white paper," Selected Air and Ground Operations in Cambodia and Laos, has transposed the numbers of Base Area 740, a target mentioned in the Menu message traffic, into Base Area 704, some 200 miles southwest of the true target.

24. Kissinger, *White House Years*, pp 284, 288.

25. E. H. Hartsook, *The Air Force in Southeast Asia: The Administration Emphasizes Air Power, 1969* (Ofc/AF Hist, Nov 71), p 4.

26. Extension of Remarks, Rep Ronald V. Dellums, "Escalation, American Options, and President Nixon's War Moves," *Congressional Record*, vol 118, pt 13, 92d Congress, May 10, 72, pp 16750–51, 16800.

27. Kissinger, *White House Years*, p 239.

28. Ibid, pp 271–72.

29. Memo, SecDef for the President, nd, subj: Trip to Vietnam and CINCPAC, Mar 5–12, 1969.

30. Memo, Gen George S. Brown for Lt Gen John B. McPherson, Asst to CJCS, Mar 8, 69, subj: Reduced U.S. Levels of Participation in SVN.

31. Memo, SecDef for the President, nd, subj: Trip to Vietnam and CINCPAC, Mar 5–12, 69.

32. Ibid.

33. Kissinger, *White House Years*, p. 272.

34. Ibid, p 1481.

35. Msg, Gen Goodpaster to Gen Abrams, 282219Z Mar 69, subj: none.

36. National Security Decision Memo 9, Apr 1, 69, subj: Vietnam.

37. Security Study Memo 36, Apr 10, 69, subj: Vietnamizing the War.

Notes to pages 137–145

38. Hartsook, *The Administration Emphasizes Air Power*, pp 14–16.
39. Brown intvw (Clement and Swenston), p 124.
40. Hartsook, *The Administration Emphasizes Air Power*, pp 16–17.
41. Msg, Gen Abrams to Adm McCain, 300316Z Mar 69, subj: Air Force Tactical Fighter Posture in SEA.
42. Msgs, Adm McCain to Gen Wheeler, 050255Z Apr 69, subj: Force Posture in SEAsia; Gen Wheeler to Adm McCain, JCS 04502, 131153Z Apr 69, subj: Tactical Aircraft Reductions; Hartsook, *The Administration Emphasizes Air Power*, p 19.
43. Msgs, Gen Abrams to Gen Goodpaster, with the President in Calif, 231554Z Mar 69, subj: none; hist, JCS, *The JCS and the War in Vietnam, 1969–1970*, pp 109–10; 7AF Background Paper on NSSM 36, nd [Jan 17, 70].
44. Kissinger, *White House Years*, p 274; hist, JCS, *The JCS and the War in Vietnam, 1969–1970*, pp 115–16.
45. Hist, JCS, *The JCS and the War in Vietnam, 1969–1970*, pp 118–19, 123–24.
46. Msg, Paul M. Kearney, Admin Asst to CJCS, to Adm McCain, Gen Abrams, JCS 10688, subj: none, retransmitting memo, JCS for SecDef, JCSM–540–69, Aug 30, 69, subj: Force Planning; 7AF Background Paper on NSSM–36, nd [Jan 17, 70].
47. Ltr, Gen George S. Brown to Lt Gen Glen W. Martin, DCS/Plans and Ops, Hq USAF, Jun 12, 69.
48. Hist, JCS, *The JCS and the War in Vietnam, 1969–1970*, pp 133–34; msg, SAC to 3d Air Div, 092252Z Aug 69, subj: Program/Budget Exercise 703.
49. Brown intvw (Clement and Swenston), p 124.
50. Hist, 7AF, Jul–Dec 69, vol I, pt 1, pp xxx–xxxix; USAF Mgt Summary, SEA, Feb 6, 70, p 1:7.
51. PACAF Summary of Air Operations, Jan 69, p 7, Dec 69, p 6; USAF Mgt Summary, Jan 9, 70, pp 2:14–15.
52. Hist, 7AF, Jul–Dec 69, pp xli–xlii; Fox, *Base Defense*, pp 110–11.
53. Msg, AFSSO Tan Son Nhut to PACAF SSO, 061105Z Oct 68, subj: none.
54. Msg, Senior Representative, SAC X-Ray, Camp H. M. Smith, Hawaii, to 3d Air Div, 181945Z Oct 68, subj: Arc Light Sortie Rate, retransmitting COMUSMACV to SAC, nd, subj; same.
55. Msg, CINCPAC to JCS, CINCSAC, et al, 191152Z Oct 68, subj: Arc Light Sortie Rate, forwarding the views of General Abrams.
56. Memo, Lt Gen K. K. Compton to CINCSAC, Oct 25, 1968, subj: Matters for Inclusion in Your Monthly Letter to CSAF-1800 Sortie Rate.
57. Msg, SAC to 3d Air Div, 162227Z Dec 68, subj: Arc Light Sortie Rate.
58. Msg, SAC to JCS, 180305Z Dec 68, subj: B–52 Sortie Rate.
59. Msg, SAC to 3d Air Div, 032346Z Jan 69, subj: Arc Light Sortie Rate retransmitting CINCPAC to SAC, 030454Z Jan 69, subj: same.
60. Hist, JCS, *The JCS and the War in Vietnam, 1969–1970*, p 64.
61. Ibid, pp 134–38; USAF Mgt Summary, SEA, Jan 5, 69, p 22; Dec 31, 69, p 2:17.
62. Hist, SAC, fiscal 69, vol I, pp 173–74; msgs, 7AF to SAC and 3d Air Div, 090925Z Dec 68, subj: Arc Light Tactics; SAC to COMUSMACV, CINCPAC, et al, 202240Z Dec 68, subj: Arc Light Bombing Tactics.
63. Hist, SAC, fiscal 69, vol I, pp 174–75; msg, 3d Air Div to 4242d Strat Wg, 4258th Strat Wg, et al, 190801Z Jan 68, subj: Azimuth Dispersion Bombing.
64. *New York Times*, Sep 26, 69, p 1.
65. Stanley Millet, ed, *South Vietnam: U.S.-Communist Confrontation in Southeast Asia*, vol IV, 1969 (New York, 1974), p 159.
66. *Public Papers of the Presidents of the United States* (Washington, 1971); *Richard M. Nixon, 1969*, p 767.
67. Ibid. p 907; Millet, *South Vietnam, 19*, pp 196–99.
68. Kissinger, *White House Years*, p 1481; Millet, *South Vietnam, 1969*, pp 203–7.

Chapter 9

1. Capt Robert F. Colwell, *Tactical Reconnaissance in Southeast Asia, July 69–*

June 71 (Hq PACAF, Proj CHECO, Nov 23, 71), pp 33–38; annex A to ACIC Sentinel Suffix/Simplex Loran OPlan, Nov 9, 70.

2. Hist, MAC, Jul 69–Jun 70, vol I, pp 25–33.

3. Cecil L. Reynolds, *MAC Aeromedical Airlift Support of U.S. SEA Operations (1964–1971)* (MAC, 1973), pp 83–85, 105.

4. 1st Lt Edward P. Brynn, *Reconnaissance in Southeast Asia* (Hq PACAF, Proj CHECO, Jul 25, 69, pp 19–23, 45, 49.

5. Brown intvw (Clement and Swentston), pp 98–99, 124.

6. Brynn, *Reconnaissance*, pp 32–33.

7. PACAF Summary of Air Operations, Jan–Dec 69, passim.

8. Ibid, Jan–Dec 68, passim.

9. Brown intvw (Clement and Swenston), p 4.

10. PACAF Summary of Air Operations, Jan–Dec 68, Jan–Dec 69, passim.

11. Ibid, Jan–Dec 69, passim.

12. Military Working Arrangement between Comdr, 7th AF and Dep Chief of Staff, Royal Australian Air Force, nd [1967]; hist data record, RAAF No 2 Squadron, Apr–Jun 68; Jan–Mar 69; hist, 25th TFWg, Jan–Mar 68, p 14; James T. Bear, *The RAAF in SEA* (Hq PACAF, Sep 30, 70), pp 6–7, 17–19, 29, 35–36, 45, 52.

13. James T. Bear, *The Employment of Air by the Thais and Koreans* (Hq PACAF, Proj CHECO, Oct 30, 70), pp 24–26, 30–31.

14. Ibid, pp 4–5, 7–11, 13–14.

15. Lt Col Bert B. Aton and E. S. Montagliani, *The Fourth Offensive* (Hq PACAF, Proj CHECO, Oct 1, 69), pp 21–24, 40–45.

16. PACAF Summary of Air Operations, Feb 69, pp 3:9–10.

17. Msgs, Gen Abrams to Gen Wheeler and Adm McCain, 261259Z Feb 69, subj: Request for Arc Light Strikes in Tri-border Area; Gen Wheeler to Gen Abrams, JCS 02439, 262357Z Feb 69, subj: none; hist, USMACV, 1969, vol I, pp V:70–71.

18. Col Fred L. Webster, Dir/Horn DASC, Resume', nd, of A Shau Valley Interdiction Campaign, Dec 9, 68–Feb 26, 69.

19. 7AF Weekly Air Intelligence Summary, 68–50, Dec 14, 68, p 2.

20. Rprt, 2d Bde, 101st Abn Div, May 25, 69, subj: Combat After Action Report, Operation Massachusetts Striker.

21. Rprt, CO, 9th Marines, to CG, 3d Mar Div, Apr 8, 69, subj: Combat After Action Rprt.

22. Intvw, Lt Col Bert Aton with Lt Col George C. Fox, CO, 2d Bn, 9th Marines, 69, Aug 3, 69.

23. Ibid; *Washington Post*, Aug 13, 73, p 1; Col Bert Aton and C. William Thorndale, *The A Shau Valley Campaign, December 1968–May 1969* (Hq PACAF, Proj CHECO, Oct 15, 69), p 16.

24. Massachusetts Striker Rprt.

25. Incl 11, Air Support, to Massachusetts Striker Rprt.

26. Aton and Thorndale, *A Shau Valley*, pp 18–19; intvw, Lt Col Bert Aton with Capt Albert W. Estes, FAC, 3d Bde, 101st Abn Div, 69, Aug 8, 69; incl, Combat After Action Rprt (Intelligence), Apache Snow, nd [Jun 69], subj: Intelligence Exploitation of "Dong Ap Bia."

27. Estes intvw; rprt, 3d Bde, 101st Abn Div (Airmobile), Jun 25, 69, subj: After Action Report, Summary, Apache Snow.

28. 22d Mil Hist Det, narrative, Operation Apache Snow, 101st Abn Div, May 10–Jun 7, 69, nd.

29. Ibid; tab B–3 to atch to ltr, Lt Gen Melvin Zais, USA, to Brig Gen James L. Collins, Chief of Military History, Jan 5, 71, subj: none.

30. Tactical Air Support, incl 8 to Apache Snow Rprt.

31. Apache Snow hist; msg, Lt Gen Stilwell, CG XXIV Corps, to Gen Abrams, 211711Z May 69, subj: none; tab B–3 to Zais ltr, cited above.

32. Hist, USMACV, 1969, vol I, p V:57.

33. *Time*, Jun 6, 1969, p 5.

34. Hartsook, *The Administration Emphasizes Air Power*, p 62.

35. *Nixon Papers*, p 767.

36. Ernie S. Montagliani, *The Siege of Ben Het* (Hq PACAF, Proj CHECO, Oct 1, 69), pp 2–4.

37. Ibid. pp 13–16; msgs, Gen Abrams to Gen Wheeler and Adm McCain, 200906Z Jun 69 and 090814Z Jul 69, subj: Operation Menu.

38. Statement, Capt Donald L. Marx, Air Ops Ofcr, DASC Alpha, 69, Jul 11, 69.

Notes to pages 158–169

39. Statement, Lt Col Thomas M. Crawford, Jr., Dir/DASC Alpha, 69, Jul 10, 69.
40. 7AF Summary, Ben Het/Dak To Campaign, May 1–July 2, 1969, nd.
41. Hist, USMACV, 1969, vol I, pp V:77–78.
42. Msgs, Adm McCain to Adm Moorer, 011510Z Dec 69, subj: Arc Light in Disputed Areas; Adm Moorer, Acting CJCS, to Gen Abrams, JCS 14943, 012024Z Dec 69, subj: Request for Operational Authority to Conduct B–52 Strikes within Disputed Area Vicinity Bu Prang; Adm Moorer, Acting CJCS, to Gen Abrams, JCS 14976, 020430Z Dec 69, subj: Arc Light Strikes; Gen Abrams to Gen Wheeler, 070933Z Dec 69, subj: Summary of Arc Light Strikes against Enemy Positions near Bu Prang CIDG Camp, Nights of 2–3 and 3–4 Dec 69.
43. 7AF Weekly Air Intelligence Summary, Aug 29–Sep 4, 69, pp 4–7.

Chapter 10

1. Msgs, COMUSMACV to CINCPAC, 290859Z Jul 68, subj: RVNAF Improvement and Modernization; VNAF Improvement and Modernization Plan, app VI to James T. Bear, *VNAF Improvement and Modernization Program* (Hq, PACAF, Proj CHECO, Feb 5, 70).
2. Msg, COMUSMACV to CINCPAC, 080425Z Oct 68, subj: RVNAF Improvement and Modernization, Phase II.
3. Msg, COMUSMACV to CINCPAC, 030610Z May 69, subj: RVNAF Improvement and Modernization.
4. Hist, JCS, *The JCS and the War in Vietnam, 1969–1970*, pp 177–78; msg, COMUSMACV to CINCPAC, 090515Z Nov 68, subj: Implementation of Phase II Plan for RVNAF Improvement and Modernization.
5. Hist, JCS, *The JCS and the War in Vietnam, 1969–1970*, pp 178–79.
6. Escalation, American Options, and President Nixon's War Moves, Extension of Remarks by Hon Ronald V. Dellums, *Congressional Record*, vol 118, pt 13, 92d Congress, 2d Session, May 10–11, 72, 16752.
7. Hist, JCS, *The JCS and the War in Vietnam, 1969–1970*, pp 181–82.
8. Msg, JCS to CINCPAC, JCS 6304, 021346Z May 69, subj: RVNAF Improvement and Modernization, quoting memo, Dep SecDef to Secretaries of the Military Departments and CJCS, Apr 28, 69, subj: RVNAF Phase II Plan for Improvement and Modernization.
9. Msg, JCS to CINCPAC, JCS 5531, 291543Z Jul 69, subj: RVNAF Improvement and Modernization.
10. Atch to memo, Chief of Staff, MACV, to CINCPAC, Jun 8, 69, subj: Republic of Vietnam Proposals, Midway Summit Meeting, 8 June 1969; hist, JCS, *The JCS and the War in Vietnam, 1969–1970*, pp 185–86.
11. Memo, SecDef for Service Secretaries and CJCS, Aug 12, 1969, subj: Government of Vietnam Proposals, Midway Summit Meeting, 8 June 1969.
12. Brown intvw (Clement and Swenston), pp 86–87, 89.
13. Ibid, p 81; Intvw, Kenneth Sams and Richard Kott with Gen George S. Brown, 7AF Comdr, 68–70, Mar 30, 70.
14. End of Tour Rprt, Brig Gen Charles W. Carson, Chief, USAF Advisory Gp, Mar 25, 68–Aug 6, 69, Aug 5, 69.
15. Ibid.; Intvw, James T. Bear and Kenneth Sams with Brig Gen Kendall S. Young, Chief, USAF Advisory Gp, 69–70, Nov 3, 1970.
16. Carson rprt; James T. Bear, *VNAF Improvement and Modernization* (Hq PACAF, Proj CHECO, Feb 5, 70), p 65.
17. Carson rprt; Notes of intvw, James T. Bear with Lt Col J. W. Woodmansee, USA, S–3, 164th CAG, 69–70, Feb 2, 70.
18. Bear, *Improvement and Modernization*, pp 66–67.
19. Language: The Key to Vietnamization, HQ USAF, Trends, Indicators, and Analyses, Oct 69; Defense Attache' Ofc, Quarterly Assessment, Oct 31, 73, p II:5.
20. Language: The Key to Vietnamization, cited above.
21. Ltr, Pacific-SEA Br, Plans Section, to DCS/Plans and Ops ([Lt] Gen [Glen W.] Martin), nd [summer 69], subj: English Language Training in SVN.

22. Bear, *Improvement and Modernization*, pp 27–31.

23. Ltr, 7AF DCS/Plans to Dir, Tactical Analysis, Jan 7, 70, subj: Inputs to CHECO Rprt; Memo, Gen George S. Brown for 7AF Chief of Staff, Sep 23, 69, subj: Nha Trang Manning Requirements.

24. End of Tour Rprt, Col Paul E. Bell, Chief USAF Advisory Gp Team 2, Dec 4–Oct 30, 69, nd.

25. End of Tour Rprt, Col H. H. D. Heiberg, Jr., Chief USAF Advisory Gp Team 1, Dec 4, 68–Oct 30, 69, nd.

26. Annex A to VNAF Plan 69–17, Air Logistics Command, Aug 1, 69.

27. Young intvw.

28. Heiberg rprt; msg, 7AF SSO to PACAF SSO, 120805Z Oct 69, subj: Vietnamizing the War; 7AF Combined Campaign Plan, FY 1/70, nd.

29. Bear, *Improvement and Modernization*, pp 54–55; End of Tour Rprt, Col Wayne G. Grooms, senior adviser to the VNAF Logistics Command, Aug 13, 69–Aug 3, 70, Jul 15, 70, p 6; USAF Advisory Gp, Vietnam, Military Assistance Program Rprt, Oct–Dec 69, nd.

30. Bear, *Improvement and Modernization*, p 59; 7AF Combined Campaign Plan Quarterly Rprt, FY 2/69, nd.

31. Heiberg rprt.

32. Ibid; USAF Advisory Gp, Vietnam, Military Assistance Program Rprt, Oct–Dec 69, nd.

33. Msg, Gen Wheeler to Gen Abrams, JCS 07380, 141457Z Jun 69, subj: none.

34. VNAF TACS ALO/FAC Upgrading Plan, Mar 69.

35. Annex B to VNAF TACS ALO/FAC Upgrading Plan, Mar 69.

36. Ibid.

37. End of Tour Rprt, Col Delbert J. Light, Chief, USAF Advisory Team 7, 68–69, nd [Aug 69].

38. Bear, *Improvement and Modernization*, p 49.

39. Brown intvw (Clement and Swenston), pp 84–85.

40. Ibid; Bear, *Improvement and Modernization*, pp 34–35.

41. Annex B to VNAF Plan 69–14, May 28, 69; Bear, *Improvement and Modernization*, pp 38–39,

42. Maj M. J. Grady, *Interdiction in III Corps Tactical Zone: Proj DART* (Hq PACAF, Proj CHECO, Aug 10, 69), pp 7–8.

43. Ltr, Gen Brown to Maj Gen Richard H. Ellis, Dir/Plans, Hq USAF, Mar 10, 69, subj: none.

44. Intvw, Maj M. J. Grady with Maj Vincent J. Evans, Comdr, Det L, 504th TASGp, 68–69, Apr 1, 69; Grady, *DART*, pp 21–22.

45. Grady, *DART*, pp 16–17; End of Tour Rprt, Col John C. O'Neill, Dir/Ops, USAF Advisory Gp, 69, Nov 3, 69.

46. DSPG Documentary Supplement I, Jun 69–Aug 70, p II:28; ltr, Asst DCS/Ops, 7AF, to DCS/Plans, Jan 7, 70, subj: 7AF OPlan 498–69, Combined Campaign Plan Quarterly Report (Your ltr, 26 Dec 69); Significant VNAF Achievements from a Headquarters Point of View, atch to End of Tour Rprt, Col William A Lafferty, Dir/Plans and Programs, USAF Advisory Gp, Jul 69–Jun 71, Jun 9, 71.

47. Young intvw.

48. Memo, Curtis W. Tarr, Asst SAF (Manpower and Reserve Affairs), for Secretary Laird, Oct 7, 69, subj: Observations on a Trip to Vietnam.

49. Hist, JCS, *The JCS and the War in Vietnam, 1969–1970*, pp 197–98.

50. Memo, Ivan Selin, Acting Asst SecDef (ISA), for SecDef, Dec 15, 69, subj: Vietnamization Progress.

51. Memo, SecDef for CJCS, Nov 10, 69, subj: Vietnamization—RVNAF Improvement and Modernization, Aspects and Related U.S. Planning.

52. Memo, David Packard for SAF, Dec 19, 69, subj: VNAF Modernization.

53. Hartsook, *The Administration Emphasizes Air Power*, p 77.

54. Intvw, Kenneth Sams and Maj Philip Caine with Gen Creighton Abrams, COMUSMACV, 68–72, Mar 3, 70.

Chapter 11

1. Kissinger, *White House Years*, p 250.

2. Ibid, p 255.

3. Ofc, Dep Asst SecDef (ISA), Regional Programs, Cambodian Contingencies, nd [summer 1970].

4. Hist, JCS, *The JCS and the War in Vietnam, 1969–1970*, pp 227–32.

5. Msg, Gen Rosson, Dep COMUSMACV, to Gen Brown, 231036Z Mar 70, subj: none.

6. Hist, JCS, *The JCS and the War in Vietnam, 1969–1970*, p 237.

7. Kissinger, *White House Years*, p 465.

8. Msg, Gen Wheeler to Gen Abrams, JCS 04182, 260126Z Mar 70, subj: Plan for Ground Strikes against Base Camps in Cambodia.

9. Msg, Gen Wheeler to Gen Abrams, JCS 04213, 261941Z Mar 70, subj: Plan for Ground Action against Base Areas in Cambodia.

10. Msgs, Gen Wheeler to Gen Abrams or Gen Rosson, JCS 04217, 261954Z Mar 70, subj: Planning for Cambodian Actions; Gen Abrams to Adm McCain, 311446Z Mar 70, quoting Saigon to State 4725, subj: Crossborder Operations and Relations with Cambodia.

11. Maj D. I. Folkman and Maj P. D. Caine, *The Cambodian Campaign, 24 April–30 June 1970* (Hq PACAF, Proj CHECO, Sep 1, 1970), pp 10–11.

12. Msgs, Gen Wheeler to Adm McCain and Gen Abrams, JCS 04372, 311441Z Mar 70, subj: Additional Cambodian Options Involving B–52s, and JCS 04447, 011716Z Apr 70, subj: Increased Menu Activities; Gen Abrams to Adm McCain, 301014Z Mar 70, subj: Plan for Ground Action against Base Areas in Cambodia; to Gen Wheeler and Adm McCain, 030025Z Apr 70, subj: Additional Cambodian Options Involving B–52s.

13. Kissinger, *White House Years*, p 495.

14. Hist, JCS, *The JCS and the War in Vietnam, 1969–1970*, pp 238–40; msgs, Gen Wheeler to Adm McCain and Gen Abrams, JCS 04424, 010041Z Apr 70, subj: Cambodian Border ROE [Rules of Engagement] Guidance; Gen Abrams to Gen Brown, Lt Gen [Frank T.] Mildren, et al, 011140Z Apr 70, subj: Operations Near Cambodian Border.

15. Msg, Adm McCain to Gen Wheeler, 310459Z Mar 70, subj; Camel Path Operations; hist, JCS, *The JCS and the War in Vietnam, 1969–1970*, pp 236–37.

16. Msg, Gen Abrams to Gen Wheeler and Adm McCain, 301242Z Mar 70, subj: Plan for Ground Action against Base Areas in Cambodia.

17. Msg, Gen Abrams to Gen Wheeler and Adm McCain, 041054Z Apr 70, subj: Salem House.

18. Msg, Paul M. Kearney, Ofc CJCS, to Adm McCain and Gen Abrams, JCS 05161, 151326Z Apr 70, subj: none, retransmitting State to Phnom Penh and Saigon, 055340, 150017Z Apr 70.

19. Msgs, Gen Abrams to Gen Wheeler, 161151Z Apr 70, subj: none; 271254Z Apr 70, subj: Additional Small Arms for Cambodian Armed Forces; to Gen Wheeler and Adm McCain, 280122Z Apr 70, subj: none.

20. Msg, Adm McCain to Gen Abrams, 282351Z Jun 70, subj: C–130 Airlift to Cambodia.

21. Hist, JCS, *The JCS and the War in Vietnam, 1969–1970*, p 236; msg, Adm McCain to Gen Wheeler, 190224Z Apr 70, subj: Request for Assistance.

22. Hist, JCS, *The JCS and the War in Vietnam, 1969–1970*, p 240.

23. DOD Rprt on Selected Air and Ground Operations in Cambodia and Laos, Sep 10, 73, p 21.

24. Hist, JCS, *The JCS and the War in Vietnam, 1969–1970*, pp 246–47.

25. Msgs, Gen Abrams to Gen Brown and Col Cavanaugh, 211154Z Apr 70, subj: Strike Authority; Gen Abrams to Gen Wheeler, 250200Z Apr 70, subj: Patio Report One.

26. Msgs, Gen Abrams to Adm McCain, 101119Z May 70, subj: Request for Strike Authorization; Adm Moorer to Adm McCain and Gen Abrams, JCS 06544, 111808Z May 70, subj: same; 7AF SSO to MACV SSO, 130758Z, subj: Intentions Regarding Special Strike Authority; 141200Z May 70, subj: Special Strike in Cambodia.

27. Memo, President Nixon to Dr. Kissinger, Apr 22, 70, in Kissinger, *White House Years*, p 1484.

28. Msgs, Gen Abrams to Adm McCain and Adm Moorer, 231436Z Apr 70, subj: Cambodian Operations; Adm Moorer, Act-

ing CJCS, to Adm McCain and Gen Abrams, JCS 05623, 232209Z Apr 70, subj: Operations in Cambodia.

29. Msg, Gen Wheeler to Gen Abrams, JCS 05711, 251802Z Apr 70, subj: none.

30. Msg, Adm Moorer to COMUSMACV and CINCPAC, 250015Z Apr 70, subj: none.

31. Msgs, Gen Abrams to Gen Wheeler and Adm McCain, 251031Z Apr 70, subj: none; 261044Z Apr 70, subj: Operation in BA 352/353 (Operation Shoemaker); Gen Abrams to Maj Gen Dixon, 7AF Vice Comdr, 290519Z Apr 70, subj: Operation Shoemaker; hist, USMACV, 1970, vol III, p C:68.

32. Msg, Col Scott G. Smith, USA, to Gen [Elvy B.] Roberts, USA, 051530Z May 70, subj: none.

33. *Public Papers of the Presidents of the United States* (Washington, 1971), *Richard Nixon, 1970*, pp 405–10.

34. Hist, JCS, *The JCS and the War in Vietnam. 1969–1970*, p 254; msgs, Gen Abrams to Gen Brown, VAdm [Elmo R.] Zumwalt, et al, 300836Z Apr 70, subj: none; Gen Wheeler to Adm McCain and Gen Abrams, JCS 06076, 022035Z May 70, subj: none.

35. Msg, Gen Wheeler to Gen Abrams and Adm McCain, JCS 05812, 281956Z Apr 70, subj: Actions to Protect U.S. Forces in South Vietnam; hist, USMACV, 1970, vol III, p C:50.

36. Msgs, Gen Abrams to Gen Wheeler, 041036Z May 70, subj: Reporting TACAIR Operations in Cambodia; Gen Wheeler to Gen Abrams, 042316Z May 70, subj: Reporting TAC Air Operations in Cambodia; DOD Rprt on Selected Air and Ground Operations in Cambodia and Laos, Sep 10, 73, pp 21–22.

37. Msgs, Gen Wheeler to Gen Abrams, Adm McCain, et al, JCS 06072, 021955Z May 70, subj: Operation Menu; JCS 07362, 272252Z May 70, subj: B–52 Strikes in Cambodia (Menu Mentioned); Gen Abrams to Gen Wheeler and Adm McCain, 280022Z May 70, subj: Operation Menu.

38. Msg, Ambassador Leonard Unger to Adm Moorer, Bangkok 1012, 020724Z May 70, subj: B–52 Support in Cambodia.

39. 7AF Study, Air Operations in Cambodia, Apr 29–Jun 21, 70, p 6.

40. Msg, Adm Moorer to Adm McCain and Gen Abrams, JCS 06037, 012239Z May 70, subj: Attack of Additional Base Areas in Cambodia.

41. 7AF Air Ops in Cambodia, p 6; hist, USMACV, 1970, vol III, pp C:57, 68–71, 76–79, 84, 88.

42. 7AF Air Ops in Cambodia, p. 6; hist, USMACV, 1970, vol III, pp C:93–94.

43. 7AF Air Ops in Cambodia, p 6; hist, USMACV, 1970, vol III, p C:97.

44. Memo for Record, Phil Odeen, Ofc of Dep Asst SecDef (Systems Analysis), Regional Programs, May 8, 70, subj: Vietnamization Meeting with Secretary Laird; hist, JCS, *The JCS and the War in Vietnam, 1969–1970*, pp 293–94, 301–2,

45. Folkman and Caine, *Cambodian Campaign*, fig 19, pp 26–27.

46. 7AF Air Ops in Cambodia, p 2.

47. Ibid; atch to rprt, USAF ALO, 22d ARVN Div, Lt Col James V. Hyland, to Hq, 7AF, Jul 10, 70, subj: CHECO.

48. Atch to rprt, Lt Col James Hyland, cited above.

49. Ibid; 7AF Air Ops in Cambodia, pp 2, 10–11.

50. Msgs, Gen Abrams to Adm McCain, 060145Z May 70, subj: Request for Authority for Overflight of Cambodia; Adm McCain to Gen Wheeler, 060259Z May 70, subj: same; Adm McCain to Gen Abrams, 060320Z May 70, subj: none; Gen Wheeler to Adm McCain, JCS 06259, 061412Z May 70, subj; Reconnaissance in Cambodia; JCS 06324, 062245Z May 70, subj; Reconnaissance Overflight of Cambodia.

51. 7AF Air Ops in Cambodia, pp 10–11.

52. Ibid, pp 11, 13; msgs, Gen Abrams to Lt Gen [Michael S.] Davison, USA, 090001Z May 70, subj: Psyop Support; 7AF to II DASC, 3d TFWg, et al, 020800Z Jun 70, subj: Operating Instructions; Adm McCain to Gen [Ralph E.] Haines [Jr.], USA, and Gen Nazzaro, 170319Z May 70, subj: Psyop Planning for Cambodia.

53. Hist, JCS, *The JCS and the War in Vietnam, 1969–1970*, pp 352–353; msgs, Gen Abrams to Gen Wheeler and Adm McCain, 020944Z May 70, subj: Interdiction of Routes 1036/1039/1032/7; 031038Z May

Notes to pages 193–202

70 and 040956Z May 70, subj: Strikes against Logistics Targets in NVN; to Adm Moorer and Adm McCain, 030203Z May 1970, subj: Interdiction of Routes 1036/1039/1032; 7AF SSO to CTF 77, 021026Z May 70, subj: none.

54. *Nixon Papers, 1970*, p 407.

55. Msg, Gen Wheeler to Adm McCain and Gen Abrams, JCS 06055, 021502Z May 70, subj: COSVN Headquarters.

56. Msg, Maj Gen [Edward] Bautz [Jr], USA, to Lt Gen Davison and Brig Gen [Francis J.] Roberts, USA, 140545Z May 70, subj: POW—COSVN Signal Unit.

57. Msg, Gen Wheeler, CJCS, to Gen Abrams and Adm McCain, JCS 07117, 212248Z May 70, subj: COSVN Headquarters.

58. Msg, Gen Abrams to Gen Brown, 221634Z May 70, subj: COSVN Headquarters.

59. Msgs, Gen Abrams to Gen Brown, 222152Z May 70, subj: none; 7AF SSO to AF SSO and COMUSMACV, 240220Z May 70, subj: 23 May 70 Special Strike against Suspected COSVN Headquarters.

60. Msgs, Gen Abrams to Lt Gen [Julian J.] Ewell, USA, U.S. Embassy, Paris, 060959Z Jun 70, subj: Rules of Engagement for Cambodia; Gen Abrams to Gen Wheeler and Adm McCain, 250647Z Jun 70, subj: B–52 Support for Ground Operations in Cambodia.

61. Hist, USMACV, 1970, vol III, pp C:45, 52–57.

62. Hist, JCS, *The JCS and the War in Vietnam, 1969–1970*, pp 298–99, 306.

63. Sir Robert Thompson, *Peace Is Not at Hand* (New York, 1974), pp 78–79.

64. William Shawcross, *Sideshow: Kissinger, Nixon, and the Destruction of Cambodia* (New York, 1979), pp 393–96.

65. *Facts on File Yearbook, 1970* (New York, 1971), pp 299–300.

66. Theodore H. White, *Breach of Faith: The Fall of Richard Nixon* (New York, 1971), p 135; Karnow, *Vietnam*, pp 611–12.

67. H. R. Haldeman with Joseph DiMona, *The Ends of Power* (New York, 1978), p. 107.

68. *Nixon Papers, 1970*, pp 414–17.

69. Hist, JCS, *The JCS and the War in Vietnam, 1969–1970*, pp 266–67; Lester A. Sobel and Hal Kosut, eds, *South Vietnam: U.S.-Communist Confrontation in Southeast Asia*, vol V, 1970 (New York, 1973), p 143.

70. Sobel and Kosut, eds, *South Vietnam, 1970*, pp 61–62, 74–77, 113, 119–20.

71. PACAF Summary of Air Operations, May 70, p 4:3; Jun 70, p 4:4; USAF Mgt Summary, Jul 16, 70, p 40.

Chapter 12

1. 7AF Rules of Engagement, Cambodia, pp 1–2; msgs, Gen Abrams to Gen Brown, 290754Z May 70, subj: Air Interdiction in Cambodia; MACV to 7AF, 311132Z May 70, subj: Air Operations in Cambodia.

2. Msg, CINCPAC to CINCPACAF, COMUSMACV, et al, 060320Z Jun 70, subj: Basic Operation Order for Air Interdiction Operations in Eastern Cambodia.

3. Msg, CJCS to CINCPAC, 240136Z May 70, subj: Air Operations in Cambodia.

4. Intvw, Maj David I. Folkman and Maj Philip D. Caine with Col Malcolm E. Ryan, 7AF staff, 70, Jun 6, 70.

5. Memo of Agreement on Rules of Engagement, Cambodia, May 29, 70; msg, 7AF SSO to MACV SSO, 131220Z Jul 70, subj: Training of Cambodian Pilots for Air/Ground Controller Employment; 7AF Study, Air Operations in Cambodia, pp 19–20.

6. Memo, Col Malcolm E. Ryan and Col [James H.] Ahmann for Gen [John W.] Roberts, May 21, 70, subj: Intelligence Targeting in Cambodia.

7. Malcolm Ryan intvw.

8. Current Ops Div, TACC, Staff Summary Sheet, w atch, May 28, 70, subj: Ivy Tree Operations.

9. Msg, Adm Moorer, Acting CJCS, to Adm McCain and Gen Abrams, JCS 08085, 092353Z Jun 70, subj: Reconnaissance in Cambodia.

10. Msg, Gen Abrams to Adm McCain, 151015Z Jun 70, subj: Extension of SAR and Recovery Authority in Cambodia; 7AF Rules of Engagement, Cambodia, Sep 30, 70, p 3.

11. 7AF Study, Air Operations in Cambodia, pp 16–17,

Notes to pages 202–208

12. Folkman and Caine, *The Cambodian Campaign*, pp 51–52.

13. 7AF Study, Air Operations in Cambodia, pp 19–20; Lt Col John F.Loye, Jr., and Maj P. D. Caine, *The Cambodian Campaign, 1 Jul–31 Oct 1970* (Hq PACAF, Proj CHECO, Dec 31, 70), pp 8–9; msgs, JCS to CINCPAC and COMUSMACV, JCS 2835, 172344Z Jun 70, subj: Employment of RVNAF in Cambodia; COMUSMACV to 7AF Comdr, 290950Z Jun 70, subj: Air Operations in Cambodia.

14. *Nixon Papers, 1970*, p 478.

15. Msg, Gen Abrams to Adm Moorer and Adm McCain, 071021Z Jun 70, subj: none.

16. Memo for Record, Phil Odeen, Ofc of Asst SecDef (Systems Analysis), Regional Programs, Jun 5, 70, subj: Vietnamization Meeting with Secretary Laird.

17. Msg, Adm Moorer, Acting CJCS, to Adm McCain and Gen Abrams, JCS 08495, 152321Z Jun 70, subj: Discussions with the President Concerning U.S. Policy toward Cambodia.

18. Folkman and Caine, *The Cambodian Campaign*, pp 52–53.

19. Msg, COMUSMACV to 7AF Comdr, 290950Z Jun 70, subj: Air Operations in Cambodia.

20. PACAF Summary of Air Operations, Jul–Dec 70, sec 4; msgs, Gen Abrams to Adm Moorer and Adm McCain, 071021Z Jun 70, subj: none; 7AF TACC to 3d TFWg, 12th TFWg, et al, 031000Z Jun 70, subj: OPREP 4 Reporting.

21. DOD Rprt on Selected Air and Ground Operations in Cambodia and Laos, Sep 10, 73, p 23.

22. *Facts on File Yearbook, 1971* (New York, 1972), p 26; *Department of State Bulletin*, vol LXIV, no 1651 (Feb 15, 1971), p 195; vol LXIV, no 1654 (Mar 8, 1971), p 281; Kissinger, *White House Years*, p 1000.

23. Msg, COMUSMACV to 7AF, 300324Z Jun 70, subj: none, retransmitting JCS to CINCPAC, 300012Z Jun 70, subj: Air Operations in Cambodia.

24. Msg, COMUSMACV to 7AF Comdr, 290950Z Jun 70, subj: Air Operations in Cambodia.

25. 7AF Rules of Engagement, Cambodia, Sep 20, 70, pp 2–3.

26. Ibid; Loye and Caine, *Cambodia 1970*, pp 20–22.

27. Msg, 7AF SSO to MACV SSO, 211010Z Jul 70, subj: Cambodian Air Operations.

28. Hist, JCS, *The JCS and the War in Vietnam, 1969–1970*, p 309.

29. Loye and Caine, *Cambodia 1970*, pp 27–28; msg, Gen Abrams to Gen Brown, 200321Z Aug 70, subj: Air Operating Authority in Cambodia.

30. Msgs, COMUSMACV to CINCPAC, 211100Z Aug 70, subj: Expansion of Air Operating Authority in Cambodia; JCS to CINCPAC, 252016Z Aug 70, subj: U.S. Air Operations in Cambodia.

31. Msgs, 7AF SSO to MACV SSO, 140227Z Aug 70, subj: Strike Authorization, and 011140Z Sep 70, subj: same; Gen Rosson to Gen [Ernest C.] Hardin [,Jr.], 7AF Dep Comdr, 141154Z Aug 70, subj: same; Gen Abrams to Gen Brown, 230332Z Aug 70, subj: same; Loye and Caine, *Cambodia 1970*, p 25.

32. Hist, JCS, *The JCS and the War in Vietnam, 1969–1970*, p 309.

33. Msgs, Gen Abrams to Adm McCain, 311142Z Aug 70, subj: Enemy Water LOCs; DOD/PRO to CINCPAC, 081303Z Sep 70, subj: [CAS Field Information Report on] Disruption of North Vietnamese Army Use of Rivers of Northeast Cambodia by Floating Mines; Loye and Caine, *Cambodia 1970*, pp 31–32.

34. Hist, USMACV, 1970, Annex B, pp III:37–40; msgs, 7AF to II DASC, 56th SOWg, et al, 181345Z Jun 70, subj: Special Operating Instructions; Adm McCain to Gen Abrams, 100410Z Jun 70, subj: Sensor Operations in Salem House.

35. Hq 7AF Evaluation of the Adequacy and Timeliness of Immediate Close Air Support, Jun 69, p 3; draft msg, 366th TFWg to 7AF, may 29, 70, subj: Fast Mover FACs.

36. Loye and Caine, *Cambodia 1970*, p 12; msg, 7AF SSO to MACV SSO, 131220Z Jul 70, subj: Training of Cambodian Pilots for Air/Ground Controller Employment.

37. Msgs, 7AF SSO, cited above; Gen Abrams to Adm McCain, 071047Z Sep 70, subj: Third Country Air Operations in Cambodia.

469

38. JCS Action Officers' Data Book on Vietnamizing the War, Jun 28, 72, p B:39.
39. Msgs, MACV SSO to 7AF SSO, 130737Z Dec 70, retransmitting Gen Abrams to Adm McCain, 111411Z Dec 70, subj: Relief of Kompong Cham; MACV SSO to 7AF SSO, 150018Z Dec 70, retransmitting Lt Gen Davison to Maj Gen [Welborn G.] Dolvin, 141110Z Dec 70, subj: III Corps Cambodian Operations as of 141600H Dec 70.
40. Brown intvw (Clement and Swenston), pp 90–91.
41. Msg, Gen Abrams to Adm McCain, 071047Z Sep 70, subj: Third Country Air Operations in Cambodia; Loye and Caine, *Cambodia 1970*, pp 13–14.
42. Loye and Caine, *Cambodia 1970*, pp 17–18; msgs, Phnom Penh to State 2297, 061345Z Sep 70, subj: Cambodian SITREP, 6 Sep, and 2388, 141203Z Sep 70, subj: Cambodian SITREP, September 14.
43. Msgs, 7AF SSO to CINCPACAF SSO and MACV SSO, 180320Z Aug 70, subj: Effective Communications and Increased Control for Air Operations over Cambodia; Gen Abrams to Adm McCain, 071047Z Sep 70, subj: Third Country Air Operations in Cambodia; hist, ADC, fiscal 1971, pp 313–15; Loye and Caine, *Cambodia 1970*, pp 33–35.
44. Ltr, Lt Col Paul D. Wagoner to Chief, Dir/Ops, 7AF, 7AF TACC, et al, Oct 30, 70, subj: Visit of Lt. Colonel Wagoner to Phnom Penh, 27–29 Oct 70; Loye and Caine, *Cambodia 1970*, p 38.

Chapter 13

1. End of Tour Rprt, Col J. R. Lilley, Chief, Advisory Team 3, Jul 29, 70–Aug 2, 71, nd [Aug 71].
2. Hist, JCS, *The JCS and the War in Vietnam, 1969–1970*, pp 373–76.
3. Msg, COMUSMACV to 7AF, USARV, American Embassy, Saigon, 160620Z Mar 70, subj: none, retransmitting JCS to CINCPAC, 142344Z Mar 70, subj: Vietnamization—Consolidated RVNAF I&M [Improvement and Modernization] Program, quoting memo, SecDef to JCS, Mar 13, 70, subj: same.
4. Msg, COMUSMACV to USARV, NAVForV, and 7AF, 102325Z, subj: none, retransmitting JCS to CINCPAC, subj: Vietnamization—Consolidated RVNAF Improvement and Modernization Program and Related U.S. Planning, quoting memo, SecDef to JCS, Jun 5, 70, subj: same.
5. Hist, USAF Advisory Gp, Vietnam, Oct–Dec 70, vol I, p 61.
6. End of Tour Rprt. Brig Gen Kendall S. Young, Chief, USAF Advisory Gp, Vietnam, Jul 31, 69–Feb 15, 71, Feb 15, 71, pp 3–4.
7. Ibid, p 37.
8. Msg, CINCPACAF to 7AF and USAF Advisory Gp, 081834Z Jul 70, subj: Management of VNAF Military Assistance Program.
9. USAF Mgt Summary, SEA, Aug 12, 70, p 51; Sep 16, 70, p i; Jan 19, 71, pp i, 54.
10. App I to Capt Drue L. DeBerry, *Vietnamization of the Air War, 1970–1971* (Hq PACAF, Proj CHECO, Oct 8, 71).
11. DeBerry, *Vietnamization, 1970–1971*, pp 7–8; hist, USAF Advisory Gp, Vietnam, Oct–Dec 70, pp 12, 16–17.
12. Maj David Roe, Maj Wayne C. Pittman, Jr., Capt Dennis K. Yee, Capt Paul D. Knobe, and Capt Drue L. DeBerry, *The VNAF Air Divisions: Reports on Improvement and Modernization* (Hq PACAF, Proj CHECO, Nov 23, 71), pp 126–28.
13. Young rprt, p 26; hist, USAF Advisory Gp, Vietnam, May 70, p 43; Jan 70, ch 4, p 1; Mar 70, ch 4, pp 1–2.
14. Hist, USAF Advisory Gp, Vietnam, Oct–Dec 70, vol I, pp 103–4.
15. Hist, USAF Advisory Gp, Vietnam, Jul–Sep 70, vol I, pp 107–8; Young rprt, pp 33–34.
16. Hist, USAF Advisory Gp, Vietnam, Oct–Dec 70, vol I, pp 92, 104–6.
17. Ibid, p 31; hist, USAF Advisory Gp, Vietnam, Apr 70, ch 2, p 4; Jun 70, p 43.
18. Hist, USAF Advisory Gp, Vietnam, Feb 70, ch 2, p 5; Apr 70, ch 7, p 1; Jun 70, p 43; Oct–Dec 70, vol I, p. 32.
19. Young rprt, pp 6–7; hist, USAF Advisory Gp, Vietnam, Mar 70, ch 1, pp 3–4; Oct–Dec 70, vol I, p 32.

Notes to pages 216–224

20. Notes of intvw, Capt Drue L. DeBerry with Col Roy D. Broadway, Chief, Air Force Advisory Team 5, 71, Aug 5, 71, p 1.

21. End of Tour Rprt, Col Nelson C. Pohl, Chief, Air Force Advisory Team 1, Aug 1 69–Jul 10, 70, Jul 7. 70.

22. Hist, USAF Advisory Gp, Vietnam, Oct–Dec 70, vol I, p 32.

23. Notes of intvw, Capt Drue L. DeBerry with Lt Col Jimmie R. Osborne, Chief Air Force Advisory Team 5, 71, Aug 5, 71, pp 1–2.

24. Young rprt, p 25.

25. Hist, USAF Advisory Gp, Vietnam, Apr 70, ch 7; May 70, pp 41–42; End of Tour Rprt, Col Cecil B. Fox, Chief Air Force Advisory Team 4, Aug 30, 69–Aug 30, 70, nd, p 23.

26. Young rprt, p 38.

27. Ibid, pp 21–23.

28. Hist, USAF Advisory Gp, Vietnam, Jun 70, p 34; Jul–Sep 70, vol I, p 70.

29. Young rprt, p 117.

30. Ibid, pp 18–19.

31. Ibid, p 28; hist, USAF Advisory Gp, Vietnam, Feb 70, ch 8, pp 1–2.

32. DeBerry, *Vietnamization, 1970–1971*, pp 13–16; Young rprt, p 18; hist, USAF Advisory Gp, Vietnam, Jul–Sep 70, pp 73–74.

33. Rprt, Tab B to 7AF OPlan 145–70, Combined Campaign Plan, Jul 21, 1970, p 10.

34. Ibid, p 12.

35. Hist, USAF Advisory Gp, Vietnam, Jul–Sep 70, vol I, p 68.

36. Ibid, p 72; hist, USAF Advisory Gp, Vietnam, Oct–Dec 70, vol I, p 66; Jan 70, ch 7, pp 1–2, May 70, p 66; Young rprt, pp 19–20.

37. Hist, USAF Advisory Gp, Vietnam, Oct–Dec 70, vol I, p 69.

38. Msgs, Gen Abrams to Adm McCain, 240352Z Jun 70, subj: Actions Related to Cambodia.

39. Msg, Brig Gen Cushman to Gen Abrams, 250850Z Nov 70, subj: VNAF Air Support.

40. Msg, Lt Gen Collins to Gen Abrams, 240900Z Nov 70, subj: VNAF Air Support.

41. Msg, Lt Gen Davison to Gen Abrams, 241040Z Nov 70, subj: VNAF Air Support.

42. Hist, USAF Advisory Gp, Vietnam, Apr 70, ch 4, p 2; Apr 70, tab C, p 3; May 70, pp 21–22.

43. Atch to memo, MACV to J–2, J–3, et al, Aug 29, 70, subj: WIEU Meeting (Commanders), 20 August 1970; hist, USAF Advisory Gp, Vietnam, Jul–Sep 70, vol I, pp 61–62.

44. Fox rprt, pp 18–19.

45. Young rprt, p 35; Comptroller, Hq USAF, *USAF Statistical Digest*, fiscal 1970, p 84.

46. Msg, Brig Gen Cushman to Gen Abrams, 250850Z Nov 70, subj: VNAF Air Support.

47. Msg, Lt Gen Sutherland to Gen Abrams, 260135Z Nov 70, subj: VNAF Air Support.

48. Msg, Lt Gen Collins to Gen Abrams, 240900Z Nov 70, subj: VNAF Air Force.

49. JCS Action Officers' Data Book on Vietnamizing the War, Apr 27, 71, p C:142.

50. Young rprt, p 12; ltr, Col Paul E. Bell to ASI, Mar 12, 71, subj: Proj Corona Harvest End of Tour Report; msg, 7AF to USAF Advisory Gp, Vietnam, and CINCPACAF, 190315Z May 70, subj: Equipage of VNAF Fighter Attack Units.

51. Hist, USAF Advisory Gp, Vietnam, Jul–Sep 70, vol I, pp 57–58; Oct–Dec 70, vol I, p 58; Young rprt, p 10.

52. Fox rprt, p 18; hist, USAF Advisory Gp, Vietnam, Jul–Sep 70, vol I, pp 58–59.

53. Hist, USAF Advisory Gp, Vietnam, Apr 70, ch 3, p 4; Fox rprt, p 24.

54. Msgs, Lt Gen Collins to Gen Abrams, 240900Z Nov 70, subj: VNAF Air Support; Lt Gen Sutherland to Gen Abrams, 260135Z Nov 70, subj: same.

55. Fox rprt, pp 5–6; msg, 7AF to CSAF and CINCPACAF, 120700Z Jun 70, subj: none.

56. Fox rprt, p 5; Young rprt, pp 40–41; DeBerry, *Vietnamization, 1970–1971*, p 74; Ofc of SecDef, *Southeast Asia Statistical Summary*, Dec 3, 1973, table 122.

57. Hist, USAF Advisory Gp, Vietnam, Jul–Sep 70, vol I, p 18; Oct–Dec 70, vol I, pp 26–27; DeBerry, *Vietnamization, 1970–1971*, pp 50–52.

58. Hist, USAF Advisory Gp, Vietnam, Feb 70, ch 1, p 3; Wright Air Development Center, Aircraft Statistics Summary, 1970.

59. Rprt, tab B to 7AF OPlan 145–70, Combined Campaign Plan, Jul 21, 70, p 4; tab B to 7AF OPlan 145–70, Combined Campaign Plan, Oct 16, 70, p 7.
60. Tab B to 7AF OPlan 145–70, Combined Campaign Plan, Oct 16, 70, pp 4, 7; hist, USAF Advisory Gp, Vietnam, Jul–Sep 70, p 57; Young rprt, p 12.
61. Young rprt, p 5; msg, CINCPACAF to CINCPAC, 160100Z Sep 70, subj: Activation of VNAF EC–47 Squadron.
62. App II to Annex A, Weapons Control Functions, VNAF Plan 69–20, AC&W Self Sufficiency, Jan 22, 70; hist, USAF Advisory Gp, Vietnam, Mar 70, ch 2, pp 1–2; Lilley rprt.
63. Lilley rprt.
64. Ibid; rprt, tab B to 7AF OPlan 145–70, Combined Campaign Plan, Jul 21, 70, p 8.
65. Hist, USAF Advisory Gp, Vietnam, Jan 70, ch 3, pp 6–7; Jul–Sep 70, vol I, p 78.
66. DeBerry, *Vietnamization, 1970–1971*, p 16.
67. Hist, USAF Advisory Gp, Vietnam, Jun 70, vol I, p 25.
68. Young rprt, p 14; tab B to hist, USAF Advisory Gp, Vietnam, Apr 70, p 11.
69. Young rprt, pp 38–39.
70. Tab A to USAF Advisory Gp, Vietnam, Update of Periodic Assessment of the Situation in Vietnam, May 27, 70, atch to hist, USAF Advisory Gp, Vietnam, May 70, vol I.
71. Young rprt, pp 30–31, 38–40.
72. Broadway intvw, pp 3–4.
73. Young rprt, pp 23, 30.
74. Tab A to USAF Advisory Gp, Vietnam, Update of Periodic Assessment of the Situation in Vietnam, May 27, 70, atch to hist, USAF Advisory Gp, Vietnam, May 70, vol I.

Chapter 14

1. *Washington Post*, Sep 25, 69; Karnow, *Vietnam*, p 597.
2. Msg, Saigon to State, 240850Z Jan 70, subj: Estimate of Enemy Strategy in 1970.
3. Memo, Phil Odeen, Dep Asst SecDef (Systems Analysis), Regional Program, for [Brig] Gen Robert E. Pursley, Aug 7, 70, subj: Presidential Statements on Vietnam.
4. 7AF Background Paper on NSSM–36, nd [Jan 70]; hist, JCS, *The JCS and the War in Vietnam, 1969–1970*, pp 382–83.
5. Brown intvw (Clement and Swenston), pp 124–25.
6. Hist, USMACV, 1970, vol I, pp IV:28–29; USAF Mgt Summary, SEA, May 13, 70, p 35; hist, 7AF, Jan–Jun 70, vol I, pt 1, p xix.
7. Msg, Gen Wheeler to Adm McCain and Gen Abrams, 312031Z Mar 70, subj: Force Planning; hist, JCS, *The JCS and the War in Vietnam, 1969–1970*, 383–84.
8. Msg, Gen Abrams to Gen Wheeler and Adm McCain, 011120Z Apr 70, subj: Force Planning.
9. Hist, JCS, *The JCS and the War in Vietnam, 1969–1970*, pp 384–85.
10. *Nixon Papers, 1970*, p 374.
11. Memo for Record, Phil Odeen, Ofc of Asst SecDef (Systems Analysis), Regional Programs, Apr 23, 1970, subj: Vietnamization Meeting with Secretary Laird.
12. Msg, Adm McCain to Gen Abrams, 250322Z Apr 70, subj: Redeployment Increment Four.
13. Msg, Gen Wheeler to Adm McCain and Gen Abrams, JCS 07202, 231854Z May 70, subj: none, forwarding memo, SecDef for CJCS and Service Secretaries, May 20, 70, subj: Troop Strength in South Vietnam.
14. *Nixon Papers, 1970*, p 479; msgs, COMUSMACV to 7AF, USARV, ComNavForV, 111137Z Jun 70, retransmitting JCS to CINCPAC, 102325Z Jun 70, subj: Vietnamization—Consolidated RVNAF Improvement and Modernization Program and Related U.S. Planning; Gen Abrams to Adm Moorer and Adm McCain, 081041Z Jun 70, subj: none.
15. Brown intvw (Clement and Swenston), pp 15–16.
16. Msg, CINCPACAF to CSAF, 090511Z Jun 70, subj: Augmentation of 523 TFSq.
17. Msg, 7AF to CINCPACAF, 100410Z Jun 70, subj: none.
18. Hist, 7AF, Jul–Dec 70, vol I, pt 1, p xxiv.
19. Ibid, pp xxv–xxvi, pt 2, p 207.
20. Brown intvw (Clement and Swenston), p 16.

21. Hist, 7AF, Jul–Dec 70, vol I, pt 1, pp xxiv, xxvii–xxviii; USAF Mgt Summary, SEA, Nov 16, 70, p 4.

22. USAF Mgt Summary, Mar 13, 70, p 3; Nov 16, 70, pp 4–5; Jan 19, 71, p 42; hist, 7AF, Jan–Jun 70, vol I, pt 1, p 72; Jul–Dec 70, vol I, pt 1, pp xix, 72.

23. Hist, 7AF, Jan–Jun 70, vol I, pt 1, p xxii; Jul–Dec 70, vol I, pt 1, p xxi; Futrell, *The Advisory Years*, p 22.

24. Msgs, COMUSMACV to CINCPAC, 060907Z Sep 69, subj: Phasedown of Herbicide Operations; 250827Z Feb 70, subj: Herbicide Operations; to CINCPAC, USARPAC, et al, 161406Z Sep 69, subj: none; Capt James R. Clary, *Ranch Hand: Herbicide Operations in SEA* (Hq PACAF, Proj CHECO, Jul 13, 71), pp 23–24.

25. Clary, *Ranch Hand*, p 28; American Embassy rprt, Herbicide Policy Review, Aug 22, 68, p 59.

26. Clary, *Ranch Hand*, pp 24–25, 29–30.

27. Memo, Gen George S. Brown, 7AF Comdr, for Chief of Staff, MACV, Jul 16, 70, subj: Herbicide Operations.

28. Clary, *Ranch Hand*, pp 31–32; William A. Buckingham. Jr., *Operation Ranch Hand: The Air Force and Herbicides in Southeast Asia, 1961–1971* (Washington, 1982), p 175; msg, 834th Air Div to 7AF, 030250Z Jan 71, subj: Deconfiguration of Herbicide Aircraft; Memo, Brig Gen John H. Herring, Jr., 834th Air Div comdr, for Gen Clay, Jan 10, 71, subj: VNAF C–123 Training; msg, COMUSMACV to CG XXIV Corps, CG FFV, et al, 161145Z Apr 71, subj: Use of Herbicides.

29. Hist, JCS, *The JCS and the War in Vietnam, 1969–1970*, pp 398–99; Kissinger, *White House Years*, pp 984–85.

30. Kissinger, *White House Years*, p 985.

31. Msg, Gen Abrams to Adm McCain, 091107Z Sep 70, subj: none.

32. Msg, Adm McCain to Adm Moorer, 090820Z Sep 70, subj: SEA Deployments.

33. USAF Mgt Summary, Dec 17, 70, p 1; Jan 19, 71, p 4; Feb 19, 71, p 44; msg, Adm McCain to Gen Westmoreland, Acting CJCS, 300258Z Sep 70, subj: Fifth Redeployment Increment.

34. Memo, SAF for Dep SecDef, Dec 3, 70, subj: Southeast Asia Forces and Activity Levels, FY 72; USAF Mgt Summary, SEA, Feb 6, 70, p 2:19; Jan 19, 71, pp 4–5.

35. Hist, USMACV, 1970, vol I, pp IV:24–25, VI:12–13.

36. Memo for Record, Phil Odeen, Ofc of Asst SecDef (Systems Analysis), Regional Programs, Jan 30, 70, subj: Vietnamization Meeting with Secretary Laird.

37. Msg, AF SSO to PACAF SSO and 7AF SSO, 272303Z Feb 70, subj: Vietnamization Phase III.

38. Msg, 7AF SSO to AF SSO and PACAF SSO, 040930Z Mar 70, subj: Vietnamization Phase III.

39. Elizabeth H. Hartsook, *The Air Force in Southeast Asia: The Role of Air Power Grows, 1970* (Washington, 1972), pp 30, 32.

40. Atch to ltr, Gen John C. Meyer to SAF, Mar 18, 70, subj: Air Operations in Southeast Asia; hist, SAC, fiscal 1970, vol I, p 165.

41. Memo for Record, Phil Odeen, Ofc of Asst SecDef (Systems Analysis), Regional Programs, Feb 2, 70, subj: Vietnam Meeting with Secretary Laird, 2 Feb 1970.

42. Hist, Dir/Plans, Jan–Jun 70, pp 124–25.

43. Msgs, 7AF to CSAF and CINCPAC, 111200Z Apr 70, subj: SEA Force Structure; Gen Abrams to Adm McCain, 011006Z May 70, subj: Future Level of Air Support Resources.

44. USAF Mgt Summary, SEA, May 13, 70, p 3; Jan 17, 71, pp 4–5; hist, Dir/Plans, Jul–Dec 70, p 88; hist, 7AF, Jul–Dec 70, vol I, pt 2, pp 225–26.

45. Memo for Record, Phil Odeen, Ofc of Asst SecDef (Systems Analysis), Regional Programs, Jul 22, 70, subj: Meeting with Secretary Laird to Discuss Vietnam, 22 Jul 70.

46. Msgs, Adm Moorer, CJCS, to Adm McCain, 061634Z Aug 70, subj: Air Support for Southeast Asia Operations; JCS to CINCPAC, 142250Z Aug 70, subj: Air Operations in Southeast Asia.

47. Hist, JCS, *The JCS and the War in Vietnam, 1969–1970*, p 343; msgs, 7AF to CINCPACAF, 311100Z Aug 70, subj: Air Operations in SEAsia; CINCPAC to CJCS, 060838Z Sep 70, subj: same.

48. Msg, CJCS to CINCPAC, JCS 12471,

Notes to pages 241–251

151532Z Sep 70, subj: Air Operations in Southeast Asia.

49. Hist, JCS, *The JCS and the War in Vietnam, 1969–1970*, pp 344–45; Memo, SAF for Dep SecDef, Dec 3, 1970, subj: Southeast Asia Forces and Activity Levels, FY 72.

50. Hist, JCS, *The JCS and the War in Vietnam, 1969–1970*, pp 63–69; hist, SAC, fiscal 1970, vol I, p 166.

51. Hist, SAC, fiscal 1970, vol I, pp 180–82.

52. Msg, COMUSMACV to CINCPAC, 100716Z Apr 70, subj: Southeast Asia Air Munitions Expenditures.

53. Hist, SAC, fiscal 1971, vol II, pp 217–19.

54. Msg, 7AF to TACC-NS, 620th TCSq, et al, 260405Z Jan 70, subj: MiG Combat Air Patrol Tactics; Staff summary sheet, Current Ops Div, TACC, Jul 5, 70, subj: Modification of OPlan 775 (Tiny Tim); ltr, Chief, Special Ops Div, 7AF, to DMX, Feb 24, 71, subj: Recon Action R–711–5201.

55. Hist, SAC fiscal 1970, vol I, pp 186–87; fiscal 1971, vol II, pp 225–26.

56. PACAF Summary of Air Operations, Jan–Dec 70; JCS Action Officers' Data Book on Vietnamizing the War, Jan 2, 71, app to draft MS, Shelley Peterson, Chronology of Significant Events in Cambodia, 1963–1973, Aug 17, 79.

57. Long-Range Forecast Requirements of the U.S. Army—Vietnam (USARV) for the Republic of Vietnam, nd, atch to hist, 1st Weather Wg, Oct–Dec 69; hist, 7AF, Jul–Dec 70, vol I, pt 1, pp xxvi–xxvii.

58. Hist, USMACV, 1970, vol I, pp III:109–10, V:6–7, VI:49–50.

59. Ibid, p VI:60.

60. Ibid, pp III:110–11.

61. Msgs, Lt Gen Sutherland to Gen Abrams, 081108Z Sep 70, subj: Air Campaign—FSB O'Reilly; Gen Abrams to Gen Sutherland, 090943Z Sept 70, subj: same.

62. Msg, Lt Gen Sutherland to Gen Abrams, 181020Z Sep 70, subj: Air Operations FSB O'Reilly.

63. Hist, USMACV, 1970, vol I, pp VI:55–56, 62, 67.

64. Hist, 7AF, Jan–Jun 70, vol I, pt 1, pp xix–xxi, xxvii; Jul–Dec 70, vol I, pt 1, pp xxi–xxv, xxviii–xxix.

65. Hist, USMACV, 1970, vol I, pp III:137–38.

66. Hist, 7AF, Jan–Jun 70, vol I, pt 1, pp xxvii–xxviii, xxx; Jul–Dec 70, vol I, pt 1, pp xxiii, xxix.

67. Hist, USAF Advisory Gp, Vietnam, Apr 70, ch 4, p 3; hist, 7AF, Jan–Jun 70, vol I, pt 1, p xxiv.

68. Hist, 7AF, Jan–Jun 70, vol I, pt 1, pp xxiv, xxvi, xxviii–xxix; Jul–Dec 70, vol I, pt 1, pp xxiii, xxvi, xxviii, xxx.

Chapter 15

1. Hist, JCS, *The JCS and the War in Vietnam, 1971–1973*, pt I, p 15.

2. Msg, Adm McCain to Adm Moorer, 100556Z Nov 70, subj; Contingency Planning for Laos.

3. Msg, Adm McCain to Gen Abrams, forwarding msg from Adm Moorer, 062130Z Dec 70, subj: Contingency Plans; Kissinger, *White House Years*, p 991.

4. U.S. Marine Corps Historical Center, *Vietnam Revisited: Conversation with William Broyles, Jr.* (Washington, 1984), pp 28–30; Maj Gen Nguyen Duy Hinh, *Indochina Monographs: Lam Son 719* (Washington, 1979), pp 10–11, 16, 32.

5. Msg, Gen Abrams to Adm McCain, 071130Z Dec 70, subj: none.

6. Hinh, *Lam Son 719*, pp 7, 53–54.

7. Kissinger, *White House Years*, p 990.

8. Msg, Adm McCain to Gen Abrams, 080435Z Dec 70, subj: Laos Contingency Planning.

9. Hist, JCS, *The JCS and the War in Vietnam, 1971–1973*, pt I, pp 16–17; msgs, Gen Abrams to Adm McCain, 120952Z Dec 70, subj: Planning for Laos; Ambassador Godley to Gen Abrams, 181234Z Dec 70, subj: none.

10. Msgs, Gen Abrams to Adm McCain, 120952Z Dec 70, subj: Cambodian Contingency Planning.

11. Col J. F. Loye, Maj G. K. St. Clair, Maj L. D. Johnson, and J. W. Dennison, *Lam Son 719, 31 January–24 March 1971: The*

South Vietnamese Incursion into Laos (Hq PACAF, Proj CHECO, Mar 24, 71), p 27; Hinh, *Lam Son 719*, pp 30–31, 57.

12. Maj Ronald D. Merrell, *Tactical Airlift in SEA* (Hq PACAF, Proj CHECO, Feb 15, 72), p 47; Hinh, *Lam Son 719*, p 35n.

13. Hinh, *Lam Son 719*, p 34.

14. Hist, JCS, *The JCS and The War in Vietnam, 1971–1973*, pt I. pp 26–27.

15. Hinh, *Lam Son 719*, pp 151–52, 156.

16. Merrell. *Tactical Airlift*, pp 47–52.

17. Loye, St. Clair, et al, *Lam Son 719*, pp 27–30.

18. Rolland V. Heiser, Dep Asst Chief of Staff, Ops, MACV J–3, After Action Rprt, Lam Son 719, Jan 12–Feb 28, 71, nd, Vietnam intvw tapes, Center of Military History; Hinh, *Lam Son 719*, pp 66–67.

19. Loye, St. Clair, et al, *Lam Son 719*, p 32.

20. Msg, Lt Gen Sutherland to Gen Abrams, 190400Z Mar 71, subj: Items of Interest to B G Haig.

21. Keith William Nolan, *Into Laos: The Story of Dewey Canyon II/Lam Son 719*; *Vietnam 1971* (Novato, Calif, 1986), p 103; hist, USMACV, 1971, vol II, pp E:19–20.

22. Capt Edward P. Brynn and Capt Michael L. Tihomirov, *Air Power against Armor* (Hq PACAF, Proj CHECO, nd, unpublished MS), p 10; Hinh, *Lam Son 719*, p 102.

23. Loye, St. Clair, et al, *Lam Son 719*, pp 15–18, 20.

24. Msgs, CINCPAC to JCS, 192121Z Jan 71, subj: Planning for Laos; JCS to CINCPAC, 262240Z Jan 71, subj: same; hist, JCS, *The JCS and the War in Vietnam, 1971–1973*, pt I, pp 21–24.

25. Merrell, *Tactical Airlift*, pp 52–53; Loye, St. Clair, et al, *Lam Son 719*, p 54.

26. End of Tour Rprt, Col Hubert W. Dean, Chief Transportation Div, MACV J–4, Sep 70–Aug 71, nd [Aug 71], p 3; msg, Gen Abrams to Gen Catton, 121012Z Mar 71, subj: Outsize Airlift.

27. Hist, JCS, *The JCS and the War in Vietnam, 1971–1973*, pt I, p 35.

28. Loye, St. Clair, et al *Lam Son 719*, pp 40–45; hist, USMACV, 1971, vol II, pp E:19–27.

29. Hinh, *Lam Son 719*, p 73.

30. Msg, Gen Abrams to Lt Gen Sutherland, 131017Z Feb 71, subj: none.

31. Kissinger, *White House Years*, p 1004; Hinh, *Lam Son 719*, p 79.

32. Hinh, *Lam Son 719*, pp 74, 79.

33. Msgs, Gen Abrams to Lt Gen Sutherland, 131017Z Feb 71, subj: none; 141220Z Feb 71, subj: none.

34. Loye, St. Clair, et al, *Lam Son 719*, pp 46–48, 50–51.

35. Hinh, *Lam Son 719*, p 81.

36. Hist, SAC, fiscal 1971, pp 219–21, 226–27; msg, CINCSAC to JCS, 192301Z Feb 71, subj: Arc Light Sortie Level; hist, JCS, *The JCS and the War in Vietnam, 1971–1973*, pt I, pp 39–40.

37. Hist, JCS, *The JCS and the War in Vietnam, 1971–1973*, pt I, pp 38–39.

38. Brynn and Tihomirov, *Air Power against Armor*, pp 11–12; Jack S, Ballard, *The United States Air Force in Southeast Asia: Development and Employment of Fixed-Wing Gunships, 1962–1972* (Washington, 1982), p 171.

39. Brynn and Tihomirov, *Air Power against Armor*, p 11; Loye, St. Clair, et al, *Lam Son 719*, pp 57–69.

40. Marine Corps Historical Center, *Vietnam Revisited*, p 27.

41. Hinh, *Lam Son 719*, pp 84–85.

42. Hist, 56th SOWg, Jan–Mar 71, vol I, pp 109–10; rprt, Capt Peter J. Ruppert, Cobra 23, Feb 25–26, and Search and Rescue Commander's Log, atchs 1 and 2 to ltr, Comdr, 1st SOSq, to Dir/Ops, Mar 9, 71, subj: SARCO Rprt for Cobra 23 A&B, supp doc to hist, 56th SOWg, Jan–Mar 71.

43. Loye, St. Clair, et al, *Lam Son 719*, p 57; hists, 12th TFWg, Jan–Mar 71, vol I, p ix; 389th TFSq, Jan–Mar 71, p vii.

44. Loye, St. Clair, et al, *Lam Son 719*, pp 62–64; Hinh, *Lam Son 719*, pp 90, 95n.

45. Msg, Lt Gen Sutherland to Gen Abrams 031230Z Mar 71, subj: none; Loye, St. Clair, et al, *Lam Son 719*, pp 93–97.

46. Msgs, Gen Abrams to Lt Gen Sutherland, 061014Z Mar 71 and 091232Z Mar 71, subj: none; Lt Gen Sutherland to Gen Abrams, 060344Z, subj: ARVN Reinforcement of Lam Son 719, and 100850Z Mar 71, subj: none; Hinh, *Lam Son 719*, pp 99–102, 103n.

47. Msgs, Lt Gen Sutherland to Gen Abrams, 061025Z Mar 71, subj: Arc Light Strikes; Gen Abrams to Lt Gen Sutherland, 091224Z Mar 71, subj: same; Gen Abrams to Lt Gen Sutherland, info Gen Holloway, 140521Z Mar 71, subj: same; Loye, St. Clair, et al, *Lam Son 719*, pp 117–21; hist, USMACV, 1971, vol II, pp E:41–42.

48. Hist, USMACV, 1971, vol II, p E:31; Loye, St. Clair, et al, *Lam Son 719*, pp 69–70; msg, Lt Gen Sutherland to Gen Abrams, 180944Z Mar 71, subj: Periodic Appraisal of Lam Son 719 for the period 110001Z to 172400Z Mar 71.

49. Msg, Lt Gen Sutherland to Gen Abrams, 181425Z Mar 71, subj: none.

50. Ibid.

51. Lt Gen Davison to Gen Abrams, 190700Z Mar 71, subj: none.

52. Brynn and Tihomirov, *Air Power against Armor*, pp 13–14; Hinh, *Lam Son 719*, p 118.

53. Loye, St. Clair, et al, *Lam Son 719*, pp 10, 76–77; Brynn and Tihomirov, *Air Power against Armor*, p 14.

54. Hinh, *Lam Son 719*, p 151; Nolan, *Into Laos*, pp 346–47.

55. Hinh, *Lam Son 719*, p 151; msgs, Lt Gen Sutherland to Gen Abrams, 250430Z Mar 71 and 251359Z Mar 71, subj: none.

56. Msg, Lt Gen Sutherland to Gen Abrams, 290600Z Mar 71, subj: none; Hinh, *Lam Son 719*, p 122.

57. Msg, Lt Gen Sutherland to Gen Abrams, 311418Z Mar 71, subj: none; Hinh, *Lam Son 719*, pp 123–24.

58. Hinh, *Lam Son 719*, pp 124–25; hist, JCS, *The JCS and the War in Vietnam, 1971–1973*, pt I, p 62.

59. Hinh, *Lam Son 719*, p 125; msgs, Lt Gen Sutherland to Gen Abrams, 300745Z Mar 71, subj: Future Plans and Operations; Lt Gen Robertson to Gen Abrams, 011050Z Apr 71, subj: none.

60. Merrell, *Tactical Airlift*, p 61.

61. "A Conversation with the President," intvw, with Howard K. Smith of the American Broadcasting Company, March 22, 1971, *Public Papers of the Presidents of the United States, Richard M. Nixon, 1971* (Washington, 1972), pp 450–52, 458.

62. Msg, Lt Gen Sutherland to Gen Abrams, 251155Z Mar 71, subj: Periodic Appraisal of Progress of Lam Son 719, 18000H to 242400H Mar 71.

63. Msg, Lt Gen Sutherland to Gen Abrams, 040740Z Mar 71, subj: Periodic Appraisal of the Progress of Lam Son 719 for the Period 250000H Feb 71 to 032400H Mar 71.

64. Hinh, *Lam Son 719*, p. 154.

65. Hist, USMACV, 1971, vol II, pp E:33–35; 7AF Rprt, Commando Hunt V, May 71, pp 82–85.

66. *Nixon Papers, 1971*, p 523.

67. Hist, USMACV, 1971, vol II, p E:15; msg, COMUSMACV to CINCPAC and JCS, 031015Z Apr 71, subj: Vietnamization.

68. Msg, Lt Gen Sutherland to Gen Abrams, 251155Z Mar 71, subj: Periodic Appraisal of Progress of Lam Son 719 for the Period 180000H Mar 71 to 242400H Mar 71.

69. Loye, St. Clair, et al, *Lam Son 719*, pp 13–14; hist, USMACV, 1971, vol II, p E:37.

70. USAF Advisory Gp, VNAF Improvement and Modernization Briefing, Apr 7, 71; hist, USMACV, 1971, vol II, p E:38.

71. Hist, USMACV, 1971, vol II, pp E:34, 41–42; Loye, St. Clair, et al, *Lam Son 719*, pp 138, 140; Hinh, *Lam Son 719*, p 132.

72. . Nolan, *Into Laos*, pp 357–58; Loye, St. Clair, et al, *Lam Son 719*, figure 17; hist, USMACV, vol II, p E:34.

73. Hinh, *Lam Son 719*, p 129.

74. Karnow, *Vietnam*, p 631.

Chapter 16

1. Hist, JCS, *The JCS and the War in Vietnam, 1971–1973*, pt I, pp 214, 219–23

2. Hist, USMACV, 1971, vol II, p F:1.

3. Msg, Adm Moorer to Adm McCain, JCS 14429, 272127Z Oct 70, subj: Cambodian Strategy.

4. Shawcross, *Sideshow*, pp 130–31.

5. Sobol and Kosut, eds, *South Vietnam*, vol 5, *1970*, pp 61, 75–76; msg, Amb Swank to Gen Abrams, Phnom Penh 531, 260955Z Oct 70, subj: Developments on the Concept to Create an Allied Air Operations Coordina-

ting Center.

6. Hist, USMACV, 1971, vol II, pp I:1–3

7. Msg, Gen Abrams to Amb Swank, 280322Z Oct 70, subj: Air Operations Coordination Center (AOCC); Capt Charles A. Nicholson, *Khmer Air Operations, Nov 70–Nov 71* (Hq PACAF, Proj CHECO, Jun 15, 72), pp 31, 33–35.

8. 7AF Briefing Paper, Rules of Engagement, May 10, 1972; memo for record, Brig Gen Richard G. Gross, Chief, Air Ops Div, Dir/Ops, USMACV, subj: Khmer Strike Clearance Authority.

9. Msg, Adm Moorer to Adm McCain, JCS 14429, 202127Z Oct 70, subj: Cambodian Strategy.

10. Denis Warner, *Certain Victory: How Hanoi Won the War* (Kansas City, 1978), pp 166–71.

11. Donald Kirk, *Wider War: The Struggle for Cambodia, Thailand, and Laos* (New York, 1971), pp 6–7, 50–55.

12. Nicholson, *Khmer Air Operations*, pp 38–41.

13. Ibid, pp 34–37.

14. Hist, USMACV, 1971, vol II, pp E:5, 7.

15. Msg, Lt Gen Davison to Gen Abrams, 210830Z Mar 71, subj: Assessment of ARVN Dry Season Campaign in Response to Request of 20 March.

16. Msgs, Lt Gen Davison to Gen Abrams, 031040Z Mar 71, subj: none; 041054Z Mar 17, subj: none; Abrams to Swank, 181037Z Nov 71, subj: none; hist, USMACV, 1971, vol II, pp E:7, 9.

17. Hist, USMACV, 1971, vol II, pp E:7, 9; Nicholson, *Khmer Air Operations*, p 29; Bowers, *Tactical Airlift*, p 507; msgs, Maj Gen John Wagstaff to Gen Abrams, 311645Z May 71, subj: none; 050425Z Jun 71, subj: Combat Effectiveness.

18. Nicholson, *Khmer Air Operations*, pp 27–29; hist, USMACV, 1971, vol II, p E:9; Shawcross, *Sideshow*, pp 202–3.

19. Msg, Gen Abrams to Lt Gen [Welborn G.] Dolvin, Mr [John Paul] Vann, et al, 260316Z Oct 71, subj: Enemy Tactics.

20. Msg, Maj Gen Wagstaff to Gen Abrams, 260115Z Oct 71, subj: Cambodian Situation Report, Personal Appraisal.

21. Msg, Maj Gen Wagstaff to Gen Abrams, 081435Z Oct 71, subj; none.

22. Ibid; msg, Maj Gen Wagstaff to Gen Abrams, 111515Z Oct 71, subj: none.

23. Msg, Maj Gen Wagstaff to Gen Abrams, 191710Z Jun 71, subj: Support of Toan Thang 01/71NB; Nicholson, *Khmer Air Operations*, p 47.

24. Bowers, *Tactical Airlift*, p 507.

25. Msgs, Lt Gen Collins to Gen Abrams, 040045Z Jan 71, subj: Employment of Helicopter Gunships; Lt Gen Davison to Gen Abrams, 081005Z Jan 71, subj: Employment of Helicopters; Gen Abrams to Lt Gen Collins, Lt Gen Davison, et al, 120119Z Jan 71, subj: none.

26. Msgs, CG, Delta Military Assistance Command, to COMUSMACV, 130910Z Jan 71, subj: Employment of Helicopter Gunships; USS *Cleveland* to 7AF TACC, 151446Z Jan 71, subj: none; Gen Abrams to Gen Clay and Maj Gen [Hal D.] McCown, 250412Z Jan 71, sub: Employment of Helicopter Gunships.

27. Capt William A. Mitchell, *Aerial Protection of the Mekong River Convoys in Cambodia* (Hq PACAF, Proj CHECO, Oct 1, 71), pp 8–9.

28. Ibid, p 6; Shawcross, *Sideshow*, p 174.

29. Mitchell, *Aerial Protection of Mekong River Convoys*, pp 6–7.

30. Msg, COMUSMACV to ComNavForV and Comdr, 7AF, 160730Z Feb 71, subj: Employment of U.S. Navy Aircraft.

31. Msg, Dep COMUSMACV for Air/Comdr, 7AF, to ComNavForV, Dep Com NavForV, et al, 241040Z Feb 71, subj; Employment of U.S. Naval Aircraft.

32. Mitchell, *Aerial Protection of Mekong Convoys*, pp 9–10, 12, 16.

33. Shawcross, *Sideshow*, pp 184–85.

34. Hist, JCS, *The JCS and the War in Vietnam, 1971–1973*, pt I, pp 85–94.

35. Msgs, Maj Gen James L. Baldwin to Gen Abrams, Lt Gen McCaffery, and Lt Gen Sutherland, 281820Z Mar 71, subj: Attack on FSB Mary Ann (AS 961988); to Gen Abrams, 071120Z Apr 71, subj: Interim Report Concerning Attack on FSB Mary Ann; hist, USMACV, 1971, vol I, p IV:21. For the details of the attack on Fire Support Base Mary Ann, see: Keith William Nolan, *Sap-

pers in the Wire: The Life and Death of Firebase Mary Ann (College Station, Tex, 1995), pt V.

36. Hist, USMACV, 1971, vol I, pp IV: 21–22; msg, Lt Gen Sutherland to Gen Abrams, 040800Z May 71, subj: Attack on Dai Loc (D), Quang Nam (P), Headquarters.

37. Msgs, Lt Gen Dolvin to Gen Abrams, 191430Z Jun 71, subj: TAC Air Allocations; Abrams to Dolvin, 231021Z Jun 71, subj: same.

38. Msgs, Lt Gen Dolvin to Gen Abrams, 071700Z Sep 71, subj: Lam Son 810; 121420Z Sep 71, subj: same.

39. Hist, USMACV, 1971, vol I, p IV:27.

40. 1st Lt Thomas G. Abbey, *Attack on Cam Ranh Bay, 25 August 1971* (Hq PACAF, Proj CHECO, Dec 15, 71), pp 7–16.

41. William Broyles, Jr., "The Road to Hill 10," *The Atlantic Monthly*, vol 255 (Apr 1985), p 102.

42. Msgs, Maj Gen [Charles P.] Brown to Gen Abrams, 051540Z Mar 71, subj: Plei Trap Operation; 071730Z Mar 71, subj: Wrap Up of Plei Trap Operations as of 062400 Mar 71.

43. Msg, Maj Gen Brown to Gen Abrams, 041600Z Mar 71, subj: none.

44. Msgs, Maj Gen Brown to Gen Abrams, 181730Z Mar 71, subj: Update on Operation Vicinity of Phu Non; 221400Z Mar 71, subj: Wrap Up of Vic Phu Non (AQ 8699).

45. Msgs, Maj Gen Brown to Gen Abrams, 010425Z Apr 71, subj: Recapitulation on Action at FSB 6; 031730Z Apr 71, subj: Update on Operations in the Highlands; 051610Z Apr 71, subj: Update on Operations in the Highlands; hist, USMACV, vol I, p IV:27.

46. Hist, USMACV, 1971, vol I, pp IV:31, 35, 37; Fox, *Base Defense*, pp 196–200.

47. E. Hartsook, *The Air Force in Southeast Asia: Shield for Vietnamization and Withdrawal, 1971* (Washington, 1976), pp 76–77; USAF Mgt Summary, SEA, Dec 31, 70, pp 6, 11; Jan 19, 71, pp 4, 9.

48. Hq PACAF, Summary of Air Operations, Southeast Asia, Dec 71, pp 5:A:1–3; hist, JCS, *The JCS and the War in Vietnam, 1971–1973*, pt I, pp 267–70.

49. Mel Porter, *Proud Deep Alpha* (Hq PACAF, Proj CHECO, Jul 20, 72), pp 2, 6, 22–23, 27–31, 50.

Chapter 17

1. Ltrs, Leonard Sullivan, Dep DDR&E (SEAM), to John Kirk, Dec 17, 69, Jul 30, 70.

2. Msg, 7AFSSO to AFSSO CSAF, 030900Z Mar 71, subj: Military Vietnamization.

3. Memo, Dep DDR&E (SEAM) for Brig Gen Fred A. Karhohs, USA, Dir, Vietnam Task Force (ISA), Feb 19, 71, subj: DDR&E Inputs on the Vietnamization of Laotian Interdiction Operations.

4. Memo, Henry A. Kissinger to Under Secretary of State, Dep SecDef, Dir/CIA, and CJCS, Apr 15, 71, subj: Assessment of the Situation in South Vietnam.

5. Memos, SecDef for the Asst to the President for National Security Affairs, Apr 16, 71, subj: Improvement and Modernization of the South Vietnamese Armed Forces; for the SecArmy, SecNav, SAF, Dir/Defense Special Projs Gp, Apr 20, 71, subj: Vietnamization of Laotian Interdiction Campaign.

6. Annex L to CINCPAC OPlan Island Tree, Aug 5, 71; hist, JCS, *The JCS and the War in Vietnam, 1971–1973*, pt I, pp 334–43.

7. Hist, USMACV, 1971, vol I, pp IV:4, 6; Annex F to Combined Campaign Plan, 1972, Oct 31, 71.

8. 7AF OPlan 732, Nov 22, 71.

9. Synthesis of remarks by Mr L. Sullivan, DDR&E (SEAM), nd.

10. Memo for Record, Frank Tapparo, Asia Div, Ofc of Asst SecDef (Systems Analysis), May 23, 72, subj: Visit to Credible Chase; Atch to memo for Col Raymond A. Boyd, Ch, AF Advisory Gp, Vietnam, Nov 16, 71, subj: CRIMP Review; msgs, COMUSMACV to CINCPAC, 211625Z Jan 72, subj: Vietnamization of Interdiction Operations; CINCPAC to JCS, 290430Z Jan 72, subj: same.

11. App to memo, CJCS to SecDef, JCSM 54–72, Feb 14, 72, Vietnamization of Interdiction Operations; Study rprt evaluating CBU–55 weapon system for the VNAF, Jun 2, 71.

12. Memo, Lt Col Deafenbaugh for 7Af Dir/Ops, Dec 14, 71, subj: VNAF Interdiction Sortie Record.

13. Msgs, State to Vietnam, State 226081, 161735Z Dec 71, subj: VNAF Interdiction in Laos; Vientiane to COMUSMACV, Vientiane 0203, 081046Z Jan 72, subj: none.

14. Memos for Record, Phil Odeen, Ofc of Asst SecDef (Systems Analysis), Oct 4, 71, subj: Vietnamization Meeting with Secretary Laird; Nov 1, 71, subj: same.

15. Hist, JCS, *The JCS and the War in Vietnam, 1971–1973*, pt I, pp 298–99, 305–6; Memo, Lt Col Watha J. Eddins, Jr., USA, Ofc of Asst SecDef (Systems Analysis), Regional Programs, for Mr McManaway, Jul 8, 71, subj: RVNAF Improvement.

16. USAF Advisory Gp, VNAF I&M [Improvement and Modernization] Briefing, Apr 7, 71.

17. Ltr, 20th TASSq, OL 201, to 20th TASSq, Apr 14, 71, subj: Special Survey.

18. End of Tour Rprt, Col Harold W. Hobbs, Comdr, 377th CSGp, Jul 70–Jul 71, Dec 18, 71, pp 3–4.

19. Atch 2 to End of Tour Rprt, Col Robert W. Slane, VComdr and Comdr, 553d Recon Wg, Sep 15, 70–Feb 1, 71, and Comdr, 6251st CSGp, Feb 2–Sep 2, 71, Nov 15, 71.

20. Atch 1 to End of Tour Rprt, Col Thomas A. Barr, Dir/Ops, Air Force Advisory Gp, Vietnam, Jul 30, 71–Jan 5, 73, nd, pp 5–6; Air Force Advisory Gp, Vietnam, I&M Briefing, Apr 7, 71; USAF Mgt Summary, May 21, 71, p i; Aug 18, 71, p iii; Jan 24, 72, p 39; Feb 22, 72, p 39; Jan 19, 73, p 39.

21. Capt Joseph G. Meeko IV, *Vietnamization of the Tactical Air Control System* (Hq PACAF, Proj CHECO, Sep 23, 74), pp 14–15.

22. Ibid, pp 38–41; ltr, I DASC to 7AF DCS/Ops, May 15, 71, subj: Night FAC Strike Certification for Close Air Support; End of Tour Rprt, Col Peter B. Van Brussel, Jr., Chief, Air Force Advisory Team 2, Aug 70–Jul 72, nd, p 2:1.

23. Atch 2 to Slane End of Tour Rprt.

24. Trip Rprt, Capt C. L. Christon, VNAF Intelligence Improvement and Modernization Program Monitor, Apr 9–16, 71, May 10, 71.

25. End of Tour Rprt, Maj Gen James H. Watkins, Chief, Air Force Advisory Gp, Vietnam, Feb 15, 71–May 16, 72, May 14, 72, p C:22.

26. Hist, USMACV, 1971, vol II, p F:7; Thomas C. Thayer, *War without Fronts: The American Experience in Vietnam* (Boulder, Colo, and London, 1985), table 4.5.

27. Hist, JCS, *The JCS and the War in Vietnam, 1971–1973*, pt I, pp 135–37.

28. *Nixon Papers, 1971*, p 524.

29. Memo for Record, Phil Odeen, Ofc of Asst SecDef (Systems Analysis), Apr 8, 71, subj: Vietnamization Meeting with Secretary Laird.

30. Hist, USMACV, 1971, vol II, fig F:1.

31. Ibid, p F–1:12; hist, JCS, *The JCS and the War in Vietnam, 1971–1973*, pt I, pp 148–49.

32. Hist, JCS, *The JCS and the War in Vietnam, 1971–1973*, pt I, pp 150–51; Hartsook, *Shield for Vietnamization and Withdrawal*, pp 68–71.

33. Hist, JCS, *The JCS and the War in Vietnam, 1971–1973*, pt I, pp 150–51, 159–61; USAF Mgt Summary, Southeast Asia, Dec 19, 70, p 5; Jan 19, 71, pp 2, 4; Dec 12, 71, pp i, 5, Jan 24, 72, pp 2, 4.

34. Hist, JCS, *The JCS and the War in Vietnam, 1971–1973*, pt I, pp 152–58.

35. Kissinger, *White House Years*, pp 1017–18; Karnow, *Vietnam*, pp 398, 633, 655; Thomas D. Boettcher, *Vietnam: The Valor and the Sorrow* (Boston, 1985), pp 246–49, 390–91, 450–51.

36. Hist, JCS, *The JCS and the War in Vietnam, 1971–1973*, pt I, pp 159–60.

37. Ibid, pt I, pp 174, 178–82.

38. JCS Action Officer's Data Book on Vietnamizing the War, Jun 28, 72, p B:37–1; Hartsook, *Shield for Vietnamization and Withdrawal*, pp 73–74.

39. Hist, JCS, *The JCS and the War in Vietnam, 1971–1973*, pt I, pp 185–207; Hartsook, *Shield for Vietnamization and Withdrawal*, pp 71–84.

Chapter 18

1. *TIG,* [The Inspector General] *Brief,* vol XX. no 6 (Mar 29, 68), p 17.

2. *TIG Brief*, vol XX, no 19 (Sep 27, 68), p 20.

3. Memo, J. William Doolittle, Asst SAF, Manpower and Reserve Affairs, for the Vice Chief of Staff, Feb 4, 69, subj: Race Relations within the Air Force; Intvw, Maj Alan Gropman with Col Hughie C. Mathews, Experiences of a Black Officer, 1945–1964, Oct 25, 73, pp 34–37.

4. Jack D. Foner, *Blacks and the Military in American History: A New Perspective*, paperback edition (New York, 1974), pp 212–13.

5. Hist, Ofc of Surgeon General, USAF, Jan–Jun 68, p 149; Jul–Dec 70, p 33.

6. End of Tour Rprt, Col Earl M. Chu, DCS/Personnel, Hq 7AF, Jun 17, 71–Jun 16, 72, June 15, 72, p 15.

7. Hobbs End of Tour Rprt, pp 2–8.

8. Atch 1 to Slane End of Tour Rprt.

9. End of Tour Rprt, Col Archie L. Henson, Staff Judge Advocate, Hq 7AF, Aug 25, 70–Aug 24, 71, Aug 15, 71, pp 2–4.

10. Slane End of Tour Rprt, pp 7–8.

11. Lt Gen Paul K. Carlton, Comdr, 15AF (SAC), speech to the graduates of the Squadron Officers' School, Aug 6, 71.

12. Intvw, Lt Col Robert G. Zimmerman with Col John E. Blake, Comdr, Travis AFB, Calif, 1970–71, Jul 24, 74. pp 54–55.

13. Intvw, Maj Richard B. Garver with Sgt "J," enrolled in drug rehabilitation program at Udorn AB, Thailand, Aug 23, 73.

14. End of Tour Rprts, Col Arden B. Curfman, Comdr, 483d CSGp, Cam Ranh Bay AB, Oct 16, 70–Oct 13, 71, nd, pp 10–11; Col Francis P. Fitzgerald, Comdr, 483d CSGp, Cam Ranh Bay, AB, Oct 13, 71–Apr 15, 72, nd, pp 2–3; OSI Rprt of Investigation, Tan Son Nhut AB, May 28–Jun 23, 71, Narcotics Investigative Survey, Jul 23, 71.

15. Slane End of Tour Rprt, p 8.

16. End of Tour Rprt, Brig Gen Walter T. Galligan, Comdr, 35th TFWg, Phan Rang AB, Aug 8, 69–Jun 10, 70.

17. OSI Rprt of Investigation, Tan Son Nhut, May–Jun 71, cited above.

18. Curfman End of Tour Rprt, p 7; PACAF Briefing Chart, Drug and Alcohol Abuse Control: Drug Incidents by Specialty, nd.

19. Sgt "J" intvw, cited above.

20. Alfred W. McCoy, with Cathleen B. Read and Leonard P. Adams, III, *The Politics of Heroin in Southeast Asia* (New York, 1972), pp 186–87; 7AF Background Paper on Drug Abuse Prevention Program, nd.

21. Hist, Ofc of the Inspector General, Jan–Jun 70, vol II, pp 14–15. Additional information supplied by Edward A. Mishler, PhD, Historian, Ofc of Special Investigations.

22. McCoy, with Read et al, *The Politics of Heroin*, pp 181–83, 185; 7AF Background Paper on Drug Abuse Prevention Program, nd.

23. Hist, Ofc of the Inspector General, Jul–Dec 70, vol II, pt 4, pp 46–47; msg, CSAF to ALMAJCOM, 081623Z Mar 71, subj: Privileged Communication for Drug Abusers, unnumbered supporting doc to hist, PACAF, Jul 70–Jun 71, vol II; Briefing chart, USAF Limited Privileged Communication Program, nd.

24. Maj Richard B. Garver, *Drug Abuse in Southeast Asia* (Hq PACAF, Proj CHECO, Jan 1, 75), pp 7–14.

25. Chu End of Tour Rprt, pp 27–28.

26. Curfman End of Tour Rprt, p 14.

27. Fitzgerald End of Tour Rprt, pp 34–35.

28. End of Tour Rprt, Col Raymond A Gailer, Comdr, 2d APGp, and Chief, Aerial Port Div, Dir/Airlift, 7AF, Jul 71–Jul 72, nd, pp 30–31; hist, Ofc of the Inspector General, Jul–Dec 70, vol II, pt 4, p 47; Jan–Jun 71, vol III, p 14; General Accounting Ofc, Review of Drug Abuse Program in Southeast Asia, nd, p 45.

29. Henson End of Tour Rprt, p 3.

30. OSI Rprt of Investigation, Tan Son Nhut, May–Jun 71.

31. OSI Rprts of Investigation, Da Nang AB, Vietnam, May 22–Jun 25, 71, Narcotics Investigative Survey, nd; Phu Cat AB, Vietnam, May 19–Jun 25, 71, Narcotics Investigative Survey, Jul 16, 71.

32. OSI Rprt of Investigation, Binh Thuy AB, Vietnam, May 21–Jul 6, 71, Narcotics Investigative Survey, Jul 19, 71.

33. Ibid.

34. OSI Rprt of Investigation, Bien Hoa AB, Vietnam, May 22–Jul 9, 71, Narcotics Investigative Survey, Jul 20, 71.

35. Ibid.

36. OSI Rprt of Investigation, Pleiku AB,

Vietnam, Jun 3–Jul 8, 71, Narcotics Investigative Survey, Jul 21, 71.

37. End of Tour Rprt, Lt Col Vaughn E. Hill, Staff Judge Advocate, 7AF, Jul 6, 72–Mar 28, 73, nd, pp 1–2.

38. Chu End of Tour Rprt, pp 24–26.

39. Slane End of Tour Rprt, pp 7, 9.

40. Hist, Ofc of the Inspector General, Jan–Jun 71, vol III, pp 12–13.

41. Hq 18th Military Police Brigade, Rprts of Investigations Concerning USARV Installation Stockade, Set 13, 68, and USARV Stockade Disturbance of 13 November 1969, Dec 11, 69; Hist Div, HQMC, Summary of Significant Racial Incidents at Marine Corps Installations, nd; Foner, *Blacks and the Military*, pp 243–48.

42. USMACV Rprt, Detailed Breakout of Disturbances, nd.

43. Maj Richard H. Bucher, Study of Black Awareness Groups, Aug 5, 70.

44. Ibid.

45. Benjamin Muse, *The American Negro Revolution: From Non-Violence to Black Power* (New York, 1970), pp 255–70; Leslie H. Fishel, Jr. and Benjamin Quarles, *The Black American: A Documentary History* (Glenview, Ill, 1970), pp 577–87.

46. OSI Rprt, Review of Racially Oriented Incidents at USAF Bases in the RVN, Apr–Jun 71, Jul 14, 71.

47. Atch 1 to Slane End of Tour Rprt.

48. End of Tour Rprt, Col Charles D. Gunn, Jr., Comdr, 377th CSGp, Jul 9 71–Jan 17, 72, and 377th ABWg, Jan 17–Jul 1, 72, nd, p 3.

49. Alan Osur, "Black–White Relations in the Military," *Air University Review*, vol XXXII, no 1 (Nov–Dec 81), pp 76–77; Blake intvw, Jul 24, 74, pp 66–87.

50. Foner, *Blacks and the Military*, pp 235–36; intvw, Shelby E. Wickham with Lt Col Thomas J. Sizemore, Chief, 2750th ABWg Social Actions Ofc, Wright-Patterson AFB, Ohio, 1974–77, Mar 3, 77, pp 16–19.

51. Gunn End of Tour Rprt, pp 2–3; End of Tour Rprt, Col Gregg F. Glick, Comdr, 6251st ABWg, Bien Hoa AB, South Vietnam, Sep 7, 71–Sep 4, 72, nd.

Chapter 19

1. Hist, JCS, *The JCS and the War in Vietnam, 1971–1973*, pt I, p 73.

2. Ibid. pt I, pp 78–79.

3. Hist, USMACV, Jan 72–Mar 73, vol I, pp 16–18, 32, 26–27, 30–31.

4. Msg, Gen Abrams to Adm Moorer, 010223Z Feb 72, subj: Unnumbered COSVN Resolution; hist, JCS, *The JCS and the War in Vietnam, 1971–1973*, pt I, pp 209–10; John M. Gates, "People's War in Vietnam," *Journal of Military History*, vol LIV, no 3 (Jul 1990), pp 337–38.

5. Msgs, Gen Abrams to Adm Moorer, 221037Z Feb 72, subj: NVN Propaganda; Maj Gen [Thomas M.] Tarpley to Gen Abrams, 070420Z Feb 72, subj: Enemy Situation.

6. Gen Bruce Palmer, Jr., USA, "U.S. Intelligence and Vietnam," *Studies in Intelligence* (Special Issue, 1984), pp 91–92.

7. Msg, Vann to Gen Abrams, 031240Z Feb 72, subj: Report of Tanks.

8. Msgs, Lt Gen [Welborn G.] Dolvin to Gen Abrams, 200430Z Feb 72, 230455Z Feb 72, and 290435Z Feb 72, subj: Commander's Daily Evaluation.

9. Eduard Mark, *Aerial Interdiction: Air Power and the Land Battle in Three American Wars* (Washington, 1994), pp 369–70.

10. Lt Gen Dolvin to Gen Abrams, 230455Z Feb 72, subj: Commander's Daily Evaluation.

11. Msg, Vann to Gen Abrams, 020235Z Feb 72, subj: Specified Strike Zone.

12. Msgs, Maj Gen Hollingsworth to Gen Abrams, 250215Z Feb 72, subj: Daily Commander's Evaluation, 241000H to 251000H Feb 72; 260206Z Feb 72, subj: Daily Commander's Evaluation, 251000H to 261000H Feb 72; 270210Z Feb 72, subj: Daily Commander's Evaluation, 261000H to 271000H Feb 72; 280205Z Feb 72, subj: Daily Commander's Evaluation, 271000H to 281000H Feb 72.

13. Capt Charles A. Nicholson, *The USAF Response to the Spring 1972 NVN Offensive: Situation and Redeployment* (Hq PACAF, Proj CHECO, Oct 10, 72), pp 25–29, 31–33.

14. Hist, SAC, Fiscal 1971, vol II, pp 235–37; msg, SSO SAC to CINCPAC,

Notes to pages 329–340

082330Z Feb 72, subj: Arc Light Deployment.

15. Msg, COMUSMACV to CINCPAC, 050055Z Feb 72, subj: Operational Plans, SEA.

16. Public Papers of the Presidents of the United States: *Richard Nixon, 1972* (Washington, 1974), pp 30, 192–193.

17. Msgs, Maj Gen [Frederick J] Kroesen [Jr.] to Gen Abrams, 240220Z Feb 72, subj: Daily Commander's Evaluation, and 260337Z Mar 72, subj: none; Lt Gen Dolvin to Gen Abrams, 090229Z Mar 72, subj: Commander's Daily Evaluation.

18. Msg, 7AF SSO to MACV SSO, 220630Z Mar 72, subj: Freedom Block.

19. Rprt, Maj David A. Brookbank, ALO Adviser, 3d ARVN Div, VNAF FACs and the Fall of Quang Tri, p 4.

20. Msg, VANN to Abrams, 270151Z Mar 72, subj: Daily Commander's Evaluation for 24 hours from 1000H, 27 Mar.

21. Hist, JCS, *The JCS and the War in Vietnam, 1971–1973*, pt I, pp 293–95.

22. Brookbank Rprt, p 3.

23. Phillip G, Davison, *Vietnam at War: The History, 1946–1975* (Novato, Calif, 1988), pp 608–11, 614, 619, 624; hist, USMACV, Jan 72–Mar 73, vol I, p 41.

24. Douglas Pike, *PAVN: People's Army of Vietnam* (Novato, Calif, 1896), pp 222–25; Ngo Vinh Long, "The Tet Offensive and its Aftermath," paper presented at *Remembering Tet: An Interdisciplinary Conference on the War in Vietnam*, Salisbury State University, Md, Nov 18–21, 1992, pp 1–3, 48–49.

Chapter 20

1. Hist, USMACV, Jan 72–Mar 73, vol II, p N:2; USAF Mgt Summary, SEA, Apr 20, 72, pp 4–6, 30, 38, Jun 21, 72, p 58.

2. Kissinger, *White House Years*, p 1098.

3. Nixon, *RN*, p 588.

4. PACAF South Vietnam Assessment, May 15, 72.

5. Peter Macdonald, *Giap: The Victor in Vietnam* (New York, 1993), p 328.

6. Hist, JCS, *The JCS and the War in Vietnam, 1971–1973*, pt I, p 457.

7. Ibid, pt I, p 353, 365–367; Kissinger, *White House Years*, p 1098; msgs, JCS to CINCPAC, 021702Z Apr 72, 031716Z Apr 72, and 042325Z Apr 72, subj: SEASIA Operating Authorities; 082259Z Apr 72, subj: Freedom Train Authorities.

8. Hist, SAC, Fiscal 1972, vol III, pp 434–35.

9. Hist, JCS, *The JCS and the War in Vietnam, 1971–1973*, pt I, pp 382–85; Kissinger, *White House Years*, pp 1169–86, 1192–94.

10. Hist, JCS, *The JCS and the War in Vietnam, 1971–1973*, pt I, pp 385–86; msgs, Adm Moorer to Adm McCain, 090247Z May 72, subj: NVN Interdiction Program, and JCS to CINCPAC, 092307Z May 72, subj: NVN Interdiction Plan; John Morrocco, *The Vietnam Experience; Rain of Fire: The Air War, 1969–1973* (Boston, 1985), pp 131–32.

11. Msg, JCS to CINCPAC, 092356Z May 72, subj: NVN Interdiction Plan.

12. Hist, SAC, Fiscal 1972, vol III, pp 423–29, 476; vol IV, p 599.

13. Ibid, vol III, pp 431–32, 481; vol IV, p 599.

14. Msg, MACV CofS to 7AF Comdr, retransmitting CINCSAC to CINCPAC and COMUSMACV, 141630Z Jun 72, subj: Arc Light Sortie Rate.

15. Hist, JCS, *The JCS and the War in Vietnam, 1971–1973*, pt I, pp 358–59; hist, CINCPAC, 1972, vol I, pp 195–97; Nicholson, *USAF Response*, pp 52–53.

16. Hist, JCS, *The JCS and the War in Vietnam, 1971–1973*, pt I, p 358.

17. Nicholson, *USAF Response*, pp 34, 36.

18. Hist, JCS, *The JCS and the War in Vietnam, 1971–1973*, pt I, p 359; Nicholson, *USAF Response*, pp 36, 53–54; Charles D. Melson and Curtis G. Arnold, *U.S. Marines in Vietnam: The War That Would Not End, 1971–1973* (Washington, 1991), pp 153–54, 157.

19. Melson and Arnold, *War That Would Not End*, p 157.

20. 1st Marine Aircraft Wing Command Chronology, Jan 1–Jun 30, 72, pt II, para 7; hist, USMACV, Jan 72–Mar 73, p B:61.

21. Nicholson, *USAF Response*, pp 35–36,

43–44.

22. Ibid, pp 40–41, 42–45.
23. Hist, TAC, Jul 71–Jun 72, vol I, p 185.
24. Nicholson, *USAF Response*, pp 40–42.
25. Ibid, pp 45–51.
26. Hist, TAC, Jul 71–Jun 72, p 184; USAF Mgt Summary, SEA, Jun 21, 72, p 6.
27. Hist, SAC, Fiscal 1972, vol II, pp 474–84; Fiscal 1973, vol I, pp 29–31.
28. Melson and Arnold, *War That Would Not End*, pp 159–160.
29. Msg, Gen Abrams to Lt Gen [William J.] McCaffrey and Maj Gen Hollingsworth, 181231Z May 72, subj: SEASIA TAC Air Augmentation; Glick End of Tour Rprt, nd, np.
30. Melson and Arnold, *War That Would Not End*, pp 165–66; Nicholson, *USAF Response*, pp 60–61; msg, Gen Abrams to Gen Vogt, 180930Z Jun 72, subj: Increment Twelve Redeployments.
31. Msgs, 7AF SSO to MACV SSO, 030100Z May 72 and 300130Z May 72, subj: Increment 12; COMUSMACV to 7AF Comdr, 070606Z May 72, subj: Increment 12 Redeployments; 7AF to PACAF, 201230Z May 72, TAC SSO to PACAF SSO, AFSSO, et al, 241915Z May 72, and AFSSO to PACAF SSO, 262215Z May 72, subj: RVN TACAIR Relocations; PACAF SSO to 7AF SSO and 13AF SSO, 070238Z Jun 72, subj: none; Nicholson, *USAF Response*, pp 54, 58, 60, 61, 63; USAF Mgt Summary, SEA, Oct 27, 72, p 4.
32. Hist, TAC, Jul 72–Jun 73, pp 217–23.
33. USAF Mgt Summary, Apr 20, 72, pp 4–5; Nov 27, 72, p 5.
34. Hist, JCS, *The JCS and the War in Vietnam, 1971–1973*, pt II, pp 442–45, 451–59.
35. Ibid, pt I, pp 375–76, 389–31.
36. *Facts on File*, vol XXXII, no 1677 (Dec 17–23, 72), p 1022G3.
37. Karnow, *Vietnam*, p 653.
38. Hist, USMACV, Jan 72–Mar 73, vol I, p C:12; Thomas D. DesBrisay, *VNAF Improvement and Modernization Program, Jul 1971–Dec 73* (Hq PACAF, Proj CHECO, Jan 1, 75), p 28.
39. Col J. L. Gardner, Background Paper on Current Status of Credible Chase, May 9, 72.

40. Hist, JCS, *The JCS and the War in Vietnam, 1971–1973*, pt II, pp 480–84; hist, USMACV, Jan 72–Mar 73, vol I, p C:14.
41. Hist, JCS, *The JCS and the War in Vietnam, 1971–1973*, pt II, pp 484–94.
42. DesBrisay, *VNAF Improvement and Modernization*, pp 32–35; Memo, SecDef to Service Secretaries and CJCS, Jun 16, 72, subj: Military Assistance to the RVN; Memo for record, Asst SecDef (I&L), Jun 16, 72, subj: same; End of Tour Rprt, Col John F. Nuding, Dir, Programs, 7AF, Jul 12, 71–May 27, 72, DCS/Plans, 7AF, May 28, 72–Jul 30, 72, nd, p 11.
43. DesBrisay, *VNAF Improvement and Modernization*, pp 35–38; hist, JCS, *The JCS and the War in Vietnam, 1971–1973*, pt II, pp 499–503; Karnow, *Vietnam*, p 648.
44. DesBrisay, VNAF, *VNAF Improvement and Modernization*, pp 49–50; hist, USMACV, Jan 72–Mar 73, p C:20–22.
45. DesBrisay, *VNAF Improvement and Modernization*, pp 50–51, 118; Point paper, Ofc of Special Asst for Vietnamization, DCS/Plans and Ops, VNAF Training for Enhance Plus Aircraft, Dec 12, 72; hist, USMACV, Jan 72–Mar 73, vol I, pp C:74, 77, 79.
46. AF Advisory Gp Rprt, VNAF Pilot Conference and FY 74 Security Assistance Workshop, Bangkok, Thailand, Feb 9–13, 73.
47. DesBrisay, *VNAF Improvement and Modernization*, pp 123–24.
48. Atch to ltr, Air Force Logistics Command to Ofc SecDef (I&L), nd [ca mid-December 72], subj: Plan for Completing U.S. Civilian and Third-Country Support of RVNAF.
49. Msg, 7602 AINTELGp, Ft. Belvoir, Va., to DIA, Washington, IR 1 502 0211 75, subj: Logistics Problems.
50. Msg, 7602 AINTELGp, Ft. Belvoir, Va., to DIA, Washington, IR 1 502 0271 75, Jul 75, subj: VNAF Logistics.
51. Msg, 7602 AINTELGp, Ft. Belvoir, Va., to DIA, Washington, IR 1 502 210 75, 221801Z Jul 75, subj: Problems Associated with VNAF Logistics.
52. Ibid.
53. Msg, 7602 AINTELGp, IR 1 502 0271 75, cited above.

483

Notes to pages 354–368

54. Rprt, Ofc SecDef Ad Hoc Panel on Technical Improvements of VNAF Capabilities, nd [ca Dec 72], pp 17, 24–25, 29–30, 32.

55. Ibid, pp 28–29.

56. Ibid, p 17; End of Tour Rprt, Col Charles E. Hammack, Chief, AF Advisory Team 1, Jun 19 72–Mar 14, 73, nd, p 3.

57. Rprt, Ofc SecDef Ad Hoc Panel on Technical Improvement of VNAF Capabilities, pp 35–36, 38–39; Hammack End of Tour Rprt, p 2.

58. End of Tour Rprt, Maj Gen James H. Watkins, Chief, AF Advisory Gp, Vietnam, Feb 15, 71–May 16, 72, p C:8; msg, 7602 AINTELGp, Ft. Belvoir, Va., to DIA, Washington, 271942Z Aug 75, subj: VNAF Reconnaissance Capabilities; DesBrisay, *VNAF Improvement and Modernization*, pp 100–101.

59. Rprt, Ofc SecDef Ad Hoc Panel on Technical Improvements of VNAF Capabilities, p 21.

60. Brookbank Rprt, p 4.

Chapter 21

1. Morrocco, *Rain of Fire*, p 102.

2. David Fulgham, Terrence Maitland, et al, *The Vietnam Experience: South Vietnam on Trial, Mid-1970 to 1972* (Boston, 1984), p 142.

3. Intvw, Lt Col Arthur W. McCants and James C. Hasdorff with Gen John W. Vogt, 7AF Comdr, Apr 72–Sep 73, Aug 8–9, 78, pp 63–64, 263–66, 271–72.

4. Brookbank rprt, pp 4–5.

5. Kissinger, *White House Years*, p 1098, 1098n.

6. Brookbank rprt, p 10; Ngo Quang Truong, *Indochina Monographs: The Easter Offensive of 1972* (Washington, 1980), pp 23–30.

7. Brookbank rprt, p 7; Morrocco, *Rain of Fire*, pp 106–7; Earl H. Tilford, *Search and Rescue in Southeast Asia, 1961–1975* (Washington, 1980), pp 118–19; 96th Cong, 1st Sess, Senate Committee on Veterans' Affairs, *Medal of Honor Recipients* (Washington, 1979); G. H. Turley, *The Easter Offensive: Vietnam, 1972* (Novato, Calif, 1985), p 202n; Melson and Arnold, *War That Would Not End*, p 71; Darrel D. Whitcomb, *The Rescue of Bat 21* (Annapolis, Md, 1988), pp 61–63, 78–82, 93–108, 120–121. For a fictionalized account of Hambleton's rescue, see William Anderson, *Bat 21*, Englewood Cliffs, NJ, Prentice-Hall, 1980.

8. Brookbank Rprt, p 9; commnets by Darrell D. Whitcomb, nd, on draft MS.

9. Tilford, *Search and Rescue*, pp 118–19.

10. Morrocco, *Rain of Fire*, pp 107, 112.

11. Turley, *The Easter Offensive*, p 203.

12. Ibid, p 123.

13. Ibid, pp 200–204; Whitcomb comments.

14. Quoted in Melson and Arnold, *War That Would Not End*, p 61.

15. Tilford, *Search and Rescue*, p 120.

16. Brookbank rprt, p 8.

17. A. J. C. Lavalle, ed, *USAF Southeast Asia Monograph Series: Airpower and the 1972 Spring Invasion* (Washington, 1985), reprint, p 41.

18. Truong, *Easter Offensive*, pp 33, 36–37.

19. Brookbank rprt, pp 6, 10.

20. Ibid, pp 6, 16–17.

21. Ibid, p 18; Tilford, *Search and Rescue*, pp 120–21; msg, MACV CofS for 7AF Comdr, 020947Z May 72, retransmitting CG FRAC to COMUSMACV, 020455Z May 72, subj: Commander's Daily Evaluation.

22. Truong, *Easter Offensive*, p 50; Davidson, *Vietnam at War*, p 618.

23. Maj David K. Mann, *The 1972 Invasion of Military Region I: Fall of Quang Tri and the Defense of Hue* (Hq PACAF, Proj CHECO, Mar 15, 73), p 56.

24. Msg, Gen Abrams to Secretary Laird, 011601Z May 72, subj: Personal Assessment of Situation in RVN.

25. Truong, *Easter Offensive*, pp 53–54, 56.

26. Msg, 7AF SSO to AF SSO and PACAF SSO, 061045Z May 72, subj: none.

27. Msgs, AF SSO to 7AF SSO, 241422Z May 72, subj: RADC [Rome Air Development Center] Artillery Locating System (RALS); Maj Gen [Howard H.] Cooksey to Gen Abrams, 140230Z Jun 72, subj: Com-

mander's Daily Evaluation; Mann, *The 1972 Invasion of Military Region I,* p 62; Whitcomb comments.

28. Msg, 7AF SSO to AF SSO and PACAF SSO, 061045Z May 72, subj: none.

29. Mann, *The 1972 Invasion of Military Region I,* pp 58, 67.

30. Msg, CG FRAC to COMUSMACV, 100300Z May 72, subj: none.

31. Truong, *Easter Offensive,* pp 56–63.

32. Hq PACAF, Summary of Southeast Asia Air Operations, Apr 72, p 5:C:2; Jul 72, p 5:C:2; Mann, *The 1972 Invasion of Military Region I,* p 74; msg, Maj Gen Cooksey to Gen Abrams, 190244Z Jun 72, subj: Commander's Daily Evaluation; Lavalle, ed, *Airpower and the Spring Invasion,* p 44; Whitcomb comments.

33. Lavalle, ed, *Airpower and the Spring Offensive,* p 58.

34. Davidson, *Vietnam at War,* pp 635–37.

35. Msgs, COMUSMACV to CG FRAC, Dir SRAG, et al, 020452Z May 72, subj: none; Gen Abrams to Vice President Agnew, 171034Z May 72, subj: Memcon of Meeting at TSN Base Operations VP Lounge.

36. Truong, *Easter Offensive,* pp 65–66.

37. CAS South Vietnam Situation Rprt, 271600Local Jun 72.

38. Truong, *Easter Offensive,* p 67.

39. Ibid, pp 70–71; hist, USMACV, Jan 72–Mar 73, vol I, pp 73–77.

40. Hammack End of Tour Rprt, p 3; CAS South Vietnam Situation Rprts, 011700Local Oct 72; 021800Local Oct 72; 281800Local Oct 72; hist, MACV, Jun 72–Mar 73, vol I, pp 78–85.

41. Truong, *Easter Offensive,* pp 75–77.

Chapter 22

1. Jeffrey J. Clarke, *The United States Army in Vietnam; Advice and Support: The Final Years, 1965–1973* (Washington, 1988), p 477.

2. Truong, *Easter Offensive,* p 82.

3. Capt Peter A. W. Liebchen, *Kontum: The Battle for the Central Highlands, 30 March–10 June 1972* (Hq PACAF, Proj CHECO, Oct 27, 72), p 2.

4. Truong, *Easter Offensive,* pp 83–84, 91; Neil Sheehan, *A Bright Shining Lie: John Paul Vann and America in Vietnam* (New York, 1988), p 755.

5. Msg, Brig Gen [George E.] Wear to Gen Abrams, 030330Z Apr 72, subj: Daily Commander's Evaluation for 24 Hours from 1000H, 2 April.

6. Liebchen, *Kontum,* pp 11–12.

7. Truong, *Easter Offensive,* pp 86–87; hist, USMACV, Jan 72–Mar 73, vol I, p 51.

8. Truong, *Easter Offensive,* pp 86–90, 93–94; Liebchen, *Kontum,* pp 17, 20–22, 36–37.

9. Msgs, Vann to Gen Abrams, 291040Z Apr 72, subj: Miscellaneous Problems Relating to Air Support; to COMUSMACV, 030340Z May 72, subj: Daily Commander's Evaluation for 24 Hours from 1000H, 2 May; to COMUSMACV, 040411Z May 72, subj: Daily Commander's Evaluation for 24 Hours from 1000H, 3 May; to COMUSMACV, 050300Z May 72, subj: Daily Commander's Evaluation for 24 Hours from 1000H, 4 May.

10. Truong, *Easter Offensive,* p 94; Intvw, Lt Col V. H. Gallacher and Maj Lyn R. Officer with Col Loyd J. King, AC–130 comdr, 71–72, Feb 8, 73.

11. Msgs, Vann to COMUSMACV, 030340Z May 72, subj: Daily Commander's Evaluation for 24 Hours from 1100H, 2 May; 070315Z May 72, subj: Daily Commander's Evaluation for 24 Hours from 1000H, 6 May.

12. Truong, *Easter Offensive,* pp 91–92.

13. Quoted in Liebchen, *Kontum,* p 34.

14. Liebchen, *Kontum,* pp 44–45, 47–48; hist, USMACV, Jan 72–Mar 73, vol II, pp K:17–18.

15. Bowers, *Tactical Airlift,* pp 566–69.

16. Leibchen, *Kontum,* pp 55, 57.

17. Liebchen, *Kontum,* pp 55–57.

18. Maj Paul T. Ringenbach, *Airlift to Besieged Areas, 7 Apr–31 Aug 72* (Hq PACAF, Proj CHECO, Dec 7, 73), p 29; Bowers, *Tactical Airlift,* pp 544–45.

19. Maj Paul T. Ringenbach and Capt Peter J. Melly, *The Battle for An Loc, 5 Apr–26 Jun 1972* (Hq PACAF, Proj CHECO, Jan 31, 73) app 2; Bowers, *Tactical Airlift,* p

Notes to pages 381–400

550.

20. Bowers, *Tactical Airlift*, p 571–572.

21. Bowers, *Tactical Airlift*, p 570.

22. Truong, *Easter Offensive*, pp 104–5; hist, USMACV, Jan 72–Mar 73, vol I, pp 87–91.

23. Truong, *Easter Offensive*, pp 107–8, 111–12, 114–15; hist, USMACV, Jan 72–Mar 73, vol II, pp J:1, 3.

24. Ringenbach, *Airlift to Besieged Areas*, pp 1–2; Ringenbach and Melly, *An Loc*, p 5.

25. Ringenbach and Melly, *An Loc*, pp 7–8, 12–13.

26. Hist, USMACV, Jan 72–Mar 73, vol II, pp J:7–9.

27. Clarke, *Final Years*, p 485.

28. Davidson, *Vietnam at War*, p 629.

29. Msg, Maj Gen Hollingsworth to Lt Gen McCaffrey, 160910Z Apr 72, subj: none.

30. Ringenbach and Melly, *An Loc*, p 15.

31. Hist, USMACV, Jan 72–Mar 73, vol II, pp J:9–10, 12–13.

32. Ibid, p J:13; Ringenbach and Melly, *An Loc*, p 17.

33. Hist, USMACV, Jan 72–Mar 73, vol II, pp J:13–14.

34. Ringenbach and Melly, *An Loc*, pp 18–19, 22–23.

35. Maj Gen Hollingsworth to Gen Abrams, 130225Z May 72, subj: Daily Commander's Evaluation Rprt, 121000H through 131000H May 72.

36. Ringenbach and Melly, *An Loc*, pp 24–25, 37–38.

37. Maj Gen Hollingsworth to Gen Abrams, 100235Z May 72, subj: Daily Evaluation Rprt, 091000H through 101000H May 72.

38. Bowers, *Tactical Airlift*, pp 550–51.

39. Ringenbach and Melly, *An Loc*, pp 27–28; Bowers, *Tactical Airlift*, pp 540, 546, 555, 596–97.

40. Bowers, *Tactical Airlift*, pp 541–48.

41. Ibid, p 546.

42. Bowers, *Tactical Airlift*, pp 549–54, 572–73.

43. Ibid, pp 555–56; Truong, *Easter Offensive*, p 133.

44. Bowers, *Tactical Airlift*, pp 555–56, 576.

45. Lavalle, *Airpower and the 1972 Spring Invasion*, p 97.

46. Msg, Maj Gen Hollingsworth to Gen Abrams, 100235Z May 72, subj: Daily Commander's Evaluation Rprt, 091000H through 101000H May 72.

47. Intvw, Lt Col Robert Zimmerman with Lt Col Stephen J. Opitz, Fire Control Officer, AC-130 Gunship, Jul 71–Jul 72, Jul 18, 72, p 43; Ringenbach and Melly, *An Loc*, p 46; Lavalle, *Airpower and the 1972 Spring Invasion*, p 97.

48. Hist, USMACV, Jan 72–Mar 73, vol II, p J:22; Vogt intvw, pp 262–67.

49. Hist, USMACV, Jan 72–Mar 73, vol II, pp J:22–23, 25; Lt Col Gerald J. Tull and Maj James C. Thomas, *Pave Aegis Weapon System (AC–130E Gunship)* (Hq PACAF, Proj CHECO, Jul 30, 73), pp 23–24.

50. Hist, USMACV, Jan 72–Mar 73, vol II, pp J: 26, 28.

51. Ringenbach and Melly, *An Loc*, p 45.

52. Msg, Maj Gen Hollingsworth to Gen Abrams, 120227Z May 72, subj: Daily Commander's Evaluation Report, 111000H through 121000H May 72.

53. Quoted in Ringenbach and Melly, *An Loc*, p 60.

54. Ringenbach and Melly, *An Loc*, p 43.

55. Lavalle, *Airpower and the Spring 1972 Invasion*, pp 85, 199; Glick End of Tour Rprt, np.

56. Truong, *Easter Offensive*, pp 137, 146, 148; Davidson, *Vietnam at War*, pp 609–10.

57. Hist, USMACV, Jan 72–Mar 73, vol I, p 63; msgs, Brig Gen Frank E. Blazey to COMUSMACV, 060215Z Apr 72, subj: TAOR [Tactical Area of Responsibility] Report; Maj Gen Tarpley to COMUSMACV, 050240Z Apr [actually May] 72, subj: same.

58. Hist, USMACV, Jan 72–Mar 73, vol I, pp 63, 65; Truong, *Easter Offensive*, pp 145–46, 148–55.

59. Truong, *Easter Offensive*, pp 146, 155.

60. Davidson, *Vietnam at War*, pp 605–8.

61. Ibid, p 608.

62. Kissinger, *White House Years*, pp 1146–47, 1352–53, 1378–92, 1402. To view the negotiating process through South Vietnamese eyes, see: Nguyen Tien Hung and Jerrold L. Schecter, *The Palace File* (New York, 1986), chapters 7–9.

63. Nixon, *RN*, p 718.
64. Ibid, pp 749–50; Karnow, *Vietnam*, pp 651–55; Kissinger, *White House Years*, pp 1459–60.
65. Vogt intvw, p 276.
66. Clarke, *Final Years*, p 520.

Chapter 23

1. Cao Van Vien, *Indochina Monographs: The Final Collapse* (Washington, 1983), pp 29–30.
2. End of Tour Rprt, Col Merrill W. Hulse, Chief, Automated Systems Div, J–3, Hq USSAG/7AF, Aug 7, 72–Aug 6, 73, Aug 6, 73, p 5.
3. Msg, PACAF SSO to USSAG SSO, 230401Z Mar 73, subj: Ten-Day Targeting Plan, retransmitting PACAF SSO to SAC SSO, 222200Z Mar 73, subj: same.
4. Msg, PACAF SSO to 7AF SSO, 282230Z Feb 73, subj: PACAF Base Reopening Plan (Commando Freight 11).
5. Msg, Nakhon Phanom SSO to CINCPAC SSO, 170250Z Apr 73, subj: Operational Procedures.
6. End of Tour Rprt, Col Frederick W. Fowler, Chief, Targets Div, J–2, USSAG, Feb 13–Aug 29, 73, Oct 11, 73, p 10.
7. Msgs, Nakhon Phanom SSO to PACAF SSO, 271040Z Apr 73, subj: Command and Control in Khmer Republic; to Phnom Penh SSO, 281015Z Apr 73, subj: SEAsia Operating Authorities; to DIA SSO, 020545Z Jul 73, subj: none; CJCS to CINCPAC and CINCSAC, 280028Z Apr 73, subj: SEAsia Operating Authorities; ltr, Gen John W. Vogt to Thomas Ostrum Enders, Dep Chief of Mission, U.S. Embassy, Phnom Penh, 1970–1974, Jul 8, 79, in Henry Kissinger, *Years of Upheaval* (Boston, 1986), tab C to app.
8. End of Tour Rprt, Col Russell F. Crutchlow, Chief, Command and Control Div, 7AF, Jun 72–Jun 73, nd [Jun 73], p 2.
9. Col William E. LeGro, *Vietnam from Cease-Fire to Capitulation* (Washington, 1981), pp 18–19; Clarke, *The Final Years*, pp 495–96; Stuart Herrington, *Peace With Honor? An American Reports on Vietnam, 1973–1975* (Novato, Calif, 1983), pp 12–14, 48–49.
10. DAO Quarterly Assessment, Oct 31, 73, pp 12:10, 12.
11. Ibid, p 12:12.
12. AFGp/XR Talking Paper, VNAF Force Structure, Jan 11, 73, DAO 201–09A, RVNAF Force Structure.
13. End of Tour Rprt, Maj Gen Jimmy J. Jumper, MACV J–5, 7AF Dir/Intelligence, and Chief, AF Advisory Gp, Jul 6, 72–Mar 28, 73, Jun 14, 73, np.
14. Atch to AF Gp/LG Working Paper, VNAF Force Structure, Jan 11, 73, DAO 201–09A RVNAF Force Structure.
15. Msg, AFGp to COMUSMACV, 110301Z Jan 73, subj: Maritime Patrol Squadron, DAO 201–09A VNAF Maritime Patrol Squadron.
16. End of Tour Rprt, Col Gerald M. Adams, Dir/Plans and Programs, AFGp, Jul 15, 72–Feb 28, 73, Feb 26, 73, pp 2–3.
17. Disposition Form, Col [Perrin W.] Gower [Jr.,] to Brig Gen [Ralph J.] Maglione [Jr.,] and Maj Gen Murray, Aug 14, 73, subj: Air Attache Visit to 6th, 2d, and 1st Air Divs, DAO 201–09A Air Attache Visit to 6th, 2d, and 1st Air Divs.
18. Disposition Form, AFGp to COMUSMACV, Jan 9, 73, subj: Non-Concurrence with JGS Recommendation That VNAF Retain Nine Excess C–47 Aircraft; ltr, Gen Fred C. Weyand to Gen Cao Van Vien, Jan 14, 73, DAO 201–09A Proj Enhance Plus, Folder 2.
19. Msg, Maj Gen Murray to Gen Vogt, 011041Z May 73, subj: Collection Capabilities in SVN—DAO vis a vis MACV.
20. DAO Quarterly Assessment, Oct 31, 73, pp 6:48–49.
21. Ibid, foreword.
22. Ibid, pp 6:35–36.
23. Ibid, p 6:31.
24. Ibid, pp 6:14, 26, 31; Memo, Maj Gen John E, Murray, USA, Defense Attache, for Gen Maglione, Aug 21, 73, subj: LSI Briefing on VNAF, DAO 201–09A, Air Attache Visit to 6th, 2d, and 1st Air Divs.
25. DAO Quarterly Assessment, Oct 31, 73, pp 6:53–56, 59, 63.
26. Msg, State to Phnom Penh, Saigon, et

487

al, State 015050, 260022Z Jan 73, subj: Cease-fire in Vietnam in Kissinger, *Years of Upheaval*, Tab A to App.

27. Msg, Brig Gen Cleland, Chief, MEDTC, to COMUSSAG, 310845Z Mar 73, quoting his msg to CINCPAC Chief of Staff, 291121Z Mar 73, subj: GKR Situation.

28. Fowler End of Tour Rprt, p 10.

29. Msg, Nakhon Phanom SSO to TAC SSO, 160440Z May 73, subj: none; Vogt intvw, pp 93–94; Earl H. Tilford, Jr., *Setup: What The Air Force Did in Vietnam and Why* (Maxwell AFB, Ala, 1991), p 276.

30. Hq PACAF, with the Support of SAC, Corona Harvest Study, USAF Air Operations in Southeast Asia, Jul 1, 72–Aug 15, 73, May 7, 75, vol III, sec VI, pp 38–39.

31. Ibid, vol III, sec VI, p 40.

32. Tilford, *Setup*, p 277.

33. Ibid, pp 276–77; msg, CINCSAC SSO to CINCPAC SSO, 251555Z Aug 73, subj: Neak Luong Short Round.

34. Ltr, Vogt to Enders, Jul 8, 1979, cited above.

35. Msg, Nakhon Phanom SSO to DIA SSO, 020545Z Jul 73, subj: none.

36. Msg, Brig Gen Cleland, Chief, MEDTC, to Adm [Noel] Gayler, CINCPAC, 091200Z Oct 73, subj: FANK Capabilities.

37. Bowers, *Tactical Airlift*, p 627.

38. Ibid, pp 627–28; msg, Brig Gen [William] Palmer, Chief, MEDTC, to Adm Gayler, Gen Vogt, et al, 181200Z Jun 74, subj: Khmer Air Force Operations.

39. Tilford, *Search and Rescue*, pp 137–41.

40. Karnow, *Vietnam*, pp 44–45.

41. Msg, Maj Gen Murray, DAO, Saigon, to Gen Vogt, 281042Z Jun 73, subj: Assessment of a Bombing Halt in Cambodia.

42. VNAF Force Structure Assessment, atch to ltr, Vice Chief of Staff, USAF, to CINCPACAF, Jun 14, 74, subj: same.

43. Defense Attache, Vietnam, Rprt, Dec 12, 72–Aug 21, 74, nd, vol I, pp 81–83, 85–88.

44. Ibid, pp 85–86.

45. DIA Military Intelligence Summary, DI–210–713–74, sec VII, Southeast Asia, Oct 1, 74.

46. Defense Attache, Saigon, Rprt, cited above, vol I, pp 87–88.

47. Defense Attache, Saigon, RVNAF Quarterly Rprt, 4th Quarter FY 74, nd, pp 2:1, 14, 21.

48. Atch to memo, Leonard Sullivan, Jr., Asst SecDef (Program Analysis and Evaluation) for SecDef, Jan 6, 75, subj: Prospects for South Vietnam—1975 and Beyond.

49. Kissinger, *Years of Upheaval*, pp 885–87; Herrington, *Peace with Honor?*, p 35.

50. Karnow, *Vietnam*, pp 660–61; *Congressional Almanac, 93d Congress, 2d Session, 1974* (Washington, 1975), p 584.

51. Cao Van Vien, *The Final Collapse*, pp 50–53.

52. End of Tour Rprt, Col David B. Ballou, Chief Advisory Team 3, Sep 12, 72–Feb 15, 73, Jan 30, 73.

53. Herrington, *Peace with Honor?*, pp 36–40, 91–93.

54. Cao Van Vien, *The Final Collapse*, pp 35–36; Karnow, *Vietnam*, pp 659–60.

55. Cao Van Vien, *The Final Collapse*, pp 58–67.

56. Karnow, *Vietnam*, pp 664–65.

57. Cao Van Vien, *The Final Collapse*, pp 75–80; Karnow, *Vietnam*, pp 665–66.

58. Herrington, *Peace with Honor?*, pp 137–40.

59. Cao Van Vien, *The Final Collapse*, pp 141–43.

60. *Public Papers of the Presidents of the United States* (Washington, 1977) Gerald R. Ford, 1975, bk I, pp 569–70. Karnow, *Vietnam*, p 667; Congressional Almanac, 94th Congress, 1st Session, 1975 (Washington, 1976), p 306.

61. Lt Col Thomas G. Tobin, Lt Col Arthur E Laehr, and Lt Col John F. Hilgenberg, *USAF Southeast Asia Monograph Series: Last Flight from Saigon* (Washington, 1978), pp 35–38.

62. Tobin, et al, *Last Flight from Saigon*, pp 50–78; Herrington, *Peace with Honor*, pp 170–71.

63. Tobin, et al, *Last Flight from Saigon*, pp 82–89.

64. Ibid, p 97; Tilford, *Search and Rescue*, pp 144–45.

65. Tilford, *Search and Rescue*, pp 144–45.

66. Tobin, et al, *Last Flight from Saigon*, pp 104, 107–8.

67. Ibid, p 111; Tilford, *Search and Rescue*, pp 145–46; John F. Guilmartin, Jr., *A Very Short War: The Mayaguez and the Battle of Koh Tang* (College Station, Tex, 1995), pp 23–24.

68. Tobin, et al, *Last Flight from Saigon*, pp 113–21.

69. See *The Role of Air Power Grows, 1970*, and *Shield for Vietnamization and Withdrawal*.

70. Cao Van Vien, *The Final Collapse*, pp 154–55.

Chapter 24

1. Guilmartin, *A Very Short War*, pp 26, 53–54; Thomas Des Brisay, *USAF Southeast Asia Monograph Series: Fourteen Hours at Koh Tang* (Washington, 1985), p 15; J. A. Messegee, "'Mayday' for *Mayaguez*: The Patrol Squadron Skipper," *U.S. Naval Institute Proceedings*, vol CII, no 11 (Nov 1976), pp 94–96.

2. Guilmartin, *A Very Short War*, pp 25–27, 36–38; *Congress and the Nation*, vol IV, 1973–1976 (Washington, 1977), pp 849–51, 898–99; Roy Rowan, *The Four Days of Mayaguez* (New York, 1975), pp 66–70, 176.

3. Guilmartin, *A Very Short War*, pp 29, 43–47.

4. Ibid, pp 39–43, 47–49.

5. Ibid, pp 49 (chart).

6. Ibid, pp 50–51, 56–57; Walter Wood, "'Mayday' for *Mayaguez*: The Company Commander," *U.S. Naval Institute Proceedings*, vol CII, no 11 (Nov 1976), p 101.

7. Guilmartin, *A Very Short War*, p 56; Wood, "The Company Commander," p 101; George R. Dunham and David A. Quinlan, *U.S. Marines in Vietnam: The Bitter End* (Washington, 1990), p 241.

8. Guilmartin, *A Very Short War*, pp 55–56; Tilford, *Search and Rescue*, pp 147–48.

9. Guilmartin, *A Very Short War*, pp 58, 99.

10. Ibid., pp 60–62, 74, 78, 85–86; J. M. Johnson, Jr., R. W. Austin, and D. A. Quinlan, "Individual Heroism Overcame Awkward Command Relationships, Confusion, and Bad Information Off the Cambodian Coast," *Marine Corps Gazette*, vol LXI, no 10 (Oct 1977), p 28.

11. Intvw, Hugh N. Ahmann with Lt Gen John J. Burns, Commanding General, US Support Activities Gp/7AF, Sep 74–Aug 75, Jun 5–8, 84, p 450; Guilmartin, *A Very Short War*, pp 71–74, 77–78, 86, 98; Robert A. Peterson, "'Mayday' for *Mayaguez*: The Destroyer Escort Skipper," *U.S. Naval Institute Proceedings*, vol CII, no 11 (Nov 1976), p 102.

12. Guilmartin, *A Very Short War*, pp 98–100; J. Michael Rodgers, "'Mayday' for *Mayaguez*: The Guided-Missile Destroyer's Skipper," *U.S. Naval Institute Proceedings*, vol CII, no 11 (Nov 1976), p 104.

13. Guilmartin, *A Very Short War*, pp 77–81, 84; Des Brisay, *Fourteen Hours at Koh Tang*, p 104; Johnson, Austin, and Quinlan, "Individual Heroism," p 29.

14. Guilmartin, *A Very Short War*, pp 88–89; Des Brisay, *Koh Tang*, p 106–109, 112.

15. Guilmartin, *A Very Short War*, pp 84–89; Dunham and Quinlan, *The Bitter End*, pp 248–49; Des Brisay, *Koh Tang*, pp 111, 113–15.

16. Guilmartin, *A Very Short War*, pp 89–93; Des Brisay, *Koh Tang*, p 119.

17. Guilmartin, *A Very Short War*, pp 44, 88, 100–104; Des Brisay, *Koh Tang*, pp 119–23, 125, 127–28.

18. Guilmartin, *A Very Short War*, p 83 (map 5).

19. Ibid, pp 91, 95, 102, 104.

20. Ibid., pp 97–98; Des Brisay, *Koh Tang*, pp 128, 130.

21. Guilmartin, *A Very Short War*, pp 105–6.

22. Msg, JCS to CINCPAC, 150455Z May 75, quoted in Guilmartin, *A Very Short War*, p 107.

23. Guilmartin, *A Very Short War*, pp 107–11.

24. Quoted in Guilmartin, *A Very Short War*, p 111.

25. Ibid, pp 111–12.

26. Ibid, pp 112–14; Dunham and Quinlan, *The Bitter End*, pp 252–57; Des Brisay, *Koh Tang*, pp 133–35.

27. Guilmartin, *A Very Short War*, pp 116–21; Des Brisay, *Koh Tang*, pp 135, 137–43; Burns intvw, p 456.

28. Guilmartin, *A Very Short War*, pp 122–24; Des Brisay, *Koh Tang*, pp 143–44; Dunham and Quinlan. *The Bitter End*, p 258.

29. Guilmartin, *A Very Short War*, pp 125–26; Des Brisay, *Koh Tang*, pp 144–45; Dunham and Quinlan, *The Bitter End*, p 264.

30. Guilmartin, *A Very Short War*, pp 127–28; Des Brisay, *Koh Tang*, p 145.

31. Guilmartin, *A Very Short War*, pp 127–28; Des Brisay, *Koh Tang*, p 146; Dunham and Quinlan, *The Bitter End*, pp 259–60; Burns intvw, p 456.

32. Guilmartin, *A Very Short War*, pp 129–30.

33. Ibid, pp 131–32; Des Brisay, *Koh Tang*, pp 146–47.

34. Guilmartin, *A Very Short War*, pp 132–33; Des Brisay, *Koh Tang*, pp 147–48.

35. Guilmartin, *A Very Small War*, pp 141–43; Des Brisay, *Koh Tang*, pp 148–49.

36. *Congress and the Nation, 1973–1976*, p 899; Dunham and Quinlan, *The Bitter End*, p 263.

37. Tilford, *Setup*, p 282; Guilmartin, *A Very Short War*, p 99.

38. Guilmartin, *A Very Short War*, pp 114, 148–50.

39. Quoted in Dunham and Quinlan, *The Bitter End*, p 265.

Glossary

A–1	The Douglas Skyraider, a piston-powered, single-engine attack plane built in one- or two-place versions. Because of its age—it saw service as the Navy's AD–1 during the Korean War—it was nicknamed the Spad, after the World War I fighter.
A–4	A single-place, single-jet attack plane built by Douglas (later McDonnell Douglas) for the Navy and Marine Corps.
A–6	The Grumman Intruder, a two-place, twin-jet attack plane flown by the Navy and Marine Corps.
A–7	A single-place, single-jet attack plane built by Ling Temco Vought and flown by the Navy and Air Force.
A–37	An attack version of the T–37 trainer.
AC–47	Gunship version of the C–47 transport.
AC–119	Gunship version of the AC–19 transport.
AC–123	A Fairchild C–123 transport fitted with sensors to locate targets at night and a bomb dispenser to attack them.
AC–130	Gunship version of the C–130.
Adm.	Admiral.
Airmobile	Tactics, developed by the U.S. Army, in which helicopters deployed, supplied, and supported with fire lightly armed combat troops.
Apache Snow	An operation in the A Shau Valley during the summer of 1969 that culminated in the fight for Ap Bia, known as Hamburger Hill.
ARVN	Army of the Republic of Vietnam.
A Shau Valley	A terrain feature that served as a conduit for enemy supplies and reinforcements destined from the Ho Chi Minh Trail in southern Laos to northwestern South Vietnam.
B–52	The Boeing Stratofortress, an eight-jet strategic bomber.
B–57	The Canberra, a British-designed, twin-jet medium bomber built in the United States by Martin.
Babylift	The spring 1975 evacuation of orphans from South Vietnam in departing American transports.
C–5	The four-turbofan Lockheed Galaxy, during the Vietnam War, the largest transport flown by the Air Force.
C–7	The twin-engine, piston-powered de Havilland Caribou; originally a U.S. Army transport, turned over to the Air Force in 1967.
C–47	A low-wing Douglas transport, designed in the 1930s and powered by two radial piston engines.
C–119	A twin-boom Fairchild transport; two radial engines powered the G model, but the K version also had two auxiliary jet engines.
C–123	A Fairchild transport originally powered by two piston engines; the K model also mounted a pair of auxiliary jets.
C–130	The Lockheed Hercules, a medium-range transport powered by four turboprop engines.
C–141	The Lockheed Starlifter, a long-range four-turbofan transport.
Capt.	Captain.
CH or HH–3	A twin-turbine, single-rotor helicopter built by Sikorsky for the Air Force and Navy.

Glossary

CH–46	A twin-turbine helicopter, with two rotors mounted in tandem, designed by Boeing-Vertol and built for the Navy and Marine Corps.
CH–47	A twin-turbine helicopter, with two rotors mounted in tandem, designed by Boeing-Vertol and built for the U.S. Army.
CH or HH–53	A twin-turbine Sikorsky helicopter, with a six-bladed overhead rotor, flown by the Marine Corps and the Air Force.
Col.	Colonel.
Combat Spyspot	A ground-based radar used to direct air strikes, especially by B–52s.
Cooper-Church Amendent	A rider to defense appropriations legislation for fiscal 1971 that forbade the introduction of American ground troops into Thailand, Laos, or Cambodia; sponsored by Senators John Sherman Cooper and Frank Church.
Comdr.	Commander.
Delaware	An attack in the A Shau Valley during April 1968.
Dewey Canyon	A probe of the A Shau Valley by Marine units in the spring of 1969 that resulted in combat patrols in Cambodia.
Dewey Canyon II	American operations in northwestern South Vietnam in preparation for Lam Son 719, the South Vietnamese attack into Laos launched in February 1971.
DOD	Department of Defense.
Eagle Pull	Designation for the withdrawal of the Americans serving at the embassy in Phnom Penh, Cambodia.
EA–6	A Grumman A–6 fitted out for electronic warfare.
EB–66	A twin-jet light bomber built by Douglas for the Navy; later acquired by the Air Force and modified to intercept or jam enemy electronic signals.
EC–47	A C–47 transport modified to intercept enemy radio traffic and locate transmitters.
EC–121	A Lockheed Superconstellation transport fitted out to relay radio traffic or interpret or relay the radio signals from sensors planted to detect hostile movement.
Enhance Plus	An American program of material aid to strengthen the armed forces of South Vietnam before a cease-fire imposed restrictions on military assistance.
F–4	The McDonnell Douglas Phantom, a twin-jet, two-place tactical fighter flown by the Navy, Air Force, and Marine Corps.
F–5	The Northrop Freedom Fighter, a lightweight, easily maintained aircraft built for use by America's allies.
F–84	An obsolete tactical fighter and reconnaissance craft, specifically the F model with a swept wing and a single jet engine, built for the Air Force by Republic and used by the reserve components.
F–100	The North American Super Sabre, a single-jet tactical fighter built in single-seat and two-place models.
F–102	The Convair Delta Dagger, a single-seat, delta-wing, single-jet interceptor flown by the Air Force.
F–105	The Republic Thunderchief, a single-jet tactical fighter; a two-place model, the F–105F, was armed with antiradiation missiles and used to suppress enemy radar.
F–111	A variable-sweep, twin turbofan, two-place fighter-bomber built for the Air Force by General Dynamics.

Glossary

FAC	Forward Air Controller.
Fishhook	Cambodian base area used by the North Vietnamese and Viet Cong.
Forces Armee Nationale Khmer	The armed forces of the Khmer Republic.
Frag	A fragmentary order—the daily operations order with portions, or fragments, applicable to various units.
Freedom Action	The authority for American air power to intervene anywhere in Cambodia where a communist victory might pose a serious military or psychological threat to the Khmer Republic.
Frequent Wind	The designation for the evacuation of Americans and some South Vietnamese from Saigon in April 1975.
Fuel-Air Munitions	A bomb employing an explosive gas like propane.
Gen.	General.
GKR	Government of the Khmer Republic.
H–34	A Sikorsky helicopter, redesignated the CH–34, with a four-bladed overhead rotor, used by the Army, Navy, and Marine Corps.
Hamburger Hill	A name given by the assaulting troops to Ap Bia, a mountain in the A Shau Valley captured in a meatgrinder-like operation that cost 56 Americans killed and 420 wounded, but then abandoned.
Ho Chi Minh Trail	A complex of roads, trails, and waterways that carried men and cargo from north Vietnam through southern Laos to South Vietnam and Cambodia.
HP–130	A C–130 transport modified to refuel helicopters and serve as a command post for rescue squadrons.
Igloo White	The air-supported, electronic, anti-infiltration system covering the Ho Chi Minh Trail and monitored from a surveillance center at the Nakhon Phanom Royal Thai Air Base.
JCS	Joint Chiefs of Staff.
Jolly Green	Call sign of the Air Force rescue helicopters, HH–3s and HH–53s.
KC–135	A four-engine, jet-powered aerial tanker sometimes employed as a transport, a communications monitoring aircraft, or a reconnaissance aircraft.
Knife	Call sign of Air Force CH–53s used in the *Mayaguez* operation.
Lam Son	A village where Le Loi, a Fifteenth Century Vietnamese leader, defeated the Chinese, a name frequently used for South Vietnamese operations like Lam Son 719, the invasion of southern Laos in 1971.
Loran	Long-Range Radio Aids to Navigation.
Khmer Rouge	The Cambodian communist movement and its armed forces.
Linebacker I	the bombing of southern North Vietnam in response to the Easter invasion of 1972.
Linebacker II	A bombing campaign in December 1972 directed at North Vietnam's heartland, especially Hanoi and Haiphong, and intended to force the communist regime to accept the cease-fire negotiated at Paris.
MACV	Military Assistance Command, Vietnam.
MAF	Marine Amphibious Force.
Maj.	Major.
Massachusetts Striker	An attack by U.S. Army troops against the A Shau Valley in the spring of 1969.
MAW	Marine Aircraft Wing.

Glossary

Mayaguez	An American-operated container ship seized by communist Cambodian forces in May 1975 and quickly recovered.
Menu	The operation, March 1969–May 1970, during which B–52s secretly bombed North Vietnamese and Viet Cong bases in Cambodia; the targets bore the nicknames Lunch, Dinner, Breakfast, Snack, and Dessert.
MiG–21	A single-engine, Soviet-built, jet interceptor flown by the North Vietnamese.
Mini-Tet	A series of Viet Cong and North Vietnamese attacks in May 1968 that American military leaders considered a pale copy of the Tet offensive early in 1968.
MR	Military Region.
Napalm Sunday	April 7, 1968, when Air Force C–130s saturated with diesel oil and jet fuel a woods concealing an enemy base; forward air controllers then ignited the mixture with rockets.
NMCC	National Military Command and Control Center.
NVN	North Vietnam.
O–1	The Cessna Bird Dog, a single-engine, piston-powered, two-place, high-wing monoplane; used by the Air Force and Marine Corps.
O–2	A two-place, twin-boom, high-wing monoplane, with piston engines mounted fore and aft of the crew compartment; built by Cessna for the Air Force.
OSI	Office of Special Investigations.
OV–1	The Mohawk, a two-place, twin-turboprop battlefield surveillance aircraft built by Grumman and flown by the Army.
OV–10	the Bronco, a two-place, twin-boom, twin turboprop counterinsurgency aircraft built by North American Rockwell for the Air Force and Marine Corps.
Parrot's Beak	The site of an enemy base in Cambodian territory just 35 miles from Saigon.
Patio	An operation that launched strikes by American aircraft against targets in certain regions of Cambodia.
Pegasus	The operation by airmobile forces in the spring of 1968 that broke the siege and provided relief for the Marines defending Khe Sanh.
Plain of Reeds	A swamp in southern South Vietnam, near the Cambodian border, that served as a communist redoubt.
Project 703	A budget-cutting exercise in preparation for the fiscal 1969 budget.
RAAF	Royal Australian Air Force.
RAND	The name—an acronym for Research and Development—of a nonprofit think tank established to conduct studies for the Air Force.
RC–47	Reconnaissance version of the C–47 transport.
RC–119G	A maritime reconnaissance version of the C–119G transport.
RF–4	Reconnaissance version of the F–4 tactical fighter.
RF–5	Reconnaissance version of the F–5 lightweight fighter.
RF–101	The single-place McDonnell Voodoo reconnaissance aircraft, a modification of the twin-jet F–101 long-range interceptor.
RVN	Republic of Vietnam.
RVNAF	Republic of Vietnam Armed Forces.
SA–7	A Soviet-developed heat-seeking, shoulder-fired antiaircraft weapon.

Glossary

Salem House	The operating area for patrols dispatched into northeastern Cambodia by the Studies and Observations Group, U.S. Military Assistance Command, Vietnam.
SEA or SEAsia	Southeast Asia.
SH–3	A Navy version of the Sikorsky CH–3 helicopter.
Shoemaker	The operation that launched American troops into Cambodia in April 1970; a reference to the name of the commander, Brig. Gen. Robert Shoemaker.
Single Management	The placing of Air Force and Marine Corps tactical combat aircraft under the direction of an Air Force officer.
SIOP	Single Integrated Operation Plan, the overall plan for a nuclear war.
Somerset Plain	A thrust into the A Shau Valley in August 1968.
Sortie	A takeoff and landing by a single aircraft; any flight by a single aircraft against the enemy.
T–37	The two-place, twin-jet, trainer built by Cessna for the Air Force.
T–41	A trainer version of the Cessna model 172, a single-engine, piston-powered, high-wing light monoplane.
TACAIR	Tactical air.
TACC	Tactical Air Control Center.
TACS	Tactical Air Control System.
Tet	The lunar new year celebrated in South Vietnam.
Thor	An operation in the summer of 1968 to neutralize through air power, naval gunfire, and artillery the North Vietnamese artillery and the antiaircraft batteries in the easternmost part of the demilitarized zone.
Toan Thang	Total Victory, a nickname used for south Vietnamese Operations against communist bases in Cambodia.
Triborder Area	The region where the borders of Laos, Cambodia, and South Vietnam converged.
Truscott White	An offensive in the western highlands during 1968.
Tropic Moon II	A Martin B–57B fitted with low-light-level television, an infrared sensor, a laser range-finder, and a computer for locating road traffic and determining the release point for weapons.
U–2	A single-place, long-range, high-altitude, single-engine, jet strategic reconnaissance craft built by Lockheed.
U–17	Military version of a piston-powered single-engine light monoplane built by Cessna.
UC–123	A Fairchild C–123 transport fitted out to spray herbicide.
UH–1	A single-rotor, single-turbine, helicopter developed by Bell as a troop carrier, gunship, and command craft for the Army.
U.S.	United States.
USA	U.S. Army.
USAF	U.S. Air Force.
USMACV	U.S. Military Assistance Command, Vietnam.
USMC	U.S. Marine Corps.
USN	U.S. Navy.
VC	Viet Cong.
VC/NVA	Viet Cong/North Vietnamese Army.
Vesuvius	An operation conducted in 1968 to develop, through aerial photography, intelligence on enemy activity in northeastern Cambodia.

Glossary

Vietnamization   The program, foreshadowed by President Johnson and conducted by President Nixon, that sought to train and arm the South Vietnamese to take over the fighting and ultimately assume responsibility for the defense of their country.

War Powers Act   Legislation adopted in 1973 that, in the absence of a declaration of war or hostile attack, requires the President to advise Congress formally of military action he may take on his own authority and obtain Congressional approval within a specified time.

Bibliographic Note

Three collections yielded the bulk of the material that formed the foundation of this book. The greatest volume of detailed information came from the largest of the three, the so-called CHECO microfilm, on which Project CHECO (initially the Contemporary Historical Evaluation of Counterinsurgency Operations, later the Contemporary Historical Evaluation of Combat Operations, and ultimately the Contemporary Historical Examination of Current Operations) preserved many of the day-to-day records of the Seventh Air Force and Seventh/Thirteenth Air Force. Two microfilmed indices hold the key to this mass of material, one dealing with material originally classified as Secret or lower and the other with items that were Top Secret.

The other two collections—the message traffic of Gen. Creighton Abrams, Commander, U.S. Military Assistance Command, Vietnam, and the historical materials prepared by or for his predecessor, Gen. William C. Westmoreland—were located at the time of my research in the Center of Military History. The Abrams documents, arranged in chronological order, had no index. The most useful of the Westmoreland material took the form of a historical diary, with commentary inserted from time to time after the event, that dealt with, among other things, the appointment of a single manager for tactical combat aviation. General Westmoreland's additions, however, could readily be separated from the original entries. The Center of Military History, besides maintaining the Abrams and Westmoreland collections, also had in its files a large number of interviews, reports, and other documents that were then being used for the writing of the Army's history of the Vietnam War.

Project CHECO, besides preserving the files of the two principal Air Force commands in Southeast Asia, produced more than two hundred reports on various aspects of the fighting. These proved most helpful, as did the end of tour reports prepared by Air Force officers in certain important assignments and the interviews conducted by the Air Force and Marine Corps oral history programs. Catalogues exist that list the CHECO reports and both collections of oral history interviews, though the revised list of Air Force interviews covering the Vietnam years is indexed exclusively by the name of the person interviewed rather than by the topics discussed. Similarly, the microfilmed index of end of tour reports refers to names rather than assignments or areas of interest.

Air Force Historical Publications and Studies

Anthony, Victor B. *The Air Force in Southeast Asia: Tactics and Techniques of Night Operations, 1961–1970.* Washington: Office of Air Force History, March 1973.

Bibliographic Note

Ballard, Jack S. *The United States Air Force in Southeast Asia: Development and Employment of Fixed-Wing Gunships, 1962–1972*. Washington: Office of Air Force History, 1982.

Berger, Carl, ed. *The United States Air Force in Southeast Asia, 1961–1973: An Illustrated Account*. Washington: Office of Air Force History, revised edition, 1984.

Bowers, Ray L. *The United States Air Force in Southeast Asia: Tactical Airlift*. Washington: Office of Air Force History, 1982.

Buckingham, William A., Jr. *Operation Ranch Hand: The Air Force and Herbicides in Southeast Asia, 1961–1971*. Washington: Office of Air Force History, 1982.

Fox, Roger P. *Air Base Defense in the Republic of Vietnam, 1961–1973*. Washington: Government Printing Office, 1979.

Gropman, Alan L. *USAF Southeast Asia Monograph Series: Airpower and the Airlift Evacuation of Kham Duc*. Maxwell AFB, Alabama: Air University, 1979.

Hartsook, Elizabeth H. *The Air Force in Southeast Asia: The Administration Emphasizes Air Power, 1969*. Washington: Office of Air Force History, November 1971.

———. *The Air Force in Southeast Asia: Air Power Helps Stop the Invasion and End the War, 1972*. Washington: Office of Air Force History, 1978.

———. *The Air Force in Southeast Asia: The Role of Air Power Grows, 1970*. Washington: Office of Air Force History, September 1972.

———. *The Air Force in Southeast Asia: Shield for Vietnamization and Withdrawal, 1971*. Washington: Office of Air Force History, July 1976.

Lane, John J. *Air War in Indochina Monograph: Command and Control and Communications Structures in Southeast Asia*. Maxwell AFB, Alabama: Air University, 1981.

Lavalle, A. J. C., ed. *USAF Southeast Asia Monograph Series: Airpower and the 1972 Spring Invasion*. Washington: Office of Air Force History, reprint 1985.

———, ed. *USAF Southeast Asia Monograph Series: The Vietnamese Air Force, 1951–1975, an Analysis of Its Role in Combat*, and *Fourteen Hours at Koh Tang*. Washington: Government Printing Office, 1977.

Mark, Eduard. *Aerial Interdiction: Air Power and the Land Battle in Three American Wars*. Washington: Center for Air Force History, 1992.

Momyer, William W. *Air Power in Three Wars*. Washington: Office of Air Force History, reprint, 1985.

Rowley, Ralph A. *The Air Force in Southeast Asia: FAC Operations, 1965–1970*. Washington: Office of Air Force History, May 1975.

Schlight, John. *The United States Air Force in Southeast Asia; The War in South Vietnam: The Years of the Offensive, 1965–1968*. Washington: Office of Air Force History, 1988.

Bibliographic Note

Thomas, James C. *Training: The Air Force in Vietnamization*. Air War College Report no. 5093. Maxwell AFB, Alabama: Air University, April 1973.

Tilford, Earl H., Jr. *Search and Rescue in Southeast Asia, 1961–1975*. Washington: Office of Air Force History, 1980.

———. *Setup: What the Air Force Did in Vietnam and Why*. Maxwell AFB, Alabama: Air University, 1991.

Tobin, Thomas G., Arthur E. Laehr, and John F. Hilgenberg. *USAF Southeast Asia Monograph Series: Last Flight from Saigon*. Washington: Government Printing Office, nd.

Van Staaveren, Jacob. *The Air Force in Southeast Asia: Toward a Bombing Halt, 1968*. Washington: Office of Air Force History, September 1970.

Wolk, Herman S. *USAF Plans and Policies: R&D for Southeast Asia*. Washington: Office of Air Force History, July 1970.

Other Government Publications and Studies

Clarke, Jeffrey J. *The United States Army in Vietnam; Advice and Support; The Final Years, 1965–1975*. Washington: Center of Military History, 1988.

Cosmas, Graham A., and Terrence P. Murray. *U.S. Marines in Vietnam: Vietnamization and Redeployment, 1970–1971*. Washington: History and Museums Division, Headquarters, U.S. Marine Corps, 1986.

Cao Van Vien. *Indochina Monographs: The Final Collapse*. Washington: Center of Military History, 1983.

Dellums, Rep. Ronald V. Extension of Remarks: Escalation, American Options, and President Nixon's War Moves. *Congressional Record*, vol 118, pt 13, 92d Congress, May 10, 1972, pp 16748–836.

Department of Defense. *The Pentagon Papers as Published by the New York Times*. New York: Quadrangle, 1971.

———. *The Pentagon Papers: The Department of Defense History of United States Decisionmaking on Vietnam, Senator Gravel Edition*. 5 vols. Boston: Beacon Press, 1971.

———. *The Pentagon Papers: United States-Vietnam Relations, 1945–1967*. 12 vols. Washington: Government Printing Office, 1971.

Dunham, George R., and David A. Quinlan. *U.S. Marines in Vietnam: The Bitter End, 1973–1975*. Washington: History and Museums Division, Headquarters, U.S. Marine Corps, 1990.

Fulton, William B. *Vietnam Studies: Riverine Operations, 1966–1969*. Washington: Department of the Army, 1973.

Kellen, Konrad. *A Profile of the PAVN Soldier in South Vietnam*. Rand memo RM 5013–1–ISA/ARPA, June 1966.

LeGro, William E. *Vietnam from Cease-Fire to Capitulation*. Washington: Center of Military History, 1981.

Melson, Charles D., and Curtis G. Arnold. *U.S. Marines in Vietnam: The War*

Bibliographic Note

That Would Not End, 1971–1973. Washington: History and Museums Division, Headquarters, U.S. Marine Corps, 1991.

Ngo Quang Truong. *Indochina Monographs: The Easter Offensive of 1972.* Washington: Center of Military History, 1980.

Nguyen Duy Hinh. *Indochina Monographs: Lam Son 719.* Washington: Center of Military History, 1979.

National Archives and Records Service. *Public Papers of the Presidents: Gerald R. Ford, 1975.* Washington: Office of the *Federal Register*, 1977.

———. *Public Papers of the Presidents: Lyndon B. Johnson, 1968–1969.* Washington: Office of the *Federal Register*, 1970.

———. *Public Papers of the Presidents, Richard M. Nixon, 1969, 1970, 1971, 1972.* Washington: Office of the *Federal Register*, 1970, 1971, 1972, 1974.

North Vietnam. *From Khe Sanh to Chepone* [Tchepone]. Hanoi: Foreign Language Publishing House, 1971.

Pearson, Willard. *Vietnam Studies: The War in the Northern Provinces, 1966–1968.* Washington: Department of the Army, 1975.

Pohle, Victoria. *The Viet Cong in Saigon: Tactics and Objectives during the Tet Offensive.* Rand memo 5799–ISA/ARPA, January 1969.

Sharp, U. S. Grant, and William C. Westmoreland. *Report on the War in Vietnam.* Washington: Government Printing Office, 1968.

Shore, Moyers S. II. *The Battle for Khe Sanh.* Washington: Headquarters, U.S. Marine Corps, 1969.

Smith, Charles R. *U.S. Marines in Vietnam: High Mobility and Standdown, 1969.* Washington: History and Museums Division, Headquarters, U.S. Marine Corps, 1988.

Tolson, John J. *Vietnam Studies: Airmobility, 1961–1971.* Washington: Department of the Army, 1973.

U.S. Marine Corps Historical Center. *Vietnam Revisited: Conversation with William Broyles, Jr.* Washington: Histories and Museums Division, Headquarters, U.S. Marine Corps, 1984.

Project CHECO Reports

Abbey, Thomas G. *Attack on Cam Ranh Bay, 25 August 1971.* December 15, 1971.

Adamic, Frank J. *Short Rounds.* July 15, 1972.

Aton, Bert B., and E. S. Montagliani. *The Fourth Offensive.* October 1, 1969.

Aton, Bert B., and William Thorndale. *A Shau Valley Campaign, December 1968–May 1968.* October 15, 1969.

Bear, James T. *The Employment of Air by the Thais and Koreans in SEA.* October 30, 1970.

———. *The RAAF in SEA.* September 30, 1970.

———. *VNAF Improvement and Modernization Program.* February 5, 1970.

Bibliographic Note

Bonetti, Lee. *USAF Civic Action in Republic of Vietnam*. April 1, 1968.
Brynn, Edward P. *Reconnaissance in SEAsia, Jul 66–Jun 69*. July 15, 1969.
——— and Tihomirov, Michael L. *Airpower against Armor*. Unpublished MS, no date.
Burch, Robert M. *The ABCCC in SEA*. January 16, 1969.
———. *Command and Control, 1966–1968*. August 1, 1969.
———. *Single Manager for Air in SVN*. March 18, 1969.
CHECO Staff. *Short Rounds and Related Incidents, 1 Jun 69–31 Dec 70*. February 15, 1971.
Clary, James R. *Ranch Hand: Herbicide Operations in SEA*. July 13, 1971.
Colwell, Robert F. *USAF Tactical Reconnaissance in Southeast Asia, July 1969–June 1971*. November 23, 1971.
DeBerry, Drue L. *Vietnamization of the Air War, 1970–1971*. October 8, 1971.
Elder, Paul W., and Peter J. Melly. *Rules of Engagement, November 1969–September 1972*. March 1, 1973.
Folkman, D. I., and Caine, P. D. *The Cambodian Campaign, 29 April–30 June 1970*. September 1, 1970.
Garver, Richard B. *Drug Abuse in Southeast Asia*. January 1, 1975.
Grady. M. J. *Interdiction in III Corps Tactical Zone: Project Dart*. August 10, 1969.
Hanks, Dorrell T., Jr. *Riverine Operations in the Delta, May 1968–June 1969*. August 31, 1969.
Harrison, Philip R. *Impact of Darkness and Weather on Air Operation in SEA*. March 10, 1969.
Leibchen, Peter A. W. *Kontum: The Battle for the Central Highlands, 30 March–10 June 1972*. October 27, 1972.
Loye, J. F., Jr., and P. D. Caine. *The Cambodian Campaign, 1 Jul–31 Oct 70*. December 31, 1970.
Loye, J. F., Jr., G. K. St. Clair, L. J. Johnson, and J. W. Dennison. *Lam Son 719, 30 January–24 March 1971*. March 24, 1971.
MacDonough, R. A. *Truscott White*. December 11, 1968.
Merrell, Ronald D. *Tactical Airlift in SEA*. February 15, 1972.
Mitchell, William A. *Aerial Protection of Mekong River Convoys in Cambodia*. October 1, 1971.
Montagliani, Ernie S. *The Siege of Ben Het*. October 1, 1969.
Nicholson, Charles A. *Khmer Air Operations, Nov 70–Nov 71*. June 15, 1972.
Penix, Guyman, and Paul T. Ringenbach. *Air Defense in Southeast Asia, 1945–1971*. January 17, 1973.
Porter, Melvin F. *The EC–47 in SEA, April 1968–July 1970*. September 12, 1970.
———. *Tactical Control Squadron Operations in SEAsia*. October 15, 1969.
Pralle, James B. *Arc Light, June 1967–December 1968*. August 15, 1969.
Ringenbach, Paul T. *Airlift to Besieged Areas, 7 Apr–31 Aug 72*. December 7,

Bibliographic Note

1973.

——— and Melly, Peter J. *The Battle for An Loc, 5 Apr–26 Jun 72.* January 31, 1973.

Roe, David H., Wayne C. Pittman, Jr., Dennis K. Yee, Paul D. Knobe, and Drue L. DeBerry. *The VNAF Air Divisions: Reports on Improvement and Modernization.* November 23, 1971.

Sams, Kenneth, and Bert B. Aton. *USAF Support of Special Forces in SEA.* March 10, 1969.

Sams, Kenneth, and A. W. Thompson. *Kham Duc.* July 8, 1968.

Schlatter, J. D. *Short Rounds, June 1968–May 1969.* August 15, 1969.

Schlight, John. *Rules of Engagement, 1 January 1966–1 November 1969.* August 31, 1969.

Seig, Louis. *Impact of Geography on Air Operations in SEA.* June 11, 1970.

Thompson, A. W. *The Defense of Saigon.* December 14, 1968.

———. *Strike Control and Reconnaissance (SCAR) in Southeast Asia.* January 22, 1969.

———. *USAF Civic Action in RVN.* March 17, 1969.

Thompson, A. W. and Thorndale, C. William. *Air Response to the Tet Offensive, 30 January–29 February 1968.* August 12, 1968.

Thorndale, C. William. *Defense of Da Nang.* August 31, 1969.

———. *Operation Delaware, 19 April–17 May 1968.* September 2, 1968.

Trest, Warren. *Khe Sanh (Operation Niagara), 22 January–31 March 68.* September 13, 1968.

Till, Jerald J., and James C. Thomas. *Pave Aegis Weapon System (AC–130E Gunship).* February 16, 1973.

Other Reports

Betts, Donzel E, Hiram Wolfe III, Raymond P. Schmidt, and Thomas N. Thompson. "Deadly Transmissions (COMSEC Monitoring and Analysis)." December 1970.

Brookbank, David A. "FACs and the Fall of Quang Tri." No date.

Bucher, Richard H. "Black Awareness Groups." August 5, 1970.

Department of Defense. "Report on Selected Air and Ground Operations in Cambodia and Laos." September 10, 1973.

1st Battalion, 501st Infantry (Airmobile), to Commanding General, 101st Airborne Division, subj: Combat Operations After Action Report [Carentan I and II]. May 28, 1968.

1st Brigade, 101st Airborne Division, to Commanding General, 101st Airborne Division, subj: Combat After Action Report, Operation Carentan II. April 29, 1968.

Foreign Broadcast Information Service. Southeast Asia Report no 1247, *Vietnam; A History of the Bulwark B–2 Theater*, vol 5: *Concluding the 30-Year*

Bibliographic Note

War. February 2, 1983.

Harp, William J., through Detachment B, 5th Special Forces Group (Airborne) to Commanding Officer, 5th Special Forces Group (Airborne), After Action Report. November 29, 1968.

Heiser, Rolland V. "After Action Report, Lam Son 719, January 12–February 28, 1971." April 1, 1971.

Headquarters, Pacific Air Forces. "Counterintelligence Digest." Recurring report.

———. "Project Corona Harvest Activity Inputs, January 1, 1965–March 31, 1968." April 1, 1968–December 31, 1969.

———. "Summary of Air Operations, Southeast Asia." Recurring report.

Headquarters, U.S. Air Force, Deputy Chief of Staff, Research and Development, Office of Science and Technology. "Ad Hoc Panel on Technical Improvements of the VNAF Capabilities." No date [summer 1972].

———. *USAF Management Summary.* Recurring report.

———. *USAF Statistical Digest.* Recurring report.

Headquarters, Seventh Air Force. "Air Operations in Cambodia, April 29–June 21, 1970."

Joint Chiefs of Staff, Director for Operations. "Action Officers' Data Book on Vietnamizing the War." Recurring report.

Meissner, Joseph P., and Leland J. Larson. "After Action Report: The Battle of Duc Lap." November 27, 1968.

Mobile Strike Forces, Company C, 5th Special Forces Group, to Commanding Officer, Company C. "After Action Report: Hgok Tavak." May 16, 1968.

Palmer, Bruce, Jr. "U.S. Intelligence and Vietnam." *CIA Studies in Intelligence*, Special Issue, 1984.

Roberts, Maj. Gen. Elvy B., Commanding General, 1st Cavalry Division (Airmobile), April 23, 1969–May 5, 1970. "Senior Officer Debriefing." April 18, 1970.

Thayer, Thomas C., ed. *A Systems Analysis View of the Vietnam War, 1965–1972.* 12 vols. Department of Defense, Assistant Secretary of Defense (Systems Analysis), 1975.

31st Military History Detachment, Headquarters, Provisional Corps, Vietnam. "Historical Study 3-68: Operation Pegasus, March 31–April 15, 1968." No date.

22d Military History Detachment. "Narrative: Operation Apache Snow, 101st Airborne Division, Maj. Gen. John M. Wright, Jr., Commanding, May 10–June 7, 1969." No date.

Recurring Official Histories

The Joint Chiefs of Staff and the War in Vietnam.
Commander in Chief, Pacific.

Bibliographic Note

U.S. Military Assistance Command, Vietnam.
U.S. Support Activities Group/Seventh Air Force.
Defense Attache Office.
Pacific Air Forces.
Seventh Air Force.
Seventh/Thirteenth Air Force.
Air Force Advisory Group, Vietnam.
Military Airlift Command.
Strategic Air Command.
Tactical Air Command.
Office of the Surgeon General.
Office of the Inspector General.

Oral History Interviews

Albright, Lt. Col. Ralph. See Connelly, Lt. Col. Daniel, USA.
Brayee, Capt. Frederick E., USA, S–2, 2d Brigade, 9th Infantry Division, 1969. June 30, 1969.
Brown, Gen. George S., Seventh Air Force Commander, 1968–1970. March 30, 1970, and October 19 and 20, 1970.
Brown, Dr. Harold, Secretary of the Air Force, 1965–1969. August 29 and 30, 1972.
Burke, Maj. Michael, Air Liaison Officer, 1st Brigade, 4th Infantry Division. No date.
Burns, Lt. Gen. John J. Commanding General, U.S. Support Activities Group/Seventh Air Force, September 1974–August 1975. June 5–8, 1984.
Carnahan, Maj. Eugene, 21st Tactical Air Support Squadron, Pleiku, South Vietnam, 1968. No date.
Carr, Lt. Comdr. James M., Jr., USN, N–2 (Intelligence), Task Force 117, 1969. No date.
Chaisson, Lt. Gen. J. R., USMC, Director, Combined Operations Center, Military Assistance Command, Vietnam, 1967–1968. March 19, 1969, and August 12, 1971.
Chapman, Gen. Leonard F., Jr., USMC, Commandant of the Marine Corps. March 28, 1979.
Connelly, Lt. Col. Daniel, USA, and Lt. Col. Maurice Williams, USA, 5th Special Forces Group, 1968; Lt Col Ralph Albright, Air Liaison Officer, Company C, 5th Special Forces Group, 1968; and Maj. Hugh D. Walker, Forward Air Controller, 5th Special Forces Group, 1968. October 16, 1968.
Cushman, Lt. Gen. R. E., USMC, Commanding General, III Marine Amphibious Force, 1967–1969. August 13, 1971.
DiEduardo, Capt. Joseph, USA, S–3 (Operations and Training), 2d Brigade, 9th Infantry Division, 1969. July 1, 1969.

Bibliographic Note

Fix, Col. Joseph E., USA, Commander, 1st Brigade, 4th Infantry Division, 1968. No date.

Flint, Maj. Dennis, USA, G–3 (Air), 9th Infantry Division, 1969. June 30, 1969.

Froid, Comdr. James C., USN, N–4 (Logistics), Mobile Riverine Force, and Commander, 9th River Assault Force, 1968–1969. June 30, 1969.

Garvin, Lt. Col. Thomas P., Air Liaison Officer, 25th Infantry Division, 1968. March 12, 1968.

Gibson, Lt. Col. Billy G, C–130 crew member, Vietnam, 1968. April 21, 1972.

Gibson, James, Forward Air Controller, 9th Infantry Division, 1968. March 9, 1968.

Ginsburgh, Maj. Gen. Robert N., Air Force member, Chairman's Staff Group, Office of Chairman, Joint Chiefs of Staff; senior staff member, National Security Council staff; and Armed Forces Aide to the President, 1966–1969. May 26, 1971.

Grant, James, Forward Air Controller, Bien Hoa Air Base, 1969. March 9, 1968.

Gropman, Maj. Alan L. Navigator, 463d Tactical Airlift Wing, 1968. April 13, 1968.

Kansfield, Maj. Donald Frank. Air Liaison Officer, 2d Brigade, 9th Infantry Division, January 2–June 30, 1969. July 2, 1969.

Laffey, Maj. Thomas P., Assistant Air Liaison Officer, 9th Infantry Division, 1968–1969. July 1, 1969.

Mathews, Col. Hughie, Air Force career 1945–1964. October 25, 1973.

McCall, TSgt John K., C–130A flight mechanic, 374th Tactical Airlift Wing, 1968. April 7, 1972.

McConnell, Gen. John P, Air Force Chief of Staff, 1965–1969. November 4, 1970.

McDonald, 1st Lt. Richard, USA, 5th Special Forces Group, 1968. October 8, 1968.

Niblack, Col. Emmett A., Chief of Standardization and Evaluation, 311th Tactical Airlift Squadron, 1968. May 3, 1972.

Parsons, Lt. Col. Donald J., Director of Operations, Horn Direct Air Support Center, 1968. October 14 and 30, 1968.

Pence, Col. A. W., Jr., USA, Airborne Advisory Detachment, Vietnam. May 17, 1971.

Probst, Capt. Lloyd J., C–130 pilot, Vietnam, 1967–1968. May 8, 1972.

Ryan, Col. Malcolm E., staff officer, Seventh Air Force, 1969–1970. January 5, 1970.

Ryan, Gen. John D., Air Force Vice Chief of Staff and Chief of Staff, 1968–1973. May 20, 1971.

Sizemore, Lt. Col. Thomas J., Chief, Social Actions Office, 2750th Air Base Wing, Wright-Patterson AFB, Ohio, 1974–1977. March 3, 1977.

Tolson, Maj. Gen. John J., Commanding General, 1st Cavalry Division (Air-

Bibliographic Note

mobile), 1968. May 27, 1968, and June 17 and 24, 1968.

Vogt, Gen. John W., Seventh Air Force Commander, April 1972–September 1973. August 8 and 9, 1978.

Walker, Maj, Hugh D. See Connelly, Lt. Col. Daniel, USA.

Wallace, Lt. Col. James L, aircraft commander, 50th Tactical Airlift Squadron, 1968. April 3, 1972.

White, Lt. Col. M. E., USMC, Deputy G–3 (Riverine War), 9th Infantry Division, 1969. July 6, 1969.

Williams, Lt. Col. Maurice, USA. See Connelly, Lt. Col. Daniel, USA.

End of Tour Reports

Adams, Col. Gerald M., Director of Plans and Programs, Air Force Advisory Group, Vietnam, July 15, 1972–February 28, 1973. February 26, 1973.

Ballou, Col. David B., Chief, Air Force Advisory Team 3, September 12, 1972–September 15, 1973. January 30, 1973.

Barr, Col. Thomas A. Director of Operations, Air Force Advisory Group, Vietnam, July 30, 1971–January 5, 1973. No date [January 1973].

Barrow, Col Sterling E., Chief, Air Force Advisory Team 7, May 1, 1970–April 11, 1971. March 12, 1971.

Bell, Col. Paul E., Chief, Air Force Advisory Teams 6 and 2, September 8, 1969–September 5, 1970. August 18, 1970.

Boyd, Col. Raymond A., Director of Plans and Programs, Air Force Advisory Group, Vietnam, July 1971–July 1972. July 14, 1972.

Chu, Col. Earl M., Deputy Chief of Staff, Personnel, Seventh Air Force, June 17 1971–June 16, 1972. June 15, 1972.

Crego, Col. John C., Deputy J–2, Military Assistance Command, Vietnam, June 2, 1971–June 5, 1972. No date [June 1972].

Crutchlow, Col. Russell, Chief, Command and Control Division, Seventh Air Force, June 1972–June 1973. No date.

Curfman, Col. Arden B., Commander, 483d Combat Support Group, October 16, 1970–October 13, 1971. No date.

Dean, Col. Hubert N. Dean, Chief, Transportation Division, J–4, Military Assistance Command, Vietnam, September 1970–August 1971. No date [August 1971].

Fisher, Col. Harold E., Chief, Air Force Advisory Team 3, September 6, 1971–September 15, 1972. August 8, 1972.

Fitzgerald, Col. Francis P., Commander, 483d Combat Support Group, October 13, 1971–April 15, 1972. No date.

Fowler, Col. Frederick W., Chief, Air Intelligence Division, J–2, Military Assistance Command, Vietnam, August 29, 1972–February 12, 1973, and Chief, Targets Division, U.S. Support Activities Group/Seventh Air Force, February 13, 1973–August 29, 1973. October 17, 1973.

Bibliographic Note

Fox, Col. Cecil E., Chief, Air Force Advisory Team 4, August 30, 1969–August 30, 1970. No date.

Galligan, Brig. Gen. Walter T., Wing Commander, 35th Tactical Fighter Wing, August 8, 1969–June 10, 1970. July 21, 1970.

Gayler, Col. Raymond H., Commander, 2d Aerial Port Group, and Chief, Aerial Port Division, Directorate of Airlift, Seventh Air Force, July 1971–July 1972. No date.

Glick, Col. Gregg F., Commander, 6251st Air Base Squadron, September 7, 1971–September 4, 1972. No date.

Grooms, Col. Wayne G., Senior Adviser to the South Vietnamese Air Force Logistics Command, August 13, 1969–August 3, 1970. July 15, 1970.

Gunn, Col. Charles D., Jr., Commander, 377th Combat Service Group, July 9, 1971–January 17, 1972, and Commander, 377th Air Base Wing, January 17, 1972–July 1, 1972. June 29, 1972.

Hammack, Col. Charles E., Chief, Air Force Advisory Team 1, June 19, 1972–March 14, 1973. No date [March 1973].

Henson, Col. Archie L., Staff Judge Advocate, Seventh Air Force, August 26, 1970–August 24, 1971. August 15, 1971.

Hill, Lt. Col. Vaughn E., Staff Judge Advocate, Seventh Air Force, July 6, 1972–March 28, 1973. No date.

Hobbs, Col. Harold W., Commander, 377th Combat Service Group, July 1970–July 1971. December 18, 1971.

Hulse, Col. Merrill W., Chief, Automated Systems Division, J–3, Military Assistance Command, Vietnam, August 7, 1972–March 1, 1973. August 6, 1973.

Hunt, Col. Senour, Chief, Air Force Advisory Team 5, November 19, 1969–November 8, 1970. December 8, 1970.

Jumper, Maj. Gen. Jimmy J., J–5, Military Assistance Command, Vietnam, and Director of Intelligence and Chief, Air Force Advisory Group, Vietnam, July 6, 1972–March 28, 1973. June 14, 1973.

Lilley, Col. J. R., Chief, Air Force Advisory Team 3, July 29, 1970–August 2, 1971. No date [August 1971].

Luby, Col. Edward W., Chief, Air Force Advisory Team 3, September 23, 1969–July 20, 1970. No date.

Pohl, Col. Nelson O., Chief, Air Force Advisory Team 1, August 1, 1969–July 10, 1970. July 7, 1970.

Saye, Col. Robert N., Jr., Chief, B–52 Operations Division, Military Assistance Command, Vietnam, and U.S. Support Activities Group/Seventh Air Force, April 15, 1972–April 11, 1973. March 21, 1973.

Slane, Col. Robert M., Vice Commander and Commander, 553d Reconnaissance Wing, September 15, 1970–February 1, 1971, and Commander, 6251st Combat Service Group, February 2–September 2, 1971. November 15, 1971.

Bibliographic Note

Slay, Maj. Gen. Alton D., Assistant Deputy Chief of Staff, Operations, and Chief of Staff, Seventh Air Force, 1971–1972. No date.

Smith, Brig. Gen Donavon F., Chief, Air Force Advisory Group, Vietnam, October 1966–March 1968. No date [March 1968].

Snyder, Col. Franklyn C., Chief, Air Force Advisory Team 4, August 22, 1970–July 26, 1971. No date. [July 1971].

Van Brussel, Col. Peter B., Jr., Chief, Air Force Advisory Team 2, August 1970–July 1972, nd [July 1972].

Wall, Col. Frank A., J-6, U.S. Support Activities Group and Deputy Chief of Staff, Communications and Electronics, Seventh Air Force, June 1, 1973–June 1, 1974. June 1, 1974.

Watkins, Maj. Gen. James H., Chief, Air Force Advisory Gp, Vietnam, February 15, 1971–May 16, 1972. May 14, 1972.

Young, Brig. Gen Kendall S., Chief, Air Force Advisory Group, Vietnam, July 31, 1970–February 15, 1971. February 15, 1971.

Books

Barrett, David M. *Uncertain Warriors: Lyndon Johnson and His Vietnam Advisers*. Lawrence: University Press of Kansas, 1993.

Boettcher, Thomas D. *Vietnam; The Valor and the Sorrow: From the Home Front to the Front Lines in Words and Pictures*. Boston-Toronto: Little, Brown, 1985.

Bonds, Ray, ed. *The Vietnam War: The Illustrated History of the Conflict in Southeast Asia*. New York: Crown, 1979.

Braestrup, Peter. *Big Story: How the American Press and Television Reported and Interpreted the Crises of Tet*. Boulder, Colorado: Westview, 1977.

Chanoff, David, and Doan Van Toan. *Portrait of the Enemy*. New York: Random House, 1986.

Cooper, Chester L. *The Lost Crusade: America in Vietnam*. New York: Dodd, Mead, 1970.

Davidson, Phillip B. *Vietnam at War: The History, 1946–1975*. Novato, California: Presidio, 1988.

Foner, Jack D. *Blacks and the Military in American History: A New Perspective*. New York: Praeger, 1974.

Fulgham, David, Maitland, Terrence, et al. *The Vietnam Experience: South Vietnam on Trial, mid-1970 to 1972*. Boston: Boston Publishing, 1984.

Gelb, Leslie H., and Richard K. Betts. *The Irony of Vietnam: The System Worked*. Washington: Brookings Institution, 1979.

Guilmartin, John F., Jr. *A Very Short War: The Mayaguez and the Battle of Koh Tang*. College Station: Texas A&M, 1995.

Haldeman, H. R., and Joseph DiMona. *The Ends of Power*. New York: *New York Times*, 1978.

Bibliographic Note

Head, William, and Lawrence E. Grinter, eds. *Looking Back on the Vietnam War: A 1990s Perspective on the Decisions, Combat, and Legacies.* Westport, Connecticut: Greenwood, 1993.

Herring, George C. *America's Longest War: The United States and Vietnam, 1950–1975*, revised edition. New York: Alfred A. Knopf, 1986.

Herrington, Stuart A. *Peace with Honor? An American Reports on Vietnam, 1973–1975.* Novato, California, Presidio, 1983.

Hoopes, Townsend. *The Limits of Intervention.* New York: David McKay, 1969.

Isaacs, Arnold R., Hardy, Gordon, Brown, MacAlister, et al. *The Vietnam Experience; Pawns of War: Cambodia and Laos.* Boston: Boston Publishing, 1987.

Johnson, Lyndon B. *The Vantage Point: Perspectives of The Presidency, 1963–1969.* New York: Holt, Rinehart and Winston.

Kalb, Marvin, and Bernard Kalb. *Kissinger.* Boston: Little, Brown, 1974.

Karnow, Stanley. *Vietnam: A History.* New York: Viking, 1983.

Kissinger, Henry. *White House Years.* Boston: Little, Brown, 1979.

———. *Years of Upheaval.* Boston: Little, Brown, 1982.

Knappman, Edward W., and Hal Kosut, eds. *South Vietnam: U.S.-Communist Confrontation in Southeast Asia, 1972–1973.* New York: Facts on File, 1973.

Lewy, Guenter. *America in Vietnam,* New York: Oxford University, 1978.

MacDonald, Peter. *Giap: The Victor in Vietnam.* New York; W. W. Norton, 1993.

Maclear, Michael. *The Ten Thousand Day War: Vietnam, 1945–1975.* New York: St. Martin's, 1981.

McCoy, Alfred W., with Cathleen B. Read and Leonard P. Adams II. *The Politics of Heroin in Southeast Asia.* New York: Harper and Row, Colophon Books, 1972.

McNamara, Robert S., with Brian VanDeMark. *In Retrospect: The Tragedy and Lessons of Vietnam.* New York: Random House Times Books, 1995.

Kirk, Donald. *Wider War: The Struggle for Cambodia, Thailand, and, Laos.* New York: Praeger, 1971.

Millet, Stanley, ed. *South Vietnam: U.S.-Communist Confrontation in Southeast Asia, 1968.* New York: Facts on File, 1974.

———. *South Vietnam: U, S.-Communist Confrontation in Southeast Asia, 1969.* New York: Facts on File, 1974.

Morrocco, John. *The Vietnam Experience; Rain of Fire: The Air War, 1969–1973.* Boston: Boston Publishing, 1985.

Nolan, Keith William. *Into Laos: The Story of Dewey Canyon II/Lam Son 719.* Novato, California: Presidio, 1986.

———. *Sappers in the Wire: The Life and Death of Firebase Mary Ann.* College Station: Texas A&M, 1995.

Bibliographic Note

Nixon, Richard M. *RN: The Memoirs of Richard Nixon*. New York: Grosset and Dunlap, 1978.

Oberdorfer, Don. *Tet!*. Garden City, New York: Doubleday, 1971.

Palmer, Bruce, Jr. *The 25-Year War: America's Military Role in Vietnam*. Lexington: University of Kentucky, 1984.

Palmer, Dave Richard. *Summons of the Trumpet: U.S.-Vietnam in Perspective*. San Rafael, California: Presidio, 1978.

Pike, Douglas. *PAVN: People's Army of Vietnam*. Novato, California: Presidio, 1986.

Pisor, Robert. *The End of the Line: The Siege of Khe Sanh*. New York: W. W. Norton, 1982.

Prados, John, and Ray W. Stubbe. *Valley of Decision: The Siege of Khe Sanh*. Boston-New York-London: Houghton Mifflin, 1991.

Rowan, Roy. *The Four Days of Mayaguez*. New York: W. W. Norton, 1975.

Schandler, Herbert. *Lyndon Johnson and Vietnam: The Unmaking of a President*. Princeton, New Jersey: Princeton University, 1983.

Shawcross, William. *Sideshow: Kissinger, Nixon, and the Destruction of Cambodia*. New York: Simon and Schuster, 1979.

Sobel, Lester A., and Hal Kosut, eds. *South Vietnam: U.S.-Communist Confrontation in Southeast Asia, 1970*. New York: Facts on File, 1973.

———. *South Vietnam: U.S.-Communist Confrontation in Southeast Asia, 1971*. New York: Facts on File, 1973.

Sorley, Lewis. *General Creighton Abrams and the Army of His Times*. New York: Simon and Schuster, 1992.

Summers, Harry G., Jr. *On Strategy: A Critical Analysis of the Vietnam War*, Novato, California: Presidio, 1982.

Thayer, Thomas C. *War Without Fronts: The American Experience in Vietnam*. Boulder, Colorado, and London: Westview Press, 1985.

Thompson, Sir Robert. *Peace Is Not at Hand*. New York: David McKay, 1974.

Thompson, W. Scott, and Davidson W. Frizell, eds. *The Lessons of Vietnam*. New York: Crane and Russak, 1977.

Truong Nhu T'ang with David Chanoff and Doan Van Toai. *A Viet Cong Memoir*. New York: Harcourt Brace Jovanovich, 1985.

Turley, G. H. *The Easter Offensive: Vietnam, 1972*. Novato, California: Presidio, 1985.

———. *The Second Indochina War: A Short Political and Military History*. Boulder, Colorado and London: Westview, 1986.

Warner, Denis A. *Certain Victory: How Hanoi Won the War*. Kansas City, Kansas: Sheed Andrew and McMeel, 1978.

Westmoreland, William C. *A Soldier Reports*. Garden City, New York: Doubleday, 1976.

White, Theodore H. *Breach of Faith: The Fall of Richard Nixon*. New York: Athenaeum, 1975.

Bibliographic Note

Articles

Brodie, Bernard. "Why Were We So (Strategically) Wrong?" *Military Review*, June 1972, pp 40–46.

Broyles, William, Jr. "The Road to Hill 10: A Veteran's Return to Vietnam." *The Atlantic Monthly*, April 1985, pp 91–118.

DeBerry, Drue L. "Vietnamese Air Force Technical Training, 1970–1971." *Air University Review*, January–February 1973, pp 43–51.

Galvin, John R. "The Relief of Khe Sanh." *Military Review*, January 1970, pp 88–94.

Garver, John W. "The Chinese Threat in the Vietnam War." *Parameters: U.S. Army War College Quarterly*, Spring 1992, pp 73–85.

Gates, John M. "People's War in Vietnam." *The Journal of Military History*, July 1990, p 325.

Gray, Colin S. "What Hath RAND Wrought?" *Military Review*, May 1972, pp 22–33.

Johnson, J. M., R. W. Austin, and D. A. Quinlan. "Individual Heroism Overcame Awkward Command Relationships, Confusion, and Bad Information Off the Cambodian Coast." *Marine Corps Gazette*, October 1977, pp 24–34.

McCutcheon, Keith B. "Marine Aviation in Vietnam." *U.S. Naval Institute Proceedings*, May 1871, pp 124–55.

Messegee, J. A. "'Mayday' for *Mayaguez*: The Patrol Squadron Skipper." *U.S. Naval Institute Proceedings*, November 1976, pp 94–97.

Ngo Vinh Long. "The Tet Offensive and Its Aftermath." A paper presented at *Remembering Tet: An Interdisciplinary Conference on the War in Vietnam*, Salisbury State University, Maryland, November 18–21, 1992.

Osur, Alan M. "Black-White Relations in the U.S. Military, 1940–1972." *Air University Review*, November–December 1981, pp 69–78.

Peterson, Robert A. "'Mayday' for *Mayaguez*: The Destroyer Escort Skipper." *U.S. Naval Institute Proceedings*, November 1976, pp 97–100.

Rodgers, F. Michael. "'Mayday' for *Mayaguez*: The Guided-Missile Destroyer's Skipper." *U.S. Naval Institute Proceedings*, November 1976, pp 108–11.

Simmons, Edwin H. "Marine Corps Operations in Vietnam." *U.S. Naval Institute Proceedings*, May 1970, pp 290–320.

Swartztrauber, S. A. "River Patrol Relearned." *U.S. Naval Institute Proceedings*, May 1970, pp 120–57.

Tilford, Earl H., Jr. "Setup: Why and How the Air Force Got Lost in Vietnam." *Armed Forces and Society*, Spring 1991, pp 327–42.

Webb, Willard J. "The Single Manager for Air in Vietnam." *JFQ: Joint Forces Quarterly*, Winter 1993–1994, pp 88–98.

Wood, Walter. "'Mayday' for *Mayaguez*: The Company Commander." *U.S.*

Bibliographic Note

Naval Institute Proceedings, November 1976, pp 100–104.
Xaioming Zhang. "The Vietnam War, 1964–1969: A Chinese Perspective." *The Journal of Military History*, October 1996, pp 731–62.
Yudkin, Richard A. "Vietnam: Policy, Strategy, and Air Power." *Air Force Magazine*, February 1973, pp 31–35.

Index

(Numerals in **bold** indicate an illustration.)

Abrams, Creighton W.: **118**
  A Shau Valley interdiction mission (1968–69): 152
  Cambodia attack plan (1970): 181–82
  Cambodia bombing proposal: 127, 129
  Cambodian threat concerns: 51–52
  force deployment decisions: 45
  Hue offense role: 25
  interpretation of Cambodia policies: 203
  Island Tree plan: 294
  opinion of senior South Vietnamese officers: 370–71
  opposition to bomber sortie cuts: 242
  opposition to force reduction: 137–38
  phase II plan for South: 162
  reevaluation of An Loc: 358
  support of B–52 sorties: 141
  truce negotiations (1968): 121
  view of single manager for tactical aviation: 114
  view on reconnaissance: 131
Acheson, Dean: 44
Acoustic sensors. *See* Sensors
Adverse-weather aerial delivery system: 380–81
Aerial interdiction
  at Ben Het: 157, 158–59
  Cambodia campaign
    close air support continuation: 203–4
    extension beyond Mekong River: 201–2
    forward air controller duties: 200
    Freedom Action: 202
    language barrier considerations: 200
    liaison officer difficulties: 200–201
    purpose of: 210
    rules of engagement: 199–200
  effectiveness in tri-border region: 76–78, **78**
  ground support role: 79–81
  intelligence gathering: 81
  lack of South Vietnamese skill in: 178
  scope in tri-border region: 79
  strike planning: 81
  Vietnamization of. *See* Vietnamization,

  aerial interdiction capability
Aerial reconnaissance
  Army dissatisfaction with Air Force efforts: 147
  in A Shau Valley: 59, 60–61
  by Australia: 150
  over Cambodia (1970): 51, 192–93
  Cambodia attack plans, lack of (1970): 182
  during Menu bombings: 131–32
  in Military Region I: 329
  in mini-Tet: 72
  photography and: 30
    for I Corps support: 117
    mapping: 145
    for Menu bombings: 131
    South Vietnamese dependence on: 356
  South Vietnamese capabilities: 224–25, 356
  Vietnamization of: 301, 356
Aeronautical Charting and Information Center: 145
Agnew, Spiro T.: 314, 370
Air America: 420–21
Airborne battlefield command and control center: 115, 120
  7th Airborne Command and Control Squadron: 342
  over Cambodia: 210, 284, 405
  over Kham Duc: 106–7
  over Khe Sanh: 96, 98
  during Lam Son 719: 254
  during *Mayaguez* incident: 430, 434–39, 441–42, 444, 448
  in Military Region I: 366
  in Military Region III: 386
  in Phnom Penh evacuation: 413
  in Saigon evacuation: 4
  during Operation Thor: 119
Aircraft, Australia
  Caribou: 150
  Canberra: **21**, 149
Aircraft, Cambodia
  AT–28: 412

513

Index

AU–24: 412
C–47: 281, 412
MiG–17: 208
O–1: 279
T–28: 208, 277, 279
Aircraft, North Vietnam (MiGs): 242, 291, 292, 415
Aircraft, South Korea (C–54): 150
Aircraft, South Vietnam
  A–1: 33, 70, 88–89, 171, 298, 333, 351
  A–37: 161, 162, **163**, 213, 222, 333, **408**
  AC–47: 34, 161, 162, 223
  AC–119: 162, 333, 355, 375, 415
  C–7: 224
  C–47: 33–34, 184, 222, 224, 299, 407
  C–119: 34, **172**, 184, 224, 299, 350, 389
  C–123: 224
  C–130: 224
  CH–47: 167, 213, 226, 282
  EC–47: 225, 350
  F–5: 33, 162, 171, 213, 225, 333, **352**
  H–34: 167, 171
  O–1: 209
  O–2: **170**
  RC–47: 214, 350, 356
  RC–119: 406–7
  RF–5: 162, 225, 299, 356, 414
  U–6: 299
  U–17: 209
  UH–1: **34**, 161, 167, **168**, 213, 223
Aircraft, Thailand
  C–123: 150–51
  O–2: 150
Aircraft, United States
  A–1
    delivery to South Vietnamese Air Force (1972): 351
    use in Cambodia: 207
    weakness due to age: 407
  A–4
    augment Constant Guard: 344
    reinforcement role: 45
  A–6
    in A Shau region: 152–53, **153**
    in Cambodia: 200
    at Thuong Duc: 86, 87
  A–7: **347**
    Constant Guard deployments: 346
    in Lam Son 719: 262
    in *Mayaguez* incident: 427, 434, 440
    Phnom Penh evacuation: 413
  A–37: 68, **137**, **408**
    anti-helicopter operations: 91
    funding reduction effects: 140
    maintenance problems (1973): 409
    in mini-Tet defense: 72
    Project Enhance Plus logistics: 406–7
  AC–47: **68, 300**
    in Ap Bia offensive: 156
    at Ben Het: 159
    Kham Duc support: 104
    in mini-Tet: 69, 72
    rocket watch role: 67
    at Thuong Duc: 86, 87
  AC–119: 88, **89, 300**
    aircrew training for South: 218–19
    in Ap Bia offensive: 156
    at Ben Het: 159
    delivery to South Vietnamese Air Force (1972): 350, 351
    funding reduction effects: 140
    transfer to South Vietnam: 285, 299
  AC–123: 88, 389
  AC–130: 88, **300, 376, 395**
    at An Loc: 394, 396
    downed by SA–7: 369
    in *Mayaguez* incident: 427, 432, 433, 440, 445, 446
    Military Region II defense (1972): 375, 376, 379–81, 385–387, 391, 396
    Phnom Penh evacuation: 413
    at Thuong Duc: 87
  B–26: 3
  B–52: 82, 244, 279, 288, 364. *See also* Operation Menu
    in Operation Alpine: 160
    at An Loc: 386, 395, 396–97
    Arc Light: 329, 364, 396
      Operating areas: 261–62, 266
      tactics during Lam Son 719: 266
    in A Shau Valley: 64, 153, 155–56, 243, 287, 325, 364, 370
    authorized sorties: 27
    at Ben Het: 158, 159
    Bugle Note procedures: 28–29
    Bullet Shot deployments: 336–37, **338**
    in Cambodia
      1970 invasion: 186–91, 194
      1971: 279–80, 282
      1972: 398
      1973: 410–11
    at Kompong Cham: 208

Index

counteroffense support role: 26
damage assessment difficulties: 28, 29, 192
debate over number of authorized sorties: 136, 141–43, 149
enemy knowledge of strike plans: 29–30
expansion outside South Vietnam: 149
over Hanoi: 348
interdiction missions: 76–78, 297–98
Kham Duc support: 105
Khe Sanh attacks by: 26–27
Kontum City defense: 378, 380
Lam Son 719 support: 254, 259, 261–62, 263, 265, 266, 270, 272
Menu bombings. *See* Operation Menu
Military Region I: 364, 368–72
Military Region II: 244, 373–74, 378, 380–81
mini-Tet defense: 72
operation modifications (1970): 242
in Operation Patio: 185, 188
Operation Pegasus role: 57
post-Tet operational sorties: 19
preparation for North Vietnam attack (1972): 328–29
reductions, 1970: 239, 241–42
sorties in 1969: 149
strain of high sortie level: 47
tandem tactics adoption: 143–44
target selection procedures: 27–28
Tet offensive sorties: 16
in Operation Thor: 118
Thuong Duc counterattack role: 87
B–57: 3, 89, 239, **240**, 304
C–5: 343, 351
replacement for C–124: 233
use in evacuations: 420
C–7: **85, 204**
A Shau Valley: 64
at Ben Het: 158, 159
Duc Lap supply drops: 86
maintenance problems (1973): 409
transferred to South Vietnam: 224, 350
withdrawal from Labansiek/Ba Kev: 202
C–47: 3, 33–34, 184, 222, 224, 299, 333, 407
C–123: 31

A Shau Valley: 64, **65**
Kham Duc evacuation: 108, 109–10
Khe Sanh relief: 56
in Lam Son 719: 253, 261
role in Tet offensive: 32–33
Thai pilots use of: 150–51
transferred to South Vietnam: 162, 224, 299, 307
withdrawal from Labansiek/Ba Kev: 202
C–124
replaced by C–5: 233
use in Lam Son 719: 258
C–130: **201**, 271
as airborne battlefield command and control center: 106, 111, 210, 342, 413, 439
adverse-weather aerial delivery system: 380–81
An Loc supply drop tactics: 390–92
in A Shau region: 62–64, **63**, 154
in Cambodia: 184, 191, 193, 224, 282–83, 412
Cam Ranh Bay: 31
Constant Guard movements: 343–44
delivery to South Vietnamese Air Force (1972): 351
Enhance Plus: 351
ground radar air delivery system use: 380–81
helicopter landing zones, bomb drops: 62, 89, 154, 189, 256, 272, 434, 443
Kham Duc evacuation: 104–10
Kontum City nighttime operations: 379
in Lam Son 719: 252–53, 258
in Military Region II: 375, 378–80
in "Napalm Sunday": 66
reduction in strength (1970): 233
role in Tet offensive: 32–33, **33**
Saigon evacuation: 421
tear gas drops: 76
Tri Ton drop: 82–83
C–133: 258
C–141: **148**
Constant Guard movements: 340, 343–44
Enhance Plus equipment transport: 351
Lam Son 719, transport relief for: 258
Mayaguez incident troop transport:

515

Index

431
  in Saigon evacuation: 421
  troop withdrawal role: 146
CH–46: 104, 236, 421–22
CH–47: 283
  Delivered to South Vietnamese: 283
  Duc Lap supply drops: 86
  Enhance Plus logistics: 406–7
  in Kham Duc evacuation: 106
CH–53
  at Koh Tang Island: 430–31, 436–47
  napalm drop: 124
  in Phnom Penh evacuation: 413
  in Saigon evacuation: 422
EB–66: **339, 340**, 341–42. *See also* Bat 21 rescue
EC–47
  over Cambodia: 209
  damaged at Pleiku: 246
  delivery to South Vietnamese Air Force (1972): 350
EC–121: 176, **209**
  as airborne battlefield command and control center: 210
  over Cambodia: 184, 209
  with Igloo White: 176
F–4: 86, 104, **146**, 151, **190, 233**, 328, **347**, 410
  1971 reinforcements: 328
  1972 reinforcements: 338–40, 342–45
  anti-helicopter operations: 90, 91
  in A Shau region: 61
  at Ben Het: 158
  over Cambodia: 192, 200, 207
  Commando Flash: 338
  Constant Guard movements: 340
  deployment after *Pueblo* capture: 39
  F–102 replacement: 92
  in Lam Son 719: 262
  during *Mayaguez* incident: 440
  in Military Region I (1972): 355, 368
  in Military Region II (1972): 375
  in Military Region III (1972): 397
  National Guard squadrons replacements for: 136–40
  North Vietnam attacks on: 291
  retention in South Vietnam (1970): 232
  Thieu requests: 164–65
F–84: 44
F–100: 33, **46**. *See also* United States Air National Guard
  in Cambodia: 186, 191, 192
  deployment after *Pueblo* capture: 39, 43–44, 45
  funding reduction effects: 140
  at Kham Duc: 107
  post-Tet deployment: 44
  reinforcement role: 45
  sorties flown during mini-Tet: 70
  use during Lam Son 719: 269
  withdrawal from South Vietnam: 232
F–102: 92
F–105: 239, **341**
  in A Shau region: 61
  Constant Guard movements: 340
  North Vietnam attacks on: 291
  Wild Weasels: 239, 339–40
F–111: 346, **347**, 410, 427
H–34: 167, 171
HC–130: 342, 413, 431, 439
HH–53: 394, **444**
  at Koh Tang Island: 430–31, 436–47
  Phnom Penh evacuation: 413
  in Quang Tri City rescue: 365–66
  Saigon evacuation use: 422
KC–135: 47, 91, 339
  in Bullet Shot deployments: 329, 337
  Constant Guard movements: 343
  in *Mayaguez* incident: 440
  sorties flown (1970): 242–43
O–1: 105. *See also* Forward air controllers
  in rocket watch: 67
  in Tet action: 23–24
  transferred to Cambodia: 279
  transferred to South Vietnam: 172, 233, 237
O–2: 30, **142**. *See also* Forward air controllers
  to Air National Guard: 233
  loss at An Loc: 397
  in A Shau Valley: 60
  Enhance Plus transfers: 351
  Mekong River convoy escorts: 284
  in mini-Tet: 69
  in Rocket watch: 67
  in Tet action: 30
OV–1: **146**, 160
  aerial photography role: 147
  in A Shau region: 153
OV–10: 90, **91**. *See also* Forward air controllers
  over Cambodia: 207

Index

in Lam Son 719: 263
in *Mayaguez* incident: 442, 445–48
Mekong River convoy escorts: 284–85
in Phnom Penh evacuation: 413
RC–47: 350
RF–4: 145, 192. *See also* Aerial reconnaissance
RF–101: **146**, 237. *See also* Aerial reconnaissance
T–28: 3
U–2: 131, 430
U–8: 148
U–21: 148, 434
UC–123. *See also* Defoliation
 conversion to transports: 31–32, 140
 funding reduction effects: 140
 herbicide spraying use: 61, 234, **235**
UH–1
 at An Loc: 394
 Phnom Penh evacuation: 421
 Saigon evacuation: 421
 transferred to South Vietnam: 167
Air Force, United States. *See* United States Air Force
Air Force Advisory Group: 166, 211, 352, 353. *See also* Vietnamization
Air Force Weapons Laboratory: 92
Air National Guard. *See* United States Air National Guard
Air Staff desire to bomb North: 133–34
Air traffic controllers in Lam Son 719: 258
Air war extension into Cambodia. *See* Cambodia
Allied Air Operations Coordinating Center: 276
Alpine (Operation): 160
A Luoi: 59, 61, 62, 259
American public opinion. *See* Anti-war sentiments
Amnesty program for drug users: 317
Anders, Lloyd J.: 430
Andersen Air Force Base, Guam: 333, 336, 337, 346
Anderson, A. V. P. III: 65
Anderson, Norman J.: 95, 102, 114
Angkor Wat: 200
An Loc
 B–52 protection for: 337
 division of strike coordination: 387
 Easter invasion (1972): 330–31, 337, 344, 370, 384–97

C–130 supply drop tactics: 390–92
end to AC–119 use: 394
high altitude delivery techniques: 392–93
high-velocity drops successes: 393–94
reluctance to fly rescue helicopters: 389
results of: 397
South Vietnam counterattack (1972): 395–96
supply drop losses: 389–90
United States command of defenses: 386–87, 389
Anti-war sentiments: 22, 144
 against bombing of North: 129
 among college students: 4–5, 197
 demonstrations (1970): 197–98
 increasing unpopularity of War (1971): 306
 influences on: 25
 Johnson's reaction to: 46
 protests of air war intensification (1972): 348–49
 reaction to reinforcement news: 43
 reaction to Tet offensive: 22, 332
 in South Vietnam: 274
 Viet Cong prisoner execution incident: 70
Apache Snow (Operation): 155–56
Ap Bia: 155–56
Arc Light. *See also* B–52
 Lam Son 719 tactics: 266
 operating areas: 261–62
Area source program: 36–37
Arends, Leslie: 129
Army, United States. *See* United States Army
Army of the Republic of Vietnam. *See* South Vietnamese Army
A Shau Valley
 aerial reconnaissance: 59–61
 Apache Snow: 155–56
 casualties: 65
 hostile fire types: 60
 interdiction mission (1968–69): 152–53
 interdiction options: 58–59
 offensive description (1968): 61–62
 political impact of offensive: 156–57
 strategic importance: 58
 supply drops: 62–64
 tactical importance: 55

Index

"A to Z" group recommendations: 43
Australia: 24
    air force. *See* Royal Australian Air Force
    force reductions (1971): 307
    HMAS *Hobart* accident: 91

Babylift (Operation): 420
Bai Thuong airfield: 335
Ban Dong: 261–62. *See also* A Luoi
Ban Me Thuot: 419
Barthelemy Pass: 193
Base Area 350: 189
Base Area 354: 189
Base Area 367: 186
Base Area 609: 152
Base Area 702: 189–90
Base Area 706: 183, 186
Bassac River: 13, 79, 181
Bat 21 rescue: 359–61
Battambang, Thailand: 205, 210
Baxter, Walter H., III: 430
Battle death reduction (1971): 275
Ben Het
    control by North Vietnam: 383
    mission description: 158–59
    offensive (1968): 152
    rules of engagement: 157
    sortie counts: 159
Bennett, Steven L.: 369, **370**
Ben Tre: 21–22
Be, Tu Van: 354
Bien Hoa Air Base
    air base transfer: 216
    casualties: 246
    Constant Guard movements: 344
    mini-Tet defense: 71
    post-Tet attacks against: 66
    Tet offensive: 31, 33, 35, 39
    Viet Cong Tet offensive: 10–12, **12, 40**
Binh Tay (operations): 189, 190, 191, 202
Binh Thuy Air Base: 13, 169–70, 215–16
Birdair: 412
Black, Reece B.: 105
Bong Son: 374, 383
Bong Son Pass: 375
Boston, USS: 90
Bowles, Chester: 49–50
Bradley, Omar N.: 44
Brezhnev, Leonid I.: 334, 350
Brookbank, David A.: 359, 361, 363, 364
Brown, George S.: **118**, 205

advisory group participation: 166
aerial photography efforts comments: 147
budget constraint comments: 238
F–4 retention (1970): 232
freedom of action for Marines: 124
opinion on herbicide spraying: 234–35
opposition to reductions: 134, 136
recommended budget savings: 140
role in Vietnamization: 212
single manager for tactical aviation arguments: 120
sortie ceiling repercussion position: 239
Brown, Leslie E.: 344
Bugle Note: 28–29
Bullet Shot deployments: 329, 336–37, **338**
Bunker, Ellsworth: 5
    discussions with Thieu: 182
    truce negotiations (1968): 121
Bu Prang: 159, **160**
Burns, John J.: 422, 429
Buse, Henry W., Jr.: 116

Calley, William F.: 306
Ca Lu: 56–58
Cambodia
    aerial interdiction, 1971
        aerial interdiction contribution: 276–77
        air power support: 281–82
        attempts to coordinate allies: 277
        lack of formal advisory group: 276
        Mekong River defense: 283–85
        motivation for support: 278–79
        rules of engagement: 277–78
    aerial interdiction, 1972: 285–86
    aerial interdiction, 1973
        end of funding for: 411
        inadequacy of Khmer forces: 412
        reliance on U.S. air power: 410
    Ben Het shelling: 152
    conflicts over bombing plans: 129
    conflicts with South Vietnam: 209
    dry season offensive (1970–71): 279–81
    efforts to expel North Vietnamese: 184
    Fishook operations: 52, 129, 133, 183, 184, 187–88
    ground war expansion (1970): 189–90
    hatred of South Vietnamese: 278
    inadequacy of Khmer forces: 412
    invasion by United States, 1970

Index

aircraft available: 208
close air support continuation: 203–4
congressional moves for withdrawal: 198
damage assessment difficulties: 192
domestic opposition to expansion: 204
expansions of invasion: 205–7
extension beyond Mekong River: 201–2
forward air controller duties: 200
Freedom Action: 202
ground invasion plans: 181–83
language barrier considerations: 200
liaison officer difficulties: 200–201
principal U.S. objective: 193–94
purpose of: 210
reconnaissance efforts: 192–93
rescue mission extension: 201–2
results evaluation: 195
rules of engagement: 199–200
sortie rate: 191
support options: 180–81
troop withdrawal: 190
Kompong Cham: 208
Labansiek/Ba Kev defensive: 202
lack of coordination with South Vietnamese: 277
Lon Nol. *See* Lon Nol
Mayaguez capture. *See Mayaguez* incident
Menu bombings. *See* Operation Menu
Military Region IV fighting: 398–99
multi-country coordination problems: 209–10
Neak Luong bombing error: 411–12
Nixon. *See* Nixon, Richard M., Cambodia
North Vietnam and
  ambushes from North: 280–82
  bases in: 51–52
  relations with (1968): 48–49
  relations with (1969): 179–80
  resupply route significance: 75–76
Operation Patio: 185–86
Operation Vesuvius intelligence: 50–51
Phnom Penh evacuation: 412–13, **414**
restoration of diplomatic ties: 133
rules of engagement
  beyond border region: 193
  buffer zone use: 194, 199–200
  cross-border firing permission: 152

noncombatant safety precautions: 191, 277–78
post-cease-fire rules: 405
prohibition to cross border: 180
U.S. advisory help: 210
secret bombings. *See* Operation Menu; Operation Patio
Sihanouk overthrown: 180
South Vietnamese ground support (1970): 183
Support Activities Group plans: 404–5
Toan Thang 43 operation: 186–90
tri-border interdiction missions: 77
Cam Lo rescue operation: 359
Camp Carroll: 359
Camp Evans: 60, 64, 69
Camp Horn: 117
Cam Ranh Bay Air Base: 13, 30–31
  casualties: 245
  drug abuse problem: 314, 317, 318
  offensives (1968): 151
  post-Tet attacks against: 66
  Viet Cong offensive (1971): 289
Cao Van Vien: **215**, 248, 250, 418, 426
Capital Military Assistance Command: 73, 74
Carey, Richard E.: 422, 423, 448
Casualties
  Ap Bia: 155–56
  A Shau Valley: 65
  Bien Hoa: 11–12, 246
  Cam Ranh Bay: 245
  civilian: 22, 24, 69, 72, 73, 79, 151, 306, 389
  Da Nang: 246
  Kham Duc: 110–11
  Koh Tang Island: 447
  Lam Son 719: 273
  mini-Tet: 70, 71–72
  Nha Trang: 245
  Phan Rang: 245
  Phu Cat: 244–45
  Pleiku: 246
  Tan Son Nhut: 10
  Tet offensive: 35
  Thuong Duc: 86
  U.S. forces in 1971: 275
  U.S. forces in Cambodia: 198
Cease-fire talks: 46
  1968 Paris: 73, 120–21, 401
  1972: 400–401
  1973: 383, 403

519

Index

truce: 401, 402
Centralized air control. *See* Single manager for tactical aviation
Central Office for South Vietnam
  December resolution: 326
  difficulties in locating: 194
  Tet offensive comments: 35
  as U.S. objective: 193
Chaisson, John R.: 26–27, 94
Chapman, Leonard F.: 99–100, 113–14, **115**
Chau Doc Province: 82, 159, 189
China
  establishment of relations with United States: 426
  importance of: 44, 426
  intervention by, concerns about: 44
  Nixon's visit to: 326
Ching Chuan Kang Air Base, Taiwan: 343, 344
Cholon District, Saigon: 20, **22**
Chu, Earl M.: 312
Chui Lang Special Forces Camp: 160
Chu Lai Air Base: 31, 42, 92
Church, Frank: 198, 276. *See also* Cooper-Church Amendment
Citadel (Hue): 13, 24–26, 35
Civilian contractors in South Vietnam: 225, 301, 352, 354, 412
  Air America: 420–21
  Birdair: 412
  civil engineering firms: 217
  Lear Sigler Incorporated: 407, 409, 416
  Pacific Architects and Engineers: 217
  Philco-Ford: 217, 301
  TransAsia: 217
Civilian population protection: 16, 26, 74, 151, 183, 194, 200, 278
Clark Air Base, Philippines: 219, 343, 344
Clay, Lucius D., Jr.: 215, 254
Claymore mines: 83
Cleland, John R.D., Jr.: 410
Cleveland, USS: 283
Clifford, Clark: 41, 46
Close air support. *See also* Aerial interdiction
  mission distribution (1968): 55
  post-Tet operational sorties: 19–20
Collins, Arthur B., Jr.: 220, 222, 283
Combat Skyspot radar: 28, **131**
  Alpine operation: 160
  in Cambodia: 200

Menu bombing role: 130
  removal from South Vietnam: 410
  tandem tactics use: 143–44
Combined Campaign Plan: 294
Combined Interdiction Coordinating Committee: 295
Commando Flash: 328, 338
Commando Fly: 328, 338
Commando Hunt operations: 293, 295, 297
Communist forces. *See* Khmer Rouge; North Vietnam; Viet Cong
Concerned Officers Movement: 313–14
Consolidated RVNAF Improvement and Modernization Program. *See* Vietnamization
Constant Guard movements: 340–41, 342, 343–44, 346
Constellation, USS: 321, 337
Cooper, John Sherman: 198, 276
Cooper-Church amendment: 250, 253, 276
Coral Sea, USS: 430
Corps Tactical Zones. *See also* Military Regions I, II, III, IV
I Corps
  force deployments: 94
  mini-Tet attacks on: 69
  new headquarters: 95
  Thuong Duc: 87
II Corps
  degree of South Vietnamese control (1969): 174
  mini-Tet fighting: 69–70
III Corps: 10
  degree of South Vietnamese control (1969): 174
  dry season offensive (1970–71): 279–81
IV Corps
  Alpine operation: 160
  civilian population in: 79
  command changes: 366
  degree of South Vietnamese control (1969): 174
  river force missions: 79–82
  Tri Ton drop: 82–83
Cost of Vietnam War
  amount requested (1975): 420
  end of funding for Cambodia: 411
  impact on troop withdrawal decisions: 236–37
  impact on Vietnamization: 236–37, 238, 295–96

520

Index

increased aid to South (1972): 349–50
Mayaguez incident: 447
Project 703: 140, 143
recommended expansion of aid to
    Cambodia: 285–86
support of South Vietnamese Air Force
    (1974): 415–16
Credible Chase: 349, 350
Cua Viet River: 119, 364
Cushman, Robert E., Jr.: **101**, 220, 222
  Hue offense role: 25
  Khe Sanh relief operation: 56–57
  post-Thor request for control: 119
  single manager for tactical aviation and:
    100–101, 114, 126
Cuu Long operations: 189

Dai Loc: 286
Dak Seang: 244
Dak To villages: 288, 374–75, 383
Da Lat: 23–24
Dambe: 280
Da Nang Air Base: 16, 286
  casualties: 246
  Constant Guard movements: 344
  housing program: 214
  lack of U.S. readiness for attack: 13–14
  mini-Tet attack: 69
  offensives (1968): 151
  Viet Cong offensive: 13
Dang Dinh Linh: 354
Dao Mong Xuan: 23
DART (deployable automatic relay
    terminal): 175–76
Davidson, Phillip B.: 399–400
Davison, Michael S.: 220, 268
Deane, John Gunther: 413
Defense Attaché Office: 405–6
Defense Race Relations Institute: 323–24
Defoliation: **235**
  Agent blue: 234
  Agent orange: 234, 235
  Agent white: 234
  missions: 31
  reduction in program: 234–35
  safety of agents: 234
Delaware (Operation). *See* A Shau Valley
Delta Military Assistance Command: 220
Deployable automatic relay terminal
    (DART): 175–76
Dewey Canyon. *See* Operation Dewey
    Canyon

Diem, Ngo Dinh. *See* Ngo Dinh Diem
Dien Bien Phu: 16, 17, 95, 233
Dillon, C. Douglas: 44
Dinh Tuong Province: 399
Direct air request network: 173–74
Direct Air Support Centers
  I: 253, 372
    Hambleton rescue: 359–61, 363
    single manager for tactical aviation
      procedures: 113
    transfer to Hue: 366
  II: 191, 194
  III: 10, 191
  IV: 81, 191
  V: 98, 113, 253, 254
  contribution to Cambodia offensives:
    191
  Horn: 117
  Khmer: 404–5
  South Vietnamese: 173, 221, 365, 366,
    372, 377
Dolvin, Welborn G.: 287, 327
Dong, Du Quoc: 254
Don Muang: 344
Doumer Bridge (Paul Doumer Bridge):
    336
Drug abuse
  amnesty program for drug users: 317
  attitude of individuals and: 314
  availability of drugs: 315–16
  contribution to theft: 320–21
  disciplinary breakdown symptom:
    312–13
  drug testing program: 320
  education and rehabilitation program:
    320
  impact of public opposition to war:
    313–14
  job tension related: 314–15
  marijuana use: 311, 315
  prevalence of: 319–20
  response to problem: 316–18
  security measures: 318, **319**
Drug smuggling: 315–16
Duc Co: 383
Duc Lap: 83, **84**, 159
Dung, Van Tieng: 419
Duong Van Minh: 424
Du Quoc Dong: 254
Dzu, Ngo. *See* Ngo Dzu

Eagle Pull (Operation): 412–13

521

Index

Easter invasion (1972)
  An Loc. *See* An Loc
  basic defensive plan, United States: 329
  battlefield strategy, United States: 401
  buildup: 373–74
  evaluation of North Vietnam effort:
    399–400
  Kontum City: 375, 377–382. *See also*
    Kontum City
  political impact of North Vietnamese
    victory (1972): 333–34
  Quang Tri City. *See* Quang Tri City
  results: 383
  scope of attacks: 330–31, 374–77,
    384–87, 398–99
  U.S. response to
    B–52 attacks: 335–37
    base overcrowding: 344–45
    electronic warfare aircraft
      deployments: 341–42
    extension of North Vietnam strike
      region: 335
    final aircraft totals: 346–47
    Haiphong harbor mining: 335–36
    logistics problems: 341, 342–43
    tactical aviation expansion: 337–41
    Thai base use: 346
    transport and tanker expansion:
      343–44
Eglin Air Force Base, Florida: 342
Eighth Air Force. *See* United States Air
  Force, Air Divisions, 3d
Electronic surveillance methods: 175–76,
  407
Elephant's Foot: 399
Ellsberg, Daniel: 306
Enthoven, Alain: 4–5
Equal Opportunity and Treatment program
  (EOT): 312
Equipment, North Vietnam
  AK–47: 184
  MiGs: 242, 291, 292, 415
  PT–76: **257**, 268–69
  SA–2: 359, **360**, 369
  SA–7: 356, 369, 393
  surface-to-air missiles: 291, 359, **360**,
    369, 393
  T–54: 268–69, 375
  T–55: 332
  wire-guided antitank missiles: 374
  ZSU–57–2: 375
Erdle, Philip: 23–24

FACs. *See* Forward air controllers
Fire bombings: 66–67
Fire Support Bases
  Bastogne: 368, 371
  Charlie-2: 286
  losses of: 263–64
  Mary Ann: 286
  North Vietnamese attacks: 262–63, 269
  O'Reilly: 244
  Ripcord: 243
Fishook operations: 52, 129, 133, 183,
  184, 187–88
Flower soldiers: 418
Force reductions
  Australia: 307
  B–52 reduction (1970): 239
  bomber sortie cuts (1970): 241–42, 243
  budget deficit impact on forces (1969):
    139–40
  budget's impact on withdrawals (1970):
    235, 236–37, 238
  F–100 withdrawal from South Vietnam:
    232
  fighter-bomber strength: 136–37
  force reduction decision (1970): 230–32
  manpower withdrawals (1971): 275
  Marine Corps: 237, 304
  New Zealand: 307
  options in 1968: 136–37
  overall effect of deployments (1972):
    346–48
  phase I plan: 161
  phase II plan: 162–63, 177–78
  phase III plan: 211
  phase IV plan: 232–34, 235–36
  phase V plan: 237
  political pressure for withdrawals
    (1971): 301–4
  Seventh Air Force: 139–41, 305
  sortie ceilings and reductions (1970):
    239–43
  South Korea: 307
  Thailand
    1970: 237, 238
    1971: 307
  troop reductions (1972): 305, 306–7
Ford, Gerald: 129
  abandonment of South Vietnam: 420
  assurances to Thieu: 417
  response to *Mayaguez* capture
    decision to act quickly: 429
    on inapplicability of War Powers Act:

Index

428–29
Foreign journalists secrecy breeches: 252
Forward air controllers
  aerial interdiction campaign in
      Cambodia: 191–92, 200
  anti-tank strategies: 364
  in A Shau region: 60, 154–55
  Ben Het contribution: 158
  dangers involved: 65
  friendly fire accidents: 64
  ground support role: 79–81
  interdiction missions: 76–77
  Lam Son 719 contribution: 253–54, 272
  limited knowledge of gunships: 385
  rocket watch: 67–68, 73
  rules of engagement in Cambodia: 284
  rules of engagement role: 26
  South Vietnamese marginal ability:
      219–20, 406
  success with arming: 207
  Tet offensive role: 30
  tri-border fighting role: 75
  use of OV–10: 90
IV Corps. *See* Corps Tactical Zones, IV
    Corps
Fracture Deep: 292
Fragmentary order
  procedures used: 98, 102
  in single manager for tactical aviation:
      114
Freedom Action: 202
Freedom Deal: 199, 200, 205
Freedom Deal Alpha: 207
Frequent Wind. *See* Operation Frequent
    Wind
Friedheim, Jerry W.: 205
Friendly fire accidents: 64, 73, 91
Fuel-air munitions: 89
Fulbright, J. William: 156

Gayler, Noel A.M.: 348, 429
Geneva Accords: 247
Giai, Vu Van. *See* Vu Van Giai
Giap, Vo Nguyen. *See* Vo Nguyen Giap
Gillem, Alvan C.: 130, 241
Ginsburgh, Robert N.: 14, **15**
Gio Linh: 69
Goodell, Charles E.: 144
Gravel mines: 76
Ground air delivery system: 390–91
Ground offensives, North Vietnamese
  325th Division in Cambodia: 75, 79

Ap Bia fortress: 155–56
armored forces in Laos: 256
artillery fire effectiveness: 367
A Shau region repair activity: 153
A Shau Valley weapons used: 60, 62–64
Ben Het: 152, 157
Bien Hoa: 151
Bu Prang: 159
Cambodia ambushes: 280–82
casualties
  Ap Bia: 155–56
  Fire Support Base O'Reilly: 244
  Lam Son 719: 273
  Thuong Duc: 86
control of Dak To-Tan Canh area: 383
Duc Lap: 84–85, 159
Easter offensive. *See* Easter invasion
    (1972)
fire support base attacks: 269, 286, 288
  O'Reilly: 244
  Ripcord: 243
Kham Duc: 104–5
Lam Son 719. *See* Lam Son 719, North
    Vietnam response to
Long Binh attack (1969): 151
Military Region I
  Camp Carroll capture: 359
  offensives (1971): 286
  Quang Tri City (1972): 286, 371–72
Military Region II
  Kontum City (1972): 377–80
  offensives (1971): 287–88
Military Region III
  An Loc loss: 384, 385–87, 396
Military Region IV
  Kompong Trach (1972): 398
  push into Mekong delta: 398–99
mini-Tet
  offensive description: 69–71
  political motives for: 71
  psychological aspects: 68
no-fire zone advantages for: 360–61
operations (1974): 416
Phu Nhon attack: 288
post-truce attacks (1974–75): 419
SA–2 use: 359, **360**, 369
SA–7 use: 356, 369, 393
Saigon capture: 420, 421
tanks and infantry use during Lam Son
    719: 262–63
Tet offensive. *See* Tet offensive
Thuong Duc attack: 86–87

523

Index

Ground offensives, South Vietnamese
　1972: 325–26
　in A Shau Valley (1971): 286–87
　Ben Het passive defense: 158
　Chau Doc ambushes: 160
　Cuu Long I operation: 189
　expansion in Cambodia (1970): 189–90
　Fire Support Base counterattacks: 288
　Fishook operations: 187–88
　Ho Chi Minh Trail attack plans
　　aerial interdiction cancellation: 336
　　code name decision: 251
　　joint phase planning: 250
　　proposal beginnings: 247–48
　　secrecy attempts: 251–52
　　strategic importance: 249
　　support of military leaders: 248–49
　　United States on air support: 250–51
　　weather considerations: 249
　Lam Son 207: 56, 57
　Lam Son 719. *See* Lam Son 719
　Lam Son 720: 286–87
　Lam Son 810: 286–87
　Plei Trap Valley offense: 287–88
　Toan Thang operations: 186, 188, 189
　training with river force: 82
Ground radar air delivery system: 380–81
Gunships, fixed-wing. *See* Aircraft, United States, AC–47, AC–119, AC–130
Gunships, helicopter: 23, 70, 79, 103, 104, 109, 149, 151, 223, 250, 259, 283, 284, 287, 384

Haig, Alexander M., Jr.: 248, 268
Haiphong: 335–36, **336**, 348, 349, 361, 403
Haldeman, H.R.: 197
Hambleton, Iceal E., rescue of: 359–61
Hamburger Hill: 156. *See also* Ap Bia
Hanoi: 56, 335, 336, 348, 349, 361, 403
Hardin, Ernest C., Jr.: 293
Harold E. Holt, USS: 430
Hassayampa, PS (Philippines): 321
Hau Nghia Province: 416
Helms, Richard M.: 41
Henry B. Wilson, USS: 430, 435, 442
Herbicide spraying. *See* defoliation
Heroin: 316, 318. *See also* Drug abuse
Herring, John H., Jr.: 235, 252
High-altitude drop delivery techniques: 392–93
High-velocity drop delivery technique: 393

Hillsboro: 254
Hinh, Nguyen Duy. *See* Nguyen Duy Hinh
Hoang Xuan Lam: 248, 364
　Lam Son 719 tactics: 264, 266, 270
　loss of command: 366
　objection to preparatory strikes: 256–57
Hobart, HMAS (Australia): 91
Hobo Woods: 328
Ho Chi Minh: 16–17
Ho Chi Minh Trail: 149, **296**
　aerial interdiction cancellation: 336
　attack designation decision: 251
　attack proposal beginnings: 247–48
　attack secrecy attempts: 251–52
　Commando Hunt operations: 293, 295, 297
　Dewey Canyon II. See Operation Dewey Canyon II
　Lam Son 719. *See* Lam Son 719
　North Vietnamese reestablishment of traffic (1974): 418–19
　strategic importance: 249
　support of military leaders for attack: 248–49
　U.S. reliance on air support: 250–51
　United States/South Vietnam joint phase planning: 250
　weather considerations: 249
Hoi An: 13, 16
Hollingsworth, James F.: 358, 394
　command of Military Region III: 386
　response to North Vietnamese attacks: 386–87
Holloway, Bruce K.: 47, 130, 241
Holt, USS: 435
Homestead Air Force Base, Florida: 342
How the Americans Killed a Vietnamese President: 418
Hue: **17**
　I Direct Air Support Center transferred to: 366–67
　communist activities in: 18
　Easter invasion (1972): 330–31
　mini-Tet attacks: 69
　rules of engagement: 24–25
　Viet Cong seizure of: 13
Hung, Le Van: 385
Huston, Tom Charles: 197

I Corps. *See* Corps Tactical Zones, I Corps
Igloo White: 176
Imperial City. *See* Citadel

Index

Initial objective of the war, United States: 3, 46, 157, 229, 306, 424
Insecticide spraying: 234. *See also* Defoliation
Interdiction campaigns. *See* Aerial interdiction
International Control Commission: 49–50, 51
Interrogation of enemy prisoners: 14, 29, 50, 51, 75, 244, 384, 395
Iosue, Andrew P.: 390
Island Tree plan: 295
Iwakuni Air Base, Japan: 339

Jackson, Joe M.: 110, **111**
Janca, R.B.: 430
Johnson, Lyndon B.: **6, 15**
    decision not to seek reelection: 45–46
    early view of the war: 5–6
    force deployment decisions: 41, 42
    hesitancy to bomb North: 128–29
    reluctance to add troops: 43–44
Joint Chiefs of Staff
    Cambodian aid expansion recommended: 285–86
    debate over B–52 sortie rate: 143
    dynamic defense strategy: 275
    Freedom Deal expansion: 206
    Menu request approval: 130
    opposition to reductions (1971): 302, 303
    phase II plan recommendations: 162–63
    phase IV ground force reductions: 235–36
    post-Tet sortie authorization: 27
    reinforcement program: 40–41, 42
    review of Vietnamization (1971): 298
    single manager for tactical aviation indecision: 99–100
    sortie requests (1972): 307–9
    South pressure on North recommended: 325
Jones, David C.: 427
Jumper, Jimmy J.: 406–7

Kadena Air Base, Okinawa: 242, 261, 329, 333, 337, 343
Karnow, Stanley: 274
Kennedy, Edward M.: 156
Kennedy, John F.: 186
Kent State University: 197, 231
Kerwin, Walter T., Jr.: 102

Kham Duc
    attack: 104
    casualties: 110–11
    communication difficulties during evacuation: 111
    defense coordination: 104–5
    evacuation description: 105–10
    mini-Tet attack: 69
    and single manager for tactical aviation: 111–12
Khang, Le Nguyen: 269–70
Khe Sanh Marine combat base: **29, 260**
    B–52 activity against: 26–27
    Dewey Canyon II plan: 257–58
    divisional tactical operations center: 253
    importance of: 16, 58
    mini-Tet attacks: 69
    relief operation: 56–57, **58**
    Tet offensive and: **15**, 15–16
Khmer Republic. *See* Cambodia
Khmer Rouge
    activities in Cambodia: 195
    growing strength: 285
    Mayaguez incident: 427, 432, 447
Kien Hoa Province: 82
Kien Phong Province: 399
Kien Tuong Province: 180, 398–99
King, Martin Luther, Jr.: 311, 312
Kissinger, Henry
    comments on weather effects: 358
    desire for dry season offensive (1970): 128–29
    force reductions: 236
    hesitancy to bomb North: 128–29
    Mayaguez advisor: 427
    political impact of North Vietnamese victory (1972): 333–34
    proposal to end war: 133
    secret negotiations with Hanoi: 335
    sortie rate study call (1971): 309
    view on Cambodia bombing proposal: 129
Kitty Hawk, USS: 321
Koh Tang Island. *See Mayaguez* incident
Komer, Robert W.: 5
Kompong Cham: 205, 208
Kompong Som: 48, 195
Kompong Thom: 202, 205, 206, 281
Kompong Trach: 398–99
Kong River truck park attack: 188
Kontum City: 16, 376
    airlift operations: 379, 380

525

Index

Easter invasion (1972): 375, 377–82
   supply drops: 380–81
Korat Air Base, Thailand: 341, 342
Korea. *See* North Korea; South Korea
Krek, Cambodia: 282
Kroesen, Frederick J.: 363
Krulak, Victor H.: 113, **115**
Ky, Nguyen Cao: 24–25, 224

Labansiek/Ba Kev defensive: 202
LaHue, Foster C.: 25
Laird, Melvin
   Cambodia attack plan (1970): 183
   debate over B–52 sortie rate: 143
   deployment decisions (1972): 339–40
   emphasis on rapid South strength buildup: 163–64
   financial ceiling support: 238
   on funding for Vietnamization: 211
   launch of improvement program: 212
   prediction of end of war: 297–98
   sortie averaging suggestion: 308
   troop withdrawal recommendations: 302
   U.S. troop reduction agreement: 134
   Vietnamization objective: 165
   view on Cambodia bombing proposal: 129
Lam, Hoang Xuan. *See* Hoang Xuan Lam
Lam Son 207: 56, 57
Lam Son 216. *See* A Shau Valley
Lam Son 719. *See also* Operation Dewey Canyon II; Ground offensives, South Vietnamese
   aircraft sorties flown: 272–73
   air support request procedures: 253–54
   Arc Light tactics: 266
   B–52 sorties: 259, 261–62
   casualties: 273
   designation as Ho Chi Minh Trail attack: 251
   equipment losses: 271
   final raids: 270–71
   fire support base abandonments: 269–70
   helicopter control: 255
   impact on North: 272
   loss of Fire Support Base 31: 263–64
   need for centralized control: 254–55
   Nixon's defense of results: 271
   North Vietnamese response to
      anti-helicopter tactics: 256
      casualties: 273
      counterattacks: 262–63
   impact of attack: 272
   Landing Zone Lolo capture: 267
   Route 9 ambushes: 268–69
   outposts: 259
   task force activities: 261
   Tchepone raid: 264–65
   Thieu's reluctance to continue: 259–60
   U.S. sorties flown: 258
   Vietnamization inadequacies shown: 274
   weather complications: 258
Lam Son 720: 286–87
Lam Son 810: 287
Landing Zone English: 375, 383
Landing Zone Lolo: 265, 267
Lang Vei: 83, 248, 270
Laos
   air attacks (1968): 149
   Dewey Canyon II. *See* Operation Dewey Canyon II
   Ho Chi Minh Trail. *See* Ho Chi Minh Trail
   Lam Son 719. *See* Lam Son 719
   Vietnamization of attacks: 297
Laser-guided bombs: 89, 257, 336
Lavelle, John D.: 328, 330, **331**
   deployment decisions (1972): 339–40
   reasons for dismissal: 357
Lear Sigler Incorporated: 407, 409
Le Duan: 229
Le Nguyen Khang: 269–70
Le Van Hung: 385
Lien, Nguyen Ba. *See* Nguyen Ba Lien
Limited Privileged Communication Program: 317
Linebacker (Operation): 336, 357
Linebacker II (Operation): 401
Linh, Dang Dinh: 354
Loan, Nguyen Ngoc. *See* Nguyen Ngoc Loan
Loc Ninh: 330–31, 384–85
Loi Phong operation: 367
Long Binh
   ammunition dump attack: 12
   North offensive (1969): 151
   racial tensions: 321
Lon Nol
   diminished health: 285
   Freedom Action comment: 202
   inability to lead: 410
   inadequacy of forces: 279
   inadequacy of government: 285

Index

restrictions set on invasions: 280
rise to power: 179–80
Loran: 145, 410
Luat, Nguyen Trong. *See* Nguyen Trong Luat

MAC. *See* Military Airlift Command
MACV (Military Assistance Command, Vietnam): 95, 235, 403
Mansfield, Mike: 144, 156
Map making: 145
Marijuana use: 311, 312, 313, 315. *See also* Drug abuse
Marine Corps, United States. *See* United States Marine Corps
Martin, Graham: 405
Massachusetts Striker (Operation): 154–55
Matak, Sisouth Sirik: 179
Mayaguez incident
  applicability of War Powers Act: 428–29, 447
  availability of ships and aircraft: 430–31
  boarding party transfer: 434–35
  casualties: 447
  command and control structure: 429–30
  cost to United States: 447
  critique of U.S. response: 447–48
  decision to act quickly: 429
  helicopter units: 430–31
  Khmer Rouge capture of ship: 427
  Koh Tang Island assault and withdrawal: **438**
    15,000-pound bomb drop: 443
    assault planning: 433–35
    assault troops offensive: 440
    landing: 435–39
    Naval fire support: 442–43
    second offensive wave: 441–42
    withdrawal: 444–47
  movement of prisoners: 432
  Naval fire support: 442–43
  rescue command structure: 439
  rescue troops: 431–32
  U.S. advisory staff: 427
McCain, John S., Jr.
  budget's impact on withdrawals (1970): 236
  Cambodian threat concerns: 51
  Ho Chi Minh Trail offensive, desire for: 247
  Island Tree plan: 294
  review of single manager for tactical aviation: 116–17
  use of Thailand bases, desire for: 304
McConnell, John P.
  criteria for Vietnamization: 135
  force reduction proposal: 137
  strategy recommendation: 48
McConnell Air Force Base, Kansas: 340
McCutcheon, Keith B.: 123, 125
McMillan, William: 66, 92
McNamara, Robert S.: 41–43
McNickle, Marvin L.: 328
Mekong River. *See also* Military Region IV
  defense of (1971): 283–85
  extension of Cambodia invasion: 201–2
  Mobile Riverine Force
    aerial support for: 79–82
    Kien Hoa mission: 82
  Operation Cuu Long I: 189
  rules of engagement: 284
Menu bombings. *See* Operation Menu
Metzger, Louis: 344
Meyer, John C.: 238–39
Midway, USS: 337, 422
Mieu Giang River: 359
MiGs
  Cambodian use of: 208
  North Vietnamese use of: 242, 291, 292, 415
Military Airlift Command
  evacuation of wounded: 147
  Saigon evacuation: 420, 421
  troop withdrawal role: 145–46
Military Assistance Command, Vietnam: 95, 235, 403
Military Equipment Delivery Team: 285
Military Region I: 213. *See also* Corps Tactical Zones, I Corps
  aircraft losses in: 369
  anti-tank successes: 364, 368
  command changes: 366
  counterattack successes: 368–69
  Easter invasion (1972). *See* Easter invasion (1972)
  impact of U.S. air power: 372
  Loi Phong operation: 367
  North Vietnamese ground offensives (1971): 286
  Quang Tri City. *See* Quang Tri City
  sorties flown (1972): 369–70
  weak South Vietnamese reconnaissance in: 329

Index

Military Region II: 213. *See also* Corps Tactical Zones, II Corps
    Easter invasion (1972). *See* Easter invasion (1972)
    Kontum City attack. *See* Kontum City
    North Vietnamese attacks (1971): 287–88
    probability of attack (1972): 327
Military Region III: 213. *See also* Corps Tactical Zones, III Corps
    An Loc. *See* An Loc
    attack on enemy bunkers: 328
    defensive plan: 373
    forward air controller contributions: 220
    Tonle Cham: 408
    Viet Cong attacks: 290
Military Region IV. *See also* Corps Tactical Zones, IV Corps
    Kompong Trach defense: 398–99
    Easter invasion (1972). *See* Easter invasion (1972)
Mines
    in Cambodian rivers: 207
    gravel: 76
    in North Vietnam harbors: 335–36
Minh, Duong Van: 424
Minh, Nguyen Van. *See* Nguyen Van Minh
Minigunships: 294, 296, 349
Mini-Tet
    casualties: 70, 71–72
    counteroffensive: 69, 70–71
    Da Nang attack: 69
    evaluation of U.S. response: 72
    mining of North Vietnam harbors: 335–36
    offensive description: 69–71
    political motives for: 71
    psychological aspects: 68
    rules of engagement: 71
    Saigon defensive moves: 70
Mobile defense plan: 48
Mobile Riverine Force
    aerial support for: 79–82
    Kien Hoa mission: 82
Momyer, William W.: **100**
    arguments for single manager for tactical aviation: 99, 103
    central authority argument: 94
    modified single manager procedures: 114–15
    rocket watch order: 67
Moore, Joseph H.: 311

Moorer, Thomas W.: 116, 187, 203
Mu Gia Pass: 291, 329
Muong Nong: 270
Murray, John E.: 405, 416
My Chanh River: 368, 369, 370
My Lai: 306

Nakhon Phanom Air Base, Thailand
    intelligence center: 175, 176, 293
    Mayaguez incident and: 431
    Support Activities Group base: 403
Nam Lyr Mountains: 51
Napalm: 62, 66, 70, 85, 107, 123, 124, 156, 262, 265, 272
Napalm Sunday: 66
National Security Council: 427
Navy, United States. See United States Navy
Nazzaro, Joseph J.: 28, 136
Neak Luong, bombing error at: 411–12
New Zealand: 149, 150, 307
Nghi, Nguyen Van: 398
Ngo Dinh Diem: 418
Ngo Dzu: 373, 377
Ngok Tavak: 104, 105, 110
Ngo Quang Truong
    command changes: 366
    comments on Military Region IV defense: 399
    counterattack successes: 368–69
    Quang Tri City counterattack: 371
Nguyen Ba Lien: 158
Nguyen Cao Ky: 24–25, 224
Nguyen Duy Hinh: 252
Nguyen Hue (Operation). *See* Easter invasion (1972)
Nguyen Ngoc Loan: 70
Nguyen Trong Luat: 268
Nguyen Van Minh: 383
Nguyen Van Nghi: 398
Nguyen Van Thieu
    abandonment of northern provinces (1975): 419–20
    discussions over Cambodia: 182
    modernization request: 164
    plans for Ho Chi Minh Trail attack: 249, 250
    reaction to cease-fire agreement (1972): 400
    reluctance to continue Lam Son 719: 259–60
    resignation: 420

Index

South Vietnamese dissatisfaction with: 418
suggested assistance from United States: 46–47
Nha Trang Air Base: 13, 16
  air base transfer: 215
  casualties: 245
  transfer to South Vietnamese: 169–70
Night operations
  attack aircraft: 88–89
  operations with C–130s: 379
Nitze, Paul: 36
  phase II plan approval: 162
  and single manager for tactical aviation: 103
Nixon, Richard M.
  Cambodia
    air strike permission: 276
    attack plan (1970): 181–82
    defense of Lam Son 719 results: 271
    invasion announcement: 193
    invasion decision: 187
    Menu bombing decision: 129
    overestimation of Cambodian leaders: 197
    policies after ground withdrawal: 202–3
    proposed bombing of: 127–28
    reversal of invasion plans: 183
    support for: 186
  cease-fire negotiations (1972): 400–401
  force reduction decision (1970): 231–32
  force reduction plans: 134–35
  instructions to Vogt: 357
  political impact of North Vietnam victory (1972): 333–34
  reaction to student demonstrators: 197
  resignation: 417
  Thieu meeting (1969): 164
  troop level objectives (1972): 348
  troop withdrawals: 306–7, 334
  Vietnamization
    criteria for: 135
    emphasis after Ap Bia: 157
    force reduction options: 136–38
    troop reductions: 138–39
Norodom Sihanouk: **181**
  difficulties of position concerning United States: 196–97
  negotiations with United States: 49–50, 51
  neutrality on Menu bombings: 132
  overthrow: 180
  restoration of diplomatic ties: 133
  returning popularity (1971): 285
  silence over Menu attacks: 179
Norris, Thomas R.: 360, **361**
North Korea: 39, 428
North Vietnam. *See also* Viet Cong
  battle tactics: 331–32
  Cambodian support of (1968): 48–49
  cease-fire conditions (1972): 400, 401
  effectiveness of tactics: 289–90
  force buildup (1971): 291–92
  goal of 1972 offensive: 334
  ground offensives, *See* Ground offensives, North Vietnamese
  helicopter operations: 90–92
  Hue occupation: 18
  knowledge of B–52 strike plans: 29–30
  lack of reaction to Menu bombings: 132–33
  leadership coalition (1970): 229
  military doctrine: 17
  preparations for invasion (1972): 329
  probability of large offensive (1972): 326–27
  refusal to leave Cambodia: 180
  relations with Cambodia: 179
  resistance to peace: 306
  Saigon offensive (1969): 151
  units/bases in Cambodia: 51
O'Donnell, Andrew W.: 345
O'Reilly Fire Support Base: 244
Office of Special Investigations. *See* United States Air Force, Office of Special Investigations
Offset aiming point: 411
Operation Alpine: 160
Operation Apache Snow: 155–56
Operation Babylift: 420
Operation Binh Tay I: 189
Operation Cuu Long I: 189
Operation Delaware. *See* A Shau Valley
Operation Dewey Canyon: 153–54
Operation Dewey Canyon II. *See also* Lam Son 719
  advance on Khe Sanh: 257–58
  attack plan preparation: 252–53
  ban on U.S. ground forces: 250, 253
  designation as Ho Chi Minh Trail attack: 251
  sorties flown: 258
Operation Eagle Pull: 412–13

529

Index

Operation Frequent Wind. *See* Saigon evacuation
Operation Lam Son 207: 56, 57
Operation Lam Son 216. *See* A Shau Valley
Operation Linebacker: 336, 357
Operation Linebacker II: 401
Operation Massachusetts Striker: 154–55
Operation Menu
   addition of tactical air strikes: 185
   bombing procedures: 129–30
   Bu Prang: 159
   duration: 133
   end to secrecy: 188
   limited effectiveness of: 195
   need for secrecy: 132
   neutrality of Sihanouk: 132, 179
   Nixon's decision on: 129
   as preparation for ground attack (1970): 182–83
   reconnaissance: 131–32
   results of: 132
   security procedures: 130–31
Operation Nguyen Hue. *See* Easter invasion (1972)
Operation Patio: 185–86, 188
Operation Pegasus: 56, 98
Operation Rolling Thunder Alpha: 336
Operation Shoemaker: 187
Operations Plan 732: 294
Operation Thor: 118–19
Operation Vesuvius: 50–51
Opium availability: 315–16
Organization of Petroleum Exporting Countries: 417

Pacific Architects and Engineers: 217
Packard, David: 164, 177–78
Pannell, William P.: 430
Parrot's Beak: 48, 51, 52, 82, 186
Partridge, Earle E.: 93
Patio (Operation): 185–86, 188
Paul Doumer Bridge: 336
Peak manpower strength: 122
Pegasus (Operation): 56, 98
Pentagon Papers: 306
People's Army of Vietnam. *See* Ground offensives, North Vietnam; North Vietnam
Pham Van Dong: **181**, 229
Phan Rang Air Base: 13
   casualties: 245

drug abuse problem: 314, 317
offensives (1969): 151
Philco-Ford: 217, 301
Philippines: 32, 219, 343, 344
Phnom Penh
   advisory group location: 276
   evacuation: 413, **414**
   fall of: 413
Photo reconnaissance. *See* Aerial reconnaissance
Phu Bai: 95, 271
Phu Cat Air Base: 13, 151, 416
Phu Nhon attack: 288
Phuoc Le: 23
Phuoc Long Province: 419
Phu Tho racetrack: 20
Pich Nil Pass: 283
Plain of Reeds: 48, 399
Pleiku Air Base: 13, 16
   air base transfer: 216
   casualties: 246
   drug abuse problem: 318
   North Vietnam offensive (1972): 374
   offensives (1969): 151
Plei Trap Valley offensive: 287–88
Polei Kleng: 376–77
Pol Pot: 410, 413
POWs release negotiations: 403, **404**, 406
Prey Veng: 190
Project 703: 140, 143
Project Enhance. *See* Vietnamization, Project Enhance
Proud Bunch: 292
Proud Deep Alpha: 292
Psychological warfare: 72
   in Cambodia: 193
   funding reduction effects: 140
Public opinion, United States. *See* Anti-war sentiments
Pueblo, USS: 27, 39, 428

Quang Tri City
   Easter invasion (1972): 330–31, 364. *See also* Easter invasion
   Camp Carroll loss: 358–59
   cost of rescue operation: 360–61
   no-fire zone rescue operation: 359–60
   recapture of: 371
   rescue of trapped personnel: 365–66
   supply drop losses: 365
   mini-Tet attacks: 69
   offensive (1971): 286

Qui Nhon Air Base: 16

Racial tensions
  Air Force
    black vs. white awareness: 321–23
    counseling and discussion efforts: 323
    disregard of surrounding problems: 311–12
    education program: 323–24
  Navy: 321
Rain of Fire: 361
RAND: 47
Reconnaissance. *See* Aerial reconnaissance
Reed, Robert R.: 430
Refugee problem: 72
Rehabilitation programs: 317, 318
Republic of Korea. *See* South Korea
Republic of Vietnam. *See* South Vietnam
Rescue operations: 342, 436–47
  Hambleton rescue: 359–61, 363
  operational command structure: 439
  performance by United States: 362–63
  Phnom Penh: 413, **414**
  Saigon fall: 420–21, 422–24, **423**
Ripcord Fire Support Base: 243
Rivers, Mendel: 129
Rocket Ridge: 374
Rocket watch
  coerced collateral damage: 73
  defensive measures: 67–68
  forward air controller duties: 73
  ground safety concerns: 72–73
Rockpile: 376
Rogers, William P.: 129
Rolling Thunder Alpha (Operation): 336
Rome Air Development Center: 367
Rosson, William B.: 117
Rostow, Walt W.: 14, **15**, 41
Route 9: 257
Royal Australian Air Force. *See also* Australia
  aerial reconnaissance: 150
  Caribou transport use: 150
  Canberra use: **21**, 149
  post-Tet operational sorties: 19
  sortie average: 149
  sorties flown (1968): 56
Royal Thai Air Force. *See* Thailand
Rules of engagement
  at Ben Het: 157
  Cambodia. *See* Cambodia, rules of engagement
  civilian population in towns: 26
  civilian structure targets in South Vietnam: 20–21
  Freedom Deal: 205
  Hue: 24–25
  Mekong River: 284
  mini-Tet: 71
  reemphasis of: 74
  rocket watch: 67
Rusk, Dean: 70
Russell, Richard: 129
Russia. *See* Soviet Union
Ryan, John D.: 226, 238, 299, 304, 330, 345

SAC. *See* Strategic Air Command
Saigon
  air offensive (1969): 151
  apathy of citizens: 17–18
  defense strategy for: 14
  evacuation
    fixed wing aircraft use: 420–21
    helicopter phase: 422–24, **423**
  mini-Tet defensive moves: 70
  Viet Cong offensive: 10
Salem House probes: 184, 206, 207
Sann, Son: 49, 50
Saratoga, USS: 337
Schlesinger, James R.: 427
Scowcroft, Brent: 427
Seamans, Robert C.: **215**, 224, 237
Search and rescue operations. *See* Rescue operations
Selective service: 349
Selin, Ivan: 136
Senate Armed Services Committee: 132
Sensors
  acoustic: 81, 367
  on aircraft: 87–89, 140, 200, 207, 339, 377, 379, 394, 396
  electronic, on ground: 160, 175–77, 207, 272, 293, 327, 329
  lacked by South Vietnamese: 294, 295, 296
  "people sniffers": 81
  seismic: 81
  shortcomings: 368, 446
Seven Mountains: 82, 244, 290
Seventh Air Force: 6. *See also* United States Air Force
  anti-tank successes: 368
  artillery location attempts: 367

Index

A Shau Valley offensive: 58
bomber sorties: 241–42, 243
Cambodia missions (1970): 190–91
change in leadership (1972): 330
changes due to reductions: 140
Fishook assistance: 188–89
force composition (1970): 230
force reductions (1970): 230
force reductions (1971): 305
ground support role: 148
harassment by Viet Cong: 244–46
headquarters location: 7
interdiction missions tactics and
    effectiveness: 76–78
Lam Son 719 sorties: 272
Lam Son 810 air support: 287
Mekong River convoy escorts: 284
Military Region I aircraft losses: 369
mission of: 90
operational control scope: 125
Operations Plan 732: 294
phase IV reductions: 232–33
post-Tet operational sorties: 19
retention of control (1971): 299
rocket watch rules of engagement: 67
single manager for tactical aviation: 98, 101
sortie bank proposal: 240–41
strike report procedures: 203–4
support strikes in South Vietnam: 191
Tactical Air Control Center: 102
tactical sortie ceiling final policy (1970): 240
Seymour Johnson Air Force Base, North Carolina: 340
Shadow. *See* Aircraft, United States, AC–119
Sharp, U.S. Grant: 28, **101**
  centralization decision: 95–96
  force deployment decisions: 44
  response to coordination request: 93
  single manager for tactical aviation concessions: 103
  view of single manager: 114
Shoemaker (Operation): 187
Sihanouk, Norodom. *See* Norodom Sihanouk
Sihanoukville: 48, 195
Single manager for tactical aviation
  A Shau Valley application: 152–53
  assessments of: 100–101
  budget cut effects: 122–23

case for centralized control for Lam Son 719: 254
centralization argument: 93–94, 95, 122
changes to: 97–98
conflicting views of: 99, 114–16
effectiveness of: 114–15, 126
Kham Duc airlift application: 111–12
Marines and
  acceptance of (1972): 357
  assessments of: 100–101
  changes to: 97–98
  criticism of: 99
  desire to circumvent: 119–20
  latitude with: 123–24
  need for air-ground coordination: 95
  rejection of: 113–14, 115–16, 117
mission direction and: 96, 112, 125
post-review procedures: 113
procedure changes: 98–99, 102–3
refinements to: 121–22
shift in I Corps forces: 94–95
Sisouth Sirik Matak: 179
Skyspot radar. *See* Combat Skyspot radar
Smith, Donavon F.: 34
Smothermon, Philip R.: 107, 109, 111
Snoul: 199, 279–82
Soc Trang Air Base: 214–15, **215**
Son Sann: 49, 50
South Korea
  contribution to air war: 150
  force reductions (1971): 307
  Pueblo crisis and: 39
South Vietnam. *See also* Ground offensives, South Vietnamese; South Vietnamese Air Force
air power emphasis: 425
air support complaints (1971): 286–87
apathy of citizens: 17–18
blame of United States for defeat: 426
Cambodia
  conflicts with: 209
  dry season offensive (1970–71): 279–81
  efforts to expel North from: 184
  ground support (1970): 183
  impact of fall: 414
  lack of coordination with: 277
  view of: 278–79
clashes with Viet Cong (1971): 289–90
corps headquarters: 173
Easter invasion (1972) defensive effort: 399–400

532

Index

inability to conduct large operations: 325–26
Krek defense: 282
military aid, increased U.S.: 349
Military Regions. *See* Military Region I, II, III, IV
reliance on United States: 264–65
self-reliance assistance from United States: 47
target selection authority: 24–26
truce negotiations (1968): 121
U.S. assessment of capabilities (1974): 414–15
U.S. troop reduction agreement: 134
Vietnamization endorsement: 138–39
Vietnamization final capabilities: 401–2
worldwide influences on economic support: 417–18
South Vietnamese Air Force. *See also* South Vietnam; Ground offensives, South Vietnamese
33d Wing: 172, 214
accident rate: 34
aircraft losses (1974): 415
Air Divisions
    1st: 213, 216
    2d: 169–70, 213, 215
    3d: 213, 216, 364–65
    4th: 213
    5th: 213–14
Air Logistics Command: 226, 409
Air Training Command: 409
Cambodian invasion participation: 208
cost of U.S. support (1974): 415–16
Defense Attaché suggested improvements: 416
Direct Air Support Center (IV): 81, 221
force composition (1972): 333
increased role (1971): 291
increase in sorties (1969): 149
Lam Son 719 sorties: 272–73
Operations Plan 732: 294
sorties flown (1968): 55–56
support role: 87–88
Tet offensive. *See also* Tet offensive
    casualties: 35
    operational sorties during: 33–34
    performance during counteroffensive: 34
    post-Tet operational sorties: 19
    response: 8–10, **9**, 33
training

aircrew: 218–19
efforts in (1969): 169, 179, 217–18, 222–23
flight crew transitions (1972): 352–53
language: 217–18
in maintenance: 226
night flight: 222–23
training and logistics problems (1973): 408–9
weaknesses in: 409–10
Tri Ton drop participation: 82–83
Vietnamization. *See* Vietnamization
withdrawal from Labansiek/Ba Kev: 202
South Vietnamese Army
    1st Infantry Division: 252, 256, 259–61, 263, 264
    1st Ranger Group: 256
    3d Infantry Division: 330, 358–59, 361, 363–65, 367, 369
    22d Infantry Division: 288
Souvanna Phouma: 258, 297
Soviet Union
    political impact of North Vietnam victory (1972): 333–34
    tanks supplied to North: 256, **257**, 268, 332
Spectre. *See* Aircraft, United States, AC–130
Spooky. *See* Aircraft, United States, AC–47
Steel-roofed shelters: 36
Stennis, John C.: 47, 129
Strategic Air Command
    Advance Echelon: 27
    Bullet Shot deployments: 329, 337
    Constant Guard movements: 343
    debate over B–52 sortie rate: 142
    reduction in forces (1970): 242–43
    strain of B–52 sortie rate: 47
Studies and Observations Group: 131–32, 184
Subic Bay, Philippines: 338
Sullivan, Leonard: 294, 295
Support Activities Group, United States
    Cambodia air strikes: 404–5
    function of: 403
    response plans for possible North Vietnamese invasion: 403–4
Surface-to-air missiles: 291
    SA–2: 359, **360**, 369
    SA–7: 356, 369, 393

533

Index

Sutherland, James W., Jr.: 123, 222
Swank, Emory: 411
Sweet, Charles: 74

Tactical Air Control Center: 102
  Marine apportionment: 123
  and single manager for tactical aviation: 98, 113
  South Vietnamese adoption of: 173
Tactical reconnaissance. *See* Aerial reconnaissance
Takhli Air Base, Thailand: 342–43
Tan Canh: 374–75, 383
Tandem targeting tactics: 143–44, 239. *See also* Arc Light
Tan Son Nhut Air Base: **322**. *See also* Tet offensive, Tan Son Nhut Air Base
  air base transfer: 170, 216
  drug abuse problem: **316**
  evacuation: 422–24
  mapping support services: 145
  mini-Tet attack: 71
  North Vietnamese air attack (1975): 421
  photo processing center: 145, 147
  post-Tet attacks against: 66
  use as training center: 218–19
Tarr, Curtis W.: 177
Tarpley, Thomas M.: 398
Task Force Oregon: 93
Tavak, Ngok. *See* Ngok Tavak
Taylor, Maxwell D.: 41, 44
Tay Ninh City: 383–84
Tchepone
  objective of Laos attack: 248, 253–54, 264, 288
  raid during Lam Son 719: 264–65
  results of failure to take: 274
  Thieu's reluctance to continue toward: 259–61
Tear gas use: 76
Tet offensive. *See also* Mini-Tet; Ground offensives, North Vietnamese
  air base defense improvements after: 35–36, **37**
  air crews trapped by: 31
  air strike allocations: 16
  apathy of Saigon citizens: 17–18
  Ben Tre destruction: 21–22
  Bien Hoa: 10–12, **12, 40**
  casualties during: 35
  characteristics of: 24
  civic action program affected by: 37–38
  Da Lat: 23–24
  Da Nang: 13
  force deployments
    "A to Z" group recommendations: 43
    new maximum: 45
    number of troops used: 4
    Pueblo crisis, impact of: 39
    reinforcement program: 40–42
    reservist mobilization: 45
    "Wise Men" ceiling recommendation: 44
  holiday cease-fire agreement: 15–16
  Hue
    communist activities in: 18
    rules of engagement: 24–25
    Viet Cong seizure of: 13
  Khe Sanh and: **15**, 15–16
  lack of U.S. readiness for attack: 13–14
  objectives of United States after: 46
  photo reconnaissance role in collapse: 30
  Phuoc Le recapture: 23
  political results: 38, 332
  post-Tet counteroffensives
    fire bombings: 66–67
    rocket watch: 67–68
  psychological impact on U.S. leaders: 38, 424
  rationale for North Vietnamese loss: 35
  Saigon: 10, **11**
  scope of attacks: 12–13
  Tan Son Nhut Air Base
    importance of: 7
    response to assault: 8–10, **9**
    results of attack on: 10
    Viet Cong offensive: 7–10
  transport sorties affected by: 31–33
  U.S. response: 19
    base defense improvements: 35–36, **37**
    civilian targets: 20–22
    intelligence role: 14–15, 36–37
Thach Han River: 365, 371
Thailand
  aircraft based in: 239, 333, 431
  air operations out of: 188
  Constant Guard movements: 340
  contribution to air war: 150–51
  force reductions (1971): 307
  force withdrawals (1970): 237, 238
  limitations on assigned manpower: 304
  U.S. aircraft deployed to: 342–44

view of Cambodia: 278–79
Thanh Hoa: 335
Theus, Lucius: 323
Thieu, Nguyen Van. *See* Nguyen Van Thieu
III Corps. *See* Corps Tactical Zones, III Corps
Thompson, Sir Robert: 195
Thor (Operation): 118–19
Thrash, William, G.: 124
Thua Thien Province: 30, 327, 329, 359
Thunder Hurricane: 367
Thuong Duc: 86–87
Tilford, Earl H., Jr.: 363, 447
Toan Thang operations: 186–91
Tolson, John: 56
Ton Duc Thang: 229
Tonkin Gulf resolution: 198, 302, 425
Tonle Bet: 280
Tonle Cham: 408, 416
Tonle Sap: 206
Tra, Tran Van: 419
Training. *See also* South Vietnamese Air Force, training
  after 1973 cease-fire: 409
  budget constraints: 228
  language barrier considerations: 167–69, 200
  Project Enhance Plus: 406–7
Tranh Van Minh: 175, **227**
Tran Van Tra: 419
Travis Air Force Base, California: 147, 314, 323
Tripartite Deputies Working Group: 277
Troop withdrawals. *See* Force reductions
Tropic Moon: 88–89
Truce: 401, 402. *See also* Cease-fire talks
Truong, Ngo Quang. *See* Ngo Quang Truong
Turley, Gerald H.: 363
Tu Van Be: 354
Tuy Hoa Air Base: 13
II Corps. *See* Corps Tactical Zones, II Corps

Ubon Air Base, Thailand: 340, 341, 345
Udorn Air Base, Thailand: 340, 345, 431
U Minh Forest: 290
Unger, Leonard: 188
Unified air control. *See* Single manager for tactical aviation
United States Air Force. *See also* Military Airlift Command; Seventh Air Force; Strategic Air Command
Advisory Group: 166, 211, 352, 353
Air Divisions
  3d: 19, 59
    Bugle Note procedures: 28–29
    Menu bombings: 130
    tandem tactics use: 143–44
    target selection role: 27–28
  834th: 31
    C–130 use in Cambodia: 282–83
    defoliation mission: 235
    Dewey Canyon II plan: 252
Air Forces
  Eight. *See* United States Air Force, Air Divisions, 3d
  Seventh. *See* Seventh Air Force
air power roles: 83
anti-tank strategies: 364
A Shau Valley offensive: 61–62
in Cambodia. *See* Cambodia
combat and logistics support: 4
decline in planned strikes (1971): 286–87
Dewey Canyon. *See* Operation Dewey Canyon
diminished resources in South Vietnam (1971): 287–88
equipment innovations
  anti-helicopter operations: 90–92
  bombs
    10,000-pound: 89, 154
    15,000-pound: 189, 256, 265, 272, 434, 443
    CBU–55: 294, 297
    cluster: 257
    fire bombings: 66–67
    fuel-air munitions: 89. *See also* CBU–55, above
    laser-guided: 89, 257, 309, 336, 368, 376
    rockeye: 89–90
  night attack aircraft: 88–89
  observation planes: 90
Enhance Plus contribution: 351
force composition (1970): 230
force composition (1972): 333
force deployment contribution: 44
force redistribution (1969): 141
force reduction options (1968): 136–37. *See also* Force reductions
force transfers due to Vietnamization:

535

Index

309
- ground support role (1969): 147
- independent strategy review: 47–48
- Kontum City airlift operations: 379–80
- *Mayaguez*. *See Mayaguez* incident
- mission distribution (1968): 55
- Office of Special Investigations
  - area source program: 36–37
  - drug abuse/racial tension investigations: 318–19
  - intelligence efforts: 289
- personnel contributions to ground forces: 18
- post-Tet strength: 45
- preparation for North Vietnamese attack (1972): 328–29
- racial tensions. *See* Racial tensions, United States Air Force
- security police
  - base defense improvements: 35–36, **37**
  - Binh Thuy defense: 13
  - defensive actions in Tet offensive: 8, 11
  - mini-Tet defense: 71
- Seventh Air Force. *See* Seventh Air Force
- single manager for tactical aviation. *See* Single manager for tactical aviation
- sortie rate approval (1972): 309–10
- sortie requests (1972): 307–9
- sorties flown (1968): 56
- sorties flown (1969): 149
- sorties flown (1971): 307
- Special Forces support
  - Duc Lap: 83–86
  - Thuong Duc: 86–87
- Squadrons
  - Aerospace Rescue and Recovery
    - 40th: 430–31
  - Airborne Command and Control
    - 7th: 342, 413
  - Air Refueling
    - 11th: 343
  - Air Rescue and Recovery
    - 39th: 342
  - Attack
    - 5th: 140
    - 8th: 232
    - 90th: 140, 232
  - Civil Engineer
    - 555th: 141
  - Reconnaissance Intelligence Technical
    - 12th: 225
  - Security Police
    - 377th: 8
    - 656th: 431
  - Special Operations
    - 4th: 140
    - 5th: 140
    - 8th: 344
    - 12th: 234
    - 21st: 430–31, 436–47
    - 71st: 45
    - 90th: 232
  - Tactical Airlift
    - 310th: 234
  - Tactical Air Support
    - 20th: 339
  - Tactical Bomber
    - 5th: 140
  - Tactical Electronic Warfare
    - 42d: 342
  - Tactical Fighter
    - 35th: 338, 345
    - 58th: 342, 346
    - 90th: 140
    - 120th: 45
    - 136th: 45
    - 174th: 45
    - 188th: 45, 46
    - 308th: 342, 346
    - 334th: 340, 341
    - 336th: 340, 341, 345
    - 388th: 340, 341
    - 390th: 345
    - 480th: 304–5
    - 510th: 140
    - 523d: 328, 338
    - 561st: 340–41
  - Tactical Reconnaissance
    - 45th: 237
- strike planning philosophy: 97
- strike planning procedures: 27–28
- tactical air strikes types: 57
- tactical aviation expansion (1972): 337–41
- tactical sortie ceiling implications (1970): 238–39
- troop reductions (1971): 304–5
- Wings
  - Special Operations

Index

  12th: 218
  Tactical Fighter
    3d: 191
    8th: 341
    12th: 7
    45th: 237
    49th: 343, 345
    347th: 434
    354th: 346
    366th: 338, 345
    432d: 434
  Tactical Reconnaissance
    432d: 342
United States Air National Guard
  force reduction plans: 136
  O-2 transferred to: 233
  post-Tet strength: 45
  Tactical Fighter Squadrons: 39
    136th: 45
    174th: 45
    188th: 45, 46
United States Army
  1st Brigade, 101st Airborne Division: 62, 66
  1st Calvary Division: 56, **58**, 122, 187
  1st Squadron, 9th Calvary: 56, 59, 61
  2d Brigade, 101st Airborne Division: 157
  3d Brigade, 101st Airborne Division: 155, 157
  9th Calvary Division: 56, 59
  9th Infantry Division river force: 79–82
  XXIV Corps: 123
    Dewey Canyon II plan: 251–52
    Lam Son 719 role: 255
    support of fire support base: 244
  25th Infantry Division: 8, 10
  82d Airborne Division: 41
  101st Airborne Division: 61, 62, 77, 155, 157
    in A Shau Valley: 59
    helicopter control in Lam Son 719: 255
    Ripcord base: 243
  aerial reconnaissance in A Shau: 59
  Air Force support of: 4
  Americal Division: 93, 104
  A Shau Valley offensive role: 64
  availability for service: 39
  comments on forward air controllers: 80
  dissatisfaction with Air Force aerial photography: 147

  helicopter sorties: 272–73
  Kham Duc support: 104
  mission coordination with Air Force: 148
  participation in interdiction efforts (1971): 283
  Provisional Corps, Vietnam
  selective service discontinued: 349
  single manager for tactical aviation procedures: 113
  Special Forces
    attacks: 84, 160, 244–46
    Chui Lang camp: 160
    Duc Lap mission
      counteroffensive: 84–85
      defenses: 83, **84**
      North Vietnamese attack on: 84
      supply drops: 85–86
    North Vietnamese attacks (1970): 244–46
    Thuong Duc: 86–87
  Task Force Oregon: 93
  Tet offensive
    Bien Hoa: 11
    Hue: 24
    Phuoc Le airstrip: 23
    Tan Son Nhut defense: 8–10
    triborder region advance: 77–78
United States Marine Corps
  1st Battalion, 4th Marines: 153–54, 431, 434
  1st Marine Aircraft Wing: 114, 123, 124, 304
  2d Battalion, 9th Marines: 431, 434, 435–39, **436**
  III Marine Amphibious Force: 100
    scope of commander's control: 125
    single manager for tactical aviation procedures: 102, 113
  3d Marine Division: 118
  9th Marines: 153–54, 431, 434
  Marine Aircraft Group 12: 344
  Marine Aircraft Group 15: 339
  27th Marines: 41
  Marine Air Refueler Transport Squadron 152
  aircraft in South Vietnam (1971): 307
  air power support role: 87–88
  An Loc defense: 396
  availability for service: 39
  Constant Guard movements: 344–45
  contribution to U.S. response (1972):

537

Index

339
  coordination with Air Force: 93–94
  daytime airborne alert procedures: 117
  deployment after Tet: 41
  Dewey Canyon: 153–54
  final aviation arm withdrawals: 304
  Fire Support Base evacuation: 269
  force composition (1970): 230
  force reductions (1970): 237
  Khe Sanh relief operation: 56–57
  Mayaguez. See Mayaguez incident
  mini-Tet counteroffensive: 69
  post-Tet operational sorties: 19
  post-Tet strength: 45
  single manager for tactical aviation. *See* single manager for tactical aviation, Marines and
  sortie ceiling (1970): 240
  sortie control (1970): 123
  sorties flown (1968): 56
  strike planning philosophy: 96–97
  tactical aviation expansion (1972): 337–41
United States Navy
  IV Corps zone flotilla: 79
  An Loc defense: 396
  availability for service: 39
  force composition (1970): 230
  forces in South Vietnam (1971): 307
  Mekong River convoy escorts: 284–85
  post-Tet operational sorties: 19
  racial tensions: 321
  share of sorties (1972): 310
  sortie ceiling (1970): 240
  sorties flown (1968): 56
  support of Military Region I operations: 372
  tactical aviation expansion (1972): 337–41
  Vietnamization of operations: 294
U-Tapao Air Base, Thailand: 188, 242, 431

Vann, John Paul: 327
  death of: 381
  Kontum City fight: 377
  Military Region II defensive plan: 373
  use of air power: 378
Van Tieng Dung: 419
Vega, USS: 430
Vesuvius (Operation): 50–51, 75, 182
Vien, Cao Van. *See* Cao Van Vien

Viet Cong. *See also* North Vietnam
  attack on Saigon: 10
  Bien Hoa attack (1969): 151
  Binh Dinh Province attacks: 375
  Cam Ranh Bay offensive (1971): 289
  Chau Doc Province operations: 159–60
  knowledge of B–52 strike plans: 29–30
  Long Binh attack (1969): 151
  Military Region IV attacks: 244–46, 290, 398–99
  mini-Tet. *See* Mini-Tet
  support of North Vietnamese: 331
  Tet offensive. *See* Tet offensive
Viet Minh: 248
Vietnamization. *See also* Force reductions
  absence of an aerial command: 406
  aerial interdiction capability
    budgetary considerations: 295–96
    equipment options: 294
    Ho Chi Minh Trail importance: 293
    Island Tree plan: 294
    lack of antipersonnel objective: 296, 297
    Laos attacks: 297
    need for B–52 substitute: 297–98
    Operations Plan 732: 295
  aircraft received in 1971: 299, 307
  aircrew performance: 226–27
  aircrew training: 218–19
  air divisions (1970): 213
  air logistics conversion: 170–71
  base security: 214
  base transfers: 169–70, 214–16, **215**, 301
  budget impact on U.S. withdrawals (1970): 236–37, 238, 295–96
  centralization issues: 213
  competency of aircrews: 221–22
  conflicting U.S. views of progress: 163
  control over tactical air strikes: 174
  credibility of air liaison officers: 174–75
  Credible Chase: 349
  criteria for: 135
  cultural/physical differences with United States: 227–28
  direct air request network: 173–74
  electronic intelligence decline: 406–7
  electronic surveillance methods: 175–76
  equipment options: 297
  final capabilities: 402, 426
  flight crew transition training: 352–53
  force acceleration program (1970):

Index

212–13
  helicopter program: 166–67, 223
  housing problems: 214
  importance in 1971: 292
  inadequacy of efforts at Cua Viet: 364–65
  intelligence and reconnaissance: 224–25
  interdiction: 295
  lack of interdiction skills: 178
  lack of technical expertise: 353–54
  lack of trained civil engineers: 216–17
  Lam Son 719 lessons learned: 274
  language barrier considerations: 167–69
  language training: 217–18
  maintenance/logistics management: 225–26, 354–55
  modernization compromise: 165
  needed scope for effort: 165
  night flight training: 222–23
  Nixon and
    criteria for: 135
    emphasis after Ap Bia: 157
    force reduction options: 136–38
    troop reductions: 138–39
  objective of: 165
  phase I plan: 161
  phase II plan: 162–63, 177–78
  phase III plan: 211
  phase IV plan: 232–37
  phase V plan: 237
  Project Enhance: 350–52
  Project Enhance Plus: 351
  reconnaissance abilities: 301, 356
  reductions in sorties flown: 142–44
  sortie counts (1969): 177
  South Vietnamese avoidance of tasks and responsibilities: 298–99
  South Vietnam budget constraints: 228
  strategy for: 164
  tactical air control responsibility: 219–20
  tactical aviation/air defense weaknesses: 355
  training efforts: 169, 179, 217–18, 222–23
  transport units: 223–24
Vinh: 335, 336
VNAF. *See* South Vietnamese Air Force
Vo Dinh: 376
Vogt, John W.: 330, **331**
  command of Support Activities Group: 403
  doubt about U.S. commitment: 401
  instructions from Nixon: 357
  scope of authority: 357
Vo Nguyen Giap
  battle tactics: 331–32
  goal of 1972 offensive: 334, 383, 399
  leadership position: 229
  strategic errors: 370
Vu Van Giai
  court-martial of: 366
  Military Region I defense: 364
  Quang Tri City defense: 359, 365

Wagstaff, Jack J.: 282
Warehouse 54: 155
War Powers Act: 428–29
Watergate: 411
Weather effects on air power: 24
  Alpine operation: 160
  in A Shau region: 59, 61–62, 64
  at Ben Het: 158
  C–130 tactics: 380–81
  considerations for Ho Chi Minh Trail attack: 249
  Hue attack: 24
  during Lam Son 719: 258, 267
  October 1970 storms: 243
  strike cancellations against North (1972): 358
  Tchepone attack: 250–51
Wells, Selmon W.: 27
Westmoreland, William C.: **100**
  I Corps headquarters established: 95
  ambiguity in reinforcement requests: 41, 42
  arguments for centralization: 95
  B–52 supervision: 27, 29
  desire to attack Ho Chi Minh Trail: 248
  early view of the war: 5
  Khe Sanh defense strategy: 15–16
  proposed control of Marines: 93–94
  reinforcement program: 40–42
  reservists bank proposal: 42–43
  rocket watch cautions: 68
  Saigon defense strategy: 14
Weyand, Frederick G.: 348
  delegation of duties: 74
  expectation of Tet attacks: 14, 16
  rocket watch cautions: 72
Wheeler, Earle G.
  Cambodian threat concerns: 51
  reinforcement offers: 39–40, 42

Index

and single manager for tactical aviation: 103
Wild Weasels. *See* F–105
Wire-guided antitank missiles: 374
"Wise Men" advisor group: 44

Xepon River: 260, 268, 269
Xuan, Dao Mong: 23

Young, Kendall S.: 166–67, 177
Young Tiger Task Force: 344

www.ingramcontent.com/pod-product-compliance
Lightning Source LLC
Chambersburg PA
CBHW060227240426
43671CB00016B/2874